Urban Economics

Urban Economics

Arthur M. Sullivan
*Graduate School of Management
and Economics Department
University of California, Davis*

IRWIN
Homewood, IL 60430
Boston, MA 02116

Publisher: John R. Black
Executive editor: Gary Nelson
Developmental editor: Melanie Murphy
Project editor: Jane Lightell
Production manager: Ann Cassady
Cover designer: Carol Chesnut
Compositor: Eastern Graphics Typographers
Typeface: 10/12 Palatino
Printer: R. R. Donnelley & Sons Company

Library of Congress Cataloging-in-Publication Data

Sullivan, Arthur M. (Arthur Morgan), 1953-
    Urban economics / Arthur M. Sullivan.
        p.   cm.
    ISBN 0-256-06834-8
    1. Urban economics.   I. Title.
    HT321.S85   1990   89–36249
    330.9173′2—dc20   CIP

Printed in the United States of America

1 2 3 4 5 6 7 8 9 0   DO   6 5 4 3 2 1 0 9

To Babe

Preface

This book uses economic analysis to explain why cities exist, where they develop, how they grow, and how different activities are arranged within cities. It also explores the economics of urban problems such as poverty, inadequate housing, congestion, pollution, and crime.

The text is designed for use in undergraduate courses in urban economics and urban affairs. It could also be used in graduate courses in urban planning, public policy, and public administration. Most of the concepts used in the book are covered in the typical introductory microeconomics course. Students who have completed such a course will be able to understand the book, although it may be useful to have a principles text handy for an occasional review of key concepts. Students who have completed an intermediate-level course in microeconomics will be able to move through the text at a faster rate.

This book uses one concept that is omitted in some introductory courses in economics. Indifference-curve analysis is used in five chapters of this book: the chapter on poverty (Chapter 12), the two chapters on housing (Chapters 13 and 14), the chapter on local revenue sources (Chapter 16), and the chapter on education (Chapter 19). The instructor's manual that accompanies this text has a brief overview of indifference-curve analysis. It is written for students without any experience with indifference-curve analysis, but it could also serve as a refresher for students with some experience with the framework. The overview is produced in a format suitable for reproduction and distribution to students.

The book covers more topics than the typical urban economics text, giving instructors several options for a one-semester course in urban economics. A course that emphasizes inter-urban location analysis would cover all six chapters in Part 1 (Market Forces in the Development of Cities), while other courses might omit some of these chapters. The prime candidates for omission are Chapter 3 (Where Do Cities Develop?), Chapter 4 (The History of Western Urbanization), and Chapter 5 (How Many Cities?). A course emphasizing intra-urban location analysis would cover all five chapters in Part 2 (Land Rent and Urban Land Use Patterns), while other courses might omit Chapter 9 (General Equilibrium Land Use) or Chapter 11 (Land Use Controls and Zoning). A course emphasizing urban problems would cover all three chapters in Part 3 (Urban Problems and the Federal Response) and several of the chapters in Part 4 (Urban Problems and Local Government). The two chapters on local government (Chapters 14 and 15) could be omitted in a course emphasizing the traditional urban problems, but would be an integral part of a course emphasizing urban public finance. The last two chapters deal with education and crime, two urban problems that receive less attention in other urban texts.

Acknowledgments

I am greatly indebted to my two mentors in urban economics. As an undergraduate at the University of Oregon, I was taught by Ed Whitelaw, whose enthusiasm for urban economics is apparently contagious. He used a number of innovative teaching techniques that made economics understandable, relevant, and even fun. As a graduate student at Princeton University, I was taught by Edwin Mills, one of the founding fathers of urban economics. He refined my mathematical and analytical skills and also provided a steady stream of perceptive insights into urban phenomena. I hope that some of what I learned from these two outstanding teachers is reflected in this book.

I am also indebted to many people who read the book and suggested ways to improve the coverage and the exposition.

John E. Anderson	Eastern Michigan University
Timothy J. Bartik	Vanderbilt University
Daniel R. Blake	California State University, Northridge
Edward Coulson	Pennsylvania State University
Philip Graves	University of Colorado
Timothy Gronberg	Texas A & M University
Robert Helsley	University of British Columbia
Arthur E. Kartman	San Diego State University
Ross M. Laroe	Denison University
Charles L. Leven	Washington University
John F. McDonald	University of Illinois, Chicago
Daniel P. McMillen	University of Oregon
Ronald L. Moomaw	Oklahoma State University
Terry Moore	University of Oregon and ECO Northwest
Roger F. Riefler	University of Nebraska
Elliott Sclar	Columbia University
Ed Whitelaw	University of Oregon and ECO Northwest

Arthur M. Sullivan

Contents

PART FOUR
Urban Problems and Local Government

CHAPTER 1
Introduction

Cities have always been the fireplaces of civilization, whence light and heat radiated out into the dark.

Theodore Parker

I'd rather wake up in the middle of nowhere than in any city on earth.

Steve McQueen

This book explores the economics of cities and urban problems. The quotes from Parker and McQueen reflect our mixed feelings about cities. On the positive side, cities facilitate production and trade, so they increase our standard of living. Unfortunately, cities also have serious problems such as poverty, congestion, pollution, and crime. Although these problems are truly urban in nature, they could be solved without abandoning our cities. One of the lessons of this book is that policies that solve urban problems will increase the vitality of cities, causing them to grow, not shrink.

Another purpose of the book is to explain broad changes in the size and spatial structure of cities. Most of the fundamental changes in urban areas have occurred in the last two centuries. In 1980, over three fourths of the U.S. population lived in urban areas, up from only 5 percent in 1800. This rapid urbanization was caused by the technological changes underlying the industrial revolution. More recently, many industrial cities have actually decreased in population, a result of a shift in the economy from traditional manufacturing activity to new types of manufacturing and services. The most important change in the spatial structure of cities has been the steady movement of economic activity from central core areas to suburbs and subcenters. Many factors have contributed to suburbanization, including increases in income and changes in transportation technology.

A third purpose of the book is to evaluate alternative means of solving urban problems. The conventional list of urban problems includes poverty, inadequate housing, congestion, pollution, and crime. All of these urban problems are affected by land-use patterns, and also influence land-use patterns. In other words, urban problems have distinct spatial features that are relevant to the discussion of alternative policy responses.

The remainder of this brief introductory chapter addresses two questions. First, what is urban economics? The answer to this question provides a

1

preview of the material covered in the book. Second, what is an urban area? The economist's definition of a city differs from the definitions used by the U.S. Census Bureau.

WHAT IS URBAN ECONOMICS?

Urban economics is the study of the location choices of firms and households. Other branches of economics ignore the spatial aspects of decision making, adopting the convenient but unrealistic assumption that all production and consumption occurs at a single point. In contrast, urban economics examines the *where* of economic activities. In urban economics, a household chooses where to work and where to live, and a firm chooses where to locate its factory, office, or retail outlet.

Urban economics explores the spatial aspects of urban problems and public policy. Urban problems such as poverty, urban decay, crime, congestion, and pollution are intertwined with the location decisions of households and firms: location decisions contribute to urban problems, and urban problems influence location decisions. For example, the suburbanization of employment opportunities contributes to central-city poverty; the resulting fiscal problems cause some wealthy households to move to the suburbs. A discussion of alternative policy options must take these spatial effects into account.

If urban economics is the study of location choices, why isn't it called *location economics* or *spatial economics*? There are three reasons for the *urban* in urban economics. First, most location decisions involve an urban choice: over three fourths of the U.S. work force live in cities, meaning that most of the action in location analysis is in urban areas. Second, urban economics is also concerned with location choices within cities. Finally, most of the pressing problems caused by location choices occur in urban areas.

Urban economics can be divided into four related areas, corresponding to the four sections of this book.

Market Forces in the Development of Cities

The first part of the book shows how the location decisions of firms and households cause the development of cities. A firm chooses the location that maximizes its profit, and a household chooses the location that maximizes its utility. These location decisions generate clusters of activity (cities) that differ in size and economic structure. The questions addressed in this part of the book include the following:

1. Why do cities exist? Why do people tolerate the dirt, noise, crime, and congestion of cities?
2. Why did the industrial revolution cause rapid urbanization?
3. Where do cities develop?

4. What were the roles of religion and defense in the development of the first cities?
5. What is the role of trade in the development of cities?
6. Why do cities differ in size and scope?
7. What causes urban economic growth and decline?
8. How do local governments encourage economic growth?

Land Rent and Land Use within Cities

The second part of the book discusses the spatial organization of activities within cities. In contrast with the first part of the book, which examines location choices from the regional perspective, the second part examines location choices within cities. Among the questions addressed in the second section are the following:

1. Why does the price of housing vary across space?
2. Why does the price of land vary across space?
3. How does government policy affect the price of land and land-use patterns?
4. Do the location decisions of households affect the location decisions of firms?
5. Why was the monocentric city of the 19th century replaced by the multicentric city of the 20th century?
6. What factors caused the suburbanization of employment and population?
7. Why are households segregated with respect to income and race?
8. Why do local governments use zoning and other land-use controls to restrict location choices?

Spatial Aspects of Poverty and Housing

The third part of the book examines the spatial aspects of two related urban problems: poverty and housing. Urban poverty has a distinct spatial dimension: the poor are typically concentrated in the central city, far from employment opportunities in the suburbs. The discussion of poverty addresses the following questions:

1. Who are the poor, and where do they live?
2. What causes poverty?
3. Why does segregation occur, and what can be done about it?
4. How does the federal government combat poverty?

5. What are the merits of recent proposals to reform the federal welfare system (e.g., negative income tax, workfare, mandated child support)?

The third part of the book also examines the spatial aspects of urban housing problems. Housing choices are linked to location choices because housing is immobile: when a household chooses a dwelling, it also chooses a location. The most important urban housing problem is the decay of dwellings and entire neighborhoods in the central city. The chapters on housing address the following questions:

1. What makes housing different from other commodities?
2. Why do the poor occupy used housing?
3. Why does central-city housing deteriorate at a faster rate than other housing?
4. How does public policy affect the supply of low-income housing and its price?
5. Should the government build new low-income housing or give money to the poor?
6. How does rent control affect the supply of low-income housing?

Local Government Expenditures and Taxes

The last part of the book explores the spatial aspects of local government policies. Under the fragmented system of local government, the typical large metropolitan area has dozens of local governments, including municipalities, school districts, and special districts. These local governments provide a wide variety of goods, including transportation systems, education, and crime protection. Firms and households "shop" for the jurisdiction that provides the best combination of services and taxes. In other words, they vote with their feet. Therefore, tax and spending policies affect the spatial distribution of activity within and between cities.

The process of shopping for a local government raises three questions about the fragmented system of local government:

1. Is the fragmented system of government efficient?
2. What is the role of intergovernmental grants in the fragmented system?
3. Who pays local taxes? If people and firms can move easily from one jurisdiction to another, who bears the burden of taxes?
4. How does the local property tax affect location choices? Does the property tax encourage segregation with respect to income and race?

One of the responsibilities of local government is to provide an urban transportation system. Most cities combine an auto-based highway system with some form of mass transit (e.g., bus, light rail, or heavy rail). Since activities are arranged within cities to facilitate interactions between different activities, any change in the transportation system that affects the relative accessibility of different sites also affects land-use patterns. The chapters on transportation address the following questions:

1. What causes congestion, and what are the alternative policy responses?
2. How does congestion affect land-use patterns?
3. What are the alternative policies for dealing with auto pollution?
4. Under what circumstances is a bus system more efficient than a fixed-rail system such as San Francisco's BART or Washington's Metro?
5. What are the costs and benefits of light-rail systems?
6. Should transit be deregulated to allow private firms to compete with transit authorities?

The last two chapters of the book deal with two local public goods: education and crime protection. The study of education fits naturally into the scheme of urban economics because education affects location decisions: a household's choice of a residence depends in part on the quality of the local schools. These location decisions also affect the provision of education: if households segregate themselves with respect to income, per-pupil spending will be relatively low in poor districts, so poor children will receive inferior education. In addition, a child's achievement level depends on (a) the income and education level of his parents and (b) the achievement level of his classmates. Therefore, a child in a poor community would receive an inferior education even if all schools spent the same amount per pupil.

The chapter on education addresses the following questions:

1. Why does spending on education vary across school districts?
2. To what extent do intergovernmental grants decrease spending inequalities?
3. How does the home environment affect educational achievement?
4. Why does educational achievement vary across school districts?
5. What are the effects of income segregation and racial segregation on educational achievement?
6. To what extent do desegregation policies decrease segregation and equalize educational achievement?
7. What are the merits of the proposal to use education vouchers to subsidize education in private schools?

The final chapter of the book explores the economics of crime and punishment. Like education, crime affects location decisions: a household's choice of a residence depends in part on the local crime rate. These location decisions also affect the provision of crime protection: if households segregate themselves with respect to income, there will be inequalities in spending on crime protection. In addition, because there is a relatively large number of potential criminals in poor areas, citizens in poor communities would experience higher crime rates even if all communities spent the same amount on crime protection.

The crime chapter addresses the following questions:

1. Are criminals rational? Do they only commit crimes for which the expected benefits exceed the expected costs? If so, what are the implications for crime-fighting policies?
2. Why are crime rates higher in central cities?
3. What is the optimum amount of crime?
4. How do the police, the courts, and the prison system deter crime?
5. What is the interaction between anti-drug policy and property crime? Do policies that control illegal drugs also increase property crime?

WHAT IS AN URBAN AREA?

To an urban economist, a geographical area is considered *urban* if it contains a large number of people in a relatively small area. In other words, an **urban area** is defined as an area with a relatively high population density. For example, suppose that the average population density of a particular county is 20 people per square mile. If a certain area of the county contains 50,000 people in a 50-square-mile area (i.e., the population density is 1,000 people per square mile), it would be considered an urban area because its population density is relatively high. This definition accommodates urban areas of vastly different size, from the small town to the large metropolitan area. The economist's definition is stated in terms of population density because the urban economy is based on frequent contact between different economic activities, and such contact is feasible only if firms and households are packed into a relatively small area.

Census Definitions

The Census Bureau has a number of definitions of geographical areas. Since most empirical work in urban economics is based on the census data, a clear understanding of these definitions is important.

Municipality or City.   A **municipality** is defined as the area over which a municipal corporation provides local government services such as sewage, crime protection, and fire protection. Another term for municipality is **city**: in this case, *city* refers to the area over which a local government exercises political authority.

Urbanized Area.   An **urbanized area** includes at least one large central city (a municipality) and the surrounding area with population density exceeding 1,000 people per acre. To be an urbanized area, the total population of the area must be at least 50,000. An example of an urbanized area is shown in Figure 1–1: The urbanized area is the large circle surrounding the municipality. The urbanized area outside the central city is called the **urban fringe**.

Metropolitan Statistical Area (MSA).   In 1984, there were 261 **metropolitan statistical areas (MSAs)**, ranging in population from just over 50,000 to over 2 million. In principle, an MSA consists of a large population nucleus and the nearby communities that are integrated, in an economic sense, with the nucleus. In the census definition, the nucleus of an MSA is the urbanized area, and the integrated communities are the surrounding counties in which a relatively large number of people commute to the nucleus.

Figure 1–1 shows the simplest type of MSA: a single county that surrounds an urbanized area. This simple case shows one of the problems with the MSA concept. To form an MSA, the Census Bureau takes an urbanized area and tacks on the rest of the county, so the MSA includes areas that are essentially rural. MSAs are defined by counties because the county is the smallest geographical unit for which a wide range of data is collected. In New England, where counties are relatively unimportant, MSAs include the urbanized area along with towns that are sufficiently integrated with the urban area.

Most MSAs include more than one county. A **central county** is defined as one in which (*a*) the majority of the population lives in the urbanized area or (*b*) at least 2,500 of its residents live in the central municipality. An adjacent county is included in the MSA if it is sufficiently integrated with the central county or counties. The degree of integration is measured in terms of commuting flows and population density. For example, a county is included in the MSA if over 50 percent of its work force commutes to a central county and its population density exceeds 25 people per square mile. As the commuting percentage drops, the threshold population density increases. For the minimum commuting percentage (15 percent), a county is included if the population density exceeds 50 people per square mile.

FIGURE 1–1   Urbanized Area and Metropolitan Statistical Area

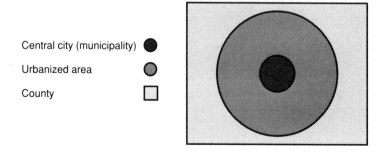

Central city (municipality)

Urbanized area

County

Figure 1–2 shows the maps of two multiple-county MSAs, Sacramento and Atlanta. The urbanized areas are the darkened areas near the centers of the MSAs. There are four counties in the Sacramento MSA, two of which stretch through rural areas to the Nevada border, about 90 miles from the city of Sacramento. The Atlanta MSA is more compact, with 18 counties surrounding an urbanized area centered on the city of Atlanta.

Some geographical areas qualify as an MSA despite the absence of an urbanized area. If the total population of the central county and the surrounding integrated counties exceeds 100,000, the area is defined as an MSA. In

FIGURE 1–2   Metropolitan Statistical Areas

Sacramento Metropolitan Statistical Area

Atlanta Metropolitan Statistical Area

FIGURE 1–3   Consolidated Metropolitan Statistical Areas

Chicago-Gary-Lake County CMSA

San Francisco-Oakland-San Jose CMSA

New England, where the town is the standard geographical unit, the population threshold is 75,000.

Consolidated Metropolitan Statistical Area (CMSA).   A **CMSA** is a large metropolitan complex composed of contiguous MSAs. In 1986, there were 20 CMSAs, ranging in population from 17.9 million (New York–Northern New Jersey–Long Island) to just over 1 million (Hartford–New Britain–Middletown). Every CMSA is split into two or more primary metropolitan statistical areas (PMSAs). For example, the New York CMSA has 12 PMSAs. Figure 1–3 shows maps of two CMSAs, Chicago–Gary–Lake County and San Francisco–Oakland–San Jose. Both of these CMSAs have six PMSAs.

The Census Bureau recently changed its terminology for metropolitan areas. Before 1983, metropolitan areas were called standard metropolitan statistical areas (SMSAs) and groups of related SMSAs were called standard consolidated statistical areas (SCSAs).

Urban versus Rural.   An **urban place** is defined as a geographical area with at least 2,500 inhabitants. The nation's **urban population** is defined as all people living in urbanized areas and urban places. According to this definition, in 1980, about three fourths of the U.S. population lived in urban areas.

Definitions Used in This Book

This book uses three terms to refer to spatial concentrations of economic activity: *urban area, metropolitan area,* and *city*. When referring to the political city, the book will use the term *central city* or *municipality*. An urban area (a city or a metropolitan area) is composed of a central city and the surrounding suburbs.

PART ONE

Market Forces in the Development of Cities

In a market economy, individuals exchange their labor for wage income, which is then used to buy other goods and services. How do these market transactions affect cities? Chapter 2 discusses the fundamental reasons for centralized production and marketing and then explores the implications for the development of cities. Chapter 3 shows how the location decisions of firms cause the development of cities in particular locations. Chapter 4 provides a brief historical sketch of urbanization, using the concepts developed in chapters 2 and 3 to explain the history of cities. Chapter 5 takes a regional perspective, showing how competition among firms leads to the development of a hierarchical system of cities. Chapter 6 explores the reasons for urban economic growth and the effects of public policy on the size of the urban economy.

CHAPTER 2

Why Do Cities Exist?

Man is the only animal that makes bargains; one dog does not change bones with another dog.

Adam Smith

Cities exist because individuals are not self-sufficient. If each of us could produce everything we consumed and we didn't want much company, there would be no need to live in dirty, noisy, crowded cities. We aren't self-sufficient, however, so we exchange our labor for other goods. Most of us live in cities because that's where the jobs are. By living in cities, we achieve a higher standard of living, but also must put up with more pollution, crime, noise, and congestion.

This chapter explores three reasons for the concentration of jobs in cities. **Comparative advantage** makes trade between regions advantageous. Under certain circumstances, interregional trade will cause the development of market cities. **Internal scale economies** in production allow firms to produce goods more efficiently than individuals. The production of goods in factories causes the development of industrial cities. **Agglomerative economies** in production and marketing cause firms to cluster in cities, and this clustering causes the development of large cities. This chapter focuses on the market forces that generate cities, ignoring the social reasons for cities (e.g., religion, companionship, and politics). Some of these nonmarket reasons for cities will be discussed later in the book.

A MODEL OF A RURAL REGION

Under what conditions would there be no cities? In other words, what set of assumptions guarantees a uniform distribution of population? This section develops a model of a rural region, that is, a region without cities. The model provides a list of assumptions that together prevent the development of cities. When these assumptions are dropped, the model predicts that cities will develop.

The model of the rural economy captures some of the essential features of England before the Norman Conquest of the 11th century. The economy was essentially rural, with only a few small market towns serving the local population. Later in the chapter, the model will be used to explain the market forces behind the development of English cities after the Norman Conquest.

Consider a region where only two commodities (wheat and wool cloth) are produced and consumed. The regional economy has the following characteristics:

1. **Inputs.** Wheat and cloth are produced with labor and land. Land is used to grow wheat and raise sheep. Residents spin the raw wool into yarn and then weave the yarn into cloth.

2. **Equal productivity.** All residents are equally productive at making cloth and producing wheat. In one hour, every person can produce either one bushel of wheat or one yard of cloth. Similarly, all land is equally productive in the production of wheat and raw wool.

3. **No scale economies.** Production is subject to **constant returns to scale**: a worker produces one yard of cloth per hour, regardless of how much cloth is produced. Similarly, wheat production per hour is independent of the volume produced.

4. **Travel time.** Travel within the region is by foot: residents walk at a speed of four round-trip miles per hour (a round trip between a home and a location four miles away takes one hour).

These assumptions are strong enough to prevent trade. Every household in the region will produce its own wheat and cloth. Because every household is equally productive in producing both goods, there are no advantages from trade between households. Because productivity is independent of the volume produced, there are no advantages from centralized production: a factory worker would be no more productive than a person working at home. The disadvantage of factory cloth is that travel to the factory takes time, so the net cost of the factory cloth (price plus travel cost) is greater than the cost of homemade cloth. To summarize, there are no advantages from trade or centralized production, so every household in the region will be self-sufficient.

The population will be distributed uniformly throughout the region. Every household will pick a plot of land and make its own wheat and cloth. Since all land is equally productive, the distribution of population will be uniform. There are no cities because the model's assumptions are strong enough to eliminate the possibility of trade.

COMPARATIVE ADVANTAGE AND URBAN DEVELOPMENT

One factor in the development of cities is comparative advantage. The model of the rural region assumes that all households are equally productive in the production of cloth and wheat. If this assumption is relaxed, one part of the region may have a comparative advantage in cloth production, and the other part may have a comparative advantage in wheat production. Under certain circumstances, comparative advantage will lead to trade and the development of cities.

Comparative Advantage

The notion of comparative advantage can be explained with a simple model of trade between two parts of the region. Suppose that the western half of the region is more productive than the eastern half. In Table 2–1, the West has an **absolute advantage** in producing both wheat and cloth: western residents produce twice as much wheat per hour and six times as much cloth per hour. The differences in productivity could be caused by differences in labor skills, weather, or soil quality.

The notion of comparative advantage is based on the principle of opportunity cost. In a one-hour period, a western worker can produce either six yards of cloth or two bushels of wheat. Therefore, the opportunity cost of cloth is one third of a bushel of wheat and the opportunity cost of wheat is three yards of cloth. An eastern worker can produce either one bushel of wheat or one yard of cloth, so the opportunity cost of wheat is one yard of cloth, and vice versa. The West has a comparative advantage in the production of cloth because the opportunity cost of cloth is one third of a bushel of wheat, compared to one bushel of wheat in the East. Similarly, the East has a comparative advantage in wheat because the opportunity cost is one yard of cloth instead of three.

Trade and Transportation Costs

Comparative advantage may lead to trade between East and West. To understand the possible advantages of trade, suppose that all households in the region are initially self-sufficient. Suppose that two households, one in the East and one in the West, agree to exchange two yards of cloth for one bushel of wheat: the price of wheat is two yards of cloth. If the western household switches one hour of work from wheat production to cloth production, it sacrifices two bushels of wheat to produce six additional yards of cloth. If it exchanges the extra cloth for three bushels of wheat from an eastern household, its net gain from trade is one bushel of wheat. If the eastern household switches one hour of work from cloth to wheat production and exchanges the extra bushel of wheat for two yards of cloth, its net gain from trade is one yard of cloth.

TABLE 2–1 Comparative Advantage

| | *Output per Labor Hour* | | *Opportunity Costs of Production* | |
	East	*West*	*East*	*West*
Wheat	1	2	1 Cloth	3 Cloth
Cloth	1	6	1 Wheat	⅓ Wheat

What about transportation costs? Trade between the two households will be beneficial only if the differences in productivity are large enough to offset the costs of shipping wheat and cloth between the two areas. To continue the example, suppose that it takes 45 minutes of travel time for the western household to execute the trade of cloth for wheat. Is trade still beneficial? The net gain from trade is the gross gain (one bushel of wheat) less the opportunity cost of 45 minutes spent executing the trade. Since the household could use the 45 minutes to produce 1.5 bushels of wheat for itself, trade is not beneficial in this case.

Trade will be beneficial if transportation costs are small relative to the differences in productivity. If the net gains from trade are positive, western households will specialize in cloth production and eastern households will specialize in wheat. The region's households will no longer be self-sufficient, but will trade to exploit their comparative advantages.

Trading Cities

Under what conditions will trade cause the development of cities? Trade will produce cities if there are scale economies in transportation services. In the absence of scale economies, each eastern household will link up with a western household to exchange cloth and wheat. If households engage in direct trade, there will be no real marketplaces. Suppose that there are scale economies in transportation: the cost per shipment rises less than proportionately with the volume shipped. Large-scale shipments of cloth and wheat will be efficient, causing the development of trading firms to collect, transport, and distribute the two goods. The trading firms will establish markets at places convenient for the collection and distribution of the goods, for example, at transshipment points such as crossroads, ports, and river junctions.

The location decisions of traders will cause the development of market cities. People who work in trading firms will live near the marketplace to economize on commuting costs and will bid up the price of land. As the price of land increases, residents will economize on land by occupying relatively small lots. In other words, the population density around the marketplace will be higher than the population density in the rest of the region. Since a city is defined as a place with a relatively high population density, the combination of comparative advantage and scale economies in transportation causes the development of a market city.

The market city develops because three conditions are satisfied. First, agricultural productivity is high enough that agricultural workers produce enough wheat and cloth for themselves and the urban traders. In other words, the agricultural surplus feeds and clothes the urban workers. Second, the differences in productivity that generate comparative advantage are large enough to offset transportation costs, so trade occurs. Third, there are scale economies in transportation, making large-scale trade and central marketplaces efficient.

INTERNAL SCALE ECONOMIES IN PRODUCTION

A second factor in the development of cities is scale economies in production. The model of the rural region assumes constant returns to scale in the production of both wheat and cloth. Because there are no advantages from centralized production in factories, all goods are produced in the home. If this assumption is dropped, factory production may replace home production, causing the development of industrial cities.

Scale Economies and the Cloth Factory

Suppose that there are advantages from the large-scale production of cloth. In other words, as the volume of production increases, the amount of labor required to produce one yard of cloth decreases. Figure 2–1 shows the average labor requirements for different amounts of factory cloth: the average labor time decreases from one hour for one yard of cloth (the same time as home production) to 15 minutes for an output of 400 yards. These scale economies arise for two reasons:

1. **Factor specialization.** In a large operation, each worker is assigned a single task. The specialization of labor increases productivity because (*a*) workers' skills increase with repetition and (*b*) workers spend less time switching from task to task. The making of woolen cloth has several steps: the raw wool is spun into yarn, the yarn is woven into

FIGURE 2–1   Scale Economies in Clothmaking

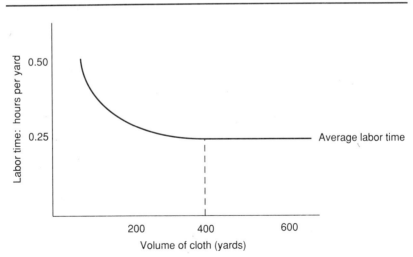

If there are scale economies in clothmaking, the average time required to make a yard of cloth decreases as the volume produced increases.

cloth, and the raw cloth is finished (cleaned, thickened, and dyed). One reason for scale economies in cloth production is that individual workers can specialize in different tasks. A group of 10 specialized workers can produce more than 10 times as much as 10 individuals working in isolation (each of whom performs all the production tasks).

2. **Indivisible inputs.** An input to the production process is indivisible if the input has a minimum efficient scale. If an indivisible input is cut in half, the total output of the two halves will be less than the output of the whole. The cloth factory uses equipment (spinning machines, power looms, thickening machines, dyeing vats) that cannot be efficiently scaled down for use by individual clothmakers. As output increases, the factory uses more of these indivisible inputs, so labor productivity increases.

If the cloth factory produces 400 yards of cloth per hour, it will employ 100 workers (400 times 0.25 hours of labor per yard of cloth).

What is the wage of factory workers? The wage must be high enough to make cloth workers indifferent between working in the factory and working at home. If consumers pay the factory workers 0.25 bushels of wheat for one yard of cloth, the factory worker will earn one bushel of wheat per hour of factory work. The worker will be indifferent between working in the factory (earning one bushel of wheat per hour) and producing his own wheat (at one bushel per hour).

A household will buy factory cloth if the net cost of factory cloth is less than the cost of home production. There are two components to the net cost of factory cloth. The first is the time required to produce enough wheat to pay the factory worker (0.25 bushels of wheat requires 0.25 hours of wheat production). The second is the time spent traveling to and from the cloth factory. The resident will buy the factory cloth as long as the net time cost of factory cloth is less than the time required to produce cloth at home (one hour). Therefore, the resident will buy factory cloth as long as the trip to the factory takes less than 0.75 hours.

Figure 2–2 shows the **market area** of the cloth factory. The market area is defined as the area over which the factory can underprice home production. The vertical axis measures the net cost of cloth, which equals the sum of the factory price (0.25 hours of wheat production), and travel time to the factory. The horizontal axis measures the distance to the factory in miles. If walking time is four round-trip miles per hour, the factory will underprice homemade cloth for residents within three miles of the factory (within 0.75 hours walking time). Therefore, the factory's market area is a circle with a radius of three miles.

Scale Economies and an Urban Area

A small urban area will develop around the cloth factory. If the output of the factory is 400 yards of cloth, it will employ 100 people. The workers will

FIGURE 2–2 Market Area of Cloth Factory

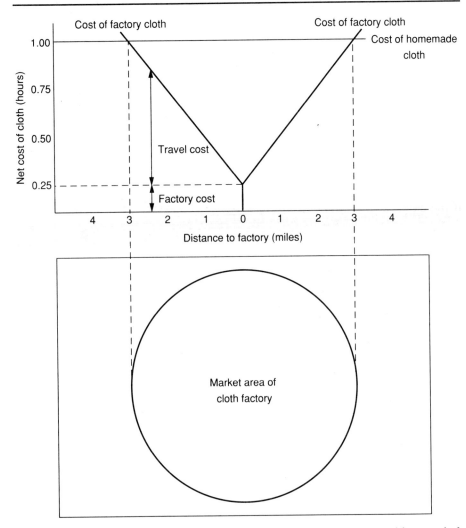

The market area of the cloth factory is the area over which the net cost of factory cloth (production time plus travel time) is less than the production time of homemade cloth (1 hour).

live near the factory to economize on commuting costs and will bid up the price of land near the factory. As the price of land increases, workers will economize on land by occupying smaller lots. In other words, the population density around the cloth factory will be higher than the population density in the rest of the region. Since a city is defined as a place with a relatively high population density, the cloth factory causes the development of a small factory city.

The factory city develops because two conditions are satisfied. First, the productivity of agricultural workers (wheat growers) is high enough that they can feed themselves and have enough left over to feed the cloth workers in the city. In other words, the agricultural surplus feeds city workers. Second, scale economies are large relative to travel costs, so the cloth factory can underprice homemade cloth.

The size of the city is determined by the number of factory workers, which in turn depends on the total output of the factory. The factory can increase its output if it manages to underprice more home producers. Therefore, output will increase as scale economies increase (decreasing the factory price) and transportation cost decrease (decreasing the net cost of factory cloth). Chapter 5 (How Many Cities?) provides a more complete analysis of the factors that determine the firm's market area.

EXAMPLES OF URBAN DEVELOPMENT

This section discusses the role of comparative advantage and scale economies in the development of cities in England and the United States. It uses some of the concepts developed in this chapter to explain the timing and the location of urban development.

The British Woolen Industry

Before the Norman Conquest in 1066, the making of wool cloth in England was an entirely local affair. Individual households and villas raised their own sheep, spun the raw wool into yarn, and wove the yarn into cloth. In other words, households were self-sufficient in cloth production, and no cities were involved in the production or trade of wool cloth. A small number of towns and small cities were involved in local trade.

The Norman Conquest increased the interactions between England and the continent, setting the stage for the development of the wool cloth trade. The barriers to trade fell, and England was able to exploit its comparative advantage in the production of wool cloth. Exports to the continent rose, causing the development of small cities and towns based on the cloth trade.

In the 12th century, there was a flourishing cloth industry in several English cities, including Lincoln, Northampton, York, and Bristol. These cities developed as both commercial and production centers. Although spinning, weaving, and finishing were still performed by hand, there were some small scale economies associated with labor specialization, so centralized production in cities was efficient.

Starting in the 13th century, the clothmaking industry moved from cities to rural areas with waterpower. The fulling process involves cleaning and thickening the wool cloth. Before the development of the fulling mill, workers stomped on wet cloth to clean and thicken it. The waterpowered fulling mill replaced foot stomping, causing producers to move their finishing operations to sites along fast-moving streams.

The move to rural fulling sites caused the replacement of urban spinners and weavers by rural workers organized under the **putting-out system**. The clothier distributed raw wool to rural households for spinning and weaving. The making of cloth (using primitive spinning wheels and hand looms) was a part-time activity, typically performed by the women of the rural household. The clothier collected the raw cloth from his rural workers, brought it to fulling mills for cleaning and thickening, and then shipped the cloth to his customers in other regions and countries.

The shift to fulling mills and a rural work force caused the decline of the traditional clothmaking cities and the development of new villages and small cities. The fulling mills provided a convenient collection point for the cloth produced by the rural households and caused the development of many small villages. Since most of the production activity was performed by rural households, most of the cities involved in the cloth industry served primarily as commercial centers. They differed from the traditional clothmaking cities, which served as both commercial and production centers.

The industrial revolution of the 19th century produced a number of innovations that increased the scale economies associated with the production of wool cloth. Mechanized spinning replaced hand spinning in the early 1800s, and power looms replaced hand looms about 1830. When the coal-fired steam engine was modified to power the spinning and weaving machinery, large factories developed on sites accessible to coal deposits (e.g., the West Riding of Yorkshire). The cloth factory integrated the production process, performing the tasks of spinning, weaving, and finishing under a single roof. The scale economies in production allowed the factory to produce wool cloth at a lower cost than home producers, so the putting-out system was replaced by factory production. The development of large factories caused the development of relatively large factory cities. The leading cities in the production of wool cloth were Bradford, Halifax, Leeds, Huddersfield, and Wakefield.

This brief history of English clothmaking cities shows how changes in transportation costs and scale economies transformed rural areas into highly urbanized ones. The opening of the European markets following the Norman Conquest allowed England to exploit its comparative advantage in clothmaking, causing the development of the traditional clothmaking cities. The industrial revolution increased scale economies in clothmaking, causing the development of clothing factories and large factory cities.

The Sewing Machine and U.S. Urbanization

The sewing machine, which was developed in the middle of the 19th century, increased scale economies in the making of clothing and contributed to the development of cities. Around the beginning of the 19th century, about four fifths of the clothing worn in the United States was hand-sewn in the home for a member of the household. The other fifth was hand-sewn by tailors. The sewing machine allowed factory producers to underprice home producers; by 1890, nine tenths of U.S. clothing was being made in factories.

As clothing factories sprung up in the United States, new cities developed around the factories.

The sewing machine also contributed to the development of U.S. cities around shoe factories. Before 1700, most shoes were produced in the home or the local village. The cost of transportation was so high that local production was efficient. Over time, transportation costs decreased, allowing the exploitation of comparative advantage in shoe production. The putting-out system was implemented in the 1700s: shoe producers distributed raw materials to cottage workers, collected their output, and finished the shoes in a central shop. As new shoemaking machines were developed, the number of operations performed in the central shop increased. The McKay sewing machine, which mechanized the process of sewing the soles to the uppers, increased scale economies in shoe production to the point at which the central shop became a genuine factory. Cities developed around the new shoe factories.

AGGLOMERATIVE ECONOMIES IN PRODUCTION

This section explores some of the reasons why cities are large. The analysis of scale economies earlier in the chapter suggests that a city will develop around a factory. This section explains why most cities have more than one factory: it explains the development of large industrial cities.

The large industrial city develops because of agglomerative economies in production. By locating close to one another, firms can produce goods at a lower cost. This is an example of a **positive externality** in production: the production cost of a particular firm decreases as the output of other firms increases. There are two types of agglomerative economies: localization economies and urbanization economies.

Localization Economies

Localization economies occur if the production costs of firms in a particular industry decrease as the total output of the industry increases. To realize these economies, a firm must be located close to other firms in the industry, so firms cluster to decrease their production costs. Localization economies occur for three principal reasons: scale economies in the production of intermediate inputs, labor-market economies, and communication economies.

Scale Economies in Intermediate Inputs.   Some clusters occur because firms in a particular industry buy an intermediate input from the same supplier. Firms cluster around a common input supplier if two conditions are satisfied:

1. The input demand of an individual firm is not large enough to exploit the scale economies in the production of the intermediate input.

2. Transportation cost is relatively high. If demanders and supplier interact in the design or fabrication of the intermediate input, face-to-face

contact between buyer and seller is necessary, so proximity to the input supplier is important. Similarly, if the intermediate input is bulky, fragile, or must be delivered quickly, proximity is important.

Vernon (1972) uses the Manhattan dressmaking industry as an example of an industry cluster caused by scale economies in the production of intermediate inputs. Because the demand for high-fashion dresses is unpredictable, a dressmaking firm cannot commit itself to large-scale production of a given type of dress, but must be prepared to quickly change to another type of dress if the first dress doesn't sell. The firm must employ inputs (capital and labor) that can (*a*) produce a wide variety of dresses and (*b*) make the transition from one dress to another quickly. As a result, specialized labor and machinery are not feasible. In addition, the manager of the firm must carefully monitor the design process, the production process, and the dress market. The dressmaking operation must be kept small enough that the manager can be involved in most decisions.

One of the intermediate inputs to dressmaking is buttons. Suppose that there are scale economies in the production of buttons, and it takes 10 dressmakers to generate sufficient button demand to exhaust these scale economies. By sharing a buttonmaker, the 10 dressmakers can get buttons at a lower cost. Because the scale economies in buttonmaking are large *relative to* the scale economies in dressmaking, the dressmakers will share a buttonmaker.

Why should dressmakers cluster around the button firm? They locate near the button producer because they must supervise the production of buttons. Because the buttons for a high-fashion dress are not standardized, they cannot simply be ordered out of a catalogue. The buttons are designed to complement the other features of the dress and the dressmaker participates in the design and fabrication of buttons to ensure that the buttons match the dress. Given the importance of face-to-face contact, dressmakers must locate close to the buttonmaker.

There are many other examples of clusters that result from scale economies in the provision of intermediate inputs.

1. **Corporate headquarters.** The corporate headquarters produces a wide variety of outputs: the executive may design an advertising campaign one week, pick a location for a new plant the next week, and develop a strategy to fend off a lawsuit the following week. Most corporations use outside advertising firms because the scale economies in the production of advertising campaigns are large relative to the advertising demand of an individual corporation. Corporate executives need to be close to the advertising firm because the executives assist in the design of the advertising campaign. In general, the clustering of corporate headquarters (usually in central business districts) allows corporations to exploit scale economies in the production of intermediate goods (advertising, economic consulting services, legal services) for which face-to-face contact is an important part of the production process.

2. **High-technology firms.** Firms producing new high-technology goods face uncertain demand for their products. Instead of producing all of their own components, they purchase electronic parts from firms that can exploit scale economies in production. The firms interact with their suppliers in the design and fabrication of the components, and they must locate close together to facilitate frequent face-to-face contact. Although the high-technology firm need not locate close to its supplier of nuts and bolts (standardized inputs that can be ordered from a catalogue), it needs to locate close to the supplier of nonstandardized electronic parts. In addition, high-technology firms exploit scale economies in product testing by sharing firms that provide testing facilities. They locate close enough to tap the testing facilities at top speed.

3. **Publishing.** Newspapers and magazines produce outputs (text and illustrations) which change in unpredictable ways from day to day. In producing their products, publishers call on a wide variety of experts, including information sources and illustrators. If each publisher uses an expert on Armenian history for one story per year, it would be inefficient for each publisher to hire a full-time Armenian expert. Instead, the publishers may share a single expert, sharing the cost of specialized information. Similarly, publishers occasionally need special illustrations and call on graphic design firms to do the illustrations. Publishers cluster around organizations that provide expert information (libraries, research institutes, universities) and illustrations (graphic design firms).

What is the role of business services in the development of firm clusters? Some industries require specialized financial services. There are scale economies in the provision of banking and insurance services, and firms in a cluster can exploit these scale economies by sharing banks and insurance agencies. Similarly, there are scale economies in the provision of transportation services, and firms can share a transportation firm. For example, a small firm can hire trucks from a trucking firm instead of purchasing its own truck fleet.

Public services also play a role in the development of firm clusters. The public sector is responsible for the development of the transportation network and the sewage system. If firms in an industry require specialized transport networks or sewage services, public-service costs will be lower if the firms cluster. The provision of public education has also played a role in the development of firm clusters. In England, some towns established spinning schools to provide specialized laborers for the textile industry. More recently, the universities and colleges in the Silicon Valley turn out a large number of engineers and computer scientists for the local computer industry.

Labor-Market Economies.   A second reason for localization economies is that a cluster of firms increases the efficiency of the labor market. Consider the computer industry, an industry with rapidly changing production processes and product demands. Every year, computer firms introduce new products; some are big sellers, and others fail. Eventually, the workers in the unsuccessful firms will move to the successful ones. A cluster facilitates the transfer of workers between computer firms for two reasons. First, workers in the cluster have relatively low search costs because (a) information about job openings is spread through informal channels (casual conversation at restaurants, bowling alleys, and baseball games) and (b) prospective employers are nearby, making formal job search relatively easy. Second, because of the physical proximity of employers, moving costs are relatively low: workers can easily switch to a different firm in the same city. Because search costs and moving costs are relatively low, firms in a cluster of computer firms can quickly fill their job vacancies and quickly increase production.

The television industry also benefits from labor-market economies. In a given season, some television programs are hits and others are failures. When it becomes clear which programs will continue to be produced, actors and technicians move from the unsuccessful programs to the successful ones. The concentrations of the television industry in Los Angeles and New York facilitate the transfer of laborers from one firm to another.

Communication Economies.   A third benefit of a cluster is that the cluster facilitates the exchange of information and the diffusion of technology. Workers from different firms exchange ideas about new products and new production techniques; the larger the number of workers in an industry, the greater the opportunity to exchange ideas in both formal and informal settings. A cluster of computer makers produces a large concentration of computer scientists and engineers who can exchange ideas while they work (e.g., the suppliers of intermediate inputs interact with the designers of new products) and play (e.g., the workers from unrelated firms "talk shop" while eating or jogging).

Where Do the Clusters Develop?   Localization economies cause the firms in some industries to locate close to one another. Most of these clusters are not isolated from other activities, but are typically in cities. As explained later in the chapter, some intermediate inputs are shared by firms in different industries, causing firms from different industries to cluster in cities. For example, the dressmaker cluster (around the buttonmaker) occurs in Manhattan because dressmakers also use business services (machine repair, banking, transportation services) utilized by nearby firms in other industries.

The Incubator Process.   Localization economies are responsible for the **incubator process**. A cluster of firms supplies a rich set of intermediate inputs and provides a nurturing environment where firms in an immature industry can develop new products and production technologies. In the early life of many industries, demand is unpredictable and production techniques are unsettled, so firms cluster to (a) exploit scale economies in the production of intermediate goods, (b) realize labor-market economies, and (c) exploit the opportunities to exchange ideas about products and production processes. As the industry matures, it develops standardized products and production processes, making large-scale production feasible. When firms internalize most of the production process, they move to locations that provide lower labor and land costs. This is also known as the **product cycle theory** of industrial location: new products are developed by small firms in clusters; when the product is standardized and produced on a larger scale, firms move to sites with lower labor and land costs.

As pointed out by Vernon (1975), a prime example of incubation is the radio industry. In the 1920s, the market for radios was unpredictable and firms were experimenting with alternative production processes. Mass production was impractical: the firms didn't know what kind of radios consumers wanted and hadn't developed efficient production techniques. Radio firms were small, agile, and nervous, and clustered in New York City to exploit scale economies in the production of intermediate goods. In the 1930s and 1940s, products were standardized and firms developed efficient methods of mass production. Firms moved their assembly facilities from New York to the Midwest, which had lower wages and better access to the national markets. Tube producers moved to the Northeast and the South, where labor costs were lower.

The computer industry is also subject to the incubation process. In the 1970s and early 1980s, the demand for computers was unpredictable and production techniques were being developed. Small computer firms clustered in the Silicon Valley in California and along Route 128 in Boston to exploit localization economies. The standardization of products and production processes allowed firms to set up large production facilities outside the clusters. Why did the clusters survive the exodus of production facilities? New products continued to be developed, and firms continued to cluster to exploit localization economies. Most firms maintained their research and development facilities in the clusters and set up branch plants for manufacturing and assembly.

Urbanization Economies

The second type of agglomerative economy in production, urbanization economies, occurs if the production costs of an individual firm decrease as the total output of the urban area increases. Urbanization economies differ from localization economies in two ways. First, urbanization economies result from the scale of the entire urban economy, not simply the scale of a particular industry. Second, urbanization economies generate benefits for firms throughout the city, not just firms in a particular industry.

Urbanization economies occur for the same reasons as localization economies. Firms from different industries share common input suppliers, allowing the realization of scale economies in the provision of business services (banking, insurance, real estate, hotels, building maintenance, printing, transportation) and public services (highways, mass transit, schools, fire protection).

Large cities also provide citywide labor-market economies: if fluctuations in the labor demands of different industries are not correlated, the large city provides a stable level of total employment. When a job disappears in one industry, it is likely to be replaced by a new job in another industry. Search costs and moving costs will be lower in large cities, so firms will be able to increase or decrease their work forces more easily.

As explained by Jacobs (1960), the urban environment also encourages innovation. Urban areas contain people with diverse backgrounds and interests. In such an environment, the exchange of ideas between people with different perspectives can lead to innovations in product design and production methods.

Empirical Estimates of Agglomerative Economies

How important are localization economies and urbanization economies? One approach to measuring agglomerative economies is to estimate the effects of changes in industry output and city size on labor productivity. The hypothesized relationship is

$$q = f(k, e, Q, N) \qquad (2-1)$$

where

q = output per worker in a particular industry
k = capital equipment per worker
e = education level of workers (a measure of labor skill and productivity)
Q = total output of the industry
N = total population of the metropolitan area

Output per worker should increase with capital per worker and the education level of the work force. If localization economies exist, output per worker will also increase with Q (industry output), and if urbanization economies exist, output per worker will increase with N (population). Statistical analysis can be used to estimate the independent effect of changes in Q on output per worker, that is, the increase in output per worker per unit change in Q, holding constant the other determinants of labor productivity (k, e, and N). Similarly, one can estimate the independent effect of changes in N on output per worker.

Henderson (1988) uses this approach to estimate both localization and urbanization economies. He measures localization economies as the elasticity of output per worker with respect to industry output (the percentage change in output per worker divided by the percentage change in industry output). For the electrical-machinery industry, the localization elasticity is 0.05, meaning that a 10 percent increase in the output of the electrical-machinery industry increases output per worker by about 0.5 percent. His elasticity estimates for other U.S. industries range from 0.02 for the pulp and paper industry to 0.11 for the petroleum industry.

Henderson also estimates the effects of changes in city size on labor productivity. His results suggest that urbanization economies are very small: the elasticity of labor productivity with respect to city size is close to zero. It appears that an increase in city size, by itself, does not increase productivity. Henderson concludes that larger cities are more productive because they have large concentrations of specific industries (localization economies), not simply because they are large (urbanization economies).

In another study, Segal (1976) uses 1967 data on manufacturers in 58 metropolitan areas to estimate the magnitude of urbanization economies. His hypothesized relationship is

$$G = f(K, L, N) \tag{2-2}$$

where

G = total output of the metropolitan area
K = total capital in the metropolitan area
L = total labor in the metropolitan area (adjusted for quality)
N = total population of the metropolitan area

In other words, he estimates a metropolitan production function, and includes city size in the production function to estimate the magnitude of urbanization economies. Segal concludes that large metropolitan areas (those with populations exceeding 2 million) are 8 percent more productive than smaller cities, meaning that urbanization economies are relatively large.

The results of Henderson and Segal are inconsistent. Henderson concludes that urbanization economies are very small, and Segal concludes that they're relatively large. Can the different results be reconciled? It's possible that Segal's estimate of large urbanization economies is actually the result of localization economies: the larger cities in his sample may have large concentrations of industries subject to localization economies. If so, it is localization economies, not urbanization economies, that make these larger cities more productive. Another possible explanation for the different results is that the two studies employ different statistical methods.

AGGLOMERATIVE ECONOMIES IN MARKETING: SHOPPING EXTERNALITIES

This section explains how agglomerative economies in marketing affect the development of cities. The preceding section of the chapter explains how agglomerative economies in production cause industrial firms to cluster, resulting in the development of large industrial cities. This section explains how agglomerative economies in marketing cause trading firms to cluster, resulting in the development of large market-based cities.

A **shopping externality** occurs if the sales of one store are affected by the location of other stores. Suppose that an isolated drug store relocates next to a grocery store. If both stores experience an increase in sales, they generate shopping externalities: each store attracts consumers to the retail cluster, generating benefits for the other store. These shopping externalities cause firms selling related products to form retail clusters. Some retail clusters cause the development of market cities. Other clusters occur within large cities, generating downtown shopping areas, malls, and shopping centers. There are two types of products that generate shopping externalities: imperfect substitutes and complements.

Imperfect Substitutes

Two goods are **imperfect substitutes** if they are similar, but not identical. Suppose that you've decided to buy a new sports car, but haven't decided whether to buy a Ford, a Chevy, or a Honda. The sports cars offered by the three companies are similar, but differ in performance, shape, color, and gadgetry. Because the differences between the cars are subtle, you must do your comparison shopping in person, spending time and money traveling to the three car dealers. If the three dealers form a cluster, they decrease the cost of comparison shopping, attracting consumers to the cluster.

There are many goods that are imperfect substitutes. Some examples are clothes, shoes, jewelry, and electronic equipment. For these goods, the clustering of firms selling similar products will decrease shopping costs and thus attract potential buyers. Some retailers cluster in the city center, while others cluster in shopping centers and malls.

Complementary Goods

Clustering also occurs when firms sell complementary goods. Complementary goods (e.g., pants and shoes) are often purchased on the same shopping trip. The shopper's travel cost will be lower if the pants store is near the shoe store. The shoe store will benefit from the presence of the pants store because together they provide one-stop shopping for consumers. Because of the benefits of one-stop shopping, firms selling complementary goods cluster in shopping centers, malls, and city centers.

Retail Clusters

The agglomerative economies associated with shopping generate several types of retail clusters. For some goods, retailers will form retail strips along arterial streets (e.g., auto rows). Other retailers cluster in shopping centers, malls, and city centers. These clusters provide a mix of both imperfect substitutes (different jewelry stores) and complements (food and drugs, clothing and shoes), allowing both comparison shopping and one-stop shopping. Retailers that choose isolated locations instead of clusters sell goods that are not subject to shopping externalities.

SUMMARY

1. Employment opportunities are concentrated in cities for three reasons: comparative advantage, internal scale economies, and agglomerative economies.

2. Comparative advantage results from differences in productivity. Trade will occur if the differences in productivity are large enough to offset transport costs. Trading firms (and urban areas) will develop if there are scale economies in transportation.

3. Internal scale economies result from factor specialization and indivisible inputs.
   a. If scale economies are large relative to transport costs, goods will be produced in factories.
   b. Factory workers will economize on travel costs by locating near factories, causing the development of factory cities.

4. The English wool industry illustrates the role of comparative advantage and scale economies in the development of cities.
   a. The Norman Conquest allowed England to exploit its comparative advantage in clothmaking, causing the development of cities involved in the production and trade of wool cloth.
   b. The development of the waterpowered fulling mill shifted production to rural areas and caused the development of villages and small trading cities.
   c. The mechanization of spinning and weaving generated scale economies that caused the development of large factories and factory cities.

5. The sewing machine increased scale economies in the production of clothing and shoes, causing home production to be replaced by factory production. Cities developed around the clothing factories and shoe factories.

6. There are three types of agglomerative economies: localization economies, urbanization economies, and shopping externalities.

7. Localization economies occur if the production costs of a particular firm decrease as industrywide output increases. There are three sources of localization economies.
   a. If there are scale economies in the production of an intermediate good for which transportation costs are relatively high, several firms will cluster around a single input supplier.
   b. If output per firm varies from year to year, a cluster of firms will facilitate the transfer of workers from one firm to another (labor-market economies).
   c. A cluster of firms improves communication, facilitating the exchange of information and the diffusion of innovations (communication economies).

8. Urban areas, with their rich set of intermediate inputs, provide a nurturing environment for immature industries (the incubator process).

9. Urbanization economies occur if the production costs of a particular firm decrease as the total output of the urban area increases. Urbanization economies result from the sharing of input suppliers (business services and public services), labor-market economies, and communication economies.

10. A shopping externality occurs if the sales of a particular store increase as other retailers move closer to the store. These agglomerative economies in marketing cause the clustering of retailers.
    a. Comparison shopping causes the clustering of firms selling imperfect substitutes.
    b. One-stop shopping causes the clustering of firms selling complementary goods.
    c. Retail clusters occur in downtowns, shopping centers, malls, and retail strips.

EXERCISES AND DISCUSSION QUESTIONS

1. In the section on comparative advantage, western workers produce twice as much wheat as eastern workers and three times as much cloth. Suppose that labor productivities change, as shown in the table below.

	Output per Labor Hour		Opportunity Costs of Production	
	East	West	East	West
Wheat	1	12		
Cloth	1	3		

   a. Complete the table: What are the opportunity costs of producing wheat and cloth in the East and the West?
   b. Assume that transport costs are zero and that the exchange rate is two bushels of wheat for one yard of cloth. If a western household switches one hour from cloth production to wheat production and exchanges half of its additional wheat for cloth, will the household be better off?
   c. Suppose that the time required to execute the trade in (b) is two thirds of an hour. Is trade still beneficial? At what transaction cost (time per trade) would the net gain from trade be zero?
   d. Under what conditions will the differences in labor productivity cause the development of cities?

2. In the section on internal scale economies, the factory produces cloth with an average labor time of 0.25 hours and travel speed is four round-trip miles per hour. Depict graphically the effects of the following changes on the market area of the cloth factory.
   a. Travel speed increases to eight round-trip miles per hour.
   b. The average labor time decreases to 0.125 hours (one eighth of an hour). The travel speed is eight round-trip miles per hour.

3. In the discussion of the cloth factory, there are no costs of capital and management: Workers are paid the entire "price" of cloth (0.25 units of wheat). Suppose instead that capital and management costs sum up to 0.25 hours per unit of cloth.
   a. What is the new price of cloth?
   b. Does the factory's market area increase or decrease? By how much?

4. Consider a region which produces and consumes fruit and ice. All resources are distributed uniformly throughout the region, and all people are equally productive in producing fruit and ice. There are scale economies in the production of ice, causing the development of an ice factory and a factory city.
   a. Suppose that the small refrigerator is introduced, decreasing the cost of producing ice at home. Explain the effects of this innovation on (i) the market area of the ice factory and (ii) the size of the city surrounding the ice factory.
   b. In the 1940s, the icebox (cooled by ice purchased from ice factories) was replaced by the refrigerator. So what?

5. Most people brew their own coffee, but purchase beer in stores. Why do grocery stores sell ready-to-drink beer, but not ready-to-drink coffee?

6. In the section on internal scale economies, scale economies in clothmaking cause the development of a factory city because workers economize on commuting costs by living close to the factory. Consider a region where most residents are retired and consume a single good (food) which is imported from another region.
   a. Will there be cities in the region?
   b. If there are cities, how will they differ from the cities that develop in regions where most people are employed?

7. Most of the dresses made in the United States are produced by large firms in suburban areas, not by small firms in city centers. Is this consistent with the notion of industry externalities and clusters? Hint: Is there a difference between a K mart dress and a dress produced by a small dressmaker?

8. Suppose that you are the economist for the city of Eggville. Describe a set of policies that will encourage the development of start-up firms in Eggville.

9. In the 1980s, a new product was introduced: video rentals. Are video rentals subject to shopping externalities? What are the implications for the location of video-rental stores?

10. Suppose that the outputs of beauty shops and pet-grooming salons are complementary, providing one-stop shopping for personal and pet maintenance. Betty is thinking about moving her beauty shop from an isolated location to a vacant building next to Peter's pet-grooming shop. In making her decision, she makes the following assumptions:
    i. If she moves, she will keep her current customers (20 people per week) and attract 25 percent of Peter's current customers.
    ii. Peter currently has 60 customers per week.
    iii. Excluding rent, Betty's profit per beauty treatment is $10.
    iv. Rent at the new location is $200 higher than her current rent.
    a. If Betty moves her beauty shop, will her profits increase or decrease?
    b. Suppose that if Betty moves next to Peter, 50 percent of her original customers will switch from George's grooming salon to Peter's. If Peter's profit per treatment is $8, how much would he be willing to bribe Betty to move in next door? Will the bribe be enough to induce Betty to make the move?

11. Suppose that you own a large mall. How would you use the lessons from question 10 to (*a*) choose tenants for the mall and (*b*) determine the rent to charge different tenants? Will you charge all tenants the same rent (per square foot of space)?

12. Another new product of the 1980s was fresh cookies served hot in cookie stores. Why did this new product (a substitute for homemade cookies) develop?

REFERENCES AND ADDITIONAL READINGS

History of the English Woolmaking Industry

Jenkins, D. T. *The West Riding Wool Textile Industry 1770–1835*. Leeds: Maney & Sons, 1975. Describes the transition of the clothmaking industry from the putting-out system to factory production.

Ponting, Kenneth G. *The Woolen Industry of South-West England*. Bath: Adams & Dart, 1971. Describes the early history of the English woolmaking industry.

Localization Economies

Clapp, J. M. "Endogenous Centers: A Simple Departure from the NUE Model." *Papers of the Regional Science Association* 54 (1984), pp. 13–24. Describes the process through which contacts between firms cause the development of a central business district and subcenters.

Hall, Peter, and Ann Markusen. *Silicon Landscapes.* Winchester, Mass.: Allen & Unwin, 1985.   Discusses the role of external scale economies in the location of high-technology industries.

Hoover, Edgar M. *Location Theory and the Shoe and Leather Industries.* Cambridge, Mass.: Harvard Univ. Press, 1937.   Discusses the role of scale economies in the location of the shoe and leather industries.

O'Hara, D. J. "Location of Firms within a Square Central Business District." *Journal of Political Economy* 85 (1977), pp. 1189–1207.   Discusses how interfirm contacts cause the development of a central business district.

Stephens, John D., and Brian Holly. "City System Behavior and Corporate Influences: The Headquarters Location of U.S. Industrial Firms 1955–1975." *Urban Studies* 18 (1981), pp. 285–300.

Tauchen, H., and Anne Witte. "An Equilibrium Model of Office Location and Contact Patterns." *Environment and Planning* 15 (1983), pp. 1311–26.   Discusses how interfirm contacts cause the development of a central business district.

Vernon, Raymond. "External Economies." In *Readings in Urban Economics, ed. M. Edel and J. Rothenberg.* New York: Macmillan, 1972.   A discussion of agglomerative economies and industry clusters.

Urbanization Economies

Carlino, Gerald A. *Economies of Scale in Manufacturing Location.* Boston: Martinus Nijhoff, 1978.

Higgs, Robert. "American Inventiveness, 1870–1920." *Journal of Political Economy* 79 (1971), pp. 661–67.

Jacobs, Jane. *The Economy of Cities.* New York: Random House, 1960.   Discusses why many innovations are developed in urban areas.

Noyelle, Thierry, and Thomas Stanback. *The Economic Transformation of American Cities.* Totawa, N.J.: Rowman and Allanheld, 1984.

Sveikauskas, L. "Interurban Differences in the Innovative Nature of Production." *Journal of Urban Economics* 6 (1979), pp. 216–27.

Empirical Estimates of Localization and Urbanization Economies

Henderson, J. V. "Efficiency of Resource Usage and City Size." *Journal of Urban Economics* 19 (1986), pp. 47–90.   Estimates the magnitude of localization and urbanization economies.

————.*Urban Development: Theory, Fact, and Illusion.* New York: Oxford University Press, 1988.   Chapter 5 provides estimates of localization economies and urbanization economies for the United States and Brazil. Other chapters discuss the theory of systems of cities and public-policy implications of localization and urbanization economies.

Moomaw, Ronald L. "Productivity and City Size: A Critique of the Evidence." *Quarterly Journal of Economics* 96 (1981), pp. 675–88.   Discusses statistical problems with the Segal and Sveikauskas analyses of urbanization economies.

Segal, David. "Are There Returns to Scale in City Size?" *Review of Economics and Statistics* 58 (1976). pp. 339–50. Estimates the magnitude of urbanization economies.

Sveikauskas, L. "The Productivity of Cities." *Quarterly Journal of Economics* 89 (1975), pp. 393–413.

Agglomerative Economies in Shopping

Eaton, B. Curtis, and Richard G. Lipsey. "Comparison Shopping and the Clustering of Homogeneous Firms." *Journal of Regional Science* 19 (1979), pp. 421–35. Discusses the role of comparison shopping in the location of retailers.

Stahl, Konrad. "Differentiated Products, Consumer Search, and Locational Oligopoly." *Journal of Industrial Economics* 31 (1982a), pp. 97–113. Discusses the effects of consumer search costs on the location of retailers.

————."Location and Spatial Pricing Theory with Nonconvex Transportation Cost Schedules." *Bell Journal of Economics* 13 (1982b), pp. 575–82. Shows that consumers are attracted to retail sites providing many goods, explaining the clustering of retailers.

CHAPTER 3

Where Do Cities Develop?

Let the river roll which way it will, cities will rise on its banks.

Ralph Waldo Emerson

Chapter 2 showed that cities develop because of comparative advantage, scale economies, and agglomerative economies. Cities develop around the concentrations of employment generated by firms, so the location choices of firms play a role in the location of cities. This chapter explores the location decisions of two types of firms. **Industrial firms** (e.g., sawmills, breweries, manufacturers, and bakeries) process raw materials and intermediate inputs into outputs. **Commercial firms** trade goods rather than producing them. The location decisions of industrial and commercial firms cause the development of different types of cities in different locations. The chapter also discusses the role of government in the location of cities.

COMMERCIAL FIRMS AND TRADING CITIES

The location decisions of commercial firms cause the development of trading cities. Trading firms collect goods from suppliers and distribute the goods to consumers, providing employment for salespeople and other intermediaries. Trading firms typically locate at transshipment points (ports, crossroads, railroad junctions, river junctions) because such locations offer convenient points for the collection and distribution of goods. Transportation firms move goods from place to place, providing employment at transshipment points for truckers, sailors, and longshoremen. Firms providing business services (banking, insurance, bookkeeping, machine repair) locate close to the trading and transportation firms that use their services.

The American fur trade was an important force in the development of cities along the Mississippi River. New Orleans, located at the mouth of the Mississippi River, provided a convenient transshipment point for American furs destined for European markets. In 1764, fur traders from New Orleans established St. Louis at the junction of the Missouri and Mississippi rivers as a central substation for the fur trade. By 1800, there were over 1,000 people in St. Louis, living in the middle of an almost unpopulated continent.

The experience of New York City illustrates the importance of trade in the development of cities. The city, which began as a fur-trading post for the Dutch, was taken over by the British in 1664. The city grew rapidly, along with other eastern cities, as a result of the flour trade with the West Indies. At the time of the war of 1812, New York and Philadelphia were about the same size. Following the war, New York grew rapidly and became the country's dominant city. Why?

The rapid growth of New York was caused by two factors that increased the volume of trade. First, New York State built the Erie Canal, which connected New York City with the Great Lakes and thus opened vast market areas to New York traders. Second, traders in New York developed innovative trading practices. One innovation was the auction sale: a British manufacturer consigned his goods to a U.S. auctioneer, who then sold the goods to U.S. merchants. The auction sale decreased prices because it eliminated the British exporter and the traditional U.S. importer. While Philadelphia and Boston passed laws that discouraged auction sales, New York allowed them. U.S. merchants responded by buying more goods from New York traders, so New York grew at the expense of Philadelphia and Boston. New York traders were also the first to establish regularly scheduled shipping across the Atlantic, which attracted more traders and shippers to the city.

Cities also developed as a result of the railroad. The spread of the railroad after 1830 gave merchants in Boston, Philadelphia, and Baltimore access to midwestern markets, so these cities diverted some trading activity from New York. In 1868, Kansas land speculators chose a site for a new city along the Chisholm Trail (the route for cattle drives from Texas to Kansas railheads), and persuaded the railroad company to extend their tracks to the site. By 1872, thousands of carloads of cattle were being shipped from the city, and Wichita was a booming cow town.

TRANSFER-ORIENTED INDUSTRIAL FIRMS

A **transfer-oriented firm** is defined as one for which transportation costs are the dominant factor in the location decision. Such a firm chooses the location that minimizes total transport costs, defined as the sum of **procurement costs** and **distribution costs.** Procurement costs are the costs of transporting raw materials from the input source to the factory. Distribution costs are the costs of transporting the firm's output from the factory to the consumer.

The classic model of a transfer-oriented firm has three assumptions:

1. **Single output.** The firm produces a fixed amount of a single good. The output is shipped from the factory to a marketplace at point M.

2. **Single transferable input.** The firm may use several inputs, but only one input is shipped from an input source (point F) to the factory. All other inputs are **ubiquitous** (available at all locations at the same price). The firm buys a fixed amount of each input.

3. **Fixed prices.** The firm is so small that it does not affect the prices of its inputs or outputs.

Under these three assumptions, the firm will maximize its profit by minimizing its transportation costs. The firm's profit equals total revenue (price times the quantity of output) less input costs and transport costs. Total revenue is the same at all locations because the firm sells a fixed amount of output at a fixed price. Input costs are the same at all locations because the firm buys fixed amounts of each input at fixed prices. The only costs that vary across space are procurement costs (input transport costs) and distribution costs (output transport costs). Therefore, the firm will choose the location that minimizes its total transport costs.

The firm's location choice is determined by the outcome of a tug-of-war. The firm is pulled toward the input source by low procurement costs, and pulled toward the market by low distribution costs. For the **resource-oriented** firm, the pull toward the input source is relatively strong, so the firm locates near its marketplace.

Resource-Oriented Firms

Table 3–1 shows the transport characteristics of a resource-oriented firm. The firm makes baseball bats, using five tons of wood to produce three tons of bats. The firm is involved in a weight-losing activity in the sense that the output is lighter than the transferable input. The **monetary weight** of the input is defined as the physical weight of the input (five tons) times the transportation rate ($1 per ton per mile) or $5 per mile. Similarly, the monetary weight of the output is three tons times $1 or $3 per mile. The firm is considered a resource-oriented firm because the monetary weight of its transferable input exceeds the monetary weight of its output.

Figure 3–1 shows the firm's transportation costs. If x is the distance from the forest to the factory, procurement costs are

$$PC = w_i \cdot t_i \cdot x \qquad (3-1)$$

that is, the monetary weight of the input (weight w_i times rate t_i) times the distance between forest and factory. The slope of the procurement-cost curve is the monetary weight of the input, so PC rises by $5 per mile, from zero at the forest to $50 at the market 10 miles away. If x_m is the distance between the forest and the market, distribution cost is

$$DC = w_o \cdot t_o \cdot (x_m - x) \qquad (3-2)$$

TABLE 3–1   Physical and Monetary Weights of a Resource-Oriented Firm

	Input (wood)	Output (bats)
Physical weight (tons)	5	3
Transport rate (cost per ton per mile)	$1	$1
Monetary weight (weight times rate)	$5	$3

FIGURE 3–1   Total Transport Costs for Resource-Oriented Firm

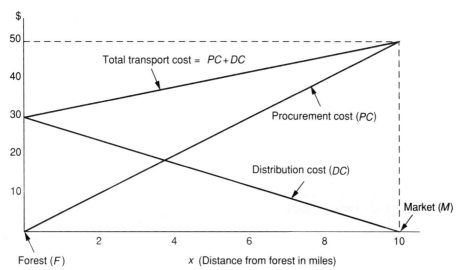

Total transport cost (the sum of Procurement cost and Distribution cost) is minimized at the forest because the monetary weight of the input ($5) exceeds the monetary weight of the output ($3). The weight-losing activity locates at its source of raw materials.

that is, the monetary weight of the output (weight w_o times rate t_o) times the distance from the factory to the market. The slope of the distribution-cost curve is the monetary weight of the output, so DC decreases by $3 per mile, from $30 at the forest (10 miles from the market) to zero at the market.

Total transport cost is the sum of procurement costs and distribution costs, as shown in Figure 3–1. Total transport cost is minimized at the forest site ($30). If the firm moves one mile away from the forest toward the market, its distribution cost decreases by $3 (the monetary weight of the output) but its procurement cost increases by $5 (the monetary weight of the input), so total transport cost increases by $2. Total cost is minimized at the forest site because the monetary weight of the input exceeds the monetary weight of the output. The resource-oriented firm will locate near its input source.

Weight-Losing Activities.   The bat firm is resource-oriented because it is a **weight-losing activity,** using five tons of wood to produce only three tons of bats. The costs of transporting wood are large relative to the costs of transporting the finished output, so the firm saves on transport costs by locating near the forest. In this case, the tug-of-war is won by the input source because there is more *physical* weight on the input side.

There are many other examples of weight-losing firms. Beet-sugar factories locate near sugar-beet farms because one pound of sugar beets generates only about 2.7 ounces of sugar. Onion dehydrators locate near onion fields because one pound of fresh onions becomes less than one pound of dried onions. Ore processors locate near mines because they use only a fraction of the materials extracted from the ground.

Other Resource-Oriented Activities. Some firms locate near input sources because inputs are relatively expensive to ship. Suppose that the physical weight of the transferable input equals the physical weight of the output but the unit cost of shipping the input exceeds the unit cost of shipping the output. The firm will locate near its input source because the monetary weight of the input will exceed the monetary weight of the output. The input will be more expensive to ship if it is more bulky, perishable, fragile, or hazardous than the output. Hoover (1975) provides several examples of such activities:

1. **Cotton baling.** The input (fluffy cotton) is more bulky than the output (baled cotton). Since the cost of shipping a ton of fluffy cotton exceeds the cost of shipping a ton of compacted cotton, the cotton baler is resource-oriented and locates near the cotton fields.

2. **Canning.** The input (raw fruit) is more perishable than the output (canned fruit). Since the cost of shipping one ton of perishable fruit (in refrigerated cars) exceeds the cost of shipping one ton of canned goods, canners locate near the fruit farms.

3. **Skunk deodorizing.** The input (fully armed skunks) is more fragile and hazardous than the output (disarmed skunks). Since the cost of shipping a ton of armed skunks exceeds the cost of shipping a ton of disarmed ones, the skunk deodorizer will locate near the skunk source.

A firm with a relatively bulky, perishable, fragile, or hazardous input will locate near its input source. The tug-of-war between input forces and output forces is won by the input source, not because the input is heavier, but because it is more expensive to ship.

Market-Oriented Firms

For a market-oriented firm, output transport costs are relatively large, so the firm locates near its output market. Table 3–2 shows the transportation characteristics of a market-oriented firm. The bottling company uses one ton of sugar and three tons of water (a ubiquitous input) to produce four tons of soft drinks.

Figure 3–2 shows the firm's transportation costs. The monetary weight of the output exceeds the monetary weight of the input by $3: as the firm moves toward the market, total transport cost decreases by $3 per mile, drop-

TABLE 3–2 Physical and Monetary Weights of a Market-Oriented Firm

	Input (sugar)	*Output (soft drinks)*
Physical weight (tons)	1	4
Transport rate (cost per ton per mile)	$1	$1
Monetary weight (weight times rate)	$1	$4

ping from $40 at the sugar plantation (point *F*) to $10 at the market. The firm is market-oriented because the monetary weight of the output exceeds the monetary weight of the input.

The bottling firm is market-oriented because it is a **weight-gaining activity.** The firm adds three tons of local water to one ton of sugar to produce four tons of soft drink, so the output is heavier than the transferable input (sugar). In this case, the tug-of-war is won by the market because there is more *physical* weight on the output side.

FIGURE 3–2 Total Transport Cost for Market-Oriented Firm

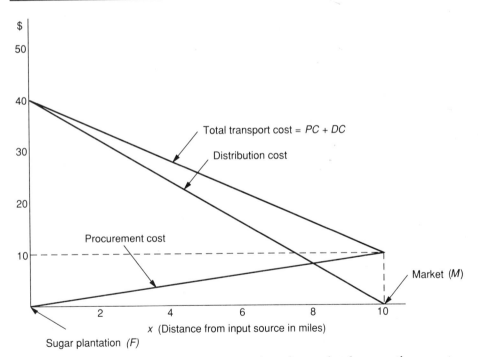

Total transport cost (*PC* + *DC*) is minimized at the market because the monetary weight of the output ($4) exceeds the monetary weight of the transferrable input ($1). The weight-gaining activity locates at its market.

Some firms locate near their markets because their output is relatively expensive to ship. If the physical weights are equal but the output is more costly to ship, the monetary weight of the output will exceed the monetary weight of the input and the firm will locate near its market. The costs of shipping the output will be relatively high if the output is relatively bulky, perishable, fragile, or hazardous. Hoover (1975) provides several examples of such firms:

1. **Automobile assembly.** The output (assembled automobiles) is more bulky than the inputs (metal, plastic, and rubber parts). The cost of shipping one ton of assembled automobiles exceeds the cost of shipping the ton of the metal, plastic, and rubber that goes into the automobiles.

2. **Bakery.** The bakery produces a relatively perishable output: although flour can be stored for months without spoiling, bread becomes stale after just a few days. A bakery locates near its market because it would be expensive to ship bread from a site near the flour mill to the marketplace in a timely manner.

3. **Weapons.** A weapons producer combines harmless inputs into a lethal output. The firm locates near its output market to avoid transporting the hazardous (or fragile) output over long distances.

A firm with a relatively bulky, perishable, fragile, or hazardous output will locate near its market. The tug-of-war is won by the output, not because it is heavier, but because it is more expensive to ship.

Intermediate Location?

The analysis of the transfer-oriented firm suggests that a firm will locate either at its input source (the resource-oriented firm) or at its market (the market-oriented firm). Will a transfer-oriented firm ever choose a location between its input source and its market?

A firm will be indifferent among all the sites between the input source and the market if two conditions are met. First, the monetary weight of the input is equal to the monetary weight of the output. Second, unit transport costs are independent of the distance shipped. If these two conditions are met, the slope of the procurement-cost curve will be equal to the slope of the distribution-cost curve, so the total-cost curve will be a horizontal line. Total transport cost will be the same at all locations, so the firm will be indifferent about all locations between its input source and the market.

The possibility of an intermediate location is eliminated by scale economies in transportation. Scale economies arise for two reasons:

1. **Terminal costs.** The fixed cost of a shipment is the sum of the costs of loading, unloading, and doing the paperwork. Because these costs are independent of the shipping distance, the average shipping cost decreases as the shipping distance increases.

2. **Line-haul economies.** The shipping cost per mile decreases as the

shipping distance increases, reflecting the efficiencies from using different modes. Firms use trucks (relatively high cost per mile) for short hauls, trains (lower costs per mile) for medium-length trips, and ships (low cost per mile) for long hauls.

Figure 3–3 shows procurement costs and distribution costs when there are scale economies in transportation. There is a fixed terminal cost per shipment, and the unit costs of shipping (t_i and t_o) decrease as the shipping distance increases. The slope of the procurement-cost curve decreases as the firm moves away from the input source, and the slope of the distribution-cost curve decreases as the firm moves away from the market. The total-cost curve is no longer a horizontal line but is bowed outward in the middle, so total costs are lower at the endpoints (the input source or the market) than at intermediate locations.

The presence of scale economies reinforces the tendency for firms to locate at input sources and markets. If there are scale economies in transporta-

FIGURE 3–3   Transport Cost with Declining Unit Costs

If there are terminal costs and declining unit transport costs, total transport cost ($PC + DC$) is minimized at either the forest or the market. Although the monetary weight of the input equals the monetary weight of the output, the firm locates at either F or M, not somewhere between the two points.

tion, it is more efficient to make one long trip (shipping either the input or the output the entire 10 miles between the input source and the market) instead of two short trips (shipping the input 5 miles and the output 5 miles).

Implications for the Development of Cities

The analysis of the transfer-oriented firm provides a simple rule for predicting the location choices of firms. If the monetary weight of the input exceeds the monetary weight of the output, the firm will locate at its input source. If the reverse is true, the firm will locate at its market. Of course, this rule is based on a simple model in which the firm has only a single transferable input and a single output. What about more complex location choices involving a firm with several input sources and markets? The general principles of this section apply to this more realistic case. The higher the costs of shipping inputs from or outputs to a particular location, the greater the pull toward that location.

The analysis of the transfer-oriented firm predicts the development of two types of cities. Resource-oriented firms locate near their raw-material sources, causing the development of **resource-based cities.** Some examples are lumber towns, steel towns, and food-processing towns. The analysis also suggests that as a city grows, it will attract market-oriented firms. The location decisions of these firms often generate cities that serve as **market centers.**

THE PRINCIPLE OF MEDIAN LOCATION

The classic model of the transfer-oriented firm assumes that the firm has a single input source and a single market. This section examines the location decisions of firms with several input sources and several markets. The most important concept is the **principle of median location.** According to this principle, the optimum location for a firm with several inputs and several markets is the **median transport location,** the location that splits the total monetary weight of the firm into two equal halves. At the median transport location, half the monetary weight comes from one direction and the other half comes from the other direction.

Location Choice with Multiple Markets

To explain the location choice of a firm with several markets, consider Ann, who makes and delivers pizzas. In choosing a site for her pizza parlor, Ann must consider the following:

   1. **Ubiquitous inputs.** All inputs (labor, dough, toppings) are ubiquitous (available at all locations for the same price), so input transport costs are zero.

2. **Pizza consumers.** Ann's customers are located along a highway. The price of pizzas is fixed, and every consumer demands one pizza per day.

3. **Delivery costs.** Ann delivers the pizza to her customers at no charge, making one trip per customer per day. The delivery cost is 50 cents per pizza per mile.

Ann will choose the location that minimizes total delivery cost.

Figure 3–4 shows the distribution of consumers along the highway. Distances are measured from the western end of the highway (point W). There are 2 customers at point W, 8 customers at point X (1 mile from W), 1 customer at Y (2 miles from W), and 10 customers at Z (9 miles from W). Since each customer buys one pizza and delivery cost is 50 cents per pizza per mile, the monetary weight of a particular location (the sales volume times the delivery cost per pizza per mile) is half the number of consumers at that location.

According to the principle of median location, Ann will minimize total transport costs at the median location. Because point Y divides the monetary weights into two equal halves, it is the median location. The monetary weight of locations to the west is $5 ($1 for W plus $4 for X), and the monetary weight

FIGURE 3–4   Pizza Delivery and the Principle of Median Location

W	X	Y	S		Z

Distance from W (miles)	0	1	2	3	9
Number of consumers	2	8	1		10
Monetary weight	$1	$4	$0.50		$5

Assumptions:

1. Every consumer purchases one pizza.
2. The delivery cost per pizza per mile is 50¢.
3. The firm delivers one pizza at a time.

Ann will locate her pizza parlor at point Y because it is the median location: she delivers 10 pizzas to consumers to the west of Y and 10 to consumers to the east of Y. A move from Y to S would decrease delivery costs for the 10 consumers at point Z (savings of $5), but would increase delivery costs for the 11 consumers at points W, X, and Y (increase of $5.50). A move in the opposite direction would also increase total transport costs.

of locations to the east is $5 ($5 for Z). The median location divides Ann's customers into two equal halves: she has 10 customers to the east and 10 to the west.

To show that the median location minimizes total transport costs, suppose that Ann starts at the median location and then moves to point S, one mile east of Y. As she moves to the east, there is good news and bad news. The good news is that she spends less on delivery to point Z: she saves 50 cents per trip to Z, saving a total of $5 in eastward delivery costs. The bad news is that westward delivery costs increase: she pays 50 cents more per trip to points W, X, and Y; since there are 11 customers to the west of S, her westward delivery costs increase by a total of $5.50 ($1 more for W, $4 more for X, and 50 cents more for Y). Since the increase in westward delivery costs exceeds the decrease in eastward costs, the move from Y to S increases total delivery costs. The same is true for a move in the opposite direction: if Ann moves from Y toward W, total delivery costs will increase.

Why does the median location minimize total transport costs? It is the minimum-cost location because it splits pizza consumers into two equal parts. At any location to the east of Y, there will be more consumers to the west of the pizza parlor than to the east. As Ann moves eastward away from Y, she moves further away from 11 customers but moves closer to only 10 customers. Similarly, a westward move will cause her to move closer to 10 customers but further from 11 customers. In general, any move away from the median location will increase delivery costs for *the majority* of consumers, so total costs increase.

It is important to note that the distances between the consumers are irrelevant to the firm's location choice. For example, if the Z consumers were located 100 miles from W instead of 9 miles from W, the median location would still be point Y. Total delivery costs would still be minimized (at a higher level of course) at point Y.

Median Location and Growth of Cities

The principle of median location provides another explanation of why large cities become larger. Suppose that a firm delivers its product to consumers in five different cities. In Figure 3–5, there is a large city at location L and

FIGURE 3–5 Median Location in the Large City

Locations	S_1	S_2	S_3	S_4		L
Demand	4	4	4	4		17

The median location is in the large city (L). Any move to the left of point L will increase travel costs for the majority of consumers, increasing total transportation costs.

four small cities at locations S_1, S_2, S_3, and S_4. The firm sells 4 units in each small city and 17 units in the large city. The median location is in the large city, even though the large city is at the end of the line. A one-mile move westward from L would decrease transport costs by $16 (as the firm moves closer to consumers in the small cities) but would increase transport costs by $17 (as the firm moves away from consumers in the large city). The lesson from this example is that the concentration of demand in large cities causes large cities to grow.

Transshipment Points and Port Cities

The principle of median location also explains why some industrial firms locate at transshipment points. A transshipment point is defined as a point at which a good is transferred from one transport mode to another. At a port, goods are transferred from trucks or trains to ships; at a railroad terminal, goods are transferred from trucks to the train.

Figure 3–6 shows the location options for a sawmill. The firm harvests logs from locations A and B, processes the logs into lumber, and then sells the lumber in an overseas market at point M. Highways connect points A and B to the port, and ships travel from the port to point M. The sawmill is involved in a weight-losing activity: the monetary weights of the inputs are $15 for point A and $15 for point B, and the monetary weight of the output is $10.

FIGURE 3–6   Sawmill Locates at Port

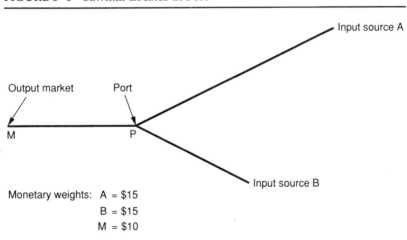

Monetary weights: A = $15
                   B = $15
                   M = $10

The firm locates its sawmill at the port (P) because it is the median transport location. A move from P toward either A or B would increase output transport costs by $10 without affecting input transport costs. A move from P toward M would increase input transport costs by $30 but decrease output transport costs by only $10.

Where will the firm locate its sawmill? Although there is no true median location, the port is closest to a median location. If the firm starts at the port (P), it could move either toward one of its input sources or to its market.

1. **Toward input sources A or B.** A one-mile move from P toward point A would cause offsetting changes in the costs of transporting logs from A and B. Because output transport costs would increase by $10, the port location is superior to locations between P and A. The same argument applies for a move from P toward B.

2. **To market (M).** Unless the firm wants to operate a floating sawmill, it would not move to points between the port and its overseas market at M. It could, however, move all the way to the market. A move from P to M would decrease output transport costs by $10 per mile of distance between M and P (the monetary weight of output) and increase input transport costs by $30 per mile (the monetary weight of the inputs). Transport costs would increase by $20 per mile, so the port location is superior to the market location.

Although the sawmill is involved in a weight-losing activity, it will locate at the port instead of one of its input sources. The port location is efficient because it provides a central collection point for the firm's inputs.

There are many examples of port cities that developed as a result of the location decisions of industrial firms. Seattle started in 1880 as a sawmill town: firms harvested trees in western Washington, processed the logs in Seattle sawmills, and then shipped the wood products to other states and countries. Baltimore was the nation's first boomtown: flour mills processed wheat from the surrounding agricultural areas for export to the West Indies. Buffalo was the midwestern center for flour mills, providing consumers in eastern cities with flour produced from midwestern wheat. Wheat was shipped from midwestern states across the Great Lakes to Buffalo, where it was processed into flour for shipment, by rail, to cities in the eastern United States. In contrast with Baltimore, which exported its output (flour) by ship, Buffalo imported its input (wheat) by ship.

Median Location and Cities

The principle of median location explains the development of several types of cities. If the median transport location is an input source, a **resource-based city** will form around the input source. If the median location is in the center of the region, a **regional center** will develop. If the median location is the transshipment point, a **port city** will develop. If the median location is in an existing city, the city will grow.

FIRMS ORIENTED TOWARD LOCAL INPUTS

An input is considered local if it cannot be efficiently transported from one location to another. Examples of local inputs are energy, labor, intermediate goods, and local public services. A firm heavily dependent on a local input bases its location decision on the availability of inexpensive local inputs: an energy-intensive firm chooses a site with inexpensive energy, and a labor-intensive firm chooses a site with inexpensive labor. Such firms ignore transportation costs because they are a relatively small part of their total costs.

Energy Inputs

In the first half of the 19th century, energy was a local input. The waterwheel was the first device used to generate nonhuman mechanical energy. The waterwheel, which was turned by waterfalls and fast-moving streams, provided power for production facilities located along rivers and streams. Textile manufacturers set up factories along small backcountry streams in New England and used waterwheels to power their machinery. Among the cities that developed as a result of the waterwheel are Lowell, Lawrence, Holyoke, and Lewiston.

The development of the steam engine in the second half of the 19th century made energy a transferable input. The steam engine could be operated anywhere, with the only constraint being the availability of coal to fuel the engine. Some energy-intensive manufacturers located near the coal mines in Pennsylvania. Others located along navigable waterways and shipped coal from the mines to their factories. The steam engine allowed New England textile firms to shift from the backcountry waterfall sites to sites along navigable waterways. Production shifted to the Fall River–New Bedford area along the south coast of New England. After the development of the railroad, firms were able to move to production sites connected by rail to the coal fields.

The development of electricity affected the location patterns of manufacturers. Because electricity can be transmitted over distances of several hundred miles, a firm can use the energy generated from waterpower without locating along a backcountry stream. Similarly, a firm can use coal resources without shipping the bulky fuel from the mine to its factory. In general, the development of electricity decreased the importance of energy considerations in location decisions. The activities for which energy considerations are still important are energy-intensive activities such as the production of aluminum and artificial abrasives. Such activities are attracted to regions that offer inexpensive energy. The Pacific Northwest, with its abundant and inexpensive hydroelectric power, attracts some energy-intensive activities.

Labor

There are practical limits on how far laborers are willing to commute, so labor is a local input. A labor-intensive firm, defined as a firm in which labor costs are a large fraction of total costs, chooses a location with low labor costs. Note that the choice is based on labor costs, not simply wages. A high-wage location will be efficient if the labor productivity is high enough to justify the higher wages. In other words, the firm bases its location decision on labor cost *per unit of output*, not simply the hourly wage.

Labor costs differ across space for four reasons. First, firms must compensate their workers for any undesirable features of the local environment. If an area has relatively dirty air or foul weather, workers will demand relatively high wages. Second, areas with strong labor unions generally have higher wages. Third, because households are not perfectly mobile, some areas will have an excess supply of labor and thus relatively low wages. Fourth, some areas have activities subject to **joint labor supply:** households move to locations that provide a job for the household's primary worker, increasing the supply of secondary workers. In colonial Massachusetts, the area north of Boston attracted men to sailing and fishing jobs. The resulting surplus of female workers decreased the wages of jobs held by women. Shoemakers moved to the area to take advantage of its low wages.

There are many examples of firms that base their location decisions primarily on labor costs. When advances in energy technology reduced their dependency on local waterpower, many textile firms moved from the high-wage New England states to low-wage southern states. More recently, apparel and shoe firms have moved overseas or to sites near the Mexican border to take advantage of inexpensive labor. The location decisions of these labor-intensive industries cause the development of cities in areas where labor is inexpensive.

Amenities, Migration, and Labor Costs

Some firms are indirectly attracted to sites that provide amenities such as good weather, high-quality schools, low crime rates, a clean environment, and cultural opportunities. If workers migrate to locations offering these amenities, the resulting excess supply of labor will decrease wages and attract labor-oriented firms to the area. In this case, the firm's location choice depends on the location choices of its work force. Instead of workers following firms, firms follow workers. Graves (1979) and Porell (1982) provide empirical support for this phenomenon.

Amenities are most important for firms that employ high-income workers. Because demands for these amenities are income-elastic, high-income workers are attracted to locations with amenities, and the firms employing these people follow. For example, research and development firms employ engineers and computer scientists, many of whom place a high value on good weather, high-quality local schools, a clean environment, and cultural opportunities. One explanation for the shift of employment from northern states to the southern and western states is that rising income has increased the demand for certain amenities, causing workers to move to areas that provide these amenities.

Intermediate Inputs—Localization and Urbanization Economies

Some firms are drawn to locations that provide intermediate inputs. As explained in Chapter 2 (Why Do Cities Exist?), localization economies generate clusters of firms in the same industry. By sharing the suppliers of intermediate inputs, firms in the cluster exploit scale economies in the production of specialized inputs. The cluster attracts both the demanders of intermediate inputs (dressmakers, corporate headquarters, research and development facilities) and the suppliers of the inputs (buttonmakers, advertising agencies, law firms, testing facilities). Firms in the cluster also exploit scale economies in the provision of specialized business services and local public services.

Urbanization economies cause firms from different industries to cluster in cities. The firms in cities exploit scale economies in the provision of business services (machine repair, banking, insurance, transportation, employment agencies) and local public services (transportation facilities, schools).

Several Local Inputs

How does a firm with several local inputs choose among the alternative locations? The firm's location choice is determined by the outcome of a tug-of-war between forces pulling the firm toward its different local inputs (labor, energy, intermediate goods). The strength of the pull toward a particular input source depends on (a) the relative importance of the input to the firm and (b) the spatial variation in the input price. The greater the importance of the input and the price variation, the stronger the pull toward a particular input source.

Consider a firm that has two local inputs: labor and energy. The firm is pulled toward city L (which has a low wage) and city E (which has inexpensive energy). The forces pulling the firm toward L will win the tug-of-war if (a) the firm's labor consumption is large relative to its energy consumption (the firm is labor intensive) and (b) the difference in the wage (controlling for productivity differences) is large relative to the difference in the price of energy.

Location Choices and Land Rent

How do the location choices of input-oriented firms affect the land market? If a particular location offers a desirable mix of local inputs, it will attract input-oriented firms. The resulting increase in the demand for land will increase the equilibrium price of land. Therefore, the advantages of a particular site (inexpensive labor, access to intermediate inputs) will be offset, in part, by higher land costs. For example, a firm in the city center can economize on intermediate inputs by locating close to banks, law firms, and advertising agencies, but it also pays more for land. Part 2 of the book will examine the factors that determine the equilibrium price of land.

TRANSPORT COSTS VERSUS LOCAL-INPUT COSTS

This chapter divides industrial firms into two types: firms that base their location decisions exclusively on transport costs (transfer-oriented firms) and firms that base their location decisions exclusively on local input costs (input firms). Table 3–3 summarizes the results of the chapter, listing the various types of transfer-oriented and input-oriented firms.

In the real world, things are not so tidy. Most firms cannot be easily classified with respect to their location orientation. For most firms, location decisions are based on both transport costs and local input costs. Since transport costs and input costs vary across space, the typical location choice requires a trade-off between transport costs and input costs.

Trade-Off between Transport Costs and Local-Input Costs

To explain the location choice of a firm that considers both transport costs and input costs, consider a decision about where to locate an auto-assembly factory. Suppose the firm has the following characteristics:

> 1. **Inputs and output.** The input source is the same as the market: as shown in Figure 3–7, point B is both the market and the source of transferable inputs.

TABLE 3–3   Summary of Location Orientation

Orientation	Relevant Characteristic	Example
Transfer orientation	Transport cost large fraction of total cost	
Resource orientation	Weight loss	Bat factory
	Bulk loss	Cotton baling
	Perishability loss	Canning
	Hazard (fragility) loss	Deodorizing skunks
Market orientation	Weight gain	Bottling
	Bulk gain	Auto assembly
	Perishability gain	Baking
	Hazard (fragility) gain	Explosives
Local-input orientation	Transport costs small fraction of total costs	
Energy	Energy-intensive production	Aluminum
Labor	Labor-intensive operation	Textiles
Intermediate inputs		
Specialized inputs	Localization economies	Dressmakers
Business services	Urbanization economies	Corporate headquarters
Amenity orientation	Workers sensitive to weather, recreation, high-quality schools, low crime rates, clean environment	Research and development

FIGURE 3–7   Transport Costs versus Labor Costs: Transfer Orientation

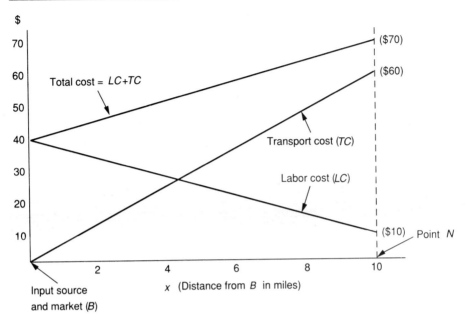

Total cost (the sum of transport cost and labor cost) is minimized at point B (the location of the input and the output market). The transfer-oriented firm locates at B because the spatial variation in transport cost is large relative to the variation in labor cost.

---

2. **Transport costs.** The monetary weights of inputs and outputs sum up to $6. Total transport costs rise from zero at point B to $60 at point N (10 miles from point B).

3. **Local input.** Labor costs vary across space. As the firm moves away from B, labor costs decrease by $3 per mile, dropping from $40 at point B to $10 at point N.

As shown in Figure 3–7, total cost (transport cost plus labor cost) is minimized at B because transport costs are large *relative to* labor costs. As the firm moves from point B toward point N, the savings in labor costs ($3 per mile) are less than the increase in transport costs ($6 per mile). Because the spatial variation in transport costs is relatively large, the firm chooses point B, close to its input sources and market.

Change in Orientation: Decrease in Transport Costs

Figure 3–8 shows the effect of a decrease in transport costs on the firm's location choice. Transport costs fall to one fourth of their original level (from

FIGURE 3–8   Switch from Transfer Orientation to Input Orientation

A decrease in transport costs causes the firm to switch from transfer orientation to input orientation. Total cost ($LC + TC$) is minimized at $x = 10$ because the spatial variation in labor cost is large relative to the spatial variation in transport cost.

$6 per mile to $1.50 per mile), decreasing the slope of the transport-cost curve from 6.0 to 1.5. The slope of the total-cost curve is negative instead of positive: a one-mile move away from B generates a net savings of $1.50 (a $1.50 increase in transport costs is combined with a $3.00 decrease in labor cost), so the firm will move to the low-wage location. In other words, the decrease in transport costs transforms the firm from a transfer-oriented firm to an input-oriented firm.

In the last several decades, many industries have switched from transfer orientation to input orientation. Firms have moved from locations close to input sources and markets to locations with inexpensive local inputs. The changes in location orientation resulted from innovations in transportation and production.

Innovations in Transportation. Improvements in transport technology decreased the costs of transporting both inputs and outputs. For example, the development of fast ocean ships and container technology (shipping freight in large, standardized containers instead of small bundles) increased the efficiency of ocean shipping and decreased the unit cost of transportation (cost per ton per mile). Similarly, improvements in rail, trucks, and planes decreased unit freight costs. For some firms, the decrease in transport costs was large enough to cause a switch from transfer orientation to local-input orientation. These firms then based their location decisions on access to inexpensive local inputs rather than access to markets or inputs. A recent example is the movement of the assembly operations of many U.S. manufacturers to sites along the Mexican border.

Innovations in Production. Improvements in production techniques decreased the physical weight of inputs. As the weight of inputs decreased, total transport costs decreased and some transfer-oriented firms became local-input firms. These firms moved from sites with low transport costs to ones with inexpensive local inputs. An example is the U.S. steel industry. Over the last several decades, the amount of coal and ore required to produce one ton of steel has decreased steadily, a result of improved steel-making methods and the use of scrap metal (a local input) instead of iron ore (a transferable input). As the physical weight of inputs decreased, transport costs decreased relative to labor costs and some firms became oriented to local inputs. Many steel plants are now located in low-wage countries (Brazil, Korea, Mexico), far from both raw materials and steel markets.

Location Orientation and Growth Patterns

Changes in transport costs affect economic growth patterns. As transport costs decrease, the relative attractiveness of a resource-rich region decreases, causing firms to move to areas with inexpensive local inputs. The steel industry has moved from the eastern United States, with its rich coal and ore deposits, to Japan and Korea, which have neither coal nor ore deposits. The steel industry made the move because the relative importance of transport costs decreased: steel firms moved to areas with lower wages because the savings in labor costs exceeded the increase in transport costs (for ore, coal, and steel). Similarly, manufacturers have moved from the United States to Asia and Mexico, far from U.S. markets, because the savings in labor costs dominate the increase in transport costs.

EMPIRICAL WORK AND CASE STUDIES

This section discusses some of the facts relating to recent location choices. The first two parts examine the location decisions of firms in two branches of the computer industry, semiconductor manufacturers and computer makers. The third part summarizes a study of the factors in the location of the electrical-equipment industry, and the fourth part discusses recent studies of the effects of taxes on location choices. The final part summarizes a case study of the decision to site GM's new Saturn plant near Nashville, Tennessee.

The Semiconductor Industry

The semiconductor industry illustrates some of the complexities of location choices in modern industry. The industry's output is light and compact relative to its value (i.e., it has a low bulk:value ratio) so transport costs are relatively unimportant in location decisions. More important are localization economies and access to different types of labor.

As explained by Castells (1988), the making of semiconductors involves several distinct operations that require three different types of labor:

1. **Research and development.** Engineers and scientists design new circuits and prepare the circuits for implantation into silicon chips.
2. **Wafer fabrication.** Skilled technicians and manual workers make the chips, which hold the circuits.
3. **Assembly into components.** Unskilled workers assemble the chips into electronic components.

Many semiconductor firms divide their operations into three parts. Some firms locate their research and development facilities in the Silicon Valley to exploit the localization economies generated by the large concentration of semiconductor firms. The Silicon Valley also provides amenities that make it a desirable location for engineers and scientists. Most advanced manufacturing (chip production) takes place located outside the Silicon Valley. For example, National Semiconductor has manufacturing facilities in Utah, Arizona, and Washington State; Intel has plants in Oregon, Arizona, and Texas; Advanced Micro Devices has a plant in Texas. These facilities are located in areas that provide (a) a plentiful supply of skilled manual laborers, (b) an environment attractive to engineers and technicians, and (c) easy access, by air transportation, to the Silicon Valley. The third operation of semiconductor firms, assembly, usually takes place overseas in locations that have a plentiful supply of low-skilled workers (e.g., Southeast Asia).

Computer Manufacturers

The splitting of manufacturing operations also occurs among computer makers. Hekman (1985) has studied the location decisions of firms producing large mainframe computers. The five largest firms, which control over 95 percent of the U.S. market, have their main research and design facilities in large metropolitan areas: Boston, New York, and Philadelphia each have one facility, and Minneapolis has two facilities. Because of the frequent design changes in mainframe computers, there is a great deal of nonroutine communication between designers and manufacturers, so proximity between the design and fabrication operations is important. Four of the five mainframe makers assemble their computers near their research and design facilities.

In contrast, peripheral equipment (terminals, tape drives, and printers) are produced in branch plants outside the home metropolitan area. Because peripherals are not subject to rapid design changes, they can be produced far from the design facilities (e.g., in Tennessee, Nebraska, South Dakota, Utah, North Carolina, Florida, and Michigan). Similarly, individual computer components are standardized inputs and are produced in Mexico, Brazil, Hong Kong, Taiwan, and Puerto Rico.

The Relative Importance of Local Inputs—Empirical Results

On a theoretical level, all local inputs (labor, energy, intermediate inputs) influence location choices. Which local inputs are the most important? A number of recent empirical studies of location decisions address this question.

Carlton (1979) examines the location choices of firms in three input-oriented industries: plastics products, electronic transmitting equipment, and electronic components. These industries have relatively low transport costs, so they are oriented toward local inputs, not output markets or natural resources. Carlton hypothesizes the following relationship between the number of new firms in a particular metropolitan area (the number of "births") and the characteristics of the metropolitan area:

$$N = f\ (W, E, Q, G, T, I, U) \tag{3-3}$$

where

N = number of new firms in a particular industry
W = metropolitan wage
E = unit energy cost
Q = metropolitanwide output of the industry
G = number of engineers in the metropolitan area
T = the tax level of the metropolitan area
I = measure of incentive programs offered by government to new business (revenue bonds, subsidized loans, tax exemptions)
U = metropolitan unemployment rate

In other words, the number of births depends on the costs of local inputs (W and E), localization economies (as measured by Q, the total output of the industry), the technical expertise of the area (as measured by G, the number of engineers), government tax policy (T and I), and the health of the local economy (as measured by the unemployment rate).

Table 3–4 shows Carlton's results for the electrical-components industry, reported as the elasticities of the number of births with respect to the various location factors. The elasticity of the number of births with respect to the wage is -1.07: a 10 percent increase in the metropolitan wage decreases the number of births by 10.7 percent. The elasticities for energy costs are lower, from -0.38 for natural gas to -0.95 for electricity. The elasticity for industry output (0.43) suggests that localization economies are important: the number of births increases as the size of the industry increases. The technical expertise of the metropolitan area (measured by the number of engineers) also affects the number of new firms.

Carlton's results suggest that tax policies do not affect the location deci-

TABLE 3–4   Relative Strengths of Location Factors

Variable	Elasticity of Number of Births with Respect to Variable
Wage	−1.07
Energy costs	−0.38 to −0.95
Output of industry	0.43
Number of engineers	0.25
Taxes	close to zero
Government incentives	close to zero

SOURCE: Dennis W. Carlton, "The Location and Employment Choices of New Firms: An Econometric Model," in *Interregional Movements and Regional Growth*, ed. William C. Wheaton (Washington, D.C.: The Urban Institute, 1979), pp. 13–50.

sions of firms producing Electronic Components. The elasticities for the tax and incentive variables are close to zero, implying that metropolitan areas with low taxes and lucrative incentive packages do not experience higher birth rates. These results are consistent with earlier studies of the influence of taxes on location decisions.

Carlton's results for the other two industries (plastics products and electronic transmitting equipment) were similar. The most important location factors were the wage, energy costs (less important for electronic transmitting equipment), industry output, and technical expertise.

Taxes and Location Choices

Do taxes affect location decisions? Until recently, the common view among economists was that taxes didn't matter. More recent evidence casts some doubt on this conclusion.

In a review of recent studies of location decisions, Newman and Sullivan (1988) cite several studies that provide evidence of a strong connection between taxes and location choices. The results of Bartik (1985) suggest that corporate and property taxes affect location choices, with the corporate tax having a stronger effect. Helms (1985) examines the effects of taxes *and* expenditures on location decisions, and found that the effect of a tax depends on how the tax revenue is spent. An increase in taxes increases the relative attractiveness of a jurisdiction if the money is spent on local public services (e.g., highways, education, public health and safety), but decreases the relative attractiveness of the jurisdiction if the money is spent on redistributional programs for the poor.

A Case Study—The Location of GM's Saturn Plant

In 1985, General Motors announced that its new Saturn plant would be located in Spring Hill, Tennessee, a crossroads community about 30 miles from Nashville. The plant, which will cost several billions of dollars to build, will employ about 3,000 workers and support thousands of jobs in the Nashville area. Why did GM choose Nashville over the dozens of other communities that sought the plant?

A case study by Bartik, Becker, Lake, and Bush (1987) suggests that the most important factor in the site choice was labor costs. A labor contract between GM and its unionized workers stipulates that the Saturn workers will be paid the same wage regardless of the plant's location, so GM would not decrease its own wage bill by locating in Tennessee, a state with low wages. However, GM will purchase a large fraction of its inputs from nearby suppliers, who will pay low wages and pass on the savings to GM.

The first step in the case study addressed the issue of transportation costs and market access. The authors estimated the costs of shipping finished cars from hundreds of alternative production sites to GM's markets in the continental United States. Based on 1984 sales figures, the cost-minimizing location (the location offering the best market access) was Indianapolis, Indiana. Based on the distribution of projected sales in the year 2000, the location offering the best market access was Terre Haute, Indiana. The shift from Indianapolis to Terre Haute reflects the shift in population and car consumers to the southern and western areas of the United States.

The second part of the study incorporated labor costs and taxes into the analysis. The authors estimated labor costs and taxes for production sites that provided reasonable access to GM's markets (a total of 130 sites in seven different states). Table 3–5 shows the costs (expressed as costs per car) for one site in each of the seven states.

    1. **Transportation costs.** The variation in transportation costs among the seven sites was relatively small. The gap between the lowest cost site (Terre Haute) and the most expensive site (Kalamazoo) was only $17 per

TABLE 3–5   Case Study of GM's Location of Saturn Plant

| | *Estimated Cost: Dollars per Car* | | | |
	Average Transport Costs (to markets)	*Labor Costs for Local Suppliers*	*State and Local Taxes (excluding subsidies)*	*Total Measured Costs*
Nashville, TN	426	159	118	703
Lexington, KY	423	186	106	715
St. Louis, MO	419	172	134	725
Bloomington, IL	417	202	162	781
Kalamazoo, MI	430	244	116	790
Terre Haute, IN	413	209	168	790
Marysville, OH	427	219	169	815

SOURCE: Timothy J. Bartik, Charles Becker, Steve Lake, and John Bush, "Saturn and State Economic Development," *Forum for Applied Research and Public Policy*, Spring 1987, pp. 29–40.

car. Nashville was ranked fifth, with transport costs only $13 per car higher than Terre Haute.

2. **Labor costs for local suppliers.** The variation in labor costs was relatively large. The difference between the lowest cost site (Nashville) and the highest cost site (Kalamazoo) was $85 per car.

3. **State and local taxes.** The table shows the tax costs per car in the absence of special subsidies and exemptions. The difference between the highest tax site (Marysville) and the lowest tax site (Lexington) was $63 per car. Nashville was ranked third, with tax costs $12 per car higher than Lexington.

The case study suggests that in the absence of special tax treatment, Nashville was the lowest cost site. The sum of its transportation, local labor, and tax costs was $12 less per car than Lexington, the second-ranked site, and $87 less than Terre Haute, the site that minimizes transportation costs. Nashville's slight disadvantage in market access is offset by its lower labor costs.

Tennessee offered three types of inducements to GM. The first was a $30 million highway project that connected the plant with Interstate 65. The second was a subsidized job-training program for Saturn workers, worth about $4 per car. The third was a program of property-tax subsidies, worth about $30 per car. Although these subsidies would not have been necessary in the absence of similar subsidies from other states, it appears that Tennessee offered them to stay competitive with the other states bidding for the plant.

THE ROLE OF GOVERNMENT IN THE LOCATION OF CITIES

Not all cities develop as a result of the location decisions of profit-seeking firms. Some cities owe their existence to government policies. Government affects the location of cities in several ways. First, governments pick the sites for administrative offices, causing concentrations of government jobs in capital cities. In the United States, many state governments chose vacant sites for their capitols, creating instant capital cities. Second, the siting of public facilities such as universities and prisons generates concentrations of jobs for guards and teachers.

Some cities develop as a result of differences in legal environments. During colonial times, several cities along the eastern seaboard thrived on illegal trade with the West Indies. Under the British Navigation Acts, trade with the French in the West Indies was restricted. The British authorities made little effort to enforce the trade regulations in the colonies, so smuggling between the colonies and the West Indies flourished. British traders complained that because colonial traders ignored the Navigation Acts, they had an unfair advantage over their British competitors.

Some state governments have exploited differences in legal environments to stimulate growth. The state of Nevada has used liberal divorce laws and legalized gambling to stimulate the growth of its cities near the California border. In 1900, the state established itself as the state with the most liberal divorce laws and kept one step ahead of other states as they liberalized their divorce laws. The divorce industry was the primary force in the early development of Reno, 12 miles from the California border. When the divorce traffic slowed during the depression, the state legalized gambling as a means of stimulating the state's economy. The gambling industry contributed to the growth of Reno, Las Vegas, and Lake Tahoe. The cities of Reno and Lake Tahoe cater to customers from Northern California, while Las Vegas caters to customers from Southern California.

SUMMARY

1. Cities develop around the concentrations of employment generated by firms, so the location choices of firms play a role in the location of cities.

2. Trading firms, which collect goods from suppliers and distribute them to consumers, locate at transshipment points. The location of trading and transportation firms explains the development of port cities and junction cities.

3. A transfer-oriented firm spends a relatively large amount on transport costs and chooses the location that minimizes total transport costs.

   a. A resource-oriented firm has relatively high transport costs for its inputs, so it locates near its input source. The location choices of resource-oriented firms cause the development of resource-based cities and port cities.

   b. A market-oriented firm has relatively high transport costs for its output, so it locates near its market. The location choices of market-oriented firms cause the development of port cities and the growth of existing cities.

4. According to the principle of median location, a market-oriented firm locates at its median transport location, defined as the location that splits its customers into two halves.

   a. This principle explains why big cities grow: the median location is often in a large city, so many market-oriented firms locate in large cities.

   b. The principle explains why some resource-oriented firms locate at transshipment points (e.g., ports): the port is often the median location for the firm because it provides a central collection point for inputs and a single distribution point for the output.

5. A local input is defined as an input that cannot be transported long distances. Examples are certain types of energy, labor, and intermediate goods.

   a. A firm is oriented toward a local input if (i) it uses a local input whose price varies across space and (ii) it spends a large fraction of its budget on the local input.

b. The input-oriented firm will locate near inexpensive local inputs, causing the development of cities near sources of inexpensive energy, labor, and intermediate goods.

6. Firms that employ people who are sensitive to amenities (e.g., good weather, high-quality local schools, low crime rates, a clean environment, cultural opportunities) are attracted to locations that offer these amenities. Instead of workers following firms, firms follow workers. Amenities are important for firms that employ high-income workers.

7. One study of the location decisions of firms producing electronic components, plastics products, and electronic transmitting equipment suggests that the most important location factors were the wage, energy costs, industry output (a measure of localization economies), and technical expertise. Taxes and incentive programs do not seem to affect location decisions.

8. Until recently, most studies of location decisions suggested that taxes were not an important location factor. Recent studies cast some doubt on this conclusion. One study suggests that the effect of a tax depends on how the tax revenue is spent: an increase in taxes increases the relative attractiveness of a city if the money is spent on local public services (e.g., highways, education, public health and safety), but decreases the relative attractiveness of the city if the money is spent on redistributional programs.

9. In the last several decades, the relative importance of transport costs has decreased, a result of innovations in transportation (which decreased unit transport costs) and production (which decreased the physical weight of inputs).
   a. Many resource-oriented and market-oriented firms have been transformed into firms oriented toward local inputs.
   b. The change in location orientation provides one reason for the shift in economic growth from resource-rich regions (e.g., the United States) to places with low labor costs (e.g., Asia).

10. Government decisions cause the development of administrative cities and cities that host public facilities such as prisons and universities. Differences in legal environments cause the development of border cities.

EXERCISES AND DISCUSSION QUESTIONS

1. Comment on the following statement by the owner of a successful plywood mill: "Firms don't use location theory to make location decisions. I chose this location for my plywood mill because it was far from my mother-in-law."

2. Depict graphically the effects of the following changes on the bat firm's cost curves (shown in Figure 3–1). Explain any changes in the optimum location.

a. The costs of shipping bats increase from $1 per ton to $4 per ton, while the costs of shipping wood remain at $1 per ton.

b. The forest at point F burns down, forcing the firm to use wood from point G, which is 10 miles east of point F (20 miles from the market).

c. The firm starts producing bats with wood and cork, using two tons of wood and two tons of cork to produce three tons of bats. Cork is ubiquitous (available at all locations for the same price).

3. Why do breweries typically locate near their markets (far from their input sources), while wineries typically locate near their input sources (far from their markets)?

4. The building of wooden ships was a weight-losing activity, as evidenced by the piles of scrap wood generated by shipbuilders. Yet shipbuilders located in ports, far from their input sources (inland forests). Why?

5. In the 1960s, the port of Oakland moved rapidly to develop facilities to take advantage of the new labor-saving containerization technology. As a result, it was able to take shipping business away from the San Francisco port (across the bay). Under what conditions will the adoption of containerization technology increase total employment in Oakland?

6. Consider a firm that delivers video rentals to its customers. The spatial distribution of customers is as follows: 10 videos are delivered to location W, 10 miles due west of the city center; 50 videos are delivered to the city center; 25 units are delivered to E, 1 mile due east of the city center; and 45 videos are delivered to point F, 2 miles east of the city center. Production costs are the same at all locations.

a. Using a graph, show where the firm should locate. Explain your location choice.

b. Suppose that point W is in a valley and point F is at the top of a mountain. Therefore, the unit cost of easterly transport (shipments from west to east) is twice the unit cost of westerly transport. If production costs are the same at all locations, where should the firm locate? Explain.

7. Figure 3–4 shows the location choice of Ann's pizza firm. Discuss the effects of the following changes on Ann's location choice.

a. A tripling of the distance between Y and Z (from 9 miles to 27 miles).

b. A doubling of the customers at point W. Instead of three customers at W, there are six.

c. Ann stops delivery service, forcing consumers to travel to the pizza parlor.

8. In Figure 3–6, the weight-losing firm is located at point P (the port). If the monetary weight of location B is $27 instead of $15, will the firm still locate at point P?

9. There is some evidence that people have become more sensitive to air pollution. In other words, people are willing to pay more for clean air. If this is true, what influence will it have on the location decision of firms?

10. Consider a firm that uses one transferable input to produce one output. The monetary weight of the output is $4, and the monetary weight of the input is $3. The distance between M (the market) and F (the input source) is 10 miles.

    a. Suppose that production costs are the same at all locations. Using a diagram like the one in Figure 3–1, explain where the firm will locate.

    b. Suppose that the cost of land (a local input) increases as one approaches the market. Specifically, suppose that the cost of land is zero at F, but increases at a rate of $2 per mile as the firm approaches M. Depict graphically the location choice of the firm.

11. Chapter 2 discusses the incubator process. When industries mature, they move from single-activity clusters to areas with lower land and labor costs. Explain this process in terms of changes in the orientation of firms as they mature.

12. Suppose that country L has a plentiful supply of labor (and a low wage), but a relatively low supply of raw materials. In contrast, H has a plentiful supply of raw materials, but a relatively low supply of labor (and a high wage). The two countries are separated by a mountain range that makes travel between the two countries very costly. Suppose that a weight-losing product is initially produced in H (close to the supply of raw materials). Suppose that a tunnel is bored through the mountain, decreasing the costs of shipping raw materials and output between the two countries. Assume that laborers do not migrate from one country to the other.

    a. How will the tunnel affect the location choices of weight-losing firms?

    b. How will the tunnel affect wages in the two countries?

    c. How might this analysis be used to explain (i) the shift in manufacturing from the United States to East Asian countries and (ii) the narrowing of the wage differential between the United States and East Asian countries?

REFERENCES AND ADDITIONAL READINGS

Location Theory of Firms

Alonso, William. "Location Theory." In *Readings in Urban Economics*, ed. by M. Edel and J. Rothenberg. New York: Macmillan, 1972. Outlines the theory of firm location, focussing on the role of transport costs. Contains a brief bibliography of the seminal works in location theory.

Hoover, Edgar M. *Regional Economics*. New York: Knopf, 1975. Chapters 2, 3, and 4 provide a concise analysis of the location decisions of firms.

Hoover, Edgar M. *The Location of Economic Activity*. New York: McGraw-Hill, 1963. Discusses the economics of industry location, urban structure, and regional development, focussing on the problems of location change and adjustment.

Richardson, Harry W. *Regional Economics*. Urbana: University of Illinois Press, 1979, pp. 37–80.

Location of People: Migration and Amenities

Graves, Phillip E. "A Life-Cycle Empirical Analysis of Migration and Climate by Race." *Journal of Urban Economics* 6 (1979), pp. 135–47. Estimates the effect of climate variables on migration patterns in the 1960s.

Greenwood, Michael. "Human Migration: Theory, Models, and Empirical Studies." *Journal of Regional Science* 25 (1985), pp. 521–44. Survey of the theoretical and empirical literature on migration.

Porell, Frank W. "Intermetropolitan Migration and Quality of Life." *Journal of Regional Science* 22 (1982), pp. 137–58. Estimates the effects of economic and quality-of-life variables on migration patterns.

Applications of Location Theory

Levy, John M. *Economic Development Programs for Cities, Counties, and Towns.* New York: Praeger Publishers, 1981. Discusses the factors affecting the location choices of firms.

Schmenner, Roger. "Energy and Location." In *Energy Costs, Urban Development, and Housing,* ed. Anthony Downs and Katherine Bradbury. Washington, D.C.: Brookings Institution, 1984. Discusses the role of energy costs in location decisions.

Storper, Michael. "Toward a Structural Theory of Industrial Location." In *Industrial Location and Regional Systems,* ed. by John Rees, Geoffrey J.D. Hewings, and Howard Stafford. Brooklyn, N.Y.: Bergin, pp. 17–40.

Empirical and Case Studies of Location Decisions

Bartik, Timothy J. "Business Decisions in the United States: Estimates of the Effects of Unionization, Taxes, and Other Characteristics of States." *Journal of Business and Economics Statistics* 3 (1985), pp. 14–22. Estimates the effects of corporate and property taxes on location decisions.

Bartik, Timothy J., Charles Becker, Steve Lake, and John Bush. "Saturn and State Economic Development." *Forum for Applied Research and Public Policy* (Spring 1987), pp. 29–40.

Brown, Stephen P. "New Directions for Economic Growth: Redesigning Fiscal Policies in Louisiana, New Mexico, and Texas." *Economic Review, Federal Reserve Bank of Dallas* (July 1987), pp. 13–20.

Carlton, Dennis W. "The Location and Employment Choices of New Firms: An Econometric Model." *In Interregional Movements and Regional Growth,* ed. Willam C. Wheaton. Washington D.C.: The Urban Institute, 1979. Estimates the effects of wages, energy costs, industry output, and taxes on location decisions.

Castells, Manuel. "The New Industrial Space: Information Technology Manufacturing and Spatial Structure in the United States." In *America's New Market Geography,* ed. George Sternlieb and James Hughes. New Brunswick: Center for Urban Policy Research, 1988. Examines the location patterns of information-technology industries (semiconductors, computers, communication equipment, electronic automated machines, and genetic engineering).

Hekman, John S. "Branch Plant Location and the Product Cycle in Computer Manufacturing." *Journal of Economics and Business* 37 (1985), pp. 89–102.

Helms, L. Jay. "The Effect of State and Local Taxes on Economic Growth: A Time Series–Cross Section Approach." *Review of Economics and Statistics* 68 (1985), pp. 574–82. Estimates effects of taxes on location decisions and growth rates; concludes that the effect of a tax increase depends on how the tax revenue is spent.

Newman, Robert J., and Dennis H. Sullivan. "Econometric Analysis of Business Tax Impacts on Industrial Location: What Do We Know, and How Do We Know It?" *Journal of Urban Economics* 23 (1988), pp. 215–34. Reviews empirical evidence of the effects of business taxes on location choices.

Schmenner, Roger W. *Making Business Location Decisions.* Englewood Cliffs, N.J.: Prentice-Hall, 1982. Discusses how firms make location decisions.

Urban and Regional Growth Patterns

Meiszkowski, Peter. "Recent Trends in Urban and Regional Development." In *Current Issues in Urban Economics,* ed. Peter Meiszkowski and Mahlon Straszheim. Baltimore: Johns Hopkins, 1979, pp. 3–39. Describes the broad patterns of urban and regional development since World War II, focussing on interregional migration, shifts in employment, and changes in regional income differentials.

Norton, R. D., and J. Rees. "The Product Cycle and the Spatial Decentralization of American Manufacturing." *Regional Studies* 13 (1979), pp. 141–51. Analyzes changes in the spatial pattern of growth in manufacturing.

Norton, R. D. *City Life Cycles and American Urban Public Policy.* New York: Academic Press, 1979. Explores the changes in the spatial pattern of growth in manufacturing and discusses the implications for public policy.

The Origins of American Cities

Boorstin, Daniel. *The Americans: The Democratic Experience.* New York: Vintage, 1974; and *The Americans: The National Experience.* New York: Vintage, 1965. American History. Discusses the influences of government on the location of cities (the siting of state capitals, county seats, and universities; the influence of divorce and gambling laws).

Boorstin, Daniel. *The Americans: The National Experience.* New York: Vintage, 1965. Part Three, "The Upstarts: Boosters," discusses some of the reasons for the development of U.S. cities, focussing on the role of local boosters.

Glaab, Charles, and A. Theodore Brown. *A History of Urban America.* 3d ed. New York: Macmillan, 1983. A textbook on American urban history. Discusses the origins of many American cities.

Transport Costs and Industry Location

Chinitz, Benjamin. "The Effect of Transportation Forms on Regional Economic Growth." *Traffic Quarterly* 14 (1960a), pp. 129–42.
———. *Freight and the Metropolis.* Cambridge, Mass.: Harvard University Press, 1960(b).

CHAPTER 4

The History of Western Urbanization

"Dost thou know how to play the fiddle?"
"No," answered Themistocles, "but I understand the art of raising a little village into a great city."

Motto on the masthead of the Emigrant Aid Journal

This chapter uses the concepts of chapters 2 and 3 to discuss the historical development of cities in the Western world. The two earlier chapters explained that four factors contribute to the development of cities: comparative advantage, internal scale economies, transportation costs, and agglomerative economies. Together, these four factors explain why cities exist and where they develop. This chapter takes an historical perspective: it shows that changes over time in these four factors caused cities to grow and shrink. In the last 200 years, changes in technology have transformed the earth from a rural world into an urban one.

THE FIRST CITIES

The first cities developed in the fertile river valleys in the Near East around 3000 B.C. The city-states that developed in the Mesopotamia Valley included Eiridu, Ur, Lagash, and Kish. Ur was the largest of these cities, with a land area of about 150 acres and a population of about 25,000. In 2000 B.C., the city of Babylon had a population of about 50,000. In the Nile River Valley, the leading cities were Memphis, Heliopolis, and Thebes.

As explained in Chapter 2, a necessary condition for the development of a city is an agricultural surplus. A number of agricultural breakthroughs preceded the development of cities in the Near East: grain was domesticated, irrigation systems were developed, and the plow replaced the hoe. Together, these innovations allowed agricultural workers to produce a surplus of food, allowing some people to pursue nonagricultural activities in cities. The food surplus was relatively low: according to Davis (1976), between 50 and 150 farmers were required to support a single city inhabitant.

Why did the first cities develop? There is some uncertainty about the social and economic characteristics of early societies, so historians can only speculate about the origins of cities. Most agree that the first cities served both defensive and religious purposes. Can the development of defensive and religious cities be explained by the same factors that explain the development of market-based cities? If scale economies are responsible for the development of market-based cities, did the first cities develop as a result of scale economies in defense and religious services?

The Defensive City

A farmer who generates an agricultural surplus will eventually use the surplus, either consuming it himself or trading it for other goods. In either case, he must store the surplus food for some period of time. The stored food provides a lucrative target for thieves. If there are scale economies in food storage and protection, farmers may be better off storing their surpluses in a central storage facility. The people working in the fortified storage facility (managers and guards) will live near the facility, generating a place with a relatively high population density, a small city. This is the theory of the defensive city: the idea is that some of the earliest cities developed because of scale economies in the storage of the agricultural surplus. Support for the theory comes from archaeologists who have uncovered the remains of fortified storage facilities in the first cities.

How does this picture of the defensive city fit into the analysis of the market-based city in Chapter 2? The agricultural surplus generated a new economic activity: the storage and protection of the surplus. This activity is subject to scale economies, meaning that a single, fortified storage facility is more efficient than a series of facilities, one for each farmer. Home storage was replaced by centralized storage, resulting in the development of a specialized labor force of managers and guards, who exchanged their services for a part of the agricultural surplus. In other words, cities developed because of scale economies in the provision of a new commodity, grain storage. Just as scale economies in cloth production caused the development of factory cities, scale economies in storage services caused the development of defensive cities.

The Religious City

According to Mumford (1961), the development of the first cities coincided with the development of large-scale religion. Before the development of cities, most people worshipped in small groups, either in the home or in the local village. Around the time that the first cities developed, the local earth gods were replaced by celestial gods, who apparently demanded worship on a grander scale. If adoration and supplication are more effective on a large scale, a doubling of the size of the shrine will more than double the religious output. To exploit these scale economies, early societies replaced the small shrines in homes and villages with large temples at central locations. The temples employed chieftains, priests, and religious workers, causing the development of a place with a relatively high population density, a city. This is the theory of the religious city: the idea is that some of the earliest cities developed because of scale economies in the provision of religion. Support for the theory comes from archeologists who have uncovered the remains of large temples in some early cities.

How does the theory of the religious city fit into the analysis of the market-based city in Chapter 2? The switch from earthen gods to celestial gods caused home production of religion to be replaced by centralized production, and a specialized labor force of religious workers exchanged their labor for a part of the agricultural surplus. In other words, cities developed because of scale economies in the provision of religion. Just as scale economies in cloth production caused the development of factory cities, scale economies in religious services caused the development of religious cities.

The Defensive and Religious City

The most prominent feature of the early city was a large temple at the city center. The temple was a large monument, with thick walls and extravagant decorations. The thick walls were presumably used to both impress the gods and protect the agricultural surplus stored in the temple. In other words, the temple served both religious and defensive purposes, and early cities served as both religious and military centers.

What came first, the central storage facility or centralized religion? Perhaps the central storage facility made worship in the central temple more convenient, causing the switch to centralized religion. Alternatively, the development of a large temple could have provided a convenient and defensible storage facility for the agricultural surplus. In other words, there were economies of scope in the provision of religion and defense: the two services were provided more efficiently if they were provided together. A third possibility is that the local chieftains used centralized religion as a subterfuge to extract the agricultural surplus from local farmers.

The military played a large role in the early cities. The development of cities increased the frequency and severity of human conflict for two reasons. First, the cities worshipped different gods and fought wars to settle religious disputes. Second, the urban societies accumulated wealth, providing lucrative targets that encouraged materialistic wars. Although cities encouraged aggressive behavior, they also provided the most effective defense against aggression. Until the development of gunpowder in the 14th century, the most effective defensive maneuver was a large but simple wall. In addition, a city contained enough people to defend itself against attack from large forces. Once the simple wall was built, there was safety in numbers.

GREEK CITIES

The next stage of western urbanization occurred in Greece. In 500 B.C., there were hundreds of independent city-states ranging in population from a few hundred to tens of thousands. Athens was the largest, with a population of about 150,000, and Sparta had a population of about 40,000. In contrast with earlier cities, which were controlled by chieftain-priests, most Greek cities were run by their citizens, who used public assemblies to make policy.

Athens was a market city, with trading activity centered in the agora. Early in its history, the city established independent colonies and traded its household crafts and olive products for food and raw materials from the colonies. Trade was facilitated by the stamping of gold and silver coins in the 7th century B.C. In this period, Athens fed itself through voluntary trade with other areas.

The Athenian empire developed in the aftermath of the successful war against Persia in the fifth century B.C. After the Greek city-states repelled the Persian invasion, they formed the Delian League to carry the war into Asia Minor. By the end of the successful campaign, Athens had assumed complete control of the league and dictated policy to the other city-states. Athens took control of the treasury, transforming the voluntary contributions of member city-states into payments of tribute to Athens.

The Peloponnesian War between the Athenian Empire and Sparta (431 to 404) devastated Greece. Because Athens continued to use the Delian League to demand homage and tribute from the lesser cities, it appears that war was inevitable. The war, which was precipitated by disputes between Athens and Corinth (an ally of Sparta) over two Corinthian cities, ended in 404 when Athens renounced control over its empire and demolished its defensive walls. The war caused large losses in manpower, and also caused many intellectuals to lose faith in the democratic system. Athens never regained its former power. Eventually, Philip of Macedonia was able to take advantage of the weakened city-states and expanded his kingdom to include most of Greece.

ROMAN CITIES

The next stage of western urbanization occurred under the Roman Empire. By the third century A.D., Rome had a population exceeding 1 million. The Romans established colonial cities throughout Northern and Western Europe. Rome fed its large population with a combination of trade and tribute, with tribute playing a relatively large role.

The Roman cities were eventually overrun by marauders from rural areas. According to Hohenberg and Lees (1985), the Roman economy emphasized the collection of the agricultural surplus and neglected production activity. Instead of exchanging urban goods for agricultural products, Rome used conquest and tribute to feed its population. In the fourth and fifth centuries, German tribes invaded from the north, disrupting the Roman collection system. It appears that there was little interest outside of Rome in restoring the "trade" routes, so the losses from successive invasions were cumulative. If Rome had relied to a greater extent on voluntary exchange, the colonies may have been more interested in maintaining the exchange network, and the Western Empire might have recovered from the Germanic raids.

LESSONS FROM ATHENS AND ROME

What are the lessons from the rise and fall of Athens and Rome? Early in its history, Athens engaged in voluntary trade with other areas by exchanging urban goods for food from the countryside. The city thrived under this system of voluntary exchange. The Athenians eventually switched to a system of conquest and tribute, which resulted in war and the decline of the city. Mumford (1961) suggests that the city of Rome should have been called "Parasitopolis" to indicate the extent to which its population lived off the labors of outsiders. The decline of Rome was caused in part by the disruption of its collection system by the Germanic raids. Perhaps the lesson is that cities based on voluntary exchange are viable, but cities based on coercive transfer payments are not.

FEUDAL CITIES

In the first few centuries following the fall of the Western Roman Empire, cities in the West declined. The Islamic conquest disrupted trade on the Mediterranean, causing the decline of port cities. Waves of marauding barbarians continued to sweep across Europe, making travel and trade dangerous. People sought safety inside city walls: once again, there was safety in numbers inside walled cities.

Table 4-1 shows the largest cities in Europe between 1000 and 1900. In 1000, most cities in western and central Europe were very small. The largest cities served the Byzantine Empire and the Muslim areas of Spain. Venice was one of the few large cities beyond the Byzantine and Muslim areas, but it was heavily dependent on trade with the Eastern Empire.

Trade on the Mediterranean increased during the 11th and 12th centuries. The Italian city-states forged agreements with the Byzantine and Islamic rulers for trade with North Africa and the East. The Europeans traded wood, iron, grain, wine, and wool cloth for medicines, dyes, linen, cotton, leather, and precious metals. The increased trade contributed to the growth of Venice, Genoa, and Pisa.

The feudal economy of the 11th through the 14th centuries was based on manorial estates and small walled cities. On the manor, the lord inherited his serfs, who worked the lord's land and served in the military in exchange for the use of small plots of land. In the small towns, workers produced handicrafts (cloth, leather goods, metal goods), which they exchanged for the agricultural surplus of the manor.

Cities in the feudal era were small and numerous. In the 11th century, London was the largest city in England, with a population of only 16,000. There were several other English cities with populations of around 5,000. The largest of the many German cities had a population of no more than 30,000.

Between the 11th and 14th centuries, the frequency of barbarian invasions decreased, and the small defensive cities gradually became market cities. The medieval cities specialized in commerce and handicrafts, and thus earned—rather than robbed—the agricultural surplus of their hinterlands. A small merchant class developed, and marketplaces were established just outside the city walls. The merchants were protected from plunder by the establishment of weekly market days: once a week, theft was outlawed in places marked by the market cross. The market peace was enforced by local chieftains, the church, and special courts with jurisdiction over traders. The markets flourished, and in many cities, the city walls were extended to include the marketplaces. The urban market was primarily a place for the exchange of local agriculture and handicrafts.

Hohenberg and Lees (1985) use Leicester, in the East Midlands of England, as an example of a medieval city in the 14th century. The city was surrounded by walls on three sides and a river on a fourth side. The town ditch was just outside the wall. The city was a regional marketplace, producing staples such as beer and bread for local consumption and woolen cloth for export. Occupations in the city included butchers, shoemakers, tailors, mercers, weavers, and bakers. Over half of the city's workers were employed in manufacturing; one quarter were employed as foodmakers; one tenth were employed as traders and merchants. The merchant guild controlled most economic activity in the city.

According to Davis (1976), the first market-based cities developed for two reasons. First, power in the feudal system was decentralized. Unlike the Greek and Roman cities, medieval cities could not simply dominate their hinterlands and demand tribute, but had to produce something in exchange for agricultural goods. Second, agricultural productivity was relatively low, so a city could not survive on the output of its immediate hinterland, but had to trade with a relatively large area. As a result, the city had to develop products that could compete with homemade products produced in its hinterland *and* products produced in other cities.

Competition among the medieval cities caused innovations in production and commerce. Urban producers developed new production techniques that allowed them to underprice their competitors. Cities invested in secular education as a means of promoting literacy and developing commercial skills. These early efforts to improve the techniques of production and commerce set the stage for the industrial revolution of the 18th and 19th centuries.

Table 4–1 shows the top 10 European cities in 1400. Paris, the largest city, was a center for trade and education, and was also the capital of the kingdom of France. Three of the top six European cities were Italian city-states. Bruges and Ghent, two cities in the Low Countries, grew rapidly in the 14th century as a result of the booming wool cloth industry.

A series of famines and plagues between 1350 and 1450 decreased Europe's population by between one third and one half. Cities suffered more than rural areas because cities had less sanitary living conditions and higher population densities (an urban sneeze transmits the germs to more people). The associated disruptions of social and economic activities caused most cities to stagnate or decline.

TABLE 4–1 European Cities, 1000–1900

1000		1400		1700		1900	
City	Population (thousands)	City	Population (thousands)	City	Population (thousands)	City	Population (thousands)
Constantinople	450	Paris	275	Constantinople	700	London	6,480
Cordoba	450	Milan	125	London	550	Paris	3,330
Seville	90	Bruges	125	Paris	530	Berlin	2,424
Palermo	75	Venice	110	Naples	207	Vienna	1,662
Kiev	45	Granada	100	Lisbon	188	St. Petersburg	1,439
Venice	45	Genoa	100	Amsterdam	172	Manchester	1,255
Regensburg	40	Prague	95	Rome	149	Birmingham	1,248
Thessalonika	40	Caffa	58	Venice	144	Moscow	1,120
Amalfi	35	Seville	70	Moscow	130	Glasgow	1,072
Rome	35	Ghent	70	Milan	124	Liverpool	940

SOURCE: P. M. Hohenberg and L. H. Lees, *The Making of Urban Europe 1000–1950* (Cambridge, Mass.: Harvard University Press, 1985), p. 11.

MERCANTILE CITIES

Starting in the 15th century, large commercial (mercantile) cities developed in Europe. Two factors contributed to the development of large cities: the centralization of power and the growth of long-distance trade.

Centralization of Power

In the 15th century, political and economic power was transferred from a large number of feudal lords to a relatively small number of princes, queens, and kings. The shift in power was caused in large part by military advances that rendered the traditional feudal defense maneuvers obsolete.

Innovations in war making increased the scale of conflict. The feudal lord used his serfs as part-time warriors. If the part-time warriors could not defeat the attackers in the field, the feudal lord could always hunker down behind his castle walls to wait out a siege. The professional army of the 15th century combined infantry (armed with pikes, crossbows, and muskets) with siege cannons and cavalry. The professional soldiers, with their sophisticated weapons and training, defeated the feudal lord's part-timers in the field. When the feudal lord retreated to his castle, the siege cannon blew holes in the castle walls. The professional armies defeated the feudal lords and centralized power in the hand of princes, queens, and kings.

The mercantile cities developed defensive maneuvers appropriate to the new level of warfare. Defense was no longer a matter of building a simple wall and dumping hot oil on the attackers. It required the building of intricate fortifications and the hiring of professional soldiers. The larger cities were able to exploit the increased scale economies in defense.

The centralization of power led to the centralization of administrative and military functions in royal cities. After the 16th century, the most rapidly growing cities were the ones that harbored a royal court. In a short period of time, over a dozen cities grew to a size attained by only a few medieval cities: London had 250,000 people, Naples 240,000, Milan 200,000, and Paris 180,000; cities with around 100,000 inhabitants included Rome, Lisbon, Palermo, Seville, Antwerp, and Amsterdam.

Long-Distance Trade

Starting in the 15th century, long-distance trade increased for two reasons. First, the consolidation of power eliminated many of the restrictions on trade (e.g., the local tariffs imposed by feudal lords). Second, the development of ocean travel led to exploration and the discovery of new markets. Cities developed along trade routes and at transshipment points. While cities with river and sea ports flourished (e.g., Naples, Palermo, Lisbon, Liverpool), inland cities like Florence declined. In Table 4–1, 4 new seaports appeared among the top 10 European cities: London, Naples, Lisbon, and Amsterdam.

URBANIZATION DURING THE INDUSTRIAL REVOLUTION

Despite the rapid spread of cities between 3000 B.C. and 1800 A.D., the world continued to be predominantly rural. Urbanization was limited by the relatively low productivity of agriculture, the high costs of transporting goods, and the relatively small advantages of centralized production. Until the early part of the 19th century, the fraction of the world's population living in cities was only about 3 percent. Between 1800 and 1970, the percentage of the population in cities increased to 39 percent. In the United States, the percentage in cities increased from 6 percent to 75 percent.

The rapid urbanization of the last two centuries was caused by the industrial revolution, which started in the 19th century. The industrial revolution produced innovations in manufacturing and transportation that shifted production from the home and the small shop to large factories in industrial cities. Table 4–1 shows the effects of the industrial revolution on the top 10 cities in Europe. Between 1700 and 1900, Manchester, Birmingham, Glasgow, and Liverpool grew from tiny towns into giant industrial cities. Most of the other cities in the top 10 combined political functions with industrial development, causing dramatic population growth. The innovations of the industrial evolution can be divided into four areas: agriculture, manufacturing, transportation, and construction.

Agriculture

The rapid urbanization of the industrial revolution was made possible by innovations that increased agricultural productivity. Farmers substituted machinery for muscle power and simple tools, increasing the output per farmer. For example, using a horse-drawn reaper, two people could harvest the same amount of grain as eight people using traditional harvesting methods. In addition, the development of agricultural science led to innovations in planting, growing, harvesting, and processing. As productivity increased, laborers were freed from food-raising responsibilities, allowing them to pursue urban activities. In the United States, the percentage of the population employed in agriculture decreased from 69 percent in 1840 to 3.6 percent in 1980.

Manufacturing

Perhaps the most visible part of the industrial revolution involved innovations in manufacturing. New machines, made of iron instead of wood, were developed for the production of most goods. Manual production by skilled artisans was replaced by mechanized production using interchangeable parts, specialized labor, and steam-powered machines. Output per worker grew, and scale economies in production increased.

The innovations in manufacturing caused the development of large industrial cities. Mass production decreased the relative cost of factory goods, causing the centralization of production and employment. In addition, many of the new production processes were subject to agglomerative economies (localization economies and urbanization economies), increasing the advantages of urban locations.

Intercity Transportation

Innovations in intercity transportation contributed to industrialization and urbanization. The steamship and the railroad decreased the costs of moving goods between cities, thus decreasing the net cost (factory price plus transport cost) of factory goods. Production became more centralized, and factory cities grew. The new transportation modes also decreased the costs of moving agricultural goods, allowing greater regional specialization in agriculture. Agricultural regions were better able to exploit their comparative advantages, so agricultural productivity increased.

Before the railroad linked eastern cities with the western parts of the United States, a large fraction of the food consumed in New England was produced by the region's farmers. Similarly, a large fraction of the goods consumed in the West (e.g., shoes) were produced by local craft workers. The coming of the railroad allowed eastern factories to underprice western craft workers, and allowed western farmers to underprice eastern farmers. The west specialized in agricultural goods and the east specialized in manufactured goods. Trade increased because the railroad allowed both regions to exploit their comparative advantages.

Industrial cities developed at points accessible to the new intercity transportation network. During the steamship era, cities developed along the rivers and lakes served by the steamship. Firms that used coal-fired steam engines located along rivers served by coal shippers. Later, the development of the railroad caused the development of cities along the rail lines. The cities that developed at transshipment points had commercial jobs (transportation, trade, business services) and manufacturing jobs.

Intracity Transportation

Innovations in intracity transportation increased the feasible size of cities. The size of a city is limited by the cost of traveling within the city. One rule of thumb is that the geographical area of the city should be small enough that the typical resident can travel from the edge of the city to the city center in an hour. Before the innovations in intracity transport, most people walked to workplaces and shops, so the radius of the city could be no more than about two miles. During the last half of the 19th century, a series of innovations in public transit increased the speed of intracity travel, increasing the feasible radius of the city.

The city of Boston provides a good example of the effects of transit innovations on city size (Boorstin, 1974). In 1850, Boston was a "walking" city with a radius of about two miles. In the 1860s, the horse-powered railroad (horses pulling cars along rails) was introduced, and the radius of the city increased to 2.5 miles in 1872 and 4.0 miles in 1887. By the 1890s, the horse railroad was replaced by the electric trolley, which traveled at twice the speed and carried three times as many passengers. As a result, the radius of the city increased to about six miles. From the 1850s to the 1890s, when walking was replaced by other modes of transportation, the radius of the city tripled and the land area increased ninefold.

The introduction of the internal-combustion engine had similar effects on the size of cities. This new engine allowed the development of relatively small vehicles for transporting people and goods. The development of the automobile decreased the cost of intracity travel, causing further increases in the feasible radius of the city. In addition, the auto freed travelers from the old fixed-rail systems that were designed to deliver people from the residential areas along the streetcar lines (the spokes) to the city center (the hub). The automobile increased the accessibility of locations throughout the city: residents could live between the spokes, and firms could locate outside the hub. As the set of feasible locations for residents and firms increased, cities grew.

The introduction of the truck had similar effects. The truck decreased the cost of intercity transportation, increasing the advantages of centralized (urban) production. In addition, the truck freed firms from their dependence on the railroad terminal and the port, allowing them to locate outside the central city. As the set of feasible production locations increased, the feasible size of the city increased. The development of the truck and the automobile also caused the suburbanization of population and employment within the urban area, a topic to be covered in Chapter 10.

Construction Methods

Innovations in construction methods also increased city sizes. The first skyscraper, a 10-story building that housed the Home Insurance Company, appeared in 1885 in Chicago. The building was revolutionary because its frame was made of steel instead of bricks. Because the steel frame was relatively light, the steel-framed building could be taller than the traditional brick building. The development of the elevator decreased the intra-building travel costs of tall buildings, increasing the advantages of the skyscraper. The skyscraper increased the intensity of land use, increasing the city's productive capacity and its feasible size.

URBANIZATION IN THE UNITED STATES

Table 4–2 shows the trend in U.S. urbanization from 1790 to 1980. In 1800, only about 6 percent of the population lived in cities. The share of population in cities increased to 15 percent by 1850, 40 percent by 1900, 64 percent by 1950, and 74 percent by 1980. Urbanization can be divided into three peri-

TABLE 4–2 Urbanization in the United States, 1790–1980

Year	Percent of U.S. Population in Cities
1790	5.1%
1800	6.1
1810	7.2
1820	7.2
1830	8.8
1840	10.8
1850	15.3
1860	19.8
1870	25.7
1880	28.2
1890	35.1
1900	39.7
1910	45.7
1920	51.2
1930	56.2
1940	56.5
1950*	59 or 64
1960	69.9
1970	73.5
1980	73.7

*Definition of urban place changed;
  Old definition = 59
  New definition = 64

SOURCE: U.S. Bureau of the Census, Census of Population.

ods. Between 1800 and 1930, the traditional port city, which was based on commerce and trade, was replaced by the industrial city. Urbanization was rapid during this period: the percentage of the population living in cities increased from 6 percent to 56 percent, and most metropolitan areas grew rapidly. The 1930s and 1940s were times of depression and war, and urbanization proceeded at a relatively slow pace. There are two urbanization figures for 1950: under the old Census definition of an urban area, 59 percent of the population lived in urban areas; under the new definition, the figure was 64 percent.

During the postwar period, urbanization has proceeded at a slower pace. The percentage of the population living in cities increased from 64 percent in 1950 to 74 percent in 1980. During the 1970s, for the first time in the nation's history, nonmetropolitan areas grew faster than metropolitan areas. Since 1970, some metropolitan areas have actually decreased in population.

From Commercial to Industrial Cities

Table 4–3 shows the population trends for the 10 largest U.S. cities in 1930. In 1810, only four cities (New York, Philadelphia, Baltimore, and Boston) had more than 10,000 residents. The rapid growth of these cities around the turn of the century was caused in large part by the Napoleonic Wars, which tied up the English and French merchant marine and caused a boom in the American shipping industry. In 1850, these four seaports were still the dominant cities, with the population of the smallest one (Philadelphia) about 2.5 times the population of the next largest city (Pittsburgh).

The industrial revolution caused dramatic growth in U.S. cities. Between 1850 and 1890, the populations of New York and Boston more than tripled, the population of Baltimore more than doubled, and the population of Philadelphia increased more than eightfold. Lurking behind these changes were large increases in urban manufacturing activity: The share of employment in manufacturing more than doubled in all of these cities, from about 9 percent of total employment to about 19 percent.

The most dramatic urban growth between 1850 and 1890 occurred away from the eastern seaboard in Chicago, Detroit, Cleveland, Pittsburgh, and Los Angeles. On average, the populations of these cities increased over eighteenfold between 1850 and 1890. Again, manufacturing growth led the way: in Chicago and Detroit, the percentage of employment in manufacturing almost quadrupled, from about 5 percent to around 19 percent; in Cleveland, the percentage in manufacturing more than doubled, from 8 percent to 19 percent. Pittsburgh was already an industrial city by 1860, so it experienced a

TABLE 4–3   Cities in the United States, 1810–1930

| | | Population in Year (thousands) | | | |
	Rank in 1930	1810	1850	1890	1930
New York	1	120	696	2,507	6,930
Chicago	2	—	30	1,100	3,376
Philadelphia	3	54	121	1,047	1,951
Detroit	4	—	21	206	1,569
Los Angeles	5	—	2	50	1,238
Cleveland	6	—	17	261	900
Baltimore	7	47	169	434	805
Boston	8	34	137	448	781
Pittsburgh	9	5	47	239	670
Washington, D.C.	10	8	40	189	487

SOURCE: U.S. Bureau of the Census, Census of Population.

relatively small increase in manufacturing employment (from 18 percent to 23 percent). Chicago was the first city to displace one of the eastern seaport cities from the top four positions, moving into the second spot by 1890.

Between 1890 and 1930, Philadelphia, Baltimore, and Boston were growing at relatively slow rates, which allowed other cities to move ahead of them in the ranking. Detroit moved to number four; Los Angeles moved to number five; and Cleveland moved to number six. By 1930, most of the largest cities were industrial cities.

The Postwar Era

As shown in Table 4–2, the pace of urbanization slowed considerably between 1950 and 1980. Using the new definition of an urban area, the percentage of the population living in cities increased by 4.9 percentage points during the 1950s, 3.6 percentage points during the 1960s, and 0.2 percentage points during the 1970s.

Metropolitan versus Nonmetropolitan Growth.   Table 4–4 provides a closer look at urbanization between 1959 and 1984. The table shows the population growth rates for metropolitan areas (areas included in an MSA) and nonmetropolitan areas (counties that are not a part of an MSA). Between 1959 and 1969, metropolitan areas grew more than four times faster than nonmetropolitan areas (1.60 percent per year compared to 0.35 percent). In contrast, during the 1970s, nonmetropolitan areas grew about 25 percent faster than metropolitan areas (1.29 percent per year compared to 1.04 percent).

Nonmetropolitan areas grew faster than metropolitan areas in the 1970s for a number of reasons:

1. **Dispersion of manufacturing employment.** Improvements in the intercity highway system increased the accessibility of nonmetropolitan locations. Some labor-intensive manufacturers moved from metropolitan areas to low-wage nonmetropolitan areas.

TABLE 4–4   Population Growth Rates for Metropolitan and Nonmetropolitan Areas

	Average Annual Growth Rate (%)		
	1959–1969	1969–1979	1979–1984
United States	1.29	1.10	1.01
Nonmetropolitan	0.35	1.29	0.84
Metropolitan	1.60	1.04	1.07

SOURCE: Daniel H. Garnick, "Local Area Economic Growth Patterns: A Comparison of the 1980s and Previous Decades," in *Urban Change and Poverty*, ed. M. G. McGeary and L. E. Lynn (Washington, D.C.: National Academy Press, 1988), p. 201.

2. **Slow decline in farm employment.** Although total employment in agriculture decreased during the decade, it decreased at a relatively slow rate. Fewer people left farms to move to cities.

3. **Growth in extractive industries.** Higher prices for energy and raw materials increased employment in oil and mining industries. For example, total mining employment increased from 626,000 in 1969 to 957,000 in 1979.

4. **Growth in recreation and retirement activities.** A large number of elderly households moved to retirement communities in nonmetropolitan areas, pulling retail and service jobs to those areas. Other urban households moved to nonmetropolitan areas with outdoor recreational opportunities.

5. **Population spillovers.** Some households moved to counties that the Census Bureau inappropriately classified as "nonmetropolitan." Some of these counties are integrated, in an economic sense, with a nearby MSA, but are still considered nonmetropolitan. Alonso (1980) suggests that this statistical problem causes a significant overestimate of the nonmetropolitan growth rate. During the 1970s, many of the fastest growing areas were nonmetropolitan counties adjacent to metropolitan areas (MSAs and CMSAs).

During the 1980s, the growth rate for nonmetropolitan areas decreased, restoring the historical pattern of relatively rapid metropolitan growth. Between 1979 and 1984, nonmetropolitan areas grew at an annual rate of 0.84 percent, compared to 1.07 percent for metropolitan areas. According to Garnick (1988), growth rates in nonmetropolitan areas decreased for three reasons. First, farm employment decreased rapidly as farm prices decreased. Second, the employment in extractive industries decreased as a result of decreases in energy and resource prices. Third, labor-intensive manufacturing employment in nonmetropolitan areas decreased as a result of increased competition from abroad.

Population Losses in Some Metropolitan Areas.   Another recent trend is the decline of some metropolitan areas. Table 4–5 shows the population growth rates for the 25 largest CMSAs and MSAs. During the 1970s, 7 of the top 25 metropolitan areas lost population: New York, Philadelphia, Detroit, Cleveland, St. Louis, Pittsburgh, and Milwaukee. The largest losses occurred in Cleveland (0.6 percent per year), Pittsburgh (0.5 percent per year), and New York (0.4 percent per year). In the early 1980s, Detroit, Cleveland, Pittsburgh, and Milwaukee continued to decrease in population.

Why have some metropolitan areas decreased in size? First, people migrated from the northern states to states with better weather, decreasing the growth rates of northeast and northcentral metropolitan areas. Given this migration pattern, the best a northern metropolitan area could hope for was a

TABLE 4–5 Population and Growth Rates for the 25 Largest Metropolitan Areas

Consolidated Metropolitan Statistical Area (CMSA) or Metropolitan Statistical Area (MSA)	Population in 1986 (thousands)	Rank in 1984	Average Annual Growth Rate (%) 1970s	Average Annual Growth Rate (%) 1980–86
New York–Northern New Jersey–Long Island CMSA	17,968	1	−0.40	0.40
Los Angeles–Anaheim–Riverside CMSA	13,075	2	1.40	2.10
Chicago–Gary–Lake County CMSA	8,116	3	0.20	0.40
San Francisco–Oakland–San Jose CMSA	5,878	4	1.20	1.50
Philadelphia–Wilmington–Trenton CMSA	5,833	5	−0.10	0.40
Detroit–Ann Arbor CMSA	4,601	6	−0.10	−0.50
Boston–Lawrence–Salem CMSA	4,056	7	0.10	0.30
Dallas–Fort Worth CMSA	3,655	8	2.20	3.50
Houston–Galveston–Brazoria CMSA	3,634	9	3.60	2.50
Washington DC–Maryland–Virginia CMSA	3,563	10	0.70	1.50
Miami–Fort Lauderdale CMSA	2,912	11	3.40	1.50
Cleveland–Akron–Lorain CMSA	2,766	12	−0.60	−0.40
Atlanta MSA	2,561	13	2.40	2.90
St. Louis MSA	2,438	14	−0.20	0.40
Pittsburgh–Beaver Valley CMSA	2,316	15	−0.50	−0.70
Minneapolis–St. Paul MSA	2,295	16	0.80	1.10
Seattle–Tacoma CMSA	2,285	17	1.30	1.40
Baltimore MSA	2,280	18	0.50	0.60
San Diego MSA	2,201	19	3.20	2.70
Tampa–St. Petersburg–Clearwater MSA	1,914	20	3.80	2.70
Phoenix MSA	1,900	21	4.40	3.70
Denver–Boulder CMSA	1,847	22	2.70	2.10
Cincinnati–Hamilton CMSA	1,690	23	0.30	0.30
Milwaukee–Racine CMSA	1,552	24	−0.02	−0.20
Kansas City MSA	1,518	25	0.40	0.90

SOURCE: U.S. Bureau of the Census, Statistical Abstract of the U.S., 1988.

small positive growth rate. Between 1980 and 1986, the average growth rate was 0.04 percent for northeast and northcentral metropolitan areas, compared to 2.51 percent for southern and western metropolitan areas. In some northern metropolitan areas, decreases in manufacturing employment generated negative growth rates. In Pittsburgh, Cleveland, and Detroit, decreases in employment in the industries producing primary metals, motor vehicles, rubber, and nonelectrical machinery caused losses in population. Although Boston experienced large decreases in its traditional manufacturing base (textiles, apparel, shoes), it was able to offset these losses with new jobs in high-technology manufacturing.

The Postindustrial City?

What does the future hold for cities? One economic trend that will affect cities and the urbanization process is the shift in employment from manufacturing to services. Table 4–6 shows the changes in distribution of employment between 1947 and 1985. The percentage of jobs in the goods-producing sector (agriculture, mining, construction, manufacturing) decreased from 45 percent in 1947 to 28 percent in 1985. The percentage in the service sectors (transportation; wholesale and retail trade; finance, insurance, and real estate; services; government) increased from 55 percent in 1947 to 72 percent in 1985. The largest increases occurred in retail trade, services, finance, real estate, and insurance.

TABLE 4–6 Distribution of Employment, 1947–1985

| | Percent of Jobs in Activity | | | | |
	1947	1959	1969	1979	1985
Goods-producing sector	45.4	39.6	35.7	32.1	28.1
Agriculture	11.6	7.4	4.0	3.3	2.9
Mining	1.7	1.2	0.8	1.0	0.9
Construction	5.2	5.5	5.4	5.9	5.7
Manufacturing	26.9	25.6	25.4	21.98	18.7
Service-producing sector	54.6	60.4	64.3	67.9	71.9
Transportation	7.4	6.4	5.7	5.4	5.1
Wholesale trade	4.6	5.2	5.1	5.6	5.6
Retail trade	14.6	13.9	13.4	14.7	15.5
Finance, insurance, real estate	3.3	4.2	4.6	5.6	6.2
Services	13.0	14.7	16.9	19.7	23.2
Government	11.8	16.1	18.6	16.9	16.3
Total	100	100	100	100	100

SOURCE: Daniel H. Garnick, "Local Area Economic Growth Patterns: A Comparison of the 1980s and Previous Decades," in *Urban Change and Poverty*, ed. M. G. McGeary and L. E. Lynn (Washington, D.C.: National Academy Press, 1988), p. 251.

How will the decrease in the relative importance of manufacturing affect cities? Most cities in the United States were built as manufacturing centers during the industrial revolution. The shift to a more service-oriented economy will certainly bring dramatic changes to metropolitan areas. The cities that are heavily dependent on traditional manufacturing activity will decline, and the cities that make the transition to the new service activities will thrive.

The move toward a service-oriented economy will affect many facets of the metropolitan economy. Chapter 6 discusses the implications for economic growth policies. Chapters 8 through 10 explore the implications of the changing economic structure for urban land-use patterns. As explained in Chapter 11, the shift to services also has implications for antipoverty policies.

SUMMARY

1. The first cities developed for religious and defense purposes.
   a. Scale economies in the storage and protection of the agricultural surplus caused the development of centralized storage facilities and cities.
   b. According to some historians, cities appeared around the time that earth gods were replaced by celestial ones, suggesting that cities developed to exploit scale economies in the provision of religious services.
2. The development of cities encouraged aggression. Cities provided the best defense against aggression (simple walls).
3. Athens started out as a market-based city, but evolved into a city based on conquest and tribute. The city declined after the Peloponnesian War with Sparta.
4. Roman cities were also based on conquest and tribute, and declined after the Germanic raids disrupted the collection system.
5. Feudal cities started as defensive cities and eventually became market cities, specializing in commerce and handicrafts.
6. Mercantile cities developed as a result of the centralization of power (caused by military innovations that eliminated the defensive advantages of the feudal castle) and the opening of new markets (caused by exploration and more efficient ocean travel).
7. The rapid urbanization of the 19th and 20th centuries was caused by the industrial revolution and the associated innovations in agriculture, transportation, manufacturing, and construction methods.
   a. Agricultural productivity increased as farmers substituted machines for laborers, freeing laborers to pursue nonagricultural activities. Transportation costs decreased, thus allowing greater regional specialization and greater productivity.
   b. The relative cost of factory goods decreased as a result of decreases in transportation costs and the realization of scale economies in production. Factory employment increased and cities developed around the factories.

c. Innovations in intracity transportation and construction techniques increased the feasible size of cities.

8. Between 1800 and 1930, the percentage of the U.S. population in cities increased from 6 percent to 56 percent. The pace of urbanization has slowed since World War II, rising from 64 percent in 1950 to 74 percent in 1980.

9. In the 1970s, nonmetropolitan areas grew faster than metropolitan areas. In the 1980s, the growth rate for nonmetropolitan areas decreased, restoring the historical pattern of more rapid growth in metropolitan areas.

10. In the 1970s and 1980s, some northern metropolitan areas decreased in population.

EXERCISES AND DISCUSSION QUESTIONS

1. Critically appraise: "Innovation in agriculture during the industrial revolution was a necessary—but not sufficient—condition for the urbanization of society."

2. One of the reasons for the decline of the feudal system was the development of professional armies. If you were a feudal lord in the 14th century, would you have hired a professional army and equipped them with crossbows, pikes, muskets, and cannons? Would you have been able to defeat the princes and kings?

3. Some societies never developed any cities. Where did these societies develop? How did they differ from the societies that developed cities?

4. Suppose that you are a citizen of Rome when the first Germanic raid occurs. You have been asked to propose a strategy to respond to the raid (and the expectation that future raids are likely). What's your strategy?

5. The Romans auctioned off the rights to tax their colonies to commercial tax-collecting agencies. In other words, the Romans sold franchises to tax collectors. Might this auction scheme have contributed to the decline of Rome? If you were in charge of the franchising system, what restrictions would you place on the tax collectors?

REFERENCES AND ADDITIONAL READINGS

Alonso, William. "The Population Factor and Urban Structure." In *The Prospective City*, ed. Arthur Solomon. Cambridge, Mass.: MIT Press, 1980.   A discussion of recent trends in urbanization.

Boorstin, Daniel, *The Americans: The Democratic Experience* (New York: Vintage, 1974).

Davis, Kingsley. "Urbanization." In *The Urban Economy*, ed. Harold Hochman. New York: W. W. Norton, 1976.   A brief history of urbanization.

Garnick, Daniel H. "Local Area Economic Growth Patterns: A Comparison of the 1980s and Previous Decades." In *Urban Change and Poverty*, ed. Michael G. McGeary and Lawrence E. Lynn. Washington D.C.: National Academy Press, 1988.   Discusses recent growth trends in metropolitan and nonmetropolitan areas and the 50 largest metropolitan areas (MSAs and CMSAs).

Hohenberg, Paul M., and Lynn H. Lees. *The Making of Urban Europe 1000–1950.* Cambridge, Mass.: Harvard Univ. Press, 1985.   Discusses the reasons for the urbanization of Europe.

Hoselitz, Bert. "Generative and Parasitic Cities." *Economic Development and Cultural Change* 3 (1955), pp. 278–94.   Discusses the effects of parasitic cities on their hinterlands.

Mumford, Lewis. *The City in History.* New York: Harcourt Brace Jovanovich, 1961.   A lengthy discussion of the history of urbanization.

Olmstead, Alan, and Eugene Smolensky. *The Urbanization of the United States.* Morriston, N.J.: General Learning Press, 1973.

Pirenne, Henri. *Economic and Social History of Medieval Europe.* New York: Harcourt Brace Jovanovich, 1961.   Discusses the role of trade in the rise and decline of medieval cities.

Rosenberg, Nathan, and L. E. Birdzell. *How the West Grew Rich.* New York: Basic Books, 1986.   Discusses the transformation of the Western world from the Dark Ages to its present state.

Sjoberg, Gideon. "The Origin and Evolution of Cities." In *Cities,* ed. by Dennis Flanagan. New York: Knopf, 1965.

CHAPTER 5

How Many Cities?

This chapter examines urban development from the regional perspective. In contrast with earlier chapters, which explore the development of individual cities in isolation, this chapter explains how cities develop as integral parts of a larger regional economy. A region supports cities of different size and scope, causing the development of a **regional system of cities**.

Table 5–1 shows the size distribution of urban places in the United States in 1986. There were only 8 urban areas with more than 1 million people, but 1,302 with between 10,000 and 25,000 people. Table 5–1 raises two questions about cities in a regional economy. First, what factors determine the equilibrium number of cities? Second, why are some cities larger than others? The answers to these questions are provided by **central-place theory**.

The chapter is divided into four sections. The first section shows how firms in a market-oriented industry carve a region into individual **market areas**, and the second shows why some industries have larger market areas than others. The third section uses central-place theory to explain how the location patterns of different industries combine to form a regional system of cities. The final section applies some of the principles of market-area analysis to decision making in the public sector, showing how policy makers could use the principles to choose the optimum number of fire stations, libraries, or hazardous-waste facilities.

THE ANALYSIS OF MARKET AREAS

Market-area analysis was developed by Christaller (translated in 1966) and refined by Losch (translated in 1954). A firm's market area is defined as the area over which a firm can underprice its competitors. The firm's net price is the sum of the price charged by the firm and the travel costs incurred by its consumers. The notion of a market area can be explained with a model of a region where consumers buy records. Consider a region with the following characteristics:

1. **Fixed store price**. All record stores have the same production technology and face the same input prices, so they charge the same price.

2. **Travel costs**. Every consumer buys one record per trip to the record store. The travel costs (the monetary and time costs of travel) are 50 cents per round-trip mile.

3. **Shape**. The region is rectangular, 60 miles long and 20 miles wide.

TABLE 5–1   Size Distribution of Urban Places in the United States, 1986

Size of Urban Place	Number of Places
More than 1 million	8
500,000 to 1 million	15
250,000–500,000	37
100,000–250,000	122
50,000–1000,000	286
25,000–50,000	563
10,000–25,000	1302

SOURCE: U.S. Bureau of the Census, *Statistical Abstract of the United States*, 1988.

Because record stores sell the same product at the same price, they differ only in location.

Pricing with a Monopolist

Suppose that there is a single record store (owned by Bob) at the center of the region. The net price per record is the sum of the store price and the consumer's travel costs. Figure 5–1 shows the net price of records for consumers living in different parts of the region. If Bob charges $8 per record, the net price rises from $8 for a household living next to the record store, to $13 for a household living 10 miles from the record store, to $23 for a household 30 miles from the store.

FIGURE 5–1   Net Price of Records under Monopoly

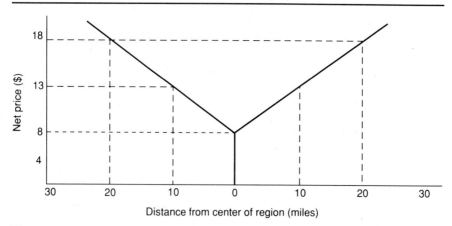

The net price of records is the sum of the store price ($8) and the cost of traveling to the record store (50¢ per round-trip mile per record).

Figure 5–2 shows how Bob the monopolist chooses the profit-maximizing output. The monopolist's demand curve is negatively sloped: as the store price increases, people buy fewer records. The negatively sloped demand curve generates a negatively sloped marginal revenue curve. Profits are maximized where marginal revenue equals marginal cost, so the monopolist produces q_m units of output. If the monopolist sells q_m records, the market-clearing price is P_m (the point on the demand curve above q_m). Total profit (revenue less cost) is shown by the shaded area.

Entry and Competition

Since Bob the monopolist is making positive economic profits, other entrepreneurs will enter the record-store business in anticipation of economic profits. Some consumers (those who live near the new record stores) will patronize the new stores, so Bob's demand curve shifts to the left: at every price, he will have fewer customers. As his demand curve and marginal-revenue curve shift to the left, his sales volume decreases and his profits fall. In other

FIGURE 5–2   Price and Quantity with Single Record Store

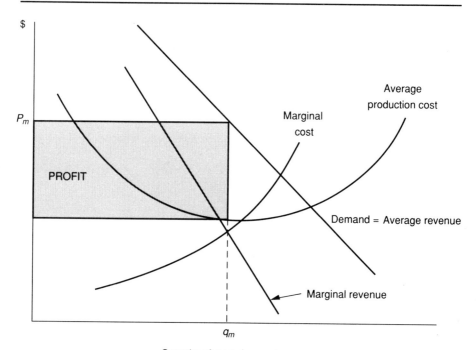

The profit-maximizing output (q_m) is the quantity at which marginal revenue equals marginal cost. The monopoly price is P_m, generating profit equal to the shaded area.

words, entry causes competition, which decreases Bob's sales volume and profits.

How long will entry and the resulting decreases in profits continue? Equilibrium occurs when two conditions are satisfied. First, every firm is maximizing its profits, producing the output at which marginal revenue equals marginal cost. Second, economic profits are zero: the store price equals the average total cost of production. Figure 5–3 shows the equilibrium situation. At an output q_e, marginal revenue equals marginal cost (firms are maximizing profits) and the store price P_e equals the average production cost (profits are zero). At the equilibrium output, the marginal revenue curve intersects the marginal cost curve, and the demand curve is tangent to the average cost curve.

This is the theory of **monopolistic competition** (covered in most intermediate microeconomics textbooks). Each record store is a monopolist within its own territory, but its monopoly power is limited by entry and competition. Each store faces a negatively sloped demand curve, and entry shifts the demand curve to the point at which profits are zero. Like a perfectly competitive firm, a firm with a local monopoly earns zero economic profits.

FIGURE 5–3 Equilibrium Price and Quantity of Records with Entry

Entry shifts the demand curve of the individual store to the left, decreasing the price and profits. Entry continues until profits are zero. The equilibrium output is q_e because $MR = MC$ (firms are maximizing profits) and $P = AC$ (profits equal zero).

Efficiency Trade-Offs

There are some efficiency trade-offs associated with entry and competition. On the one hand, entry decreases output per firm, so individual firms move upward along their average cost curves. Scale economies are lost: output is divided among a larger number of firms, each of which produces at a higher average cost. On the other hand, the increase in the number of stores decreases travel distances for consumers, so it decreases travel costs.

Figure 5–4 shows the trade-offs between production and travel costs. The average total cost of records is defined as the sum of average production cost (from Figure 5–3) and average travel cost. Average travel cost is the travel cost incurred by the typical record consumer. As the output of the record stores increases, the market area increases and the typical consumer travels a longer distance to buy records. Therefore, the average travel cost increases with the output of the store. Average total cost (production plus travel costs) reaches its minimum point at q_t, far below the output that minimizes average production cost (q_c).

Entry decreases output per firm, generating bad news and good news.

FIGURE 5–4   Trade-Offs with Entry: Production Costs versus Travel Costs

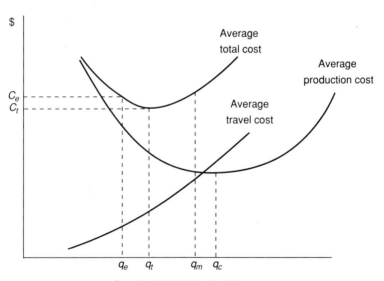

Entry increases the number of firms and decreases output per firm. As output falls, average production cost increases and average travel cost decreases. In this case, entry goes "too far" in the sense that average total cost is higher than the feasible minimum (C_t).

The bad news is that the average production cost increases as firms move up the average production-cost curve. The good news is that the average travel cost decreases as firms move down the average travel cost curve. Starting from q_m in Figure 5–4, the good news dominates the bad news until output per firm reaches q_t. From that point on, further entry increases production costs by more than it decreases travel costs, so average total cost increases. In equilibrium, the output per firm drops to q_e, meaning that the entry process goes too far in the sense that average total cost is higher than the feasible minimum.

Figure 5–4 shows only one possible equilibrium outcome. For different sets of cost and demand curves, the equilibrium output per firm might be greater than q_t or equal to q_t. In other words, unless one knows something about the demand and cost curves, it's impossible to predict exactly where on the average total cost curve the firm ends up. However, we do know that (a) entry decreases output per firm and (b) in equilibrium, the firm does *not* produce at the minimum point of its average production-cost curve, but at some point to the left of the minimum point.

Market Areas

Figure 5–5 shows the market areas for record stores under the assumption that there are three stores in equilibrium. Tammy and Dick set up record stores 20 miles from Bob and charge the same price for records ($6). Tammy underprices Bob for the western third of the region, and Dick underprices Bob for the eastern third of the region. The three record stores split the region into three equal market areas, so every store has a circular market area with a 10-mile radius.

The market arrangement in Figure 5–5 has two implications for record consumers. First, if the spaces between the circular market areas are ignored, the maximum net price is $11—the sum of the price charged by record stores ($6) and the maximum travel cost ($5). Second, every household patronizes the record store closest to its home. All stores charge the same price for the same product, so a household will patronize the store with the lowest travel costs.

DIFFERENCES IN MARKET AREAS

What factors determine the market areas of market-oriented firms? The size of the market area depends on travel costs, per capita demand, population density, and scale economies. This section uses a simple algebraic model to identify the determinants of market areas. The first part of the section assumes that the demand for records is perfectly inelastic, and the second part drops this assumption.

FIGURE 5–5   Equilibrium Market Areas

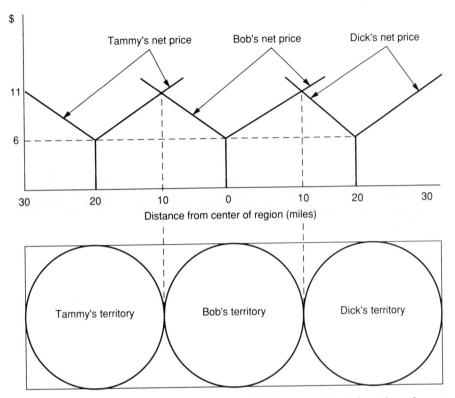

Each store's market area is the area over which its net price is less than the net prices of other stores. Each store has a circular territory with a 10-mile radius.

Determinants of Market Area—Fixed Demand

An expression for the size of the market area can be derived with some simple algebra. The following symbols represent the market for records in a region:

   d = monthly per capita demand (number of records)
   e = population density (people per square mile)
   A = land area of the region (in square miles)
   q = output of the typical record store (records sold per month)
   Q = total (regionwide) demand for records

To simplify matters, per capita demand (d) is assumed to be independent of the net price of records: the individual consumer demands a fixed number of records regardless of the net price. In other words, the individual demand curve is perfectly inelastic. Later in the chapter, this assumption will be relaxed.

What is the equilibrium number of record stores? The total demand for records (Q) equals the product of per capita demand (d), population density (e), and the land area of the region (A):

$$Q = d \cdot e \cdot A \qquad (5\text{--}1)$$

Table 5–2 provides a numerical example that shows how to compute the equilibrium number of stores. Per capita demand is 4 records and population density is 50 people per square mile, so **demand density** (record demand per square mile, equal to d times e) is 200. The region has an area of 300 square miles, so total demand is 60,000 records (200 times 300). The number of record stores in the region (N) is total demand divided by the output per store:

$$N = \frac{Q}{q} \qquad (5\text{--}2)$$

Output per firm is 1,000 records, so there will be 60 stores in the region (60,000 divided by 1,000).

How large is the market area of record stores? The size of the market area (M) equals the land area of the region divided by the number of stores:

$$M = \frac{A}{N} \qquad (5\text{--}3)$$

If the region has a land area of 300 square miles and there are 60 stores, the market area of the typical store is 5 square miles. Using the expressions for N and Q, the expression for M can be rewritten as

$$M = \frac{q}{d \cdot e} \qquad (5\text{--}4)$$

TABLE 5–2   Numerical Example of Number of Stores and Market Area

Variable	Symbol	Numerical Example
Per capita demand	d	4
Population density (people per square mile)	e	50
Demand density (records per square mile)	$d \cdot e$	200
Land area (square miles)	A	300
Output per store	q	1,000
Total demand	$Q = d \cdot e \cdot A$	60,000
Number of stores	$N = Q/q$	60
Market area (square miles)	$M = q/(d \cdot e)$	5.0

FIGURE 5–6 Increase in Scale Economies Increases Output per Firm

An increase in scale economies shifts the average production-cost curve downward, shifting the average total-cost curve downward. The minimum points of both curves move to the right. If the record store produces at the minimum point of its average total-cost curve, output per store increases from q_1 to q_2.

In other words, the size of the market area is determined by output per store (q), per capita demand (d), and population density (e). In Table 5–2, $q = 1,000$, $d = 4$, and $e = 50$, so the market area is 5.0 square miles.

The algebraic model identifies three factors that determine the size of the firm's market area: per capita demand, population density, and output per store. Output per store is affected by both scale economies and transportation costs. How do changes in each of these variables affect market areas?

Market Area and Scale Economies.   Figure 5–6 shows the effects of an increase in scale economies on the firm's costs curves. An increase in scale economies means that the average production-cost curve is negatively sloped over a larger range of output. The average production cost is minimized at q_4 instead of q_3. Since average total cost equals average production cost plus average travel cost, an increase in scale economies also shifts the average total-cost curve. Average total cost is minimized at q_2 instead of q_1.

The shifts of the cost curves increase output per firm. Although it's not possible to predict exactly how much the firm will produce, it's safe to say that its output will increase. One possibility is that the firm starts at q_1 (the minimum point of the original average total-costs curve) and moves to q_2 (the new minimum point). If the firm starts with an output close to q_1, it is likely to switch to an output close to q_2. In general, an increase in scale economies increases the advantages of large-scale operations: starting from q_1, the benefit of increasing output (the savings in production costs) will exceed the costs (increase in travel costs), so output per firm will increase.

An increase in scale economies increases the market area of the typical record store. As output per store increases, fewer stores are required to serve the region. Using the numbers in Table 5–2, if output per store increases from 1,000 to 1,200, the number of stores will decrease from 60 to 50 (60,000/1,200). The decrease in the number of stores increases the market area from 5 square miles to 6 square miles (300 divided by 50). Because an increase in scale economies increases output per store, every store needs a larger market area to exploit its scale economies. Note that his result depends on the assumption that per capita demand is fixed, an assumption to be relaxed later in the chapter.

Market Area and Travel Costs.   How does a decrease in travel costs affect the output per store? Suppose that the development of a faster and cheaper travel mode decreases the monetary and time costs of travel. In Figure 5–7, travel costs are cut in half, narrowing the gap between the average

FIGURE 5–7 Decrease in Travel Costs Increases Output per Firm

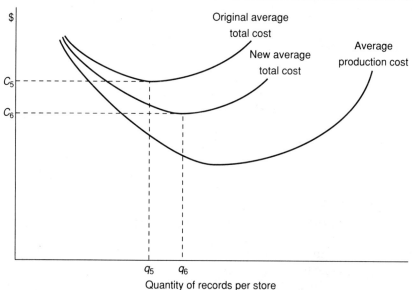

A decrease in travel costs shifts the average travel-cost curve downward, shifting the average total-cost curve downward. The minimum point on ATC moves to the right. If the record store produces at the minimum point of its average total-cost curve, output per store increases from q_5 to q_6.

total cost and average production cost by one half. The minimum point of the total-cost curve moves to the right, increasing the cost-minimizing output from q_5 to q_6. A decrease in travel costs decreases the relative importance of travel costs, so the minimum point of the total-cost curve moves closer to the minimum point of the production-cost curve.

The shift of the average cost curve increases output per firm. Again, it's impossible to predict exactly how much the firm will produce, but it's safe to say that output increases. If the firm starts with an output close to q_5 (the minimum point on the original average total-cost curve), it is likely to switch to an output close to q_6. In general, a decrease in transport costs increases the advantages of large-scale operations: starting from q_5, the cost of increasing output will be less than the benefit, so output per firm will increase.

The decrease in travel costs increases the market area because every store needs a larger territory to sell its output. Using the numbers in Table 5–2, if output per store increases from 1,000 to 1,250, the number of stores will decrease from 60 to 48 (60,000/1,250). The decrease in the number of stores increases the market area per store from 5 square miles to 6.25 square miles (300 divided by 48). Because a decrease in travel costs increases output per store, every store needs a larger market area to exploit its scale economies. Again, this result depends on the assumption that per capita demand is fixed, an assumption to be relaxed later in the chapter.

Market Area and Per Capita Demand.   How does an increase in per capita demand affect the size of the market area? An increase in per capita demand increases the demand density (the number of records sold per square mile, or d times e). If output per store is fixed, each store needs a smaller market area to exhaust its scale economies. For example, a doubling of per capita demand doubles total demand, so it doubles the number of stores. If there are twice as many stores in the region, the market area per store will be cut in half (from 5 square miles to 2.5 square miles).

Market Area and Population Density.   How does an increase in population density affect the market area? Like an increase in per capita demand, an increase in population density increases demand density. If output per store is fixed, each store needs a smaller market area to exhaust its scale economies. For example, a quadrupling of population density quadruples total demand for records, so it quadruples the number of stores. If there are four times as many stores in the region, the market area per store decreases to one fourth its original size (from 5 square miles to 1.25 square miles).

Will output per store be affected by an increase in population density? An increase in population density decreases the average travel distances for consumers (the typical consumer is closer to the nearest store), decreasing average travel costs. To explain this, suppose that density is so high that everyone lives within a one-minute walk of a record store. Obviously, travel costs will be lower in this high-density area. In Figure 5–7, the slope of the average travel-cost curve decreases, increasing output per store. The decrease in transport costs increases the advantages of large-scale operations, so output per firm will increase. If output per store increases with population density, an increase in population density may either increase or decrease the market area.

Market Area and Income.   How do differences in income affect the size of the market area? Consider a region with the following characteristics:

1. There are two cities, a poor one and a wealthy one.
2. A record is a "normal" good (positive income elasticity of demand).
3. Land is a "normal" good (positive income elasticity).

The city with the larger demand density will have a smaller market area for record stores. Since both records and land are "normal" goods, the wealthy city has higher per capita demands for both records and land; its residents consume more records per capita, but also live in relatively low-density housing. For example, the wealthy may live in single-family homes and the poor may live in apartment buildings. In the wealthy city, the larger per capita demand for records (which increases demand density) is offset in part by a lower population density (which decreases demand density), so demand density may be either higher or lower. Therefore, the wealthy city may have a smaller or a larger market area. The relationship between income and market area is ambiguous because income affects both per capita demand and population density.

Under what circumstances will the wealthy community have a larger market area? Suppose that the income elasticity of demand for land is large relative to the income elasticity of demand for records. If so, the density effect (increased income decreases population density) will dominate the demand effect (increased income increases per capita demand) and the wealthy city will have a lower demand density and a larger market area. Record stores will need larger market areas because although each household consumes more records, there are many fewer households per square mile.

Table 5–3 shows a simple example of the effects of differences in income on the size of the market area. The income elasticity of demand for records is assumed to be 0.50. In the wealthy city, where per capita income is 20 percent higher, the per capita demand for records is 10 percent higher. In the middle column, the income elasticity of demand for land is assumed to be 1.0. Therefore, the wealthy city has a 20 percent higher demand for land and a 20 percent lower population density (40 instead of 50). Given these assumptions, the wealthy city has a lower demand density, so record stores need larger market areas to exploit their scale economies (5.68 square miles instead of 5 square miles).

This result depends, of course, on the numerical assumptions. If the de-

TABLE 5–3   Income and Market Area with Different Income Elasticities of Demand for Land

	Poor City	Wealthy City	
		Low Income Elasticity	High Income Elasticity
Income elasticity for land	1.0	1.0	0.25
Per capita income	$1,000	$1,200	$1,200
Per capita demand for records (d)	4	4.4	4.4
Population density (e)	50	40	47.5
Demand density (d times e)	200	176	209
Output per store (q)	1,000	1,000	1,000
Market area in square miles ($q/d \cdot e$)	5	5.68	4.78

mand for land were relatively income-inelastic, the difference in population density would be relatively small. The demand effect would dominate the density effect, so the wealthy city would have a smaller market area. In the third column of Table 5–3, the income elasticity of demand for land is assumed to be 0.25: population density in the wealthy city is 47.5 (a 5 percent difference) instead of 40; demand density is 209 instead of 176; and the market area is 4.78 instead of 5.68. In general, if the income elasticity for land is small relative to the income elasticity for records, the wealthier city will have a smaller market area.

Market Areas and the Law of Demand

Up to this point, the discussion of the market area has assumed that per capita demand is fixed. What happens if consumers obey the law of demand, increasing the quantity of records demanded as the net price decreases?

Travel Costs.   If consumers obey the law of demand, a decrease in travel costs has an ambiguous effect on the market area. As explained earlier in the chapter, a decrease in travel costs increases the output per store because the minimum point on the average total-cost curve moves to the right. The market area increases because each store needs a larger territory to sell its output. This is the output effect of a decrease in travel costs. The decrease in travel costs also decreases the net price of records: in Figure 5–7, the net cost decreases from C_5 to C_6. If consumers obey the law of demand, per capita demand will increase, so each firm will need a smaller territory to sell a given output. This is the demand effect of a decrease in travel costs.

The net effect of a decrease in travel costs depends on the relative strengths of the output effect and the demand effect. The expression for the size of the market area is

$$M = \frac{q}{d \cdot e} \qquad (5\text{--}5)$$

Suppose that the output effect increases q from 1,000 to 1,500 and population density (e) is 50. If the demand effect is relatively weak and d increases from four to five, the market area will grow from five square miles (1000/200) to six square miles (1500/250). Alternatively, if the demand effect is relatively strong and d increases from 4 to 10, the market area will shrink from 5 square miles to 3 square miles (1500/500). The strength of the demand effect depends on the price elasticity of demand for records: the more elastic the demand for records, the stronger the demand effect. Therefore, a decrease in travel costs is more likely to decrease the market area if the price elasticity is large.

For an example of the effects of changes in travel costs on market areas, consider the effects of parcel post on farm communities. Before the introduction of parcel post in 1913, most farmers purchased most of their goods, including clothing and tools, in general stores in small farm communities. The introduction of parcel post decreased the costs of shipping goods from big-city merchants to farmers. Mail order houses (Sears Roebuck, Montgomery Ward) underpriced the local general store, and farmers started buying clothing and tools from the mail-order houses. In the year following the introduction of parcel post, the sales of Sears and Montgomery Ward quintupled and many general stores disappeared.

The introduction of parcel post decreased the costs of transporting clothes and tools, increasing the market area of the typical firm. The general store with its small market area was replaced by Sears and Wards with their large market areas. In this case, the output effect was stronger than the demand effect, so the market area grew. Although farmers consumed more trousers and shovels as the net prices fell, the increases in per capita demands were not large enough to offset the output effect.

Scale Economies.   If consumers obey the law of demand, an increase in scale economies has an ambiguous effect on the size of the market area. As explained earlier in the chapter, an increase in scale economies increases the output per store, which in turn increases the market area required to exhaust scale economies (the output effect). If the net price falls as a result of the increased scale economies, the per capita demand for records will increase, generating a demand effect that provides downward pressure on the market area: the firm needs a smaller territory to sell a given output. The net effect of an increase in scale economies depends on the relative strengths of the output effect and the demand effect. If the demand for the good is relatively inelastic, an increase in scale economies will increase the market area.

The Demise of Small Stores

The demise of the small store illustrates the effects of changes in population density and transportation costs on market areas. Before the late 1800s, most goods in the United States were purchased in small stores: people bought food in small "mom and pop" grocery stores and purchased other goods in small general stores. The traditional merchant was involved in every transaction, playing two roles:

1. **Huckster**. The merchant assisted customers in their choice of goods, providing information on alternative products and persuading reluctant customers to buy the good. The merchant was an effective huckster because he knew the features of every good in the store and was a trusted source of information about his products.

2. **Haggler**. The merchant negotiated with each customer over the price of the good. The merchant was an effective haggler because he knew the cost of every good in his store and could quickly compute his profit margin as he negotiated with the customer. In addition, the merchant was skillful in assessing his customers' willingness to pay for various goods.

Since huckster and haggler skills were not easily transferred to low-skilled employees, the merchant was involved in every transaction, so the traditional store was relatively small.

The replacement of the small general store with larger stores suggests that the optimum store size increased. The optimum size increased for a number of reasons, two of which are related to transportation costs. First, in the late 1800s and early 1900s, innovations in urban transit increased the speed and decreased the monetary costs of intracity travel. Second, rapid urbanization during this same period increased population density, decreasing average travel distances (from home to store). As travel costs decreased, merchants expanded to exploit scale economies in marketing.

As merchants developed larger stores, they adopted new marketing techniques. New advertising and display techniques made the goods "sell themselves." Some stores, such as Macy's and Marshall Fields, used newspaper advertising to inform and persuade consumers. Woolworth's used plate-glass windows to display goods and attract customers. Grocery stores displayed their goods in such a way that consumers could do their own comparison shopping. A grocery store named Piggly Wiggly developed a floor plan that forced customers to walk through a maze from the entrance to the exit. In following the prescribed path from the entrance to the exit, customers were exposed to every commodity in the store, allowing them to make their own choices. These marketing techniques freed the merchant from huckster responsibilities. Another new feature was the single-price policy, under which the merchant charged each customer the same price. The single-price policy freed the merchant from haggling responsibility.

These two new marketing techniques freed the merchant from being involved in every transaction, allowing an increase in the size of the store. The merchant hired low-skilled laborers to perform the simple tasks of stocking shelves, wrapping goods, and collecting money. A single merchant could run a store with dozens of low-wage employees, so the self-service store could underprice the small traditional store.

Market Areas of Different Industries

Market areas vary from industry to industry, reflecting differences in travel costs, per capita demand, and scale economies. If scale economies are large *relative* to per capita demand, the industry will have a small number of firms, each of which has a large market area. In constrast, if scale economies are small relative to per capita demand, there will be a large number of firms with small market areas.

Consider the market areas of pizza parlors and Tibetan restaurants. Suppose that both activities are subject to the same sort of scale economies, so the optimum output for both types of restaurants is 200 meals per day. If the total (regionwide) demand for pizza is 10,000 meals per day, the region will have 50 pizza parlors (10,000/200). If the total demand for Tibetan food is 200 meals per day, a single Tibetan restaurant will serve the entire region. The market area is not determined by scale economies *per se*, but by scale economies *relative* to per capita demand.

CENTRAL-PLACE THEORY

Central-place theory, which was developed by Christaller (1966) and refined by Losch (1954), is used to predict the number, size, and scope of cities in a region. The theory is based on a simple extension of market-area analysis. Market areas vary from industry to industry, depending on scale economies and per capita demand, so every industry has a different location pattern. Central-place theory shows how the location patterns of different industries combine to form a regional system of cities. The theory answers two questions about cities in a regional economy:

1. How many cities will develop?
2. Why are some cities larger than others?

A Simple Central-Place Model

Consider a region with three consumer products: records, pizzas, and jewelry. The region has the following characteristics:

1. **Population density**. The initial distribution of population is uniform. The total population of the region is 80,000.
2. **No shopping externalities**. As explained in Chapter 2, shopping externali-

ties normally occur with complementary goods (one-stop shopping) and imperfect substitutes (comparison shopping). The simple central-place model assumes that there are no shopping externalities.

3. **Ubiquitous inputs**. All inputs are available at all locations at the same prices.

4. **Uniform demand**. For each product, per capita demand is the same throughout the region.

5. **Number of stores**. The three goods have different per capita demands and scale economies:

   a. **Jewelry:** scale economies are large relative to per capita demand. Every jewelry store requires a population of 80,000, so a single jeweler will serve the entire region.

   b. **Records:** scale economies are moderate relative to per capita demand. Every record store requires a population of 20,000, so there will be four record stores in the region.

   c. **Pizza:** scale economies are small relative to per capita demand. Every pizza parlor requires a population of 5,000, so there will be sixteen pizza parlors in the region.

The central-place model is a model of **market-oriented** firms, defined in Chapter 3 as firms that base their location decisions exclusively on access to their consumers. Because all inputs are ubiquitous, the firms ignore input costs in their location decision.

The single jeweler will locate at the center of the region. Because production costs are the same at all locations (all inputs are ubiquitous), the jeweler will minimize total costs by minimizing travel costs. According to the principle of median location (discussed in Chapter 3), travel costs are minimized at the median location. Because population density is uniform, the median location is the center of the region.

A city will develop around the jewelry store. Jewelry workers will locate near the store to economize on commuting costs. The population density near the jeweler will increase, generating a city (a place of relatively high density) at the center of the region. In Figure 5–8, a city develops at point L.

The record stores will carve up the region into market areas, causing the development of additional cities. If the region's population density were uniform, record firms would carve out four equal market areas. However, because there is a city surrounding the jeweler in the center of the region, there will be enough demand to support more than one record store near city L. If city L has enough people to support two record stores, the two other record stores will split the rest of the region into two market areas. In Figure 5–8, two more cities develop at the locations marked with an M.

The pizza parlors will also carve up the region into market areas, causing the development of more cities. Because the population density is higher in the cities that develop around the jewelry and record stores, there will be more than one pizza parlor in L and each of the M cities. If L will support four

FIGURE 5–8   The Central-Place Hierarchy

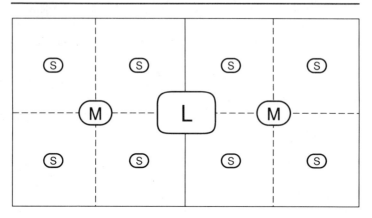

City L	M Cities	S Cities
1 Jeweler	1 Record store	1 Pizza parlor
2 Record stores	2 Pizza parlors	
4 Pizza parlors		

There are 11 cities in the region: one large city (L), two medium-sized cities (M), and 8 small cities (S). The larger the city, the greater variety of goods sold.

pizza parlors and each of the M cities will support two pizza parlors, a total of eight pizza parlors will locate in cities L and M. The remaining eight pizza parlors will divide the rest of the region into eight market areas, causing the development of eight additional cities (the places marked with S in Figure 5–8).

The rectangular region has a total of 11 cities. The large city at the center of the region sells jewelry, records, and pizza. City L has a population of 20,000, meaning that it is large enough to support four pizza parlors (5,000 people per pizza parlor). The city sells records to consumers from the four surrounding S cities, so the total number of record consumers is 40,000 (20,000 from L and 5,000 each from the four S cities), enough to support two record stores. The two medium-sized cities sell records and pizza. Each of the M cities has a population of 10,000, so each city is large enough to support two pizza parlors. Each city sells records to consumers from two nearby S cities, so the total number of record consumers in each M city is 20,000 (10,000 from L and 5,000 each from two S cities), enough to support one record store per M city. The eight small cities sell only pizza. Each of the S cities has a population of 5,000, meaning that each city can support one pizza parlor.

Figure 5–9 shows the size distribution of cities in the region. The vertical axis measures city size (population), and the horizontal axis measures the rank of the city. The largest city (L) has a population of 20,000; the second

FIGURE 5–9   Size Distribution of Cities with the Simple Central-Place
Model

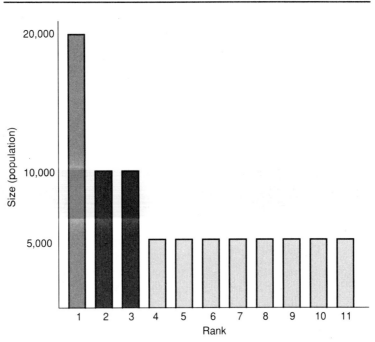

The simple central-place model generates one large city (L) with a
population of 20,000, two medium-sized cities (M) each of which has
a population of 10,000, and eight small cities (S), each of which has a
population of 5,000.

and third largest cities (M cities) have populations of 10,000; and the fourth
through the eleventh largest cities (S cities) have populations of 5,000.

The simple central-place model generates a **hierarchical system of cities**.
There are three distinct types of cities: L (high order), M (medium order), and
S (low order). The larger the city, the greater the variety of goods sold. Each
city imports goods from higher-order cities and exports goods to lower-order
cities. Cities of the same order do not interact. For example, an M city imports
jewelry from L and exports records to S cities, but does not interact with the
other M city. Similarly, an S city imports jewelry from L and records from either L or an M city, but does not trade with other S cities. The system of cities
is hierarchical in the sense that there are distinct types of cities and distinct
patterns of trade dominance.

There are three lessons from the simple central-place model:

1. **Diversity and scale economies.** The region's cities differ in size
and scope. This diversity occurs because the three consumer products
have different scale economies relative to per capita demand, so they

have different market areas. To explain the importance of differences in relative scale economies, suppose that the three goods have the same scale economies relative to per capita demand, so the region has 16 jewelers, 16 record stores, and 16 pizza parlors. The market areas of the three goods would coincide, so the region would have 16 identical cities, each of which would provide all three goods. In other words, if there are no differences in scale economies relative to per capita demand, the region's cities will be identical.

2. **Large means few.** The region has a small number of large cities and a large number of small cities. Why isn't there a large number of large cities and a small number of small cities? A city is relatively large if it provides more goods than a smaller city. The extra goods provided by a large city are those goods that are subject to relatively large scale economies. Since there are few stores selling the goods subject to relatively large scale economies, few cities can be large. In the simple central-place model, L is larger than an M city because L sells records, pizza, *and* jewelry. Since there is only one jewelry store in the region, there is only one city larger than the M cities.

3. **Shopping paths.** Consumers travel only to bigger cities. For example, consumers from an M city travel to L to buy jewelry, but do not travel to the other M city or an S city to consume records or pizza. Instead, they buy records and pizza in their own city. Similarly, consumers in S cities travel to larger cities for jewelry and records, but do not shop in other S cities.

Relaxing the Assumptions

Several of the assumptions of the simple central-place model are unrealistic. This section relaxes some of the assumptions and addresses two questions. First, does a more realistic model generate the same hierarchical pattern of cities? Second, does a more realistic model have more or fewer cities?

Scale Economies, Market Areas, and the Number of Firms. Suppose that the equilibrium number of pizza parlors decreases from 16 to 8. As explained earlier in the chapter, this would occur if scale economies increased relative to per capita demand, increasing the market area of pizza parlors. The decrease in the number of pizza parlors would decrease the equilibrium number of cities in the region: there would be two pizza parlors in city L and one parlor in each of the M cities, leaving four pizza parlors for the S cities. The equilibrium number of cities would decrease from 11 to 7 because there are fewer cities that provide only pizzas. The hierarchical pattern of cities persists: each city still provides a subset of the goods sold in larger cities.

Shopping Externalities—Imperfect Substitutes. Suppose that consumers buy used records instead of new ones. Used records are imperfect substitutes: consumers engage in comparison shopping, comparing the used records from several stores before buying. Therefore, record stores will cluster to facilitate comparison shopping. If the optimum cluster is four record stores, the stores will cluster at the center of the region. The region will have only two types of cities, large ones (with jewelers, record stores, and pizza parlors) and small ones (with pizza parlors). The presence of imperfect substitutes reduces the equilibrium number of cities from 11 to 9 because record stores compromise on their ideal (central-place) locations to exploit shopping externalities. Although comparison shopping decreases the number of cities, it does not disrupt the hierarchical pattern of cities.

Shopping Externalities—Complements.   Suppose that pizza and records are complementary goods, so that the typical consumer purchases a record and a pizza on the same shopping trip. If so, record stores and pizza parlors will pair up to facilitate one-stop shopping. If pizza parlors cannot survive without a companion record store, there will be only two types of cities in the region: large (with jewelry, records, and pizza) and medium (with records and pizza). Pizza parlors compromise on their ideal (central-place) locations to exploit the shopping externalities associated with one-stop shopping, so the equilibrium number of cities decreases from 11 to 3. The presence of complementary goods does not, however, disrupt the urban hierarchy.

Variation in Demand.   One of the assumptions of the simple central-place model is that per capita demand does not vary with city size. Systematic variation in per capita demand may disrupt the urban hierarchy.

Consider first the possibility that the per capita demand for pizza decreases as city size increases. In other words, per capita demand is large in small cities, moderate in medium-sized cities, and zero in large cities. Alternatively, pizza could be replaced in the example with grits, a good for which per capita demand is higher in small cities. Since there will be no pizza parlors (or grits restaurants) in the large city, the urban hierarchy will be disrupted: the medium and the small cities supply goods that are not available in the large city. The variation in demand may also increase the equilibrium number of cities: if the region has the same total pizza demand, all 16 pizza parlors will be outside the largest city (instead of 12), so there will be more than 8 small (pizza-only) cities.

What if the per capita demand increases with city size? Pizza parlors will be more concentrated in medium and large cities: there may be 6 pizza parlors in L, 3 in each type-M city, leaving only 4 of the 16 pizza parlors for small cities. Therefore, there will be a total of 7 cities instead of 11. This type of variation in demand does not, however, disrupt the hierarchy of cities.

Other Types of Industry

Central-place theory is applicable to market-oriented firms. The objective of a market-oriented firm is to minimize the travel costs of its consumers. The market-oriented firm is not concerned about (a) the costs of transporting its inputs or (b) the costs of local inputs. Central-place theory predicts the pattern of cities that would result if all firms were market oriented.

As explained in Chapter 3 (Where Do Cities Develop?), there are two other types of firms, resource-oriented firms and firms oriented toward local inputs. For the resource-oriented firm (e.g., the producer of baseball bats), the costs of transporting raw materials are relatively high, so the firm locates near its input sources. For the input-oriented firm, the costs of local inputs vary across space and the firm locates near sources of inexpensive labor, energy, or intermediate goods.

The location decisions of resource-oriented firms may disrupt the central-place hierarchy. Suppose that a bat factory is located near the coastal forests of the region. Once the coastal city is established, it may attract some market-oriented firms (e.g., pizza parlors). In addition to the three types of cities described above (large [L], medium [M], and small [S]), there will be a coastal city with a bat factory and pizza parlors. The urban hierarchy is disrupted because the coastal city has one activity (bat production) not available in the largest city.

It is possible that the bat factory will not disrupt the region's urban hierarchy. Suppose that the coastal city grows to the point at which it becomes the median location for the jeweler. If so, the coastal city will have all four types of goods (jewels, bats, records, pizza). The medium-sized cities will have two goods (pizza and records), and the small cities will have only one good (pizzas). In this case, the hierarchy is preserved because the coastal city takes the place of city L.

The same arguments apply to input-oriented activities such as textile firms (labor oriented), aluminum producers (energy oriented), corporate headquarters (oriented to intermediate inputs), and firms engaging in research and development (oriented to amenities valued by engineers and scientists). If the input-oriented firm locates near its input source, the resulting city will have some goods that are not available in the largest city. If, however, the city becomes the median location in the region, it may replace city L as the largest city in the region.

Central-Place Theory and the Real World

While central-place theory does not literally apply to many regions, it provides a useful way of thinking about a regional system of cities. The theory identifies the market forces that generate a hierarchical system of cities. It explains why some cities are larger than others and why the set of goods sold in a particular city is typically a subset of the goods sold in a larger city. Exceptions to the hierarchical pattern result from (a) systematic variation in per capita demand and (b) the location decisions of firms oriented toward raw materials and local inputs.

Empirical Studies of Central-Place Systems.   Table 5–4 shows the results of an empirical study of central-place theory. Berry and Garrison (1958) examined the economic activities of urban places in Snohomish County, Washington. They concluded that the dozens of communities could be divided into three distinct types of urban places: town (high order), village (medium order), and hamlet (low order). The largest urban place, a town, was about twice as large as a village, which was in turn about twice as large as a hamlet. There were about half as many towns as villages and about half as many villages as hamlets. As one moves down the hierarchy, the number of establishments and the number of functions per settlement decrease, which is exactly what is predicated by central-place theory. Berry and Garrison concluded that the system of urban places was indeed hierarchical, with individual communities exporting to lower order places and importing from higher order places.

Most of the empirical studies of central-place theory examine systems of small towns in agricultural regions. Such regions have little industrial activity, so most firms are oriented toward the local market, not toward natural resources or local inputs. What about the national economy? As explained earlier, the central-place hierarchy is disrupted by the location choices of resource-oriented firms and input-oriented firms. Since a large fraction of national employment comes from resource-oriented and input-oriented activities, it would be quite surprising if a study of the national economy provided much support for the simple central-place model.

Size Distribution of Cities—The Rank-Size Rule.   Figure 5–10–A shows the size distribution of the 25 largest metropolitan areas in the United States in 1986. Metropolitan size (population) decreases from about 18 million in the largest metropolitan area (New York CMSA) to 1.5 million in the 25th largest (Kansas City MSA). Figure 5–10–B shows the size distribution for the 26th through the 131st largest metropolitan areas. Note that the vertical scale is different from the scale in Figure 5–10–A. Population decreases from 1.4

TABLE 5–4   The Urban Hierarchy in Snohomish County, Washington

	Type of Place		
	Town	*Village*	*Hamlet*
Number of places	4	9	20
Average population	2433	948	417
Average number of establishments per place	149	54.4	6.9
Average number of functions per place	59.8	32.1	5.9
Average number of establishments per function	2.5	1.7	1.2

source: Brian J. L. Berry and William Garrison, "The Functional Bases of the Central Place Hierarchy," *Economic Geography*, April 1958, pp. 145–54.

FIGURE 5–10–A   Size Distribution of 25 Largest U.S. Metropolitan Areas

FIGURE 5–10–B   Size Distribution of 26th through 131st Largest U.S. Metropolitan Areas

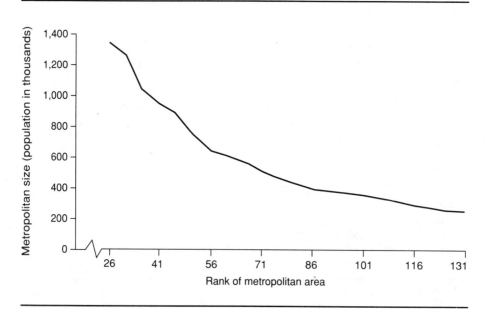

SOURCE: U.S. Bureau of the Census, *Statistical Abstract of the United States*, 1988.

million in the 26th largest metropolitan area (Portland, Oregon CMSA) to 251,000 in the 131st largest (Columbus, Georgia MSA).

How does the U.S. size distribution of cities compare to the size distribution generated by the simple model of central-place theory? To compare the two size distributions, compare Figure 5–9 to Figure 5–10. Both figures show a small number of large cities and a large number of small cities. In addition, as one moves down in the ranking (to smaller cities), the size difference between two successive cities decreases.

Geographers and economists have estimated the relationship between city size and rank. The relationship is approximated by the **rank-size rule:**

$$\text{Rank} \cdot \text{Size} = \text{Constant} \qquad (5\text{–}6)$$

This rule suggests that the product of rank and size is the same in all cities in a region. For example, if the largest metropolitan area has a population of 18 million, the rank-size rule suggests that the second largest city has a population of 9 million, the third largest city has a population of 6 million, and the 18th largest city has a population of 1 million.

Empirical evidence concerning the rank-size rule comes from statistical studies of city-size distributions. The hypothesized relationship between rank and size is

$$\text{Size} = \frac{\text{Constant}}{\text{Rank}^\beta} \qquad (5\text{–}7)$$

The rank-size rule is a good approximation of the relationship between rank and size if β (the exponent of rank) is close to 1.0. Rosen and Resnick (1980) estimate the rank-size relationship for 44 countries. Although the value of β was 1.0 for the United States (supporting the rank-size rule), there was substantial variation in β across other countries, with an average value of 0.88. This result suggests that population is more evenly distributed than would be predicted by the rank-size rule. Rosen and Resnick conclude that the rank-size rule is only a first approximation to the relationship between rank and size.

APPLICATION—OPTIMUM NUMBER OF FIRE STATIONS

This final section applies the concepts underlying market-area analysis to decision making in the public sector. A city government could use these concepts to determine the optimum number of public facilities (fire stations, police stations, schools, and public libraries).

The General Case

Figure 5–11 shows how a city government could use the concepts of market-area analysis to determine the optimum number of fire stations. The horizontal axis measures the number of fire stations, and the vertical axis measures the average cost of fire protection. The average production-cost curve is positively sloped: because of scale economies in fire fighting (indivisible inputs and labor specialization), a large number of small fire stations is more expensive, on average, than a small number of large stations. The average transportation-cost curve is negatively sloped: as the number of stations increases, travel time from the nearest station to a fire decreases, so the damage from fire decreases. The average total cost equals the sum of the average production cost and average travel cost. As shown in Figure 5–11, the average total cost curve is U-shaped.

Suppose that the city's objective is to minimize the average total cost of fire-protection service. Starting from a single station, the city should increase the number of stations as long as the decrease in average transportation cost exceeds the increase in average production cost. The city trades off scale economies in production (which favor a small number of large stations) and transportation costs (which favor a large number of small stations). In Figure 5–11, the cost minimizing number of stations is N^* and the average total cost of fire protection is C^*.

A Numerical Example

This section provides a numerical example that shows how market-area analysis could be used to choose the number of fire stations. Consider a city with the following characteristics:

1. **Frequency of fires.** The city expects 10 fires per year, distributed evenly throughout the city.

2. **Fire station options.** The city has three policy options: it will build 1, 4, or 10 fire stations.

The costs of the three options are listed in Table 5–5. The total operating cost of the city's fire-protection program increases with the number of fire stations, from $10,000 for 1 station to $40,000 for 10 stations. The average operating cost, equal to total operating cost divided by the expected number of fires, rises from $1,000 for 1 station to $4,000 for 10 stations.

Consider next the costs of property damage from fires. The response time of the fire department is the amount of time between the call for help and the arrival of the fire truck. An increase in the number of fire stations means that every house is closer to a fire station, so the average response time decreases. In Table 5–5, the response time drops from 11 minutes for 1 station to 2 minutes for 10 stations. Suppose that the typical fire generates property damage of $300 per minute of burning. If the city has a single station, the average property damage (property damage per fire) is $3,300 (11 minutes times $300). The average property damage drops to $1,500 for 4 stations and $600 for 10 stations.

Suppose that the city's objective is to minimize the average total cost of

FIGURE 5–11   Optimum Number of Fire Stations

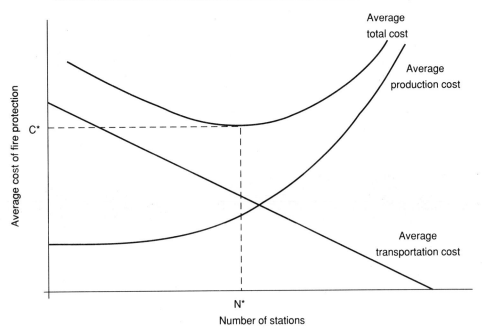

The average total cost of fire protection (the sum of average production cost and average transportation cost) is minimized with N* facilities.

TABLE 5–5   Costs of Different Fire-Station Schemes

	1 Station	4 Stations	10 Stations
Total operating cost ($)	10,000	20,000	40,000
Average operating cost ($)	1,000	2,000	4,000
Response time (minutes)	11	5	2
Average damage per fire ($)	3,300	1,500	600
Average total cost ($)	4,300	3,500	4,600

Definitions
1. Average operating cost = total operating cost divided by 10 fires per year.
2. Average damage per fire = response time times $300 property damage per minute.
3. Average total cost = average operating cost plus average damage per fire.

fires. The average total cost is the sum of the average operating cost and the average property damage. Given the assumptions about operating costs, response times, and property damage, the four-station option has the lowest average total cost ($3,500). As the city moves from the one-station option to the four-station option, there is good news and bad news. The good news is that the faster response time cuts property damage from $3,300 to $1,500, generating a savings of $1,800. The bad news is that the average operating cost increases by $1,000. Because the savings in property damage exceeds the increase in operating cost, the four-station option is more efficient than the one-station option. As the city moves from the 4-station option to the 10-station option, the savings in property damage ($900) is smaller than the increase in operating cost ($2,000), so the 4-station option is more efficient than the 10-station option.

Using Market-Area Analysis

Suppose that a policy analyst wants to estimate the optimum number of other public facilities. How would the analyst compute the average transportation costs for other public services? For police services, the average transportation cost is determined by the response time of police: the larger the number of stations, the quicker the response and the lower the social costs of crime. In the case of libraries, the average transportation cost is the average travel cost for library patrons. As the number of libraries increases, the average distance from patrons' houses to libraries decreases, so travel costs increase.

Do cities really base their facility decisions on this kind of formal analysis of average production costs and average transportation costs? Perhaps not. They do, however, consider the trade-offs between production costs and accessibility, usually in an informal way. The purpose of this section is to show how a formal analysis would proceed, providing a framework for addressing the issue of the optimum number of facilities.

SUMMARY

1. The net price of a retail product is the sum of its price and the consumer's travel costs. The market area is the area over which a particular firm offers the lowest net price.
2. Market-oriented firms are involved in monopolistic competition. Each has a local monopoly, but its monopoly power is limited by entry and competition from other firms.
   a. In equilibrium, every firm makes zero economic profits.
   b. The entry process decreases travel costs but increases average production costs.

  c. In equilibrium, each firm produces along the negatively sloped portion of its average production-cost curve.

3. The size of a firm's market area depends on output per firm, per capita demand, and population density. The market area increases as
  a. Output per firm increases.
  b. Per capita demand decreases.
  c. Population density decreases.

4. Because an increase in scale economies increases both output per firm (the output effect) and per capita demand (demand effect), it has an ambiguous effect on market area.

5. A decrease in transportation costs increases both output per firm and per capita demand. The market area will grow if the price elasticity of demand is relatively small.

6. Central-place theory, which is based on market-area analysis, predicts that a regional system of cities will be hierarchical, with a small number of large cities and a large number of small cities. The set of goods sold in smaller cities will be a subset of the goods sold in larger cities.

7. If the assumptions of the simple central-place theory are relaxed to allow imperfect substitutes (comparison shopping) and complements (one-stop shopping), the equilibrium number of cities may decrease, but the urban hierarchy will not be disrupted.

8. If the assumptions of the simple central-place theory are relaxed to allow variation in per capita demand, the equilibrium number of cities may change and the urban hierarchy may be disrupted.

9. Central-place theory is not applicable to resource-oriented firms and firms oriented toward local inputs. The introduction of such firms into the central-place model may disrupt the urban hierarchy.

10. The rank-size rule suggests that the product of rank and size is constant. It is an accurate predictor of city sizes in the United States, but does not perform so well elsewhere.

11. The concepts of market-area analysis could be used by policy makers to determine how many public facilities (fire stations, public libraries, schools, police stations) to provide. Market-area analysis shows the trade-offs between production costs and scale economies.

EXERCISES AND DISCUSSION QUESTIONS

1. The discussion of the market area of record stores assumed that Bob, Tammy, and Dick had the same production costs. As a result, each household patronized the store nearest its home. Suppose that Bob discovers a new way of marketing records that cuts his production costs (and store price) in half, from $6 to $3. Tammy and Dick continue to sell records for $6.
  a. How does the decrease in production costs affect Bob's market area?

     b. What is the net price at the border between Bob's and Tammy's market area?

     c. Will each household still patronize the firm closest to its residence?

2. Consider the market area of food stores in a region described by the following assumptions:

     i. The per capita demand for food is 30 units.

     ii. Population density is 40 people per square mile.

     iii. The land area of the region is 100 square miles.

     iv. The output of the typical food store is 6,000 units.

     a. How many food stores will there be in the region?

     b. How large is the market area of the typical food store?

3. Consider the market areas of hardware stores in two independent regions, Low and High. The average production-costs (APC) curves of the two regions reach their minimum points at the same level of output (1,000 units), but because Low has lower input costs, the minimum point of its APC curve has a lower average cost (the average costs of 1,000 units is $1 instead of $2).

     Will the market area in Low be larger, smaller, or the same as the market area in High? If you don't have enough information to answer the question, indicate what additional information you need, and how you would use it.

4. Suppose that you intend to purchase the franchise rights for a pizza parlor. The franchiser has divided your region into two areas of equal size: H is a high-income area, and L is a low-income area. Suppose that the income elasticity of demand for pizza is zero: the consumption of pizza is independent of income. The income elasticity of demand for land is 1.0. Your objective is to maximize the quantity of pizzas sold.

     a. Which of the two franchises will you choose?

     b. How would your response to (*a*) change if the income elasticity of demand for pizza is 1.5?

5. In the example based on the data in Table 5–3, the implicit assumption is that travel costs were the same in the two cities. Suppose that the opportunity cost of travel is higher in the wealthy city. How might this change the market areas in the wealthy city?

6. In 1930, most rural children walked to school. By 1980, most of them rode school busses. Would you expect the average "market area" of rural schools to increase or decrease as a result of the school bus?

7. The introduction of parcel post decreased transportation costs and increased the market area of the typical firm. Can you think of any good for which a decrease in transportation costs is likely to decrease the market area?

8. In the city of Metro, retail firms locate either in the central area of the city or in one of the suburban subcenters. Two retail goods (A and B) are sold

in the city. The per capita demands for the two goods are equal. The scale economies associated with the production and sale of A are large relative to the scale economies associated with B. Where in the city will firms selling A and B locate?

9. Consider a city with a uniform distribution of population where every household consumes the same number of video rentals. The city is two miles long and two miles wide. The mayor recently stated her policy for the location of video rental outlets:
   "A video outlet reaches the minimum point of its average production-costs curve at an output of 1,000 units. Since the total demand for video rentals is 4,000 units, we should have four video outlets. Since the distribution of population is uniform, the video outlets should be distributed uniformly throughout the city, with every outlet at the center of a one-square mile market area."
   Comment on the mayor's policy. Will it lead to an efficient distribution of video outlets?

10. Mr. Wizard, a regional planner, recently made the following statement:
    "If my assumptions are correct, all cities in this region will eventually be identical. They will be the same size and will sell the same set of goods."
    a. Assuming that Mr. Wizard's reasoning is correct, what are his assumptions?
    b. Are Mr. Wizard's assumptions realistic?

11. In the example based on the data in Table 5–5, the city had three fire-station options (1, 4, or 10 fire stations). Suppose that two additional options appear. If the city builds 6 stations, the total operating cost will be $28,000 and the response time will be three minutes. If the city builds 3 stations, the total operating cost will be $15,000 and the response time will be six minutes.
    Given these two additional options, how many fire stations should the city build?

12. Consider a city that must decide how many libraries to provide. The city assumes the travel cost is $0.10 per library trip per mile. The table below lists the average production costs (APC) and average distances to library patrons (AD) for different numbers of libraries.

Number of Libraries	APC	AD
1	$0.30	20
3	$0.40	10
5	$0.50	7
9	$0.90	4
11	$1.20	2

  a. If the objective is to minimize the average total cost of a library trip and the city must choose from the options listed in the table, how many libraries should it provide?

  b. If the unit travel cost were to double, how many libraries should the city provide?

13. In Figure 5–11, the optimum number of facilities is N^* and the average total cost of public services is C^*. Use graphs to explain the effects of the following events on the optimum number of facilities and the average cost of public services.

  a. Transportation costs are cut in half.

  b. The city discovers a way to avoid the duplication of some equipment. The slope of the average production-cost curve decreases.

14. Some people claim that state capitals (e.g., Sacramento, California; Salem, Oregon; Olympia, Washington) are boring cities. Specifically, people say that these cities have fewer goods than one finds in other cities of equal size. After checking a map to see where each of these capital cities is located, use central-place theory to explain why they might be considered boring.

REFERENCES AND ADDITIONAL READINGS

General Discussions of Central-Place Theory

Beckmann. M. J. "City Hierarchies and the Distribution of City Size." *Economic Development and Cultural Change* 7 (1958), pp. 243–48.

Christaller, Walter. *Central Places in Southern Germany*, trans. C. W. Baskin. Englewood Cliffs, N.J.: Prentice-Hall, 1966.   The classic on central-place theory.

Hoover, Edgar M. *An Introduction to Regional Economics*. New York: Knopf, 1975. Chapter 6, "The Location of Urban Places".

Hoover, Edgar M. "Transport Costs and the Spacing of Central Places." *Papers of the Regional Science Association* 25 (1970), pp. 255–74.   Discusses the effects of changes in transport costs on the size of the market area.

King, Leslie J. *Central Place Theory*. Beverly Hills, Calif.: Sage, 1984.   A thorough discussion of central-place theory and its implications. Includes a careful discussion of the origins of central-place theory.

Losch, August. *The Economics of Location*. Translated by W. H. Woglom and W. F. Stolper. New Haven, Conn.: Yale University Press, 1954.   A refinement of central-place theory.

Losch, August. "The Nature of Economic Regions." In *Regional Development and Planning: A Reader*, ed. John Friedman and William Alonso. Cambridge, Mass.: MIT Press, 1964.   Discusses the roles of scale economies and transport costs in determining the market area of the firm.

Noyelle, Thierry, and Thomas Stanback. *The Economic Transformation of American Cities.* Totawa, N.J.: Rowman and Allanheld, 1984.   Discusses exceptions to the central-place framework.

Parr, John B. "Growth Poles, Regional Development, and Central Place Theory." *Papers of the Regional Science Association* 3 (1973(a)), pp. 173–212.

————. "Structure and Size in the Urban System of Losch." *Economic Geography* 49 (1973(b)), pp. 185–212.

Parr, J. B., and K. G. Denike. "Theoretical Problems in Central Place Analysis." *Economic Georgraphy* 46 (1970), pp. 568–80.

Philbrick, Allen. "Areal Functional Organization in Regional Geography." *Papers of the Regional Science Association* 3 (1957), pp. 87–98.   Describes the hierarchy of urban places.

Shape of Market Areas

Mills, Edwin S., and Michael R. Lav. "A Model of Market Areas with Free Entry." *Journal of Political Economy* 72 (1964), pp. 278–88.   Discusses the shapes of market areas.

Empirical Tests of Central-Place Theory

Berry, Brian J. L., and William L. Garrison. "The Functional Bases of the Central Place Hierarchy." *Economic Geography* 34 (1958), pp. 145–54.   An empirical analysis of central-place theory.

Berry, Brian J. L. *Geography of Market Centers and Retail Distibution.* Englewood Cliffs, N.J.: Prentice-Hall, 1967.   Discusses central-place theory, including a review of empirical tests of the theory.

Lloyd, Peter E., and Peter Dicken. *Location in Space: A Theoretical Approach to Economic Geography.* New York: Harper & Row, 1977.   Reviews empirical work on central-place theory.

Preston, Richard E. "The Structure of Central Place Systems." In *Systems of Cities,* ed. L. S. Bourne and J. W. Simmons. New York: Oxford University Press, 1978.   Empirical analysis of central-place theory in the Pacific Northwest.

Rosen, Kenneth T., and Mitchell Resnick. "The Size Distribution of Cities: An Examination of the Pareto Law and Primacy." *Journal of Urban Economies* 8 (1980), pp. 165–86.   Estimates the rank-size relationship and concludes that the rank-size rule is a poor approximation to the true size distribution.

Central-Place Theory and Intraurban Distribution of Activity

Carol, H. "The Hierarchy of Central Functions within the City." *Annals of the Association of American Geographers* 50 (1960), pp. 419–38.   Applies central-place theory to the location of activities within cities.

Proudfoot, M. J. "The Outlying Business Centers of Chicago." *Journal of Land and Public Utility Economics* 13 (1937), pp. 57–70.   Applies central-place theory to the location of activities within cities.

Weiss, Leonard. "The Geographic Size of Markets in Manufacturing." *Review of Economics and Statistics* 54 (1972), pp. 245.

Technology and the Urban Hierarchy

Berry, Brian J. L. "Hierarchical Diffusion: The Basis of Developmental Filtering and Spread in a System of Growth Centers." In *Growth Centers in Regional Economic Development*, ed. N. M. Hansen. New York: Free Press, 1972.   Discusses how innovations (e.g., television) are first utilized in large cities and then spread down the urban hierarchy.

Huang, J. C., and P. Gould. "Diffusion in an Urban Hierarchy: The Case of Rotary Clubs." *Economic Geography* 50 (1974), pp. 333–40.   Discusses how new organizations (e.g., Rotary Clubs) are first established in large cities and then spread down the urban hierarchy.

Public Facilities

Dear, Michael. "Planning for Mental Health Care: A Reconsideration of Public Facility Location." *International Regional Science Review* 3 (1978), pp. 93–111.

Getz, Malcolm. *The Economics of the Urban Fire Department*. Baltimore: The Johns Hopkins Press, 1979.   Estimates the relationship between the density of stations and losses from fires. The elasticity of losses with respect to the number of stations per square mile is -0.70.

CHAPTER 6

Urban Economic Growth

An economic forecaster is like a cross-eyed javelin thrower: he doesn't win many accuracy contests, but he keeps the crowd's attention.

Anonymous

Earlier chapters have shown why cities exist and where they develop. This chapter takes a closer look at the economy of a particular city, exploring the market forces that determine the size of the city's economy. The first section uses a simple model of the urban labor market to describe the economic growth process. If economic growth is defined as an increase in total employment, growth results from an increase in the demand for labor (caused by an increase in the demand for the goods produced in the city) or an increase in labor supply (caused by migration to the city).

This chapter defines urban economic growth as an increase in the city's total employment. Alternatively, economic growth could be defined as an increase in real income per capita. The purpose of this chapter is to explain the factors that determine the size of the urban economy, so it is natural to use the simplest measure of city size (total employment) to explain the growth process. A more thorough analysis of economic growth would consider the effects of employment growth on per capita income.

An understanding of the urban growth process is useful for two reasons. First, if policy makers understand the reasons for urban economic growth, they can develop policies to encourage or discourage growth. The second part of the chapter discusses various growth policies. Second, if firms and policy makers understand the growth process, they can more accurately predict future growth patterns. Firms use economic forecasts to project the demands for their products, and local governments use forecasts to project the demand for local public services. The third section of the chapter describes two forecasting techniques: the **economic-base study** and the **input-output study**.

THE URBAN LABOR MARKET AND ECONOMIC GROWTH

Consider a city that is part of a larger regional economy. In the long run, households and firms can move freely between cities in the region. A household lives in the city that maximizes its utility, and a firm locates in the city that maximizes its profits. In long-run equilibrium, households and firms

121

have no incentive to change cities: households will be indifferent among all cities in the region and firms will make zero economic profits in all cities.

Suppose that the size of an urban economy is defined in terms of total employment. Figure 6–1 shows the city's labor-supply and labor-demand curves. The equilibrium wage is $1,000 per month and equilibrium employment is 50,000 laborers. Economic growth, defined as an increase in total employment, results from either an increase in demand (a rightward shift of the demand curve) or an increase in supply (a rightward shift of the supply curve).

The Demand for Labor

Labor demand comes from two types of activities. The **export** or **basic sector** sells its products to consumers outside the city. Examples of export firms are steel producers and computer manufacturers. In contrast, the **local** or **nonbasic sector** sells its products to consumers within the city. Examples of local producers are bakeries, bookstores, and local schools. Before discussing the city's labor-demand curve, it will be useful to explain the relationship between these two employment sectors.

FIGURE 6–1   Urban Labor Market

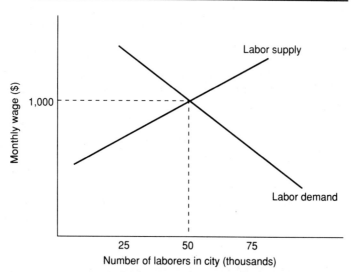

The labor market is in equilibrium if supply equals demand. The equilibrium wage is $1,000 per month, and the equilibrium number of laborers is 50,000.

The Multiplier Process.   Because export workers spend part of their income on local goods, an increase in export sales increases local sales. Table 6–1 shows the **multiplier effects** of a $100,000 increase in export sales. In Round 1, the increase in export sales is paid out to workers, capitalists, and landowners in the form of wages, interest, and land rent, so local income increases by $100,000. If 60 percent of the increased income is spent on local goods, local consumption increases by $60,000. The first-round increase in local consumption is the second-round increase in local income: local producers pay the $60,000 to their workers, capitalists, and landowners, who in turn spend 60 percent of the increased income on local goods. In other words, the second-round increase in local consumption is $36,000. The spending and respending of income continues forever, but every spending round is smaller than the previous one because 40 percent of income is spent on imports.

The increase in the city's total income exceeds the original increase in export income. The marginal propensity to consume locally (m) is defined as the fraction of income spent locally (0.60 in Table 6–1). If the original change in export sales is ΔX, the increase in total income is the sum of the income changes from a series of spending rounds:

$$\Delta \text{Total income} = \Delta X + m \cdot \Delta X + m^2 \cdot \Delta X + m^3 \cdot \Delta X + m^4 \cdot \Delta X + \ldots \quad (6\text{–}1)$$

The change in total income is the sum of an infinite series and can be rewritten as

$$\Delta \text{Total income} = \Delta X \cdot \frac{1}{1 - m} \quad (6\text{–}2)$$

The **income multiplier** is defined as the change in total income per unit change in export sales:

$$\frac{\Delta \text{Total income}}{\Delta X} = \frac{1}{1 - m} \quad (6\text{–}3)$$

If $\Delta X = 100$ and $m = 0.60$, the multiplier is

$$\frac{\Delta \text{Total income}}{\Delta X} = \frac{1}{1 - 0.60} = 2.5 \quad (6\text{–}4)$$

For every additional dollar of export sales, total income increases by 2.5 dol-

TABLE 6–1   Increase in Local Spending and Employment from Increased Exports

Increase in	Round 1	Round 2	Round 3	Total
Local income	$100,000	$60,000	$36,000	$250,000
Local consumption	60,000	36,000	21,600	150,000
Import consumption	40,000	24,000	14,400	100,000

lars. In Table 6–1, export sales increase by $100,000, so local production increases by $150,000 and total income increases by $250,000.

The multiplier process also affects employment. The **employment multiplier** is the change in total employment per unit change in export employment. If there is one job per $1,000 of sales, an increase of $100,000 in export sales will increase export employment by 100 jobs. Similarly, the additional $150,000 in local sales will increase local employment by 150 jobs. Total employment in the city will increase by 250, meaning that the employment multiplier is 2.5.

The employment multiplier is the same as the income multiplier because sales volume per job is assumed to be the same in both sectors. If sales volume per job is lower in the local sector, the employment multiplier will exceed the income multiplier because more local jobs will be supported by a given amount of sales. For example, if sales volume per local job is $500 instead of $1,000, local employment would increase by 300 instead of 150 and the employment multiplier would be 4.0 instead of 2.5. Conversely, if sales volume per local job exceeds $1,000, the employment multiplier would be less than the income multiplier.

A second method for computing the employment multiplier uses data on the composition of the work force. If B is the number of jobs in export industries and L is the number of jobs in local industries, total employment in the city is $B + L$, or T. The ratio (L/B) indicates how many local jobs are "supported" by each export job. For example, if $B = 20,000$ and $L = 30,000$, an economic "base" of 20,000 jobs supports 30,000 local jobs: each export job supports 1.5 local jobs. The employment multiplier (the change in total employment per unit change in export employment) is

$$\frac{\Delta T}{\Delta B} = \frac{T}{B} = 2.5 \tag{6–5}$$

Every additional export job increases total employment by 2.5 jobs, one additional export job plus 1.5 "support" jobs in local industry.

The Labor-Demand Curve.   The city's labor-demand curve is negatively sloped for two reasons. First, as the city's wage increases, both exporters and local producers substitute capital for the relatively expensive labor. This is the **substitution effect**: an increase in the wage causes factor substitution that decreases the quantity of labor demanded. Second, as the city's wage increases, production costs increase, increasing the prices charged by the city's firms. As the prices of export goods increase, the quantity demanded decreases, so exporters need fewer workers. As the price of local goods increase, city residents substitute imports for the relatively expensive local goods, so local firms need fewer laborers. This is the **output effect**: an increase in the city's wage increases prices and decreases output, thus decreasing the quantity of labor demanded. The demand curve is negatively sloped because an increase in wages generates both a substitution effect and an output effect.

Under what conditions will the demand curve shift? The following factors determine the position of the curve:

1. **Demand for exports.** An increase in the demand for the city's exports will increase export production, so exporters will need more workers: the labor demand curve will shift to the right.

2. **Labor productivity.** An increase in labor productivity decreases production costs, allowing firms to cut their prices and increase output. Although firms need fewer workers to produce a given amount of output, they also sell more output. If the increase in the output is relatively large (if the price elasticity of demand for the city's output is relatively large), the demand for export workers will increase: the demand curve will shift to the right. Similarly, local producers will underprice importers, increasing the demand for local workers.

3. **Local business taxes and public services.** Suppose that a city increases business taxes without changing its public services (water, sewage, transportation network). Production costs will increase, increasing the prices of exports and local goods. Labor demand will decrease as exporters lose customers to their competitors in other cities and local producers lose customers to importers. In contrast, if the city uses the additional tax revenue to improve its public services in an efficient way, prices will fall, increasing output and labor demand.

Figure 6–2 shows the multiplier effect of an increase in export sales. Suppose that an increase in the demand for exports increases the demand for export workers by 10,000. The city's demand curve will shift to the right from D_1 to D_2: at a wage of $1,000 per month, an additional 10,000 export workers will be demanded. This is the **direct effect** of an increase in export demand. If the employment multiplier is 2.5, every export job supports 1.5 local jobs, so the demand curve will shift to the right by an additional 15,000 workers (from D_2 to D_3). This is the multiplier effect of an increase in export demand. Total labor demand increases by 25,000 (2.5 times the increase in the demand for export laborers).

The Supply Curve

Consider next the supply side of the urban labor market. The supply curve is positively sloped because of the **migration effect**: an increase in the wage increases the relative attractiveness of the city, causing migration from other cities in the region.

What determines the slope of the supply curve? In other words, by how much will the wage increase as total employment increases? As total employ-

FIGURE 6–2   Direct and Multiplier Effects of an Increase in Export Employment

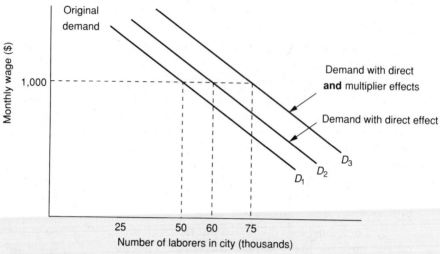

If export employment increases by 10,000 jobs, the demand curve shifts to the right in two steps. The shift from D_1 to D_2 is the direct effect of the increase in export employment: At a fixed wage, total employment rises from 50,000 to 60,000. The shift from D_2 to D_3 reflects the multiplier effect of the increase in export employment: if the employment multiplier is 2.5, local employment increases by 1.5 times the increase in export employment, thus increasing labor demand by an additional 15,000 jobs.

ment and population in a city increase, the total demands for housing and land increase, increasing the prices of these two goods. A growing city must offer a higher wage to compensate its workers for its higher cost of living. The more rapidly the cost of living increases with population, the steeper the supply curve.

A number of empirical studies have estimated the relationship between the wage and labor supply. Henderson (1988) estimated an elasticity of local labor supply (the percentage change in the number of workers in the city divided by the percentage change in the wage) of about 2.0: a 10 percent increase in the wage increased labor supply by about 20 percent. Other studies have generated similar results. It's important to note that this is the supply elasticity for an individual city. The elasticity is relatively high because workers migrate to cities that offer relatively high wages. The national labor supply elasticity is much lower than the local supply elasticity because there is less migration between nations.

Under what conditions will the supply curve shift? The position of the supply curve is determined by the following factors:

1. **Environmental quality.** An increase in the quality of the environment (better air or water quality) increases the relative attractiveness of the city, causing migration to the city. The supply curve will shift to the right: at every wage, more workers will be willing to work in the city.

2. **Residential taxes and public services.** Suppose that the city increases taxes without a corresponding increase in public services (e.g., schools, parks, police). The tax increase will decrease the relative attractiveness of the city, causing migration from the city: the supply curve will shift to the left. Alternatively, if the increase in tax revenue is used to improve the city's public services in an efficient manner, the relative attractiveness of the city will increase, shifting the supply curve to the right.

Equilibrium Effects of an Increase in Exports

Figure 6–3 shows the effects of an increase in export sales on the urban labor market. The labor-demand curve shifts to the right by 25,000 workers,

FIGURE 6–3 Equilibrium Effects of an Increase in Export Employment

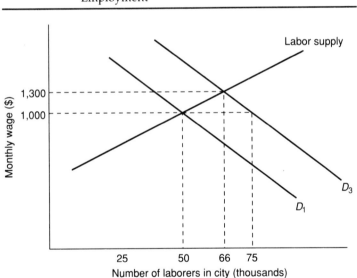

An increase in exports shifts the demand curve to the right by 25,000. As the city grows, the prices of housing and land increase, requiring a higher wage to compensate workers for the higher cost of living. The equilibrium wage increases from $1,000 to $1,300, and the equilibrium number of laborers increases by only 16,000.

reflecting both the direct effect and the multiplier effect of an increase of 10,000 export jobs. As the population of the city increases, the prices of housing and land increase, requiring an increase in the wage to compensate workers for the higher cost of living. In other words, the city moves up its supply curve. The equilibrium wage rises from $1,000 per month to $1,300, and the equilibrium number of laborers increases from 50,000 to 66,000.

Figure 6–3 suggests that predicting the effects of an increase in export employment is tricky. The simple approach is to use the employment multiplier to predict the change in total employment from a projected change in export employment. In the numerical example, the predicted change in total employment from this method would be 25,000 (2.5 times 10,000). This approach provides an estimate of the horizontal shift of the demand curve, not the change in equilibrium employment. To accurately predict the change in total employment, one must also know the slopes of the supply and demand curves. The slope of the supply curve indicates how rapidly the wage increases with city size, and the slope of the demand curve indicates how rapidly the quantity of labor demanded decreases as the wage increases.

Benefits and Costs of Economic Growth

Urban economic growth generates several types of benefits. As a city grows, it can exploit scale economies in production, retailing, and some local public services. As explained in Chapter 2, urbanization economies decrease production costs as citywide output increases, so wages are higher and prices are lower in large cities. As explained in Chapter 5, a large city can support activities that have relatively large scale economies, so a larger city has a wider variety of goods and services. Finally, there are scale economies in the provision of some local public goods, so an increase in population decreases the average costs of some public goods.

Urban economic growth is not costless. An increase in population increases the demands for housing and land, so it increases the prices of housing and land. Because landowners benefit at the expense of some residents, it is not surprising that landowners are often the strongest advocates of economic growth. A large city also has relatively high commuting costs: as the land area of the city increases, the average commuting distance increases, thus increasing average commuting costs. Larger cities often have greater problems with pollution and traffic congestion. Finally, large cities typically have higher crime rates.

It's important to note that the problems of congestion, pollution, and crime are not caused by city size *per se*. They are caused by market failures that become worse as the city grows. As explained later in the book, there are a number of policies that address these problems directly. Therefore, these problems can be solved (or decreased to their optimum levels) without decreasing city size. In fact, a city that solves its market failures is likely to grow, not shrink.

PUBLIC POLICY AND ECONOMIC GROWTH

Public policy affects the equilibrium number of workers by shifting the city's supply and demand curves. This section discusses several types of public policies, including education, job training, public safety, infrastructure, zoning, subsidy programs, and pollution abatement.

Consider first the effect of public policy on the demand side of the labor market. If public policy decreases the production costs of exporters, the labor-demand curve will shift to the right, increasing wages and total employment. The decrease in production costs allows exporters to sell their products at a lower price, so they sell more output and hire more workers. The multiplier effect means that total employment will increase by perhaps two or three times the increase in export employment.

Public policy can also affect employment in the local sector. A policy that decreases the production costs of the local sector encourages households to purchase goods locally instead of importing them: it encourages **import substitution.** Such a policy has the same multiplier effect as an increase in exports. Imports are negative exports, so a decrease in imports (a smaller negative number) has the same effect as an increase in exports. For example, if the multiplier is 2.5 and import substitution increases local consumption by an amount large enough to support 100 additional local jobs, total employment will increase by 250 jobs.

Local government can decrease the production costs of its firms in a number of ways:

1. **Public education and job training.** If education and training programs increase the productivity of the local work force, production costs will fall and total employment will rise. Exporters will expand their markets in other cities, and local producers will sell more output locally.

2. **Infrastructure.** The provision of roads, mass transit, and airports affects intercity and intracity transportation costs, and the provision of public utilities (gas, water, sewage) affects production costs. Improvements in the public infrastructure decrease costs, allowing firms to charge lower prices and sell more output. A recent study by Aschauer (1988) suggests that infrastructure has a profound effect on productivity. There is a striking similarity between the trends in infrastructure investment and productivity growth: from 1950 to 1970, public infrastructure expanded at a rate of 4.3 percent per year and productivity increased 1.8 percent per year; from 1970 to 1985, public infrastructure expanded at a rate of only 1.5 percent and productivity increased only 0.8 percent per year. According to Aschauer, the similarity is not a coincidence: investment in public infrastructure increases productivity and stimulates economic growth.

3. **Land-use policies.** Industrial firms require production sites that (*a*) are accessible to the intracity and intercity transportation networks

and (*b*) have a full set of public services (water, sewage, electricity). By coordinating its land-use and infrastructure policies to ensure an adequate supply of industrial land, a city can encourage the expansion of existing firms and the development of new ones.

Public policy also affects the supply side of the urban labor market. As discussed in Chapter 3, some households are attracted to cities that provide high-quality education, efficient commuting systems, and low crime rates. Improvements in these public services will increase the relative attractiveness of the city, shifting the labor-supply curve to the right. This is shown in Figure 6–4: the shift of the supply curve decreases the equilibrium wage and increases the equilibrium number of laborers. Workers are willing to accept lower wages because the city provides a superior mix of local public goods. The effects of environmental policies are discussed later in the chapter.

Subsidy Programs

Many cities try to attract export firms by offering special subsidies for new firms. Levy (1981) describes several types of subsidy programs, including the following:

1. **Tax abatement.** In some cities, new firms are exempt from local property taxes for a fixed period (e.g., 10 years). Some cities offer tax abatements to all new developments, while others offer abatements only to firms that are particularly sensitive to tax differentials.

2. **Industrial bonds.** Some cities issue tax-free industrial bonds to finance property developments. The local government uses the revenue from the bonds to purchase land and then leases the property to a private firm. Because the interest income from industrial bonds is not subject to federal taxes, the bond buyer accepts a relatively low interest rate (e.g., 9 percent instead of 12 percent). Therefore, the lessee pays less than the market interest rate on the money borrowed to finance the project. The use of industrial bonds was sharply curtailed by the tax reform act of 1986.

3. **Government loans and loan guarantees.** Some cities loan money to developers, and others guarantee loans from private lenders to developers. In both cases, developers borrow money at a relatively low interest rate: either the city charges an interest rate below the market rate, or the city decreases the risk associated with a private loan, allowing the developer to borrow private money at a relatively low interest rate.

4. **Site development.** Some cities subsidize the provision of land and public services for new development. The city purchases a site, clears the land, builds roads and sewers, and then sells the site to a developer at a fraction of the cost of acquiring and developing the site.

FIGURE 6-4   Improvement in Public Services Shifts the Supply Curve and Increases Total Employment

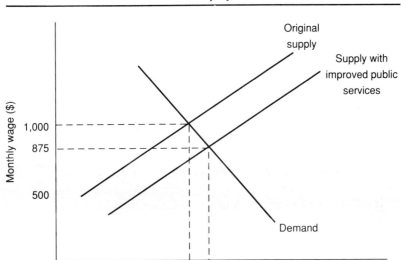

An improvement in local public goods increases the relative attractiveness of the city, shifting the supply curve to the right. The equilibrium number of laborers increases to 55,000, and the equilibrium wage falls to $875 per month. Workers accept a lower wage because the city provides a more efficient set of local public services.

These subsidy programs raise three questions. First, do the subsidies increase total employment in the city? Second, do the local benefits from the subsidies exceed the local costs? Third, are the subsidies efficient from the national perspective?

Employment Effects of Subsidy Programs.   Any policy that decreases production costs will increase total employment, everything else being equal. In the case of tax subsidies, not everything else is equal. Tax revenue supports local public services, so a community with low taxes may also have inferior public services. The empirical evidence cited in Chapter 3 suggests that if a city cuts taxes and decreases its spending on public services (e.g., highways, education, public safety), the city is unlikely to grow, and may in fact shrink. In contrast, if the city cuts taxes and decreases its spending on redistributional programs to the poor, the city is likely to grow. In other words, the effect of a tax cut depends on what type of services are cut along with taxes. If taxes are used to finance public services used by businesses, a tax cut is unlikely to stimulate economic growth.

Local Benefits and Costs.   Local governments provide subsidies for a number of reasons. Some cities subsidize development in an attempt to decrease the local unemployment rate. Are the additional jobs worth the loss in local tax revenue? There is no guarantee that jobs in new firms will be filled by the city's unemployed workers. In fact, it is likely that a large fraction of new jobs will be filled by new residents. Summers (1976) studied the effects of new plants in small towns. He concluded that over 75 percent of the jobs in new firms were filled by newcomers, leaving less than 25 percent of the new jobs for the town's unemployed workers. Of course, the city's unemployed workers may benefit from the increase in local employment caused by the new export jobs.

Another objective of a subsidy program is to decrease the local tax burden. If a tax cut or a subsidy makes the city more attractive to firms, the city's tax base will increase, thus increasing total tax revenue. As the city grows, it will also spend more on local public services (roads, schools, police, fire protection). The subsidy program will be beneficial from the fiscal perspective if the increase in tax revenue exceeds the increase in the costs of public services.

Efficiency—The National Perspective.   Local subsidy programs may cause inefficient location choices. Most subsidy programs promote the growth of one city at the expense of another. Cities bid for firms in a sort of zero-sum game: the gain of one city is equal to the loss of another city.

The bidding process is often a negative-sum game. In other words, the gain of the winner is less than the loss of the loser, so the bidding process decreases national welfare. Consider a computer firm that initially locates in city E instead of S because transport costs are $10 lower in E. Suppose that city S offers the firm a subsidy of $11, causing the firm to move to the city. From the national perspective, the move to S is inefficient: although the firm may produce the same number of computers, it spends more on transportation, using up more resources (e.g., labor, capital, fuel) in the process. In general, local subsidies cause firms to choose inefficient locations, generating net losses to the national economy.

How can local governments stimulate export growth without distorting location choices? Instead of bribing firms with tax subsidies, a city could provide efficient public services or a more productive work force. If the city improves the efficiency of the local public sector or the productivity of its work force, it will grow because it can produce goods at a lower cost, not because it can pay a larger bribe.

Urban Growth and Environmental Quality

Is there a trade-off between environmental quality and economic growth? This section uses the model of the urban labor market to explore the effects of a pollution-abatement program. The principal question is: Will an abatement program increase or decrease the city's total employment?

Consider a city with two industries, a polluting steel industry and a relatively clean assembly plant. If the city imposes an effluent tax of $100, steel producers will pay $100 for every ton of pollution generated. The tax affects both sides of the urban labor market.

1. **Shift of demand curve.** The tax increases the production costs of steel producers. In addition to paying for labor, capital, and land, a firm pays $100 for every ton of pollution. The increase in production costs increases the price of steel, so it decreases steel production and the demand for labor. In Figure 6–5, the demand curve shifts to the left: at every wage, less labor is demanded.

2. **Decrease in pollution.** The tax decreases air pollution for two reasons. First, steel producers will install pollution-control equipment to decrease their pollution taxes, so the amount of pollution generated per

FIGURE 6–5   Pollution Tax Increases Total Employment

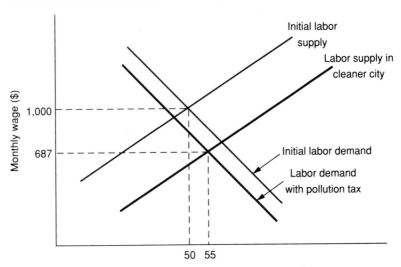

A pollution tax increases production costs, decreasing the demand for labor. It also improves environmental quality, increasing the supply of labor and decreasing the wage. The rightward shift of the supply curve is large relative to the leftward shift of the demand curve (people are relatively sensitive to air pollution), so total employment increases. The increase in employment in the clean industry more than offsets the decrease in employment in the polluting industry.

ton of steel will decrease. Second, the increase in the price of steel decreases total steel production.

3. **Shift of supply curve.** The improvement of the city's air quality will increase the relative attractiveness of the city. People sensitive to air quality will move to the city, shifting the supply curve to the right.

Figure 6–5 shows one possible outcome of the abatement program. Because supply increases and demand decreases, the program decreases the equilibrium wage. Because the rightward shift of the supply curve is large relative to the leftward shift of the demand curve, the city's equilibrium employment increases. The supply shift will be relatively large if households are relatively responsive to changes in environmental quality, that is, if a large number of households migrate to the city as air quality improves.

How does the abatement program affect the distribution of employment between the polluting industry and the clean industry? As the wage falls, the production costs of both industries decrease. For the steel industry, the decrease in the wage partly offsets the increase in pollution taxes. The abatement program is likely to generate a net increase in production costs, so the polluting industry is likely to decrease its total work force. In contrast, the clean industry will simply pay lower wages, so its production costs will decrease and its total employment will increase. In Figure 6–5, the increase in employment in the clean industry more than offsets the decrease in employment in the steel industry, so total employment increases. This occurs because households are relatively sensitive to pollution, so migration to the cleaner city causes a large decrease in the wage.

Figure 6–6 shows another possible outcome of the abatement program. In this case, households are less responsive to changes in environmental quality, so the increase in supply is small relative to the decrease in demand, and the equilibrium number of laborers decreases. Because the supply curve shifts by a relatively small amount, the wage decreases by a small amount. Therefore, the increase in employment in the clean industry is not large enough to offset the decrease in employment in the steel industry.

The lesson from Figures 6–5 and 6–6 is that an abatement program may either increase or decrease total employment. Total employment will increase if the supply response (migration that decreases wages) is large relative to the demand response (the decrease in labor demand from the polluting industry). Total employment will decrease if the demand response is relatively large.

PREDICTING ECONOMIC GROWTH

This section discusses two techniques that are used to predict the economic future. The economic-base study is a simple, low-cost method for projecting employment growth. The input-output study provides a more sophisticated approach to economic forecasting. Both techniques are designed to estimate the increase in total labor demand from an increase in export sales.

FIGURE 6–6   Pollution Tax Decreases Total Employment

A pollution tax decreases the demand for labor and increases the supply of labor. The rightward shift of the supply curve is small relative to the leftward shift of the demand curve (people are relatively insensitive to air pollution), so total employment decreases.

The Economic-Base Study

According to economic-base theory, the export industries form the economic base of the urban economy. Like a household, a city earns its livelihood by producing goods for others. Exports bring money into the local economy, increasing local income and employment through the multiplier process. The ultimate purpose of an economic-base study is to estimate the increase in total employment generated by an increase in export employment. In algebraic terms,

$$\Delta T = \text{multiplier} \cdot \Delta B = \frac{T}{B} \cdot \Delta B \qquad (6\text{--}6)$$

that is, the predicted change in total employment (ΔT) equals the employment multiplier (T/B) times the change in export employment (ΔB). To predict the change in total employment, the economic forecaster needs an estimate of the multiplier and a projection of the change in export employment.

To compute the employment multiplier, the economic forecaster estimates how much of the city's work force is involved in export production. The most precise method of estimating B is to collect information on the actual shipments of goods to other cities. This approach is costly, so most cities use less expensive and less precise methods to estimate export employment.

The simplest method is to classify each industry as either an export industry or a local industry. For example, if the mitten industry is assumed to be an export industry, all the employees of mitten producers would be counted as export workers. If restaurant meals are assumed to be local goods, all the employees of restaurants would be counted as local workers. The problem with this crude method is that some mittens may be consumed locally and some meals may be eaten by nonresidents. In other words, since few industries are exclusively exporters or local producers, it is inappropriate to classify them as such.

Location-Quotient Approach.   The location-quotient approach recognizes that each industry produces partly for export and partly for local consumption. The trick is to estimate what portion of each industry's output is exported. The mitten industry's true **location quotient** is

$$L_1 = \frac{\text{Mitten production in the city}}{\text{Mitten consumption in the city}} \qquad (6\text{--}7)$$

A quotient of 1.0 (the city's mitten production equals its mitten consumption) would indicate that all of the city's production is consumed within the city, so none of the mitten workers produce for export. If $L_1 = 5.0$, mitten production is five times local consumption, so only one fifth of mitten workers produce for the local market, and four fifths produce for export.

Data limitations prevent the direct estimation of the true location quotient. Instead, a proxy for the true location quotient is

$$L_2 = \frac{\dfrac{\text{City's mitten employment}}{\text{City's total employment}}}{\dfrac{\text{Nation's mitten employment}}{\text{Nation's total employment}}} \qquad (6\text{--}8)$$

The denominator (the share of national employment in mitten production) provides a measure of how much local production is needed to satisfy the local demand for mittens. For example, if 1 percent of national employment is in mitten production (the denominator is 0.01), the city is assumed to need 1 percent of its work force to satisfy its local mitten demand. If the city actually employs 6 percent of its workers in mitten production (if the numerator is 0.06), one sixth of the workers are assumed to produce for local consumption and five sixths are assumed to produce for export.

There are three problems with the location-quotient approach. The first two are related to the choice of the national economy as the reference point, and the third results from grouping consumer goods into broad categories.

1. **Uniform consumption patterns.** The approach assumes that every city in the nation has the same per capita demand for mittens. Of course, mitten consumption depends on weather, fashion, and the tastes for outdoor winter sports (skiing, ice fishing, snow shoveling). If a city's resi-

dents consume a relatively large amount of mittens, the location quotient L_2 will overestimate the number of export workers. Conversely, if city residents consume a relatively small amount of mittens, L_2 will underestimate the number of export workers.

2. **National self-sufficiency.** Another assumption of the location-quotient approach is that the nation neither imports nor exports mittens, so the share of national employment in mitten production is the share required for local self-sufficiency. If the nation in fact exports mittens, the share of national employment in mitten production will overstate the share required for self-sufficiency, so the location quotient will underestimate the number of export workers. Conversely, if mittens are imported, the location quotient will overestimate the number of export workers.

3. **Industry grouping.** The location quotient is typically computed for a set of consumer goods, not for a particular product. For example, a city might compute a location quotient for the apparel industry, which includes mittens, pants, dresses, and children's clothes. Suppose that all the city's apparel workers produce mittens for export: no other apparel products are produced in the city. Suppose that the mitten industry is large enough that the city's location quotient for apparel is 1.0: the city uses the same share of its work force in mitten production as the nation uses in apparel production. The city's location quotient suggests that the city does not export apparel products when in fact it exports mittens and imports other apparel. The grouping of goods into broad categories causes the location quotient to underestimate export employment.

Tiebout (1962) showed that location quotients systematically underestimate export employment. He compared estimates of export employment derived from location quotients to the estimates generated by direct surveys of manufacturers. His results, shown in Table 6–2, suggest that the location-quotient approach performs poorly in estimating export employment.

Estimating the Multiplier.   The second step in an economic-base study is to compute the city's employment multiplier. For each industry, the location quotient generates an estimate of export employment. If T_i is total employment in industry i and L_i is the industry's location quotient, export employment in the industry is

$$B_i = \frac{L_i - 1}{L_i} \cdot T_i \qquad (6\text{–}9)$$

For example, if L_i is 4.0 and T_i is 800, B_i is 600: three fourths of the industry's workers produce for export. The city's total export employment is estimated by summing up the export employment across individual industries. The employment multiplier is total employment divided by export employment.

TABLE 6–2 Percentages of Exports Estimated from Surveys and Location Quotients, 1955–56

Manufacturing Industry	Decatur		Ft. Wayne		Indianapolis	
	Survey	Location Quotient	Survey	Location Quotient	Survey	Location Quotient
Food	87	71	67	26	63	24
Chemicals	98	44	—	—	100	50
Primary metals	97	20	99	20	99	0
Nonelectrical machinery	97	74	91	40	98	38
Transportation equipment	100	45	100	68	100	68

SOURCE: Charles M. Tiebout, *The Community Economic Base Study* (New York: Committee for Economic Development, 1962), p. 49.

Projecting Growth in Export Industries.   The third step in an economic-base study is to project the growth of the basic industry, that is, to estimate ΔB in equation (6–6). Given the uncertainties associated with predicting future events, export projection is more of an art than a science. One approach is to (a) estimate the national trend in the demand for a particular good and (b) assess the city's relative attractiveness to the firms producing that good. The city's economic forecaster could estimate the national demand for mittens for the next decade by looking at the trends in weather, winter sports, and fashion. If the city's relative attractiveness is not expected to change, the city's mitten production should increase at the same rate as national mitten consumption: a doubling of mitten consumption should double the city's mitten production and employment. If the city's relative attractiveness increases over time, its mitten production and employment should increase at a relatively fast rate.

Using the Economic-Base Study.   Economic-base studies are used to project population growth and the demand for public services. Suppose that a city projects that its mitten industry will grow by 1,000 jobs. If the city's employment multiplier is 2.5, the economic-base approach suggests that total employment will increase by 2,500 jobs. If there are 3 residents per job, the population of the city will increase by 7,500 people, increasing the demand for all public services. For example, if there is 1 school-age child for every 5 residents, total enrollment in schools will increase by 1,500 students.

Local firms use the employment projections from the economic-base study to predict the demand for their products. Suppose that the city's economic-base study projects an increase in population of 7,500 people. If it takes 3,750 people to support a barber, there will be room for two more barbers in the city. If the city grows by 7,500 people per year and it takes 30,000 people to support a shopping center, there will be enough demand to support a new shopping center in four years.

Local governments also use economic-base studies to guide their growth-management policies. If a local government can affect the sales and employment of its basic industry, it can control the city's population. Suppose that the city has a growth target of 15,000 additional people: it wants to increase its population by 15,000 people in the next 20 years. If there are three residents per job, the city will meet its population target if it allows an additional 5,000 jobs. If the employment multiplier is 2.5, the city will meet its employment and population targets if it allows 2,000 additional export jobs.

Input-Output Analysis

An alternative to an economic-base study is an input-output study. Unlike the economic-base study, the input-output study generates a complete accounting of the transactions between firms and households in the economy. This approach has two advantages over the economic-base study. First, instead of assuming that every industry has the same multiplier, it derives a multiplier for each export industry. Second, instead of using the location-quotient approach to guess the volume of exports, it measures exports directly.

Consider a city that produces and consumes three goods: computers, electrical wire, and local consumer goods. Computers and wire products are produced for both export and local consumption. By definition, local merchants (restaurants, dry cleaners, grocery stores) produce goods for local consumption.

Transactions Table and Input Coefficients.   Table 6–3 shows the transactions in the city's economy. The first column of numbers shows the input usage of firms in the computer industry. To produce computers, they buy $400 of electrical wire, $1,000 of labor from city residents, and $600 of imported inputs (raw materials and intermediate inputs). The sum of these input costs equals the total output of the computer industry ($2,000). The next column shows the input usage of wire producers, who use computers, labor, and imported inputs to produce $1,000 of wire. The third column shows the input usage of local merchants, who use computers, labor, and imports to produce $2,500 of output. The household column shows how households divide their total income ($3,600) between computers ($180), local goods ($2,500), and imports ($920). The export column shows the exports of computers ($1,370) and wire ($600). The total column shows the sum of the items in each row. Note that the figures in the total column match the figures in the total row.

Table 6–4, which is derived from Table 6–3, provides a summary of the interactions between firms and households. The first column shows the **input coefficients** for the computer industry: for every dollar's worth of computer production, the computer industry uses 20 cents' worth of input from the wire industry, 50 cents' worth of labor, and 30 cents' worth of imported materials (e.g., silicon chips and plastic). The second and third columns show the

TABLE 6–3   Transactions Table from Input-Output Study

| | Producers | | | | | |
Inputs	Computer Firms	Wire Producer	Local Merchants	Households	Exports	Total
Computers	0	300	150	180	1370	2000
Wire	400	0	0	0	600	1000
Local	0	0	0	2500	—	2500
Labor	1000	600	2000	0	0	3600
Imports	600	100	350	920	—	1970
Total	2000	1000	2500	3600	1970	—

TABLE 6–4   Input Coefficients Table

	Producers			
Inputs	Computer Firms	Wire Producer	Local Merchants	Households
Computers	0.00	0.30	0.06	0.05
Wire	0.20	0.00	0.00	0.00
Local	0.00	0.00	0.00	0.69
Labor	0.50	0.60	0.80	0.00
Imports	0.30	0.10	0.14	0.26
Total	1.00	1.00	1.00	1.00

input coefficients for wire producers and local merchants. The fourth column shows that households spend 5 percent of their income on home computers, 69 percent on local goods, and 26 percent on imports.

   The Multiplier Process.   The information in Table 6–4 can be used to estimate the multiplier effects of an increase in computer exports. Suppose that computer exports increase by $100. The increase in computer sales will increase local spending, precipitating a series of spending rounds. The first three spending rounds are shown in Figure 6–7.

Round 1. The increase in computer sales increases wire production by $20 (0.20 times $100) and wages by $50 (0.50 times $100).

Round 2. The $20 increase in wire production increases computer sales by an additional $6 (0.30 times $20) and wages by an additional $12 (0.60 times $20).
   The first-round increase in wages ($50) increases home-computer

FIGURE 6–7   Multiplier Effects of a $100 Increase in Computer Exports

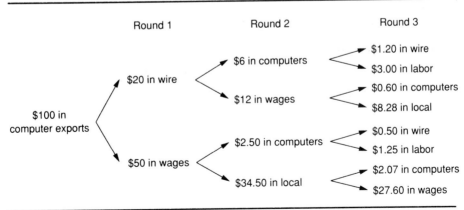

sales by $2.50 (0.05 times $50) and local consumption by $34.50 (0.69 times $50).

Round 3. The increases in computer sales, wages, and local sales cause additional increases in wire sales, wages, computer sales, and local consumption.

Because of the multiplier process, an increase in computer exports increases spending on all three goods.

The spending and respending of income continues forever, but every spending round is smaller than the previous one. The multiplier process eventually peters out because both producers and consumers spend some of their budgets on imports. As shown in the fifth row in Table 6–4 (Imports), there is a leakage of 30 percent in computer production, 10 percent in wire production, 14 percent in local-goods production, and 26 percent from consumers. These leakages weaken the multiplier process, causing each spending round to be smaller than the previous round.

The input coefficients from Table 6–4 can be used to compute spending multipliers for the two export industries. For a description of the techniques used to derive the spending multipliers, see the references at the end of the chapter. In Table 6–5, the first column shows the multiplier effects of a one-dollar increase in computer exports. Total computer sales increase by $1.23, wire production increases by $0.25, and local sales increase by $1.17. The total multiplier effect is the sum of the effects on the three industries: a one-dollar increase in computer sales increases total sales by $2.65. Because the wire industry has a smaller import leakage (10 percent compared to 30 percent for the computer industry), it has a larger multiplier (3.04 versus 2.65).

Limitations of Economic-Base and Input-Output Studies

The economic-base study and the input-output study share a number of defects that limit their applicability. The three most important problems are as follows:

TABLE 6–5   Spending Multipliers from Input-Output Example

	Added Sales Per Dollar of Additional Export Sales of	
	Computer Industry	Wire Industry
Computers	1.23	0.52
Wire	0.25	1.10
Local	1.17	1.42
Total	2.65	3.04

Constant Multipliers.   The multipliers derived from both types of studies are assumed to be constant. In fact, a city's multipliers will change over time for three reasons.

1. City size and consumer products. Multipliers increase with city size, reflecting the ability of a larger city to support a wider variety of firms. As explained in Chapter 5, a larger city has enough demand to support activities with relatively large scale economies. For example, if a city grows to the point at which it can support its own Mexican restaurant, city residents will patronize the local restaurant instead of traveling to another city. A larger fraction of increases in income will be spent locally, so the income and employment multipliers will increase.

2. City size and intermediate inputs. As the city grows, the demand for intermediate inputs increases, so more of these inputs will be provided locally instead of being imported. For example, if the computer industry grows to the point at which the city can support its own silicon-chip maker, computer firms will spend less on imported inputs and more on locally produced inputs. Therefore, a given increase in computer exports will generate a larger increase in total income.

3. Changes in input prices. Changes in input prices cause factor substitution that change the interactions among the city's economic sectors. Suppose that the city's wage increases, causing computer firms to substitute imported capital equipment for laborers. If the input coefficient for labor decreases from 0.50 to 0.40, only $40 of a $100 increase in computer exports will be paid to laborers. Because a smaller fraction of export income will be spent locally, the multiplier effect of an increase in exports will decrease.

Constant Wage.   The economic-base study and the input-output study assume that the city's wage is fixed. In other words, they estimate the horizontal shift of the city's labor-demand curve, not the equilibrium change in employment. If an economic-base study estimates a multiplier of 2.5 and an increase in export employment of 10,000, it would predict an increase in total employment of 25,000 jobs. This is incorrect because the supply curve is positively sloped, meaning that the increase in demand increases the city's wage, which decreases the quantity of labor demanded. In Figure 6–3, total employment increases by only 16,000 jobs. Because the economic-base study and the input-output study assume that the wage is fixed, they overestimate the stimulative effect of increases in exports. For small changes in export employment, the errors from assuming a fixed wage will be relatively small.

The Demand Side of the Economy.   Both types of studies focus attention on the demand side of the urban economy. The implication is that growth occurs when outsiders buy more of the city's exports. In other words, the city's economic fate is in the hands of outsiders. This is incorrect for two reasons.

First, local government policies can stimulate economic growth by decreasing the production costs of exporters and local producers. Some supply-side policies decrease production costs directly: improvements in the education system increase worker productivity, thus decreasing labor costs, and improvements in infrastructure (roads, highways, ports, sewers) decrease freight costs and utility costs. Other supply-side policies make the city a more attractive place for workers, causing migration that decreases wages and labor costs. For example, a city can increase its relative attractiveness by offering a clean environment, safe neighborhoods, and high-quality public schools.

Second, growth does not necessarily require an increase in exports. The most compelling counterexample to the export-oriented theories of urban economic growth is the world economy. The world economy has grown despite the absence of exports to other worlds. Growth has occurred because technological advances have increased output per person and increased real income per capita. The same phenomenon occurs at the urban level: an increase in labor productivity increases per capita income, so an increase in exports is not necessary for an increase in the standard of living.

PLANT-CLOSURE LEGISLATION

In recent years, a total of 24 states have considered various types of laws that would impose penalties on firms that close unprofitable plants. These proposed plant-closing laws share three features:

1. Notification requirement. The firm would be required to give advance notification of a plant closing. The notification requirement may be as short as 30 days or as long as 2 years. Many of the proposed laws specify a notification period in excess of the federally mandated 60-day period (passed in 1988).

2. Severance pay. In some states, firms would be required to provide a lump-sum payment to each of its workers, the size of which would depend on the worker's wage and the length of employment. In other states, firms would be required to continue paying a former employee until the worker found another job.

3. Severance tax. When a plant closes, the firm would be required to pay a special tax to the local government. The severance tax is meant to replace the taxes that the firm would have paid if it had stayed open.

What are the benefits and costs of these features of plant-closure legislation?

Notification Requirement

The notification requirement may increase the number of plant closures. Suppose that your firm is in trouble: there is a 40 percent chance that your plant will close in the next year. Will you explain your troubles to your cus-tomers, creditors, and workers? If you do, your troubles may get worse in-stead of better. Your customers may look for more reliable suppliers. Your creditors, realizing the risk of lending money to a troubled firm, may be reluc-tant to lend you money. Your best workers may look for other jobs. Although you stand a 60 percent chance of survival if you retain your customers, credi-tors, and best employees, you may have only a 30 percent chance of survival if you lose them. Because the notification requirement forces the marginal firm to disclose its troubles to everyone, it increases the likelihood that the plant will close.

On the positive side, the notification requirement gives workers a head start in the search for new jobs. Suppose that the plant closing is inevitable: the plant will close even if advance notification is not given, and advance no-tification does not affect the timing of the closure. In this case, advance notice promotes efficiency because workers can plan ahead, so they will be unem-ployed for shorter periods of time. An unannounced plant closure idles pro-ductive workers, generating substantial opportunity costs in the form of de-creased production. Advance notification decreases the opportunity costs because it shortens unemployment spells. If the plant closing is unavoidable, more information is clearly better than less.

Severance Pay and Workers

The requirement for severance pay will decrease wages. In equilibrium, a worker's total compensation (wages plus fringe benefits) is determined by the worker's productivity. If workers are granted severance pay (one type of fringe benefit), firms will decrease workers' wages to compensate for the in-crease in fringe benefits. The closure law will not increase total compensation, but will increase severance pay at the expense of wages.

Will the closure law impose an undesirable compensation package on workers? Before the closure law was passed, workers in unionized firms had the opportunity to negotiate a compensation package with low wages and high severance pay. The fact that they chose wages over severance pay sug-gests that they may be worse off under the closure law. Most workers are not in unions, however, so negotiations over severance pay and wages are often difficult and costly. For such workers, a plant-closure law places the govern-ment in the role of a labor negotiator, and generates a compensation package with more severance pay and lower wages. One problem with this approach to labor policy is that the mandated package is the same for all workers, re-gardless of their preferences for wages and severance pay.

The Efficiency of the Labor Market

Does plant-closing legislation promote efficiency in the labor market? Proponents argue that the closure of a plant generates externalities because it idles productive workers and decreases production, imposing substantial opportunity costs on society. According to this line of reasoning, plant-closure legislation internalizes these external costs by forcing the firm to pay its idle workers until they find new jobs.

This reasoning ignores the fact that a plant closure sometimes increases employment elsewhere. Some firms close a plant in one city to open or expand a plant in another city. In fact, most closure legislation is motivated by the perception that firms are moving their operations from the Rustbelt to the Sunbelt. Even if a firm does not relocate its plant, the plant closure frees up resources that can be used elsewhere. Therefore, a plant closure may generate external benefits (an increase in Sunbelt employment) as well as external costs (a decrease in Rustbelt employment). To defend plant-closure laws on efficiency grounds, one must show that the external costs of a plant closure exceed its external benefits.

Plant-Closure Legislation and the Tax Base

How will a closure law affect the city's tax base? The good news is that the law may delay the closure of some plants. The bad news is that the law may increase the number of marginal plants that eventually shut down. In addition, the closure law may discourage the development of new plants. In weighing alternative plant sites, a firm includes in its calculations the expected costs of eventually closing the plant. A city that requires severance pay and severance taxes will have relatively high plant costs, so firms are less likely to locate there. The short-run gains from keeping marginal plants on the tax rolls may be offset by long-term losses in employment and capital investment.

Alternative Policies

What should a city with a declining industry do? First, if the city wants to save a troubled industry, it could develop policies that decrease the industry's production costs. The city can decrease production costs by providing more efficient public service (e.g., schools, roads, and utilities). Second, the city could let marginal plants close and then encourage the development of new industries. In a dynamic economy, changes in product demand and production technology are inevitable. If these changes make an industry obsolete, rescue attempts will be futile. On the positive side, the death of one industry frees up resources (capital, labor, land) that can be used to produce other goods. One option for a local government is to focus its economic-development efforts on facilitating the transition from old industries to new ones.

A third policy option is to attack the unemployment problem directly. Subsidized education and training will prepare workers for new employment opportunities. Subsidized job information and relocation assistance will encourage the unemployed to move to areas with better job opportunities.

SUMMARY

1. Urban economic growth results from changes in the urban labor market.
   a. The demand for labor comes from exporters and local producers. An increase in export sales increases local sales through the multiplier process. The employment multiplier is defined as the change in total employment per unit change in export employment.
   b. An increase in demand increases total employment and the wage. The demand curve shifts as a result of changes in the costs of producing exports and local goods.
   c. The supply of labor comes from city residents. The supply curve is positively sloped because an increase in city size increases housing and land prices, forcing firms to pay higher wages to compensate workers for the increased living costs. An increase in supply (caused by improvements in environmental quality or public services) increases total employment and decreases the wage.

2. Economic growth generates benefits and costs. The larger city can exploit scale economies in production, retailing, and public goods. On the cost side, the larger city has higher housing prices, longer commuting distances, and more pollution, congestion, and crime.

3. Public policy can stimulate economic growth by decreasing the production costs of exporters and local producers. Direct policies include public education and training programs (which increase labor productivity) and the efficient provision of public services and infrastructure. Indirect policies improve the quality of life of the city, thus attracting workers and decreasing wages.

4. Some cities try to attract firms by offering subsidies (tax abatement, industrial bonds, government loans, and subsidized site development).
   a. Because taxes support local public services, a tax cut may decrease spending on public services, making the city less attractive to firms.
   b. Subsidy programs that attract new firms often generate relatively small benefits for local workers because many of the new jobs are filled by newcomers.
   c. Subsidy programs often promote the growth of one city at the expense of another, causing inefficient location choices.

5. A pollution-abatement program may increase total employment. The abatement program decreases labor demand and increases labor supply. If people are relatively sensitive to pollution, the increase in supply will be large relative to the decrease in demand, and the city will grow.

6. An economic-base study predicts trends in urban income and employment. It is based on the notion that a city must earn its livelihood by exporting. An economic-base study has three steps:
   a. Estimate the amount of export employment. Location quotients provide inaccurate estimates of export employment.

    b. Compute the multiplier. The multiplier equals the ratio of total employment to export employment.

    c. Project growth in export sales or employment.

7. Economic-base studies are used by local governments to predict the demands for local public goods (schools, sewage, fire protection) and by firms to predict the demands for private goods.

8. An input-output study is a sophisticated version of the economic-base study. It is based on a complete accounting of the economy's transactions, so it more accurately measures export and local activities. Input coefficients, which summarize the interactions between different sectors of the economy, are used to derive income multipliers for each industry.

9. The economic-base study and the input-output study share a number of defects that limit their applicability.

    a. The multipliers are assumed to be constant. The actual multiplier is likely to change with factor prices and city size.

    b. The two approaches assume that the city's wage is fixed. They estimate the horizontal shift of the city's demand curve, not the change in equilibrium employment.

    c. Both approaches focus attention on the demand side of the economy, suggesting that the city's economic fate is determined by outsiders. In fact, local governments can stimulate growth through the provision of public services.

10. Plant-closure laws include provisions for advance notification of closure and severance pay.

    a. The notification requirement may increase the likelihood that a marginal plant will be closed. On the benefit side, advanced notice gives workers an opportunity to look for alternative employment, so it shortens unemployment spells.

    b. The requirement for severance pay (an additional fringe benefit) will decrease wages. Some workers will be forced to accept an undesirable compensation package.

    c. Because a plant closure sometimes increases employment elsewhere, there are external benefits as well as external costs.

    d. A city with a declining industry could focus its development efforts on facilitating the transition from old industries to new ones.

EXERCISES AND DISCUSSION QUESTIONS

1. Consider a city where the only export industry is a toaster manufacturer. For every $1 of income, citizens save 10 cents and spend 15 cents on imports. If toaster sales increase by $3 million, by how much will total income in the city increase?

2. Consider a city where 10,000 people are employed in export industries and 20,000 people are employed in local industries. Suppose that a new export firm, employing 100 people, opens up.
   a. Is it possible to accurately predict the change in equilibrium employment? If so, what is the change in local and total employment? If not, why not?
   b. How would your answer to (a) change if the new firm employed 2,000 people instead of 100?

3. Consider a city that finances all of its public goods with taxes on residents. Suppose that the city discovers a way to organize its public services that cuts the costs of local services in half. Depict graphically the effects of this change on the city's labor market.

4. Consider a city that uses a business tax to finance the provision of industrial services (roads, water, sewers). If the city does not provide these services, the individual firms must supply their own roads, water, and sewers. Suppose that the city decides to cut business taxes and expenditures on industrial services by the same amount.

   Evaluate the effects of the new tax-expenditure policy on the city's labor market. Will total employment in the city increase or decrease?

5. Suppose a city eliminates all taxes on residents and replaces them with taxes on business. Depict graphically the effects of the change in tax policy on equilibrium city size.

6. Suppose that a new machine cuts the costs of pollution abatement in half, causing a resident of a city with a polluting steel industry to make the following statement: "I used to oppose the proposed $100 pollution tax because I figured that it would decrease total employment. With this new machine, the $100 tax will increase total employment, so I support the tax."

   Under what circumstances is this statement correct? Illustrate your answer with a graph.

7. The section on environmental quality suggests that a pollution tax may increase total employment. Suppose that instead of using a pollution tax to reduce citywide pollution by a total of 25 percent, the city requires that *each* polluting firm decrease its pollution by 25 percent.
   a. Is the uniform-reduction policy more or less efficient than the pollution-tax program? In other words, will the total costs of abatement be larger or smaller under the uniform-reduction policy?
   b. Is the city more or less likely to grow under the uniform-reduction policy? Demonstrate by using a graph.

8. Consider the trade-offs associated with choosing a reference region for defining a city's location quotient. The traditional approach (see equation 6.8) is to compare the city economy to the national economy. What if the

denominator of the location quotient is defined as the percentage of state employment in mitten production? Would the measured location quotient be closer to or farther from the city's true location quotient?

9. In Figure 6–2, the shift of the demand curve from D_2 to D_3, which reflects the multiplier process, is parallel. The implicit assumption is that the employment multiplier is constant. Draw the demand curves under the assumption that the multiplier increases with city size.

10. Suppose that you have been given the following data on transactions within a city's economy:

| | Producers | | | | | |
Inputs	Computer Firms	Wire Producer	Local Merchants	Households	Exports	Total
Computers	0	350	?	300	?	2000
Wire	500	0	0	0	500	1000
Local goods	0	0	0	2500	—	?
Labor	1000	600	2000	0	0	3600
Imports	?	?	300	?	—	1650
Total	2000	?	?	3600	?	—

a. Fill in the blanks (shown by ?) in the transactions table.

b. Will this city have larger or smaller export multipliers than the city with the transactions listed in Table 6–3? Explain.

11. Suppose that wire production in the city with the input coefficients shown in Table 6–4 increases by $100.

a. Compute the first, second, and third rounds of spending that result from the increase in wire sales, using the format of Figure 6–7 to report your results.

b. By how much does spending on wire, computers, and local goods eventually increase?

c. What is the ultimate increase in total sales?

12. Consider a city that estimates its export multipliers from the input coefficients from a 1965 input-output study.

a. Will the city overestimate or underestimate the stimulative effects of exports?

b. If your answer to (a) is that "it depends on . . .", make a list of questions that you would ask Ms. Information, the most knowledgeable person in the city. Note: She does not know the current input coefficients.

13. Suppose that you are a landowner in a city where several firms have recently closed their plants. The city council is considering a law that would impose heavy penalties on firms that close their plants. Should you support or oppose the proposed law? Distinguish between the short-run and long-run effects of the law.

14. Suppose that a city adopts a plant-closure law with the following provision:

    For every dollar of wages paid to an employee, the firm must deposit $0.10 in an interest-bearing bank account for the employee. The funds in the bank account are to be paid to the employee if (*i*) the firm closes its plant or (*ii*) the employee quits or is fired.
    a. Will the law affect the labor costs of the firm?
    b. Will the law make workers better or worse off?
    c. How does the bank-account policy differ from the severance-pay provision of a normal plant-closure law?

REFERENCES AND ADDITIONAL READINGS

The Urban Labor Market

Henderson, J. V. *Urban Development: Theory, Fact, and Illusion.* New York: Oxford University Press, 1988.   Chapter 6 estimates the relationships between wages and city size, environmental quality, weather, and crime rates.

Rosen, Sherwin. "Wage-based Indexes of Urban Quality of Life." In *Current Issues in Urban Economics*, ed. Peter Mieszkowski and Mahlon Straszheim. Baltimore: The Johns Hopkins Press, 1979.   Estimates the relationships between wages and city size, environmental quality, weather, and crime.

Demand-Side versus Supply-Side Growth

Chinitz, Benjamin. "Contrasts in Agglomeration: New York and Pittsburgh." In *Readings in Urban Economics*, ed. Matthew Edel and Jerome Rothenberg. New York: Macmillan, 1972.   A discussion of the supply side of the urban economy.

North, Douglass C. "Location Theory and Regional Economic Growth." In *Regional Policy: Readings in Theory and Application*, ed. John Friedmann and William Alonso. Cambridge, Mass.: MIT Press, 1975.   States the case for the export-driven model of regional growth.

Tiebout, Charles M. "Exports and Regional Economic Growth." In *Regional Policy: Readings in Theory and Application*, ed. John Friedmann and William Alonso. Cambridge, Mass.: MIT Press, 1975.   Critiques the standard export-driven growth model.

Public Policy and Economic Growth

Aschauer, David A. "Rx for Productivity: Build Infrastructure." *Federal Reserve Bank of Chicago Letter* 13 (September 1988), pp. 1–3. Discusses the relationship between investment in infrastructure and productivity, suggesting that under-investment in public infrastructure during the 1970s and 1980s caused productivity to grow at a relatively slow rate.

Blinder, Alan. "Are Crumbling Highways Giving Productivity a Flat?" *Business Week* (August 1988), p. 16. Discusses Aschauer's study of the connection between sluggish productivity growth and investment in public infrastructure.

Harrison, Bennett, and Sandra Kanter. "The Political Economy of Job-Creation Business Incentives." *Journal of the American Institute of Planners* 44 (October 1978). pp. 424–435.

Levy, John M. *Economic Development Programs for Cities, Counties, and Towns.* New York: Praeger Publishers, 1985. Detailed discussion of programs for economic development.

Mishan, E. J. *The Costs of Economic Growth.* London: Staples Press, 1967. Discusses the costs and benefits of regional growth.

Morris, David. *Self Reliant Cities.* San Francisco: Sierra Club Books, 1982. Describes city programs for economic development.

Peltz, Michael, and Marc Weiss. "State and Local Government Roles in Industrial Innovation." *Journal of the American Planning Association* 50 (1984), pp. 270–279.

Rasmussen, David W.; Marc Bendick; and Larry Ledebur. "Evaluating State Economic Development Incentives from a Firm's Perspective." *Business Economics* 10 (1982), pp. 23–29.

Schmenner, Roger. "Industrial Location and Urban Public Management." In *The Prospective City*, ed. Arthur Solomon. Cambridge, Mass.: MIT Press, 1980. A discussion of the ways that local government can encourage economic development.

Schmenner, Roger W. *Making Business Location Decisions.* Englewood Cliffs, N.J.: Prentice-Hall, 1982. Discusses how firms make location decisions.

Senia, Al, and George Weimer. "The War Between the States for High Technology." *Iron Age* (September 5, 1983). Discusses competition between states over high-technology industries.

Summers, Gene. *The Invasion of Non-Metropolitan America by Industry: A Quarter Century of Experience.* New York: Praeger Publishers, 1976. Describes the experiences of small towns that have attracted new industry.

City Size and Environmental Policy

Henderson, J. Vernon. "Effect of Taxation of Externalities on City Size." In *Urban Growth Policy in a Market Economy*, ed. George S. Tolley, Philip E. Graves, and John L. Gardner. New York: Academic Press, 1979. pp. 91–97.

Izraeli, Oded. "Externalities and Intercity Wage and Price Differentials." In *Urban Growth Policy in a Market Economy*, ed. George S. Tolley, Philip E. Graves, and John L. Gardner. New York: Academic Press, 1979. pp. 159–94.

Economic-Base Theory and Input-Output Analysis

DiPasquale, Denise,and Karen Polenske. "Output, Income, and Employment Input-Output Multipliers." In *Economic Impact Analysis: Methodology and Applications,* ed. Saul Pleeter. Boston: Martinus Nijhoff, 1980. pp. 85–113.

Hoover, Edgar M., and Frank Giarratani. *An Introduction to Regional Economics.* New York: Knopf, 1985, Chapter 11.   A discussion of the forecasting techniques (economic-base analysis and input-output analysis).

Isserman, Andrew M. "Estimating Export Activity in a Regional Economy: A Theoretical and Empirical Analysis of Alternative Methods." *International Regional Science Review* 5 (1980), pp. 155–84.   Discusses the location quotients and other methods for measuring the region's exports.

Miernyk, William H. *The Elements of Input-Output Analysis.* New York: Random House, 1965.   Describes the nuts and bolts of input-output analysis.

Pleeter, Saul. "Methodologies of Economic Impact Analysis: An Overview." In *Economic Impact Analysis: Methodology and Applications,* ed. Saul Pleeter. Boston: Martinus Nijhoff, 1980. pp. 7–31.

Richardson, Harry W. *Input-Output Analysis and Regional Economics.* New York: John Wiley & Sons, 1972. pp. 1–52.

Plant-Closing Legislation

Edel, Matthew. "People versus Place in Urban Impact Analysis." In *The Urban Impacts of Federal Policy,* ed. Norman J. Glickman. Baltimore: The Johns Hopkins Press, 1980. pp. 175–91.   Discusses the issue of whether policy should be directed toward people or places.

Hekman, Hohn S., and John S. Strong. "Is There a Case for Plant Closing Laws?" *New England Economic Review* (July/August 1980), pp. 34–51.   Discusses the pros and cons of closing laws, and describes Sweden's policies for plant closures. Explores some of the evidence concerning the effects of plant closures in the Frostbelt.

McKenzie, Richard. *Plant Closings: Public or Private Choices.* Washington, D.C.: Cato, 1982.   A discussion of plant-closure laws.

Winnick, Louis. "Place Prosperity vs. People Prosperity." In *Essays in Urban Land Economics,* ed. James Gillies. Los Angeles: University of California, 1966.

Trends in Regional Growth

Chinitz, Benjamin. "The Regional Transformation of the American Economy." *American Economic Review* 76 (1986), pp. 300–303.   Discusses recent trends in regional growth, documenting the migration from the Frostbelt to the Sunbelt.

Glickman, Norman J. *Econometric Analysis of Regional Systems: Explorations in Model Building and Policy Analysis.* New York: Academic Press, 1977, Chapter 2.

Hill, Richard C. "Economic Crisis and Political Response in the Motor City." In *Sunbelt-Snowbelt: Urban Redevelopment and Regional Restructuring,* ed. New York: Oxford University Press, 1984.   Describes city programs for economic development.

Hirsch, Werner Z. "Interindustry Relations of a Metropolitan Area." *Review of Economics and Statistics* 41 (1959), pp. 368–83.

Luria, Dan, and Jack Russell. "Motor City Changeover." In *Sunbelt-Snowbelt: Urban Redevelopment and Regional Restructuring*, ed. Larry Sayers and William Tebb. New York: Oxford University Press, 1984. Describes city programs for economic development.

Meiszkowski, Peter. "Recent Trends in Urban and Regional Development." In *Current Issues in Urban Economics*, ed. Peter Meiszkowski and Mahlon Straszheim. Baltimore: The Johns Hopkins Press, 1979. Describes the patterns of regional development in the postwar period, with emphasis on interregional migration, interregional shifts in employment, and changes in regional income differentials.

Norton, R. D., and J. Rees. "The Product Cycle and the Spatial Decentralization of American Manufacturing." *Regional Studies* 13 (1979), pp. 141–51.

Perloff, Harvey, and Lowdon Wingo. "Natural Resource Endowment and Regional Economic Growth." In *Regional Policy: Readings in the Theory and Applications*, ed. John Friedman and William Alonso. Cambridge, Mass.: MIT Press.

Small Businesses and Economic Growth

Armington, Catherine, and Marjorie Odle. "Small Business—How Many Jobs?" *Brookings Review* (Winter 1982), pp. 14–17.

Birch, David. "Who Creates Jobs?" *The Public Interest* (Fall 1981), pp. 3–14. Discusses the role of small business in economic development.

U.S. Small Business Administration. *The State of Small Business: 1984.* Washington, D.C.: U.S. Government Printing Office, 1984. Chapters 1, 2, and 4 discuss the debate over David Birch's work.

PART TWO

Land Rent and Urban
Land-Use Patterns

The first part of this book explained why cities exist and where they develop, but did not explain how activities are arranged within the city. This second part examines the spatial structure of cities, taking a close look at land use within cities. It explores the market forces and government policies that determine the equilibrium pattern of land use.

This part is divided into five chapters. Chapter 7 develops the basic concepts of land rent and land use: it explains the factors that determine the equilibrium price of land and shows how land is allocated among alternative land uses. Chapter 8 discusses land rent and land use in the traditional monocentric city of the 19th century and explains why commercial and industrial activity was concentrated in the central core area. It also explains why the poor tend to locate in central cities. Chapter 9 uses general-equilibrium analysis to explore the interactions between the residential land market, the business land market, and the urban labor market. This is a challenging chapter, and could be skipped without disrupting the flow of the rest of the book. Chapter 10 explains land use in modern cities and explains why the traditional monocentric city was replaced with the modern multicentric city. Chapter 11 discusses the role of local government in the urban land market, exploring the market effects of zoning and other land-use controls.

CHAPTER 7

Introduction to Land Rent and Land Use

The trouble with land is that they're not making it anymore.

Will Rogers

This chapter introduces some basic concepts of land rent and land use, setting the stage for the discussion of urban land use in chapters 8 through 11. This chapter addresses three questions about the land market. First, what determines the price of land? Second, who benefits from public policies that increase the fertility or accessibility of land? Third, does the land market allocate land efficiently?

DEFINITIONS: RENT, VALUE, AND PRICE

It will be useful to define two terms, land rent and market value. Like other assets, land yields a stream of marketable services and thus a stream of income. For example, agricultural land yields a stream of agricultural output (bushels of corn), generating a stream of income for the farmer. Similarly, a parking lot in the city yields a stream of parking services, generating income for the parking firm. When a landowner grants the rights to use his land to another individual or firm, he charges **land rent**. If a corn farmer is granted the right to grow corn on a plot of land, the rent might be $1,000 per acre per year. If a parking firm is granted the right to operate a parking lot, the rent might be $5,000 per acre per year.

What determines the market value of land? The **market value** of land equals the **present value** of the stream of rental income from the land. To explain the concept of present value, consider an asset that generates R_t of income in time period t and is expected to generate this income for N years. If the market interest rate is i, the present value of the stream of earnings from the asset is

$$PV = \sum_{t=1}^{N} \frac{R_t}{(1+i)^t} \tag{7–1}$$

The annual income from most assets (e.g., buildings, machines) decreases over time as the asset deteriorates. The income stream from agricultural land

157

may also decrease over time if the soil deteriorates. In contrast, land used for residential, commercial, and industrial activities yields a constant stream of rental income because the land never wears out. If the annual rental income (R_t) is constant and lasts forever, the income stream is like a perpetuity, and the present value formula simplifies to

$$PV = \frac{R}{i} \tag{7-2}$$

The market value of land equals the present value of the stream of rental income. For example, if the annual rent is $5,000 per acre and the market interest rate is 10 percent, the market value of land will be $50,000 per acre. The market value of land makes an investor indifferent between buying the land (spending $50,000 to earn $5,000 per year in land rent forever) and putting the $50,000 in a bank account with a 10 percent interest rate.

This book uses land rent—not market value—as the **price of land**. Most economic variables are defined as streams of revenue or costs. For example, a household earns an annual income; a firm computes its annual profits as its annual revenue less its annual costs. To be consistent, the price of land will be defined as the annual payment in exchange for the right to use the land: the price of land is synonymous with land rent. Given the simple relationship between rent and value, it's easy to make the translation from land rent to market value: just divide the annual rent by the market interest rate.

LAND RENT AND FERTILITY

David Ricardo (1821) is credited with the idea that the price of agricultural land is determined by its fertility. The more productive the land, the more a tenant farmer will be willing to pay to use the land. Ricardo's fertility analysis demonstrates the most important concepts of land rent in a simple and compelling way.

Consider an agricultural county where tenant farmers use land of varying fertility to grow corn. The characteristics of the local economy are as follows:

1. **Fixed prices.** The prices of the output (corn) and inputs (labor, seed, fertilizer, capital) are determined in national markets, so local farmers take the prices as given. The prices are the same at all locations in the county.

2. **Zero economic profits.** There is free entry into farming, so all farmers make zero economic profits ("normal" accounting profits).

3. **Fertility of land.** There are three types of land: H (high fertility), M (medium), and L (low).

4. **Land to highest bidder.** Landowners rent their land to the highest bidder.

5. **Zero transport costs.** Transport costs are assumed to be so small that they can be ignored. Later in the chapter, this assumption will be relaxed.

Figure 7–1 shows the conventional cost curves for one-acre plots of the three types of land. The marginal-cost curves (*MC*) are positively sloped and pass through the U-shaped average total-cost curves (*ATC*) at the minimum points of the average-cost curves. The cost curves include all the nonland costs of production, including the costs of raw materials (seeds and fertilizer), capital (tractors), and labor. They also include the opportunity costs of being a farmer (e.g., the money the farmer gives up by being a farmer instead of a steelworker).

The positions of the cost curves depend on the fertility of the land. A farmer on relatively fertile land can produce the same amount of corn with smaller quantities of nonland inputs. Because the farmer spends less money on seeds, fertilizer, tractors, and labor, his average-cost curves are lower. In general, the higher the fertility, the lower the cost curves.

How much are farmers willing to pay for the three types of land? In Figure 7–1, the national corn market generates an equilibrium price of $10: supply intersects demand at a price of $10. Farmers are price takers and maximize profits where price equals marginal cost. The profit-maximizing output on the high-fertility land is 220 bushels per acre, generating a profit equal to the shaded area. In this example, profit is $1,320 per acre per year (total revenue of $2,200 less total costs of $880). A farmer would be willing to pay up to $1,320 per year to use one acre of the high-fertility land. Similarly, a farmer would be willing to pay up to $320 per year for the medium-fertility land. For the low-fertility land, production costs are so high that corn production is not profitable at a price of $10, so a corn farmer would not be willing to pay anything for the low-fertility land.

Competition and Land Rent

Competition among prospective farmers will bid up the price of land to the point at which economic profits are zero (accounting profits are normal). Farmers are willing to pay up to $1,320 for the high-fertility land and will be forced by competition to do so: at any rent less than $1,320 per acre, the landowner will be able to find another farmer willing to pay slightly more to use the land. Similarly, the equilibrium rent on the medium-fertility land will be $320. Because the equilibrium land rents make economic profits equal to zero, farmers will be indifferent between the alternative plots of land. Although the high fertility land has lower production costs, the savings in production costs are offset by higher land costs.

In equilibrium, land rent equals the excess of total revenue over nonland costs. This is the **leftover principle**: because of competition among farmers

FIGURE 7–1 Fertility and Land Rent

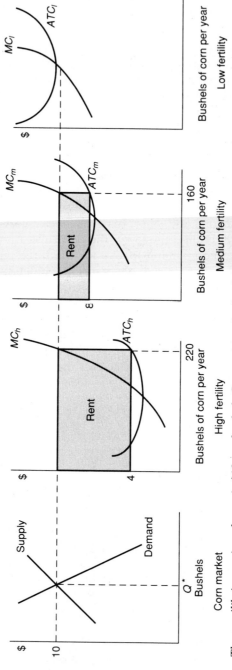

The equilibrium price of corn is $10 per bushel. Competition for land forces farmers to pay their surplus (total revenue less total nonland cost) to landowners. The high-fertility land has lower production costs and higher pre-rent profits, so farmers are willing to pay more rent. The medium-fertility land earns less rent because it has higher production costs. The low-fertility land generates no profits, so its rent is zero.

for land, the landowner gets the leftovers. This principle is based on the assumption that individual plots of land have unique characteristics, but farmers are all the same. Competition among a large number of farmers, each of whom has the same cost curves, bids up the price of high-fertility land to the point at which economic profits are zero. If the farmer on the high-fertility land pays less than the excess of total revenue over nonland costs, the farmer would be evicted and replaced with another farmer willing to pay the leftovers (total revenue less nonland costs) for the opportunity to earn normal accounting profits.

The leftover principle does not hold if there are restrictions on entry and competition. One restriction on entry comes from patents. If farmer Tom holds the patent for a particular farming technique, he will have lower production costs than all other farmers. For example, suppose that Tom can produce an acre's worth of corn for a pre-rent profit of $2,000 while other farmers, using inferior techniques, generate a pre-rent profit of only $500. The landlord will be unable to charge Tom a rent of $2,000 because the threat of eviction is a hollow one: there are no other farmers with the same production costs, so there are no farmers willing to pay $2,000 per acre. Instead, Tom will be charged only $500, allowing him to make economic profits of $1,500. The landowner will not get the leftovers because the patent restricts competition. Once the patent expires and all farmers have access to the same technology, the landowner will increase land rent and convert the economic profits into higher land rent.

Land Rent and Public Policy

Fertility analysis can be used to predict the effects of public policy on land rent. Suppose that an agricultural county builds an aqueduct and provides free irrigation water to farmers. Who will benefit from the irrigation project?

Consider first the possibility that the irrigation project does not affect the equilibrium price of corn. The irrigation project will decrease farmers' production costs, shifting the cost curves downward, as shown in Figure 7–2. For all three types of land, pre-rent profits increase: production on high-fertility land and medium-fertility land becomes more profitable, and low-fertility land now generates a positive profit. As profits increase, competition among farmers will bid up land rent to the point at which economic profits are zero. The savings in production costs will be paid to landowners in the form of higher rent, so the benefits of the irrigation project go to landowners.

Will the price of corn be affected by the irrigation project? The project increases the supply of corn for two reasons. First, the project shifts the marginal-cost curves downward, increasing the profit-maximizing outputs of the high-fertility and medium-fertility farms. Second, marginal land (low-fertility land) is brought into production. For these two reasons, the supply curve shifts to the right, decreasing the equilibrium price of corn, so corn consumers benefit from the irrigation project. As the price of corn decreases,

FIGURE 7–2 Effects of Irrigation Project on Land Rent and Corn Price

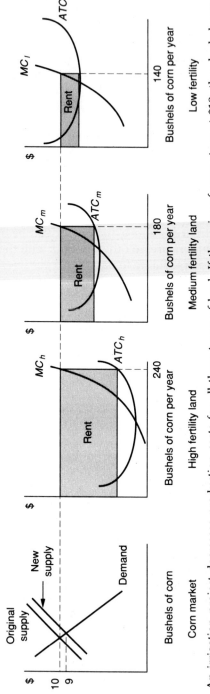

An irrigation project decreases production costs for all three types of land. If the price of corn stays at $10, the shaded areas show land rent on the three types of land. The supply of corn will increase because land is used more intensively (output increases on the high-fertility and medium-fertility land) and marginal (low-fertility) land is brought into production. The increase in supply decreases the equilibrium price of corn, so rent on each plot of land is actually less than the shaded area.

the pre-rent profits of farmers decrease, decreasing land rent. In other words, consumers gain at the expense of landowners.

What determines the distribution of benefits between landowners and corn consumers? The general rule is that the smaller the geographical area covered by the irrigation program, the larger the share of the benefits that go to landowners. Consider first an irrigation project that decreases the production costs of a single 50-acre plot of land. The project will cause a trivial increase in supply and virtually no change in the price of corn. Therefore, virtually all the benefits will go to the landowner. Consider next a national irrigation project that decreases the production costs of all corn farmers. The project will cause a large increase in supply (existing land will be cultivated more intensively and more land will be brought under production), so it will decrease corn prices significantly. In this case, a large share of the benefits will go to consumers.

The benefits of the irrigation project are **capitalized** into the market value of land. Since the project increases the annual rent, it increases the present value of the stream of earnings from land, so it increases the market value of land. Therefore, the benefits of the irrigation project go to the person who owns the land when the irrigation project is announced. Future landowners can charge higher rent after the project is completed, but also pay a higher price for the land. For example, suppose that the annual rent on high-fertility land increases from $1,320 per acre per year to $1,500. If the market interest rate is 10 percent, formula (7–2) suggests that the market value of land will increase from $13,200 per acre to $15,000 per acre.

LAND RENT AND ACCESSIBILITY

This section uses a model developed by Von Thunen (in 1826) to explain why land rent increases with the accessibility of land. In the Von Thunen model, accessibility replaces fertility as the determinant of land rent. The Von Thunen approach will be used in Chapter 8 (Land Use in the Monocentric City) to discuss urban land rent and land use.

Consider a county where all land is used to grow carrots. The characteristics of the economy are as follows:

1. **Fixed prices.** The prices of the output (carrots) and inputs (land, seed, fertilizer, capital) are determined in national markets, so farmers take the prices as given. The prices are the same at all locations.

2. **Marketplace.** All carrots are transported from farms to a central marketplace at a cost of $t per ton per mile.

3. **Competitive markets.** There is free entry into carrot farming. In equilibrium, all farmers make zero economic profits (normal accounting profits).

4. **Fertility of land.** All land is equally fertile, so production costs are the same at all locations.

Linear Land-Rent Function

Suppose that carrots are produced with fixed factor proportions. In other words, farmers do not engage in factor substitution as the relative prices of inputs change. The typical farmer occupies one acre of land and produces Q tons of carrots, which are sold at a price of P per ton. If the unit transport cost is $ t per ton per mile, total transport cost for a farm located u miles from the marketplace is

$$TC = t \cdot Q \cdot u \qquad (7\text{-}3)$$

For example, if unit transport cost (t) is $4 per ton per mile and the farmer produces 20 tons per acre, transport cost is $80 for a farm one mile from the market, $160 for a farm two miles from the market, and so on. If the farmer spends $C on nonland production costs (labor, raw materials, and the opportunity costs of farming time) and land rent is R, the profit per acre is

$$\pi = P \cdot Q - C - t \cdot Q \cdot u - R \qquad (7\text{-}4)$$

For zero economic profits, the bid rent for land (the amount the farmer is willing to pay for an acre of land) is

$$R = P \cdot Q - C - t \cdot Q \cdot u \qquad (7\text{-}5)$$

Because land near the marketplace (small u) has relatively low transport costs, the farmer will be willing to pay more for this land.

Figure 7-3 shows the **bid-rent function** of the typical farmer. The numerical assumptions are listed below the graph. Total revenue per acre (shown by the horizontal line) is the same at all locations because price and quantity do not vary across space. Total cost is the sum of nonland cost per acre and transport costs. The total-cost curve is positively sloped because transport costs increase with distance to the market; the slope of the cost curve is $(t \cdot Q)$. The farmer's bid rent for a particular location is total revenue less total costs, so the bid-rent function is negatively sloped. The bid rent is $250 at the marketplace and falls by $80 per mile.

The **land-rent function** shows the equilibrium land rent for different locations. Farmers compete for land, bidding up land rent to the point at which economic profits are zero at every location. If all farmers are identical (they all have the same production costs and transport costs), the land-rent function is the same as the bid-rent function of the typical farmer. The land-rent function makes farmers indifferent among all land in the county: as the farmer approaches the market, the savings in transport costs are exactly offset by increases in land rent.

Factor Substitution—Convex Land-Rent Function

The bid-rent function in Figure 7-3 is linear because the farmer is assumed to be inflexible. The farmer produces 20 tons of carrots with one acre of land and $50 worth of nonland inputs, regardless of the relative price of

FIGURE 7–3 Revenue, Costs, and Bid Rent for the Carrot Farmer

Assumptions:

1. Price (P) = $15
2. Output per acre (Q) = 20 tons
3. Unit transport costs (t) = $4 per ton per mile
4. Nonland cost per acre = $50

Rent equals total revenue less nonland costs and transport costs. The farmer's total revenue is $300 and nonland cost is $50. Transport cost increases by $80 for every mile from the marketplace, so the slope of the bid-rent function is $80.

land. This section shows that if farmers engage in factor substitution, the bid-rent function will be convex instead of linear.

Consider a flexible farmer, defined as one who changes input proportions as the relative price of land changes. If the farmer moves to relatively expensive land, he substitutes nonland inputs (capital, labor, raw materials) for land, so he can produce 20 tons of carrots on a smaller plot of land. The farmer's production isoquant, mapped in Figure 7–4, shows the different input combinations that will produce 20 tons of carrots: the possibilities include points B (0.80 acres of land and $60 of nonland inputs) and C (0.60 acres and $80 of nonland inputs).

Table 7–1 shows how to compute the farmer's bid-rent function for different distances from the market. If the farmer uses T acres of land, the new expression for profit is

TABLE 7–1 Costs and Land Rent for the Flexible Farmer

Distance to Market	Farm Size (acres)	Total Revenue	Nonland Costs	Transport Cost	Pre-Rent Profits	Rent per Acre
0	0.4	300	120	0	180	450
1	0.6	300	80	80	140	233
2	0.8	300	60	160	80	100
3	1.0	300	50	240	10	10

Assumptions:
  Output = 20 tons
  Price = $15
  Transport cost = $4 per ton per mile
  Pre-rent profits = Total revenue – Nonland costs – Transport cost

$$\text{Rent} = \frac{\text{Pre-rent profits}}{\text{Farm size}}$$

$$\pi = P{\cdot}Q - C - t{\cdot}Q{\cdot}u - R{\cdot}T \tag{7–6}$$

Economic profits will be zero if the total payment for land is

$$R{\cdot}T = P{\cdot}Q - C - t{\cdot}Q{\cdot}u \tag{7–7}$$

Dividing each side by T gives the bid-rent per acre:

$$R = \frac{P{\cdot}Q - C - t{\cdot}Q{\cdot}u}{T} \tag{7–8}$$

At a location three miles from the market, the flexible farmer uses the same input combinations as the inflexible farmer (one acre of land and $50 worth of nonland inputs) and is willing to pay the same amount in land rent ($10). As the farmer moves toward the marketplace, the price of land increases, causing movement up the isoquant in Figure 7–4, from point B (two miles), to C (one mile), to D. For each location, the pre-rent profit equals total revenue less nonland costs and transport costs (the right-hand side of equation (7–7)). The bid rent per acre equals the pre-rent profit divided by the size of the farm (in acres). For a farm two miles from the market, pre-rent profit is $80 on 0.80 acres of land, so the farmer is willing to pay $100 per acre ($80/0.80). The bid rent increases as the farmer approaches the market, rising to $450 for a farm close to the marketplace.

Figure 7–5 shows the bid-rent functions of the flexible and inflexible farmers. The flexible bid-rent function lies above the inflexible one for all locations except $u = 3$: the flexible farmer outbids the inflexible one for all land except at $u = 3$. To explain the ability of the flexible farmer to outbid the inflexible one, suppose that both farmers start at $u = 3$. At $u = 3$, both farmers have the same bid rent ($10) because they use the same input combination (1 acre

FIGURE 7–4   Isoquant for 20 Tons of Carrots

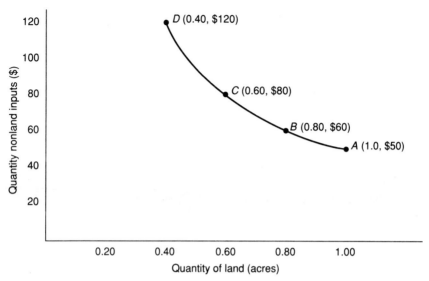

The isoquant shows the different combinations of land and nonland inputs needed to produce 20 tons of carrots. As the farmer moves toward the market, the price of land increases, so the farmer moves up the isoquant, substituting nonland inputs for land.

of land and $50 of nonland inputs). Suppose that each farmer considers a one-mile move toward the marketplace, which would decrease transport costs by $80. Because the inflexible farmer does not change his input combinations, his bid rent would increase by $80. In contrast, the flexible farmer would substitute nonland inputs for the relatively expensive land (moving up the isoquant from point A to B in Figure 7–4). Given the higher price of land at $u = 2$, point B is more efficient than point A, so the flexible farmer has lower production costs. The decrease in production costs from factor substitution increases the bid rent for land, so the flexible farmer outbids the inflexible farmer.

Figure 7–6 shows the general shape of the bid-rent functions of flexible and inflexible farmers. Because the inflexible farmer uses the same input combination at all locations, the bid-rent function simply reflects differences in transport costs: the bid-rent function is linear, with a slope equal to the transport cost per mile. In contrast, the flexible farmer engages in factor substitution, generating savings in both transportation costs and production costs as the farmer moves toward the city center. As a result, the flexible bid-rent function is convex, as shown by R_f. The two bid-rent functions are tangent at the point at which the two farmers choose the same input combination (u^*).

FIGURE 7–5   Bid-Rent Functions of Inflexible and Flexible Farmers

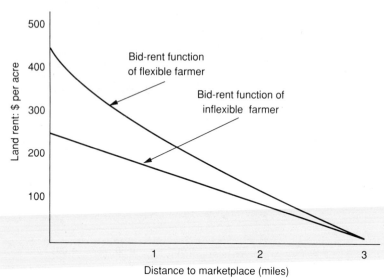

The bid-rent function of the inflexible farmer is linear because carrots are produced with fixed factor proportions. In contrast, the flexible farmer substitutes nonland inputs for land as the price of land increases. The flexible farmer is more efficient, so the farmer has lower production costs and is able to pay more rent.

Will landowners rent land to inflexible farmers? For most plots of land, flexible farmers will outbid inflexible farmers. The inflexible farmer will get land only if he is lucky enough to choose the efficient input combination. In general, inflexibility means inefficiency, so the competition for land will eliminate inefficient farmers.

Decrease in Transport Costs and Land Rent

How does a decrease in transport costs affect the bid-rent function? In Figure 7–7, the original bid-rent function is R_0 and the radius of the carrot farming district is u_0 miles. For land beyond u_0, transport costs are so high that carrot farmers are not willing to pay anything for land. Suppose that a new highway is built, decreasing the costs of transporting carrots to the market. The decrease in transport costs will decrease the slope of the bid-rent function. If the price of carrots is fixed, the bid-rent function will shift from R_0 to R_1, so the radius of the carrot district increases from u_0 miles to u_1 miles. In this case, the benefits of decreased transport costs go to landowners: land within the original farm district commands a higher rent, and marginal land (between u_0 and u_1) now commands a positive rent.

FIGURE 7–6   Flexible versus Inflexible Bid-Rent Functions

The flexible firm is more efficient than the inflexible one and is therefore able to pay more for land. The rent functions are tangent at the
point at which the inflexible firm is lucky enough to choose the efficient input combination.

The decrease in transport costs will increase the supply of carrots for two
reasons. First, land in the original carrot district will be used more intensively.
As land rent rises, farmers will economize on land by substituting nonland
factors for land. As farmers move up their isoquants, output per acre will increase. Second, marginal land (between u_0 and u_1) will be brought into production, increasing the total acreage of carrot production.

What are the implications of the increased carrot supply for the bid-rent
function? If the increase in supply is large enough to decrease the equilibrium
price of carrots, total revenue per acre will decrease, thus decreasing the
amount farmers are willing to pay for land. As shown in Figure 7–7, the decrease in the price of carrots shifts the bid-rent function downward from R_1 to
R_2. The downward shift of the bid-rent function decreases the radius of the
carrot district from u_1 to u_2.

The benefits of the highway will be shared by landowners and consumers. Most landowners can charge a higher rent because their land is more accessible. People who own land close to the market lose because the benefits of
the project (increased accessibility and higher land rent) are dominated by
the costs (decreased corn prices and lower land rent). Carrot consumers face
lower prices because there is a greater supply of carrots. As explained earlier
in the example of the irrigation project, the distribution of benefits between
landowners and consumers depends on the geographical extent of the public

FIGURE 7–7   Effect of Decreased Transport Costs on Bid-Rent
Function

Distance to marketplace (miles)

A decrease in transport costs decreases the slope of the bid-rent
function. If the price of carrots is fixed, the function shifts from R_0
to R_1. If the supply of carrots increases and the market price drops,
the bid-rent function shifts downward from R_1 to R_2.

works program. If a single county improves its road to increase the accessibility of its carrot-growing land, the supply of carrots will increase by a trivial amount, so the price will decrease by a trivial amount. Therefore, most of the benefits to the highway will go to landowners. In contrast, a national highway program is likely to increase supply and decrease price by relatively large amounts, so a larger fraction of the benefits of new highways will go to consumers.

Two Land Uses

Figure 7–8 shows how land is allocated between two competing users. Because land is allocated to the highest bidder, land within u' miles of the market is occupied by activity E, and land beyond u' is occupied by activity C. The equilibrium land-rent function (the thick line in Figure 7–8) shows the market rent for different locations. For u less than u', E outbids C, so the land-rent function is the same as E's bid-rent function. For u greater than u', the land-rent function is the same as C's bid-rent function.

Activity E occupies the land closest to the market because it has a relatively steep bid-rent function. The bid-rent function is negatively sloped be-

FIGURE 7–8   The Activity with the Steeper Bid-Rent Function
                  Locates Near the Market

Distance to marketplace (miles)

Because activity E's bid-rent function is steeper than C's, E occupies
land closer to the marketplace. E has a relatively steep bid-rent function because it has relatively high transport costs, a result of either
higher unit transport costs (eggs versus carrots) or more tons per
acre (eggplant versus cotton). The equilibrium land-rent function is
the thick line (the E bid-rent function for $u<u'$, and the C bid-rent
function for $u>u'$). Land is allocated to the highest and best use.

cause of transport costs, so the higher the transport costs, the steeper the bid-
rent function. Transport costs will be relatively high if the output is relatively
heavy or relatively costly to ship.

    1. More output per acre: eggplant and cotton. Because eggplant
farmers produce more tons per acre than cotton farmers, they have
higher transport costs and a steeper bid-rent function (everything else
being equal).

    2. Higher unit transport costs: eggs and carrots. Although carrots
can be thrown in the back of a truck, eggs must be carefully placed in egg
cartons. A ton of eggs takes up more space than a ton of carrots, so eggs
have a higher unit transport cost. Egg producers will have higher total
transport costs and thus a steeper bid-rent function (everything else being equal).

In general, the activity with higher transport costs (higher transport rate or
greater weight) will occupy the central land.

    Does the land market allocate land efficiently? The market allocates central land to the activity with the higher transport costs, that is, the activity with the most to gain from proximity to the market. Suppose that an eggplant farmer starts at a location one mile from the market and then swaps locations with a cotton farmer three miles from the market. Since the eggplant farmer has higher transport costs per acre of production, the land swap will increase eggplant transport costs by more than it decreases cotton transport costs, so total transport costs will increase. In general, because the market allocates central land to the activity with relatively large transport costs, it minimizes total transportation costs. In the terms used by land developers, land is allocated to its "highest and best use."

The conclusion that land is allocated efficiently rests on the assumption that there are no externalities in land use. In other words, the analysis assumes that all the benefits and costs of using a particular plot of land are confined to the individual who rents or owns the land. If there are externalities, the market allocation may be inefficient and government intervention may be justified on efficiency grounds. The issue of land-use externalities will be examined in detail in later chapters.

MARKET INTERACTIONS

The demand for land is derived from the demand for outputs (corn, carrots, housing, retail goods, manufactured goods). This section examines the interactions between the land market and the output market. The discussion addresses a sort of chicken-and-egg question about the land market: Is the price of land high because the price of output is high, or is the price of output high because the price of land is high?

The Corn Laws Debate

The British Corn Laws of the 1800s restricted grain imports to Britain. The decrease in the supply of imported grain increased the demand for domestically produced corn. Figure 7–9 shows the effects of the corn laws on the corn market and the land market.

    1. Corn market. The corn laws shifted the demand curve from d_1 to d_2. The price of domestic corn increased from P_1 to P_2, and the quantity of corn produced increased from C_1 to C_2.

    2. Land market. As domestic corn production increased, the demand for land increased. In Figure 7–9, the increase in corn production shifted the demand curve for land from D_1 to D_2. Because the supply curve is perfectly inelastic ("they aren't making land any more"), the increase in demand increased the price of land from R_1 to R_2.

To summarize, the price of land is high because the price of corn is high. The corn laws increased the price of corn, which stimulated the production of corn

FIGURE 7-9   The Corn-Laws Debate

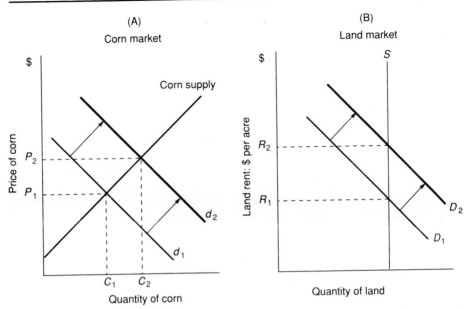

The corn laws restricted grain imports, increasing the demand for domestic corn and its price. Corn production increased from C_1 to C_2, increasing the demand for land from D_1 to D_2 and increasing the price of land from R_1 to R_2. The price of land is high because the price of corn (and the production of corn) is high.

and the demand for corn-growing land. Landowners responded by increasing the price of land to allocate the fixed resource among competing land uses. The lesson is that high land prices are the result of high corn prices, not the reason for high corn prices.

Housing Prices and Land Prices

The lesson from the corn laws debate is applicable to the urban housing market. Consider the following statement: "Greedy landowners in the San Francisco Bay Area have increased the price of land, increasing the price of housing." In fact, the price of land is high because the demand for housing (and the demand for land on which to build housing) is high. As the demand for housing increases, the price of housing increases, causing builders to buy more land to build more houses. The increase in the demand for land increases the price of land. Or consider the following: "The price of land in Boston is so high that few people can afford to live there." In fact, the price of land in Boston is high because so many people *can* afford to live there. The large demand for housing generates a large demand for land and a high price for land. The high price of land is the result—not the cause—of high housing prices.

THE SINGLE TAX

In 1880, Henry George proposed a 100 percent tax on rental income in the United States. The proposed tax was dubbed the "single tax" because in George's time it would have generated enough revenue to support all levels of government. The spirit of the single tax is best expressed by George himself. The following is from an interview with David Dudley Field (in the *North American Review* in 1885):

Field:

Then suppose A to be the proprietor of a thousand acres on the Hudson, chiefly farming land, but at the same time having on it houses, barns, cattle, horses, carriages, furniture; how is he to be dealt with under your theory?

George:

He would be taxed on the value of his land, and not on the value of his improvements and stock. . . . The effect of our present system, which taxes a man for values created by his labor and capital, is to put a fine upon industry, and repress improvement. The more houses, the more crops, the more buildings in the country, the better for us all, and we are doing ourselves an injury by imposing taxes upon the production of such things.

Field:

Then you would tax the farmer whose farm is worth $1000 as heavily as you would tax the adjoining proprietor, who, with the same quantity of land, has added improvements worth $100,000; is that your idea?

George:

It is. The improvements made by the capitalist would do no harm to the farmer, and would benefit the whole community, and I would do nothing to discourage them.

Field:

A large landlord in New York, owns a hundred houses, each worth say $25,000 (scattered in different parts of the city); at what rate of valuation would you tax him?

George:

On his houses, nothing. I would tax him on the value of the lots.

Field:

As vacant lots?

George:

As if each particular lot were vacant, surrounding improvements remaining the same.

Field:

Well, what do you contemplate as the ending of such a scheme?

George:
> The taking of the full annual value of land for the benefit of the whole people. I hold that land belongs equally to all, that land values arise from the presence of all, and should be shared among all.

George proposed the single tax for both equity and efficiency reasons. On the equity issue, George argued that land rent is determined by nature and society, not by the efforts of landowners. As discussed earlier in the chapter, agricultural land rent is determined by the fertility of the soil and its accessibility to markets. Similarly, the urban land rent is determined by its accessibility to other activities. In George's time, cities were growing rapidly, causing rapid increases in land rent and value. George argued that the windfall gains from urban growth should be taxed away.

On the efficiency issue, George argued that the land tax would eliminate the need for taxes on improvements. The elimination of improvement taxes would stimulate investment in houses, crops, and buildings. The land tax would not affect the supply of land because the supply of land is fixed. Therefore, the replacement of the improvement tax with the land tax would increase the total wealth of society.

The single tax has been criticized for three reasons. First, the single tax would decrease the net return to the landowner (net land rent) to zero, making the market value of land zero. In other words, the government would essentially confiscate the land. This strikes many people as inequitable. Second, if the net return on land is zero, landowners will abandon their land and leave government bureaucrats to decide who uses the land. Unlike the private owner, who receives more income if the land is used efficiently, the bureaucrat has nothing to gain from the efficient use of land. Therefore, a government land market would be less likely to allocate land to its highest and best use. The third criticism is that it is difficult to measure land rent (and the appropriate tax). Most land has structures or other improvements, and it is difficult to separate the value generated by the raw land from the value generated by the improvements.

An alternative to the single tax is a **partial land tax**. Under a partial tax, land is taxed at less than 100 percent of its value. A partial land tax would be less confiscatory than the single tax: like conventional taxes on labor and capital, the partial tax would confiscate only a portion of the taxpayer's resources. In addition, because a partial tax leaves landowners with a positive net return, the land market will continue to be run by those who have a private interest in allocating land to its highest bidder.

Another alternative to a pure land tax is the **two-rate tax** or the **split tax**. Under the conventional property tax, land and improvements are taxed at the same rate: a 3 percent property tax is actually a 3 percent tax on land and a 3 percent tax on improvements. Under a split tax, the tax rate on land may be 9 percent, while the tax rate on improvements may be 1 percent. The split tax is widely used in Australia and New Zealand. It is also used in some cities in Pennsylvania: Pittsburgh implemented a split tax in 1913, and 6 other cities, including Scranton and Harrisburg, have adopted the split tax in recent years.

The replacement of the conventional property tax with the split tax would stimulate capital investment. The switch to the split tax would decrease the tax rate on capital, encouraging capital improvements. Suppose that Rhonda would like to add a recreation room to her house, which would increase the assessed value of her house by $20,000. Under a conventional 3 percent property tax, her tax liabilities would increase by $600 per year. Under a split tax with a 1 percent rate on improvements, her tax liabilities would increase by only $200 per year. The tax penalty from the home improvement would be lower under the split tax, so Rhonda would be more likely to improve her house.

The same argument applies to investment in commercial and industrial property. Under the split tax, the tax liability of the property owner is only 1 percent of market value, so investments that increase the market value of the property will have smaller tax penalties. The owner of an apartment building is more likely to install a new roof if the roof (and the associated increase in assessed value) increases his tax liability by a relatively small amount.

SUMMARY

1. According to the leftover principle, the bid rent for land equals the difference between total revenue and total cost. Competition for land ensures that the landowner gets the excess of total revenue over total cost.

2. Land that is relatively fertile has relatively low production costs, so it commands a higher rent.

3. A policy that increases fertility (e.g., an irrigation project) generates benefits for both landowners and consumers.
   a. The project will decrease production costs, increasing land rent.
   b. If the supply of the agricultural good increases, the price will fall, thus generating benefits for consumers.
   c. The distribution of benefits between landowners and consumers depends on the geographical extent of the program: the smaller the geographical area affected by the project, the smaller the price decrease and the larger the rent increase.
   d. The benefits of an irrigation project are capitalized into the market value of land: the increase in rent increases the present value of rental income, so it increases the market value of land.

4. The bid-rent function shows how much a firm is willing to pay for land at different distances from the market. The function is negatively sloped: transportation costs are lower near the market, so rent is higher. The rent function is convex—not linear—if firms substitute nonland inputs for land as the price of land increases.

5. A decrease in transport costs decreases the slope of the bid-rent function. If the resulting increase in supply of agricultural goods decreases agricultural prices, the bid-rent function will shift downward. The benefits of increased accessibility are shared by consumers and landowners.

6. If there are two land uses, the activity with the higher transport costs will have a relatively steep bid-rent function and will occupy the land closest to the market.

   a. The bid-rent function will be relatively steep if (*i*) output per acre is relatively large or (*ii*) unit transport costs are relatively high.

   b. The market allocates central land to the activity with the most to gain from proximity.

7. The demand for land is derived from the demand for output (e.g., corn, housing). The price of land is high because the demand for output is high. Expensive land is the result—not the cause—of expensive output.

8. Henry George proposed the single tax, a 100 percent tax on rental income, for efficiency and equity reasons. Because the supply of land is fixed, the land tax will not distort behavior. If the land tax decreases taxes on improvements, the supply of improvements would increase.

EXERCISES AND DISCUSSION QUESTIONS

1. In the state of California, rice growers burn their field stubble to sanitize their fields. The field burning causes serious air pollution. The alternative sanitizing method costs $150 per acre.

   Consider a county where rice farmers are currently willing to pay $500 per acre for land and corn farmers (who do not sanitize their fields) are willing to pay $300 per acre. The total output of the county is small enough that the prices of rice and corn are unaffected by events in the county. Suppose that field burning is outlawed in the county, forcing rice farmers to switch to the alternative sanitizing method.

   a. How does the field-burning law affect rice consumers, corn consumers, farmers, and landowners? In other words, who bears the costs of the pollution-control program?

   b. How would your answer to (*a*) change if the cost of the alternative method is $250 per acre?

   c. How would your answer to (*b*) change if field burning is outlawed in the entire state of California?

2. Suppose that Mr. Greengenes, a farmer and genetic engineer, develops a new method for growing corn that decreases the cost of growing corn by $300 per acre. Greengene's landlord rejoices, saying, "According to the leftover principle, you will pay me $300 more in rent." Is the landlord correct? If not, is he applying the leftover principle incorrectly or is the principle wrong?

3. Consider a county where farmers produce with fixed factor proportions and truck their output to a central marketplace. Draw the land-rent function under the following circumstances.

   a. Unit transport cost is a constant $*t* per ton per mile.

   b. Unit transport cost increases as the farmer approaches the marketplace (a result of traffic congestion).

c. Unit transport cost decreases as the farmer approaches the market-place.

4. Using the information in Table 7–1, recompute the land-rent function for the following events. Assume that the farm size at each location is fixed (0.4 acres at $u=0$, 0.6 acres at $u=1$, et cetera).
   a. A herd of rabbits invades the county, stealing $50 worth of carrots per acre.
   b. The unit cost of transport increases from $4 to $5.
   c. The price of carrots increases from $30 to $40.
   d. Is the assumption of a fixed farm size at each location realistic? If not, how would your answer to (c) change if farm sizes could change?

5. Consider a flexible carrot farmer. Complete the following table, assuming that (i) the farmer produces 10 tons of carrots, (ii) the price of carrots is $40, and (iii) transport cost per ton per mile is $5.

Distance to Market	Farm Size (acres)	Total Revenue	Nonland Costs	Transport Cost	Pre-Rent Profits	Rent (per acre)
0	0.70		66			
1	0.80		52			
2	0.90		40			
3	1.00		30			

6. Consider the input combinations listed in Table 7–1. As the price of land increases, the farmer substitutes nonland inputs for land. As the farmer uses less and less land, the trade-off between land and nonland inputs becomes less favorable.
   a. In what sense does the trade-off become less favorable?
   b. Why does the trade-off become less favorable?

7. Suppose that two activities, F and R, compete for land. Activity R produces a good that requires fixed factors of proportion: factor substitution is impossible. Activity F engages in factor substitution: as the relative price of land increases, the firm substitutes nonland inputs for land.
   a. Draw a pair of bid-rent functions showing F occupying the land closest to the market. In what sense is it efficient for F to occupy central land?
   b. Draw another pair of bid-rent functions showing F occupying land close to the market and far from the market, and R occupying intermediate land. In what sense is it efficient for F to occupy land close to and far from the market?

8. Pick the word in parentheses that makes the following statement correct: "As a firm's isoquant changes in shape gradually from a straight line to an

L-shaped curve, the firm's bid-rent function becomes (*less, more*) curved." Note: Less curved means closer to a straight line.

9. Consider Euphoric County, where a large share of the arable land is used to grow M. The production of M is illegal: there are severe penalties imposed on M growers, but no penalties imposed on M consumers. Suppose that M is a competitive industry with equilibrium profits equal to zero: total revenue equals total costs. Included in the costs are the costs associated with engaging in illegal activities (the opportunity costs of time spent in jail, legal costs, concealment costs).

    a. Depict graphically the effects of legalization on the equilibrium price and quantity of M. Explain your graph.

    b. Depict graphically the effects of legalization on the price of land in Euphoric County. Explain your graph.

10. The residents of mobile-home parks own their dwellings and rent land from absentee landowners. Consider a city in which all land is currently occupied by mobile-home parks. Suppose the city imposes a 50 percent tax on land to be paid (in legal terms) by the person who occupies the land (the tenant, either a mobile home owner or some other user). Who will actually pay the tax?

11. What would be the effect of a partial land tax ($100 per acre) on land rent, land values, and corn prices?

12. As the flexible farmer approaches the marketplace, the farmer substitutes nonland inputs for land. As a result, the bid-rent function of the flexible farmer is steeper than the bid-rent function of the inflexible farmer. What happens as the flexible farmer moves *away* from the marketplace? Is the flexible bid-rent function steeper or flatter than the inflexible function? Explain.

REFERENCES AND ADDITIONAL READINGS

Alonso, William. "A Theory of the Urban Land Market." In *Readings in Urban Economics,* ed. Matthew Edel and Jerome Rothenberg. New York: Macmillan, 1972. Extends the standard model of agricultural land rent to the urban land market.

Alonso, William. *Location and Land Use.* Cambridge, Mass.: Harvard Univ. Press, 1964.

George, Henry. *Progress and Poverty.* New York: Schalkenbach Foundation, 1954. Discusses George's theory of land rent and explains the single-tax proposal.

Mills, Edwin S. "The Value of Urban Land." In *The Quality of the Urban Environment,* ed. H. Perloff. Washington, D.C.: Resources for the Future, 1969. Traces the theory of land rent from Ricardo's fertility analysis to the modern theory of urban land rent.

Ricardo, David. *Principles of Political Economy and Taxation.* 1821. Reprint. London: John Murray, 1886. Explains fertility analysis and Ricardo's views on other matters.

CHAPTER 8

Land Use in the Monocentric City

The outcome of the city will depend on the race between the automobile and the elevator, and anyone who bets on the elevator is crazy.

Frank Lloyd Wright

This chapter uses the concepts developed in Chapter 7 to discuss land rent and land use in the monocentric or core-dominated city. The monocentric city was the dominant urban form before the development of the automobile and the truck in the early part of the 20th century. In the monocentric city, commercial and industrial activities were concentrated in the central core area. During the last 70 or 80 years, most large metropolitan areas have become multicentric, with suburban subcenters that complement and compete with the central core area. This chapter explains the market forces behind the development of the monocentric city, and Chapter 10 discusses the market forces behind the transformation of monocentric cities to multicentric ones.

Why study the monocentric city? Although few of today's large cities are monocentric, the analysis of the monocentric city is important for four reasons. First, the monocentric city was the dominant urban form until the early part of the 20th century, so urban history is largely a history of the monocentric city. Second, many of today's small and medium-sized cities are still monocentric. Third, to understand the transition from the traditional monocentric city to the modern multicentric city, one must understand the forces behind the development of the monocentric city in the first place. Fourth, many of the lessons from the monocentric model can be extended to the modern multicentric city.

The discussion of the various land users in the monocentric city will start with the city center and then proceed outward. The first section derives the bid-rent functions of three business sectors (manufacturers, office firms, retailers) and uses the bid-rent functions to discuss land-use patterns in the central business district. The second section examines the location choices of households and derives the bid-rent function for residential land. The third section explains why employment is concentrated in the city center (why the city is monocentric). The final two sections address three empirical questions. First, why do poor households tend to locate in the central city while wealthy households tend to locate in the suburbs? Second, how rapidly does land rent fall as distance to the city center increases? Third, what is the relationship between population density and distance to the city center?

The traditional monocentric city has the transportation technology of the 19th century. The monocentric model has four key assumptions:

1. **Central export node.** All manufacturing output is exported from the city through a railroad terminal at the city center (a central export node).

2. **Horse wagons.** Manufacturers use horse-drawn wagons to transport their freight from their factories to the export node.

3. **Hub-and-spoke streetcar system.** Commuters and shoppers travel by streetcar from the residential areas to the central business district (CBD). The streetcar lines are laid in a radial pattern: the lines form spokes that lead into the CBD (the hub).

4. **Agglomerative economies.** The office industry is dependent on face-to-face contact: employees from different office firms meet in the city center to transact business.

Under these assumptions, the city center is the focal point of the entire metropolitan area: manufacturers are oriented toward the export node; office firms are oriented toward the central market area; retailers are oriented to the hub of the streetcar system; and households are oriented toward employment and shopping opportunities in the central core area.

COMMERCIAL AND INDUSTRIAL LAND USE

This section discusses land rent and land use in the central business district (CBD) of the monocentric city. Three types of firms occupy the central core area: manufacturers, office firms, and retailers.

The Bid-Rent Function of Manufacturers

Suppose that manufacturers in the monocentric city produce baseballs. The firms in the baseball industry have the following characteristics:

1. **Production.** Firms produce baseballs with land, labor, capital, and wood. Every firm produces B tons of baseballs per month.

2. **Fixed prices.** The prices of baseballs and nonland inputs (labor, capital, and wood) are determined in national markets, so firms take these prices as given. The prices are the same at all locations in the city.

3. **Competitive markets.** There is free entry into the industry. In equilibrium, all firms make zero economic profits (normal accounting profits).

4. **Baseball freight costs.** Baseballs are shipped by horse-drawn wagon from the factory to the central railroad terminal, where they are exported to other cities.

5. **Raw-material freight costs.** Wood is imported to the city by railroad. The intracity freight costs of wood are small enough to be ignored.

6. **Factor substitution.** Baseball makers engage in factor substitution: as the price of land increases, firms substitute nonland inputs for land.

For the purposes of choosing a location within the city, baseball firms are market-oriented. The intracity freight cost of wood is assumed to be negligible, and the costs of other inputs (capital and labor) are assumed to be the same at all locations within the city. Because input costs are the same throughout the city, a firm's location decision is based on access to its market. Once a firm decides to locate somewhere in the city, the relevant market is the destination of baseballs *within* the city (the central railroad terminal).

The firm's profits equal total revenue less the costs of inputs, intracity freight, and land. Total revenue is the price of baseballs (P_b) times the quantity produced (B). C is the cost of all nonland inputs (capital, labor, wood). If freight cost is t per ton per mile, total freight cost for a location u miles from the export node is t times B times u. If R is land rent per acre and T is the acreage of the factory site, the profit at a location u miles from the export node is

$$\pi = P_b \cdot B - C - t \cdot B \cdot u - R \cdot T \qquad (8\text{--}1)$$

All markets are perfectly competitive, so the firm's economic profits are zero. According to the leftover principle, the firm is willing to pay its landowner the excess of total revenue over the cost of nonland inputs and freight costs.

TABLE 8–1   The Bid-Rent Function of Baseball Manufacturers

Miles to Export Node	Size of Site (acres)	Total Revenue	Nonland Costs	Freight Costs	Pre-Rent Profits	Rent per Acre
0	0.4	800	360	0	440	1100
1	0.6	800	240	200	360	600
2	0.8	800	180	400	220	275
3	1.0	800	150	600	50	50

Assumptions

1. Output = 5 tons of baseballs
2. Price = $160 per ton
3. Transport costs = $40 per ton per mile
4. Pre-rent profits = total revenue − nonland costs − freight cost

5. Rent = $\dfrac{\text{pre-rent profits}}{\text{size of factory site}}$

As shown in Chapter 7, the expression for the bid rent is derived by setting $\pi = 0$, adding $R \cdot T$ to both sides of the profit equation, and dividing by T. The firm's bid rent per acre is

$$R = \frac{P_b \cdot B - C - t \cdot B \cdot u}{T} \qquad (8\text{-}2)$$

that is, pre-rent profit divided by land consumption.

The bid-rent function shows how much the typical firm is willing to pay per acre for different production sites in the city. Table 8–1 shows how to compute the bid rent for different distances from the city center, given values for P_b, B, C, t, T, and u. The bid-rent function, shown in Figure 8–1, is negatively sloped because freight costs increase as the firm moves away from the city center.

The bid-rent function is convex because firms engage in factor substitution. As the firm approaches the city center, with its higher land costs, the firm substitutes nonland inputs (capital and labor) for land, producing the same

FIGURE 8–1   Bid-Rent Function of Baseball Firms

The bid-rent function of baseball firms is negatively sloped because freight costs increase with distance to the city's central export node. It is convex (not linear) because firms substitute nonland inputs for land as the price of land increases.

tonnage of baseballs with less land and more of the other inputs. From Table 8–1, the firm uses one acre of land and $150 worth of other inputs for a location three miles from the city center, and 0.40 acres and $360 worth of nonland inputs for a location near the city center. The bid-rent function of the typical baseball firm will be used to represent the bid-rent function of the entire manufacturing sector.

The Bid-Rent Function of Office Firms

Although firms in the office sector provide a wide variety of goods and services, all office firms share two important characteristics. First, they gather, process, and distribute information. Because information becomes obsolete quickly, office firms must be able to quickly collect and distribute information. Second, office firms rely on face-to-face contact in the collection, processing, and distribution of information. For example, accountants explain and interpret the information in accounting reports. The loan officers of banks meet with prospective borrowers to appraise their credit worthiness. The investment advisors of finance firms meet with clients to assess their attitudes toward risk and investment. In general, office firms rely on speedy face-to-face contact in the collection and distribution of information. In contrast to baseball manufacturers, who throw their baseballs into the back of a horse-drawn wagon, office firms transmit their output in the minds and the briefcases of their employees.

Suppose that office firms in the monocentric city provide financial services. The finance industry has the following characteristics:

1. **The office.** Every finance firm is based in an office. The nonland cost of the office (capital and labor cost) is C per month. The "output" of the firm is investment consultations, and each firm produces A consultations per month.

2. **Travel to city center.** The manager of each firm travels from the office to the city center (the hub of the streetcar system) to consult with clients. Every consultation requires one trip to the city center.

3. **Fixed prices.** The prices of financial advice and nonland inputs are determined in national markets, so finance firms take the prices as given. The prices are the same at all locations in the city.

4. **Competitive markets.** There is free entry into the industry. In equilibrium, all firms make zero economic profits (normal accounting profits).

5. **Factor substitution.** Finance firms engage in factor substitution: as the price of land increases, they substitute nonland inputs for land.

The travel cost of an office firm equals the opportunity cost of the manager's travel between the office and the clients in the city center. Suppose that the manager takes t minutes to walk one block and the wage is W per minute. If the office is u blocks from the city center, the travel cost per consultation is

$$t \cdot W \cdot u \tag{8–3}$$

For example, if $t = 3$ minutes per block and $W = \$4$ per minute, travel cost per consultation per block is $12, so a firm located 10 blocks from the city center will incur a travel cost of $120 per consultation. If the firm provides A consultations per month, the monthly travel cost for a location u blocks from the city center is

$$TC = t \cdot W \cdot A \cdot u \tag{8–4}$$

If $A = 200$ consultations per month, the monthly travel cost is $2,400 for a location one block from the city center, $4,800 for a location two blocks from the city center, and so on.

The firm's total profit equals total revenue less the costs of nonland inputs, land, and travel. If the price of a consultation is P_a, rent per acre is R, and the firm occupies T acres of land, total profit is

$$\pi = P_a \cdot A - C - R \cdot T - t \cdot W \cdot A \cdot u \tag{8–5}$$

Since markets are perfectly competitive, economic profits will be zero in equilibrium. According to the leftover principle, the firm will be willing to pay the landlord the excess of total revenue over nonland costs. The bid rent per acre of land is

$$R = \frac{P_a \cdot A - C - t \cdot W \cdot A \cdot u}{T} \tag{8–6}$$

that is, pre-rent profit divided by the amount of land consumed.

The bid-rent function indicates how much the office firm is willing to pay for different office sites. Table 8–2 shows how to compute the bid rent for different distances from the city center, given values for P_a, A, C, t, W, T, and u. The bid-rent function, shown in Figure 8–2, is negatively sloped because travel costs increase as the firm moves away from the city center.

The bid-rent function is convex because finance firms engage in factor substitution. As a firm approaches the city center, it substitutes nonland inputs (capital and labor) for the relatively expensive land and produces the same number of consultations with less land and more of its nonland inputs. In other words, finance firms near the city center occupy taller buildings. The bid-rent function of the typical finance firm will be used to represent the bid-rent function of the entire office sector.

Land Use in the Central Business District

In the monocentric city, manufacturers and office firms are oriented toward the central business district. Manufacturers are attracted by the central export node, and office firms cluster around the city center to facilitate face-

TABLE 8–2 The Bid-Rent Function of Office Firms

Blocks to City Center	Size of Site (Acres)	Total Revenue	Nonland Costs	Travel Costs	Pre-Rent Profits	Rent per Acre
0	0.40	9,600	3,600	0	6,000	15,000
1	0.60	9,600	2,400	2,400	4,800	8,000
2	0.80	9,600	1,800	4,800	3,000	3,750
3	1.00	9,600	1,500	7,200	900	900

Assumptions
 1. Output = 200 consultations (A)
 2. Price = $48 per consultation
 3. Travel time per block (t) = 3 minutes
 4. Opportunity cost per minute (W) = $4
 5. Travel cost per block = $t \cdot A \cdot W$ = $2,400
 6. Pre-rent profits = total revenue − nonland costs − travel costs

 7. Rent = $\dfrac{\text{pre-rent profits}}{\text{size of office site}}$

to-face contact. How is CBD land allocated between the two types of firms?

Figure 8–3 shows the bid-rent functions of manufacturers (R_m) and office firms (R_o). Figure 8–3 also shows the bid-rent function of city residents (R_h), which is derived later in the chapter. Because land is allocated to the highest bidder, office firms outbid manufacturers for land within u_o miles of the city center, generating an office district with a radius of u_o miles. Manufacturers outbid office firms and residents for land between u_o and u_m miles of the city center, generating a manufacturing district with a width of ($u_m − u_o$) miles. The central area of the city is occupied by the office industry because the office bid-rent function is steeper than the manufacturing bid-rent function.

The office bid-rent function is relatively steep because the office industry has relatively high transportation costs. Office firms rely on frequent face-to-face contact, using high-priced financial consultants to transport their output to clients in the city center. In contrast, the manufacturing industry ships its output by horse-drawn wagon, so its transport costs are relatively low. In the numerical example shown in Tables 8–1 and 8–2, the baseball manufacturer has monthly freight costs of $200 per mile while the finance firm has monthly travel costs of $2,400 *per block*. The bid-rent functions are negatively sloped because of transportation costs, so the larger the transportation costs the larger the slope.

Does the land market allocate land efficiently? In the terms used by land developers, is land allocated to its "highest and best use?" The office industry, with its higher transportation costs, occupies the land closest to the city center. This allocation is efficient because the office industry has the most to gain from proximity to the city center. Suppose that a finance firm located

FIGURE 8–2   The Bid-Rent Function of Office Firms

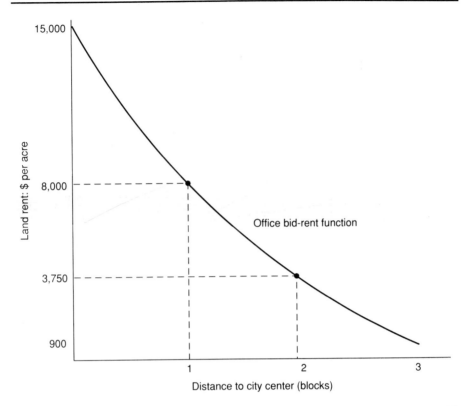

The office bid-rent function is negatively sloped because travel costs increase with distance to the central marketplace. It is convex because firms substitute nonland inputs for land as the price of land increases.

one block from the city center swaps locations with a manufacturer three blocks (one fifth of a mile) from the city center. The land swap will increase the finance firm's travel costs by $7,200 (three blocks times $2,400 per block), but decrease the baseball firm's freight costs by only $40 (one fifth a mile times $200 per mile). Office travel costs will increase by more than freight costs decrease, so total transportation costs will increase. The market allocation, which gives central land to the office industry, minimizes total transportation costs.

Location of Retailers

Where in the monocentric city do retailers locate? Central-place theory, which is used in Chapter 5 to explain the regional distribution of retailers, is also applicable to the intracity distribution of retailers. Retailers carve up the

FIGURE 8–3   Bid-Rent Functions and Land Use in the Central Business District

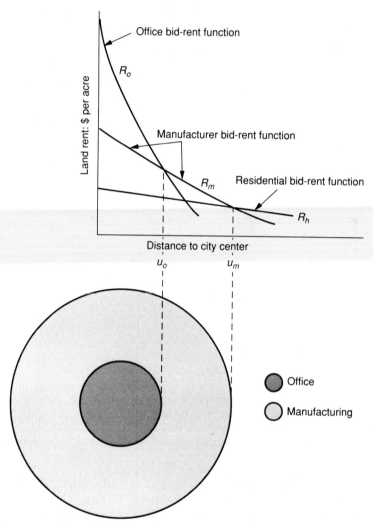

The office industry has a relatively steep bid-rent function because the travel cost of people is large relative to the travel cost of freight. The office industry outbids manufacturers for land near the city center. Central land is occupied by the activity with the most to gain from proximity (decreased transportation costs).

city into market areas, with the size of the market areas being determined by scale economies, per capita demand, and transportation costs.

Large Scale Economies—Glove Sellers.   Consider first an activity for which scale economies are large relative to per capita demand (e.g., a glove store). The glove market has the following characteristics:

1. **Single glove store.** The scale economies of glove selling are exhausted only at outputs that are large *relative* to the total demand for gloves, so there will be a single glove store in the city. The efficient size for the glove seller is 5,000 pairs of gloves per month, and total demand for gloves is 5,000 per month.

2. **Glove consumers.** Consumers are distributed uniformly throughout the city.

3. **Perfect competition.** Although there is a single glove seller, entry into the glove market is not very costly. Given the threat of entry, economic profits will be zero.

The retailer's profit at a particular location is total revenue less total costs. Suppose that the profit margin (price less average cost) is constant. If P_g is the price of gloves, G is the quantity sold, and AC_g is the average cost, pre-rent profit is

$$\pi = G \cdot (P_g - AC_g) \tag{8–7}$$

For example, if P_g is $9 and AC_g is $5, the profit margin is $4. If G is 5,000, total profit would be $20,000.

At what location will the glove store earn the most profit? If the profit margin is constant, the firm will maximize total profit by maximizing sales volume (G). As shown in Chapter 5, sales volume is maximized at the center of the market area (the median location) for the simple reason that the central location is accessible to the most consumers. Since the glove store sells to people throughout the city, profit will be maximized at the city center. The benefit of the central location is reinforced by the hub-and-spoke streetcar system of the monocentric city, which delivers suburban commuters and shoppers to the city center.

Because there is free entry into the glove-selling business, the glove store will make zero economic profits. Competition for the best glove-selling site will bid up the price of land to the point at which economic profits are zero. If the glove store refuses to pay its economic profits to the landowner, the landowner will rent the site to another glove seller.

Moderate Scale Economies—Hat Sellers.   Consider next an activity for which scale economies are moderate relative to per capita demand (e.g., hat stores). The hat industry has the following characteristics:

1. **Five hat stores.** The scale economies of hat selling are moderate relative to the total demand for hats, so there will be five hat stores in the urban area. The efficient sales volume for the hat store is 4,000 hats per month, and the total demand is 20,000 hats per month.

2. **Hat consumers.** Consumers are distributed uniformly throughout the monocentric city.

3. **Perfect competition.** Entry into the hat market is not very costly. Given the threat of entry, economic profits will be zero.

The pre-rent profit of an individual store equals total revenue less total costs. If H is the number of hats sold, P_h is the price of hats, and AC_h is the average cost, total profit is

$$\pi = H \cdot (P_h - AC_h) \tag{8-8}$$

For example, if P_h is \$8 and AC_h is \$5, the profit margin is \$3. If H is 4,000, total profits would be \$12,000.

According to the simple version of central-place theory, hat sellers will divide the city into five equal market areas and each hat seller will locate at the center of a market area. This result can also be expressed in terms of bid-rent functions. The bid-rent function of a particular hat store depends on where the other stores locate. Locations close to other hat stores will have lower sales volumes, so the hat sellers will be willing to pay less in rent. The bid-rent function of the hat industry will have five peaks, one at the center of each market area.

Will hat sellers adopt the location pattern predicted by the simple version of central-place theory? The simple version of the theory assumes that unit travel cost (the cost per mile) is the same in all directions. In the mono-centric streetcar city, this assumption is violated: the hub-and-spoke streetcar system collects people along the suburban spokes and delivers them to the central hub. Travel along the spokes into the city is cheaper than travel between the spokes, so a trip from a house in the suburbs to a downtown hatter may be easier than a trip to a suburban hatter. If so, most—if not all —of the hat sellers will locate in the downtown core area.

The tendency for hat sellers to cluster in the core area is reinforced by **shopping externalities** (explained in chapters 2 and 5). If hats from different stores are **imperfect substitutes**, hat consumers will go to several stores to compare hats, and shopping costs will be lower if the stores are clustered. Since the core (the hub of the streetcar system) is accessible to the entire urban area, hat retailers are likely to cluster in the city center. If hats and gloves are **complementary goods**, consumers will save on shopping costs if hat stores are near glove stores. Stores selling complementary goods are likely to cluster in the city center. In terms of central-place theory, hat sellers will compromise on their central-place locations to exploit shopping externalities. Given the hub-and-spoke streetcar system, the retail clusters will be in the downtown core area.

RESIDENTIAL LAND USE

This section uses a simple model of the residential sector to explore residential land use in the monocentric city. According to the leftover principle, the bid rent for land equals total revenue less total costs. The first step in the analysis of residential land rent examines the revenue side of housing production. The housing-price function shows the relationship between housing prices and distance to the city center.

The simple model of the residential sector has a number of simplifying assumptions. Later in the chapter, each of these assumptions will be dropped.

1. One member of each household commutes to a job in the central business district (CBD).
2. Noncommuting travel is insignificant.
3. Public services and taxes are the same at all locations.
4. Air quality is the same at all locations.
5. All households have the same income and tastes for housing.
6. The opportunity cost of commuting time is zero.

The first four assumptions make the CBD the focal point of city residents. All jobs are in the CBD, and all the other things that people care about (public services, taxes, air quality) are distributed uniformly throughout the city. Given the fifth assumption, the choices of the typical household can be used to represent the choices of all households in the city. The sixth assumption means that the simple model ignores the time costs of commuting.

The Housing-Price Function

As explained later in the book, the price of housing is usually defined as the price per unit of housing service generated by a dwelling. For the purposes of this chapter, the **price of housing** will be defined as the price *per square foot* of housing per month. If a household rents a 1,000 square-foot house for $250 per month, the price of housing is 25 cents per square foot ($250 divided by 1,000 square feet). The **housing-price function** shows how much a household is willing to pay for dwellings at different locations in the city. There are two types of housing-price functions, linear and convex.

Linear Housing-Price Function—No Consumer Substitution. Figure 8–4 shows the housing-price function for a simple case described by the following set of assumptions:

1. **Identical dwellings.** Every dwelling in the city has 1,000 square feet of living space.

2. **Fixed budget.** The typical household has a fixed budget of $300 per month to spend on commuting and housing costs.

3. **Commuting cost.** The monthly cost of commuting is $20 per mile per month: the household pays $20 per month in commuting costs for a residence one mile from the city center, $40 per month for a residence two miles from the city center, and so on.

How much is the household willing to pay for dwellings at different locations in the city? At the city center, commuting costs are zero, so the household can spend its entire $300 budget on housing. For a 1,000 square-

FIGURE 8–4   Housing-Price Function for a City with Identical 1,000 Square Foot Dwellings

The price of housing drops from 30 cents per square foot at the city center to 6 cents per square foot 12 miles from the city center. The price increases as commuting costs decrease (as distance to the center decreases), making households indifferent among all locations within the city.

foot house, the price will be 30 cents per square foot. At a distance of six miles from the center, commuting cost is $120, so the household has $180 left to spend on housing (18 cents per square foot).

The negatively sloped housing-price function is necessary for **locational equilibrium**. Locational equilibrium exists when all households are satisfied with their location choices, so that no household wants to change its location.

One way to explain the negatively sloped housing-price function is to see what happens if we start with a horizontal function. If the price of housing is 15 cents per square foot throughout the city, the household can get a 1,000 square-foot dwelling anywhere in the city for $150 per month. Suppose that a household starts out in a house 10 miles from the city center. A move toward the city center will increase utility because such a move will decrease commuting costs without affecting housing costs. Therefore, the household will move closer to the city center. Other households have the same incentive to move closer to the center, so the demand for housing near the city center will increase (increasing prices), and the demand for suburban housing will decrease (decreasing prices). In other words, the movement of households toward the city center will transform a horizontal housing-price function into a negatively sloped function.

The equilibrium housing-price function makes residents indifferent among all locations because differences in commuting costs are offset by differences in housing costs. Consider the effects of a one-mile move toward the city center. The good news is that commuting costs will decrease by t (the unit commuting cost). The bad news is that housing costs will increase by ΔP (the change in the price per square foot) times H (housing consumption in square footage). The household will be indifferent between the two locations if the decrease in commuting costs equals the increase in housing costs:

$$t = -\Delta P \cdot H \qquad\qquad (8\text{–}9)$$

If t = $20 and H = 1,000 square feet, the household will be indifferent between the two locations if the price of housing increases by two cents per square foot. In Figure 8–4, the price of housing increases by two cents per mile as the household moves toward the city center.

Convex Function—Consumer Substitution.   The housing-price function in Figure 8–4 is linear because the city's dwellings are identical: everyone lives in a 1,000 square-foot house, regardless of the price of housing. A more realistic assumption is that housing consumption depends on the price of housing. In other words, households obey the law of demand, decreasing the quantity demanded as the price increases. As a household moves toward the city center, it will pay a higher price for housing, so it will occupy a smaller dwelling. As the relative price of housing increases, the household will substitute nonhousing goods (pizza, hot dogs, stereo equipment) for housing.

Figure 8–5 shows the effects of consumer substitution on the housing-price function. The assumed pattern of housing consumption is shown below the graph. Suppose that a household moves 3 miles closer to the city center, from a distance of 12 miles (where the price of housing is six cents per square foot) to 9 miles. If housing consumption is fixed at 1,000 square feet, the household would be willing to pay an additional $60 for housing (the decrease in commuting cost), or six cents more per square foot. Because its housing consumption drops from 1,000 square feet to 750 square feet, however, the household is willing to pay more than an additional six cents per square foot to offset the $60 decrease in commuting costs. In general, as a household moves toward the high-priced city center, it occupies smaller dwellings, requiring progressively larger increases in the price *per square foot* of housing to offset the fixed $20 per mile decrease in commuting costs. The lesson from Figure 8–5 is that if consumers obey the law of demand, the housing-price function will be convex, not linear.

The slope of the housing-price function can be expressed in simple algebraic terms. Since both the price of housing (P) and housing consumption

FIGURE 8–5   Housing-Price Function with and without Consumer Substitution

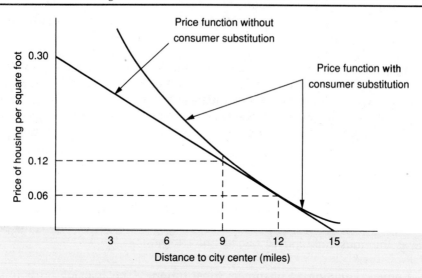

Assumed Consumption Pattern

Distance from city center (miles)	3	6	9	12
Housing consumption (square feet)	400	600	750	1000

As the household approaches the city center, the price of housing increases. If the household substitutes other goods for housing, the housing-price function is convex, not linear.

(*H*) vary with distance to the city center (*u*), the trade-off between commuting and housing costs can be rewritten as

$$\Delta u \cdot t = -\Delta P(u) \cdot H(u) \qquad (8\text{–}10)$$

For a small change in distance to the city center (Δu), the change in commuting costs (the change in *u* times the commuting cost per mile) equals the change in the housing price times housing consumption. The equation can be rearranged to show the slope of the housing-price function:

$$\frac{\Delta P(u)}{\Delta u} = -\frac{t}{H(u)} \qquad (8\text{–}11)$$

In the numerical example, *t* is $20 and *H*(9) is 750, so the slope of the housing-price function at $u=9$ is $0.0267 (20/750), compared to a slope of $0.02 under the assumption of fixed housing consumption. Since *H*(6) is 600, the slope at $u=6$ is $0.033 (20/600). As the household moves toward the city center, housing consumption decreases, increasing the slope of the housing-price function.

How rapidly should the price of housing decrease as distance to the city center increases? The **housing-price gradient** is defined as the percentage change in the price of housing per mile. Dividing both sides of equation (8–11) by P,

$$\frac{\Delta P/P}{\Delta u} = - \frac{t}{H \cdot P} \qquad (8\text{–}12)$$

In words, the housing-price gradient equals commuting cost per mile divided by housing expenditures. If the full cost of commuting (including monetary and time costs) is $1 per round-trip mile, the monthly commuting cost (for 20 work days per month) will be $20 per round-trip mile. If the household spends $500 per month on housing, the rent gradient will be 4 percent per mile (20/500).

The Residential Bid-Rent Function

The **residential bid-rent function** indicates how much housing producers are willing to pay for land at different locations in the city. According to the leftover principle, housing producers will be willing to pay land rent equal to total revenue less total costs. There are two types of bid-rent functions: one that occurs if housing is produced with fixed factor proportions, and one that occurs if housing firms engage in factor substitution.

The Bid-Rent Function with Fixed Factor Proportions.   Consider first the possibility that housing is produced with fixed factor proportions. Suppose that firms in the housing industry have the following characteristics:

1. **Production.** Each firm produces Q square feet of housing, using land and other inputs. Once the firm erects a building, it can be used as a single dwelling (with Q square feet of space) or divided into x units, each of which has (Q/x) square feet of living space.

2. **Nonland costs.** Firms use K worth of nonland inputs for each building.

3. **Fixed factor proportions.** Each firm produces its Q square feet of housing with T acres of land and K worth of other inputs, regardless of the price of land.

4. **Housing prices.** The housing-price function is negatively sloped and convex.

5. **Perfect competition.** The markets are perfectly competitive, so every firm makes zero economic profits.

According to the leftover principle, the bid-rent for land equals the excess of total revenue over total nonland costs. Total revenue equals the price of housing (P) times Q, and total cost is nonland costs (K) plus land costs (R times T). Since P varies with the distance to the city center (u), the bid for land is

$$R(u) = \frac{P(u) \cdot Q - K}{T} \qquad (8\text{–}13)$$

If the price of housing decreases as u increases, the residential-rent function will be negatively sloped.

Figure 8–6 maps the residential bid-rent function. The horizontal line is nonland cost per acre, assumed to be the same at all locations. Since the bid rent equals total revenue less nonland costs, the bid-rent function lies below the revenue function, with the distance between the two functions equal to the costs of nonland inputs. At u^*, total revenue equals nonland costs, so the bid rent for land is zero. The bid-rent function is convex because the housing-price function is convex.

FIGURE 8–6   Housing Prices and the Bid-Rent Function

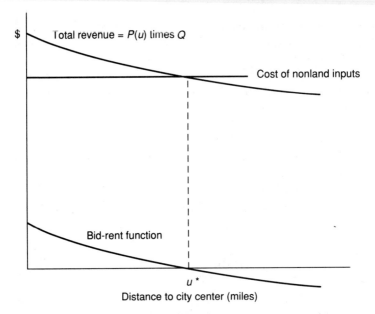

The bid-rent of the housing firm equals total revenue per acre less the cost of nonland inputs. Total revenue (the price of housing times square footage produced) decreases as the distance to the city center increases because the housing-price function is negatively sloped. The cost of nonland inputs is the same at all locations. The bid-rent function is convex because the housing-price function (and the revenue function) is convex. At u^*, the cost of nonland inputs equals total revenue, so the bid-rent equals zero.

The Bid-Rent Function with Factor Substitution.   The bid-rent function shown in Figure 8–6 is based on the assumption that housing is produced with fixed factor proportions. Housing firms use the same input combination at all locations, regardless of the price of land. What happens if firms substitute other inputs for land as the price of land increases?

Figure 8–7 shows the bid-rent functions for inflexible and flexible housing producers. The inflexible firm uses the same input combination throughout the city. In contrast, the flexible firm substitutes nonland inputs for land as the price of land increases, building progressively taller buildings as the firm approaches the city center. The flexible rent function lies above the inflexible rent function at every location except $u = 6$. At this location, the input combination of the inflexible firm is, by chance, the efficient combination, so the two builders use the same input combination. While the inflexible firm's input ratio is efficient for $u = 6$, it is inefficient for other locations: it is too low for locations closer to the city center, and too high for locations farther from the city center. For all locations except $u = 6$, the flexible firm produces housing for a lower cost and thus outbids the inflexible firm.

Summary—The Convex Bid-Rent Function.   There are two lessons from the analysis of residential land rent. First, the bid-rent function is negatively sloped because the housing-price function is negatively sloped. Second, the bid-rent function is convex because of both consumer substitution (which makes the housing-price function convex) and factor substitution (which increases the convexity of the rent function).

FIGURE 8–7   The Residential Bid-Rent Function with Factor Substitution

Factor substitution (substituting nonland inputs for land as the price of land increases) increases the convexity of the bid-rent function.

How rapidly should the price of residential land decrease as distance to the city center increases? The **rent gradient** is defined as the percentage change in the land rent per mile. The gradient depends on (a) the housing-price gradient and (b) the relative importance of land in the production of housing. In Table 8–3, the housing-price gradient is 4 percent (a one-mile move away from the city center decreases the market value of housing by 4 percent, from $150,000 to $144,000) and the value of land is assumed to be 20 percent of the total property value. Because the price of capital is the same at all locations, land value absorbs the entire $6,000 decrease in market value, dropping from $30,000 to $24,000, a 20 percent decrease. In this example, the rent gradient is 20 percent, five times the housing-price gradient.

The relationship between the housing-price gradient and the rent gradient can be stated algebraically as

$$\text{Rent gradient} = \frac{1}{\text{Land's share of house value}} \cdot \text{Housing-price gradient} \quad (8\text{–}14)$$

The smaller the land's share of house value, the larger the percentage decrease in land rent needed to absorb a given decrease in the price of housing. For example, if land's share of house value is only 10 percent, the rent gradient will be ten times the housing-price gradient.

Residential Density

How does population density vary within the monocentric city? Table 8–4 shows how to compute population density at different locations in the city. The first step is to compute the lot size (the amount of land occupied per household). Lot size increases with distance to the city center for two reasons:

1. **Consumer substitution.** The price of housing decreases as the distance to the city center increases, and households respond to lower

TABLE 8–3   Land Rent Gradient

	Location	
	A	B
Distance to city center (miles)	4	5
Market value of housing ($)	150,000	144,000
Land value ($)	30,000	24,000
Capital value ($)	120,000	120,000

Assumptions
1. Land value = 20% of market value of housing.
2. Housing-price gradient = 4% per mile.

housing prices by consuming more housing. In Table 8–4, housing consumption rises from 1,404 square feet for a household 0.20 miles from the city center (location A) to 3,000 square feet for a household four miles from the center (location B).

2. **Factor substitution.** The price of land decreases as the distance to the city center increases, and housing firms respond to lower land prices by using more land per unit of housing. In Table 8–4, at a distance of 0.20 miles from the city center, every square foot of living space comes with 0.33 square feet of land. In other words, people live in three-story apartment buildings. At a distance of four miles from the center, the amount of land per square foot of housing is 2.20: households live in one-story houses with lot sizes 2.2 times the "footprint" of the house.

Lot size equals housing consumption (in square feet of living space) times the amount of land per unit of housing. Because of consumer substitution and factor substitution, the lot size decreases as distance increases: a household located 0.20 miles from the center uses only 468 square feet of land (sharing the 1,404 square feet under the three-story apartment building with two other households), while a household located five miles from the center uses 6,600 square feet of land.

Population density is the number of people per square mile. Lot size, which is defined as the number of square feet used per household, can be converted to population density in three steps:

1. Divide lot size by the number of square feet per mile (27,878,400) to re-define lot size as square miles of land per household.

2. Invert the new lot size (square miles per household) to get the number of households per square mile.

TABLE 8–4   Population Density at Different Locations

	Location	
	A	B
Distance to city center (miles)	0.2	4.0
Housing consumption (square feet)	1,404	3,000
Land per square foot of housing (square feet)	0.33	2.2
Lot size (square feet)	468	6,600
Household density (households per square mile)	29,793	2,112
Population density (people per square mile)	59,586	4,224

Assumptions
1. Lot size = housing consumption times land per unit of housing
2. Number of people per household = 2.0
3. 50% of land used for nonresidential activities

3. Multiply the number of households per square mile by the number of people per household to give the number of people per square mile.

The computations in Table 8–4 are based on two assumptions: first, there are two people per household; second, half of the city's land is used for non-residential activities. Population density drops from around 60,000 people per square mile at a location 0.20 miles from the city center to about 4,200 per square mile at four miles from the city center.

FIGURE 8–8   Bid-Rent Functions and Land Use in the Monocentric City

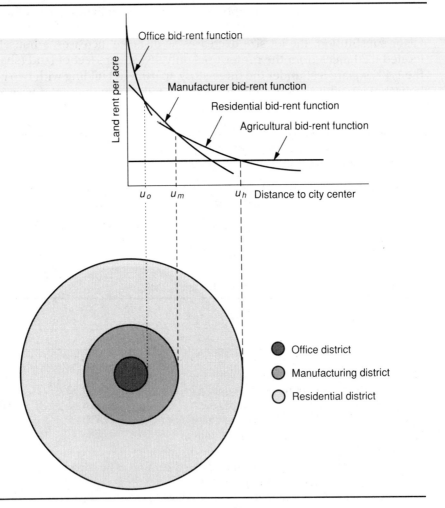

LAND USE IN THE MONOCENTRIC CITY

Figure 8–8 shows the land-use pattern of the monocentric city. The office bid-rent function intersects the manufacturing function at a distance of u_o miles from the city center, so the office district is a circle with a radius of u_o miles. The manufacturing bid-rent function intersects the residential function at a distance of u_m miles from the city center, so the manufacturing district is a ring of width $(u_m - u_o)$ miles. The residential bid-rent function intersects the agricultural bid-rent function at a distance of u_h miles, so the residential district is a ring of width $(u_h - u_m)$ miles. The retail bid-rent function is omitted from this diagram in the interest of simplicity. As explained earlier, most retailers congregate at the center of the monocentric city.

Land users in the monocentric city are arranged according to their transportation costs: the higher the transportation costs, the closer the activity is to the city center. As explained in Chapter 7, the firm with relatively high transport costs will have a relatively steep bid-rent function and will locate closer to the marketplace. In the monocentric city, the market is the city center, where office workers meet with clients and manufacturers load their output onto ships or trains. The office sector, with the highest transport costs and the steepest bid-rent function, occupies land closest to the center. Manufacturing, with the next highest transport costs and the next steepest bid-rent function, occupies the next ring of land. The residential sector, with relatively low transport costs and a relatively flat bid-rent function, occupies the land farthest from the city center.

This spatial arrangement has two interesting features. First, office firms occupy the central area of the CBD. As explained earlier in the chapter, office firms have relatively high transport costs and thus a relatively steep bid-rent function because office output is transmitted by office workers, while manufacturing output is transported by horse-drawn wagon.

The second feature of the monocentric city is that employment is concentrated in the CBD, not distributed throughout the city. Why do all the manufacturers and office firms locate in the CBD? Consider a baseball firm that is considering a move from the CBD to a suburban location. What are the trade-offs associated with a move to the suburbs?

1. **Higher freight costs**. The firm will be farther from the central export node, so it will pay higher freight costs.

2. **Lower wages**. The firm will be closer to its work force, so workers will commute shorter distances. The wage compensates workers for commuting costs: the longer the commuting distance, the higher the wage. When the firm moves closer to its work force, it decreases its workers' commuting costs, so the firm can pay a lower wage.

The firm's location decision is determined by the outcome of a tug-of-war. On one side is the central export node, which pulls the firm toward the CBD.

On the other side is its suburban work force, which pulls the firm toward the low-wage suburbs.

In the monocentric city, the tug-of-war was won by the CBD because the costs of moving freight were large relative to the costs of moving workers. Freight traveled by horse-drawn wagon, a relatively slow and expensive travel mode. In contrast, workers traveled by streetcar, a relatively fast and inexpensive travel mode. Although the wage was lower in the suburbs, the wage differential was relatively small because commuting by streetcar was fast and efficient: workers demanded a relatively small premium to commute to CBD jobs. If a firm moved from the city center to the suburbs, the small savings in wages would be more than offset by the increase in the costs of shipping freight to the central export node. In the monocentric city, it was cheaper to bring the workers from the suburbs to the central-city factory than to bring the output from a suburban factory to the central export node.

The same analysis applies to office firms. Although a move from the CBD to the suburbs would decrease the wage, it would also increase the costs of travel between the office and the central market area: managers would spend more time traveling between the suburban office and the firm's clients in the city center. Given the frequency of travel to clients in the central market area, the increase in travel costs would dominate the savings in wage costs. In the monocentric city, it was cheaper to bring the workers from the suburbs to a central-city office than to bring the output (in the minds and briefcases of managers) from a sururban office to clients in the city center.

RELAXING THE ASSUMPTIONS

The simple monocentric model has a number of unrealistic assumptions about residential land use. This section derives the residential bid-rent function under more realistic sets of assumptions. The assumption that the city is monocentric is maintained: all employment is assumed to be in the CBD.

Changes in Commuting Assumptions

The simple model is based on a number of simplifying assumptions about commuting. What happens if these assumptions are dropped?

1. **Time costs of commuting.** The simple model assumes that the only costs of commuting are monetary costs: money spent on cars (for gasoline and maintenance) or public transit (bus tickets). In fact, commuting time comes at the expense of work or leisure time, so there is an opportunity cost associated with commuting. The unit cost of commuting (t) is actually the sum of the monetary *and* time costs per mile of travel. Studies of commuting behavior suggest that most people value commuting time at between one third and one half the wage rate. For a worker with a wage of $10, the time cost of commuting is between $3.33

and $5.00 per hour. Commuting costs are discussed in greater detail in chapters 17 (Autos and Highways) and 18 (Mass Transit).

2. **Noncommuting travel: uniform distribution of destinations.** The simple model assumes that noncommuting travel is insignificant. This assumption is unrealistic because households in fact travel to different destinations within the city for shopping and entertainment. Suppose that shopping and entertainment destinations are distributed uniformly throughout the urban area. For example, suppose that the household commutes northward to a job in the city center and also travels north to a museum, south to a grocery store, west to a disco, and east to the shore. If the frequency of travel to the four sites is about the same, any change in residence will cause a relatively small change in total noncommuting travel time. For example, if the household moves south, the costs of museum trips will increase, but the costs of the grocery trips will decrease. If the household travels in all directions for shopping and entertainment, changes in noncommuting costs will usually offset one another, and it is appropriate to focus on commuting costs as the primary factor in location decisions.

3. **Noncommuting travel: concentrated destinations.** Consider next the possibility that shopping and entertainment sites are concentrated rather than dispersed. Suppose that members of a household travel to the city center for work, shopping, and entertainment. As the household moves closer to the city center, it will save on travel costs for commuting, shopping, and entertainment, so the savings in travel costs will be relatively large and the housing-price function will be relatively steep. In general, the more frequent the travel to the city center, the steeper the housing-price function and the residential bid-rent function.

4. **Two-earner households.** The simple model assumes that a single person from each household commutes to the city center. Suppose that all the households in a city are suddenly transformed into two-earner households. What happens to the housing-price function? If two members of each household commute to the CBD, a household that moves closer to the city center will experience double the savings in commuting costs. In equilibrium, the housing-price function will be steeper in the two-earner city, reflecting the greater savings associated with living closer to central-city jobs. Therefore, the residential bid-rent function will be steeper.

Variation in Tastes for Housing

The simple model assumes that every household has the same tastes for housing. The housing-price function of the typical resident is used to represent the housing-price function of the entire city. Suppose that there are two types of households in the city, large and small. The "tastes" for housing are dictated by the number of children: the small households live in small dwellings, and large households live in large dwellings.

Where in the city will the two types of households live? Because land is rented to the highest bidder, the division of residential land between the two household types is determined by the bid-rent functions of the two groups. As shown in Chapter 7, the land user with the steeper bid-rent function occupies land closer to the city center. Since the residential bid-rent function is determined by the housing-price function, the user with the steeper housing-price function will have a steeper bid-rent function.

Which household has the steeper housing-price function? The expression for the housing-price function is

$$\frac{\Delta P(u)}{\Delta u} = \frac{-t}{H(u)} \tag{8--15}$$

If the two households have the same commuting cost per mile (t), the small household will have a steeper housing-price function because it consumes less housing (smaller H). Because the small household consumes a smaller amount of housing (in square feet), it takes a larger change in the price of

FIGURE 8–9   Bid-Rent Function and Family Size

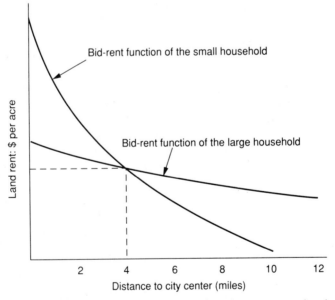

The slope of the bid-rent function decreases as housing consumption increases, so large households, who live in large houses, have a relatively flat bid-rent function. Large families have the most to gain from low suburban housing prices, so they outbid small households for suburban housing.

housing per square foot to compensate for a given change in commuting costs.

Figure 8–9 shows the bid-rent functions for the two types of households. The bid-rent function for small dwellings is steeper because the small household has a steeper housing-price function. The two functions intersect at a distance of four miles from the city center, so small households occupy small dwellings within four miles of the city center and large households occupy large dwellings outside the four-mile radius. Large households occupy low-price suburban housing because they live in large houses and thus have more to gain from inexpensive suburban housing.

Spatial Variation in Public Goods and Pollution

The simple model has a number of assumptions that make the city center the focal point of the city. Except for jobs in the CBD, all the things that people care about (public services, taxes, pollution, amenities) are distributed uniformly throughout the city. What happens if these things are not distributed uniformly?

Public Goods and Taxes.   Taxes and public services usually vary within a metropolitan area. Suppose that the quality of public schools varies within the city, but the costs of schools (tuition and taxes) are the same throughout the city. In equilibrium, the price of housing will be higher in the communities with better schools. Parents pay for better public schools indirectly: instead of paying higher taxes, they will pay more for housing and residential land. Similarly, the prices of housing and land will be higher in communities with lower crime rates. The same argument applies to variation in taxes. If two communities have the same level of public services but one community has higher taxes, the price of housing will be higher in the low-tax community.

Pollution and Scenic Views.   The simple model assumes that environmental quality is the same at all locations in the city. Suppose that a polluting factory moves into the center of a previously clean city. If the smoke and smell from the factory are heaviest in the central area of the city, the factory will decrease the relative attractiveness of dwellings near the city center and decrease the price of central-city housing. In addition, the factory will increase the relative attractiveness of more remote dwellings, so it will increase the price of suburban housing.

Figure 8–10 shows the effects of the polluting factory on the housing-price function. P_c is the price function in the absence of pollution (the clean city), and P_s is the price function with a small amount of pollution. The pollution from the central-city factory decreases the slope of the housing-price function. As a household moves toward the city center, there are costs (more pollution) as well as benefits (lower commuting costs), so the increase in the price of housing will be smaller in the polluted city. If the city has a relatively high level of pollution, the housing-price function may be positively sloped,

FIGURE 8–10   Pollution in the Central City and Housing Prices

Distance to city center (miles)

Air pollution from a central-city factory decreases housing prices near the city center and increases housing prices far from the city center. The more severe the pollution, the greater the change in housing prices.

as shown by P_d. In this case, central-city pollution is so obnoxious that the advantages of a central city dwelling (lower commuting costs) are dominated by its disadvantages (greater exposure to pollution). As a result, people will live near the city center only if they are compensated in the form of lower housing prices.

Changes in the housing-price function cause similar changes in the residential bid-rent function. A relatively flat housing-price function (P_s) will generate a relatively flat bid-rent function. Similarly, a positively sloped housing-price function (P_d) will generate a positively sloped residential bid-rent function.

The same arguments apply to locations that have positive locational attributes (amenities) such as scenic views or access to parks. If people get utility from scenic views or park access, they will be willing to pay more for dwellings that provide such amenities.

INCOME AND LOCATION

In U.S. cities, the wealthy tend to locate in the suburbs and the poor tend to locate near the city center. In other words, average household income increases as one moves away from the city center. Because the most expensive land is near the city center, this location pattern is puzzling: why should the poor occupy the most expensive housing and land? There are several theories of this observed pattern of income segregation. The first is based on the simple monocentric model, and the others are based on extensions of the monocentric model.

Trade-Off between Housing and Commuting Costs

According to the simple monocentric model, a household chooses the location that provides the best trade-off between housing costs and commuting costs. One theory of income segregation, developed by Alonso (1964) and Muth (1969), suggests that central locations provide the best trade-off for the poor, while suburban locations provide the best trade-off for the wealthy.

Figure 8–11 shows the trade-offs between land costs and commuting costs. The marginal cost of distance (the horizontal line) is defined as the in-

FIGURE 8–11   Location Choices: The Trade-Offs between Housing and Commuting Costs

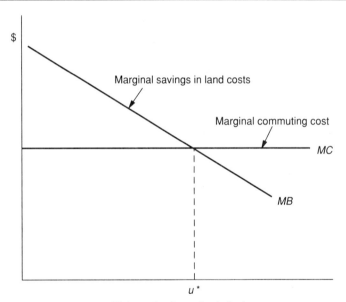

The optimum location is where the marginal benefit of distance (*MB*) equals the marginal cost (*MC*). The marginal benefit equals the savings in land costs generated by the decrease in the price of land. The marginal-benefit curve is negatively sloped because the residential bid-rent function is convex. The marginal cost equals the increase in commuting costs per mile.

crease in commuting cost resulting from a one-mile move away from the city center. The marginal-cost curve is horizontal because the marginal commuting cost (t) is assumed to be constant. The marginal benefit of distance (the negatively sloped line) is defined as the decrease in land cost resulting from a one-mile move away from the city center. As the household moves away from the center, land rent falls, and the decrease in land costs equals the change in land rent (per acre) times the amount of land consumed (in acres). The marginal-benefit curve is negatively sloped because the bid-rent function is convex: as distance increases, land rent decreases at a slower rate, so the marginal savings in land costs decreases.

The optimum location is where the household's marginal cost of distance (the increase in commuting cost) equals its marginal benefit (the savings in land costs). The position of the marginal-benefit curve is affected by land consumption: the larger the consumption of land (the larger the lot), the larger the benefit associated with lower land prices. In Figure 8–11, an increase in land consumption would shift the marginal benefit (MB) upward and increase the optimum distance.

What are the effects of income on the residential location decision? Figure 8–12 shows the benefit and cost curves underlying the Alonso-Muth theory

FIGURE 8–12   The Alonso-Muth Theory of Income Segregation

If the income elasticity of demand for land is large relative to the income elasticity of commuting costs, the gap between the marginal-benefit curves will be larger than the gap between the marginal-cost curves. Therefore, the poor will live in the central city, and the wealthy will live in the suburbs.

of income segregation. The figure shows the cost and benefit curves for a wealthy household (MC_w and MB_w) and a poor one (MC_p and MB_p). The wealthy household has a higher marginal-benefit curve because it consumes more land: land is a normal good, so consumption increases with income. The wealthy household has a higher marginal-cost curve because it sacrifices more income per minute of travel time: the wealthy household has a higher opportunity cost of commuting. In Figure 8–12, the optimum location for the wealthy household is u_w and the optimum location for the poor household is u_p. In this case, the poor occupy housing near the city center and the wealthy occupy suburban housing.

What are the assumptions underlying this theory of income segregation? The benefit and cost curves in Figure 8–12 are drawn under the assumption that the income elasticity of demand for land (the percentage change in land consumption divided by the percentage change in income) is large relative to the income elasticity of commuting costs (the percentage change in unit commuting cost divided by the percentage change in income). Although both land consumption and commuting costs increase with income, the increase in land consumption is assumed to be relatively large. Therefore, the gap between the two marginal-benefit curves is larger than the gap between the marginal-cost curves, so the poor will occupy central-city housing.

FIGURE 8–13   Location Choices Using Wheaton's Results

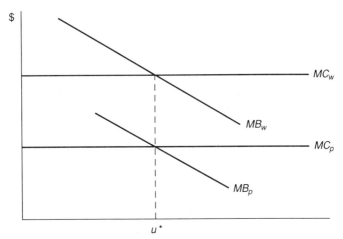

Distance to city center (miles)

If the income elasticity of demand for land equals the income elasticity of commuting costs, the gap between the marginal-benefit curves will be equal to the gap between the marginal-cost curves. Therefore, the simple monocentric model predicts that income will not affect location choices: both wealthy and poor will choose the same location.

Wheaton (1977) provides empirical evidence that questions the validity of the Alonso-Muth model of income segregation. His results suggest that both income elasticities (for land and commuting costs) are about 0.25. Therefore, an increase in income shifts the benefit and cost curves upward by about the same amount. In Figure 8–13, the gap between the benefit curves is the same as the gap between the costs curves, so the simple monocentric model predicts that rich and poor households will choose the same location (u^*). In other words, the observed locational pattern (poor central-city residents and wealthy suburbanites) cannot be explained by the trade-off between commuting costs and housing costs. Wheaton's results suggest that one must look beyond the simple monocentric model to explain the observed pattern of income segregation.

Other Explanations

The alternative explanations of income segregation are based on factors excluded from the simple monocentric model:

1. **New suburban housing.** Suppose that the utility generated from a particular dwelling decreases over time as the dwelling deteriorates and becomes obsolete. In other words, people get less utility out of an older house because it is less fashionable, has higher maintenance costs, and is equipped with fewer modern gadgets. The wealthy, who demand high-quality housing, will occupy new housing instead of used housing. As an urban area grows, it expands outward and developers build new housing for high-income households in the peripheral areas. The poor are left with old houses in the central city.

2. **Fleeing central-city problems.** As explained later in the book, poverty contributes to three urban problems. First, crime rates are higher among the poor, in part because the poor face relatively low opportunity costs of committing crime. Second, fiscal problems are more likely in a jurisdiction with a large fraction of low-income citizens. Third, students from poor families have relatively low achievement levels and pull down the achievement levels of other students. To escape these problems, some wealthy households flee to the suburbs, leaving large concentrations of poor households behind.

3. **Suburban zoning.** As explained in Chapter 11 (Land-Use Controls and Zoning), suburban governments use zoning to exclude low-income households. Therefore, only the wealthy have the opportunity to escape the problems of the central city.

Income and the Residential Bid-Rent Function

The issue of income segregation can also be explained with the housing-price function and the residential bid-rent function. As explained earlier in the chapter, the activity with the steeper bid-rent function will occupy land closer to the city center. Since the residential bid-rent function is determined by the housing-price function, the poor will occupy central land if they have a steeper housing-price function. Figure 8–14 shows two residential bid-rent functions, one for low-income housing and one for high-income housing. The low-income function is steeper because the poor have a steeper housing-price function.

Why do the poor have a steeper housing-price function? In the simple monocentric model, the expression for the slope of the housing-price function is

$$\frac{\Delta P}{\Delta u} = -\frac{t}{H(u)} \tag{8–16}$$

An increase in income increases both t (the opportunity cost of commuting increases) and H (housing consumption increases), so rising income has an ambiguous effect on the slope of the housing-price function. If the increase in H exceeds the increase in t (if the income elasticity of demand for housing exceeds the income elasticity of unit commuting cost), the wealthy will have a flatter housing-price function and a flatter residential bid-rent function. This is the Alonso-Muth theory of income segregation.

Wheaton's results suggest that the slope of the housing-price function will be independent of income. If H and t increase at the same rate as income

FIGURE 8–14   Bid-Rent Function and Income

The poor occupy central land (land less than u^* miles from the city center) because the bid-rent for low-income housing is relatively steep (a result of a relatively steep housing-price function for poor households).

increases, the two housing-price functions will have the same slope, so the two residential bid-rent functions will have the same slope. Therefore, if the poor have a relatively steep bid-rent function, it is not because of the trade-off between commuting costs and housing costs.

The alternative explanations of income segregation suggest that the slope of the residential bid-rent function is affected by other factors. Specifically, if central cities have higher taxes, inferior schools, and more pollution and crime, households will be willing to pay more for housing and land in the suburbs. In other words, the problems of the central city decrease the slopes of the housing-price function and the bid-rent function. The wealthy will have a flatter housing-price function if the income elasticities of demand for safety, clean air, and education are relatively large, that is, if the wealthy are willing to pay more for safety, clean air, and superior education. Wasylenko (1984) summarizes the empirical evidence supporting these alternative explanations of income segregation.

Policy Implications

These alternative theories of income segregation suggest that public policy can affect the location choices of wealthy and poor households. A housing policy that encourages the renovation of the central-city housing stock may cause some high-income households to return to the central city. Policies that decrease poverty will decrease crime rates, reduce fiscal problems, and improve central-city schools, thus encouraging high-income households to live in the central city. Similarly, policies that address the crime and education problems directly will increase the relative attractiveness of central-city locations. Finally, policies that control exclusionary zoning will allow poor households to move to the suburbs.

EMPIRICAL ESTIMATES OF RENT AND DENSITY FUNCTIONS

This section discusses empirical studies of land rent and land use in the monocentric city. The studies are based on data from the early 20th century, during the heyday of the monocentric city. Chapter 10 (Suburbanization of Employment and Residence) will discuss empirical work that is based on more recent data.

Estimates of the Land-Rent Function

A number of researchers have estimated the relationship between land rent and distance to the city center. Mills (1969) used data collected by Homer

Hoyt to estimate the relationship between land *value* and distance. As explained in Chapter 7, land value is the present value of land rent, so it's easy to make the translation from value to rent. Mills assumes the following relationship between value and distance:

$$V(u) = B \cdot e^{-c \cdot u} \tag{8–17}$$

where

    $V(u)$ is the value of land u miles from the city center

    B is a parameter to be estimated from the data

    e is the base of the natural logarithm

    c is a parameter to be estimated from the data

Figure 8–15 shows the estimated relationship for Chicago in 1928, a time when the city was monocentric. The value of land drops from about $140,000 per acre at the city center to about $114,000 1 mile from the center, to about $17,000 10 miles from the city center. The value of land falls by 21 percent per mile: the rent gradient is 21 percent.

FIGURE 8–15   Value of Land in Chicago in 1928

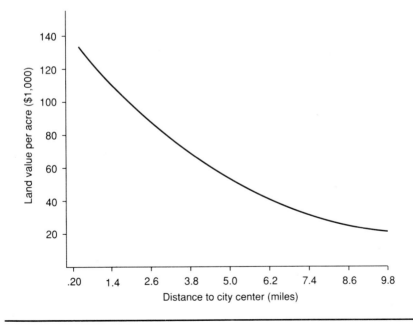

SOURCE: Edwin S. Mills, "The Value of Urban Land," in *The Quality of the Urban Environment*, ed. H. Perloff (Washington, D.C.: Resources for the Future, 1969), pp. 231–253.

Estimates of the Population-Density Function

How does population density vary within the monocentric city? The **density function** describes the relationship between population density and distance to the city center. Mills (1972) has estimated the density functions for 18 metropolitan areas for different years. The assumed relationship between density and distance is

$$D(u) = A \cdot e^{-g \cdot u} \qquad (8\text{–}18)$$

where

$D(u)$ is population density (people per square mile) u miles from the city center

A is a parameter to be estimated from the data

e is the base of the natural logarithm

g is a parameter to be estimated from the data

Figure 8–16 shows the estimated relationship for Baltimore in 1920, a time when the city was monocentric. Population density drops from about 60,000 people per square mile at a distance of 0.20 miles from the city center, to about 34,000 per square mile at a distance of one mile, to about 4,200 per square mile at a distance of four miles. The density gradient, defined as the percentage change in population density per mile, is about 70 percent.

SUMMARY

1. The monocentric city has the following characteristics:
   a. All manufacturers export their output through a central export node.
   b. Manufactured goods are transported within the city by horse-drawn wagon.
   c. Office workers travel by foot from offices to a central market area to exchange information.
   d. Commuters and shoppers travel on a hub-and-spoke streetcar system.
2. The manufacturing bid-rent function is negatively sloped because transport costs are lower near the export node. It is convex because of factor substitution.
3. The office bid-rent function is negatively sloped because travel costs are lower near the central market area, and it is convex because of factor substitution.
4. Transport costs in the monocentric city are relatively high for office firms, so the office bid-rent function is relatively steep and office firms occupy the central area of the city.
5. The location choices of retailers depend on scale economies, per capita demand, and shopping externalities. In the monocentric city, the hub-

FIGURE 8–16   Population Density in Baltimore in 1920

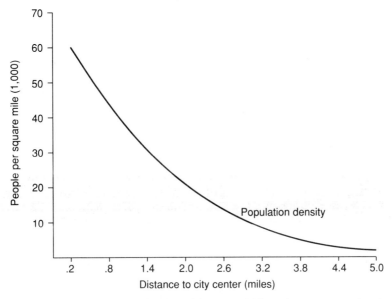

The density function is negatively sloped because (*a*) housing consumption increases with *u* (a result of declining housing prices) and (*b*) land per unit of housing increases with *u* (a result of declining land prices).

SOURCE: Edwin S. Mills, *Studies in the Structure of the Urban Economy* (Baltimore: The Johns Hopkins Press, 1972), derived from Table 15, p. 48.

and-spoke streetcar system makes central locations accessible to the entire urban area, causing most retailers to locate there.

6. In the simple monocentric model, all employment is in the CBD, and other things that residents care about (e.g., public services, taxes, pollution) are the same at all locations within the city.

7. The housing-price function shows the price of housing (per square foot of living space) for different locations in the city. The function is negatively sloped because commuting costs increase with the distance to the city center. It is convex because of consumer substitution: as the price of housing rises, consumers substitute other goods for housing.

8. The residential bid-rent function shows the amount housing producers are willing to pay for land at different locations in the city. It is negatively sloped because the housing-price function is negatively sloped. It is convex because of consumer substitution (which makes the housing-price function convex) and factor substitution.

9. The density function shows the number of people per acre for different locations in the city. It is negatively sloped for two reasons.

a. Housing prices are higher near the city center, so housing consumption is lower (fewer square feet of living space per household).

b. Land prices are higher near the city center, so the amount of land per square foot of housing is lower.

10. Activities in the monocentric city are arranged according to their transportation costs: the higher their transportation costs, the closer they locate to the city center.

a. The city center is occupied by the office sector rather than the manufacturing sector because office output is transmitted by high-cost office workers while manufacturing output is transported by horse-drawn wagon.

b. Employment is concentrated in the CBD because the cost of commuting (from the suburbs to the CBD factories and offices) is low relative to the costs of moving output (from the suburbs to the city center). Freight traveled by horse-drawn wagon, a relatively slow and expensive travel mode. In contrast, workers traveled by streetcar, a relatively fast and inexpensive travel mode.

11. If the assumptions of the simple monocentric city are dropped, the housing-price function and the residential bid-rent change.

a. The opportunity cost of commuting is the value of forgone work or leisure time. The typical commuter values commuting time at between one third and one half of his wage. The unit cost of commuting is the sum of time and monetary costs.

b. Noncommuting travel to the CBD increases the slopes of the housing-price and bid-rent functions because total travel costs increase more rapidly as the household moves away from the CBD.

c. The two-earner household has a relatively steep housing-price function if both earners commute to the CBD.

d. The prices of housing and land are higher in communities with superior local public goods and low taxes.

e. The prices of housing and land are higher in communities with clean air, scenic views, and access to parks.

12. The slopes of the housing-price and land-rent functions depend on housing consumption. A household that occupies a relatively large house has a relatively flat housing-price function and a relatively flat bid-rent function, so the household will live relatively far from the city center. Such a household has more to gain from inexpensive suburban housing.

13. In U.S. cities, the wealthy tend to locate in the suburbs and the poor tend to locate near the city center. One theory of income segregation suggests that the location choices of wealthy and poor households are based on different trade-offs between commuting and housing costs. This theory has been refuted by empirical evidence, which suggests that the observed pattern of segregation is caused by other factors, such as the demand for new suburban housing, the desire to escape central-city problems associated with poverty, and exclusionary zoning in the suburbs.

EXERCISES AND DISCUSSION QUESTIONS

1. The discussion of the baseball industry assumes that the intracity freight costs of raw materials (which come through the central railroad terminal) are small enough that they can be ignored. Draw a firm's bid-rent function under the assumption that intracity freight costs are zero and label it A. Suppose that the raw-material freight costs are large enough to matter. Draw a new bid-rent function and label it B. Explain the differences between the two curves.

2. In the city of Trekburg, manufacturers have two options for intracity freight. They can use a conventional transportation system (the truck) or a matter transmitter. The transmitter instantly transports the output from the factory to the central export node ("Beam it over, Scotty"). It costs $C to install the transmitter, but running the machine is costless once it is installed. The transmitter can transport output up to a distance of two miles. All manufacturing output goes through the export node.
   a. Draw the bid-rent function for a firm that uses the matter transmitter and label it M.
   b. On the same graph, draw the bid-rent function for a firm that uses the truck and label it T.
   c. Will every manufacturer use the matter transmitter? If not, where will the firms using the truck be located?

3. Complete the following table, given the following assumptions:
   a. The office firm produces 100 consultations per month.
   b. The consultation fee is $75.
   c. Travel time is five minutes per block.
   d. The opportunity cost of travel time is $3 per minute.
   e. Every consultation requires one trip to the city center.

Distance to City Center	Size of Site (acres)	Total Revenue	Nonland Input Costs	Travel Costs	Pre-Rent Profits	Rent per Acre
0	0.40		3600			
1	0.70		2000			
2	0.90		1200			
3	1.00		900			

4. Consider an office firm with the following characteristics. The wage of executives is $120 per hour, and the executive takes four minutes to walk one block. The price of output is $150 per consultation, and the firm produces 50 consultations (requiring 50 trips to the city center). At a location four blocks from the city center, the firm occupies a one-acre site and spends $1000 on nonland inputs.
   a. What is travel cost per block?
   b. How much is the firm willing to pay for land four blocks from the city center?

   c. Given the available information, is it possible to compute how much the firm is willing to pay for land one block from the city center? If not, what additional information do you need?

5. Suppose that a monocentric city imposes a tax on capital used in the office industry. Draw the office bid-rent functions before and after the imposition of the capital tax for the following two cases:
   a. Office firms do not engage in factor substitution.
   b. Office firms engage in factor substitution.

6. Depict graphically the effects of the following changes on the division of CBD land between office firms and manufacturers.
   a. Freight costs decrease.
   b. The price of office output increases.
   c. The opportunity cost of executive travel decreases.

7. Choose the word in parentheses that makes the following statement correct: As the curvature of a firm's isoquant increases, the curvature of the bid-rent function (*increases, decreases*).
   Hint: Compare the shape of the bid-rent function for a firm with a linear isoquant to the shape of a bid-rent function for a firm with an L-shaped isoquant.

8. Consider an industry that makes Ping-Pong balls and competes with the baseball makers for land near the central export node. Each Ping-Pong firm produces the same volume of output as a baseball firm (five tons of balls), sells for the same price ($160 per ton), and has the same production isoquants.
   Which activity will locate closer to the export node?

9. Consider a monocentric city in which the unit cost of commuting is $10 per mile per month. A household located eight miles from the city center occupies a dwelling with 1200 square feet, at a monthly rent of $600. Nonland costs per dwelling are $200, and there are four houses per acre.
   a. What is the price (per square foot) of housing at $u=8$? What is the bid rent at $u=8$?
   b. Assume that the demand for housing is perfectly inelastic. What is the price of housing at $u=5$?
   c. Assume that housing firms do not engage in factor substitution. What is the bid rent at $u=5$?
   d. How would your answers to (*b*) and (*c*) change if the demand for housing depends on the price and firms engage in factor substitution? Would the prices of housing and land be higher or lower?

10. Consider a city in which all employment is in the city center. Suppose that the work week is shortened from five days per week to four days per week. Depict graphically the effects of the shorter work week on the housing-price function and the residential bid-rent function.

11. In the section where the assumptions of the monocentric model were relaxed, the introduction of two-earner households doubled the housing-

price function. Suppose that couples ride to work together. Using a graph, show the housing-price function before and after the introduction of two-earner households.

12. Suppose that a city restricts the heights of residential structures. The maximum height is four stories, the height that would normally occur at a distance of five miles from the city center. Draw two residential bid-rent functions, one for the city in the absence of height restrictions and one with height restrictions.

13. Consider a CBD worker with the following characteristics:
    i.   The wage is $10 per hour.
    ii.   The monthly monetary cost of commuting is $10 per mile.
    iii. The monthly commuting time is four hours per mile.
    iv.   The opportunity cost of commuting time is one half the wage.
    v.   The worker consumes 1,000 square feet of land.
    vi.   The bid-rent function for land (price per square foot) is

Distance	1	2	3	4	5	6	7
Price	90¢	70¢	60¢	65¢	62¢	60¢	59¢

    a. After reviewing Figure 8–11, draw the worker's marginal-cost curve (marginal commuting cost) and marginal-benefit curve (marginal savings in land costs). What is the optimum location?
    b. Suppose that the wage doubles, but land consumption does not change. Draw the new marginal-cost and marginal-benefit curves. What is the new optimum location?
    c. How would your answer to (b) change if the worker doubled his land consumption when the wage doubled?
    d. What is the lesson from this exercise?

14. Between 1940 and 1965, the average household size increased dramatically.
    a. Draw two housing-price functions (one for 1940 and one for 1965) and explain the differences between the two functions.
    b. Could the increase in household size explain part of the suburbanization that occurred between 1940 and 1965?

15. Suppose that the demand for housing (H = square feet of housing space per capita) and the demand for land (T = square foot of land per square foot of housing space) are described by the following equations (P is the price of housing, and R is land rent per square foot):

$$H = 1500 - 500 \cdot P$$

$$T = \frac{1}{10000} \cdot (15{,}000 - R)$$

Compute land consumption per capita for the following locations:
    a. Location A: $P = 1.5$ and $R = 12{,}000$
    b. Location B: $P = 1.0$ and $R = 10{,}000$
    c. Location C: $P = 0.30$ and $R = 3{,}000$

16. In Figure 8–5, the introduction of consumer substitution increases the price of housing at all locations. Comment on the following: "Something is wrong here. As we move from a world without substitution to a world with substitution, overall demand for housing decreases. Yet Figure 8–5 shows an increase in the price of housing. How can the price rise when the demand falls?"

REFERENCES AND ADDITIONAL READINGS

Location of Office Firms

Clapp, J. M. "Endogenous Centers: A Simple Departure from the NUE Model." *Papers of the Regional Science Association* 54 (1984), pp. 13–24. Describes the process through which contacts between firms cause the development of a CBD and subcenters.

David, Philip. *Urban Land Development* Homewood, Ill.: Richard D. Irwin, 1970. Discusses the rent function of commercial firms.

O'Hara, D. J. "Location of Firms Within a Square Central Business District." *Journal of Political Economy* 85 (1977), pp. 1189–207. Discusses how interfirm contacts cause the development of a central business district.

Tauchen, H., and Anne Witte. "An Equilibrium Model of Office Location and Contact Patterns." *Environment and Planning* 15 (1983), pp. 1311–26. Discusses how interfirm contacts cause the development of a central business district.

Tauchen, H., and Anne Witte. "Socially Optimal and Equilibrium Distributions of Office Activity: Models with Exogenous and Endogenous Contacts." *Journal of Urban Economics* 15 (1984), pp. 66–86. Discusses two sources of market failure in the location decisions of office firms: agglomeration economies and transaction externalities.

Transportation, Land Rent, and Land Use

Alcaly, Roger E. "Transportation and Urban Land Values: A Review of the Theoretical Literature," *Land Economics* 52 (1976), pp. 42–53. Discusses the effects of changes in transport costs on land rent.

Meyer, J.; John Kain; and M. Wohl. *The Urban Transportation Problem*. Cambridge, Mass.: Harvard Univ. Press, 1965. Discusses the effects of the trend toward two-earner households and noncommuting travel on the residential-rent function.

Housing-Price Function

Jackson, Jerry. "Intraurban Variation in the Price of Housing," *Journal of Urban Economics* 6 (1979), pp. 465–79. Estimates the housing-price function and finds that housing prices fall by about 2 percent per mile.

Kain, John F. and John M. Quigley. "Measuring the Value of Housing Quality." *Journal of the American Statistical Association* 65 (1970), pp. 532–38. Estimates the relationship between various housing characteristics (including location) and the price of housing.

King, Thomas, "The Demand for Housing: Integrating the Roles of Journey to Work, Neighborhood Quality, and Prices." In *Household Production and Consumption*, ed. Nester Terleckyj. New York: National Bureau of Economic Research, 1975. Estimates the relationship between various housing characteristics (including location) and the price of housing.

Quigley, John M. "Housing Demand in the Short Run: An Analysis of Polytomous Choice." *Explorations in Economic Research* 3 (1976), pp. 76–102. Estimates the effects of location on the implicit prices of different components of housing.

Straszheim, Mahlon. *An Economic Analysis of the Urban Housing Market*. New York: National Bureau of Economic Research, 1975. Estimates the effects of location on the implicit prices of different components of housing.

Empirical Studies of Population Density and Land Rent

Mills, Edwin S. *Studies in the Structure of the Urban Economy*. Baltimore: The Johns Hopkins Press, 1972. Chapter 3 estimates population- and employment-density functions for U.S. cities.

Mills, Edwin S. "The Value of Urban Land." In *The Quality of the Urban Environment*, ed. H. Perloff. Washington, D.C.: Resources for the Future, 1969. Estimates the land-rent function in Chicago for various years between 1836 to 1959.

Muth, Richard. *Cities and Housing*. Chicago: University of Chicago Press, 1969. A classic study of residential location decisions in Chicago. Chapter 7 estimates the density function for several U.S. cities.

Income and Location

Alonso, William. *Location and Land Use*. Cambridge, Mass.: Harvard Univ. Press, 1964. Extends the Von Thunen land use model to include the location decisions of households.

Downs, Anthony. *Urban Problems and Prospects*. Chicago: Markham, 1970. Suggests that the building of new housing on the peripheral area of the metropolitan area contributes to the suburbanization of high-income households.

LeRoy, Stephen, and Jon Sonstelie. "Paradise Lost and Regained: Transportation Innovation, Income, and Residential Segregation." *Journal of Urban Economics* 13 (1983), pp. 67–89. Discusses the effects of different transport modes on the location patterns of different income groups.

Muth, Richard. *Cities and Housing*. Chicago: University of Chicago Press, 1969. A classic study of residential location decisions in Chicago. Chapter 2 models the location decision, and Chapter 10 provides empirical evidence that suggests that the tendency for higher-income households to locate farther from the city center is caused by differences in the trade-offs between housing and commuting costs.

Wasylenko, Michael J. "Disamenities, Local Taxation, and the Intrametropolitan Location of Households and Firms." In *Research in Urban Economics* vol. 4, ed. Robert Ebel. Greenwich, Conn.: JAI Press, 1984. Reviews the empirical evidence concerning the effects of income on location. Also reviews the evidence concerning the intrametropolitan location choices of firms.

Wheaton, William. "Income and Urban Residence: An Analysis of Consumer Demand for Location." *American Ecnomic Review* 67 (1977), pp. 620–31.   Suggests that the income elasticity of demand for land is close to the income elasticity of commuting costs, meaning that the tendency for the poor to locate near the city center cannot be explained by the simple monocentric model.

Miscellaneous

Clawson, Marion. "Urban Sprawl and Speculation in Suburban Land." In *Urban Economic Issues*, ed. Stephen Mehay and Geoffrey Nunn. Glenview, Ill.: Scott, Foresman, 1984, pp. 47–52.   Analyzes the market for undeveloped land and suggests that urban sprawl is efficient.

Eberts, Randall. "An Empirical Investigation of Intraurban Wage Gradients." *Journal of Urban Economics* 10 (1981), pp. 50–60.   Estimates the variation in wages within a metropolitan area.

Modeling the Monocentric City

Mills, Edwin S. "Planning and Market Processes in Urban Models." In *Public and Urban Economics*, ed. Ronald Grieson. Lexington, Mass.: Lexington Books, 1976.   A model of urban land use that uses linear and nonlinear programming to allocate land to alternative activities.

Mills, Edwin S. *Studies in the Structure of the Urban Economy*. Baltimore: The Johns Hopkins Press, 1972.   Chapter 5 derives the conditions under which the monocentric city is more efficient than a city with dispersed employment.

Wheaton, William. "Monocentric Models of Urban Land Use: Contributions and Criticisms." In *Current Issues in Urban Economics*, ed. Peter Meiszkowski and Mahlon Straszheim. Baltimore: The Johns Hopkins Press, 1979.   Discusses several renditions of the traditional monocentric model.

CHAPTER 9

General-Equilibrium Land Use

Everything should be explained as simply as possible, but not more so.

Albert Einstein

This chapter uses general-equilibrium analysis to explore the interactions between different parts of the urban economy. In contrast with partial-equilibrium analysis, which examines a single market in isolation, general-equilibrium analysis recognizes that markets are interdependent, and explores the effects of changes in one market on related markets.

Urban general-equilibrium analysis explores the interactions between the residential land market, the business land market, and the urban labor market. It is used to predict the effects of changes in one part of the urban economy on land use throughout the urban area. This chapter will use general-equilibrium analysis to explore the effects of three changes in the monocentric city: an increase in export sales, the introduction of a streetcar system, and an increase in the residential property tax. Later in the book, general-equilibrium analysis will be used to explore the land-use effects of other changes in technology and public policy. Chapter 10 (Suburbanization of Employment and Population) explores the land-use effects of the truck and the automobile. Chapter 11 (Land-Use Controls and Zoning) examines the general-equilibrium effects of various land-use controls. Chapter 17 (Autos and Highways) explores the effects of highway congestion on land-use patterns.

GENERAL-EQUILIBRIUM CONDITIONS

Figure 9–1 shows the equilibrium land-use pattern of a monocentric city. The bid-rent function of the business sector (office firms and manufacturers) is negatively sloped, reflecting the benefits of locating near the central market area and the central export node. The bid-rent function of the housing sector (residents) is negatively sloped, reflecting the benefits of living close to jobs in office and manufacturing firms. The central business district (CBD) is the area over which office firms and manufacturers outbid residents, so the radius of the CBD is u_b miles. The suburban residential district (SRD) is the area over which residents outbid firms and farmers, so the SRD is a ring of width $(u_h - u_b)$ miles. For land beyond u_h, farmers outbid residents, so the radius of the city is u_h miles.

The monocentric city is assumed to be one of hundreds of cities in a regional economy. The city is "open" in the sense that households and firms

FIGURE 9–1   Equilibrium Land-Use Pattern in a Monocentric City

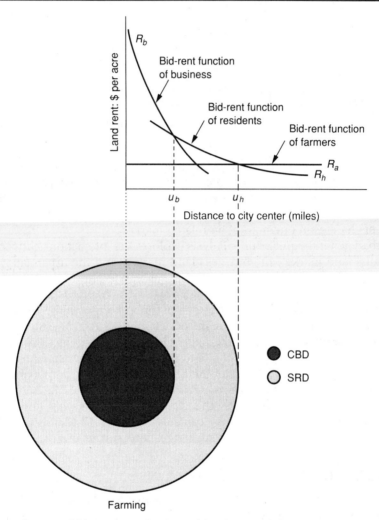

Business firms outbid residents for central land, generating a CBD with radius u_b. The SRD is the area over which residents outbid firms and farmers, that is, a ring with width $(u_h - u_b)$.

can costlessly enter or leave the city. The city is "small" in the sense that it is a trivial part of the regional economy, small enough that changes in the city do not affect the common utility level of the region's residents. Any change that increases the utility level of the city's residents will cause migration from the rest of the region. This migration will bid up the prices of housing and land (increasing the cost of living) and decrease the utility level of the city's residents. Migration will continue until the original utility level is restored.

The urban economy will achieve general equilibrium when four conditions are satisfied simultaneously:

1. **Locational equilibrium for firms.** If all firms make zero profits at all locations, there will be no incentive to change locations. This condition is guaranteed by the business bid-rent function R_b: competition for land bids up the price of land at locations with relatively low transportation costs, so firms will be indifferent among all locations in the city.

2. **Locational equilibrium for households.** If all households achieve the same utility level at all locations in the city, there will be no incentive to change locations. This condition is guaranteed by the residential bid-rent function R_h: competition for land will bid up the price of land at locations with relatively low commuting costs, so households will be indifferent among all locations in the city.

3. **Competitive bidding.** Land is allocated to the highest bidder. This condition will be satisfied if landowners, like other people in a competitive economy, seek the highest return on their assets.

4. **Labor-market equilibrium.** The total demand for labor (from office firms and manufacturers in the CBD) equals the total supply of labor (from residents in the SRD).

To summarize, general equilibrium requires that both the land market and the labor market be in equilibrium at the same time.

NUMERICAL EXAMPLES OF GENERAL-EQUILIBRIUM ANALYSIS

This section uses two numerical examples to explain the principles of general-equilibrium analysis. An increase in export sales has a direct effect on the CBD land market, and the introduction of a streetcar system has a direct effect on the SRD land market.

Initial Equilibrium

Table 9–1 shows the numbers associated with the monocentric city depicted in Figure 9–1. The CBD radius is two miles, and the city radius is six miles. The land area of the CBD is computed with the formula for the area of a circle:

$$\text{CBD land area} = \pi \cdot (u_b)^2 \tag{9–1}$$

TABLE 9–1   General-Equilibrium Effects of an Increase in Export Price

	Initial Equilibrium	*Partial Equilibrium*	*General Equilibrium*
Radius of CBD (u_b) (miles)	2.0	2.5	2.2
Area of CBD (square miles)	12.56	19.63	15.20
Width of SRD ($u_h - u_b$) (miles)	4.0	3.5	4.3
Land area of SRD (square miles)	100.48	74.58	117.47
Radius of city (u_h) (miles)	6.0	6.0	6.5
Land area of city (square miles)	113.04	113.04	132.67
Wage ($ per hour)	10.0	10.0	13.0
Average labor density (per square mile)	20,000	22,000	21,000
Total labor demand	251,200	431,750	319,150
Average household density (per square mile)	2,500	2,500	2,717
Total labor supply	251,200	186,438	319,150

Because u_b is 2 miles, the CBD land area is 12.56 square miles. The land area of the city is

$$\text{City land area} = \pi \cdot (u_h)^2 \tag{9-2}$$

Because u_h is 6 miles, the land area of the city is 113.04 square miles. The land area of the residential district is the difference between the land areas of the city and the CBD, or 100.48 square miles.

The city is in general equilibrium because total labor supply equals total labor demand. Total labor demand equals the land area of the CBD times the average number of workers per square mile:

$$\text{Total labor demand} = \text{CBD land area} \cdot \text{Average employment density} \tag{9-3}$$

In Table 9–1, the average employment density is 20,000 workers per square mile, so total labor demand is 251,200. Total labor supply equals the land area of the SRD times the average household density (assuming that there is one worker per household):

$$\text{Total labor supply} = \text{SRD land area} \cdot \text{Average household density} \tag{9-4}$$

In Table 9–1, the average household density is 2,500 per square mile, so total labor supply is 251,200. Labor supply equals labor demand, so the land-use allocation shown in Figure 9–1 is an equilibrium allocation.

Increase in Export Price and Export Sales

Suppose that the price of baseballs (the city's export good) increases. What are the effects of the price increase on the city's land and labor markets?

Consider first the partial-equilibrium effect of the price increase, that is, the effect on the CBD land market. In the short run, the increase in price will increase the profits of baseball firms. The demand for CBD land will increase as *(a)* existing baseball firms increase their output and *(b)* new firms enter the baseball industry. The increase in the demand for land will shift the bid rent for business land upward, as shown in Figure 9–2. The upward shift of R_b is consistent with the leftover principle: at the higher baseball price, firms have a greater excess of revenue over costs, so they are willing to pay more for land. As the business bid-rent function shifts upward, the CBD expands at the expense of the residential area: the radius of the business district increases from 2.0 miles to 2.5 miles, and the SRD shrinks from a width of 4.0 miles to 3.5 miles.

How does the upward shift of the business bid-rent function affect the urban labor market? Total labor demand increases for two reasons:

1. **CBD territory effect.** Table 9–1 shows an increase in CBD land area from 12.56 square miles in column one to 19.63 square miles in column two.

2. **Employment-density effect.** The increase in the relative price of land causes baseball firms to substitute nonland inputs (capital and labor) for land, increasing employment density (workers per square mile). Table 9–1 shows an increase in employment density from 20,000 in column one to 22,000 in column two.

FIGURE 9–2   Partial-Equilibrium Effects of an Increase in Export Price and Export Sales

An increase in the price of exports shifts the business bid-rent function upward. The CBD expands (the radius increases from 2.0 miles to 2.5 miles) at the expense of the SRD (the width decreases from 4.0 miles to 3.5 miles).

In combination, these two effects increase total labor demand from 251,200 to 431,750. The upward shift of the business bid-rent function also decreases total labor supply: the CBD encroaches on SRD land, decreasing total supply from 251,200 to 186,438. Because labor demand increases and labor supply decreases, there is excess demand for labor.

The increase in the price of baseballs increases labor demand while it decreases labor supply, and the resulting excess demand for labor will increase the city's wage. The increase in the wage will increase the quantity of labor supplied for two reasons:

1. **SRD territory effect.** An increase in the wage increases the relative attractiveness of the city. Laborers will move to the city, bidding up the prices of housing and residential land. R_h will shift upward, increasing the size of the SRD as residents outbid farmers (for land near the city border) and firms (for land near the CBD border). As the residential district expands, total labor supply increases.

2. **Household-density effect.** As the price of housing increases, households will substitute nonhousing goods for housing, so housing consumption per household will decrease. In addition, as the price of residential land increases, housing producers will substitute capital for land, so the amount of land per unit of housing will decrease. In combination, these two changes decrease land consumption per household: every household occupies a smaller lot. The decrease in land consumption increases household density (the number of households and laborers per square mile), thus increasing total supply.

To summarize, the increase in the wage increases the quantity of labor supplied because both the size and the density of the residential district increase.

How does the increase in the wage affect the demand side of the labor market? The increase in the wage decreases the quantity of labor demanded for two reasons:

1. **CBD territory effect.** An increase in the wage will increase production costs. Some firms will decrease their output, and other firms will shut down. The decrease in production activity decreases the demand for land, so the business bid-rent function will drop. As the CBD loses territory to the residential district, total labor demand will decrease.

2. **Employment-density effect.** The relative price of labor will increase because the wage increases and land rent decreases. As the relative price of labor increases, firms will substitute capital and land for the relatively expensive labor. Employment density (the number of workers per square mile) will decrease.

To summarize, the increase in the wage decreases the quantity of labor demanded because both the size and the density of the business district decrease.

These two changes in the labor market narrow the gap between labor supply and labor demand. The wage will continue to rise until general equilibrium is restored. Figure 9–3 shows the new equilibrium allocation of land, and the third column of Table 9–1 shows numbers behind the new allocation. The new equilibrium wage is $13 (up from $10). The CBD radius is 2.2 miles and employment density is 21,000 workers per square mile, so total labor demand is 319,150. The SRD is 4.3 miles wide and household density is 2,717 per square mile, so total labor supply equals total demand. In other words, general equilibrium is restored with a wage of $13. For a lower wage, labor demand would exceed supply; for a higher wage, supply would exceed demand.

There are four lessons from the general-equilibrium analysis of the increases in the export price:

> 1. **Market interactions.** Changes in the CBD (the business land market) affect the city's labor market and its residential land market. The upward shift of the business bid-rent function (precipitated by the increase in the export price) increases the size and the density of the CBD, causing excess demand for labor. The resulting increase in the wage shifts the bid-rent function of residents upward, increasing the size and density of the SRD.

FIGURE 9–3 General-Equilibrium Effects of an Increase in Export Price and Export Sales

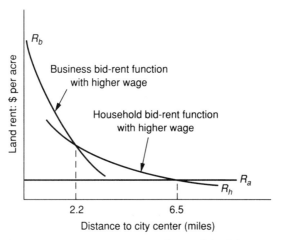

The increase in the export price causes excess demand for labor, increasing the city's wage. The increase in the wage shifts the business bid-rent function downward and shifts the residential bid-rent function upward. The net effect is a larger CBD (the radius increases from 2.0 miles to 2.2 miles) and a larger SRD (the width increases from 4.0 miles to 4.3 miles).

2. **Shifts in bid-rent functions.** The increase in the export price causes an upward shift of the business bid-rent function (a partial-equilibrium effect). The resulting increase in the wage causes a downward shift of the business bid-rent function (a general-equilibrium effect).

3. **Land rent.** The increase in the export price increases land rent throughout the city. The increase in export production increases the demand for land in both the CBD and the residential district, so landowners throughout the city benefit from the increase in export sales.

4. **Welfare effects of increased export sales.** In general equilibrium, the city's residents are no better off in the larger city. The increase in the wage is offset by higher costs of housing and land, leaving the utility level unchanged. The increase in export sales increases the number of people in the city, not their utility. In addition, export firms are no better off: they sell more output, but still make zero economic profits.

A Streetcar System

As a second illustration of general equilibrium analysis, suppose that the city installs a streetcar system. The streetcar will decrease the time and monetary costs of commuting, causing a number of changes in the urban economy.

How does the streetcar system affect the residential bid-rent function? As explained in Chapter 8 (Land Use in the Monocentric City), the slope of the bid-rent function is determined by commuting costs: the lower the unit cost of

FIGURE 9–4 The Partial-Equilibrium Effect of the Streetcar System

The streetcar system decreases commuting costs, decreasing the slope of the residential bid-rent function. The width of the SRD increases from 4 miles to 6 miles, and the city radius increases from 6 miles to 8 miles.

commuting, the flatter the bid-rent function. In Figure 9–4, the streetcar system decreases the slope of the bid-rent function, which increases the width of the SRD from four to six miles. The streetcar system makes peripheral areas accessible to CBD jobs, allowing residents to outbid farmers for land near the city's edge. This is the partial-equilibrium effect of the streetcar system.

The upward tilt of the residential bid-rent function increases total labor supply for two reasons.

1. **SRD territory effect.** The expansion of the residential district increases labor supply. Table 9–2 shows an increase in the land area of the residential district from 100.48 square miles in column one to 188.40 square miles in column two.

2. **Household density effect.** The streetcar system increases the prices of housing and land, causing consumer substitution (consumers substitute nonhousing goods for housing) and factor substitution (housing producers substitute nonland inputs for land). The lot size per household decreases, increasing population density. Table 9–2 shows an increase in household density from 2,500 in column one to 2,700 in column two.

To summarize, the streetcar system increases the quantity of labor supplied because it increases both the size and the density of the residential district. The streetcar system increases the relative attractiveness of the city, causing migration that bids up the price of land. People migrate from other cities because workers in the streetcar city have shorter commuting times and higher net income (gross labor income less the time costs of commuting).

Because the streetcar system does not initially affect the demand side of the labor market, it causes an excess supply of labor. The excess supply of labor will decrease the city's wage, causing changes on both sides of the labor

TABLE 9–2   General-Equilibrium Effects of a Streetcar System

	Initial Equilibrium	Partial Equilibrium	General Equilibrium
Radius of CBD (u_b) (miles)	2.0	2.0	2.3
Area of CBD (square miles)	12.56	12.56	16.61
Width of SRD ($u_h - u_b$) (miles)	4.0	6.0	4.8
Land area of SRD (square miles)	100.48	188.40	141.68
Radius of city (u_h) (miles)	6.0	8.0	7.1
Land area of city (square miles)	113.04	200.96	158.29
Wage ($ per hour)	10.0	10.0	6.0
Average labor density (per square mile)	20,000	20,000	22,000
Total labor demand	251,200	251,200	365,433
Average household density (per square mile)	2,500	2,700	2,579
Total labor supply	251,200	508,680	365,433

market. On the demand side, the business bid-rent function will shift upward, increasing both the territory and the employment density of the CBD. On the supply side, the residential bid-rent function will shift downward, decreasing both the territory and the density of the residential district.

These two changes in the labor market narrow the gap between labor supply and labor demand. The wage will continue to drop until general equilibrium is restored. Figure 9–5 shows the new equilibrium allocation of land, and the third column of Table 9–2 shows numbers behind the new equilibrium: the new equilibrium wage is $6 (down from $10); the CBD radius is 2.3 miles; the SRD is 4.8 miles wide; the equilibrium number of laborers is 365,433. There are three basic lessons from the general-equilibrium analysis of the streetcar system:

1. **Tilt and shift of the residential bid-rent function.** The streetcar system affects the residential bid-rent function in two ways. The upward tilt (or flattening) of the function is the partial-equilibrium effect, which occurs because the streetcar system decreases commuting costs. The downward shift is the general-equilibrium effect, which occurs because the streetcar system causes an excess supply of labor and decreases the city's wage.

FIGURE 9–5   The General-Equilibrium Effect of the Streetcar

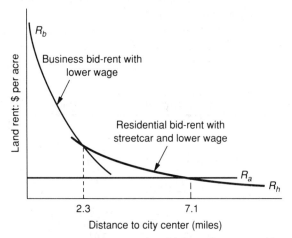

The streetcar system causes excess supply of labor, decreasing the city's wage. The business bid-rent function shifts upward and the residential bid-rent shifts downward. The CBD grows, and the SRD shrinks. General equilibrium is restored with a larger CBD (the radius increases from 2.0 miles to 2.3 miles), a larger SRD (the width increases from 4.0 miles to 4.8 miles), and a larger city (the radius increases from 6.0 miles to 7.1 miles).

2. **Land rent.** The streetcar system increases land rent in both the SRD and the CBD. The system increases the accessibility of residential land, so residents are willing to pay more for land. The streetcar system also decreases wages and production costs, so firms are willing to pay more for land in the CBD. Landowners throughout the city benefit from the streetcar.

3. **Welfare effects of the streetcar.** In general equilibrium, the city's residents are no better off with the streetcar system. Because the city is "open," the system causes migration from the rest of the region that decreases wages and increases the prices of housing and land. The benefits of the streetcar system (faster and cheaper commuting) are offset by a lower wage and a higher cost of living.

THE GENERAL-EQUILIBRIUM EFFECTS OF THE PROPERTY TAX

Consider a city that initially finances all of its public services with a land tax. If all the land in the city is owned by people living outside the city, the city's public services are initially financed by a tax on absentee landowners. Suppose that the city replaces its land tax with a tax on residential capital (improvements such as houses and apartments), and the capital tax is paid by the city's residents. Under the new tax policy, city residents pay more taxes but do not receive more public services.

How will the property tax affect the city's economy? There are two ways to answer this question. First, a graph can be used to show the partial-equilibrium effects of the tax. Second, a computer can be used to show the general-equilibrium effects of the tax.

Figure 9–6 shows the partial-equilibrium effect of the residential property tax. As explained in Chapter 8 (Land Use in the Monocentric City), the capital:land ratio increases as one approaches the city center because housing producers substitute capital for relatively expensive land. Because the amount of improvements per acre is higher closer to the city center, the tax liability per acre will increase as one approaches the city center. For example, an apartment building on a one-acre site two miles from the city center will face a higher tax liability than a single-family home on a one-acre site five miles from the city center. Therefore, the closer the site to the city center, the larger the downward shift of the bid-rent function. This is shown in Figure 9–6: the gap between the pretax and posttax bid-rent functions increases as one approaches the city center.

The residential property tax will disrupt the labor market. The downward shift of the residential bid-rent function will decrease the territory and the density of the residential district, causing excess demand for labor. The city's wage will increase, causing responses in the CBD and SRD that narrow the gap between supply and demand. In the CBD, the increase in the wage

FIGURE 9–6   Partial-Equilibrium Effects of the Residential Property Tax

Distance to city center (miles)

The residential property tax is partly a tax on improvements, so it generates a larger tax burden on locations with large capital:land ratios. Therefore, the gap between the pretax and the posttax residential bid-rent functions increases as one approaches the city center.

will increase production costs and decrease the bid rent for business land. The resulting decreases in the size and the density of the CBD will decrease the quantity of labor demanded. In the SRD, the increase in the wage will shift the residential bid-rent function upward. The resulting increases in the size and the density of the residential district will increase the quantity of labor supplied. The wage will continue to rise until general equilibrium is restored.

What will the city look like after general equilibrium is restored? One way to answer this question is to use a computer to generate two pictures of the urban economy, one before the property tax is imposed and one after the economy has adjusted to the new tax. An urban general-equilibrium computer model allocates different plots of land in a hypothetical city to firms (labor demanders) and households (labor suppliers). If a particular allocation of land does not satisfy the conditions for general equilibrium, the computer tries a different allocation. This groping process continues until an equilibrium allocation is found. The computer model can be designed to compute a pretax equilibrium and a posttax equilibrium. By comparing the before and after snapshots of the urban economy, one can identify the general-equilibrium effects of the property tax.

Sullivan (1985) used a computer model to simulate the effects of a 1.7 percent residential property tax. The results of the study are listed in Table 9–3. The hypothetical city has an initial work force of about 250,000 and a population of about 500,000. The property tax decreases the city's land area, pop-

TABLE 9–3   General-Equilibrium Effects of the Residential Property Tax

	Initial Equilibrium	General Equilibrium
Number of households	250,038	225,853
Territories		
Radius of CBD (miles)	2.916	2.85
Width of SRD (miles)	3.582	3.378
Radius of city (miles)	6.498	6.228
Input prices		
Wage ($ per hour)	10.00	10.02
Median CBD land rent ($ per acre per year)	28,999	26,016
Median SRD land rent ($ per acre per year)	2,886	2,761
Density		
Average labor density (per square mile)	9,360	8,851
Average household density (per square mile)	2,359	2,344
Land Rent		
CBD land rent ($ per week)	7,053,134	6,258,973
SRD land rent ($ per week)	3,580,168	3,163,577
Total land rent ($ per week)	10,633,302	9,422,550

SOURCE: Arthur M. Sullivan, "The General Equilibrium Effects of the Residential Property Tax: Incidence and Excess Burden," *Journal of Urban Economics* 18 (1985), pp. 235–50.

ulation, employment density, and population density. Although the tax applies only to residential property, it ultimately affects land rent and land use throughout the city. Land rent at the median CBD location decreases 11 percent (to $26,016 per acre per year), and land rent at the median SRD location decreases 4 percent (to $2,761 per acre per year). Employment density decreases 5.7 percent, and household density decreases 1 percent. The decrease in total land rent is about 160 percent of the total revenue from the property tax. The computer model provides a comprehensive view of the general-equilibrium effects of the property tax.

SUMMARY

1. In the small, open city, the utility level of residents is fixed: any change that increases the relative attractiveness of the city will cause migration that increases housing and land prices, decreasing utility to its original level.

2. The urban economy will achieve general equilibrium if four conditions are met.

   a. Firms make zero economic profits at all locations (guaranteed by the bid-rent functions).

    b. Households achieve the same utility level at all locations (guaranteed by the bid-rent functions).

    c. Land is rented to the highest bidder.

    d. Total demand for labor (from firms in the business district) equals total supply (from residents in the residential district).

3. An increase in the export price shifts the business bid-rent function upward, thus increasing labor demand as the size and the density of the CBD increase.

    a. The excess demand for labor increases the wage.

    b. The increase in the wage shifts the residential bid-rent function upward, thus increasing the quantity of labor supplied as the size and the density of the SRD increase.

    c. The increase in the wage also shifts the business bid-rent function downward, decreasing the quantity of labor demanded as the size and the density of the CBD decrease.

    d. The wage continues to rise until labor supply equals labor demand.

4. The streetcar system decreases the slope of the residential bid-rent function, tilting it upward. The size and the density of the residential district increases, thus increasing total labor supply.

    a. The excess supply of labor decreases the wage.

    b. The decrease in the wage shifts the business bid-rent function upward, increasing the quantity of labor demanded as the size and the density of the CBD increase.

    c. The decrease in the wage shifts the residential bid-rent function downward, decreasing the quantity of labor supplied as the size and the density of the SRD decrease.

    d. The wage continues to drop until labor supply equals labor demand.

5. In general equilibrium, city residents are no better off with the streetcar. Migration to the open city decreases wages and increases the prices of housing and land, thus offsetting the benefits of the streetcar.

6. The property tax decreases the slope of the residential bid-rent function, decreasing the supply of labor as the residential district decreases in size and density. In general equilibrium, the property tax decreases the city's size, density, and total land rent.

EXERCISES AND DISCUSSION QUESTIONS

1. Suppose that the intracity truck is introduced into the traditional monocentric city, decreasing the costs of intracity freight. Depict graphically the partial-equilibrium and general-equilibrium effects of the truck.

2. Suppose that a city subsidizes the construction of radial highways. How

will such a policy affect land rent, land use, and wages in a small, open city?

3. Suppose that the government subsidizes the production of agricultural products. How will such a policy affect land rent, land use, and wages in a small, open city?

4. Suppose a city builds a streetcar and passes a law that prevents any outsiders from moving to the city. In other words, the city keeps its population at its pre-streetcar level, so it is a "closed" city instead of an open one. Depict graphically the partial-equilibrium and general-equilibrium effects of the streetcar in the closed city.

5. Chapter 6 (Urban Economic Growth) uses a supply-demand model to depict the urban growth process.
   a. Use the supply-demand model to depict the general-equilibrium effects of the streetcar system shown in Table 9–2. Be sure that your graph matches the numbers in the table.
   b. Use your graph to compute the elasticity of labor demand with respect to the wage.

6. Use a graph to show the partial-equilibrium effect of a tax on business property. Outline the general-equilibrium effects of the business property tax. How do the general-equilibrium effects differ from the effects of the residential property tax?

7. Consider a rectangular city with the following characteristics:
   i. The city is two miles wide.
   ii. The CBD is on a harbor, and the SRD is east of the CBD.
   iii. Manufacturers transport their output from factories to the CBD docks by horse-drawn wagon.
   iv. Labor demand is a fixed 2,000 per square mile (no factor substitution).
   v. Labor supply is a fixed 500 per square mile (no consumer or factor substitution).
   vi. In the initial equilibrium, the wage is $10, the CBD is one mile long, and the SRD is four miles long.
   a. Draw the bid-rent functions consistent with the characteristics above.
   b. Show that the city is in equilibrium with a one-mile CBD and a four-mile SRD.
   Suppose that the intracity truck replaces the horse-drawn wagon. The partial-equilibrium effect of the truck is to increase the length of the CBD by 0.50 miles.
   c. Depict graphically the partial-equilibrium effect.
   d. What is the partial-equilibrium effect on the labor market: by how much does labor demand exceed labor supply?
   e. Will the wage increase or decrease?
   f. The table on page 238 lists the length of the CBD and the length of the city for different wages. What is the new equilibrium wage for the city?

Wage	CBD Length	SRD Length	City Length
10.0	1.50	4.0	5.50
11.0	1.42	4.3	5.75
12.0	1.33	4.7	6.00
13.0	1.25	5.0	6.25
14.0	1.17	5.3	6.50

REFERENCES AND ADDITIONAL READINGS

Theoretical General-Equilibrium Models

Brueckner, Jan K. "Labor Mobility and the Incidence of the Residential Property Tax." *Journal of Urban Economics* 10 (1982), pp. 173–82. Uses a theoretical general-equilibrium model to explore the effects of the residential property tax on the urban labor market.

Mills, Edwin S. "An Aggregative Model of Resource Allocation in a Metropolitan Area." *American Economic Review, Papers and Proceedings* (May 1967), pp. 197–210. Reprinted in *Readings in Urban Economics,* ed. Matthew Edel and Jerome Rothenberg. New York: Macmillan, 1972. The first general-equilibrium model of the urban economy.

Polinski, A. M., and D. L. Rubinfeld. "The Long Run Effects of a Residential Property Tax and Local Public Services." *Journal of Urban Economics* 5 (1978), pp. 241–62. A theoretical model that explores the interactions between a city's land markets and its labor market. Discusses the general-equilibrium effects of the property tax on a number of city characteristics.

Wheaton, William. "Monocentric Models of Urban Land Use: Contributions and Criticisms." In *Current Issues in Urban Economics,* ed. Peter Meiszkowski and Mahlon Straszheim. Baltimore: The Johns Hopkins Press, 1979. Discusses several renditions of the traditional monocentric model.

Computer Models of Urban Land Use

Birch, David, Reilly Atkinson, Sven Sundstrom, and Linda Stack. *Patterns of Urban Change.* Lexington, Mass.: Lexington Books, 1974. A simulation model that predicts the location patterns of housing and employment.

Mills, Edwin S. "Planning and Market Processes in Urban Models." In *Public and Urban Economics,* ed. Ronald Grieson. Lexington, Mass.: Lexington Books, 1976. A model that uses linear and nonlinear programming to allocate land to different activities.

Sullivan, Arthur M. "The General Equilibrium Effects of the Residential Property Tax: Incidence and Excess Burden." *Journal of Urban Economics* 18 (1985), pp. 235–50. Uses a computational model of a monocentric city to simulate the general-equilibrium effects of the residential property tax.

Computer Models of Residential Land Use

Arnott, R. J., and J. G. MacKinnon "The Effects of the Property Tax: A General Equilibrium Simulation." *Journal of Urban Economics* 4 (1977), pp. 389–407. Uses a general-equilibrium model of the residential sector to compute the effects of the property tax on residential land rent and land use.

Carlton, D. W. "The Spatial Effects of a Tax on Housing and Land." *Regional Science and Urban Economics* 11 (1981), pp. 509–27.

Grieson, Ronald. "The Economics of Property Taxes and Land Values: The Elasticity of Supply of Structures." *Journal of Urban Economics* 1 (1974), pp. 367–81.

Leroy, S. F. "Urban Land Rent and the Incidence of Property Taxes." *Journal of Urban Economics* 3 (1976), pp. 167–79.

Mills, Edwin S. *Studies in the Structure of the Urban Economy.* Baltimore: The Johns Hopkins Press, 1972. A general-equilibrium model is used to simulate the effects of transportation congestion on residential land rent and land use. The demand side of the urban labor market is not included in the model.

Solow, Robert M. "Congestion, Density, and the Use of Land in Transportation." *Swedish Journal of Economics* 74 (1972), pp. 161–73. Uses a general-equilibrium model of the residential sector to simulate the effects of congestion externalities on residential land use and the use of land for streets.

Solow, Robert M. "Congestion Costs and the Use of Land for Streets." *Bell Journal of Economics and Management Science* 4 (1973), pp. 602–18. Uses a general-equilibrium model of the residential sector to simulate the effects of congestion externalities on residential land use and the use of land for streets.

CHAPTER 10

Suburbanization of Population and Employment

A suburb is a place where a developer cuts down all the trees to build houses, and then names the streets after the trees.

Bill Vaughn

This chapter explains the decline of the traditional monocentric city and the rise of the modern multicentric city. In the monocentric city of the 19th century, most economic activity was concentrated in the central core area. The entire metropolitan area was oriented toward the employment and shopping opportunities in the central city. In the modern multicentric city, a large fraction of employment is in suburban areas, with much of the employment in suburban subcenters. People who live in metropolitan areas no longer rely on the central city for employment and shopping.

What are the facts on the suburbanization of employment and population? Figure 10–1 shows the distribution of population and employment between central cities and suburbs in 1948 and 1980. The percentage of the metropolitan population in central cities dropped from 64 percent in 1948 to 43 percent in 1980, and the percentage of manufacturing employment in central cities dropped from 67 percent to 43 percent. The losses in trade and service employment were even larger: the share of employment in central cities dropped from over three fourths in 1948 to less than one half in 1980.

It's important to note that part of the measured increase in suburbanization results from urban growth with fixed central-city boundaries. As an urban area grows, most growth occurs on the periphery. As the metropolitan area expands outward, an increasing share of population will live outside the fixed boundaries of the central city. If the suburban population is assumed to be the population outside the central-city border, growth causes suburbanization.

Table 10–1 provides a closer look at the history of suburbanization in eight large metropolitan areas. The table shows the growth rates of population and employment between 1940 and 1970. In the 1940s, the suburbs grew faster than the central cities, with the largest difference between them being in population growth rates. During the 1950s and 1960s, the central cities of the eight metropolitan areas decreased in population and employment, while the suburbs grew rapidly.

FIGURE 10–1 Percent of Metropolitan Population and Employment in Central Cities, 1948 and 1980

SOURCES: 1948 Data from John F. Kain, "The Distribution and Movement of Jobs and Industry," in *The Metropolitan Enigma*, ed. James Q. Wilson (Cambridge, Mass.: Harvard Univ. Press, 1968). 1980 Data from U.S. Bureau of Census, 1980 Census of Population.

Table 10–2 provides a closer look at the current distribution of employment between central cities and suburbs. The employment sectors are listed in decreasing order of importance. Service employment is divided almost equally between central cities and suburbs. The most suburbanized services are education, business services, and other professional services (legal and

TABLE 10–1 Annual Growth Rates for Employment and Population, Central Cities and Suburbs of Eight Metropolitan Areas, 1940–1970

	Central City			Suburbs		
Decade	*Population*	*Manufacturing*	*Retailing*	*Population*	*Manufacturing*	*Retailing*
1940s	0.8	10.39	4.74	4.19	12.16	8.4
1950s	−0.21	−1.13	−0.52	6.78	5.02	7.69
1960s	−0.54	−0.04	−1.33	3.35	4.21	7.48

Metropolitan areas: Baltimore, Boston, Cleveland, Denver, New Orleans, New York, Philadelphia, St. Louis.

SOURCE: Thomas Stanback and Richard Knight, *Suburbanization and the City* (Montclair, N.J.: Allanheld, Osmun and Company, 1976), p. 56.

TABLE 10–2   Distribution of Employment between Central City and Suburbs by Type of Employment, 1980

	Employment in SMSAs (thousands)	Employment in Central Cities (thousands)	Percent in Central Cities	Percent in Suburbs
Total	62,406	29,001	46	54
Services	19,008	9,411	50	50
Education	5,213	2,518	48	52
Health services	4,942	2,528	51	49
Business services	2,187	1,012	46	54
Other professional services	1,611	752	47	53
Personal services	1,563	822	53	47
Social services	1,461	781	53	47
Manufacturing	13,300	5,714	43	57
Retail trade	10,355	4,718	46	54
Transportation, public utilities	4,756	2,213	47	53
Finance, insurance, real estate (FIRE)	4,468	2,111	47	53
Public administration	3,515	1,731	49	51
Wholesale trade	2,922	1,272	44	56

SOURCE: U.S. Bureau of Census, 1980 Census of Population, General Social and Economic Characteristics, PC80-1-cl, Table 104.

engineering services). The only employment sectors with a majority of employment in the central cities are health services, personal services, and social services. For the other sectors, the similarities in the distributions of employment are striking: every sector has between 51 percent and 57 percent of its employment in the suburbs. The most suburbanized sectors are manufacturing (57 percent) and wholesale trade (56 percent), and the least suburbanized is public administration (51 percent). The remaining three sectors (retail trade, transportation and utilities, and FIRE) have between 53 percent and 54 percent of their employment in the suburbs.

SUBURBANIZATION OF MANUFACTURING

As shown in Figure 10–1, the share of metropolitan manufacturing employment in central cities decreased from about two thirds in 1948 to just over two fifths in 1980. Mills (1972) provides evidence that the suburbanization of manufacturing started long before 1948. What caused the suburbanization of manufacturing employment?

The Intracity Truck

Moses and Williamson (1972) explain how the intracity truck encouraged the suburbanization of manufacturing. In the monocentric city of the 19th and early 20th centuries, freight was shipped within cities by horse-drawn wagons. Starting about 1910, manufacturers switched from the horse-drawn wagon to the truck. The truck was both faster and cheaper than the horse-drawn wagon: around 1920, the truck was half as costly ($0.15 per ton per mile versus $0.33) and at least twice as fast. Once the intracity truck was introduced, its use spread rapidly: for example, the number of trucks in the city of Chicago increased from 800 in 1910 to 23,000 in 1920.

As explained in Chapter 8 (Land Use in the Monocentric City), the location decision of a manufacturing firm is determined by the outcome of a tug-of-war. On one side is the central export node, which pulls the firm toward the city center because freight costs are lower near the export node. On the other side is the suburb, which pulls the firm toward low-wage suburban locations. In the era of the horse-drawn wagon and the streetcar, the cost of moving freight was large relative to the cost of moving people, so manufacturers located in the city center. It was cheaper to ship the workers from the suburbs to the central-city factory than to ship the output from a suburban factory to the export node. The intracity truck decreased freight costs, weakening the pull toward the central export node, so the tug-of-war was more frequently won by the suburb. Although a suburban location was inefficient with the horse-drawn wagon, it was efficient with the truck.

How did the intracity truck affect the bid-rent function of manufacturers? The bid-rent function is negatively sloped because of freight costs. The truck decreased freight costs, so it decreased the slope of the bid-rent function. This is shown in Figure 10–2: the bid-rent function tilts upward, allowing manu-

FIGURE 10–2   The Partial-Equilibrium Effects of the Intracity Truck

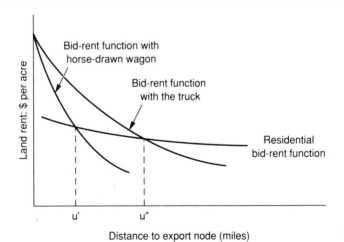

The replacement of the horse-drawn wagon with the truck decreased freight costs, decreasing the slope of the manufacturing bid-rent function. The radius of the manufacturing district increased from u' to u''.

facturers to outbid residents for suburban land. As a result, the radius of the manufacturing district increases from u' to u''.

Figure 10–2 shows the partial-equilibrium effects of the intracity truck. As explained in Chapter 9 (General-Equilibrium Land Use), the expansion of the manufacturing district will increase total labor demand, causing excess demand for labor and an increase in the city's wage. The increase in the wage will shift the residential bid-rent function upward (increasing the quantity of labor supplied as the size and the density of the residential district increase) and shift the manufacturing bid-rent function downward (decreasing the quantity of labor demanded as the size and the density of the manufacturing district decrease). These changes in the labor and land markets will continue until general equilibrium is restored.

The Intercity Truck

Two decades after the truck was first introduced, manufacturers started using the truck for intercity transport. Improvements in the truck made long-distance travel feasible, and the expansion of the intercity highway system facilitated intercity truck traffic. Eventually, the truck became competitive with the train and ship for intercity freight. As manufacturers switched from trains and ships to trucks, they were freed from their dependence on the railheads and ports in city centers and moved to sites near intercity highways, many of which were in the suburbs. The intercity truck decreased the freight costs associated with suburban production sites, allowing manufacturers to move closer to their suburban workers.

In the 1950s, the interstate highway system was developed. The highway system decreased the relative cost of shipping by truck, causing more manufacturers to switch their freight operations from ships and trains to trucks. More recently, cities have built circumferential highways (beltways) that are connected to the interstate highway system. Manufacturers locate close to the suburban beltways because they provide easy access to the interstate highway system.

Figure 10–3 shows the manufacturing bid-rent functions in a beltway city. The beltway circles the city at a distance of u' miles from the city center. R_r is the bid-rent function for firms that still use a central railroad terminal to export their output by train. R_t is the bid-rent function for firms that use the beltway to export their output by truck. Manufacturers are likely to outbid other land users for land near the suburban beltway.

The Automobile

The automobile contributed to the suburbanization of manufacturers. Consider a firm with a highly skilled work force: only 1 in 1,000 people has

FIGURE 10–3   Manufacturing Bid-Rent Function in the Beltway City

If the city has a central export node and an urban beltway at u', manufacturers can export by train or by truck. The manufacturing bid-rent function has peaks at the city center and u'.

the skills required to work for the firm. Suppose that the firm employs 100 people and is located in a streetcar city of 100,000. Where in the city will the firm locate? Because the firm draws laborers from the entire metropolitan area, it will locate at a point that is accessible to the entire urban area. In the hub-and-spoke streetcar city, the city center (the hub) is the most accessible location.

Where will such a firm locate in a modern automobile city? In the modern city, employees can easily drive their cars from their homes to any location in the urban area. Although the firm might still locate in the city center, it could also locate along an urban highway or a suburban beltway because such sites are accessible to residents throughout the metropolitan area. In general, the automobile loosened the firms' ties to the streetcar nodes in the core area, allowing the suburbanization of firms with specialized labor forces.

THE SUBURBANIZATION OF POPULATION

As shown in Figure 10–1, the share of metropolitan population living in central cities dropped from about two thirds in 1948 to just over two fifths in 1980. Mills (1972) provides evidence of suburbanization as far back as 1880. As explained in Chapter 8 (Land Use in the Monocentric City), the **density function** describes the relationship between population density and distance to the city center. Mills estimated the density functions for four metropolitan areas (Baltimore, Milwaukee, Philadelphia, and Rochester) between 1880 and 1963. The assumed relationship between density and distance is

$$D(u) = A \cdot e^{-g \cdot u} \qquad (10-1)$$

where

$D(u)$ is population density (people per square mile) u miles from the city center

A is a parameter estimated from the data

e is the base of the natural logarithm

g is a parameter to be estimated from the data

Table 10–3 shows the average density gradient (defined as the percentage change in population density per mile) for the four cities between 1880 and 1963. The gradient decreased over time, meaning that the population density function flattened out over time. The third column of the table uses the estimated density gradients to compute the percentage of the metropolitan population living within three miles of the city center. Between 1880 and 1963, the percentage dropped from 88 percent to 24 percent.

This section discusses five possible reasons for the suburbanization of population:

1. Increases in real income.
2. Decrease in commuting costs.

TABLE 10–3   Average Density Gradients for Four Metropolitan Areas, 1880–1963

Year	Average Gradient	Percent of Population within 3 Miles of City Center
1880	1.22	88%
1890	1.06	83
1900	0.96	78
1910	0.80	69
1920	0.69	61
1930	0.63	56
1940	0.59	53
1948	0.50	44
1954	0.40	34
1958	0.35	28
1963	0.31	24

Metropolitan Areas: Baltimore, Milwaukee, Philadelphia, Rochester

SOURCE: Edwin S. Mills, *Studies in the Structure of the Urban Economy* (Baltimore: The Johns Hopkins Press, 1972), p. 49.

3. Central-city problems: race, crime, taxes, education.
4. Following the firms to the suburbs.
5. Public policy.

Increases in Real Income

Did income growth contribute to the suburbanization of population? As explained in Chapter 8 (Land Use in the Monocentric City), an increase in income has an ambiguous effect on the relative attractiveness of the suburbs because it has two conflicting effects on the relative costs of a suburban location.

1. **Increase in commuting costs.** An increase in real income increases the amount of income sacrificed per minute of travel time: it increases the opportunity cost of commuting. Therefore, an increase in income increases the relative attractiveness of dwellings close to workplaces. For someone who works in the CBD, an increase in income increases the relative attractiveness of central-city housing. This is the opportunity-cost effect: an increase in income increases the opportunity cost of commuting, pulling households toward the central city.

2. **Increase in land consumption.** Because land is a normal good, an increase in income increases land consumption (increases lot size). Income growth increases the relative attractiveness of locations with low-priced land (the suburbs). A household that occupies a large lot is willing to commute long distances to occupy low-cost suburban land. This is the consumption effect: an increase in income increases lot size, pulling households toward inexpensive suburban land.

Given these conflicting effects, it is not possible to predict, on theoretical grounds, whether income growth will contribute to suburbanization. Income growth will cause suburbanization if the consumption effect dominates the opportunity-cost effect. This will occur if the income elasticity of demand for land exceeds the income elasticity of commuting costs. As explained in Chapter 8 (Land Use in the Monocentric City), the land elasticity is close to the commuting-cost elasticity, so the two effects almost cancel each other out. Therefore, it does not appear that income growth contributed very much to the suburbanization of population.

Decrease in Commuting Costs

Over the last 140 years, technological innovations have decreased the monetary and time costs of commuting. In the 1800s, the development of new transit systems decreased the costs of commuting from the suburbs to the central city. The most important innovations were the horse streetcar (developed in the 1850s) and the conventional streetcar (developed in the 1890s). In the last 60 years, improvements in the automobile and the intracity highway network have increased travel speeds and decreased the costs of personal commuting.

Chapter 9 (General-Equilibrium Land Use) explains the partial- and general-equilibrium effects of the streetcar. The same analysis applies to other changes that decrease commuting costs (e.g., the automobile). The sequence of changes in the urban economy is as follows:

1. The slope of the residential bid-rent function decreases (the function tilts upward), increasing total labor supply as the size and density of the residential district increase.
2. The increase in the supply of labor decreases the city's wage.
3. The decrease in the wage shifts the business bid-rent function upward, increasing the quantity of labor demanded as the size and the density of the CBD increase.
4. The decrease in the wage shifts the residential bid-rent function downward, decreasing the quantity of labor supplied as the size and the density of the residential district decrease.
5. The wage continues to drop until labor supply equals labor demand.

In equilibrium, the streetcar (or automobile) increases the population and land area of the monocentric city. The increase in the relative accessibility of suburban locations increases the share of population in the suburbs.

Figure 10–4 shows the bid-rent functions of a metropolitan area before and after a decrease in commuting costs. Suppose that the central city is a circular area with a radius of three miles: locations beyond three miles from the city center are considered suburban. Before the streetcar (or automobile), the CBD radius is one mile, the metropolitan radius is four miles, and a relatively small fraction of the population lives in the suburban area. The decrease in commuting costs shifts the bid-rent functions outward, increasing the radius of the metropolitan area. The fraction of the population living outside the central-city border increases for two reasons. First, the suburban area grows: the width of the suburban ring increases from one mile to three miles. Second, the price of suburban land increases, so the population density within the suburban area increases.

In the late 1800s and early 1900s, many landowners profited from the introduction of streetcars. In a number of cities, speculators bought large tracts of undeveloped land just outside the city's borders and patiently awaited the extension of streetcar service to their land. Other investors took a more active role. In Cleveland, the Von Sweringen brothers bought a large parcel of undeveloped land from the local society of Shakers. When the Cleveland State Railways refused to extend their streetcar service to the undeveloped area, the Von Sweringen brothers built their own streetcar line to the area that became known as Shaker Heights. The brothers' land, which was appraised at $240,000 in 1900, increased in value to $80 million by 1930.

FIGURE 10–4   Suburbanization Caused by a Decrease in Commuting Costs

A change in technology that decreases the unit cost of commuting (e.g., streetcar or automobile) causes suburbanization: a larger fraction of the population lives beyond the central city border (e.g., 3 miles from the city center).

Central-City Problems

Other theories of suburbanization focus on the negative locational attributes (disamenities) of central cities. The following factors may encourage some households to move from the central city to the suburbs:

1. **Old housing.** The deterioration of the central-city housing stock encourages households to move to the suburbs, where newer housing is available.

2. **Race and income.** Some households move to the suburbs to escape racial conflict; others move to avoid living near low-income households.

3. **Central-city fiscal problems.** Many central cities have relatively high taxes, encouraging households to move to low-tax suburbs. The causality goes both ways: fiscal problems cause suburbanization, and suburbanization contributes to central-city fiscal problems.

4. **Crime.** Most central cities have relatively high crime rates, encouraging households to move to the suburbs. The reasons for the relatively high central-city crime rates are discussed in Chapter 20 (Crime and Punishment).

5. **Education.** Suburban schools are typically superior to central-city schools, encouraging households to relocate in suburban school districts.

The reasons for the inferiority of central-city schools are explained in Chapter 19 (Education).

Empirical studies of the suburbanization process provide support for the theory that central-city problems encourage suburbanization. The empirical literature is reviewed by Wasylenko (1984). Bradbury, Downs, and Small (1982) tested various theories of suburbanization using a sample of 121 SMSAs for the period 1970–75. They found that a metropolitan area experienced relatively rapid suburbanization if its central city had (a) a relatively old housing stock, (b) relatively high taxes, and (c) a relatively large black population. Another factor in suburbanization was the number of suburban local governments: the larger the number of suburban governments to choose from, the more rapid the suburbanization. Frey (1979) found that metropolitan areas with high taxes, high crime rates, and low spending on education experienced relatively rapid suburbanization.

Following Firms to the Suburbs

As explained earlier in the chapter, the development of the truck and the building of circumferential highways shifted manufacturing employment from the central city to the suburbs. As explained later in the chapter, employment in retailing and office firms has also shifted to the suburbs. The suburbanization of employment contributed to the suburbanization of population because some workers followed their employers to the suburbs.

In the multicentric city, workers commute to jobs in suburban subcenters. Table 10–4 shows commuting patterns within metropolitan areas in 1980. In the United States, 40 percent of workers commute between suburbs, about twice the percentage who commute from the suburbs to the central city. In the Northeast, the number of workers commuting within the suburbs is over three times the number commuting from the suburbs to the central city.

TABLE 10–4 Commuting Patterns within Metropolitan Areas for Different Regions, 1980

Region	Percentage of Total Work Trips within SMSAs			
	Central City to Central City	Central City to Suburb	Suburb to Central City	Suburb to Suburb
Total United States	33.1	6.7	20.1	40.1
Northeast	32.2	4.7	15.3	47.8
North Central	30.7	7.0	20.3	49.0
South	36.1	6.1	23.7	40.1
West	32.4	9.3	19.9	38.4

SOURCE: U.S. Bureau of the Census. 1980 Census of Population: Journey to Work, Metropolitan Commuting Flows (Washington D.C.: Government Printing Office, 1984).

How does the suburbanization of employment affect the residential bid-rent function? Workers are willing to pay more for housing near suburban subcenters because such locations have relatively low commuting costs. In the modern multicentric city, the housing-price function has several peaks, one at the city center, and one for each suburban subcenter. The residential bid-rent function will look like the housing-price function, with a series of peaks, one at the city center and one for each subcenter.

Public Policy and Suburbanization

A number of public policies affect the intraurban location choices of households, encouraging households to live in the suburbs. Among the public policies to be discussed later in the book are the following.

1. **Subsidies for home ownership.** The federal tax code allows the deduction of interest paid on home loans, providing an implicit subsidy for home ownership. Federal mortgage programs (e.g., FHA guaranteed mortgages) also decrease the cost of ownership. These housing subsidies encourage suburbanization because they increase housing consumption and thus increase the relative attractiveness of the suburbs, where housing is relatively inexpensive.

2. **Commuting externalities.** Because commuting generates congestion externalities and pollution externalities, the marginal private cost of commuting is less than the marginal social cost. As explained in Chapter 17 (Autos and Highways), the internalization of these externalities would increase the relative cost of suburban living, thus encouraging commuters to live closer to their workplaces.

3. **Fragmented system of local government.** Some households move to the suburbs to flee central-city fiscal problems. The fragmented system of local government encourages suburbanization because it provides alternatives to the central-city government. Chapter 15 (Decision-Making in Local Government) explores the effects of metropolitan consolidation (a switch to a metropolitan government) on the location decisions of households. The issue is whether consolidation would discourage suburbanization.

4. **Highway construction.** The building of the highway system decreased commuting costs, increasing the relative attractiveness of the suburbs.

Gentrification: Return to the City?

In the 1970s and 1980s, the popular press publicized the renovation of central-city housing by wealthy households. To many people, the efforts of these households signalled a change in residential location patterns: it appeared that many high-income households were abandoning the suburban lifestyle to embrace an urban one. The process is labeled gentrification because the wealthy households often displaced poor households.

What are the facts on gentrification? The most important fact is that gentrification is a relatively small factor in the urban housing market. In most cities, the number of renovations is a small fraction of the number of dwellings abandoned. Kern (1984) describes the characteristics of renovators. The typical renovator is wealthy, young, highly educated, and either single or married with less than two children. Such households are attracted to central-city locations because the households (a) patronize cultural establishments in the central city, (b) have relatively high commuting costs, and (c) have relatively low demands for housing and land. Most of the renovators move from one part of the central city to the area being renovated, not from the suburbs back to the central city. These facts suggest that gentrification involves a relatively small number of households and does not signal a fundamental change in residential location patterns.

SUBURBANIZATION OF RETAILERS

As shown in Figure 10–1, the suburban share of retail employment increased from one fourth in 1948 to over one half in 1980. There are three principal reasons for the suburbanization of retailing.

Following the Consumers

The suburbanization of population caused some retail activity to move to the suburbs. According to the simple version of central-place theory (Chapter 5: How Many Cities?), a retailer locates at the center of its market area. If scale economies are small relative to per capita demand, market areas will be small. A retailer with a relatively small market area is likely to follow its consumers to the suburbs. In contrast, a retailer with relatively large scale economies would not necessarily follow its customers to the suburbs: if a single store serves the entire metropolitan area, the most accessible location might still be in the city center.

The more sophisticated version of central-place theory considers the effects of shopping externalities on location choices. If there are external benefits from one-stop shopping and comparison shopping, retailers may compromise on their ideal (central-place) locations to exploit these shopping externalities. The more sophisticated theory predicts that some retailers with relatively small scale economies will not follow their consumers to the suburbs, but will stay in the city center to exploit shopping externalities.

The Automobile

The automobile, which replaced the hub-and-spoke streetcar system, loosened the ties to the city center. Before the development of the automobile, a retailer with relatively large scale economies was tied to the CBD because that's where the streetcar delivered all the consumers. If shoppers use the auto instead of the streetcar, they can easily travel from their homes to any point in the metropolitan area, so even a suburban store can draw consumers from the entire metropolitan area. After the development of the automobile, retailers no longer had to locate in the city center to be accessible to consumers throughout the metropolitan area, and many retailers moved to the suburbs.

What about a retailer with moderate scale economies? In the hub-and-spoke streetcar city, travel from the suburb to the city center (along the spokes) was fast and inexpensive, while travel within the residential areas (between the spokes) was costly. A suburban store could not survive in this environment because intra-suburban travel costs were high: if the firm located its store at the geographical center of its suburban market area, few consumers would show up. If shoppers use the auto instead of the streetcar, however, travel costs within the residential area will be lower, and the store can locate at the center of its suburban market area.

Population Growth

The third reason for retail suburbanization is population growth. As the population of a metropolitan area increases, the total demand for retail goods increases, so the equilibrium number of stores will increase. Some of the new stores will locate in suburban areas.

This idea can be explained with a simple example of the market for wigs. Suppose that scale economies in wig retailing are exhausted with an output of 500 wigs per store per month and the per capita demand for wigs is 0.01 wigs per person per month. For example, a city with a population of 50,000 will have a total demand of 500 wigs per month, so it will support a single wig store in the city center. If the city grows to 500,000 and the demand for wigs *per capita* remains constant, the city will support 10 wig stores. If wig shopping is not subject to shopping externalities (comparison shopping and one-stop shopping), the wig stores will divide the metropolitan area into 10 market areas and each wig store will locate in the center of a market area. Some of the market areas will be centered in the suburbs, so some of the new wig stores will locate in the suburbs. If there are shopping externalities, wig stores may compromise on their ideal (central-place) locations, but some wig stores are still likely to locate in the suburbs.

SUBURBANIZATION OF OFFICE EMPLOYMENT

Before the early 1970s, most office firms were still located in the city center because they were dependent on face-to-face contact with other firms, and the CBD provided a central meeting place for workers from different firms. Although some office activities had moved to the suburbs by the early 1970s, these were typically the "back-office" operations of insurance firms and banks (operations involving paper processing rather than face-to-face contact). For such operations, a CBD location was unnecessary. For most office activities, the advantages of the CBD (opportunities for timely contact with other firms) outweighed the disadvantages (high wages and rents).

Table 10–5 shows the changes in central-city and suburban office employment during the 1970s for the United States and selected cities. Nationwide, suburban office employment grew over seven times faster than central-city office employment (115.9 percent versus 15 percent). According to Cervero (1986), the most rapid growth in suburban office employment occurred in medium-sized metropolitan areas (population between 250,000 and 1 million). In all five of the cities in the table, suburban office employment more than doubled. Other cities experienced rapid growth in suburban office employment: it increased by 112 percent in Des Moines, 126 percent in Norfolk-Virginia Beach, 154 percent in Memphis, and 166 percent in Tulsa.

The suburbanization of office employment was caused in part by several advances in communications technology (satellites, fiber-optics, and solid-state electronics) that have decreased the cost of transmitting data, voices, and pictures. The new technology has generated three new methods of communication: electronic mail, teleconferencing, and telecommuting. These new communication methods made some office firms less dependent on face-to-face contact and thus less likely to choose a CBD location.

TABLE 10–5   Growth in Office Employment, Central Cities and Suburbs, 1970–1980

	Percent Change in Office-Related Employment, 1970–1980	
	Central City	Suburban
All U.S. metropolitan areas	15.0	115.9
Atlanta	−16.4	109.2
Denver	19.4	110.8
Houston	60.4	120.6
Phoenix	59.5	124.7
Tampa	19.2	134.8

SOURCE: Robert Cervero, *Suburban Gridlock* (New Brunswick, N.J.: Center for Urban Policy Research, 1986), p. 27.

Electronic Mail

Office firms use electronic mail to send messages, documents, and data over computer lines. Electronic mail decreases the need for face-to-face contact because information can be sent over computer lines instead of being delivered by employees. Electronic mail allows the suburbanization of firms involved in the rapid turnaround of documents and reports.

To explain the effects of electronic mail, consider Abby, who runs an accounting firm. Abby gets 50 pages of data from her client (another firm) and condenses the information into an income statement. The client demands that the income statement be ready within 24 hours. In the absence of electronic mail, Abby would locate near her CBD customers to ensure the timely pickup of her client's data and the timely delivery of her income statement. The development of electronic mail allows Abby to move to the suburbs. Her inputs (the client data) and her output (the income statement) can be sent over telephone lines, so she can do her accounting in the suburbs, far from her CBD clients. Because Abby is not dependent on face-to-face contact, but on report-to-face contact, electronic mail allows her to escape the high wages and high rent of the CBD.

Electronic mail has caused the **decoupling** of some CBD firms. Many firms have split their operations into suburban activities and CBD activities. Suppose that a firm has a large number of accountants, whose only task is to condense information into reports: they compute bottom lines. The accountants do not interact with people outside the firm, but simply provide condensed information to the firm's executives, who then use the information in their interactions with other firms.

In the absence of electronic mail, the firm's accountants and executives will be in the same location to facilitate the rapid turnaround of information. Given the need for face-to-face interactions among the executives of different firms, the firm will locate in the CBD. If the accounting information can be transmitted electronically, however, the accounting division can move to the suburbs and the firm can send information between the suburban accountants and the CBD executives over telephone lines. Because electronic mail facilitates intrafirm communication, it allows the firm to decouple its operations, moving its support staff to the suburbs while keeping its executives in the CBD.

Teleconferencing

The second new communication method, the teleconference, is essentially a video meeting. The teleconference is superior to the telephone conference because it allows both visual and verbal communication. The teleconference decreases the need for face-to-face contact within and between firms:

instead of sending employees across town to another office, the firm can send them down the hall to the video room.

Because the video camera does not transmit as much information as a face-to-face encounter, the teleconference is not a perfect substitute for face-to-face contact. While the video camera focuses on one or two people in a meeting, a person who is physically present can watch everyone in the room, picking up verbal and nonverbal cues from a large number of people. In addition, the video camera cannot transmit tactile information. The tactile information provided by face-to-face encounters is sometimes useful: a firm, enthusiastic handshake sends a message than cannot be easily conveyed through a video camera.

Because the teleconference is not a perfect substitute for face-to-face contact, it is unlikely to cause substantial suburbanization of office firms. Most of the face-to-face contact that occurs in the CBD is between employees of different firms. The subtle interactions between people from different firms often require face-to-face contact. When people from different firms meet, one of the purposes of the meeting is to establish trust. Because it is easier to establish trust in a face-to-face encounter, a video meeting is inappropriate for some types of interactions.

The teleconference approach will be inefficient for firms whose interactions are infrequent and unpredictable. If two firms contact each other once or twice a year, it may be inefficient for each of them to incur the fixed costs of establishing a video link. If a firm has a small number of encounters with a large number of firms, it may be more efficient to locate near the other firms in the CBD and rely on face-to-face contact.

Telecommuting

Telecommuting refers to a system under which employees work at home and use personal computers and telephone lines to interact with people in the office. Telecommuting decreases commuting costs because it allows workers to travel to work fewer days per week. As a result, CBD office workers will demand a smaller premium to compensate for commuting costs, so the labor costs of CBD locations will decrease. Because telecommuting decreases the relative costs of a CBD location, it is likely to prevent some office firms from moving to the suburbs.

Summary—Suburban Subcenters

Many office firms have moved from the CBD to suburban subcenters. The firms moved to the suburbs because new communication methods provided cost-effective alternatives to face-to-face contact. Many of the firms clustered in subcenters to exploit agglomerative economies (localization economies) in the provision of business services. In an office cluster, the total demand for some intermediate inputs will be large enough to support external suppliers, who can produce the inputs at lower costs. For example, if there are scale economies in printing glossy brochures and reports, a large cluster of office firms can support a printing firm, allowing each firm to save on printing costs. The same principle applies to restaurants and hotels: one rule of thumb is that a 250-room hotel can be supported by 2.5 million square feet of office space.

In most urban areas, office employment occurs in both the CBD and suburban subcenters. The CBD contains activities for which face-to-face contact is still important (negotiation, design, marketing, and research); suburban subcenters contain activities for which electronic communication is a good substitute for face-to-face contact.

THE MODERN CITY—URBAN VILLAGES?

The monocentric, core-dominated city was gradually replaced with the multicentric, suburbanized city. The modern city, with its suburban subcenters, has been called a system of **urban villages.** The suburban subcenters have midrise office buildings, hotels, shopping malls, and entertainment facilities. People in the surrounding area travel to the subcenter for work, shopping, and play. In other words, the subcenter is the core of an urban village.

The best example of the urban-village phenomenon is the Los Angeles area. In recent years, the metropolitan area has experienced the development of sixteen subcenters, including Burbank, Irvine, Century City, the area around the Los Angeles Airport, Pasadena, and Westwood. As a result of the growth of these subcenters, the share of office employment in downtown Los Angeles decreased from 60 percent in 1960 to 34 percent in 1987. Many of the subcenters have established their own identities: the aerospace industry is concentrated near the airport, and the entertainment industry is moving to Burbank.

The Atlanta area is also experiencing the urban-village phenomenon. In 1980, most office employment in the Atlanta area was concentrated in the city center. By 1985, a large fraction of office employment was located in two subcenters along Interstate 285: the Perimeter Center north of the city center, and the Cumberland–Galleria Center northeast of the city center. Between 1980 and 1985, the city center gained 4.3 million square feet of office space, while the Perimeter Center gained 7.6 million square feet and the Cumberland–Galleria Center gained 10.6 million square feet. If the present trends continue, the office space in each of the subcenters will exceed the office space in the city center by 1990. Among the activities in the subcenters are corporate headquarters and business services. The city's most important accounting and law firms have offices in the two subcenters.

Most cities in the United States are experiencing the urban-village phenomenon. Subcenters are developing in the rapidly growing Sunbelt cities (e.g., Atlanta, Phoenix, Dallas, Houston, and San Francisco) as well as in cities with less rapid growth (e.g., St. Louis, Detroit, and Kansas City). Subcenters are also developing in the nation's oldest cities (e.g., New York, Boston, Chicago, and Baltimore). In most urban areas, the fraction of office and retail employment in suburban subcenters is increasing.

The development of urban villages is explained by the suburbanization of retailers and office firms. Retailers moved to the suburbs to be close to their customers and clustered in malls and subcenters to exploit shopping externalities. Some office firms moved to the suburbs to save on labor costs and clustered in subcenters to exploit agglomerative economies in the provision of business services, restaurants, and hotels.

SUMMARY

1. The truck contributed to the suburbanization of manufacturing employment for two reasons.
   a. The intracity truck replaced the horse-drawn wagon, decreasing freight costs relative to commuting costs. Some firms moved to the low-wage suburbs.
   b. The intercity truck replaced the boat and train for intercity freight, freeing manufacturers from central export nodes. Some firms moved closer to their suburban workers.

2. The automobile replaced the streetcar as the principal means of commuting, making locations throughout the urban area accessible to workers. Some firms with specialized labor forces moved to the suburbs.

3. Because the income elasticity of demand for housing is close to the income elasticity of commuting costs, it appears that income growth did not contribute very much to suburbanization.

4. The suburbanization of population occurred for five reasons.
   a. Decreases in commuting costs (from the streetcar and the auto) increased the accessibility of suburban locations.
   b. Central-city problems (racial tensions, deteriorating housing, high taxes, high crime rates, inferior schools) encouraged households to flee to the suburbs.
   c. The suburbanization of employment opportunities contributed to the suburbanization of population because some households followed the firms to the suburbs.
   d. The underpricing of commuting (congestion and pollution externalities) decreases the relative costs of suburban locations.
   e. The fragmented system of local government allows households to escape central-city housing problems.

5. In the modern multicentric city, workers commute to jobs in both the CBD and suburban subcenters. Workers are willing to pay more for housing near employment centers (everything else being equal), so the housing-price function has several peaks, one near the CBD and one near every

subcenter. Similarly, the residential bid-rent function has several peaks, one for the city center and one for each subcenter.

6. Retailers moved to the suburbs for three reasons.

   a. Some retailers followed consumers to the suburbs.

   b. The replacement of the streetcar with the automobile increased the accessibility of noncentral locations.

   c. Population growth increased the equilibrium number of retailers. Some of the new retailers located in the suburban areas.

7. The suburbanization of office firms is a fairly recent phenomenon. Advances in communication technology decreased the need for face-to-face contact, allowing some firms to move to the low-wage suburbs, and allowing others to decouple their operations into CBD activities and suburban activities.

8. The development of suburban subcenters (urban villages) is explained by the suburbanization and clustering of retailers and office firms. Retailers moved to the suburbs to be closer to their customers and clustered in subcenters to exploit shopping externalities. Office firms moved to the suburbs to be closer to their work forces and clustered to exploit agglomerative economies.

EXERCISES AND DISCUSSION QUESTIONS

1. Consider a manufacturing firm that exports some of its output by train (through a central export node) and the rest by truck (the truck exits the metropolitan area using a suburban beltway). Suppose that production costs are the same at all locations. The unit cost of transporting output inward (toward the central export node) is t_i, and the unit cost of transporting output outward (toward the beltway) is t_o. The volume of output going to the central export node is w_i, and the volume going to the beltway is w_o.

   a. Under what conditions will the firm's bid-rent function be positively sloped?

   b. How would your answer to (a) change if wages were lower in the suburbs?

2. Consider a city with a 10-mile radius. Two members of the Dink household work: Mr. Dink commutes to the city center $(u = 0)$, and Ms. Dink commutes to a suburban subcenter four miles due east of the city center. Depict the household's housing-price functions for two cases:

   a. The unit cost of commuting is the same in both directions (toward the city center and away from the city center).

   b. Because the bulk of workers commute to the city center, the unit cost of inward commuting (toward the city center in the morning rush hour and away from the center in the evening rush hour) exceeds the unit cost of outward commuting (away from the city center in the morning rush hour and toward the center in the evening rush hour).

3. Consider a city where a single store sells pet rocks, a good with a large income elasticity of demand. The store is located in the central shopping area of the city. Suppose that households in the city experience an increase in income.

   a. Assume that the number of pet-rock stores is fixed at one. How will the increase in income affect the store's bid rent for land at the city center?

   b. Is it realistic to assume that the number of pet-rock stores will remain constant?

   c. If the number of stores is allowed to vary, what will be the effect of the increase in income on the retail bid-rent functions?

4. Comment on the following statement:
   "Instead of investing money in traditional, radial mass-transit systems (hub-and-spoke systems), we should be investing in circumferential transit systems. We should build a circular transit system along the urban beltways."

5. The traditional core-dominated city was segregated in the sense that all employment was in one area (the core) and all residents lived in another area (the satellite or suburban area). The modern city is less segregated in the sense that employment is dispersed throughout the city, with some employment areas along beltways that pass through residential areas. Mr. Wizard recently made the following statement:

   If my assumptions are correct, the segregation of employment and residence will soon end. In less than 30 years, land use in the city will be completely integrated. Instead of having separate areas for manufacturing, offices, and housing, every area of the city will have manufacturers, office firms, and residents. I predict that manufacturers and office firms will leave the beltways and locate closer to their workers. Every manufacturing and office firm will locate in the middle of a residential area and will be surrounded by its work force. That's integration.

   a. Assume that Mr. Wizard's reasoning is correct. What are his assumptions? In other words, under what set of assumptions will manufacturers and office firms be surrounded by their workers?

   b. Are Mr. Wizard's assumptions realistic?

6. The development of the internal-combustion engine caused fundamental changes in urban land-use patterns. The transformation from the core-dominated city to the modern suburbanized city took only about 50 years. Given the rapid pace of technological change, it seems likely that some future innovation will cause another transformation of cities. Given your knowledge of science fiction and fact, describe an innovation that would cause fundamental changes in the spatial structure of cities.

REFERENCES AND ADDITIONAL READINGS

General Suburbanization

Chinitz, Benjamin. *City and Suburb*. Englewood Cliffs, N.J.: Prentice-Hall, 1965. A collection of essays on the causes and effects of suburbanization.

Greenwood, Michael. "Metropolitan Growth and the Intrametropolitan Location of Employment, Housing, and Labor Force." *The Review of Economics and Statistics* 62 (1980), pp. 491–501.

Harrison, B. *Employment and Economic Development*. Washington D.C.: Urban Institute, 1974. Discusses the interdependence of the location decisions of firms and households, showing that the suburbanization of residents contributed to the suburbanization of retailers and service establishments.

Mills, Edwin S. *Studies in the Structure of the Urban Economy*. Baltimore: The Johns Hopkins Press, 1972. Documents the suburbanization of employment and population between 1880 and 1963.

Stanback, Thomas, and Richard Knight. *Suburbanization and the City*. Montclair, N.J.: Allanheld, Osmun and Company, 1976. Documents suburbanization trends and discusses the implications for the metropolitan economy.

Central-City Problems and the Suburbanization of Population

Bradbury, Katharine L.; Anthony Downs; and Kenneth A. Small. *Urban Decline and the Future of American Cities*. Washington, D.C.: Brookings Institution, 1982. Discusses the reasons behind the decline of central cities.

Frey, W. H. "Central City White Flight: Racial and Non-Racial Causes." *American Sociological Review* 44 (1979), pp. 425–88. Tests various theories of suburbanization, focusing on the effects of central-city problems on suburbanization.

Grubb, W. N. "The Flight to the Suburbs of Population and Employment, 1960–1970." *Journal of Urban Economics* 11 (1982), pp. 348–67. Examines the role of taxes, education, and crime rates on suburbanization.

Kern, Clifford R. "Upper Income Residential Revival in the City." In *Research in Urban Economics* vol. 4, ed. Robert Ebel. Greenwich, Conn.: JAI Press, 1984. Discusses the facts on gentrification, including the characteristics of renovators.

Laska, Shirly, and Daphne Spain. *Back to the City: Issues in Neighborhood Renovation*. New York: Pergamon Press, 1980. Case studies of gentrification.

Reschovsky, A. "Residential Choice and the Local Public Sector: An Alternative Test of the Tiebout Hypothesis." *Journal of Urban Economics* 6 (1979), pp. 501–20. Examines the role of taxes, local expenditures, and school quality on suburbanization.

Wasylenko, Michael J. "Disamenities, Local Taxation, and the Intrametropolitan Location of Households and Firms." In *Research in Urban Economics* vol. 4, ed. Robert Ebel. Greenwich, Conn.: JAI Press, 1984. Reviews the empirical evidence concerning the effects of income on location.

Suburbanization of Manufacturers

Erickson, R., and M. Wasylenko. "Firm Location and Site Selection in Suburban Municipalities." *Journal of Urban Economics* 8 (1980), pp. 69–85. Examines the influences of labor markets, land prices, transportation facilities, fiscal variables, and agglomeration economies on the intrametropolitan location decisions of firms.

Hoover, Edgar M., and Raymond Vernon. *Anatomy of a Metropolis.* Cambridge, Mass.: Harvard Univ. Press, 1959. Discusses the suburbanization of manufacturers in the New York area.

Kitigawa, Evylyn M., and Donald Bogue. *Suburbanization of Manufacturing Activity within Standard Statistical Metropolitan Areas.* Oxford, Ohio: Scripps Foundation, 1955. Discusses the suburbanization of manufacturing before World War II.

Moses, Leon, and Harold Williamson. "The Location of Economic Activity in Cities." In *Readings in Urban Economics,* ed. Matthew Edel and Jerome Rothenberg. New York: Macmillan, 1972. Discusses the role of the intraurban and interurban truck on the suburbanization of manufacturing.

Struyk, Raymond. "Evidence on the Locational Activity of Manufacturing Industries in Metropolitan Areas." *Land Economics* 48 (1972), pp. 377–82.

Wasylenko, Michael J. "Disamenities, Local Taxation, and the Intrametropolitan Location of Households and Firms." In *Research in Urban Economics* vol. 4, ed. Robert Ebel. Greenwich, Conn.: JAI Press, 1984. Reviews the evidence concerning the intrametropolitan location choices of firms.

Suburbanization of Office Firms and Services

Cervero, Robert. *Suburban Gridlock.* New Brunswick, N.J.: Center for Urban Policy Research, 1986. Discusses the recent growth in office employment and its implications for transportation planning.

Clapp, J. M. "Endogenous Centers: A Simple Departure from the NUE Model." *Papers of the Regional Science Association* 54 (1984), pp. 13–24. Describes the process through which contacts between firms causes the development of a CBD and suburban subcenters.

Hughes, James W., and George Sternlieb. "The Suburban Growth Corridor." In *America's New Market Geography,* ed. George Sternlieb and James W. Hughes. New Brunswick, N.J.: Center for Urban Policy Research, 1988. Discusses the market forces behind the recent office construction boom in suburbs.

Mills, Edwin S. "Service Sector Suburbanization." In *America's New Market Geography,* ed. George Sternlieb and James W. Hughes. New Brunswick, N.J.: Center for Urban Policy Research, 1988. Discusses the recent trends in the suburbanization of services and compares the spatial distributions of employment and residences.

Effects of Beltways

Bone, A. J., and Martin Wohl. *Economic Impact Study: Massachusetts' Route 128.* Cambridge, Mass.: MIT Transportation Engineering Division, 1958.

Bureau of Population and Economic Research. *The Socio-Economic Impact of the Capital*

Beltway on Northern Virginia. Charlottesville, Va.: Bureau of Population and Economic Research, University of Virginia, 1968. Discusses the effects of beltways in the Washington, D.C. metropolitan area.

Levitan, Don. "Massachusetts Route 128: A Nonemulative Enigma." *Transportation Research Record* #583 (1976), pp. 45–54. Discusses the effects of Boston's beltway.

Mills, Florence. "Effects of Beltways on the Location of Residences and Selected Workplaces." *Transportation Research Record* #812 (1981), pp. 26–33. Compares changes in population and employment in metropolitan areas with and without beltways. Concludes that beltways did not have a significant effect on central-city employment.

Payne-Maxie Consultants. *The Land Use and Urban Development Impacts of Beltways: Case Studies.* Washington, D.C.: U.S. Department of Transportation and U.S. Department of Housing and Urban Development, 1980. Discusses the effects of beltways in eight different metropolitan areas.

Telecommunications and Land Use

Chinitz, Benjamin. "The Influence of Communication and Data Processing Technology on Urban Form." In *Research in Urban Economics* vol. 4, ed. Robert Ebel. Greenwich, Conn.: JAI Press, 1984, pp. 67–77. Discusses the effects of new communications technology on the location decisions of office firms.

Moss, Mitchell. "Telecommunications: Shaping the Future." In *America's New Market Geography,* ed. George Sternlieb and James W. Hughes. New Brunswick, N.J.: Center for Urban Policy Research, 1988. Discusses the effects of new communication technologies on location patterns.

Salomon, I. "Telecommunications and Travel Relationships: A Review." *Transportation Research A* 20A (1986), pp. 223–38. Discusses the effects of telecommunications technology on location patterns.

Future Location Patterns

Anas, Alex, and Leon Moses. "Transportation and Land Use in the Mature Metropolis." In *The Mature Metropolis,* ed. Charles L. Leven. Lexington, Mass.: Lexington Books, 1978.

Macrae, Norman. "Tomorrow's Agglomeration Economies." In *The Mature Metropolis,* ed. Charles Leven. Lexington, Mass.: Lexington Books, 1978. Predicts future development patterns based on predictions about agglomeration economies.

CHAPTER 11

Land-Use Controls and Zoning

That's not a regular rule; you invented it just now.

Lewis Carroll in *Alice in Wonderland*

This chapter discusses the government's role in the urban land market. The analysis of chapters 7 through 10 assumes that land is allocated to the highest bidder. In other words, it assumes that the government is not involved in the urban land market. In fact, local governments use a number of policies to control land use. Most cities have zoning plans that limit the location choices of most activities. Some cities use zoning and other land-use controls to limit population growth.

This chapter discusses various types of land-use controls and addresses three basic questions. First, why do cities control land use? Second, what are the market effects of land-use controls? Third, what are the legal foundations for zoning and other land-use controls?

CONTROLLING POPULATION GROWTH

Some local governments use land-use policies to limit population growth. The purpose of a growth-control policy is to control the undesirable side effects of growth (e.g., pollution, congestion, crime, the loss of a small-town atmosphere). This section discusses two growth-control policies: urban service boundaries and limits on the number of building permits.

Urban Service Boundary

One way to control population growth is to limit the land area of the city. If a city refuses to extend urban services (e.g., sewers, roads, schools, parks) beyond an **urban service boundary**, it limits growth to the area within the boundary.

Figure 11–1 shows the equilibrium land-use pattern in a monocentric city. The residential bid-rent function intersects the agricultural bid-rent function at a distance of eight miles from the city center, so the radius of the city is eight miles. An implicit assumption of this model is that the city government provides urban services to all areas where city residents outbid farmers (out to a distance of eight miles from the city center). The business bid-rent function intersects the residential bid-rent function at a distance of two miles from the city center, so the equilibrium radius of the CBD is two miles.

FIGURE 11–1   Partial-Equilibrium Effect of an Urban Service Boundary

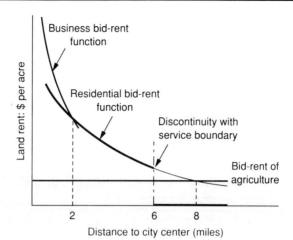

In the market equilibrium, the CBD radius is 2 miles and the city radius is 8 miles. An urban service boundary prevents residential development beyond 6 miles, so the residential bid-rent drops to zero between 6 and 8 miles from the city center. This is the partial-equilibrium effect of the service boundary.

Suppose that the city refuses to extend urban services beyond six miles from the city center. Unless residents can provide their own roads, sewage systems, and schools, residential development outside the boundary will be impossible. Therefore, the residential bid rent will fall to zero at a distance of six miles from the city center. This is shown in Figure 11–1 as a discontinuity in the residential bid-rent function at a distance of six miles. This is the partial-equilibrium effect of the urban service boundary: land beyond $u = 6$ is rendered uninhabitable, so the market rent on land outside the boundary drops to the agricultural bid rent.

What are the general-equilibrium effects of the urban service boundary? The service boundary decreases the size of the residential district, so it decreases the city's total labor supply. The excess demand for labor will increase the city's wage. The increase in the wage increases the relative attractiveness of the city, causing migration that bids up the prices of housing and land. The quantity of labor supplied will increase for two reasons:

1. **Increased population density.** The increases in housing and land prices will decrease lot sizes: households will occupy smaller dwellings, and housing producers will use less land per unit of housing. The number of households (and workers) per acre will increase.

2. **Increased residential territory.** The upward shift of the residential bid-rent function allows households to outbid businesses for land

near the CBD border. Therefore, the residential district will expand inward toward the city center.

The increase in the wage also affects the market for business land. Production costs will increase, decreasing the relative attractiveness of the city as a production site. The demand for CBD land will decrease, causing a downward shift of the business bid-rent function. The quantity of labor demanded will decrease for two reasons:

1. **Decreased employment density.** The increase in the relative price of labor will cause factor substitution (firms will substitute capital and land for labor) that decreases the city's employment density (the number of laborers per acre).

2. **Decreased business territory.** The CBD will shrink as businesses lose land to the residential district.

The city's wage will continue to rise until general equilibrium (labor supply equal to labor demand) is restored.

Figure 11–2 shows the new equilibrium allocation of land. The CBD radius is 1.5 miles (down from 2 miles), and the city radius is 6 miles (the radius dictated by the urban service boundary). The service boundary has different effects in the city's two land markets. In the residential district, the service

FIGURE 11–2   General-Equilibrium Effect of an Urban Service Boundary

The urban service boundary decreases the supply of labor, increasing the city's wage. The increase in the wage shifts the residential bid-rent function upward (increasing the quantity of labor supplied) and shifts the business bid-rent function downward (decreasing the quantity of labor demanded). General equilibrium is restored with a smaller, less dense CBD, and a more dense residential district.

boundary increases the prices of housing and land, so it increases population density. In contrast, the service boundary decreases both land rent and employment density in the CBD.

Who gains and who loses from the service boundary? People who own land outside the service boundary lose: for land between $u = 6$ and $u = 8$, the market rent drops to the agricultural bid rent, decreasing the market value of land. People who own residential land within the service boundary win: the increase in the wage and the resulting increased demand for residential land bids up the price of land within the boundary. People who own land within the CBD lose: the increase in the wage and the resulting decrease in the demand for CBD land decreases the price of business land.

Building Permits

Some cities control residential growth by limiting the number of building permits issued. By limiting the number of new dwellings built per year, a city can control its growth rate.

Consider a city which initially has no limit on the number of building permits issued. Figure 11–3 shows the city's market for new housing: the supply curve AG intersects the demand curve at point F, generating an equilibrium quantity of 100 houses per year and an equilibrium price of $50,000 per house. To accommodate the housing market, the city will issue 100 free permits per year, which will be used to build houses with a market value of $50,000. If the housing market is perfectly competitive, developers will make zero economic profits (normal accounting profits), meaning that the cost of producing each house (the sum of land, labor, and capital costs) will be $50,000.

Suppose that the city limits the number of building permits to 60 per year. The new supply curve for housing is ACE: the maximum number of new houses is 60, so the supply curve becomes vertical at 60 dwellings. The new supply curve intersects the demand curve at an equilibrium price of $70,000. In other words, the permit policy increases the equilibrium price of housing by $20,000.

The permit policy also decreases the costs of producing housing. The permit policy decreases the number of houses built, so it decreases the demand for land. For example, if houses are built on quarter-acre lots, the permit policy will decrease the demand for land from 25 acres per year (100 times 0.25) to 15 acres per year. The decrease in the demand for land will decrease the market price of land, decreasing the costs of producing housing. This is shown by the housing-supply curve: if 100 houses are built, the production cost is $50,000 per house; if only 60 houses are built, the cost drops to $40,000 per house. Because the permit policy decreases the number of houses built, it decreases the price of land, allowing developers to build houses at a lower cost.

The city must decide how to allocate the 60 building permits among its developers. One option is to auction the permits to the highest bidders. What

FIGURE 11–3   Market Effects of Building Permits

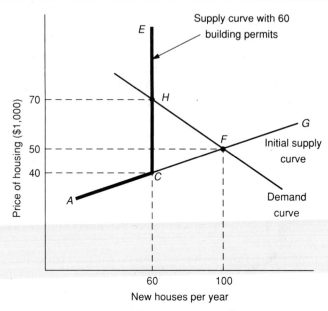

New houses per year

If the city decreases the supply of building permits from 100 to 60, the supply curve for housing shifts from *AG* to *ACE*. The new equilibrium is point *H* (price of housing = $70,000). Point *C* shows the cost of producing 60 houses ($40,000 per house). The difference between the price and the cost per house is the equilibrium price of the building permit ($30,000).

is the monetary value of a building permit? A person with a building permit can make a profit equal to the difference between the market price of a house ($70,000) and the cost of producing the house ($40,000), so the monetary value of a permit is $30,000. If the city auctions the building permits, the market price would be $30,000.

Some cities allocate their building permits to development projects that promote their development objectives. If the city is interested in high-density housing, it could allocate the permits to a high-density housing project. Alternatively, the city could allocate the permits to a project in an area targeted for development. Many cities use sophisticated point systems to rate and rank alternative development proposals. Among the criteria for which points are assigned are various design features (the exterior appearance of the dwellings, the amount of open space within the project), density, and the proximity of the project to public infrastructure (roads, schools, sewer lines).

LAND-USE ZONING—TYPES AND MARKET EFFECTS

A zoning plan designates a set of admissible land uses for each plot of land in a city. In theory, the purpose of zoning is to promote public health, safety, and welfare. Zoning is often used to separate incompatible land uses.

The first zoning ordinances were used by the wealthy to exclude the poor. In the 1880s, the city of San Francisco passed laws that restricted its Chinese population to certain areas. When this explicit segregation was declared unconstitutional, the city passed a zoning law that banned laundries from certain neighborhoods. The zoning law did not violate the constitution because it promoted public welfare by keeping an undesirable land use (laundries) out of some residential areas. Because the Chinese operated most of the city's laundries, the zoning law provided a legal means of segregation. In New York City in 1916, the rapid growth of employment in offices and garment factories increased the number of low-wage women on the streets of midtown Manhattan. The owners of exclusive Fifth Avenue stores feared that the increased traffic of poor women would be bad for business, so they proposed zoning laws that limited building sizes and heights. The law limited the growth of office buildings and garment factories, so it decreased the number of clerical and garment workers walking along Fifth Avenue. The zoning law was declared constitutional because it also promoted public welfare by controlling the nuisances created by tall buildings (shadows, blocked light, disruption of views).

There are many types of zoning, each of which has at least one purpose. This section divides zoning into three types. The purpose of **nuisance zoning** is to separate incompatible land uses. Cities use **fiscal zoning** to exclude households that would not pay their share of the costs of local government. **Design zoning** is a sort of macro-architecture: planners arrange activities within the city to promote the efficient use of the city's infrastructure.

Nuisance Zoning

Nuisance zoning (or externality zoning) is the practice of separating land uses that are considered incompatible. The classic example is the glue factory: one way of dealing with the air pollution generated by the glue factory is to move the factory into an industrial zone, far from residential areas. Similarly, the externalities generated by retailers (traffic congestion and noise) can be controlled by establishing a retail zone. High-density housing also generates externalities: apartment buildings cause traffic and parking problems, and also block views and light. These externalities can be controlled by establishing a zone for high-density housing.

Industrial Nuisances.   Industrial firms generate several types of externalities, including noise, glare, dust, odor, vibration, and smoke. Zoning separates residential and industrial land uses, reducing the exposure to air and noise pollution by isolating the polluters. Zoning is appealing as an environmental policy because of its simplicity: the easiest way to limit exposure to pollution is to separate polluters from their potential victims. The problem with zoning as an environmental policy is that zoning does not reduce the total amount of pollution; it just moves it around. Because zoning does not provide firms with the incentive to decrease pollution, it is less effective than other environmental policies.

Alternative to Industrial Zoning—Spatial Effluent Fees. When economists hear the word *pollution*, their knee-jerk response is "effluent fees." An effluent fee is a tax on pollution. For efficiency purposes, the fee should be set equal to the marginal external cost of pollution, that is, the cost to society of an additional unit of pollution. For example, if one ton of sulfur dioxide generates an external cost of $2, the effluent fee should be $2 per ton. The effluent fee "internalizes" the pollution externality, forcing polluters to pay for pollution in the same way that they pay for labor, capital, and raw materials. The firm has an incentive to decrease its pollution because by doing so, it decreases its effluent tax bill. If the effluent fee equals the marginal external cost of pollution, firms will generate the optimum level of pollution.

In theory, a system of effluent fees would generate both the optimum level of pollution and the optimum spatial distribution of pollution. If the effluent fee varies across space, a firm would pay a higher effluent fee for pollution generated near sensitive areas (e.g., residential areas). For example, the effluent fee might be $2 per ton of pollution if the firm is 10 miles from the residential area and $5 per ton if the firm is 4 miles from the residential area. Under a system of spatial effluent fees, the firm would base both its production decisions and its location decision on effluent fees. If the effluent fees are set equal to the marginal external cost of pollution at different locations, the firm would choose both the optimum location and the optimum level of pollution.

The differences between zoning and effluent fees can be explained with a simple model of a polluted city. Consider a rectangular city with the following characteristics:

1. Residents live in the western part of the city and commute eastward to a polluting steel mill.
2. The longer the distance between the residential area and the mill, the higher the wage: workers are compensated for commuting costs in the form of higher wages. The firm's total labor cost equals the wage ($ per worker) times the total quantity of labor.
3. The longer the distance between the mill and the residential area, the lower the effluent fee. The firm's total pollution cost equals the effluent fee ($ per ton) times the amount of pollution.
4. The city starts with an industrial zoning policy under which the steel mill is located 10 miles from the residential area.

Figure 11–4 shows the total costs of producing steel at different locations. The positively sloped curve shows labor costs, which increase from $20 for a location adjacent to the residential district to $63 in the industrial zone (10 miles from the residential area). The negatively sloped curve shows pollution costs which decrease from $60 at a location adjacent to the residential district to $5 in the industrial zone. The variation in pollution costs reflects the variation in the effluent fee. The U-shaped curve shows total costs, the sum of labor costs and pollution costs, which decrease from $80 for a location adjacent to the residential district to $53 for a location 4.2 miles from the residential area and then increase to $68 in the industrial zone.

Suppose the firm starts in the industrial zone. As the firm moves toward the residential district, there are benefits and costs. On the benefit side, labor costs decrease as the firm moves closer to its work force. On the cost side, the effluent fee increases because the firm's pollution affects more people, so pollution costs increase. Given the shapes of the labor-cost and pollution-cost curves, total cost is minimized at a location 4.2 miles from the residential district. If the city switches from a zoning policy to an effluent-fee policy, the steel producer would move from the industrial zone to a location 4.2 miles from the residential district, decreasing its total costs from $68 to $53.

FIGURE 11–4   Spatial Effluent Fees and Optimum Location

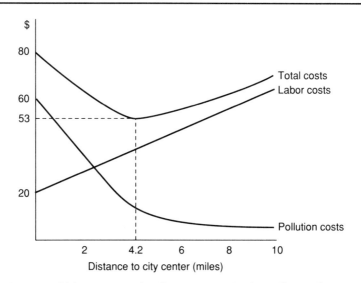

Total costs are the sum of labor costs and pollution costs. As the polluting firm moves toward the residential district, pollution costs increase (more residents are affected by pollution, so the effluent fee increases), but labor costs decrease (commuting distances decrease, so the wage decreases). Total costs are minimized at a distance of 4.2 miles from the residential area.

The effluent-fee policy is more efficient than the zoning policy for two reasons. First, the effluent policy allows the firm to choose the location that minimizes production costs. From the social perspective, the new location is more efficient because the decrease in commuting costs (as indicated by the labor-cost curve) exceeds the increase in pollution costs (as indicated by the pollution-cost curve). Second, the effluent-fee policy forces the firm to pay for pollution, so pollution decreases to its optimum level.

Will all the polluting firms leave the industrial zone when the city switches from industrial zoning to effluent fees? A firm will stay in the industrial zone if its pollution-cost curve is steeper than its labor-cost curve. In this case, a move toward the residential district increases pollution costs by more than it decreases labor costs, so total production costs increase. Nonetheless, the effluent-fee policy is still more efficient than industrial zoning because the effluent-fee policy decreases pollution to its optimum level.

Why do cities use zoning instead of effluent fees to control industrial pollution? There are two principal reasons. First, industrial zoning is simple compared to a system of spatial effluent fees. To set the effluent fees, the city would have to estimate the marginal external cost of pollution for different locations in the city; to collect the fees, the city would have to monitor the polluting firms. It would certainly be easier to put all the polluters in an industrial zone. Second, a switch from zoning to effluent fees may increase pollution in some neighborhoods. Although the factory will produce less pollution under the effluent-fee policy, if the factory locates closer to the residential district, some neighborhoods may become more polluted. The fact that air pollution is at its optimum level is small consolation to those who breathe the dirty air. The switch to effluent fees would improve efficiency and generate a net gain for society, so it would be possible, in principle, to compensate those who breathe dirtier air. In fact, compensation is rarely attempted, so local opposition to effluent fees remains.

Performance Zoning.   Traditional zoning is based on a zoning map and a land-use list. The zoning map shows the zoning classification for each plot of land in the city, and the list shows the admissible land uses for each zoning classification. If an activity is designated *heavy industry*, every firm involved in this activity must locate in the heavy-industry zone, regardless of how much noise, odor, or smoke the individual firms actually generate. The alternative to traditional zoning is **performance zoning**, under which the city sets performance standards for each zone. For industrial uses, performance standards typically set upper limits on the amount of noise, glare, odor, vibration, gas, and smoke to be emitted by firms. Performance zoning is a sort of compromise between traditional zoning and effluent fees: although performance zoning does not force firms to pay for pollution, it does encourage abatement by giving cleaner firms more location options.

Retail Nuisances.   Retailers generate a number of externalities that affect nearby residents. The traffic generated by retailers causes congestion, noise, and parking problems. The establishment of retail zones decreases the exposure to these externalities. For example, zoning prevents the invasion of quiet residential neighborhoods by shoppers and delivery trucks.

The alternative to traditional zoning is performance zoning. Under performance zoning, the city allows retailers in a particular zone as long as they satisfy performance standards for parking, traffic, and noise. For each area, the city may specify a minimum number of parking places, a minimum rate of traffic flow, and a maximum noise level. These performance standards force commercial developments to provide off-street parking to control parking problems, street improvements to control traffic problems, and berms and landscaping to control noise problems. Performance zoning allows the mixing of commercial and residential land uses because retailers can take steps that shield residents from the undesirable effects of commercial development.

Residential Nuisances.   Most residential externalities are generated by high-density housing. Suppose that a developer builds a four-story apartment complex in a neighborhood with single-family homes. The apartment complex will increase traffic volume, causing congestion and noise, and increase the demand for on-street parking, causing a shortage of parking spaces. In addition, the tall apartment building is likely to deprive neighbors of scenic views and sunlight.

Under traditional zoning, the apartment building would be excluded from the low-density neighborhood. Conventional zoning shields the residents of single-family homes from externalities by excluding high-density housing.

The alternative to conventional zoning is performance zoning. Under a performance-based zoning policy, the apartment complex would be allowed if the developer took the following steps.

1. **Off-street parking.** The developer provides enough off-street parking to prevent parking problems.

2. **Street improvements.** The developer pays for street improvements that prevent congestion problems.

3. **Building design.** The building is designed to prevent loss of views and sunlight. The developer uses landscaping to establish a buffer between the apartment building and the single-family houses.

The idea behind performance zoning is that the apartment building should be judged on the basis of its actual effects on the neighborhood, not on the simple fact that it is high-density housing. If a high-density project does not generate externalities, it would be allowed in the neighborhood.

Income-Related Residential Externalities.   Three types of residential externalities encourage wealthy households to exclude poor ones.

1. **Education.** As explained in Chapter 19 (Education), the students from poor families have low achievement levels and pull down the

achievement levels of other students. By excluding poor households, wealthy households may improve the quality of neighborhood schools.

2. **Crime.** As explained in Chapter 20 (Crime and Punishment), crime is more prevalent among the poor because they have lower opportunity costs of crime (fewer legal opportunities) and punishment (lower opportunity cost of prison time). By excluding poor households, wealthy households may decrease the neighborhood crime rate.

3. **Housing externalities.** Housing is a normal good, so the poor consume less housing. In addition to consuming fewer square feet of living space, they also spend less on upkeep and the external appearance of their houses and lots. Because the market value of a particular house depends on the external appearance of neighboring houses, property values are typically lower in neighborhoods with a large number of poor households. By excluding poor households, wealthy households may keep their property values high.

Fiscal Zoning

The second type of zoning occurs because local governments finance public services with the property tax. Under **fiscal zoning**, a city excludes households that would impose fiscal burdens on local government. Suppose that a household consumes $3,000 worth of local services but pays only $2,000 in local property taxes. Such a household generates a fiscal burden because its tax contribution is less than the costs of its local public services. Fiscal burdens are sometimes generated by *(a)* households living in high-density housing, *(b)* households living in the fringe areas of the city, and *(c)* new commercial and industrial development.

High-Density Housing.   As explained in Chapter 16 (Local Government Revenue), the most important source of local revenue is the property tax. Because a household's tax liability increases with its housing consumption, a household in a small house or apartment pays a relatively small amount in taxes, and is therefore more likely to impose a fiscal burden on local government. Local governments exclude households by zoning land for low-density (high-value) housing.

Large-lot zoning establishes a minimum lot size for residential development. Land and housing are complementary goods, so the city can use restrictions on lot size to indirectly establish a minimum house value. Suppose that a city breaks even on a house worth $125,000: the tax liability of such a house equals the cost of supplying public services to the household living in the house. According to one rule of thumb, the market value of land is about 20 percent of the total property value (the value of the structure and the land). If the price of land is $50,000 per acre, a half-acre lot ($25,000 worth of land) will produce a house worth $125,000 (five times $25,000). A minimum lot size of one half of an acre will ensure that the government breaks even on all new houses.

How does large-lot zoning affect the urban land market? Consider an unzoned city with 120 acres of undeveloped land. As shown in Figure 11–5, the market is in equilibrium with points A and B, and the equilibrium price of land is $20,000 per acre. At this price, the total demand for land equals the fixed supply, and land is divided equally between single-family homes (SFH) and apartments (60 acres in each).

Suppose that the city passes a zoning ordinance that limits apartment buildings to a total of 40 acres of land. What happens to the equilibrium price of land? In Figure 11–5, the city moves up the demand curve for apartment land from point B to point E: since only 40 acres are available for apartments, developers are willing to pay $40,000 per acre for apartment land. At the same time, the city moves down the other demand curve from point A to point C: there are now 80 acres available for single-family homes, and the surplus of land decreases the price from $20,000 to $10,000.

This example shows the effects of large-lot zoning on landowners and housing consumers. Zoning makes land for apartments a relatively scarce commodity, so the owners of apartment land gain from large-lot zoning. In contrast, zoning makes land for single-family homes a more plentiful commodity, so the owners of land destined for single-family homes lose. What about housing consumers? The increase in the cost of apartment land in-

FIGURE 11–5   Large-Lot Zoning and the Price of Land

A fixed amount of land (120 acres) is divided between single-family homes (SFH) and apartments. In the absence of large-lot zoning, the price of land is $20,000 per acre, and land is divided equally between apartments and homes (60 acres for each type of housing, i.e., points A and B). If apartment acreage is limited to 40 acres (point E), 80 acres are left for single-family homes (point C). The price of apartment land rises to $40,000, and the price of land of single-family homes drops to $10,000.

creases the costs of apartments, so apartment dwellers lose. In constrast, the land cost of single-family homes decreases, so home buyers gain.

Exclusionary and Inclusionary Zoning.   Large-lot zoning is often labeled **exclusionary zoning** because it excludes low-income households. The exclusion is both direct and indirect. In the example shown in Figure 11–5, large-lot zoning prevented the construction of 20 acres of apartments. Because low-income households are more likely to occupy apartments, the decrease in the number of apartment buildings decreases the number of low-income residents in the city. In addition, the zoning policy increases the price of apartments, so it excludes low-income households indirectly: the apartments that are built will be too expensive for many poor households.

In response to the exclusion problem, many cities have developed **inclusionary zoning** policies. Under an inclusionary housing program, the local government forces local developers to build dwellings for low-income households. The dwellings are typically sold to low-income households for less than the costs of construction. By providing subsidized dwellings for low-income residents, the local community partly offsets the exclusionary effects of fiscal zoning. Many of the dwellings built for inclusionary purposes are not typical low-income dwellings, but are medium-income dwellings provided to the poor at the price of low-income dwellings.

Who pays for inclusionary zoning? The requirement of subsidized housing has the same effect as a development tax. Suppose that a developer builds five inclusionary units and loses $10,000 per unit, generating a total loss of $50,000. If the developer is allowed to build 50 houses for the open market, the effective tax per market dwelling would be $1,000 ($50,000 divided by 50). If the housing market is perfectly competitive, the developer will make zero economic profits (normal accounting profits) with or without inclusionary zoning, so the implicit tax is passed on to consumers (housing prices increase) and landowners (the price of vacant land decreases). In other words, housing consumers and landowners pay for inclusionary zoning.

Fringe Land Use.   New housing is usually built on the fringe of the metropolitan area. If the costs of supplying public services are higher in fringe areas, the tax contribution of new housing may be less than the costs of public services. Therefore, new housing may impose a fiscal burden on the city.

The fiscal burden of fringe housing can be explained with a simple example. Consider a city with the following characteristics:

1. The current average cost of public services is $500 per household per year.
2. The typical household owns a house worth $50,000 and pays a property tax of $500 per year (1 percent of market value).
3. A developer has proposed a new residential development on fringe land. The market value of the new houses is the same as existing houses ($50,000).

4. The new development would require the expansion of the city's public services (widening of streets, expansion of the sewage system, extension of bus routes). The full cost of serving the new houses would be $600 per house per year.

Given these assumptions, every new house generates a fiscal burden of $100 per year ($600 - $500). A simple way to prevent the new development and the associated fiscal burden is to zone the vacant land for agricultural use. If the city sets a minimum lot size of 20 acres, no additional houses will be built on the land, so the expansion of city services will be unnecessary.

An alternative to low-density zoning is a tax surcharge for new development. Suppose that the city imposes an annual surcharge of $100 per new house. The annual tax liability of new housing would be $600 ($500 in property tax plus the $100 surcharge), and the occupants of new housing would pay the full costs of the new public services. The surcharge would eliminate the fiscal burden of new housing, so the city would be more likely to approve the development project.

An alternative to an annual tax surcharge is a one-time **impact fee** or **development tax**. By paying an impact fee, the developer compensates the local government for the fiscal burden of new housing. If the city collects a $1,000 impact fee from the developer and invests the money in the bank at a 10 percent interest rate, it can use the annual interest earnings ($100) to cover the difference between the tax contribution and the public-service costs of new housing. Who pays the impact fee? If the housing market is perfectly competitive, the developer will make zero economic profits, so the fee will be passed on to consumers (housing prices increase) and landowners (land prices decrease).

Commercial and Industrial Development.   In some cities, commercial and industrial development generates fiscal burdens. If the city cannot pass on the costs of new infrastructure to new firms and employees, it may restrict development by (a) limiting the supply of commercial and industrial land and (b) restricting building heights.

The city of San Francisco recently adopted a zoning plan that restricts building heights in its downtown area. The objective of the policy is to limit the number of people working downtown. By limiting the number of downtown workers, city officials hope to control the volume of traffic on the bridges into the city, all of which are already highly congested. An alternative to the zoning policy would be to increase the carrying capacity of the bridges, with the costs of the capacity expansion imposed on new employers. Since this is impractical, the city has decided to use its zoning policy to limit total employment.

Some cities impose impact fees on commercial and industrial developers, using the revenue from the fees to expand local transportation networks. For example, in the Westchester area of western Los Angeles, developers pay a one-time fee of $2,010 for each additional rush-hour trip generated by new office buildings. The revenue from the impact fee is used to widen the roads used by the employees of the new office buildings. Impact fees can reduce the fiscal burden of new development, decreasing the opposition to development.

Design Zoning

The third type of zoning is a form of macro-architecture. Just as an architect designs an individual house, the planner designs a city, arranging activities to promote the efficient use of the city's infrastructure (streets, sewage systems, water systems). Residential and employment growth is directed to areas where infrastructure can be efficiently provided. Design zoning is also used to preserve open space.

Directed Development.   Some cities use zoning to direct residential development to particular areas. Consider a metropolitan area with the following characteristics:

1. There are 50 acres of vacant land: 25 acres to the north of the city and 25 acres to the south.
2. The city wants to accommodate 500 new households on its vacant land.
3. Under the initial zoning ordinance, both areas are zoned for 10 dwellings per acre: 250 households would live in the north, and 250 would live in the south.

Suppose that the city changes its zoning policy. It decides to preserve the north area and accommodate all 500 of the new households in the south area. One way to accomplish this would be to zone the north area for agriculture and the south area for 20 dwellings per acre. What are the effects of this rezoning on land prices? The rezoning will decrease the demand for northern land, decreasing its price, and increase the demand for southern land, increasing its price. The change in zoning policy is clearly inequitable: southern landowners gain at the expense of northern landowners.

An alternative to rezoning is a system of **transferrable development rights** (TDRs). Under a TDR policy, the city establishes a **preservation zone** (the north area) and a **development zone** (the south area). The south area is zoned for 10 dwellings per acre, giving Mr. South (the southern landowner) the right to build a total of 250 dwellings. Ms. North (the northern landowner) is not allowed to develop her land, but is issued 250 development coupons instead. These development coupons can be used to override zoning restrictions in the development zone. If South wants to build 20 dwellings on one acre of land, he must purchase 10 development coupons from North. The TDR policy gives each landowner development rights (the right to build 250 houses) and allows the owners of preserved land to transfer their development rights to other areas of the city. When the northern landowner sells her coupons, she is at least partially compensated for the losses in property value caused by the rezoning of her land.

Figure 11–6 shows the effects of zoning and TDRs on the prices of southern and northern land. In the initial equilibrium (both areas zoned for 10 dwellings per acre), land sells for P_2 per acre. Suppose that northern land is zoned for preservation, but southern land is still zoned for 10 dwellings per acre. The rezoning of northern land will decrease its price to P_1 because the landowner has fewer development options. When northern land is taken off the residential market, the resulting shortage of residential land will increase the price of southern land to P_3. Under a TDR policy, northern landowners receive development coupons that can be used to override the density limit (10 dwellings per acre) in the development zone. The relaxation of density limits gives southern landowners more development options, increasing the market value of their land from P_3 to P_4. Southern landowners are willing to pay up to $(P_4 - P_3)$ for an acre's worth of development coupons, so the market value of one acre's worth of development coupons is $(P_4 - P_3)$.

What determines the market value of the development coupons? The

FIGURE 11–6   Market Effects of Rezoning and Transferrable Development Rights

In the initial equilibrium, the price of land is P_2 per acre. If the north area is rezoned for preservation, the demand for southern land will increase (increasing its price to P_3) and the demand for northern land will decrease (decreasing its price to P_1). Under a TDR policy, northern landowners receive development coupons that can be used to override density limits in the development zone. The relaxation of density limits increases the market value of southern land from P_3 to P_4, so southern landowners are willing to pay up to $(P_4 - P_3)$ for an acre's worth of development coupons.

coupons have a positive price because they allow landowners in the development zone to exceed the normal density restrictions. The market price depends on the power of the coupons to override density restrictions: if the coupons allow a 100 percent increase in density, they will obviously be more valuable than if they allow only a 15 percent increase in density. The market price also depends on the underlying demand for high-density housing in the development zone. If households in the development demand low-density housing, developers won't need the development coupons and the market price of the coupons will be relatively low. In contrast, if there is a strong demand for high-density housing in the development zone, the market price of the coupons will be relatively high.

Open-Space Zoning.   Some cities zone parcels of land as "open space," "green belts," or "agricultural preserves." This type of zoning provides city dwellers with open space by denying landowners the full use of their land.

Is open-space zoning efficient? The alternative to zoning is the outright purchase of land for open space. If the city were to purchase land instead of zoning it for open space, the city would preserve land only if the marginal benefit of open space exceeds the marginal cost. In other words, if the city faces the full cost of open space, it will choose the optimum amount of open space. In contrast, if the city simply zones the land for open space, the city is likely to consume too much open space.

Figure 11–7 shows the costs and benefits of open space. The marginal-benefit curve is negatively sloped, reflecting the diminishing marginal utility of open space. The marginal-benefit curve shows how much citizens are willing to pay for different amounts of open space. The marginal cost of open space is the opportunity cost of using the land for open space instead of residential development. For example, if housing developers are willing to pay $20,000 for undeveloped land, the marginal cost of open space is $20,000 per acre. If the city purchases land for open space, it will outbid developers for 60 acres of land. This is an efficient allocation of land: for the first 60 acres of open space, the value of land as open space (citizens' willingness-to-pay for open space) exceeds the value of land in housing. For the 61st through the 100th acres, the value of land in housing exceeds the value as open space, so 40 acres will be developed.

Suppose that the city simply zones land for open space. From the perspective of city officials, the marginal cost of open space will be zero. The city will preserve land as long as the marginal benefit is positive, so it will zone for 100 acres of open space instead of 60. This is inefficient because the 61st through the 100th acres are more valuable as housing land.

A CITY WITHOUT ZONING?

What would an unzoned city look like? Would glue factories and pizza parlors invade quiet residential neighborhoods? Would land use be disorderly and ugly?

FIGURE 11–7   Inefficiency of Open-Space Zoning

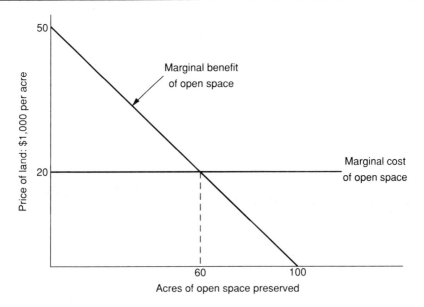

The opportunity cost of open space is the value of land in an alternative use (housing). The optimum amount of open space is 60 acres (where the marginal-benefit curve intersects the marginal-cost curve). If the government does not compensate landowners for open-space zoning, it will preserve 100 acres (the point at which the marginal benefit of open space is zero).

Some tentative answers to these questions come from Siegen's (1972) analysis of Houston, the only metropolitan area in the United States without zoning. Land use in the city is controlled by **restrictive covenants**, voluntary agreements among landowners that limit land uses and structures. The covenants governing residential subdivisions (over 7,000 in number) are typically more strict than conventional zoning. They have detailed restrictions on architectural design, external appearance, and lot maintenance. The covenants for industrial parks limit the activities that can locate in the park.

How does Houston compare to zoned cities? Although a rigorous comparison of land-use patterns may be impossible, some tentative observations can be made.

1. **Dispersion of industry.** The spatial distribution of Houston's industrial firms is similar to those of zoned cities. As in other cities, Houston's industrial firms locate close to the transportation network (near railroads and highways) and tend to cluster to exploit localization economies.

2. **Retailers.** Like retailers in most cities, most retailers in Houston locate along major thoroughfares in strip developments and shopping

centers. Few of the city's retailers locate in quiet residential neighborhoods. Retailers locate along major thoroughfares because such locations provide large volumes of foot and auto traffic. Many retailers are subject to shopping externalities (from the benefits of one-stop shopping and comparison shopping), so they cluster in shopping centers, malls, and downtown areas.

3. **Strip development.** Houston appears to have more strip development (retail and commercial establishments along arterial routes) than zoned cities.

4. **Apartments.** Low-income housing is more plentiful in Houston than in zoned cities and is relatively inexpensive. There is a wide range of densities among apartment projects: the projects occupied by the wealthy have more open space and lower density, while the projects occupied by the poor have higher density.

5. **Single-family homes.** In some areas, Houston homes have relatively small backyards; in other areas, lot sizes are similar to those in zoned cities.

There are two lessons from Houston's experience without zoning. First, in the absence of zoning, landowners have the incentive to negotiate restrictions on land use. It seems that neighborhood externalities are large enough to justify the costs of developing and enforcing restrictive covenants. This is the **Coase solution** to externalities (named after R. H. Coase): the parties affected by externalities negotiate a contract to solve the externality problem. Second, in the absence of zoning, most industrial firms cluster in locations accessible to the transportation network, and most retailers cluster in shopping centers and retail strips. If a city were to drop its zoning plan, it is unlikely that glue factories and pizza parlors would invade quiet residential neighborhoods.

THE LEGAL ENVIRONMENT OF LAND-USE CONTROLS

Local governments, which are creatures of state governments, derive their power to control land use from the states. In most states, enabling legislation for zoning is patterned after the Standard State Zoning Enabling Act, which was developed by the U.S. Department of Commerce in 1926. Section 1 of the Enabling Act states:

> Grant of Power. For the purpose of promoting health, safety, morals, or the general welfare of the community, the legislative body of cities and incorporated villages is hereby empowered to regulate and restrict the height, number of stories, and size of buildings and other structures, the precentage of the lot that may be occupied, the size of yards, courts, and other open spaces, the density of population, and the location and use of buildings, structures, and land for trade, industry, residence, or other purposes.

The model legislation grants local governments broad powers in the regulation of land use. Zoning is considered a legitimate exercise of the **police power** of local government if it promotes the public health, safety, and welfare.

Current zoning laws are the result of over 60 years of legal decisions. In the last six decades, individuals affected by specific zoning laws have sued local governments, forcing state and federal courts to rule on the constitutionality of zoning ordinances. If a particular type of zoning is declared unconstitutional, all cities get the message from the courts and rewrite their zoning ordinances to drop the illegal practices. On the other hand, if a zoning practice is upheld as constitutional, the practice spreads to other local governments. In other words, zoning law is evolutionary. Early court decisions established three criteria for the constitutionality of zoning: substantive due process, equal protection, and just compensation.

Substantive Due Process

The case of *Euclid* v. *Ambler* established the standards for **substantive due process.** According to the due-process criterion, zoning must be executed for a legitimate public purpose using reasonable means. In the early 1920s, the city of Euclid, Ohio, enacted a zoning ordinance that restricted the location, size, and height of various types of buildings. Ambler Realty had purchased some property between the railroad tracks and a major thoroughfare and expected to sell the land to an industrial developer. When the city zoned its land for residential use, Ambler sued, claiming that the separation of industrial and residential land uses did not serve a legitimate public purpose. The Supreme Court ruled against Ambler, concluding that the zoning ordinance satisfied the standards for substantive due process because it had some "reasonable relation" to the promotion of "health, safety, morals, and general welfare." In other words, nuisance zoning (the separation of different land uses) is a legitimate use of the city's police power because it promotes public health and safety.

One interpretation of the *Euclid* decision is that a zoning ordinance is constitutional as long as it generates some benefit for the local community. The court did not say that the benefits of zoning must exceed the costs of zoning, but simply that the benefits must be positive. Fischel (1985) calls this *benefit* analysis, as opposed to *benefit-cost* analysis. The court defined the possible social benefits from zoning in broad terms—to include monetary, physical, spiritual, and aesthetic benefits.

Equal Protection

The second criterion for the constitutionality of zoning is **equal protection.** The equal-protection clause of the Fourteenth Amendment requires that all laws be applied in an impersonal (nondiscriminatory) fashion.

Recent court cases have tested whether fiscal zoning violates the principle of equal protection. Fiscal zoning excludes households that do not pay their share of the costs of local public services. Local governments have been sued by people outside the city, who claimed that fiscal zoning systematically excludes some types of people from the city. The plaintiffs argued that zoning laws are not applied in an impersonal manner, but instead treat some people differently than others: rich and poor are treated differently, as are whites and blacks.

The federal courts have upheld the constitutionality of exclusionary zoning. In the *Euclid* decision, the Supreme Court suggested that a zoning ordinance must generate some benefit for insiders (citizens of the community), and the effects of zoning on outsiders are unimportant. In *Warth* v. *Selden*, the court dismissed the claims of outsiders because they did not prove that the zoning ordinance caused specific personal damage. In *Village of Arlington Heights* v. *Metropolitan Housing Corporation*, the court dismissed the claims of outsiders because they did not prove discriminatory intent on the part of zoning officials. In *Ybarra* v. *Town of Los Altos Hills*, the court ruled that although zoning laws that discriminate on the basis of race are unconstitutional, zoning laws that discriminate on the basis of income are legal. In general, the federal courts have adopted a noninterventionist approach to exclusionary zoning.

Some state courts have adopted a more activist role. In *Southern Burlington County NAACP* v. *Mount Laurel*, the New Jersey Supreme Court ruled that Mount Laurel's exclusionary zoning harmed low-income outsiders. The court directed the city to develop a new zoning plan under which the city would accommodate its "fair share" of low-income residents. The implication from *Associated Home Builders Inc.* v. *City of Livermore* (California Supreme Court) is that the courts will judge zoning on the basis of its effects on both insiders and outsiders. If a zoning ordinance does not represent a reasonable accommodation of the competing interests of insiders and outsiders, it may be declared unconstitutional. In Oregon, state law requires municipalities to plan and zone land for a diversity of housing types and income levels. Despite these state rulings, in most states, exclusionary zoning is still considered legal.

Just Compensation

The third criterion for the constitutionality of zoning is **just compensation**. The Fifth Amendment states ". . . nor shall private property be taken for public use, without just compensation." This is the **taking clause**: if the government converts land from private to public use, the landlord must be compensated.

How is the taking clause applied to zoning? Most zoning ordinances do not actually convert land to public use, but merely restrict private use. For example, nuisance zoning prevents a landowner from building a factory in a residential area, and large-lot zoning prevents a landowner from building high-density housing. By restricting the private use of land, zoning decreases the market value of the property. The policy issue is whether landowners should be compensated for the loss of property value caused by zoning. For example, if large-lot zoning decreases a landowner's property value by $5,000, should the local government pay $5,000 in compensation?

According to Fischel (1985), the courts have provided mixed and confusing signals to local zoning authorities. The courts routinely uphold zoning laws that cause large losses in property values. In general, it appears that as long as landowners are left with some profitable use of their land, compensation is not required. The courts have developed four rules to determine whether compensation is required.

1. **Physical invasion.** Compensation is required if the government occupies the land. When the government merely restricts private land use, this rule is inapplicable.

2. **Diminution of value and reasonable beneficial use.** The origin of this rule is *Pennsylvania Coal* v. *Mahon*, in which Justice Holmes states, ". . . while property may be regulated to a certain extent, if regulation goes too far it will be recognized as a taking." In other words, compensation is required if zoning decreases the property value by a sufficiently large amount. Unfortunately, the courts have not indicated how far zoning must go before compensation is required. A related rule is **reasonable beneficial use**: if zoning leaves the landowner with options that provide a *reasonable* rate of return, no compensation is required.

3. **Balancing means (Benefit-Cost).** According to this rule, compensation is required if the cost of a zoning ordinance (the loss in property value) exceeds the benefit to the local community. Because this rule requires compensation for inefficient zoning ordinances, it discourages inefficient zoning practices. For example, suppose that a zoning ordinance decreases property values by $50 and generates a $30 benefit to the community. According to the balancing-means rule, compensation must be paid. Taxpayers will oppose the ordinance because the cost of compensating landowners would exceed the benefit generated by the ordinance. If the balancing-means rule were used, voters would approve only efficient zoning ordinances.

4. **Harm prevention.** According to this rule, compensation is not required if the zoning ordinance prevents a harmful use of the land. In other words, zoning is not a "taking" if it prevents landowners from using their land in ways that are detrimental to the general public. The harm-prevention rule suggests that landowners, like car owners, have limited property rights. Car owners have the right to drive their cars, but they must stop at red lights. Should drivers be compensated for the opportunity cost of time spent waiting for traffic lights to turn green? Since

traffic lights prevent a harmful use of cars, compensation is not required. Similarly, landowners have limited property rights: if zoning prevents landlords from building a polluting factory in a residential district, compensation is unnecessary because nuisance zoning prevents a harmful use of the land. Most zoning ordinances are judged by a broad interpretation of the harm-prevention rule: if an ordinance promotes public health, safety, or welfare, compensation is usually not required.

SUMMARY

1. Some cities use land-use regulations to control population growth.
   a. An urban service boundary controls population growth by decreasing the supply of land available for development. Land prices within the boundary increase, and prices outside the boundary decrease.
   b. A limit on building permits decreases the number of houses that can be built, so it increases housing prices and decreases land prices.
2. A zoning plan designates a set of admissible land uses for each plot of land in the city. There are three types of zoning: nuisance zoning, fiscal zoning, and design zoning.
3. Nuisance zoning decreases the exposure to pollution, noise, and congestion externalities.
   a. An alternative to industrial zoning is a system of spatial effluent fees.
   b. An alternative to industrial and commercial zoning is performance zoning, under which the city develops performance standards for noise, odor, smoke, parking, and traffic.
   c. High-density housing produces congestion, noise, and parking problems and sometimes blocks light and views. Performance zoning can be used to shield low-density housing from these effects, allowing high-density housing to locate near single-family homes.
   d. In the absence of conventional residential nuisances (traffic, blocked views, and light) and fiscal problems, the wealthy will still have the incentive to exclude the poor. By doing so, they may increase school achievement, decrease crime rates, and protect property values.
4. Fiscal zoning excludes households that impose a fiscal burden on the city. Fiscal burdens are sometimes generated by high-density housing, fringe housing, and new commercial and industrial development.
5. Local governments use large-lot zoning to exclude high-density (low-income) housing.
   a. Zoning decreases the supply of high-density housing and excludes the poor in two ways: there are fewer low-income dwellings, and the available dwellings are relatively expensive.
   b. The price of land zoned for high-density housing increases, and the price of land zoned for low density housing decreases.

6. Under an inclusionary zoning policy, developers provide subsidized new dwellings to low-income residents. The costs of inclusionary housing are borne by housing consumers (higher housing prices) and landowners (lower land prices).

7. Fringe development often imposes a fiscal burden on the city: the taxes from new development fall short of the costs of extending public services to the urban fringe.

    a. Cities prevent fringe development by zoning vacant land for low-density use (e.g., agriculture).

    b. The alternative to fiscal zoning is a system of impact fees or development taxes.

8. Commercial development sometimes generates fiscal burdens. If the city cannot pass the costs of new infrastructure on to new firms and employees, it may limit the supply of land and restrict building heights. Some cities use impact fees to pay for new infrastructure.

9. Design zoning is a form of macro-architecture: zoning promotes the efficient use of infrastructure and provides open space.

    a. Some cities use zoning to direct development to particular areas and use transferable development rights to prevent horizontal inequities.

    b. In the absence of compensation, open-space zoning will produce an inefficient amount of open space.

10. The market value of a development coupon is determined by (a) the power of the coupon to override density restrictions and (b) the underlying demand for high-density housing in the development zone.

11. The zoning authority of local governments comes from state governments. There are three criteria for the constitutionality of zoning: due process, equal protection, and just compensation.

    a. Zoning decreases the supply of high-density housing and excludes the safety, and welfare.

    b. Federal courts have rejected the claims that fiscal (exclusionary) zoning violates the equal-protection clause of the U.S. Constitution. In contrast, some state courts have declared fiscal zoning unconstitutional.

    c. Zoning is one of the police powers of local government, so compensation is generally not required.

EXERCISES AND DISCUSSION QUESTIONS

1. In Figure 11–3, the equilibrium price of building permits is $30,000. Suppose that the demand curve shifts down and intersects the supply curve at a quantity of 50 dwellings per year. What is the new equilibrium price of permits?

2. Most cities do not auction building permits to the highest bidder. Instead, they allocate the permits on a first-come, first-served basis. Discuss the ef-

ficiency effects and distributional consequences of this allocation scheme.

3. Use Figure 11–4 to show the effects of the following changes on the optimum location of the polluting factory. Do the following changes cause the optimum location to move closer to or farther from the residential area?
   a. The unit commuting cost (cost per mile) increases.
   b. Residents become more sensitive to pollution.
   c. The polluting firm discovers a new method of pollution abatement that cuts abatement costs in half.

4. Consider a city where a polluting industry is separated from the residential area by a five-mile buffer. The table below lists the wages and effluent fees for different locations within the buffer zone: the closer the firm is to the residential district, the lower the wage and the higher the effluent fee.

Commute Distance	Effluent Fee	Wage
5	1.0	10.0
4	2.5	9.9
3	4.5	9.8
2	7.0	9.7
1	10.0	9.6

Suppose that the firm produces 500 units of output per week, uses 1,000 hours of labor per week, and generates 20 units of pollution per week.
   a. Assume that the quantities of output and inputs are constant. What is the optimum location for the firm?
   b. What is the social cost of the segregation zoning policy? In other words, if the city prevents the firm from locating at its optimum location, what is the cost to society?

5. Suppose that a city eliminates all zoning. What types of retailers will move from the retail zones to the residential zones?

6. Suppose that all local taxes are eliminated and all funding for local public services comes from state governments. Would you expect any changes in local zoning practices?

7. Suppose that you are a member of the zoning board in a growing city. A residential developer appears before the board with a proposal to develop a parcel of land at the city's edge. The proposed development would increase the population of the city by 5 percent. The developer makes the following statements:
   i. Because the development will increase the population of the city by 5 percent, it will increase tax revenue by 5 percent.

      ii. Because the development will increase the population of the city by 5 percent, it will increase the total costs of public services by 5 percent.

     iii. Given (*i*) and (*ii*), the development will not create a fiscal burden on the city, so it should be approved.

    a. How would you respond to statements (i) and (ii)? Are the developer's calculations correct?

    b. What additional information would you need to evaluate the fiscal effects of the proposed development?

8. In a certain city, all new housing is built on the city's edge (10 miles from the city center). The city institutes the following policy: Every new house will be subject to a $1,000 impact fee. The fee is paid by the firm that builds the house.

    a. Who will actually pay the development tax?

    b. Will the development tax affect the radius of the city? Illustrate your answer with a graph.

    c. Would you expect the implementation of the development tax to change the city's zoning practices?

9. In Figure 11–5, large-lot zoning increases the price of apartment land and decreases the price of land for single-family homes. Under what circumstances (what values of the relevant elasticities) will the zoning policy increase the total value of land in the city?

10. Suppose that a city has recently proposed the rezoning of a 10-acre parcel of land from low-density use (1 dwelling per acre) to high-density use (20 dwellings per acre).

    a. Who will support the zoning change? Who will oppose the rezoning?

    b. Describe a policy under which all parties will agree to the rezoning if the rezoning is efficient.

11. Ollie recently bought the Notel Hotel in downtown Portland and intends to demolish the hotel and replace it with an office building with 100,000 square feet of office space. When the city planner hears about Ollie's plans, he quickly rezones the hotel site as a historical preserve, preventing the demolition of the hotel.

    a. You have been asked to estimate Ollie's loss from the rezoning of his land. What information would you collect, and how would you use it?

    b. The city offers Ollie development coupons (TDRs) that permit the development of 100,000 square feet of office space somewhere else in the city. What determines the market value of the coupons?

    c. Under what circumstances will Ollie be worse off as a result of the zoning and TDR policy?

12. Suppose that city U establishes an urban service boundary five miles from the city center. People who own land outside the boundary object and demand compensation. Design a practical scheme under which those who are harmed by the service boundary will be compensated for their losses. Be specific. How will the money for compensation be raised? Who will ac-

tually pay for the compensation package? How will you determine the amount of compensation per landowner?

13. Using Figure 11–7, compute the total welfare loss caused by a switch from the optimum policy (purchase of land for open space) to open-space zoning.

14. Suppose that a city provides open space by purchasing land from land-owners, not by zoning land for open space. When someone suggests that the city buy another plot of land for open space, the mayor appears on lo-cal television and solicits contributions to the city's open-space fund. The city will purchase the land for open space if the total contributions exceed the market price of the land. If the contributions do not cover the cost of the land, the city will return the contributions to the individual donors and not buy the land.

    Will the city provide the optimum amount of open space?

15. Consider the following quote:

    "Depending on the variable one controls, a zoning policy may either in-crease or decrease the price of undeveloped land within and around the zoned city."

    Explain this statement, using examples of the various variables that are controlled by the various zoning policies.

16. Consider two of the compensation rules developed by the courts: the diminution-of-value rule and the balancing-means rule. Will these rules promote horizontal equity (the equal treatment of equals)?

17. Comment on the following statement:

    "The courts should not be involved in overseeing local zoning practice. Such matters are the responsibility of the legislative branch of govern-ment. Let democracy work."

18. Houston uses private covenants (private zoning) to regulate land use. Which do you think is more efficient, public zoning or private zoning?

REFERENCES AND ADDITIONAL READINGS

General Readings on Land-Use Controls and Zoning

Bosselman, Fred; David Callies; and John Banta. *The Taking Issue*. Washington, D.C.: Council on Environmental Quality, 1973.   A history of zoning that focusses on the issue of compensation.

Delafons, John. *Land Use Controls in the United States*. Cambridge, Mass.: MIT Press, 1969.   A history of zoning and other land-use controls.

Fagin, Henry. "Regulating the Timing of Urban Development." *Management and Con-trol of Growth* vol. 1. Washington, D.C.: Urban Land Institute, 1975.   Discusses the reasons for design zoning.

Fischel, William. *The Economics of Zoning Laws*. Baltimore: The Johns Hopkins Press, 1985.   A comprehensive economic analysis of land-use zoning, including discussions of the legal foundations of zoning and the effects of zoning on housing prices and location patterns.

Mills, Edwin. "Economic Analysis of Urban Land-Use Controls." In *Current Issues in Urban Economics*, ed. Peter Mieszkowski and Mahlon Straszheim. Baltimore: The Johns Hopkins Press, 1979.   A discussion of the use of zoning as a means of controlling externalities. Includes a historical sketch of land-use controls.

Patterson, T. *Land Use Planning: Techniques of Implementation.* New York: Van Nostrand Reinhold, 1977.   Chapter 2 describes the basic features of zoning policies.

Siegan, Bernard. *Land Use Without Zoning.* Lexington, Mass.: D.C. Heath, 1972.   A discussion of land-use in Houston, a city without zoning.

Growth Controls

Alonso, William. "Urban Zero Population Growth," In *The Urban Economy*, ed. Harold M. Hochman. New York: Norton, 1976.

Cooley, Thomas F., and C. J. LacCivita. "A Theory of Growth Controls," *Journal of Urban Economics* 12 (1982), pp. 129–45.   Explores the factors that lead communities to control population growth, including rising costs of public services and limitations on the property tax.

White, Michelle. "Self Interest in the Suburbs: The Trend toward No-Growth Zoning." *Policy Analysis* 4 (1978), pp. 185–204.   Discusses the reasons for no-growth zoning and suggests public policies that might reverse the no-growth trend.

Nuisance Zoning and Performance Zoning

Kendig, Lane. *New Standards for Nonresidential Uses.* Report 405. Chicago: American Society of Planning Officials, 1987.   Shows how performance zoning can be used to control externalities from nonresidential uses.

Kendig, Lane. *Performance Zoning.* Chicago: American Planning Association, 1980. Discusses performance zoning as a means of controlling residential nuisances.

Meshenberg, Michael J. *The Administration of Flexible Zoning Techniques.* Report 318. Chicago: American Society of Planning Officials, 1976.   Discusses various types of flexible zoning, including planned unit development, special permits, floating zones, overlay zoning, contract zoning, and transfer of development rights.

Moore, Terry. "Why Allow Planners to Plan." *American Institute of Planners Journal* vol. 44 (1978) pp. 387–98.   Describes the reasons for planning and zoning in terms of externalities and market failure.

Porter, Douglas R.; Patrick L. Phillips; and Terry J. Lassar. *Flexible Zoning: How It Works.* Washington, D.C.: The Urban Land Institute, 1988.   Contrasts traditional zoning with more flexible approaches developed in recent years. Discusses the effects of flexible zoning in seven communities.

Fiscal Zoning and Inclusionary Zoning

Brooks, Mary E. "Housing Trust Funds: Lessons from Inclusionary Zoning." In *Inclusionary Zoning Moves Downtown*, ed. Dwight Merriman, David J. Brower, and Philip

D. Tegeler. Chicago: American Planning Association, 1985, pp. 7–22. Describes housing trust funds, which use money collected from office and commercial developers to subsidize new housing.

Davidoff P., and L. Davidoff. "Opening the Suburbs: Toward Inclusionary Controls." *Management and Control of Growth* 1 (1975), pp. 540–50.

Dowall, David E. "The Effects of Tax and Expenditure Limitations on Local Land Use Policies." *Perspectives on Local Public Finance and Public Policy* 1 (1983), pp. 69–87. Suggests that fiscal limitations (e.g., Proposition 13) will make fiscal zoning more prevalent. Discusses the implications of fiscal zoning for housing costs and the imbalance between jobs and residents.

Franklin, H. M.; D. Falk; and A. Levin. *In-Zoning: A Guide for Policy Makers on Inclusionary Land Use Programs.* Part I discusses the legal reasons for inclusionary zoning. (Washington, D.C.: The Potomac Institute, 1974).

Schwartz, Seymour I., and Robert A. Johnston. "Inclusionary Housing Programs." *American Planning Association Journal* 49 (1983), pp. 3–21. Describes inclusionary programs in several California cities.

Transferable Development Rights

Roddewig, Richard J., and Cheryl A. Inghram. *Transferrable Development Rights Programs: TDRs and the Real Estate Marketplace.* Report 401. Chicago: American Society of Planning Officials, 1987. Case studies of TDR programs in four cities (New York City, Denver, Seattle, San Francisco) and two counties. Also explores the legal foundations of TDRs.

Schnidman, F. "TDR: A Tool for More Equitable Land Management?" *Management and Control of Growth* 4 (1978), pp. 52–57.

The Administration of Zoning

Babcock, Richard R. *The Zoning Game.* Madison: University of Wisconsin Press, 1966. Discusses the political and legal aspects of zoning.

Babcock, Richard R., and Charles Siemon. *The Zoning Game Revisited.* Boston: Oelgeschlager, Gunn, and Hain, 1985. Accounts of 11 zoning conflicts.

Hinds, Dudley; Neil Carn; and Nicholas Ordway. *Winning at Zoning.* (New York: McGraw-Hill, 1979). Gives practical tips for dealing with zoning authorities.

Market Effects of Zoning

Babcock, Richard. "The Spatial Impact of Land-Use and Environmental Controls." In *The Prospective City,* ed. Arthur Solomon. Cambridge, Mass.: MIT Press, 1980.

Courant, Paul N. "On the Effect of Fiscal Zoning on Land and Housing Values." *Journal of Urban Economics* 3 (1976), pp. 84–94. Explores the effect of fiscal zoning on total land value, reaching conclusions different from Ohls, Weisberg, and White (1974).

Dowall, David E. "Reducing the Cost Effects of Local Land Use Controls." *Journal of the American Planning Association* 47 (1981), pp. 145–53. Discusses the effects of land-use controls on the prices of housing and land. Proposes a monitoring system to control the inflationary effects of land-use controls.

Dowall, David E. "The Suburban Squeeze: Land-Use Policies in the San Francisco Bay Area." *Cato Journal* 2 (1982), pp. 709–33. Discusses local land-use policies and their effects on the regional economy.

Grieson, Ronald E., and James R. White. "The Effects of Zoning on Structures and Land Markets." *Journal of Urban Economics* 10 (1981), pp. 271–85. Explores the effects of three types of zoning (restrictions on density, lot size, and allowable uses) on the prices of housing and land.

Lustig, Morton, and Janet Rothenberg Pack. "A Standard for Residential Zoning Based Upon the Location of Jobs." *Journal of the American Institute of Planners* 40 (1974), pp. 333–45. Proposes that residential zoning be used to match labor supply (residential land use) with labor demand (commercial and industrial land use).

Ohls, James C.; Richard C. Weisberg; and Michelle J. White. "The Effect of Zoning on Land Value." *Journal of Urban Economics* 1 (1974), pp. 428–44. Discusses the effect of fiscal zoning on (*a*) the value of land zoned for different uses and (*b*) total land value. Also discusses the trade-offs associated with nuisance zoning.

Ohls, James C.; Richard C. Weisberg; and Michelle J. White. "Welfare Effects of Alternative Models of Zoning." *Journal of Urban Economics* 3 (1976), pp. 95–96. Discusses the reasons for the different conclusions of Courant (1976).

White, Michelle J. "The Effect of Zoning on the Size of Metropolitan Areas." *Journal of Urban Economics* 2 (1975), pp. 279–90. Explores the effect of large-lot zoning on the land area and total land value of a metropolitan area, showing that the effects of zoning on both variables are ambiguous.

PART THREE

Urban Problems and the Federal Response

This third part of the book discusses two urban problems that are addressed by the federal government: poverty and housing. The federal government uses a number of policies to combat poverty, including cash assistance, education and training programs, and payments in kind (food stamps, medical care, housing assistance). The problem of inadequate housing is related to the poverty problem in the sense that increases in income would allow families in inadequate housing to move to better dwellings. Most housing policies, like poverty policies, are redistributional in nature.

The federal government is responsible for income redistribution because local redistributional efforts are weakened by the mobility of taxpayers and transfer recipients. Suppose that a city imposes a tax on its wealthy citizens and uses the tax revenue to finance transfer payments to the poor. Some wealthy households would leave the city to escape the tax, and some poor households would enter the city to get the transfer payment. In combination, the fleeing of the wealthy and the migration of the poor would weaken the city's redistribution program: there would be less money to transfer to more poor households. A national redistribution program will be more effective because there is less mobility between nations than between cities.

There are three chapters in this part. Chapter 12 discusses the causes of poverty and explores the effects of several types of poverty policies. It also discusses several proposals to reform the current welfare system. Chapter 13 explains why housing is different from other goods. Chapter 14 takes a detailed look at several types of housing policies, including public housing, housing vouchers, and community-development programs.

Poverty and Public Policy

Now, too much of nothing
Can make a man ill at ease.
One man's temper might rise
While another man's temper might freeze.

Bob Dylan

Although there are poor people in every segment of society, the incidence of poverty is greatest among women, children, racial minorities, and central-city residents. This chapter explores the various causes of poverty, including slow macroeconomic growth, racial segregation and discrimination, and increases in the number of female-headed households. It also discusses several programs designed to reduce poverty, including education and training programs, cash assistance, and in-kind transfers (food stamps and medical care). The principal question is: How effective are these policies in decreasing poverty and welfare dependence? The chapter also evaluates various welfare-reform proposals, including the negative income tax, workfare, and a recent proposal that would combine child support from absent fathers with subsidies for poor working mothers. A final issue concerns the special problems of the central city. The question is: What causes central-city poverty, and what can be done to increase the income and decrease the welfare dependence of central-city residents?

In the passionate debates over poverty, the facts on poverty are often overlooked, misunderstood, or manipulated to support a particular position. In the words of Mark Twain, some people "use the facts like a drunk uses a lamp post—for support, not illumination." An informed discussion of poverty policies must be preceded by a careful discussion of the facts. The first section of the chapter discusses the facts on poverty, many of which are in conflict with the popular images of poverty and the facts used in public debates.

POVERTY FACTS

What is poverty? The U.S. government defines a poor household as one whose total income is less than the amount required to satisfy the "minimum needs" of the household. The government estimates a minimum food budget for each type of household and multiplies the food budget by three to get the official **poverty budget**. A household with income less than the official poverty budget is considered poor. In 1989, the poverty budget was $6,250 for a single person, $12,560 for a four-person household, and $21,100 for an eight-person household.

Who and Where Are the Poor?

Table 12–1 shows the composition of the poor population in 1987. For each type of household, the poverty rate equals the percentage of households with incomes less than the official poverty budget. Several facts stand out from the table.

1. **Race.** The number of poor whites was over twice the number of poor blacks, and about four times the number of poor Hispanics. Nonetheless, the black poverty rate was over three times the white rate, and the Hispanic poverty rate was just under three times the white rate.

2. **Male versus female.** The poverty rate for female-headed households was over five times the rate for male-headed households (38.3 per-

TABLE 12–1   The Poverty Population in 1987

Group	Persons in Poverty (1,000)	Poverty Rate (percent)
All persons	32,546	13.5
Race		
White	22,409	10.5
Black	9,683	33.1
Hispanic	5,470	28.2
Sex of household head		
Male	12,903	7.3
Female	12,076	38.3
Age		
Aged persons (over 65)	3,419	12.2
Children	13,016	20.6
Location		
In metropolitan areas	23,423	12.5
In central cities	13,893	18.6
In suburban rings	9,530	8.5
Outside metropolitan areas	9,123	16.9
Education of household head		
Elementary school	1,642	22.8
High school dropout	1,406	18.8
High school graduate	2,132	6.3
College (1 year or more)	899	3.7

SOURCE: U.S. Bureau of the Census, *Current Population Reports*, Series P-60.

cent versus 7.3 percent). The table does not show the poverty rate for households headed by a black female, which was over 50 percent.

3. **The aged.** One of the successes in the war on poverty has been the decrease in poverty among the aged: their poverty rate dropped from 35 percent in 1959 to 12.2 percent in 1987, largely as a result of increased Social Security benefits.

4. **Children.** Over one fifth of children lived in poverty in 1987. Figure 12–1 provides a closer look at poverty among black and white children. Over half of black children spent more than 4 of their first 10 years in poverty, compared to only 8 percent of white children. Only about a

FIGURE 12–1   Years of Pretransfer Poverty from Birth to Age 10 for White and Black Children

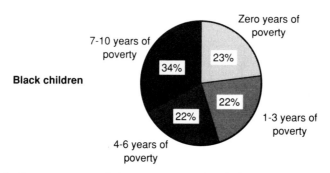

Pretransfer Poverty: Income below the poverty line before counting government transfer payments.

SOURCE: David T. Ellwood, *Poor Support* (New York: Basic Books, 1988), Figure 6.2, p. 201.

quarter of black children escaped poverty altogether, compared to about three quarters of white children.

5. **Location.** The poverty rate of central cities is more than twice the suburban rate. The poverty rate outside metropolitan areas is about one third higher than the metropolitan rate.

6. **Education.** Poverty rates are negatively related to the level of education. The poverty rate of high-school dropouts is three times the rate of high-school graduates and five times the rate of those who attend at least one year of college.

Where Do the Poor Get Their Money?

Table 12–2 shows the distribution of work effort of poor household heads in 1987. Over half of the poor household heads worked at least part time for part of the year, and over 1 million worked full time for the entire year. Because the typical poor household has four members, this means that over 4 million poor people were in households with a full-time worker. If one assumes that part-time workers averaged 20 hours per week, over 2 million household heads worked at least the equivalent of 20 full-time weeks (800 hours for the year). In other words, about a quarter of the poor (8 million of 32 million) were in households in which the household head worked the equivalent of 20 weeks per year. The implication is clear: half-time employment is not enough to escape poverty.

The working poor receive relatively low wages. Among poor household heads who work full time, the typical wage is between $3.50 and $4.00. The annual income from a $4 wage is $8,320, which falls short of the poverty bud-

TABLE 12–2   Work Effort of Poor Nonaged Household Heads, 1987

Weeks Worked	Full-Time Workers (1,000)	Part-Time Workers (1,000)	Total (1,000)
50–52	1,024	309	1,333
40–49	254	110	364
27–39	236	128	391
14–26	361	212	573
1 to 13	371	278	649
Total 1–52	2,273	1,037	3,310
Did not work	—	—	2,961
Total			6,271

SOURCE: Bradley Schiller, *The Economics of Poverty and Discrimination*, 5th ed. (Englewood Cliffs, N.J.: Prentice-Hall, 1989), p. 66.

get for a 3-person household by $1,480. For the poor who work part time, the gap between market income and the poverty level is even larger.

Table 12–3 provides a closer look at the income sources of poor households. Male-headed households receive a large share of their income from earnings (63 percent) and a small share from welfare programs (23 percent). Female-headed households are more dependent on welfare programs: they receive 26 percent of their income from earnings and 60 percent from welfare. The differences are explained in large part by the greater child-care responsibilities of women, which limit their working time.

CAUSES OF POVERTY

Tables 12–2 and 12–3 suggest that there are two principal reasons for poverty. The first is the lack of employment: most poor households lack a full-time worker. The second is low wages: a full-time job at a wage of $4.00 per hour does not generate enough income to lift a household out of poverty. To escape poverty, the household head must earn more than the minimum wage. This section explores the reasons why some workers have low employment rates and low wages.

Economic Growth and Stagnation

Perhaps the most important reason for poverty is slow macroeconomic growth. Stated another way, the most powerful means of decreasing poverty is through economic growth. According to the **queuing theory** of unemployment, prospective workers form an employment line (a queue) outside the factory or office building. A worker's position in the line is determined by his

TABLE 12–3   Income Sources of Poor Households

	Male-Headed		Female-Headed	
	Amount ($)	Percent of Total	Amount ($)	Percent of Total
Earnings	5,136	62.63	1,722	25.70
Welfare programs	1,909	23.28	4,049	60.43
Cash benefits	1,110	13.54	2,398	35.79
Food stamps	666	8.12	1,106	16.51
Housing assistance	133	1.62	545	8.13
Social security	562	6.85	414	6.18
Unemployment	340	4.15	91	1.36
Other	253	3.09	424	6.33
Total	8,200	100.00	6,700	100.00

SOURCE: Bradley Schiller, *The Economics of Poverty and Discrimination*, 5th ed. (Englewood Cliffs, N.J.: Prentice-Hall, 1989), pp. 40 and 42.

productivity: the lower the productivity, the further down the line the worker is positioned. Because employers draw workers from the front of the line, the least productive workers are the last to be hired. When economic growth increases the demand for labor, firms hire workers further down the employment queue (low-productivity workers who would normally be unemployed). Because economic growth generates jobs for marginal (low productivity) workers, it decreases poverty. In contrast, a recession decreases the demand for labor, and the least productive workers are the first fired.

There is conclusive evidence that economic growth decreases poverty. Ellwood (1987) predicted poverty rates for different years using two macroeconomic variables (the unemployment rate and median earnings) and compared the predicted rates with the actual poverty rates. His results for male-headed households are shown in Figure 12–2. The predicted rates are very close to the actual poverty rates, suggesting that the state of the economy has a strong influence on the poverty rates of male-headed households: an increase in the unemployment rate increases the poverty rate, and vice versa. In contrast, economic growth plays a less important role in the poverty of female-headed households. Because fewer female household heads work, they are less affected by changes in the demand for labor.

A number of studies have estimated the effects of recessions on poor households. Gramlich and Laren (1984) estimated the effects of changes in unemployment rates on the earnings of different types of households. The

FIGURE 12–2   Expected versus Actual Poverty

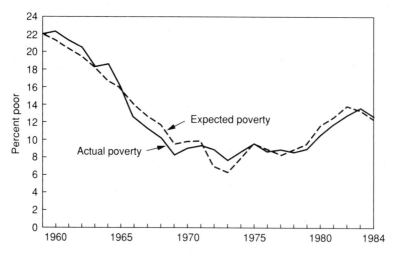

Expected poverty is based solely on the median earnings of full year, full-time male workers, and the unemployment rate.

SOURCE: David Ellwood, *Divide and Conquer* (New York: Ford Foundation, 1987), p. 16.

earnings of both poor and middle-income households decreased as the unemployment rate rose, but the relative loss of poor households was about three times the loss of middle-income households. In terms of racial differences, a one-point increase in the unemployment rate decreased the income of white males by 1.2 percent, but decreased the earnings of nonwhite males by 2.0 percent. The implications are clear: because recessions impose relatively large costs on the poor, policies that promote macroeconomic growth reduce poverty.

Blank and Blinder (1986) examined the effects of changes in unemployment and inflation on poverty rates. They concluded that rising unemployment between 1973 and 1983 added over five percentage points to the poverty rate: if the 1983 unemployment rate had been equal to the 1973 rate, the 1983 poverty rate would have been 10.1 percent instead of 15.2 percent. Stated another way, a one-point increase in the prime-age male unemployment rate increased the poverty rate by 0.70 percentage points. Although inflation also increases the poverty rate (the real income of poor households decreases), the relationship is a relatively weak one: the poor are harmed more by unemployment than by inflation.

Residential Segregation

As shown in Table 12–1, the black poverty rate is over three times the white poverty rate. One reason for the greater poverty among black households is residential segregation. In most metropolitan areas, blacks are concentrated in central cities: in 1980, about 74 percent of metropolitan blacks lived in central cities, compared to only 35 percent of whites (Kain 1985). In other words, only 26 percent of blacks lived in the suburbs, compared to 65 percent of whites.

What does racial segregation have to do with poverty? As discussed in Chapter 10 (Suburbanization of Employment and Population), the majority of jobs in manufacturing, retailing, and offices are now in suburban areas: in 1980, 54 percent of metropolitan employment was in suburban areas. Because only 26 percent of blacks lived in the suburbs, blacks had limited access to suburban employment opportunities. According to the **spatial mismatch theory**, the segregation of blacks in the central city, far from suburban employment opportunities, contributes to black poverty. The suburbanization of employment in recent decades has increased poverty because blacks have not followed jobs to the suburbs.

Why don't central-city blacks commute to suburban jobs? Commuting is costly for central-city residents because (*a*) most transit systems are designed to deliver suburban residents to the city center and are ill-suited for bringing central-city residents to suburban jobs and (*b*) relatively few central-city households own cars. Even if commuting were feasible, finding a suburban job would be difficult because much of the information about job openings is transmitted through informal channels: many workers find out about job openings from their neighbors and friends. As long as blacks live in the central city, they will not have access to this informal information network.

Poverty and Changes in Central-City Employment.   The employment problems of central-city blacks have been exacerbated by changes in the structure of the central-city economy. Table 12–4 shows the changes in central-city employment between 1959 and 1985 for five cities (New York, Philadelphia, Boston, Baltimore, and St. Louis). Total employment in jobs requiring relatively low skills and education has decreased: in 1985, manufacturing employment was 40 percent of its 1953 level, and retail and wholesale employment was 70 percent of its 1953 level. In contrast, employment in jobs requiring higher skills and education has increased: total employment in white-collar services more than doubled between 1953 and 1985.

Kasarda (1988) provides further evidence of the increased educational requirements of central-city employment. Figure 12–3 shows employment changes between 1970 and 1985 in two groups of cities. In the five northern and eastern cities, the number of jobs requiring less than a high-school education dropped by over 900,000, while the number of jobs requiring some college education increased by 428,000. In the four growing southern and west-

TABLE 12–4   Employment in Five Central Cities by Sector, 1953–1985

	1953		1985	
Employment Sector	Number (1,000)	% of Total	Number (1,000)	% of Total
Total employment	4,940	100	4,662	100
Manufacturing	1,867	38	743	16
Retail and wholesale	1,335	27	954	20
White-collar services	925	19	2,218	48
Blue-collar services	577	12	561	12
Other	236	5	186	4

Central Cities: New York, Philadelphia, Boston, Baltimore, and St. Louis

Definitions
1. Total employment: total classified employment excluding government employment and sole proprietors.
2. White-collar services: service industries (excluding government, retail, wholesale) in which more than half of employees hold executive, managerial, professional, or clerical positions.
3. Blue-collar services: service industries (excluding government, retail, wholesale) in which less than half of employees hold executive, managerial, professional, or clerical positions.

SOURCE: John Kasarda, "Jobs, Migration, and Emerging Urban Mismatches," in *Urban Change and Poverty*, ed. Michael McGeary and Laurence Lynn (Washington, D.C.: National Academy Press, 1988), pp. 70–71.

FIGURE 12–3 Change in Number of Jobs with Different Education Requirements, 1970–1985

Cities in North and East: New York, Philadelphia, Boston, Baltimore, St. Louis
Cities in South and West: Atlanta, Houston, Denver, San Francisco

SOURCE: John Kasarda, "Urban Change and Minority Opportunities," in *The New Urban Reality*, ed. Paul Peterson (Washington, D.C.: Brookings Institution, 1985). p. 177.

ern cities, employment growth was more rapid in jobs requiring some college education.

Because the average education level of blacks is relatively low, they are unable to take full advantage of the new employment opportunities in white-collar industries. Most of the new white-collar service jobs in central cities require at least some college education. Nationwide, the black high-school dropout rate is twice that of whites (20 percent versus 10 percent). As shown by Kasarda (1988), only about 27 percent of central-city blacks complete at least one year of college, compared to 40 percent of central-city whites.

Why Segregation?   Why are blacks concentrated in central cities? Kain (1985) discusses several possible reasons for segregation.

1. **Voluntary segregation.** Perhaps blacks prefer to live in segregated neighborhoods. The evidence from attitudinal surveys suggests the opposite: most blacks would in fact prefer to live in integrated neighborhoods (Kain 1985).

2. **Lower incomes.** Perhaps blacks cannot afford suburban housing and are forced to live in low-cost housing in the central city. Several studies have explored this idea without finding much support for it (Kain 1977; Schnare 1977). Kain (1985) poses the following question: if location decisions were based strictly on nonracial characteristics (income, family type, age of household head), how many black households would live in the suburbs? His answer is that 3.6 million black households would live in the suburbs, about twice the actual number of black suburban households. Kain's results suggest that the low rate of black suburbanization is caused by factors other than income.

3. **Racial prejudice.** It appears that many whites prefer to live in segregated neighborhoods and that the actions of real-estate agents promote racial segregation. A 1979 study by the Department of Housing and Urban Development estimated that 27 percent of rental agents and 15 percent of house sellers discriminated against blacks. Discrimination was defined as "failing to provide important, necessary information to rent or purchase a home" to a person of a particular race. In particular, discrimination occurs when blacks are (*a*) falsely informed that a particular dwelling has already been rented or sold or (*b*) actively discouraged from looking for a dwelling in certain neighborhoods (steering). Black home buyers who inquired about four different advertised homes had a 48 percent chance of encountering discriminatory treatment for at least one home, and renters had an 85 percent chance of encountering discriminatory treatment for at least one of four rental properties.

4. **Exclusionary zoning.** As explained in Chapter 11, suburban governments use zoning to exclude low-income households from their jurisdictions. Exclusionary zoning is motivated in part by fiscal concerns: if low-income households do not pay their "fair share" of the costs of local public services, they are excluded by suburban governments. Since the average income of blacks is lower than that of whites, exclusionary zoning has a larger effect on black households. Exclusionary zoning is also motivated by concerns over crime and education: the wealthy exclude the poor in an attempt to keep crime rates low and educational achievement high.

There is some evidence that racial segregation decreased during the 1970s. According to Kain (1985), the fraction of black households living outside central cities increased from 18.1 percent in 1970 to 25.8 percent in 1980. Most of the increase in the number of black suburbanites was caused by (*a*) the expansion of central-city ghettos across central-city lines and (*b*) the growth of suburban concentrations of blacks. There was, however, a small movement of blacks into previously white suburban neighborhoods. In the San Francisco Bay area, the number of suburban communities with between 50 and 1,000 black households increased from 22 in 1970 to 40 in 1980. In

Chicago, the number of such neighborhoods increased from 11 to 39. Although these changes are relatively small, they may suggest that the forces that inhibit black suburbanization are weakening.

Evidence on the Spatial Mismatch Theory.   The spatial mismatch theory suggests that racial segregation in central cities increases black poverty. Evidence in support of this theory comes from a number of sources. In the first study of the connection between housing segregation on black employment, Kain (1968) estimated that racial segregation in Chicago decreased employment opportunities for blacks by over 20,000 jobs. More recently, Straszheim (1980) found that blacks received higher wages for suburban jobs than for central-city jobs. In other words, blacks require compensation for commuting from the central city to suburban jobs. If blacks lived in the suburbs, they would demand a lower wage, so they would be more attractive to employers and more of them would be employed. Kain and Zax (1983) show that when an integrated firm moves from the central city to the suburbs, black employees are unlikely to follow. Mills and Price (1985) estimated that the average earnings of the typical central-city black male would increase by 9 percent if he moved to the suburbs. Kasarda (1985) shows that the segregation of blacks in central cities increases unemployment rates, decreases labor-force participation rates, and increases welfare dependency.

Some researchers question the importance of the spatial mismatch phenomenon. Using data from Chicago, Ellwood (1986) suggests that the spatial mismatch is a relatively small factor in black youth unemployment. Although jobs are moving to the Chicago suburbs faster than black teenagers, most teenagers (both black and white) do not work in their own neighborhoods anyway, so the location of jobs is relatively unimportant. The unemployment rates of blacks in Chicago seem to be unrelated to their proximity to jobs. For example, the West Side of Chicago, where jobs are plentiful, has about the same black teenage unemployment rate as the South Side, where jobs are scarce. Ellwood concludes that the high unemployment rates and low participation rates of black teenagers are caused by racial factors, not by a spatial mismatch between residence and work places.

What conclusions can be drawn from the conflicting evidence concerning the spatial mismatch theory? First, there is a consensus that even if the spatial mismatch theory is correct, discrimination in the labor market (discussed later in the chapter) is probably a more important factor in black poverty. Second, as pointed out by Leonard (1986), there are a number of problems with the data used by Ellwood, so his results must be interpreted with caution. Nonetheless, his work provides a useful framework for testing the spatial mismatch theory, and could be used to test the theory in other cities. Future empirical work will presumably shed more light on the relative importance of segregation in explaining black unemployment and poverty.

The Policy Response.   The government could promote the suburbanization of blacks in three ways. First, by enforcing the fair-housing laws, the federal government could reduce the discriminatory treatment of blacks in the suburban housing market. Second, local governments could change their zoning laws to allow the suburbanization of blacks and other minorities. Third, if state governments provided more support for local-government services, the incentives for exclusionary zoning would decrease.

Education and Poverty

As shown in Table 12–1, the poverty rate depends on the education level of the household head: the lower the education level, the greater the poverty rate. Table 12–5 provides a closer look at the effects of education on employment and earnings. The unemployment rate of high-school dropouts is over six times the rate for college graduates and almost twice the rate for high-school graduates. The lower labor-force participation rate among less educated people is evidence of "discouraged workers": because these people have a more difficult time finding jobs, they are more likely to stop looking for work.

How does education affect employment and earnings? The theory of human capital stresses the effects of increased education on worker productivity. The idea is that schools teach skills that (*a*) can be directly applied to tasks on the job and (*b*) allow workers to learn more quickly on the job. Education is also a signalling device: a diploma shows a prospective employer that the person is sufficiently smart and dedicated to survive a rigorous educational program and is thus likely to be a good worker.

The National Bureau of Economic Research (NBER) completed a comprehensive study of black youths in the inner-city areas of Boston, Chicago, and Philadelphia (Freeman and Holzer, 1986). The study explored the various factors that contribute to the inner-city unemployment problem, including inadequate education. Some of the conclusions of the study are as follows:

1. Graduation from high school increased earnings in two ways: it increased wages by 15 percent and increased hours worked by 6 percent.

TABLE 12–5   Education and Success in the Labor Market

	High School Dropouts	High School Graduates	College Graduates
Unemployment rate	15.4%	8.6%	2.5%
Labor-force participation rate	61	81	88
Full-time workers	57	76	84
Average earnings	$15,266	$18,370	$28,519

SOURCE: Bradley Schiller, *The Economics of Poverty and Discrimination*, 5th ed. (Englewood Cliffs, N.J.: Prentice-Hall, 1989), p. 121.

2. An increase in the number of years in school increased wages, decreased participation in crime, and decreased the amount of time spent in nonproductive activities (activities other than schooling and employment, such as hanging out, watching TV, and getting high).
3. An increase in school performance (measured by grades) increased wages, decreased the likelihood of dropping out, and improved work habits.

The general conclusion of the study is that education has a strong effect on the employment prospects of inner-city youths.

The Title I programs of the federal government are special programs for disadvantaged youths. In 1984, the federal government spent $3.4 billion on these programs. A total of 5 million children were served by the programs, with an average cost per child of about $700 (Glazer, 1986). What are the effects of these programs?

A recent study of the Perry Preschool Program in Ypsilanti, Michigan, suggests that the program is a resounding success (Berrueta-Clement et al. 1984). The study compares teenagers who participated in the preschool program to those who did not. Compared to the control group, program participants had higher high-school completion rates (67 percent versus 49 percent), lower arrest rates (by a margin of 40 percent), and half the teenage pregnancy rate. The estimated benefit-cost ratio of the program was 7.0. This study suggests that preschool programs may generate substantial long-term benefits.

Glazer (1986) summarizes the results of several other studies of Title I programs. One comprehensive study suggests that Title I programs have increased achievement in mathematics and reading, with the largest gains in the early grades. Other studies by the National Assessment of Educational Progress (NAEP) show that Title I programs have narrowed the achievement gaps between black and white students, with the largest relative gains at the elementary level (NAEP 1981; National Center for Education Statistics 1982).

Labor-Market Discrimination

Discrimination in the labor market takes two forms, employment discrimination and wage discrimination. Employment discrimination refers to the practice of systematically hiring one racial group over the other, despite the fact that both groups are equally productive and are paid the same wage. Wage discrimination is defined as paying different wages to equally productive workers. Both types of discrimination have the potential to increase poverty among racial minorities, because either minority workers will not be hired or they will be hired at a lower wage.

Differences in Earnings. Table 12–6 shows the median earnings for white, black, and Hispanic men. For all workers, the gap between white and black earnings is $7,776 and the gap between white and Hispanic earnings is $9,179. Part of this gap is caused by differences in education. The gaps for

TABLE 12–6   Median Annual Earnings by Race and Education, Men Aged 16 and Over, 1986

Education Level	White Workers	Black Workers	Hispanic Workers
All Workers	$25,890	$18,114	$16,711
High school drop-out	18,547	14,681	13,816
High school graduate	23,524	16,629	17,984
Some college time	26,206	21,182	22,254
College graduate	32,789	27,345	28,332

SOURCE: Bradley Schiller, *The Economics of Poverty and Discrimination*, 5th ed. (Englewood Cliffs, N.J.: Prentice-Hall, 1989), p. 156.

workers of particular educational levels are slightly smaller: the black-white gap for high school graduates is $6,895, and the gap for college graduates is $5,544. Because blacks typically receive inferior education, a simple comparison based on years of schooling is deceptive. According to Schiller (1989), the typical black high school graduate has the same educational preparation as the typical white high school dropout, so the gap for a black high school graduate and a white person with the same educational preparation is only $1,918. Schiller concludes that a black worker earns about 90 percent of the wages of a white worker with an equivalent educational background.

The earnings gap is decreased further if one controls for other factors such as age, labor skills, and location. The general conclusion from research on race differences in earnings is that about three fourths of the earnings gap can be explained by differences in education, age, skills, and location, leaving one quarter of the gap unexplained. The unexplained portion is presumably caused by racial discrimination.

Theories of Discrimination.   There are two theories of labor-market discrimination. The first theory, developed by Becker (1957), explains the competitive forces that limit discrimination. The second theory, developed by Phelps (1972) and Arrow (1973), explains why discrimination may persist.

Becker's theory suggests that market forces will limit the extent of wage discrimination. Consider a city with black and white workers. Suppose that all workers have the same **value of marginal product** (VMP), defined as the marginal physical product of labor times the market price of the product produced. Suppose that white workers are paid their VMP ($6) but blacks are paid only $5. If you were a profit-maximizing firm, what would you do? If you hire black workers, you will have lower production costs than your all-white competitors, so your sales and profits will increase. What's good for you is good for other capitalists, so other firms will hire the under-valued black workers and fire the over-valued white workers. As the demand for blacks increases and the demand for whites decreases, the gap between black and white wages will decrease. In equilibrium, whites and blacks will have the same wage.

Under what conditions will wage discrimination persist? If a white firm can keep other firms from entering its industry, it can protect itself from the competition of color-blind firms. Bigotry is not costless, however. The white firm will pay relatively high wages to its white workers, and its higher production costs will force its consumers to pay a relatively high price for its output. In addition, profits will be lower, so stockholders will pay for bigotry in the form of lower dividends and stock prices. Job discrimination may persist if (a) bigoted firms are protected from competition and (b) consumers and stockholders are willing to pay for their bigotry.

The same arguments apply to sex discrimination. If the female wage is less than the male wage and men and women are equally productive, profit-seeking firms will hire women and fire men, thus narrowing the wage gap. In equilibrium, one would expect equally productive men and women to earn the same wage. Job discrimination may persist if (a) sexist firms are protected from competition and (b) consumers and stockholders are willing to pay for their sexism.

As explained earlier, the empirical evidence does not support this simple theory of discrimination. After controlling for all non-discriminatory factors, there is still a large gap between the wages of whites and blacks. Obviously, there is something wrong with the simple model.

The theory of **statistical discrimination** shows that the black-white wage differential will persist if there is imperfect information about worker productivity. Suppose that an employer must hire one of two workers, a black or a white. If the firm knew which worker had the higher VMP, it would obviously hire the more productive worker. Such information is not available, however, so the employer must guess which worker has the higher VMP. Suppose that because of differences in education and work experience, the average black is less productive than the average white, although some blacks are more productive than some whites. If the employer has no other information on the productivities of the applicants, the best choice, in a statistical sense, is the white worker. The white worker will be chosen over the equally productive (or more productive) black worker because black workers are less productive *on average*. In this case, discrimination occurs because of imperfect information, not bigotry.

Demographic Change—Female-Headed Households

As shown in Table 12–1, the poverty rate of female-headed households is over three times the poverty rate of male-headed households. Female-headed households are more likely to be poor for three reasons. First, most of these households are single-parent households, so the woman must juggle employment and child-care responsibilities. For many women, especially those with preschool children, full-time work is not feasible. Second, women earn lower wages than men, so a given amount of work generates less income. Third, only one third of female-headed households receives child-support payments from absent fathers.

The number of female-headed households has increased rapidly in the last few decades. Between 1970 and 1985, the percentage of white households headed by a female increased from 9.6 percent to 13.4 percent (U.S. Census 1986). For blacks, the percentage of households headed by a female increased from 31.8 percent to 43.9 percent. According to Sawhill (1985), the increase in the number of female-headed households between 1967 and 1985 added between one and two percentage points to the overall poverty rate.

Why did the number of female-headed households increase? One theory, popularized by Murray (1984), suggests that the welfare system is responsible for the increase in female-headed households. Murray argues that generous payments from Aid to Families with Dependent Children (AFDC) made it possible for women to raise children outside of marriage: because women could rely on AFDC for support, they had less need for a husband. On a theoretical level, this is a sensible notion: if we decrease the cost of single parenthood, we should expect an increase in the number of single mothers. The issue is really an empirical one: by how much does AFDC increase the number of single parents?

There have been dozens of studies of the effects of welfare programs on family structure and out-of-wedlock births. Wilson and Neckerman (1986) review the literature and come to the following conclusions:

1. There is no evidence that welfare payments affect the number of out-of-wedlock births. States with relatively generous welfare programs did not have higher birth rates among unmarried women.

2. There is some evidence that welfare encourages divorce and separation. States with relatively generous welfare programs have higher rates of marital dissolution. Ellwood and Bane (1984) estimate that a $100 increase in monthly AFDC benefits would cause a 10 percent increase in the number of divorced or separated mothers.

In general, it appears that AFDC encourages women to set up independent households, but does not encourage them to bear more children. McLanahan, Garfinkel, and Watson (1988) suggest that rising AFDC benefits between 1960 and 1975 increased the number of female-headed households by between 9 percent and 14 percent. Because the actual number of female-headed households increased by over 100 percent, it is clear that AFDC played only a small role in the growth of female-headed households.

Wilson and Neckerman (1986) propose an alternative theory for the increase in female-headed households. They compute a "marriageability index" for black men, which shows the number of men who have the financial means to support a household. A man is assumed to be capable of supporting a household if he holds a full-time job. Between 1960 and 1980, the number of young black men (age 20–24) capable of supporting a household decreased rapidly. In 1960, there were 70 employed young black men for every 100 young black women; by 1980, there were only 47 employed men per 100 women. Given the small number of men capable of supporting a family, the large number of black female-headed households is understandable.

PUBLIC POLICY—EMPLOYMENT AND JOB-TRAINING PROGRAMS

As explained earlier in the chapter, the federal government can use macroeconomic policies to stimulate economic growth and decrease poverty. Since the early 1960s, the federal government has supplemented its macroeconomic policies with employment and job-training programs. Employment programs operate on the demand side of the market, providing direct employment for the poor. These programs are sometimes used when the government fears that the stimulation of the national economy through macroeconomic policies would increase the inflation rate. Job-training programs operate on the supply side of the labor market: they increase the labor skills of the poor, making them more attractive to private industry. Spending on employment and training programs increased during the 1960s and 1970s, and then fell during the 1980s: real spending per capita (in 1972 dollars) rose from 2.9 cents in 1965 to 29 cents in 1979 and then fell to 6.4 cents in 1984 (Bassi and Ashenfelter, 1986).

Since the early 1960s, there have been dozens of employment and training programs. Bassi and Ashenfelter (1986) and Schiller (1989) outline the history of the various programs and summarize the results of many of the benefit-cost studies of the programs. Some of the most important programs are the following:

1. **Manpower Development and Training Act (1962).** Although the original purpose of this program was to provide training to experienced workers displaced by changes in the labor market (typically male heads of households), it evolved into a program to assist the hard-core unemployed. The program increased the earnings of male participants by about $200 per year and increased the earnings of women by about $500 per year.

2. **Job Corps (1965).** The Job Corps program is an intensive training and counseling program for disadvantaged youths (low-income and minority youths between age 6 and 12). In 1980, the cost per participant was $13,000. The program increases employment rates and earnings and decreases welfare dependence, out-of-wedlock births, and criminal activity. The estimated benefit-cost ratio of the program is about 1.45.

3. **Work Incentive Program (WIN) (1965).** The purpose of WIN was to encourage AFDC recipients to get jobs. The program provided day-

care, transportation, counseling, and job-placement services to welfare mothers. Funding for this program decreased sharply during the 1980s, and the program was eventually dropped in 1987.

4. **Public Employment Program (PEP) (1971).** Under PEP, the federal government subsidized employment in state and local governments. A small amount of money was also provided for training. After they left the program, women and minorities earned significantly more than they did before the program. In contrast, the program did not increase the earnings of men.

5. **Comprehensive Employment and Training Act (CETA) (1974).** The CETA program was a mixture of employment and training programs. The federal government gave money to local "prime sponsors" to run employment and training programs. Between 1974 and 1982, CETA served a total of 30 million people, with most of the participants coming from low-income and minority households: in 1983, about 95 percent of the participants came from disadvantaged households. Researchers have examined the effects of CETA on the earnings of participants after they left the program. There are four basic results:

a. The earnings of women increased, but the earnings of men did not. Three years after participation, women were earning between $600 and $1,200 more as a result of the program, a large increase relative to their preprogram earnings ($2,700).

b. The earnings of women increased as a result of increases in hours worked, not increases in wages.

c. The largest gains were experienced by the most disadvantaged workers.

d. The most effective components of CETA were classroom training, on-the-job training, and public-service employment. The least effective component was a program that acclimated participants to the work environment without giving them much training or actual work.

6. **National Supported Work Demonstration (NSWD) (1975).** This experimental program enrolled several "problem" groups (long-term AFDC recipients, reformed drug addicts, ex-offenders, and high-school dropouts) in a highly structured program with counseling and work experience. For AFDC recipients (most of whom were women), the program increased both wages and hours worked. For ex-addicts, the program generated a large decrease in crime rates but only a small increase in earnings. The estimated benefit-cost ratio was over 2.0 for AFDC recipients and about 1.9 for ex-addicts. The program had relatively small effects on youths and ex-offenders, so the benefit-cost ratios for these groups were less than 1.0.

7. **Youth Employment Demonstration Projects Act (YEDPA) (1977).** This program was similar to the Job Corps program, and it generated

similar results. The most effective parts of the YEDPA program were re-medial education, job training, and training in job-search skills.

8. **Job Training Partnership Act (JTPA) (1982).** JTPA replaced CETA, bringing two basic changes in employment and training policies. First, JTPA does not provide any public employment, but instead focuses on job training. Second, JTPA enrolls disadvantaged people *and* dislocated workers (people who have lost jobs because of plant closures and permanent layoffs). In 1988, about 1 million people participated in JTPA job-training and job-search programs (Schiller, 1989).

There are four general conclusions from the benefit-cost studies of employment and job-training programs. First, programs that focus on youths (e.g., Job Corps and YEDPA) are successful. Second, programs that stress classroom teaching and on-the-job training often increase the earnings of women, particularly those with little prior work experience. Third, the successful job-training programs increase earnings by increasing the number of hours worked, not by increasing wages. Fourth, training programs have relatively small effects on the earnings of adult men.

DIRECT INCOME TRANSFERS—AFDC AND SSI

Table 12–7 shows spending on various transfer programs in 1987. Total spending was over $100 billion. About one quarter of this sum was spent on direct income transfers: Aid to Families with Dependent Children (AFDC), Supplemental Security Income (SSI), and General Assistance. The bulk of AFDC money went to female-headed households. SSI is a special program for the aged, the blind, and the permanently disabled. General Assistance is a program for poor people who do not qualify for AFDC or SSI.

Total spending on AFDC was $16 billion in 1987. AFDC payments went to a total of 11 million people, with an average payment of $123 per recipient per month. The federal government provides about half the funds of AFDC, with state and local governments contributing the other half. State governments set the eligibility requirements and the benefit levels. In most states, eligibility for AFDC is limited to families in which one parent is either absent or disabled. In 1987, the average monthly payment for a three-person household ranged from $114 in Alabama to $553 in California. Nationwide, the average monthly payment for a three-person household was $359.

AFDC and SSI are "means-tested" programs in the sense that the payment to a household depends on its earnings (its market income). Under AFDC, the first $30 of monthly market income does not affect the AFDC payment, but every additional dollar decreases the AFDC payment by 1 dollar.

TABLE 12–7   Spending on Transfer Programs in 1987

Program	Number of Recipients (millions)	Average Monthly Benefit ($)	Annual Costs ($ billion)
Income transfers			
Supplemental Security Income (SSI)	4	252	9.9
Aid to Families with Dependent Children (AFDC)	11	123	16.3
General Assistance (GA)	1	144	1.4
In-kind transfers			
Food stamps	21	46	12.5
Medicaid	23	179	49.3
Housing assistance	4	57	11.2
School lunch program	24	11	3.2
Total			103.8

SOURCE: Bradley Schiller, *The Economics of Poverty and Discrimination*, 5th ed. (Englewood Cliffs, N.J.: Prentice-Hall, 1989), pp. 172 and 183.

Under SSI, the recipient can earn $65 of market income per month without affecting the SSI grant, and every additional dollar decreases the SSI payment by only 50 cents.

AFDC and Work Incentives

How does AFDC affect the labor supply of recipients? Figure 12–4 shows the trade-offs between income and leisure time for Judy, a potential AFDC recipient. The horizontal axis measures the number of leisure (nonworking) hours per week, and the vertical axis measures her weekly income. Suppose that Judy's wage is $4 per hour and she has 100 hours per week to allocate between work and other activities. One option is point A (zero income and 100 hours of free time). As her work time increases, Judy moves up her budget line (AB), increasing her income by $4 per hour of work: the opportunity cost of leisure time is $4 per hour.

Judy's negatively sloped indifference curves reflect her preferences for income and nonworking time. For example, she is indifferent between points C and F: point F has less income but more leisure time, and the lower income is offset by more nonworking time. Given her budget line and the shapes of her indifference curves, she maximizes utility at point C: she chooses 80 hours of leisure time, 20 hours of work (100 minus 80), and $80 of income ($4 times 20).

Suppose that Judy is offered an AFDC payment of $100 per week. The cash payment adds point D to her budget set: she can have 100 hours of leisure time (zero hours of work) and an income of $100. If her AFDC payment is reduced by one dollar for every dollar of market income, her new budget line is $ADEB$: starting from point D, a one-hour reduction in leisure time (a

FIGURE 12–4   AFDC Decreases Hours Worked from 20 to Zero

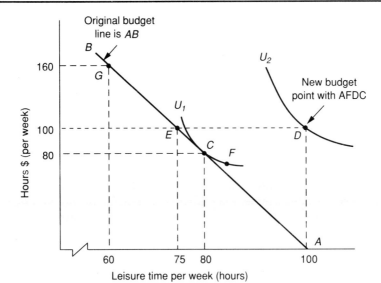

Given her original budget line, Judy maximizes utility at point C (20 hours of labor and $80 income). AFDC (payment of $100) adds point D to the budget set. Utility is higher at point D because Judy gets more leisure time and more income. Therefore, AFDC decreases work effort from 20 hours to zero.

one-hour increase in labor time) increases her labor income by $4, but also decreases her AFDC payment by the same amount. This dollar-for-dollar trade-off continues until she exhausts her AFDC payment. Therefore, for up to 25 hours of work (75 hours of leisure), her net wage is zero.

Given the shapes of Judy's indifference curves, utility is maximized at point D, so she will accept the AFDC payment. Under the AFDC program, she can have both more income and more leisure time, so her choice is an easy one. The AFDC program decreases Judy's labor supply from 20 hours per week to zero.

For some workers, the choice between working and AFDC is not so straightforward. Suppose that before the offer of AFDC, Judy worked full time (40 hours per week). In Figure 12–4, she starts at point G, with an income of $160 per week. Will she enroll in an AFDC program offering $100 per week? If she joins the AFDC program, she would sacrifice $60 of income (the difference between her market income and the AFDC payment) to get 40 hours of extra nonworking time. She will accept AFDC if the value of the extra time is large relative to the value of lost income.

AFDC will be attractive to single mothers with low wages or small children. If the wage is low, the income sacrificed by accepting AFDC (and quitting the job) will be relatively small. For many poor households, wages are so low that the acceptance of AFDC increases household income. The presence of preschool children encourages participation in AFDC because (*a*) many mothers want to participate in their child's development and (*b*) the costs of child care decrease the net wage. For example, if Judy pays $1 per hour for someone to take care of her children, her net wage will be only $3, so she will sacrifice less income by accepting the AFDC payment.

What are the actual effects of AFDC on labor supply? A number of studies have shown that AFDC decreases the labor supply of recipients (see Blank 1986). The reasons are rather simple. First, recipients have relatively low wages, so their market incomes either exceed the AFDC payment by a small amount or are less than the AFDC payment. AFDC is a good deal because (*a*) it increases the opportunities for nonwork activities and (*b*) either increases total income or decreases it by a small amount. Second, for income above $30 per month, the net wage of an AFDC recipient is zero (AFDC falls by one dollar for every dollar of market income), so there is little incentive to work more than a few hours per week. Given the combination of low market earnings, child-care responsibilities, and a 100 percent tax rate, it is not surprising that few AFDC recipients work.

The Negative Income Tax

The alternative to the conventional welfare program is a **negative income tax.** Figure 12–5 shows labor-income trade-offs under a negative income tax. The wage of the household's worker is $4 per hour. The negative income tax has a basic grant of $100 and a marginal tax rate of 50 percent. In other words, a household with zero market income receives the basic grant ($100), and every additional dollar of market income (every quarter hour of work), decreases the grant by 50 cents. For example, if the household works 10 hours per week and earns $40, the grant decreases by $20, from $100 to $80, so the household's total income would be $120. The grant is exhausted at a market income of $200 (50 hours of work).

The Response of Recipients.   Figure 12–6 shows the effect of the negative income tax on Mary, an AFDC recipient with a wage of $4 per hour. In the absence of income assistance, she works 30 hours per week and earns $120 (point *F*). Under AFDC, utility is maximized at point *D*, so Mary quits her job and collects $100 in AFDC. Under a negative income tax with a basic grant of $100 and a tax rate of 50 percent, her budget line is *ADB*: the grant is $100 for zero market income and decreases by 50 cents for every dollar of market income. The grant runs out when her market income reaches $200 (labor time equals 50 hours). Under the negative income tax, Mary will maximize utility at point *K*, with 80 hours of leisure, 20 hours of labor (100 minus 80), $80 of market income ($4 times 20), a grant of $60 ($100 minus half of $80), and a total income of $140 ($80 plus $60).

FIGURE 12–5   Labor-Income Choice under a Negative Income Tax

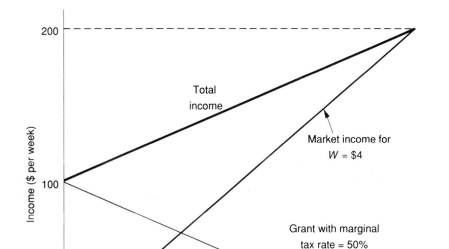

The wage is $4 per hour, the basic grant under the negative income tax is $100, and the marginal tax rate is 50%. The grant is exhausted when labor equals 50 hours per week (market income is $200). Total income is the sum of market income and the grant.

The switch from AFDC to the negative income tax decreases Mary's grant but increases her total income. Because her net wage increases from zero to $2, she increases her hours worked from zero to 20 and keeps half of her market income. As a result, her total income increases from $100 (the AFDC grant) to $140 (market income plus the $60 grant). The switch in welfare policy saves taxpayers money because every $1 of market income decreases Mary's grant by 50 cents: Mary earns $80 in market income and saves taxpayers $40.

The Negative Income Tax and Work Effort.   The negative income tax has been proposed as an unconditional grant. In other words, it would be available to all households, not just households who are currently eligible for AFDC. How would it affect the work effort of different types of households?

FIGURE 12–6   Negative Income Tax Increases Recipient Income and Decreases the Transfer

Leisure time per week (hours)

Given her original budget line, Mary maximizes utility at point F (30 hours of labor and $120 income). AFDC (payment of $100) adds point D to the budget set, and Mary maximizes utility at point D. Under a negative income tax with a grant of $100 and a 50% marginal tax rate, the budget line is ADB. Utility is maximized at point K, with 20 hours of leisure time, $80 of market income, and $60 of grant income. The switch from AFDC increases Mary's income by $40 and saves taxpayers $40.

Three types of households would be eligible for support under a negative income tax:

    1. Current AFDC recipients. As shown in Figure 12–6, the switch from AFDC to the negative income tax increases Mary's work effort from zero hours to 20 hours.

    2. Poor households ineligible for AFDC, with persons capable of working. This type of household may start at point F in Figure 12–6. Under the negative income tax, the household moves from point F to point K, decreasing work effort from 30 hours to 20 hours.

    3. Households without persons capable of working (the elderly, the disabled, and households with very young children). This type of household will be eligible for some type of support (AFDC or SSI), so it will be at point D before and after the negative income tax. Since working is not an option for this type of household, the negative income tax has no effect on work effort.

To summarize, the negative income tax is likely to increase work effort among current AFDC recipients and decrease work effort among households that are currently ineligible for AFDC.

What are the facts on the labor-supply effects of the negative income tax? The federal government ran a series of experiments in the 1960s and 1970s to test the effects of a negative income tax. Poor households were divided into two groups: one group was eligible for a negative-income tax program, and the other group continued to receive conventional welfare payments. The negative-income tax program was more generous than existing programs, with basic grants between 95 percent and 140 percent of the official poverty level. The marginal tax rates were all above 50 percent. The negative income tax decreased labor supply of men, women, and youths: the average reduction in hours worked was 10 percent for men, 14 percent for female household heads, and 24 percent for youths. These supply responses were large enough to disturb most policy makers. As a result, the negative income tax has dropped off the welfare-reform agenda.

The basic problem with the negative income tax is that it enrolls two different types of households in a single program. For a household in which no one is capable of working, the basic grant should be high enough to provide adequate support. For a household with people capable of working, the marginal tax rate should be low enough to encourage work effort. The government is unlikely to adopt a program with both a large basic grant and a low marginal tax rate because such a program would be extremely expensive. If the government chooses a large basic grant and a high marginal tax rate, it would provide adequate support for workerless households, but would also discourage work effort. If it chooses a small basic grant and low tax rate, work effort would be encouraged, but workerless households would receive inadequate support. One response to this problem would be to have one redistributional program for workerless households and another program for households with people capable of working.

PUBLIC POLICY—IN-KIND TRANSFERS

As shown in Table 12–7, spending on in-kind transfer programs exceeded $76 billion in 1987, about three times the total spending on direct income transfers. The three largest in-kind programs are medicaid ($49.3 billion), food stamps ($12.5 billion), and housing ($11.2 billion). This section discusses medicaid and food stamps. Housing programs will be discussed in Chapter 14 (Housing Policies).

Medicaid provides free medical care to the recipients of AFDC and SSI. It is essentially a free medical insurance policy: the government agrees to cover all the recipient's medical expenses, just as a private insurer would. The difference is that medicaid is free. In 1987, two thirds of medicaid funds went to aged and disabled households (SSI recipients). In a comprehensive evaluation of the medicaid program, Starr (1986) suggests that the program was responsible for increases in life expectancy and decreases in infant mortality among the poor.

Under the food-stamp program, poor households are given coupons that can be exchanged for food. The food-stamp allotment depends on household income. Every additional dollar of market income decreases the food-stamp allotment by 30 cents, so the effective marginal tax rate is 30 percent.

Figure 12–7 shows the effects of a $100 food-stamp allotment on the recipient. The food-stamp program shifts the budget line from AB to AGD. Ann starts at point R (spending $50 on food) and moves to point G under the food-stamp program. In contrast, Bill moves from point P ($300 on food) to Q. For Bill, the food-stamp program is equivalent to a cash transfer of $100 because he uses the food stamps to free up part of his own $300 food budget. In contrast, Ann initially spends only $50 on food, so she can use food stamps to re-

---

FIGURE 12–7   The Equivalence of Food Stamps and Cash

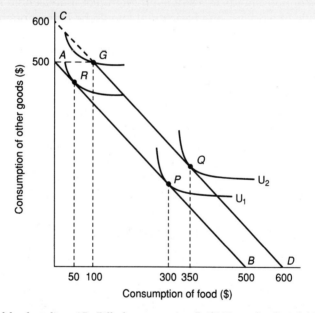

With original budget line AB, Bill chooses point P ($300 on food and $200 on other goods). The budget line with $100 worth of food stamps is AGD, and Bill moves to point Q. Food stamps are equivalent to a $100 cash transfer (budget line DC) because Bill uses the stamps to decrease his own food expenditures, freeing up $100 to spend on either food or other goods. If Ann starts at point R, she spends less than $100 on food, so she cannot use the food stamps to replace her own food expenditures. Therefore, she would prefer $100 in cash to $100 worth of food stamps.

place only $50 worth of food spending. For Ann, the food stamp program is equivalent to a cash transfer of less than $100.

Most food-stamp recipients are like Bill: their desired spending on food exceeds the food-stamp allotment. Therefore, the value of food stamps to recipients is close to the market value of the stamps. According to Smeeding (1982), 1 dollar of food stamps is worth about 97 cents to the typical recipient. Evidence from welfare experiments supports the idea that food stamps are equivalent to cash transfers. In one experiment, the replacement of food stamps with cash payments did not affect the food consumption of recipients (Blanchard, Butter, Doyle, Jackson, Ohls, and Posner, 1982).

EFFECTS OF CASH AND IN-KIND TRANSFERS ON POVERTY

This section addresses two questions about the effects of government transfer programs. First, how do the transfer programs affect the typical poor household? Second, to what extent do the programs decrease poverty?

Effects of Transfer Policies on the Typical Poor Household

Table 12–8 shows an example of the options faced by the typical poor household, a female-headed household with two children. It shows annual disposable income for different amounts of work and wages, taking into account the effects of market income on income transfers and in-kind transfers. If the household head does not work, her disposable income equals the sum of AFDC and food stamps ($6,284). As her income increases, her benefits from transfer programs decrease.

If the woman accepts a minimum-wage job, there is bad news and good news. The bad news is that she spends money on day care and also receives less from AFDC and food stamps. The good news is that she earns income and also gets an earned income tax credit. Poor households receive a 14 percent tax credit on earned income, with a maximum credit of $868. The net result of these changes in day-care costs, welfare payments, wages, and tax credits is an increase in disposable income of $872 for part-time work and $532 for full-time work.

Working is slightly more lucrative at higher wages. Although a higher wage generates more earnings, it also increases taxes (the earned income tax credit is eventually dominated by income and payroll taxes) and decreases the AFDC payment and the food-stamp allotment. Even if the woman worked a full-time job at a wage of $6, her income would still be below the poverty line ($9,800). An added problem is that she eventually loses her medicaid coverage. For a low-wage single mother, the benefits of working are relatively small.

TABLE 12–8 Earnings, Benefits, and Income for Single Parent with Two Children

Level of Work and Wages	Earnings	Day Care	Taxes + EITC	AFDC + Food Stamps	Disposable Income	Medicaid
No work	0	0	0	6,284	6,284	Yes
Half time at minimum wage	3,350	–1,000	229	4,577	7,156	Yes
Full time at minimum wage	6,700	–3,000	373	2,744	6,816	Yes
Full time at $4.00 per hour	8,000	–3,000	171	1,624	6,795	Yes
Full time at $5.00 per hour	10,000	–3,000	–172	970	7,798	No
Full time at $6.00 per hour	12,000	–3,000	–515	538	9,023	No

Taxes + EITC include:
  1. Social security tax of 7.15%
  2. EITC: refundable credit of 14% of earned income to maximum of $868.

source: David T. Ellwood, *Poor Support* (New York: Basic Books, 1988), p. 139.

Effects of Transfer Programs on Poverty

Table 12–9 shows the effects of various programs on poverty rates. In the absence of transfer payments, the overall poverty would have been over 20 percent and the poverty rate for aged persons would have been over 55 percent. Social security and other nonwelfare transfers cut the poverty rate for the aged to 15 percent and decreased the poverty rate for families by about 2 percentage points. Cash transfers decrease the poverty rates of nonaged households by an additional percentage point. Finally, food stamps and housing programs cut poverty rates of aged persons and families by an additional two percentage points.

WELFARE REFORM

The Family Support Act of 1988 is the most recent attempt to reform the U.S. welfare system. The legislation is designed to move people off the welfare rolls into productive employment. The legislation directs states to enroll their welfare recipients in programs offering remedial education, job training, work experience, and assistance with job search. By 1995, 20 percent of welfare recipients are supposed to be enrolled in these self-help programs. Parents with small children (less than three years old) are not required to participate in the training and job-search programs. The legislation also directs the states to require 16 hours of community service per month from two-parent welfare households.

Workfare

Workfare is defined as a program under which welfare recipients are forced to participate in various employment and training programs. Wiseman (1987) describes workfare as a process, a series of steps that a potential wel-

TABLE 12–9 Effects of Transfer Programs on Poverty, 1988

	Percent of Group in Poverty			
	Income before Transfers	After Social Security and Nonwelfare Transfers	After Cash Welfare Transfers	After Cash, Food Stamps, Housing
All persons	20.8	14.5	13.6	12.2
Families with children	19.5	17.4	16.5	14.6
Aged persons	55.8	15.3	13.9	11.8

SOURCE: U.S. Congress, Committee on Ways and Means, Background Material and Data on Programs within the Jurisdiction of the Committee on Ways and Means (Washington, D.C.: U.S. Government Printing Office, 1988), Appendix I.

fare recipient must go through to qualify for support. Figure 12–8 shows Wiseman's model of the workfare process.

    1. **Preliminary assessment.** A social worker gathers information about the applicant's skills and employment record and finds out what kind of assistance will be needed (e.g., child care, transportation) to get the person back to work.

    2. **Job search.** After developing a job-search strategy, the applicant searches for a job under the close supervision of a search supervisor. If the applicant finds a job, she drops out of the workfare process; if the job pays enough, she will also drop out of the welfare system.

    3. **Counseling.** If the applicant does not find a job after several weeks, she moves into a counseling program. The counselor determines the reasons for the unsuccessful job search and designs a program to enhance the applicant's employability.

    4. **Skill enhancement program.** Some of the enhancement options are unpaid work experience (community service), on-the-job training (public or private), or classroom training for specific skills.

    5. **Job search.** When the enhancement program is completed, the applicant searches again and hopefully finds a job and drops out of the workfare process. If not, she is recycled (sent back to counseling).

This model of workfare differs from the popular view of workfare in one important respect. The "work" in workfare is often assumed to be mandatory community service for no pay. In fact, community service is but one of the options under the skill-enhancement step of the program. Participants can also work in the classroom or earn money while acquiring on-the-job training.

    What happens if the applicant refuses to go through the workfare pro-

FIGURE 12–8 The Workfare Process

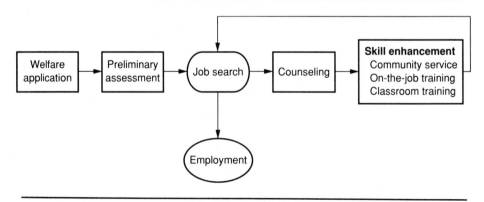

SOURCE: Michael Wiseman, "How Workfare Really Works," *The Public Interest*, Fall 1987, p. 39.

cess? A mild form of punishment is to remove some of the applicant's discretion in spending her welfare check. For example, the agency might pay her landlord and deduct the rent from her welfare check. A more severe punishment is to cut the welfare payment.

The experiments with workfare suggest that it may move a small number of people off the welfare rolls. In a widely cited experimental program in San Diego, 47 percent of workfare participants were receiving public assistance nine months after enrolling in the program, compared to 53 percent of a control group that did not go through the workfare process. In other words, workfare decreased the welfare caseload by a relatively small amount.

Reform Proposal—Child Support and Earned Income Credit

Garfinkel (1984) and Ellwood (1988) have proposed several changes in welfare policy. Their reform proposals have four features:

1. **Child-support requirements.** Absent fathers would be required to pay child support. For example, an absent father of two children would be required to pay one quarter of his income for child support. Under the current system, only about one third of female-headed households receive child support.

2. **Minimum child support.** The federal government would guarantee a minimum level of child support, for example, $1,750 per child per year. The federal government would make up the difference between the father's contribution and the minimum support level. The minimum child-support program would replace AFDC.

3. **Increased earned income tax credit.** The current EITC, which is 14 percent of earned income with a maximum credit of $868, would be increased to 25 percent of earned income with a maximum credit of $2,000.

4. **Child-care tax credit.** Poor families would receive a 30 percent tax credit for child care.

Table 12–10 shows the effects of such a scheme on the typical poor household. The figures are based on the assumption that the mother receives only the minimum level of child support. Many poor, female-headed households would in fact receive greater child-support payments from the absent father. The proposed scheme allows a single working mother to keep more of her earned income because (a) the earned income tax credit is more generous, (b) the cost of day care is reduced by the child-care credit, and (c) the child-support payment does not decrease as her income increases.

The proposal has several desirable features. First, if the absent father earns enough income, the 25 percent support payment will lift many female-headed households out of poverty. For example, if the father's income is $21,260, the child-support payment will be $5,315. If the mother works a half-time job at the minimum wage, her disposable income would be $9,800, just

TABLE 12–10 Earnings, Benefits, and Income for Single Parent with Two Children under Increased Earned Income Tax Credit and Guaranteed Child Support

Level of Work and Wages	Earnings	Day Care	Taxes + EITC	Child Support	Disposable Income
No work	0	0	0	3,500	3,500
Half time at minimum wage	4,400	−1,000	+1,085	3,500	7,985
Full time at minimum wage	8,800	−3,000	+1,511	3,500	10,811
Full time at $5.00 per hour	10,000	−3,000	+1,185	3,500	11,685
Full time at $6.00 per hour	12,000	−3,000	+642	3,500	13,142

Minimum wage assumed to be 4.40 per hour.
Taxes and EITC include:

1. 30% child-care tax credit
2. Social security tax of 7.15%
3. EITC of 25% up to $8,000; reduced by 20¢ per dollar above $8,000

SOURCE: David T. Ellwood, *Poor Support* (New York: Basic Books, 1988), p. 167.

above the poverty line. Second, because the working woman keeps more of her earnings, it encourages work effort. Finally, it may actually save taxpayers some money. According to Garfinkel, if the collection rate from absent fathers is 80 percent and the minimum child-support benefit is $2,000 per child, the program would cost less than the current welfare system. The program is sufficiently attractive that it is being tried in the state of Wisconsin.

THE PROBLEMS OF THE CENTRAL-CITY ECONOMY

One of the most difficult problems in the urban economy is the concentration of poverty in the central city. Particularly disturbing is the continued concentration of poor blacks in certain areas of central cities. In 1983, less than half of inner-city blacks in Boston, Philadelphia, and Chicago were employed (Freeman and Holzer 1986). In contrast, 61 percent of U.S. blacks and 76 percent of U.S. whites were employed. Along with low employment rates, central cities have high crime rates and widespread drug abuse.

The reasons for central-city poverty are discussed earlier in the chapter. Although the majority of jobs are now in the suburbs, the vast majority of blacks continue to live in central cities. Moreover, an increasing share of central-city jobs requires a college education, so most blacks are unable to take advantage of new job opportunities in the central city. Racial discrimination contributes to the black poverty problem: segregation inhibits the movement of blacks to the suburbs, and job discrimination limits their employment options. Education problems also contribute to poverty: central cities have inferior schools, so the average black teenager emerges from the education system with lower skills than the average white teenager.

The National Bureau of Economic Research (NBER) completed a comprehensive study of the black youth unemployment problem. Freeman and Holzer (1986) summarize the findings of the study and come to the following conclusions:

1. **Local labor market.** Cities with relatively strong labor markets had relatively high black teenage employment rates. For example, the employment rate in Boston (a city with a relatively healthy economy) was 10 percentage points above the employment rates in Chicago and Philadelphia. This finding is consistent with the notion that the most effective way to reduce poverty is through macroeconomic growth.

2. **Spatial mismatch.** Blacks who lived relatively close to jobs did not have lower unemployment rates: physical proximity to jobs did not decrease unemployment rates. This conclusion is based on Ellwood's (1986) study of Chicago (discussed earlier in the chapter). Blacks on the West Side, where jobs are plentiful, did not have lower unemployment rates than blacks on the South Side, where jobs are scarce. In addition, whites hold most of the jobs in the border areas between white and black neighborhoods.

3. **Competition with women.** Cities with the highest proportion of women in the labor market had the worst labor market for black teenagers (the lowest wages and participation rates). It seems that increases in female participation rates have decreased employment opportunities for young blacks.

4. **Discrimination.** Prospective employers treated black applicants differently than white ones. In general, employers were less courteous to black applicants.

5. **Family experience.** Black youth were more likely to be employed if other members of the family were employed. This suggests that adult joblessness increases youth unemployment, meaning that employment problems are passed from generation to generation.

6. **Reservation wage.** Black and white youths had comparable reservation wages (defined as the lowest acceptable wage). Because employers assumed that blacks were less productive, the black reservation wage was high relative to the assumed productivity, so employers systematically chose whites over blacks.

7. **Illegal opportunities.** Crime rates were higher in cities with fewer legal opportunities. Crime rates were also affected by the perceived risks and returns of crime: teenagers were more likely to commit crime if they perceived that the risks were low and the returns were high.

8. **Welfare involvement.** Teenagers from welfare families had more trouble in the labor market, even after controlling for differences in income and family structure. Youths living in public housing did worse than youths living in private housing.

9. **Education.** Employment and wages were affected by the amount of schooling and school performance. Youths with more years of schooling and higher grades had higher wages, more work hours, and lower crime rates.

The NBER study suggests that the problems of black inner-city teenagers are caused by many factors, including weak labor markets, competition with women, discrimination, opportunities for crime, and inadequate education. It suggests that a comprehensive approach will be required to decrease youth unemployment.

One approach to solving the inner-city poverty problem is based on the spatial mismatch theory. The idea is that poverty is caused by racial segregation and can be solved by one of two spatial policies: dispersal of the central-city population or economic development of the inner-city economy.

Dispersal Policies

Under a dispersal policy, central-city blacks would be moved to suburban communities. The idea behind dispersal is that blacks should live near suburban employment centers. As discussed earlier in this chapter, the government could promote black suburbanization with fair-housing laws, less restrictive zoning, and state support of local governments.

The critics of the dispersal option raise four questions:

1. **Integration.** Will dispersal cause real integration or the development of smaller, more numerous concentrations of racial minorities (mini-ghettos)?

2. **Black underclass.** Will dispersal allow the most mobile and wealthy blacks to move to the suburbs, leaving immobile and poor blacks in the central city? When middle-income blacks (e.g., clerical workers and midlevel managers) leave the central city, it becomes a less attractive location for employers, so employment opportunities for poor blacks (e.g., janitors) will decrease. In addition, the departure of middle-income blacks will decrease the demand for retail goods, decreasing the employment opportunities for low-skill retail workers. Some people fear that the departure of middle-income blacks will cause more poor blacks to slip into the underclass, defined as the group of people dependent on crime, drugs, and welfare.

3. **Cultural disruption.** Will the dispersal of blacks disrupt black culture and society?

4. **Spatial mismatch?** If the spatial mismatch theory is incorrect and geographical access to jobs is not an important factor in the black unemployment problem, simply moving blacks to the suburbs will not solve the problem. If poverty is caused by job discrimination, inferior education, and low skills, these problems must also be addressed.

The Development Option

The alternative to dispersal is the development of the central-city economy. In contrast to the dispersal policy, which brings workers to suburban jobs, the development policy bring jobs to central-city residents.

There are three approaches to central-city development. First, under the **black capitalism** approach, the government encourages the development of black businesses. The experiences with black capitalism have not been encouraging (see Bates and Bradford 1979). Second, **community development corporations** (CDCs) assist black businesses, oversee large development projects, and run various community projects (housing assistance, job training). Third, the government can establish **enterprise zones**, areas of the city where firms (*a*) pay lower taxes, (*b*) receive subsidies for worker training, and (*c*) are exempted from many local regulations. Given the limited experience with enterprise zones, it is too early to say whether they will decrease central-city poverty.

The critics of the development option raise four questions:

1. **Viable location.** Is the central city a viable location for firms? The suburbanization of jobs was caused by fundamental changes in the economy (e.g., the development of the auto and the truck, innovations in information technology). Given the advantages of a suburban location, a firm in the central city may be unable to compete with its suburban counterparts.

2. **Zero-sum employment changes.** Will the gain in central-city employment come at the expense of employment elsewhere in the metropolitan area?

3. **Low skills.** Do central-city residents have the education and skills to work in new stores, factories, and offices?

4. **Migration.** How many of the new central-city jobs will be filled by current residents of the central city? How many will be filled by newcomers?

5. **Spatial mismatch?** If the spatial mismatch theory is incorrect and geographical access to jobs is not the principal reason for the black unemployment problem, bringing jobs to the central city will not solve the problem. Other reasons for poverty (job discrimination, inferior education, and low skills) must be addressed.

The debate over dispersal versus development has been going on for decades. The issues are complex, and the questions raised by each side are not easily answered. In recent years, several states have experimented with enterprise zones. The information from these experiments will provide valuable information on the merits of the development option.

CONCLUSION—WHAT CAN BE DONE ABOUT POVERTY?

There is no single policy that will eliminate poverty. Nonetheless, there are many policies that could be used to whittle the problem down to a more manageable size. Title I education programs have increased the achievement level of disadvantaged students, increasing their earning potential. Job-training programs have increased the earnings of the most disadvantaged workers. The reform of child-support laws would increase support from absent fathers and decrease poverty among female-headed households. An increase in the earned income tax credit would decrease poverty and increase the incentives for welfare recipients to work. Finally, workfare may increase the employment opportunities of welfare recipients. Each of these policies may have a small effect on the poverty problem, but together they could decrease poverty significantly.

SUMMARY

1. A poor household is defined as one whose total income is less than three times the minimum food budget. Poverty rates are greatest among racial minorities, women, and central-city residents.

2. Economic growth decreases poverty because the poor are the last hired and the first fired.

3. One theory of black poverty is that blacks have been confined to the central city while employment has shifted to the suburbs. Critics of the spatial mismatch theory suggest that segregation plays a relatively small role in black poverty.

4. The poverty rate depends on the education level of the household head: the unemployment rate of high school dropouts is over six times the rate for college graduates and about twice the rate for high school graduates. A study of inner-city youths suggests that increased education increases wages and earnings and decreases crime rates.

5. Studies of education programs suggest that some programs increase achievement.
   a. The Perry Preschool program increased high school completion rates and decreased arrest rates.
   b. Studies of Title I programs suggest that they have increased achievement, with the largest gains at the elementary level.

6. Job discrimination contributes to poverty: in some circumstances, blacks are paid less than whites and women are paid less than men. Although market forces limit the extent of job discrimination, wage differences persist because of statistical discrimination.

7. Economic growth is a necessary—but not sufficient—condition for reducing poverty: because the poor are the last hired, it is necessary; because the poor must have the skills for the new jobs and must live near the new jobs, it is not sufficient.

8. The number of female-headed households has increased rapidly in the last few decades, thus increasing poverty rates.
   a. It appears that AFDC has increased the number of female-headed households by a small amount.
   b. The increase in male joblessness played a major role in the increase in female-headed households.

9. Some government job-training programs have been successful for some participants.
   a. Youth programs (Job Corps and YEPTA) increased earnings and decreased crime rates.
   b. Programs that stress classroom teaching and on-the-job training increased the earnings of women, particularly those with little work experience.

10. Because AFDC recipients have low wages, AFDC increases the opportunities for nonwork activities (e.g., child care) and either increases income or decreases it by a small amount. AFDC discourages work effort because the marginal tax rate is close to 100 percent.

11. The alternative to AFDC is a negative income tax, under which recipients would keep a large fraction of their market income. The problem with

such a program is that some households (those not eligible for AFDC) would decrease their labor supply.

12. The two largest in-kind transfer programs are medicaid and food stamps.
    a. Medicaid is equivalent to a private medical insurance policy. Medicaid has improved the health of the poor.
    b. Food-stamp allotments typically fall short of the food consumption of recipients, so food stamps are equivalent to cash payments.

13. Federal transfer programs decreased the overall poverty rate from 20.8 percent to 12.2 percent.

14. Under workfare, welfare recipients participate in various employment and training programs. The Family Support Act of 1988 has a workfare component that is designed to move people off the welfare rolls into productive employment.

15. One reform proposal combines required child-support payments from the absent father, a minimum child-support payment from the government, a tax credit for day care, and an increase in the earned income tax credit. Such a program would eliminate the need for AFDC and would encourage work effort.

16. One of the most difficult problems in the urban economy is the concentration of poverty among blacks in the central city. A study of the black youth unemployment problem suggests that low employment rates are caused by weak labor markets, competition with women, discrimination, opportunities for crime, and inadequate education.

17. Under a dispersal policy, blacks would be moved closer to suburban employment centers. The critics of the dispersal approach suggest that the suburbanization of employable blacks will contribute to the development of a permanent underclass in the central city.

18. Under a development policy, jobs would be moved closer to central-city blacks. Development strategies include black capitalism, community development corporations, and enterprise zones. The critics of the development approach suggest that the central city is not a viable location for most firms and that any central-city employment gains will come at the expense of other areas of the city. If central-city residents do not have the skills for the new jobs, the new jobs will be filled by newcomers.

EXERCISES AND DISCUSSION QUESTIONS

1. The section on job discrimination suggests that the market penalizes racist and sexist firms because such firms are underpriced by color-blind and sex-blind firms. As a result, there are limits on the extent of wage discrimination.
    a. What if all firms (capitalists and managers) are color-blind, but white laborers refuse to work with black laborers? Will wage discrimination (lower wages for blacks) persist?

    b. What if firms and employees are color-blind, but white consumers refuse to purchase goods produced by blacks? Who bears the cost of bigotry? Will wage discrimination persist?

2. Suppose that industries A and B together employ all workers in the economy. Initially, wage rates for all workers, male and female, are equal. Suppose that Congress passes a law that denies women the right to work in industry A.

    a. Under what circumstances will the law not affect the wages of men and women?

    b. Under what circumstances will the law decrease the wages of women and increase the wages of men?

    c. What are the implications for the effects of occupational discrimination on the wages of women?

3. Suppose that a comparable-worth law is enacted, requiring a 20-percent increase in the wages of female-dominated occupations. Who will bear the costs of this policy? How will the policy affect nonworking women and women who work in male-dominated occupations?

4. Comment on the following: "Black central-city residents are poor because they do not have access to suburban employment opportunities. I propose that we supply each central-city household with a car. Such a plan will reduce poverty at a relatively low cost."

5. Figure 12–4 shows the budget line for AFDC as if every dollar of market income decreases the AFDC payment by one dollar. Under current policy, the first $30 of market earnings do not affect the AFDC payment. Draw a budget line consistent with the current AFDC policy.

6. Explain why the food-stamp program can have the same effect on the consumption pattern and well-being of recipients as an outright cash transfer of the same cost.

7. Until 1979, food stamps were sold to recipients at a fraction of their market value. Consider a household with an income of $500. Suppose that the government charges $1 for a food stamp with a market value of $2, with a maximum of 100 food stamps per household.

    a. Draw the household's budget line with and without the food-stamp program.

    b. Under what circumstances will the food-stamp program be equivalent to a $100 cash payment?

8. Suppose that the government replaces AFDC with a refundable earned income tax credit of 25 percent. The government pays every current AFDC recipient 25 cents for every dollar of wage income. Consider the effects of the wage subsidy on the welfare recipient whose choices are shown in Figure 12–4.

    a. Draw the budget line for AFDC and the refundable tax credit.

    b. How does the policy affect the hours of labor? Is she more or less likely to continue working?

c. Suppose that the recipient's elasticity of supply of labor is 0.50: a 10 percent increase in the wage increases the number of hours worked by 5 percent. By how much will labor supply increase?

d. How does the policy change affect the government's welfare budget?

REFERENCES AND ADDITIONAL READINGS

Poverty Facts

U.S. Bureau of the Census. *Current Population Reports Series P-60*. Washington, D.C.: U.S. Government Printing Office.   Estimates poverty rates by status of household head and place of residence. Reports unemployment rates for different races and education levels.

U.S. Office of Management and Budget. *Budget of the United States Government, Fiscal Year 1987*. Washington, D.C.: U.S. Government Printing Office, 1986.   Projects spending on antipoverty programs.

General References

Ellwood, Daniel T. *Poor Support*. New York: Basic Books, 1988.   A detailed description and analysis of poverty among two-parent families, single-parent families, and residents of inner-city neighborhoods.

Freeman, Richard B., and Harry J. Holzer. "The Black Youth Employment Crisis: Summary of Findings," in *The Black Youth Employment Crisis*, ed. Richard B. Freeman and Harry J. Holzer. Chicago: University of Chicago Press, 1986. Summarizes the results of a series of studies that explore the reasons for the high unemployment among black youths.

Sawhill, Isabel V. "Poverty in the U.S.: Why Is It So Persistent?" *Journal of Economic Literature* 26 (1988), pp. 1073–119.   Explores the reasons for the persistence of poverty between the middle 1960s and 1988. Examines the influence of five factors: demographic changes (increased number of female-headed households), sluggish macroeconomic growth, inadequate investment in human capital, work disincentives of the welfare system, and the growing underclass. Concludes that the most important factors were demographic changes and rising unemployment.

Schiller, Bradley. *The Economics of Poverty and Discrimination*, 5th ed. Englewood Cliffs, N.J.: Prentice-Hall, 1989.

Poverty and Economic Growth

Blank, Rebecca M., and Alan S. Blinder. "Macroeconomics, Income Distribution, and Poverty." In *Fighting Poverty: What Works and What Doesn't*, ed. Sheldon H. Danziger and Daniel H. Weinberg. Cambridge, Mass.: Harvard Univ. Press, 1986.   Explores the relationship between macroeconomic conditions (unemployment and inflation) and poverty. Concludes that the poor suffer more from unemployment than inflation.

Danziger, Sheldon, and Peter Gottschalk. "Do Rising Tides Lift All Boats? The Impact of Secular and Cyclical Changes on Poverty." *American Economic Review* 76 (1986), pp. 405–410.

Gottschalk, Peter, and Sheldon Danziger. "Macroeconomic Conditions, Income Transfers, and the Trend in Poverty." In *The Social Contract Revisited*, ed. D. Lee Baudeng Washington, D.C.: Urban Institute, 1984.

Gramlich, Edward, and Deborah Laren. "How Widespread Are Income Losses in a Recession?" In *The Social Contract Revisited*, ed. D. Lee Bauden. Washington, D.C.: Urban Institute, 1984.   Estimates the distributional effects of recessions.

Segregation and Poverty: The Spatial Mismatch Theory

Ellwood, David T. "The Spatial Mismatch Hypothesis: Are There Teenage Jobs Missing in the Ghetto?" In *The Black Youth Employment Crisis*, ed. Richard B. Freeman and Harry J. Holzer. Chicago: University of Chicago Press, 1986, pp. 147–185. Provides evidence from Chicago that questions the validity of the spatial mismatch hypothesis.

Kain, John. "Black Suburbanization in the Eighties: A New Beginning or a False Hope?" In *American Domestic Priorities*, ed. John Quigley and Daniel Rubinfeld. Berkeley and Los Angeles: University of California Press, 1985.   Describes recent trends in the suburbanization of blacks.

Kain, John F., and J. Zax. "Feets don't fail me now: The Impact of Residential Segregation on Racial Employment Patterns." Working Paper.

Kain, John F. "Housing Segregation, Negro Employment, and Metropolitan Decentralization." *Quarterly Journal of Economics* 82 (1968), pp. 175–97.

Kain, John F. "Housing Segregation, Negro Employment, and Metropolitan Decentralization: A Retrospective View." In *Patterns of Racial Discrimination Volume I: Housing*, ed. George Von Furstenburg, Bennett Harrison, and Ann R. Horowitz. Lexington, Mass.: Lexington Books, 1974.   Kain's response to Mooney (1969).

Kasarda, John. "Urban Change and Minority Opportunities." In *The New Urban Reality*, ed. Paul Peterson, Washington, D.C.: Brookings Institution, 1985.   Discusses the effects of changes in the spatial distribution of employment on central-city blacks. Also discusses the mismatch between central-city employment opportunities and the labor skills of central-city residents.

Leonard, Jonathan. "Comment." In *The Black Youth Employment Crisis*, ed. Richard B. Freeman and Harry J. Holzer. Chicago: University of Chicago Press, 1986, pp. 185–190. Critiques the Ellwood (1986) paper.

Mills, Edwin S., and Richard Price. "Race and Residence in Earnings Determination." *Journal of Urban Economics* 17 (1985). pp. 1–8. Estimates the wage differentials caused by racial segregation and discrimination.

Mooney, Joseph D. "Housing Segregation, Negro Employment: An Alternative Perspective." *Quarterly Journal of Economics* 84 (1969), pp. 299–311.   Critique of Kain's (1968) results.

Orr, Larry L. *Income, Employment, and Residential Location*. New York: Academic Press, 1975.   A study of the spatial mismatch theory.

Pettigrew, Thomas. "Racial Change and the Intrametropolitan Distribution of Black Americans." In *The Prospective City*, ed. Arthur P. Solomon. Cambridge, Mass.: MIT Press, 1980.

Straszheim, Mahlon R. "Discrimination and the Spatial Characteristics of the Urban Labor Market for Black Workers." *Journal of Urban Economics* 7 (1980).   pp. 119–140. Shows that black wages are higher in the suburbs than in the central city, reflecting the segregation of blacks in central cities.

U.S. Department of Housing and Urban Development. *Measuring Racial Discrimination in American Housing Markets*. Washington, D.C.: U.S. Government Printing Office, 1979.

U.S. Department of Housing and Urban Development. *Recent Evidence on Discrimination*. Washington, D.C.: U.S. Government Printing Office, 1984.

Yinger, John. "Prejudice and Discrimination in the Urban Housing Market." In *Current Issues in Urban Economics*, ed. Peter Meiszkowski and Mahlon Straszheim. Baltimore: The Johns Hopkins Press, 1979.

Education and the Evaluation of Title I Programs

Aaron, Henry J. *Politics and the Professors—The Great Society in Perspective*. Washington, D.C.: Brookings Institution, 1978.   Discusses the uncertainty about the relationship between education and poverty.

Berrueta-Clement, John R., et al. *Changed Lives: The Effects of the Perry Preschool Programs on Youths Through Age 19*. Ypsilanti, Michigan: High-Scope Press, 1984.   Reports the results of a successful preschool program.

Glazer, Nathan. "Education and Training Programs and Poverty." In *Fighting Poverty. What Works and What Doesn't*, ed. Sheldon H. Danziger and Daniel H. Weinberg. Cambridge, Mass.: Harvard Univ. Press, 1986.   Discusses the effects of compensatory education on poverty, suggesting that preschool and elementary-school programs are most effective.

Jenks, Christopher. "Comment." In *Fighting Poverty: What Works and What Doesn't*, ed. Sheldon H. Danziger and Daniel H. Weinberg. Cambridge, Mass.: Harvard Univ. Press, 1986.   Discusses the effects of compensatory education on poverty; concludes that our understanding of the relationship between education and poverty is limited.

National Assessment of Educational Progress. *Has Title I Improved Education for Disadvantaged Students? Evidence from Three National Assessments on Reading*. Washington, D.C.: Department of Education, 1981.   Reports the results of NAEP tests showing increasing relative scores for minority students participating in Title I programs.

National Center for Educational Statistics. *The Condition of Education: A Statistical Report*. Washington, D.C.: Department of Education, 1982.   Reports the results of NAEP tests showing increasing relative scores for minority students participating in Title I programs.

Labor-Market Discrimination

Arrow, Kenneth. "The Theory of Discrimination." In *Discrimination in Labor Markets*, ed. Orley Ashenfelter and Albert Rees. Princeton, N.J.: Princeton University Press,

1973.   Describes the phenomenon of statistical discrimination, which explains the persistence of wage differentials.

Becker, Gary S. *The Economics of Discrimination.* Chicago: University of Chicago Press, 1957.   Describes the market theory of discrimination, which suggests that competition will limit the extent of wage discrimination.

Phelps, Edmund. "The Statistical Theory of Racism and Sexism." *American Economic Review* 62 (1972), pp. 659–61.   Explains the theory of statistical discrimination.

Smith, James P., and Finis Welch. "Race Differences in Earnings: A Survey and New Evidence." In *Current Issues in Urban Economics*, ed. Peter Meiszkowski and Mahlon Straszheim. Baltimore: The Johns Hopkins Press, 1979.   Summarizes the evidence on wage discrimination.

Thurow, Lester C. *Poverty and Discrimination.* Washington, D.C.: Brookings Institution, 1969.   Discusses the link between poverty and racial discrimination (unequal pay for equal work, denied access to high-paying jobs).

U.S. Commission on Civil Rights. Unemployment and Underemployment Among Blacks, Hispanics, and Women. Washington, D.C.: U.S. Government Printing Office, 1982.   Discusses labor-market discrimination against minority groups.

Increase in Female-Headed Households: Reasons and Effects on Poverty

Bane, Mary Jo. "Household Composition and Poverty." In *Fighting Poverty: What Works and What Doesn't*, ed. Sheldon H. Danziger and Daniel H. Weinberg. Cambridge, Mass.: Harvard Univ. Press, 1986.   Discusses the effects of changes in family structure on poverty rates, suggesting that such changes between 1959 and 1979 increased the 1979 poverty rate by two percentage points.

Ellwood, David T., and Lawrence H. Summers. "Poverty in America: Is Welfare the Answer or the Problem?" In *Fighting Poverty: What Works and What Doesn't*, ed. Sheldon H. Danziger and Daniel H. Weinberg. Cambridge, Mass.: Harvard Univ. Press, 1986.   Discusses the effects of AFDC on family structure, addressing the issue of whether AFDC causes the breakup of families.

Ellwood, David T., and Mary Jo Bane. "The Impact of AFDC on Family Structure and Living Arrangements." *Research in Labor Economics*, 7 (1985).   pp. 137–208. Explores the relationship between welfare benefit levels and family structure.

Moffit, Robert. "Work Incentives in the AFDC System: An Analysis of the 1981 Reforms." *American Economic Review* 76 (1986), pp. 219–23.

Murray, Charles. *Losing Ground: American Social Policy, 1950–1980.* New York: Basic Books, 1984.   Argues that welfare policy was a large factor in the growth of female-headed households.

Wilson, William Julius, and Kathryn Meckerman. "Poverty and Family Structure: The Widening Gap Between Evidence and Public Policy Issues." In *Fighting Poverty: What Works and What Doesn't*, ed. Sheldon H. Danziger and Daniel H. Weinberg. Cambridge, Mass.: Harvard Univ. Press, 1986.   Examines changes in fertility rates and family structure and the effects of welfare policy on the number of female-headed households. Concludes that male joblessness is the most important factor in the increase in female-headed households.

Evaluation of Employment and Job Training Programs

Bailey, Thomas R. "Market Forces and Private Sector Processes in Government Policy: The Job Training Partnership Act." *Journal of Policy Analysis and Management* 7 (1988), pp. 300–15.

Bassi, Laurie, and Orley Ashenfelter. "The Effect of Direct Job Creation and Training Programs on Low-Skilled Workers." In *Fighting Poverty: What Works and What Doesn't*, ed. Sheldon H. Danziger and Daniel H. Weinberg. Cambridge, Mass.: Harvard Univ. Press, 1986.   Discusses the history of employment and job-training programs and summarizes the conclusions from several studies of these programs.

Bloom, Howard S., and Maureen A. McLaughlin. *CETA Training Programs: Do They Work for Adults?* Washington, D.C.: Congressional Budget Office, 1982.   Analysis of the costs and benefits of the CETA program.

Haveman, Robert. *A Decade of Federal Anti-Poverty Programs: Achievements, Failures and Lessons.* New York: Academic Press, 1977.   Discusses the programs initiated under the Economic Opportunity Act of 1964 (the "war on poverty").

Manpower Demonstration Research Corporation. *Summary and Findings of the National Supported Work Demonstration.* Cambridge, Mass.: Ballinger, 1980.   Estimates benefit-costs ratios for participants in work-experience programs.

Schiller, Bradley. *The Economics of Poverty and Discrimination*, 5th ed. Englewood Cliffs, N.J.: Prentice-Hall, 1989.   Chapter 12 provides a historical sketch of employment and training programs.

The Negative Income Tax

Aaron, Henry J. "Six Welfare Questions Still Searching for Answers." *Brookings Review* (Fall 1984) pp. 1–20.   Summarizes the results of the negative income tax experiment.

Robins, Philip K.; Robert G. Spiegleman; and Samuel Weiner. *A Guaranteed Annual Income: Evidence from a Social Experiment.* New York: Academic Press, 1980.

Rossi, Peter, and Katherine Lyall. *Reforming Public Welfare: A Critique of the Negative Income Tax Experiment.* New York: Sage Foundation, 1976.

In-Kind Transfers: Food Stamps and Medicaid

Aaron, Henry J. "Six Welfare Questions Still Searching for Answers." *Brookings Review* (Fall 1984), pp. 1–20.   Discusses the political feasibility of converting from in-kind to cash programs.

Blanchard, Lois; J. S. Butler; T. Doyle; R. Jackson; J. Ohls; and Barbara Posner. *Final Report, Food Stamp SSI/Elderly Cash-Out Demonstration Evaluation.* Princeton, N.J.: Mathematica Policy Research, 1982.   When food-stamp recipients were given cash instead of food stamps, expenditures on food did not change. This suggests that food stamps are equivalent to cash payments.

Smeeding, Timothy M. "Alternative Methods for Evaluating Selected In-Kind Transfer Benefits and Measuring Their Effect on Poverty." U.S. Bureau of the Census, Technical Paper no. 50. Washington, D.C.: U.S. Government Printing Office, 1982.   Estimates the value of in-kind transfers to the recipients. Estimates that $1 of food stamps is worth 97 cents to the typical recipient, $1 of medicaid is worth 44 cents, and $1 of public housing is worth 80 cents.

Starr, Paul. "Health Care for the Poor: The Past 20 Years." In *Fighting Poverty: What Works and What Doesn't*, ed. Sheldon H. Danziger and Daniel H. Weinberg. Cambridge, Mass.: Harvard Univ. Press, 1986.   Discusses the effects of medicaid on the health of the poor.

Effects of Government Transfer Programs on Poverty

Danziger, Sheldon H.; Robert H. Haveman; and Robert D. Plotnick. "Anti-Poverty Policy: Effects on the Poor and the Non-Poor." In *Fighting Poverty: What Works and What Doesn't*, ed. Sheldon H. Danziger and Daniel H. Weinberg. Cambridge, Mass.: Harvard Univ. Press, 1986.   Estimates the combined effects of cash and in-kind transfers on poverty. Concludes that these programs decreased the number of people in poverty by about 46 percent.

Paglin, Morton. "Poverty in the United States: A Reevaluation." *Policy Review* 8 (1979), pp. 7–24.   Discusses the effects of in-kind transfers on poverty rates.

U.S. Congress Committee on Ways and Means. *Background Material and Data on Programs within the Jurisdiction of the Committee on Ways and Means*. Washington, D.C.: U.S. Government Printing Office, 1988.   Estimates the effects of different transfer programs on poverty rates.

Reform Proposal: Child Support

Ellwood, Daniel T. *Poor Support*. New York: Basic Books, 1988.   Chapter 5 discusses poverty among female-headed households and describes a reform proposal based on requirements for child support by absent fathers.

Garfinkel, Irwin, and Elizabeth Uhr. "A New Approach to Child Support." *Public Interest* 75 (Spring 1984), pp.111–122.   Proposes a scheme under which absent parents would pay a child-support tax.

Garfinkel, Irwin. "Child Support Assurance: A New Tool for Achieving Social Security." Unpublished paper, University of Wisconsin, 1985.

Reform Proposal: Workfare

Frielander, Daniel; Barbara Goldman; Judith Gueron; and David Wong. "Initial Findings from the Demonstration of State Work-Welfare Initiatives." *American Economic Review, Papers and Proceedings* 76 (2) (1986), pp. 224–29.   Discusses the effects of a program under which AFDC recipients receive work experience and job training. Concludes that workfare may decrease the number of welfare recipients.

Gideonse, Sarah K., and William R. Meyers. "Why Workfare Fails." *Challenge* 31 (January-February 1988), pp. 44–49.   Argues that the poor will not escape poverty unless they receive basic education and job skills. Discusses some of the reasons for the failure of the Work Incentives Program (WIN) and the implications for workfare.

Long, David A. "The Budgetary Implications of Welfare Reform: Lessons from Four State Initiatives." *Journal of Policy Analysis and Management* 7 (1988), pp. 289–99.

Mead, Lawrence M. "The Potential for Work Enforcement: A Study of WIN." *Journal of Policy Analysis and Management* 7 (1988), pp. 264–88.

Wiseman, Michael. "How Workfare Really Works." *Public Interest* 89 (Fall 1987), pp. 36–47. Describes the features of the typical workfare system and discusses the key questions to be asked in the evaluation of a workfare program.

Transfer Policy

Bane, Mary Jo, and David T. Ellwood. "Slipping into and out of Poverty: The Dynamics of Spells." *Journal of Human Resources* 21 (1986), pp. 1–23. Discusses the fact that many families stay on welfare for long periods of time.

Danziger, Sheldon, and Daniel Fester. "Income Transfers and Poverty in the 1980's." In *American Domestic Priorities*, ed. John Quigley and Daniel Rubinfeld. Berkeley and Los Angeles: University of California Press, 1985. Reviews the recent history of income-transfer programs.

Smolensky, Eugene. "Is a Golden Age in Poverty Policy Right Around the Corner?" *Focus* (Spring 1985), pp. 3–18. Discusses means of preventing the development of a permanent underclass of welfare dependents.

Development versus Dispersal

Banfield, Edward C. "Why Government Cannot Solve the Urban Problem." In *The Urban Economy*, ed. Harold M. Hochman. New York: Norton, 1976, pp. 257–72.

Bateman, Worth, and Harold M. Hochman. "Social Problems and the Urban Crisis: Can Public Policy Make a Difference?" In *The Urban Economy*, ed. Harold M. Hochman. New York: Norton, 1976, pp. 283–93.

Bates, Timothy, and William Bradford. *Financing Black Economic Development*. New York: Academic Press, 1979. Describes experiences with subsidized loans for black capitalism.

Brimmer, Andrew F., and Henry S. Terrell. "The Economic Potential of Black Capitalism." In *The Urban Economy*, ed. Harold M. Hochman. New York: Norton, 1976, pp. 239–56. Discusses the problems associated with the black-capitalism approach. Concludes that the approach is unlikely to substantially improve the economic position of blacks.

Butler, Stuart M. "Free Zones in the Inner City." In *Urban Economic Development* vol. 27, *Urban Affairs Annual Reviews*, ed. Richard D. Bingham and John P. Blair. Beverly Hills: Sage, 1984.

Edel, Matthew. "Development versus Dispersal: Approaches to Ghetto Poverty." In *Readings in Urban Economics*, ed. Matthew Edel and Jerome Rothenberg. New York: Macmillan, 1972, pp. 307–25.

Garn, Harvey A.; Nancy L. Tevis; and Carl E. Snead. *Evaluating Community Development Corporations: A Summary Report*. Washington, D.C.: Urban Institute, 1976. Describes experiences with CDCs.

Harrison, Bennett. "Ghetto Economic Development." *Journal of Economic Literature* 12 (1974), pp. 1–37.

Kain, John F., and Joseph J. Persky. "Alternatives to the Guilded Ghetto." *Public Interest* (Winter 1969), pp. 74–87. Reprinted in *The Urban Economy*, ed. Harold M. Hochman. New York: Norton, 1976, pp. 211–25.

Orfield, Gary. "Ghettoization and Its Alternatives." In *The New Urban Reality*, ed. Paul Peterson. Washington, D.C.: Brookings Institution, 1985.

Urban Underclass

Auletta, Ken. *The Underclass.* New York: Random House, 1982.

Lemann, Nicholas. "The Origins of the Underclass." *Atlantic Monthly* (June and July 1986), pp. 31–55; 54–68.   Discusses the development of a black underclass in central cities.

Ricketts, Erol R., and Isabel V. Sawhill. "Defining and Measuring the Underclass." *Journal of Policy Analysis and Management* 7 (1988), pp. 316–25.

Wilson, William Julius. "The Urban Underclass in Advanced Industrial Society." In *The New Urban Reality*, ed. Paul Peterson. Washington, D.C.: Brookings Institution, 1985.   Discusses the special problems of the urban underclass.

CHAPTER 13

Why Is Housing Different?

This is the first of two chapters on urban housing. This chapter explains why housing is a unique commodity, focusing on five characteristics that make housing different from other goods. First, the housing stock is heterogeneous: dwellings differ in size, location, age, floor plan, interior features, and utilities. Second, housing is immobile: it is impractical to move a dwelling from one location to another. Third, housing is durable: if a house is maintained properly, it can be used for several decades. Fourth, housing is expensive: to purchase a dwelling, a household must borrow a large sum of money. Finally, moving costs are relatively high: in addition to the substantial monetary costs of moving, there are also costs associated with leaving the old neighborhood—with its schools, stores, and friends—behind. Although other goods have some of these five characteristics, housing is unique because it has all five characteristics.

The chapter explains how these five characteristics affect the housing market. The first section shows that because housing is heterogeneous and immobile, the housing market is split into a set of distinct but related housing submarkets. The second section explores the effects of durability. It describes the "filtering" process (through which housing is passed from one type of household to another) and explains the special features of the market for used housing. The filtering model explains how subsidies for new housing benefit poor households in used housing. The second section also discusses the market forces behind the abandonment of older housing in central cities and the effects of public policy on abandonment. The third section explains that the high cost of housing forces consumers to choose between renting and owning. It explores the relative costs of owning and renting, as well as the effects of public policy on the choice between renting and owning. The final section discusses the effects of moving costs on housing consumption.

HETEROGENEITY AND IMMOBILITY

The housing stock is heterogeneous in the sense that each dwelling offers a different combination of features, that is, a different bundle of housing services. There are two types of housing features: dwelling characteristics and site characteristics.

Consider first the features of the dwelling itself. Dwellings differ in size (square footage of living space) and layout (the arrangement of rooms within the dwelling). They also differ in the quality and efficiency of kitchen equipment and utility systems (heating, air-conditioning, plumbing, electrical).

Other differences occur in interior design (type of flooring, windows, cabinets) and structural integrity (the durability of the foundation and the roof). To summarize, every dwelling offers a different bundle of size, layout, utilities, structural integrity, and interior design.

Because housing is immobile, one component of the housing bundle is the residential location. In other words, a house buyer purchases both a dwelling and a set of site characteristics. One site characteristic is accessibility: sites differ in their access to jobs, shopping, and entertainment. Another site characteristic is the provision of local public services: metropolitan areas have dozens of local governments, each of which provides a different combination of taxes and public services (schools, fire protection, police). A third characteristic is environmental quality: sites differ in air quality, noise levels, and scenic views. A final site characteristic is the appearance of the neighborhood (the exterior features of neighboring houses and lots). To summarize, housing is consumed along with a residential site, so the housing bundle includes several site attributes, including access to different activities, public services, environmental quality, crime rates, and neighborhood characteristics.

The Price of Housing—The Hedonic Approach

What determines the equilibrium price of a dwelling? The hedonic approach is based on the notion that a dwelling is composed of a bundle of individual components, each of which has an implicit price. The market price of a dwelling is the sum of the prices of the individual components.

The hedonic approach can be explained with a model of a housing market in which dwellings differ in only three ways. Suppose that dwellings differ in location (the distance to jobs in the city center) the number of bedrooms, and the age of the roof. A hedonic study of the market might generate the following information:

1. **Base price.** The average house has three bedrooms and a six-year-old roof. It is located five miles from the city center and sells for $70,000.

2. **Location price.** The price of housing drops by $1,000 for every additional mile from the city center: more accessible dwellings have higher prices.

3. **Bedroom price.** The price of housing increases by $10,000 for every additional bedroom: larger dwellings have higher prices.

4. **Roof price.** The price of housing decreases by $100 for every additional year of roof age: an older roof means that the roof must be replaced sooner, so the market price of the dwelling is lower.

To predict the price of a particular dwelling, one needs information on location, the number of bedrooms, and the age of the roof. For example, consider a four-bedroom house located seven miles from the city center that has a two-year-old roof. Such a house would sell for $78,400 (the base price of

$70,000 plus $10,000 for the extra bedroom, less $2,000 for the extra two miles, plus $400 for the four extra years of roof life).

Kain and Quigley (1975) used data from the St. Louis housing market in the 1960s to estimate the dollar values of different housing attributes. Table 13–1 shows some of their results. There are three types of housing characteristics: the quality of the dwelling itself, the size of the dwelling, and site characteristics. The numbers in the table show the increases in monthly rent (for rental housing) and market value (for owner-occupied housing) resulting from one-unit increases in the various housing attributes. For example, a one-unit increase in interior quality (a measure of the quality of floors, windows, walls, ceilings, stairways) increased the monthly rent by $1.31 (about 2.1 percent of the average monthly rent of $61.34) and increased the market value by $818 (about 5.6 percent of the average market value of $14,596). Rental units with central heating rented for $4.44 more per month, and older dwellings had lower rent and market value. The price of housing is also affected by dwelling size: a second bathroom added $9.07 to monthly rent and $769 to market value. The exterior quality of nearby dwellings was measured on a scale of 1 (bad) to 5 (excellent). A one-unit increase in the quality of dwellings on the block increased rent by $3.17 and market value by $419. The final variable is distance to the central business district: a one-mile increase in distance

TABLE 13–1   Change in Housing Prices from One-Unit Increases in Housing Attributes: A Hedonic Study of the St. Louis Housing Market

	Rental Market Increase in Monthly Rent ($)	Owner-Occupied Market Increase in Market Value ($)
Dwelling quality		
Interior	1.31	818
Central heating	4.44	—
Age	−0.29	−100
Size of dwelling		
Number of rooms	22.63	1,453
Number of baths	9.07	769
Site characteristics		
Exterior quality of adjacent dwellings	1.86	777
Exterior quality of dwellings on block	3.71	419
Miles from CBD	−0.30	−354
Average monthly rent = $61.34		
Average market value = $14,596		

SOURCE: John F. Kain and John M. Quigley, *Housing Markets and Racial Discrimination: A Microeconomic Analysis* (New York: National Bureau of Economic Research, 1975), Table 8.2, p. 200.

to the employment center decreased the monthly rent by $0.30 and the market value by $354.

Choosing a Dwelling

How does a household choose among alternative dwellings, each of which provides a different bundle of characteristics? The household must find the dwelling with the best combination of features at the best price. Most consumers do not have access to a hedonic study of their housing market. As they shop, they gather their own information about the implicit prices of location, size, and design features. Eventually, the household chooses a bundle that maximizes the household's utility subject to its budget constraints.

The household chooses the dwelling that provides the best affordable combination of features. Consider a housing market in which dwellings differ in only two respects: size (square feet of living space) and quality (of floors, walls, and roof). Figure 13–1 shows the housing choices for three different households. There are two budget lines: AB is the budget line for middle-

FIGURE 13–1   Households with Different Income and Preferences Choose Dwellings of Different Size and Quality

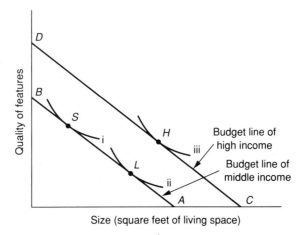

The household's choice of a combination of size and quality reflects the household's subjective trade-off between size and quality (as represented in indifference curves *i, ii, iii*), the market trade-off (as shown in the slope of the budget line), and household income (which determines the position of the budget line). Households S and L (both middle-income households) choose different combinations because they have different tastes for housing: L chooses a large, low-quality dwelling, while S chooses a small, high-quality dwelling. The high-income household (H) chooses a large, high-quality dwelling.

income households S and L, and CD is the budget line for H, a high-income household. The position of the budget line is determined by the household's housing budget. The slope of the budget line is determined by the implicit prices of size and quality: the larger the price of quality relative to the price of size, the flatter the budget line. The indifference curves show the different combinations of quality and size that generate the same utility. Three indifference curves are shown: S's indifference curve is labeled "i"; L's is "ii"; H's is "iii." The indifference curves are negatively sloped, reflecting the household's subjective trade-off between quality and size: as quality decreases, the household needs a larger dwelling to achieve the same utility level.

Housing choices reflect the household's preferences and income. Given the shape of its indifference curves, household L (a middle-income household) chooses a large, low-quality dwelling. Although household S has the same income and housing budget as L, S chooses a smaller, higher-quality dwelling. Its choice is rational because S has relatively strong preferences for quality, as shown by the shape of its indifference curve. Household H has a higher income and a larger housing budget, so it chooses a large, high-quality dwelling. The high-income household faces the same monetary trade-off between size and quality (the same opportunity cost) but it has more money to spend on both size and quality.

Segmented but Related Markets

The heterogeneity of the housing stock means that a city's housing market is composed of a number of submarkets. The housing market is segmented with respect to size, location, and quality. For example, some households look for small dwellings, while others look for large ones. Therefore, there will be one market for small dwellings and another market for large ones. Similarly, some households look for houses accessible to central-city jobs, while others look for houses in high-quality school districts. Finally, some households look for new houses, full of modern conveniences, while others look for older houses with old-world charm.

Although the housing market is segmented into submarkets, the submarkets are related because consumers have some flexibility in their housing choices. As the relative price of three-bedroom houses increases, some households will switch from the three-bedroom market to the two-bedroom market. Similarly, as the price of older houses increases relative to the price of new ones, some households will switch to the new-housing market. In other words, dwellings from different submarkets are imperfect substitutes, so households move between the submarkets in response to changes in the relative prices of different types of housing. The implications of the segmented housing market will be discussed later in the chapter.

Neighborhood Effects

The quantity of housing services produced by a particular dwelling depends not only on the characteristics of the dwelling, but also on the characteristics of its neighborhood. When one home owner improves the appearance of his house by painting it or repairing its broken windows, the neighborhood becomes a more desirable place to live, so the market values of surrounding houses increase. This is the **neighborhood effect**: changes in the exterior appearance of one house cause spillover benefits (increases in market value) for surrounding houses. Although there is no doubt that neighborhood effects exist, there is some question as to their magnitude and geographical extent.

Economists use the hedonic approach to estimate the magnitude of neighborhood effects (see Crecine, Davis, and Jackson 1967; and Kain and Quigley 1975). In Table 13–1, a one-unit increase in the quality of adjacent dwellings increased monthly rent by $1.86 and increased market value by $777. Similarly, improvements to other dwellings on the block increased rent and market value. The evidence from hedonic studies suggests that neighborhood effects are highly localized: the spillover benefits from changes in the exterior appearance of one house are confined to dwellings within a few hundred feet of the house.

DURABILITY OF HOUSING

Housing is more durable than most goods. If a dwelling is maintained properly, it can last a hundred years or more. Although dwellings deteriorate over time, they do so at a relatively slow rate. The durability of housing has three implications for the housing market. First, the landlord can control the rate of physical deterioration by spending money on repair and maintenance. Second, there is a large supply of used housing on the market every year. The general rule of thumb is that new construction in a given year is between 2 percent and 3 percent of the total housing stock. Over the course of a decade, new dwellings provide about 20 percent to 30 percent of the housing stock, so between 70 percent and 80 percent of households live in dwellings that are at least 10 years old. The final implication is that the supply of housing is relatively inelastic: the market is dominated by the stock of used housing, so changes in price cause relatively small changes in the quantity supplied.

Deterioration and Maintenance

A property owner can control the rate of physical deterioration by spending time and money on repair and maintenance. Landlords have the incentive to maintain and repair their property because these activities increase the quantity of housing services (Q) generated by the dwelling. Consumers are willing to pay more for a dwelling that generates a larger quantity of housing services, so an increase in maintenance increases rent and market value. The question for the landlord is: How much should I spend on maintenance?

Figure 13–2 shows the benefits and costs of maintenance. The horizontal axis measures the quantity of housing service generated by the dwelling (Q), which the landlord can affect by repairing broken windows and leaky roofs, maintaining the heating and plumbing systems, and painting the house. The total-cost curve shows the sum of fixed costs (independent of Q) and variable costs. The fixed cost ($100) includes taxes and the costs of managing the property (collecting rent, advertising for tenants). The variable costs include repair and maintenance costs. The total-cost curve is positively sloped because variable costs increase with Q: it costs more to maintain a dwelling at a higher Q. The cost curve is convex from below, a result of diminishing returns to maintenance: as Q increases, it becomes progressively more costly to maintain the property at the given Q. The straight line in Figure 13–2 shows the relationship between total revenue (rent per month) and Q. The implicit assumption

FIGURE 13–2   Optimum Quantity of Housing Service

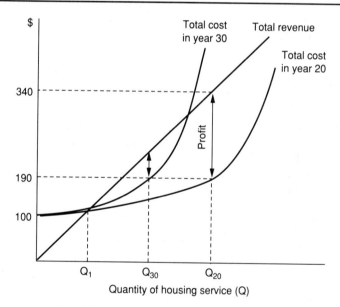

The optimum quantity of housing services is the Q at which profit (total revenue less total cost) is maximized. In year 20, profit is maximized at Q_{20}. The aging of the dwelling increases maintenance costs, shifting the cost curve upward and decreasing the optimum Q.

is that the price per unit of Q is constant: a dwelling with twice the quantity of housing services commands twice the rent.

The landlord's profit equals the difference between total revenue and total costs. In year 20 (20 years after the dwelling was built), the landlord has the lower of the two cost curves. Profit is positive above Q_1 and reaches its maximum level at Q_{20}. At Q_{20}, the slope of the revenue curve equals the slope of the cost curve, that is, the marginal benefit (change in total revenue per unit change in Q) equals marginal cost (the change in total cost per unit change in Q). Therefore, the profit-maximizing landlord will choose an output of Q_{20} units of housing services.

The optimum quantity of housing service will change over time, a result of changes in variable costs or changes in demand.

1. **Change in variable costs.** As the dwelling ages, it becomes progressively more costly to maintain at a given quantity of housing service level. In Figure 13–2, between year 20 and 30, the fixed cost does not change, but maintenance costs increase, causing an upward tilt of the total-cost curve. By year 30, the optimum quantity drops from Q_{20} to Q_{30}, and the landlord's profit falls.

2. **Change in demand.** Suppose that the demand for housing in a particular area decreases, decreasing the equilibrium price of rental housing. In Figure 13–2, the total-revenue function would tilt downward (pivoting from the origin), decreasing the profits associated with every Q. As the revenue function tilts downward, the optimum Q decreases.

The Retirement Decision

What happens when the profit from rental housing is negative? Suppose that because of changes in costs or demand, the total-cost curve lies above the total-revenue curve for all values of Q. Rental housing will clearly be unprofitable, leaving the landlord with three options: conversion, boarding up, and abandonment.

1. **Conversion.** A dwelling can be converted to nonresidential use such as an office, a store, or a parking lot. Conversion will be profitable if the alternative activity generates enough profit to offset the costs of conversion to the nonresidential use. If conversion would require the demolition of the dwelling and the construction of a new building, conversion costs will be relatively high and conversion may be unprofitable.

2. **Boarding up.** A dwelling can be boarded up and taken off the market temporarily. The board-up option will be profitable if two conditions are met. First, if the landlord expects the market rent to increase sometime in the future, expected profits will eventually be positive. Second, if the landlord's carrying costs (the opportunity cost of keeping his

money in housing instead of a bank account) are relatively low, there will be relatively low costs associated with waiting for the market rent to increase. This type of temporary retirement was common during the Great Depression.

3. **Abandonment.** The owner can disown the dwelling and walk away from the property. Abandonment will be profitable if the alternative uses (retail, commercial, industrial) do not generate enough profit to cover the costs of converting the property from residential to nonresidential use. If conversion costs are high, the market value of the property will be zero, so there will be no reason to keep title to the property.

Retirement results from three types of changes that decrease the profitability of rental housing. On the demand side of the market, a decrease in average income or a decrease in population will decrease the demand for housing in certain areas. As the market rent falls, the total-revenue curve tilts downward, decreasing profits. On the supply side, an increase in the supply of rental housing will decrease market rents and profits. Finally, as the dwelling ages, increases in maintenance costs will decrease the profits generated from a given total-revenue curve, increasing the likelihood of conversion or abandonment.

Abandonment and Public Policy

How does tax policy affect abandonment? White (1986) shows that the property tax increases the frequency of abandonment. Because old, low-quality dwellings have relatively high tax liabilities, landlords have less incentive to keep title to their properties. Some landlords abandon their property to avoid taxes.

Figure 13–3 shows the effects of the property tax on the landlord's revenues and costs. Given the initial total-revenue curve, the optimum quantity of housing services is Q_0; total revenue is $340; total cost is $190; and profit is $150 per month. Suppose that the assessed value of the rental property is $24,000 and the tax rate is 3 percent of assessed value per year, or $720 per year ($60 per month). If so, the posttax profit will be $90 ($150 − $60).

Suppose that the demand for housing decreases, tilting the total-revenue curve downward. The profit-maximizing Q will drop to Q_2, and pretax profit will drop to $48 ($210 − $162). The decrease in profit will lower the market value of the property: an investor will be willing to pay less for the property because it yields less profit. In a perfect tax world, the government would decrease the assessed value of the property to reflect its lower market value, thus decreasing the landlord's tax liability. If the tax stays at $60, however, the posttax profit will be negative ($48 − $60 = − $12), so the landlord is likely to abandon the property. To prevent abandonment, the government would have to cut the tax liability to less than $48.

White (1986) explores the effects of various factors on abandonment in

FIGURE 13–3   A Fixed Property Tax of $60 Encourages Abandonment

If the property tax is fixed at $60 per month, posttax profit is $90 instead of $150. A decrease in demand tilts the revenue curve downward, decreasing the optimum service level to Q_2. Pretax profit is $48, but posttax profit is $-$12. A fixed property tax will cause abandonment despite the fact that pretax profit is positive. If the property were reassessed after the decrease in demand, its tax liability would decrease, making abandonment less likely.

New York City and concludes that the property tax is by far the most important factor. She estimated that the elasticity of abandonment with respect to the property tax is 1.65: a 10 percent increase in the property tax increased the frequency of abandonment by 16.5 percent. For example, if the average assessed value of properties in the Brownsville section of Brooklyn were cut by $1,000 (a 6 percent reduction), the resulting decreases in property taxes would decrease the abandonment rate from 17 percent per year to 14.8 percent. Given this large elasticity, a tax cut would generate a fiscal surplus for the city: although the tax liability per property would decrease, the direct revenue loss would be offset by (a) an increase in the number of properties on the tax rolls and (b) a decrease in the number of properties that the city must either take over or demolish.

Because abandonment is the ultimate neighborhood externality, it contributes to the problems of central-city neighborhoods. Abandoned buildings provide targets for vandals and graffiti artists, and quickly become eyesores.

Even worse, they often become the temporary homes and retail outlets for transients and drug dealers and thus contribute to crime. For these reasons, abandonment decreases the relative attractiveness of the neighborhood and decreases the rent that other landlords can charge for their properties. Abandonment feeds on itself, transforming livable neighborhoods into unlivable ones.

Durability and Supply Elasticity

The durability of housing also has important implications for the market supply curve. Consider the response to an increase in the demand for housing. In the short run, the supply of housing is fixed, so the increase in demand will increase the equilibrium price. In the long run, suppliers will respond to the increase in market price by increasing the quantity of housing supplied. The questions are: By how much will supply increase, and how soon will it increase?

There are three types of supply responses to an increase in price:

1. **Build new dwellings.** As the price rises, new housing will become more profitable, so more dwellings will be built. Most of the new dwellings will be built on vacant land in the suburbs.

2. **Slower deterioration of used dwellings.** As the price of housing increases, the benefits of maintaining dwellings will increase. Landlords will spend more on maintenance and repair, slowing the deterioration rate and decreasing the number of dwellings retired from the housing stock.

3. **Remodel used dwellings.** Some landlords will upgrade their dwellings, increasing the quantity of housing services generated.

Because the bulk of housing is used housing, the supply response will be relatively large only if the second and third responses (the used-housing responses) are relatively large.

How responsive is the supply of used housing to an increase in price? Although an increase in price slows down the deterioration process, the process is slow in the first place, so the supply response is relatively small. In addition, remodeling is extremely expensive, so it takes a very large price hike to make modifications worthwhile. For these two reasons, housing supply will be relatively inelastic for relatively long periods of time. In other words, the supply side of the housing market is sluggish: it takes suppliers a long time to respond to an increase in the demand for housing. In the meantime, the price of housing will remain relatively high.

The same argument applies to a decrease in housing demand and the resulting decrease in the market price. A decrease in price decreases the incentives for maintenance, so dwellings will deteriorate at a faster rate and more dwellings will be retired. Even the fastest deterioration rate is relatively slow, so the decrease in the quantity supplied will be relatively small for relatively long periods of time. Although dwellings can be converted to other uses, the high cost of conversion inhibits this response. Because a decrease in price causes relatively small changes in a large part of the market, supply will be relatively inelastic for a long period of time. Therefore, the lower price of housing will prevail for a long period of time.

What is the price elasticity of the supply of housing? Unfortunately, economists have been unable to answer this question. It is difficult to estimate the supply elasticity because it is difficult to measure the quantity of housing services. The existing studies of housing supply suffer from a number of statistical problems (see Olson 1985; and Quigley 1979), so their results must be interpreted with caution. Ozanne and Struyk (1978) estimate that the supply elasticity of used housing is between 0.20 and 0.30. In other words, a 10 percent increase in the market price increases the quantity of used housing on the market by between 2 percent and 3 percent. Over a 10-year period, new construction provides only about 30 percent of the housing stock, so their estimate applies to 70 percent of the housing stock over a 10-year period. De Leeuw and Ekanem (1971) estimate that the long-run supply elasticity for rental housing is between 0.30 to 0.70. In other words, the available evidence, which is of questionable validity, suggests that the supply of housing is relatively inelastic over relatively long periods of time.

The Filtering Model of the Housing Market

The filtering model captures some of the essential features of the market for used housing. It describes the interactions between different housing submarkets and explains the process through which a dwelling passes from one use to another. The filtering process has two basic features:

1. **Decrease in housing service.** The quantity of housing service produced by a particular dwelling decreases over time. The decrease in Q results from physical deterioration, technological obsolescence, and changes in housing fashion.

2. **Decrease in occupant income.** The dwelling is occupied by households with progressively lower incomes. As Q decreases, the dwelling is occupied by households that demand progressively lower quantities of housing service, typically households with lower incomes.

The filtering model can be used to address two questions. First, why do the poor occupy used housing instead of new housing? Second, do the poor benefit from policies that subsidize the construction of new housing for the wealthy?

Why Do the Poor Occupy Used Housing?   Consider a city with the following characteristics:

1. **Three income groups.** There are three income groups (wealthy, middle-income, and poor).

2. **Rising income.** Real income is increasing over time, causing increases in the desired quantities of housing service for all three income groups.

3. **Costly upgrading.** It is relatively costly to upgrade dwellings: increases in quality and size are relatively expensive.

4. **Deterioration.** Houses are built every decade and deteriorate by five units of housing service per decade.

Figure 13–4 shows the city's housing market in 1980. The wealthy demand 160 units of housing service and occupy new houses (point f). The middle-income households demand 135 units of service (point d), occupying houses built in 1970 (which produced 140 units of service when they were new and 135 units one decade later). The middle-income households occupy smaller and lower quality dwellings than the wealthy. The poor households demand 110 units of service and live in houses built in 1960 (point b).

Suppose that the real incomes of all three groups increase between 1980 and 1990. The desired quantities of housing service increase to 180 for the rich, 155 for the middle-income households, and 130 for the poor. Figure 13–4 shows one possible arrangement of the 1990 housing market. New dwellings with 180 units of service are built for the wealthy, so the wealthy move from

FIGURE 13–4   Filtering: The Allocation of Housing in 1980 and 1990

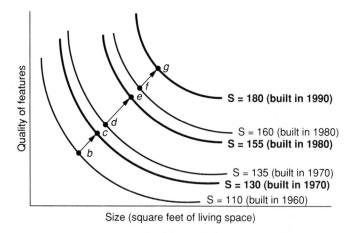

In 1980, the poor are at point b, the middle-income households are at point d, and the wealthy are at point f. Rising income increases the housing consumption of the rich, and they move into new housing in 1990 (point g). The middle-income households move into the 1980 housing vacated by the wealthy (from point d to e), and the poor move into the 1970 housing vacated by the middle-income households (point b to c).

point f to g. The middle-income households occupy the dwellings vacated by the rich, moving from point d to e (the dwellings built in 1980 generate 155 units of housing service one decade later). The poor occupy the dwellings vacated by the middle-income households, moving from point b to c.

Why should the wealthy live in new houses? If the wealthy did not occupy new housing, they could be accommodated by upgrading the 1980 houses. Because a 1980 house would normally produce only 155 units of housing service in 1990, substantial modifications would be required to increase its service level to 180 units. Rooms would be added, the roof and plumbing would be upgraded, and the house would be remodeled to accommodate changes in housing tastes. Since these modifications would be costly, it is usually more efficient to build new housing for the wealthy.

If new housing is built for the wealthy, there will be a plentiful supply of used housing for middle-income households. When the wealthy vacate the 1980 dwellings, the market values of the leftover houses will decrease. Because the market value of a used 155-unit dwelling will be less than the cost of building a new 155-unit dwelling, the middle-income households will live in leftover houses. As the middle-income households vacate the 1970 dwellings, their prices fall, making the used 130-unit dwellings a bargain for the poor. Since there is a plentiful supply of used housing (with unfashionable design and old pipes), a used, low-quality dwelling is less expensive than a new one.

Who Benefits from Construction Subsidies.   New housing is typically occupied by the wealthy. Does this mean that all of the benefits of construction subsidies go to the wealthy?

The effects of construction subsidies can be explained with a model of a city with two housing submarkets. Consider a city with the following characteristics:

1. **Fixed number of households.** There are 120 households in the city.
2. **Housing submarkets.** There are two submarkets: the market for high-quality housing and the market for medium-quality housing.
3. **Quality level.** Landlords respond to changes in relative prices by moving their dwellings between the two submarkets: dwellings can be upgraded to the high-quality submarket or downgraded (by decreasing maintenance) to the medium-quality submarket.
4. **Imperfect substitutes.** The two types of housing are imperfect substitutes: consumers move between the two markets in response to changes in market prices.

Figure 13–5 shows the initial equilibrium in the housing market. In the high-quality submarket, there are 40 dwellings at a price of $30 per square foot. In the medium-quality submarket, there are 80 dwellings at a price of $20 per square foot.

Suppose that the city subsidizes the construction of new, high-quality housing. In Figure 13–5, the subsidy shifts the supply curve to the right from S_1 to S_2, increasing the quantity supplied at every price: at the original price of $30, there would be 80 dwellings instead of 40. Since the quantity supplied exceeds the quantity demanded, the price of high-quality housing will decrease. As the price of high-quality housing decreases, two things happen.

1. **Demand effect.** The decrease in the relative price of high-quality housing increases the quantity demanded: some households move from medium-quality dwellings into high-quality dwellings, causing movement downward along the demand curve D_1.

2. **Supply effect.** As the price of high-quality dwellings decreases, the quantity supplied decreases as some landlords downgrade their dwellings to the more lucrative medium-quality submarket: the market moves downward along the supply curve S_2, decreasing the quantity of high-quality housing supplied.

FIGURE 13–5   Effects of Construction Subsidy on High-Quality and Medium-Quality Submarkets

Construction subsidies shift the supply curve for high-quality (new) dwellings outward, from S_1 to S_2. In equilibrium, the price drops from $30 to $24, and the number of high-quality dwellings increases from 40 to 60.

The decrease in the price of high-quality dwellings increases the supply of medium-quality dwellings as some landlords move their dwellings from the high-quality to the medium-quality market. The decrease in the price of high-quality dwellings also decreases the demand for medium-quality dwellings because some consumers switch from the medium-quality market to the high-quality market. The equilibrium price drops from $20 to $13, and the quantity drops from 80 to 60.

In equilibrium, the subsidy increases the quantity of high-quality housing and decreases its price. In Figure 13–5, the number of high-quality dwellings increases from 40 to 60 and the price decreases from $30 to $24.

The changes in the high-quality submarket cause two types of changes in the medium-quality submarket.

   1. **Substitution effect.** As some consumers of medium-quality dwellings move into high-quality dwellings, the demand curve for medium-quality dwellings shifts to the left. This is shown in Figure 13–5 as a shift from D_3 to D_4. Because the two types of housing are substitutes, a decrease in the price of high-quality housing decreases the demand for medium-quality housing.

   2. **Filtering effect.** The downgrading of some dwellings from the high-quality submarket to the medium-quality submarket shifts the supply curve of medium-quality housing to the right. This is shown in Figure 13–5 as a shift from S_3 to S_4.

The new equilibrium occurs where the new demand curve (D_4) intersects the new supply curve (S_4). The subsidy program for high-quality housing decreases the price of medium-quality housing from $20 to $13 and decreases the quantity of medium-quality dwellings from 80 to 60.

The construction subsidies also cause the retirement of 40 dwellings. Since the city's population is fixed at 120 households, every new house causes one retirement. The number of households in the high-quality submarket increases by only 20 (from 40 to 60), leaving 20 of the 40 new houses to filter down to the medium-quality market. The number of households in the medium-quality submarket decreases by 20 (from 80 to 60), so there will be 40 extra houses in the medium-quality submarket. Therefore, the 40 lowest-quality houses in the medium-quality submarket will be retired from the housing stock.

Summary—Filtering and Public Policy.   The benefits of housing subsidies are not confined to the households who occupy the subsidized dwellings. Other households benefit for two reasons. First, the subsidies decrease the price of high-quality houses, allowing some of the occupants of medium-quality houses to move into high-quality dwellings. Second, houses filter down from the high-quality submarket to the medium-quality submarket and decrease the price of medium-quality housing.

What about the market for low-quality housing? In a model with three submarkets (high-quality, medium-quality, and low-quality), some medium-quality housing would filter down to the low-quality submarket, decreasing the price of low-quality housing. Therefore, the poor would benefit from construction subsidies: some poor households would be able to move into less expensive medium-quality housing, and others would pay less for low-quality housing. In general, the filtering process transmits the benefits of construction subsidies to middle-income and poor households.

The same analysis applies to policies that decrease the supply of high-quality dwellings. Suppose that growth controls restrict the supply of new, high-quality houses. The decrease in supply will increase the price of high-quality housing, increasing the benefits of maintaining dwellings for the high-quality market. Landlords will spend more on maintenance and repair, slowing the filtering process and decreasing the supply of medium-quality housing. At the same time, some consumers will be unwilling to pay the higher prices in the high-quality submarket and will switch to the medium-quality submarket. Growth controls on new, high-quality housing will increase the price of medium-quality housing because they decrease the supply *and* increase the demand for these dwellings. The price of low-quality housing will increase for the same reasons. Consequently, some of the costs of growth control are borne by middle-income and low-income households.

THE HIGH COSTS OF HOUSING

When a household buys a home, it typically spends between two and four times its annual income on the house. The large cost of housing has two implications for the housing market. First, given the large investment required for home ownership, a large fraction of households rent instead of owning. In the United States, about one third of households are renters. Second, most middle-income households use home ownership to accumulate wealth. In other words, a large fraction of the savings of middle-class households is tied up in housing. This section explores the household's choice between renting and owning and the effects of public policy on this choice.

The Cost of Renting

The cost of renting a dwelling is simply the rent paid to the landlord. In a competitive market, landlords will make zero economic profits (normal accounting profits), so the annual rent will equal the landlord's annual costs. In the absence of taxes, the landlord has three types of costs:

1. **Capital cost.** If the landlord borrows money to purchase the dwelling, the capital cost is the annual interest cost, which is equal to the market interest rate (i) times the purchase price of the dwelling (V). If the landlord uses his own money to purchase the house, the capital cost is the opportunity cost of investing money in housing instead of a bank account earning an interest rate of i.

2. **Depreciation.** If the market value of the house decreases by d per dollar of dwelling value per year, the annual depreciation cost is d times V.

3. **Maintenance costs.** If the annual cost of routine maintenance is m per dollar of dwelling value per year, the annual maintenance cost is m times V. The maintenance cost includes the opportunity cost of the landlord's time.

The expression for the annual cost of a rental dwelling is

$$C_r = V \cdot (i_r + d_r + m_r) \tag{13-1}$$

where i_r is the interest rate paid by the landlord, d_r is the depreciation rate for rental housing, and m_r is the maintenance cost per dollar of dwelling value. Suppose that $V = \$50,000$, $i_r = 0.10$, $d_r = 0.01$, and $m_r = 0.04$. If so, the annual cost is $7,500$, the sum of $5,000 in capital costs, $500 in depreciation costs, and $2,000 in maintenance costs. In a taxless world, the landlord will charge an annual rent of $7,500, thus covering his costs and making zero economic profits.

What happens if the market value of the dwelling increases over time? If the dwelling appreciates over time instead of depreciating, d_r will be a negative number. For example, if the market value increases by 8 percent per year, d_r will be -0.08 instead of $+0.01$ and the landlord will earn $4,000 per year in appreciation. What is the new equilibrium rent? Economic profits will be zero if total cost (for capital and maintenance) equals the sum of rent and appreciation. Total cost is $7,000, so the equilibrium rent will be $3,000 ($7,000 = $4,000 in appreciation plus $3,000 in rent). The equilibrium rent is lower because the landlord earns money by owning the property, and therefore needs less rental income to generate zero economic profits.

The Costs of Home Ownership

Consider next the costs of owning a home. In the absence of taxes, the home owner incurs the same types of costs as the landlord (capital, depreciation, and maintenance). If the household borrows money to buy its home, the capital cost is the annual mortage-interest payment. If the household pays cash for the house, the capital cost is the opportunity cost of investing money in a house rather than a bank account. In either case, the capital cost is the market interest rate (i) times the value of the house (V). The home owner also incurs depreciation costs (d times V) and maintenance costs (m times V). The maintenance cost includes the opportunity costs of time spent fixing faucets, painting walls, and keeping the books. The annual cost of ownership is

$$C_o = V \cdot (i_o + d_o + m_o) \tag{13-2}$$

where i_o is the interest rate paid by the home owner, d_o is the depreciation rate for owner-occupied housing, and m_o is the maintenance cost for owner-occupied housing. If the dwelling appreciates over time, d_o will be a negative number and the net cost of ownership will be lower.

Indifference between Renting and Owning?

Under what circumstances will a household be indifferent between owning and renting? The household will be indifferent between the two options if $C_r = C_o$. If homeowners and landlords face the same interest rate and depreciation rate and incur the same maintenance cost, the annual cost of renting will be equal to the annual cost of home ownership. The cost of renting is often higher for three reasons.

The **renter externality** causes the depreciation rate on rental property to be relatively high. Because renters have no long-term stake in the dwelling, they have little incentive to participate in everyday maintenance. As long as the tenants are not inconvenienced by small problems (e.g., a leaky pipe), they are unlikely to report the problem to the landlord. Although the landlord would benefit from finding out about the problem (he could prevent the small problem from becoming a big one), the tenant does not have the proper incentive to inform the landowner. The externality occurs because the tenant does not directly benefit from better care of the property. In contrast, the home owner receives all the benefits from everyday maintenance, so he is more likely to fix a leaky pipe immediately to prevent long-term damage to the dwelling. If tenants do not keep their landlords fully informed about the condition of the house, rental property will have higher maintenance costs and higher depreciation rates. In other words, the renter externality increases the market rent on residential property.

The cost of renting is relatively high for two other reasons. First, rental property is a riskier investment (it has a higher default rate), so lenders charge higher interest rates on loans for rental property. Second, some home owners use work on the house (maintenance, repair, and yardwork) as a hobby, so they have lower maintenance costs than a landlord. For these reasons, the annual cost of home ownership is often less than the annual rent on an equivalent rental dwelling, even without considering the tax advantages of home ownership.

What type of household will rent instead of owning? Three factors tend to push some households toward renting. The first is low income: to qualify for a home loan, the household must have enough income to pay the mortgage. The second is mobility: given the substantial transactions costs of executing a home loan, frequent movers tend to rent rather than own. The third is a distaste for work on the home and yard: if a person is unwilling to do everyday maintenance and small repairs, renting will be relatively attractive.

Taxes and Housing

The federal government provides a number of tax breaks for both rental and owner-occupied property. The tax breaks for rental property decrease the landlord's costs, and these costs are passed on to consumers in the form of lower rent. The tax breaks for home owners are more explicit: home owners deduct interest costs from their gross income, so they pay lower taxes. What are the net effects of these tax breaks? Do they encourage or discourage home ownership?

Rental Tax Break—Rapid Depreciation. The tax code allows the landlord to deduct the full value of his property before the property actually wears out. In other words, the tax code allows the **rapid depreciation** of property (also called accelerated depreciation). Suppose that the landlord builds a dwelling at a cost of $60,000. If the dwelling has a useful life of 60 years and deteriorates at a constant rate, the economic cost of depreciation is $1,000 per year. Under a system of rapid depreciation, the dwelling may have a "tax life" of only 15 years, meaning that the deduction for depreciation is $4,000 per year for the first quarter of the dwelling's life and zero for the rest of its life.

Rapid depreciation does not change the total deductions for depreciation, but simply allows landlords to deduct depreciation costs sooner and thus pay taxes later. If rapid depreciation defers a $100 tax bill for eight years, the landlord can place the $100 in a bank and earn interest for eight years. When the tax comes due, the landlord pays the tax bill with the $100 principal and keeps the interest. The deferral of taxes decreases the landlord's net tax liability because the landlord can earn interest on the deferred taxes. In other words, rapid depreciation decreases the **present value** of the landlord's tax liability. In a competitive environment, all landlords make zero economic profits, so the decrease in taxes will be passed on to renters in the form of lower rent.

Ownership Tax Break—Mortgage Deduction.   The federal tax code also decreases the cost of home ownership. Taxpayers can deduct mortgage-interest payments from their gross income, so every dollar of mortgage interest decreases the federal tax liability by the taxpayer's marginal tax rate. For example, if the taxpayer's marginal tax rate is 28 percent, every dollar spent on mortgage interest decreases the tax liability by 28 cents. Table 13–2 shows the tax benefits of home ownership for three households. The poorest household does not have enough deductions to justify itemizing its deductions, so it receives no benefit from the mortgage deduction. Household B, an itemizer with a marginal tax rate of 15 percent, receives a 15 cent subsidy, and household C, with a marginal tax rate of 28 percent, receives a subsidy of 28 cents.

The tax benefit increases with household income for two reasons. First, under a progressive tax system, the marginal tax rate increases with income, so the tax benefit per dollar of mortgage payment increases with income. Second, because the demand for housing increases with income, wealthier households have larger mortgage payments and thus larger deductions. In 1985, the mortgage deduction decreased federal tax revenue by about $34 billion (U.S. Census Bureau 1985).

TABLE 13–2   Tax Benefits of Home Ownership and Income

Household	Income	Marginal Tax Rate	Mortgage Interest	Tax Benefit	Benefit as % of Income
A	20,000	Non-itemizer	5,000	0	0
B	30,000	15%	7,000	1,050	3.50%
C	50,000	28	11,000	3,080	6.16

The mortgage deduction increases housing consumption because it decreases the net costs of housing. Figure 13–6 shows the effect of the subsidy on the housing consumption of a household with a 28 percent marginal tax rate. The demand curve shows the marginal benefit of housing consumption (the willingness to pay for housing). The horizontal line at $1 shows the marginal social cost or opportunity cost of housing: by spending $1 on housing, society forgoes $1 worth of investment in other capital goods (e.g., factories, machines, schools). The optimum housing consumption is H^* (the amount such that the marginal social benefit equals the opportunity cost). For consumption above H^*, the marginal benefit is less than the opportunity cost: the money would be more efficiently spent on factories, machines, or schools.

The mortgage deduction causes inefficiency because it creates a gap between the marginal private cost and the marginal social cost of housing. In the absence of the subsidy, the household pays $1 per unit of housing and chooses the point where the demand curve intersects the marginal social cost

FIGURE 13–6   Mortgage Subsidy Increases Housing Consumption

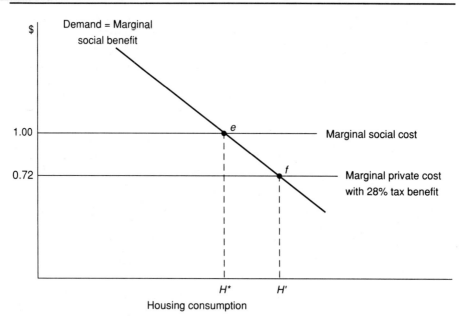

The optimum housing consumption occurs at point e, where the marginal social benefit (shown by the demand curve) equals the marginal social cost. If the marginal tax rate is 28%, the mortgage subsidy decreases the marginal private cost of housing from $1 to 72¢, increasing housing consumption from H^* to H'. Consumers pay less than the marginal social cost of housing, so they consume too much housing and divert investment from other uses.

curve (point e). When the private cost drops from \$1 to 72 cents, the household increases its housing consumption from H^* to H'. This is inefficient because the household's benefit from increased housing consumption (from the demand curve) is less than the opportunity cost of spending on housing (from the marginal social cost curve). By spending more on housing, society has less to spend on factories, machines, and schools. The household makes an inefficient choice because the government pays 28 percent of its housing bill.

Struyk and Tuccillo (1983) suggest that the mortgage deduction has contributed to recent declines in U.S. productivity. Because the deduction encourages the investment in housing at the expense of industrial investment, there is less capital equipment (factories and machines) per worker. Rosen (1979) estimated the effect of the mortgage deduction on housing consumption in the 1970s, before the 1981 and 1986 tax changes. He estimated that the deduction increased housing consumption by about 14 percent, suggesting that a substantial amount of capital was diverted to residential uses.

Mortgage Deduction and Imputed Rental Income.   Under the federal tax code, both landowners and home owners can deduct their interest costs in computing their taxable incomes. Does this mean that the mortgage deduction for home owners is neutral with respect to the consumer's choice between owning and renting?

The bias toward ownership created by the mortgage deduction can be explained with a simple numerical example. Fred the home owner and Barney the landlord live in city B, where all dwellings are identical rock hovels that sell for \$2,000. Fred has two housing options. First, he can borrow \$2,000 from the bank to purchase a home. If the interest rate is 10 percent, the mortgage-interest payment for a perpetual loan will be \$200 per year, so the cost of ownership in the absence of tax benefits will be \$200. Second, he can rent an identical dwelling from Barney. Since the houses are made of stone, there are no maintenance or repair costs, so Barney's only expense is the capital cost of \$200 per year. The market rent (\$200) is the same as the cost of ownership, so Fred will be indifferent between owning and renting.

The mortgage deduction creates a bias toward home ownership because it allows Fred the homeowner to deduct expenses that do not generate taxable income. Contrast the mortgage deduction for Fred (home owner) with the mortgage deduction for Barney (landlord). Barney's deduction is sensible because Barney declares his rental income as taxable income. He declares \$200 of rental income per house and deducts \$200 in mortgage costs. His taxable income from his property is zero because his deduction equals his rental income. In contrast, Fred does not declare any rental income from his property, but still deducts his mortgage costs. Fred's mortgage deduction does not offset rental income, but simply subsidizes home ownership.

The government could eliminate the tax bias toward home ownership in one of two ways. The simple and obvious one is to eliminate the interest deduction for home owners. An alternative is to force Fred to declare his **im-**

puted rental income as taxable income. The imputed rental income is the income earned from owning a dwelling and renting it to yourself. Alternatively, it is the money you could earn if you rented your dwelling to someone else. Fred's imputed rental income is $200 per year. If he were to declare $200 of imputed rental income and then deduct his $200 mortgage cost, the two items would cancel one another and the ownership bias would disappear. His taxable income would be the same whether he rents or owns, so he would be indifferent between renting and owning.

Rationale for the Favorable Treatment of Home Ownership.   Because the mortgage deduction favors ownership over renting, it increases home ownership rates. In 1980, 66 percent of U.S. households were owner-occupiers, up from 48 percent in 1945. According to Hendershott and Shilling (1982), about one quarter of the increase in the ownership rate was caused by the favorable tax treatment of home ownership.

The principal rationale for the tax breaks for home ownership is the renter externality. If renters do not have the proper incentive to participate in everyday maintenance, a subsidy for home ownership may be justified on efficiency grounds: the subsidy discourages renting, decreasing the inefficiencies resulting from the renter externality. This rationale raises two questions. First, how large is the renter externality, and how large must the ownership subsidy be to counteract the externality? Second, what is the appropriate form for the ownership subsidy? Does the present system, under which the wealthiest households receive the largest subsidies, internalize the externality in the most efficient manner?

There have been a number of proposals to modify the mortgage deduction. One option is to replace the deduction with a tax credit equal to a fixed percentage of the household's mortgage costs. For example, if the tax credit is 15 percent, every household would receive a tax cut equal to 15 percent of its mortgage costs. Under a tax credit, all taxpayers would receive the same percentage subsidy for home ownership. A second option is to place a ceiling on the amount of mortgage interest that can be deducted. This would decrease the subsidy to the wealthiest households.

The Net Effects of the Tax Code—Renting versus Owning.   What is the net effect of the federal tax code on the choice between renting and owning? For renters, rapid depreciation decreases the costs of supplying rental housing and decreases market rents. For owner-occupants, the mortgage deduction decreases the costs of ownership. Does the tax code decrease the cost of renting by more than it decreases the cost of ownership?

The net effect of the tax code depends on a number of factors. One factor is the generosity of depreciation allowances: the more rapidly rental property can be depreciated, the larger the tax benefits and the lower the market rent on rental property. Two studies in the early 1980s suggested that the tax code decreased the relative cost of renting, causing a bias toward rental housing

(King and Fullerton 1984; Gordon, Hines, and Summers 1986). Since 1986, however, depreciation rules have become less generous. For example, the tax life of rental property increased from 15 years to 27.5 years: the allowable depreciation rate dropped from an average of 6.7 percent per year to about 3.6 percent. As a result, the tax liabilities of rental property have increased, increasing market rents and decreasing the bias toward rental housing.

Inflation and Home Ownership

How does inflation affect the costs and benefits of home ownership for a household that has a fixed-rate mortgage? Consider first the effect of unanticipated inflation. Suppose that the inflation rate unexpectedly increases from 4 percent to 10 percent. The increase in inflation will increase the appreciation rate of residential property from 4 percent to 10 percent, so the benefits of home ownership will increase. For a household holding a fixed-rate mortgage, the increase in the inflation rate does not affect the monthly mortgage payment, so it does not affect the costs of ownership. If inflation is anticipated, however, mortgage lenders will build the expected inflation rate into the mortgage interest rate. For example, if the expected inflation rate increases from 4 percent to 10 percent, the interest rate might increase from 8 percent to 14 percent. In this case, the home purchaser pays a higher mortgage interest rate to get the higher appreciation rate.

An alternative to a fixed-rate mortgage is one in which the mortgage interest rate is adjusted periodically to reflect changes in market interest rates. Under an adjustable-rate mortgage, an increase in the inflation rate will increase the monthly mortgage payment because the mortgage interest rate rises with the inflation rate. As a result, unanticipated inflation increases both the benefits and costs of ownership.

LARGE MOVING COSTS

For most households, a change in housing consumption requires a move to a different dwelling. Moving costs are substantial: in addition to the large costs of moving furniture, clothes, and kitchen equipment, there are also large costs associated with leaving the old neighborhood—with its people, schools, and stores—behind. In other words, a move to a new neighborhood disrupts social and consumption patterns, imposing large costs on the household. A household will change its housing consumption only if the benefits of moving (the opportunity to live in a dwelling with a better combination of housing services and cost) exceed the costs of moving.

Figure 13–7 shows the choices faced by a household that experiences an increase in income. The household starts with income I_1 and chooses point b (the point at which its indifference curve is tangent to its initial budget line), so it lives in a house with S_1 square feet of living space. An increase in income to I_2 shifts the budget line upward, giving the household two choices. One

FIGURE 13–7   Moving Costs and Responses to Increases in Income

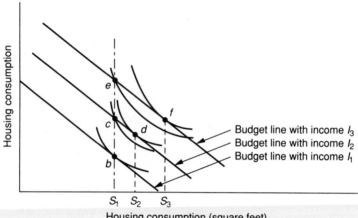

An increase in income shifts the budget line upward. In the absence of moving costs, the household would move from point *b* to point *d*, moving to a larger house (S_2 square feet of living space). If moving is costly, the household will stay in its present house, choosing *c* instead of *d*. If income increases again and the household does not move, it will choose point *e*. The household will move to a larger dwelling (going to point *f*) if the resulting increase in utility is large enough to offset moving costs.

option is to stay in its original house and spend all the extra income on non-housing goods (point *c*). Alternatively, the household could move to a larger house (S_2 square feet instead of S_1 square feet), choosing point *d*. In the absence of moving costs, utility would be higher at point *d* (point *d* lies on a higher indifference curve), but the question is whether the increase in utility is large enough to justify the costs of moving. If moving costs are relatively high, the household will stay in its original house and choose point *c*. If income increases to I_3, the budget line will shift upward again and the household is faced with the same choice: stay put (point *e*) or pay the moving costs and move to a larger house (point *f*). Because the gap between the initial housing consumption (S_1) and the desired housing consumption (S_3) is relatively large, the household is more likely to move than it was in the first case, when the gap was relatively small ($S_2 - S_1$).

There are two lessons from Figure 13–7. First, a small change in income (or price) is unlikely to change housing consumption. Most households tolerate some dissatisfaction with their housing circumstances because moving is costly. A household will move to a different dwelling only if the change in income or price is large relative to moving costs. Second, when a household changes houses, it is likely to make a large change in its housing consumption. A household moves when its dissatisfaction with its current dwelling is large enough to justify the costs of moving.

Permanent Income and Income Elasticity

Because moving costs are large, households base their consumption choices on permanent, or long-run, income. Given the costs of moving, the household makes a long-term commitment to living in a particular dwelling. The commitment is based on the household's expected income over several years. Therefore, to estimate the income elasticity of demand for housing (the percentage change in housing consumption divided by the percentage change in income), one must use a measure of the permanent (long-run) income of the household, not its income in any particular year.

The proper estimation of income elasticity can be explained with a simple example. Suppose that Lucky has a steady wage income of $20,000. In 1991, she wins $10,000 at a bingo game. As a result of her windfall, she increases her housing consumption by 5 percent, moving to a slightly larger rental apartment. If her income elasticity is computed using her income in 1990 and 1991, the elasticity would be computed as 0.10 (a 5 percent increase in housing consumption divided by a 50 percent increase in income). To correctly estimate the income elasticity, one must use a measure of her permanent income, defined as her average income over some period of time. One approach is to translate the windfall into an equivalent annual income. If Lucky invests her $10,000 prize in a bank account yielding 10 percent interest, her annual income from the prize would be $1,000, meaning that the bingo prize increases her permanent annual income by 5 percent. The income elasticity would then be computed as 1.0 (the 5 percent increase in housing consumption divided by the 5 percent increase in permanent income).

What is the income elasticity of demand? There have been dozens of studies of housing demand, and there is a consensus on three points. First, the overall income elasticity is about 0.75 (Ellwood and Polinski 1979): a 10 percent increase in income will increase housing consumption by about 7.5 percent. Second, the income elasticity for renters is less than the income elasticity for owner-occupants. Third, the income elasticity increases with income. According to Ihlanfeldt (1982), the elasticity for low-income households is between 0.14 and 0.62 and the elasticity for high-income households is between 0.72 and 1.10.

Price Elasticities

What is the price elasticity of demand for housing? Most estimates of the price elasticity fall between -0.75 and -1.20 (Ellwood and Polinski 1979). The consensus is that demand is slightly price-inelastic (an elasticity slightly less than 1.0 in absolute value). This means that an increase in price will increase total expenditures on housing by a small amount: an increase in price decreases the quantity demanded by a slightly smaller percentage amount, so total expenditures (price times quantity) increase by a small amount.

SUMMARY

1. Housing is different from other commodities because it is heterogeneous, immobile, and durable. Housing is costly in two senses: housing is a large part of the household budget, and changes in housing consumption are costly.

2. Housing is heterogeneous in the sense that every dwelling provides a different bundle of features. Dwellings differ in size, layout, the quality of utility systems, and interior design. Sites differ in access, tax liabilities, local public goods, environmental quality, and neighborhood appearance.
   a. The hedonic approach is based on the notion that a dwelling is composed of a bundle of individual components, each of which has an implicit price.
   b. Housing consumers choose the dwelling that provides the best combination of features at the best price, trading off quality, size, location, and other attributes.
   c. The heterogeneity of the housing stock means that a city's housing market is segmented with respect to size, location, and quality: the market is composed of a number of submarkets.
   d. Changes in the exterior appearance of one house increase the market value of surrounding houses (the neighborhood effect).

3. Housing is durable, and the landlord can control the rate of physical deterioration by spending money on repair and maintenance.
   a. Spending on maintenance and repair determines the quantity of housing services generated by the dwelling (Q). At the optimum quantity, the marginal benefit (the change in total revenue) equals marginal cost (the change in total cost).
   b. When the profit from housing is negative, the dwelling is retired from the housing stock. There are three types of retirement: conversion to another use, boarding up, and abandonment.
   c. Retirement results from decreases in market price (from a decrease in demand or an increase in supply) or an increase in maintenance costs.
   d. A recent study suggests that an inflexible property tax encourages abandonment.

4. The supply of housing is relatively inelastic for relatively long periods of time because the bulk of the housing stock is used housing. There are no reliable estimates of the price elasticity of supply.

5. According to the filtering model, the quantity of housing services generated by a dwelling decreases over time, so the dwelling is occupied by households with progressively lower income. The filtering model explains

why the poor occupy used housing and shows that the poor benefit from the subsidization of new housing for the wealthy.

6. The costs of rental housing and owner-occupied housing are determined by the cost of capital (the opportunity cost of money invested in housing), depreciation, and maintenance costs. Three factors push many households toward home ownership: the renter externality (tenants have little incentive to inform landlords of maintenance problems), higher interest rates for rental property loans, and the hobby aspect of home repair and maintenance.

7. The federal tax code has special tax breaks for rental and owner-occupied housing.

   a. Rapid depreciation of rental property defers taxes, increasing the profitability of rental property and decreasing monthly rent.

   b. The deductibility of mortgage interest decreases the cost of home ownership and increases ownership rates and housing consumption.

   c. The net effect of the tax code on home ownership depends on marginal tax rates and the generosity of depreciation allowances, both of which have changed over time.

8. Moving costs are relatively large, so households change their housing consumption infrequently and make large changes when they do move.

9. The income elasticity of demand for housing is about 0.75, and the price elasticity is between -0.75 and -1.20.

EXERCISES AND DISCUSSION QUESTIONS

1. Consider an apartment building that does not generate enough rental revenue to cover the landlord's costs.

   a. Use a graph to show this situation (see Figure 13–2).

   b. Suppose that the government provides a 50 percent subsidy for operating, maintenance, and repair costs. Show the effects of the subsidy program on your graph. What happens to the optimum Q and the likelihood of retirement?

2. Suppose that you own an apartment building that does not generate enough rental revenue to cover your costs. You have two options: first, you could demolish the building and set up a parking lot; second, you could abandon the building. Suppose that the cost of demolition is $20,000 and the annual profit from the parking lot would be $1,500. Should you demolish or abandon? If you don't have enough information to answer this question, list the information you need and explain how you would use it.

3. Dwellings are eventually retired from the housing stock as a result of either decreases in market rent (a downward tilt of the total-revenue curve in Figure 13–3) or rising maintenance costs (an upward tilt of the total-cost curve).

a. Use a graph like Figure 13–3 to prove or disprove the following statement: "A dwelling that leaves the market as a result of decreases in market rent leaves the market at a higher quantity of housing services (a larger Q) than one that leaves as a result of increases in maintenance costs."

b. Explain why this statement is true or false.

4. In city E, all households have the same income, and real income is constant over time. Will there be filtering in the city?

5. Consider city B, which has a fixed population. In an attempt to decrease total residential energy consumption, the city has adopted the following policy:
Policy E: All new housing in the city must be equipped with an energy-saving device that decreases the dwelling's energy consumption by 10 percent.

a. Evaluate the effects of Policy E on the city's new and used housing markets. What happens to the prices of new and used housing?

b. What happens to the quantities of new and used housing?

c. Under what circumstances will total energy consumption in the city increase?

d. Describe and analyze a more effective conservation policy.

6. The real-estate brokers in city F are baffled. Although dwellings are subject to the normal physical and fashion deterioration over time, there is little filtering. In contrast to most cities, in which the typical house changes hands every 7 years (usually going to a household with a lower income than the previous owner), the typical house in this city changes hands every 50 years. Explain this phenomenon.

7. Compute the annual cost of renting and home ownership under the following set of assumptions:

i. The market interest rate is 12 percent for rental property and 10 percent for owner-occupied property.

ii. The market value of the typical house is $100,000.

iii. Maintenance cost is 5 percent per year on rental property and 2 percent per year on owner-occupied property.

iv. The marginal tax rate of the typical household is 28 percent.

v. Both types of properties are appreciating by 4 percent per year.

vi. Rapid depreciation decreases the annual cost of rental property by 25 percent.

8. Comment on the following statement: "Property values in this city are increasing rapidly, rising at an annual rate of about 20 percent. This will cause many households to switch from renting to owning."

9. The owners of rental property can deduct routine maintenance costs from their gross income, and homeowners cannot. Does the deductibility of maintenance costs decrease the relative cost of renting, thus creating a bias toward renting?

10. Consider a city where the demand for housing for the typical household
    is

$$Q = 1000 - 1000 \cdot P$$

where Q is the square footage of housing demanded and P is the price per
square foot.
   a. Draw the demand curve for housing.
   b. At a price of $0.50, how many square feet of housing does the typical
      household demand?
   c. What is the consumer surplus associated with a price of $0.50?
   d. Suppose that the price of housing decreases to $0.40.
      What is the consumer surplus at the new price, assuming that the
      household does not move to a new residence?
   e. What is the consumer surplus at the new price, assuming that the
      household moves to a new residence?
   f. If the cost of moving is $25, will the typical household move to a new
      residence?

11. In city D, landlords charge a security deposit of $900 and do not refund
    the money when the tenant leaves. Suppose that a new deposit law is
    passed. The law requires that all landlords refund 100 percent of the secu-
    rity deposit unless the landlord can prove that the tenant damaged or
    dirtied the dwelling. Comment on the following statement: "The new law
    will save the typical tenant $900."

12. Comment on the following statement: "I live in an apartment complex
    that was built in a year when interest rates were relatively low. My rent is
    lower than the rent on other apartments because the cost of financing the
    complex is relatively low."

REFERENCES AND ADDITIONAL READINGS

Overview

Arnott, Richard. "Economic Theory and Housing." Chapter 24 in *Handbook of Regional
and Urban Economics* vol. 2, ed. Edwin S. Mills. New York: North Holland, 1987.
Reviews various models of the urban housing market and suggests future directions
for research.

Olsen, Edgar "A Competitive Theory of the Housing Market." *American Economic Review* 59 (1969), pp. 612–22.

Olsen, Edgar O. "The Demand and Supply of Housing Service: A Critical Survey of
the Empirical Literature." Chapter 25 in *Handbook of Regional and Urban Economics*
vol. 2, ed. Edwin S. Mills. New York: North Holland, 1987. Reviews empirical
studies of housing supply and demand.

Quigley, John M. "What Have We Learned About Housing Markets?" In *Current Issues
in Urban Economics*, ed. Peter Meiszkowski and Mahlon Straszheim. Baltimore:

The Johns Hopkins Press, 1979.   A review of theoretical and empirical research in housing.

Supply of New Housing

Follain, James R. "The Price Elasticity of the Long-Run Supply of New Housing Construction." *Land Economics* 55 (1979), pp. 190–99.

Muth, Richard. "The Demand for Non-Farm Housing." In *The Demand for Durable Goods*, ed. Arnold C. Harberger. Chicago: University of Chicago Press, 1960.   Estimates the elasticity of supply of new housing.

Supply of Used Housing

Farb, Warren E. "An Estimate of the Relative Supply and Demand for Substandard Rental Housing in Major US Cities." Ph.D. dissertation, Washington University, St. Louis, 1971.   Suggests that the supply of low-quality housing is highly elastic.

Ingram, Gregory K., and Yitzhak Oron. "The Behavior of Housing Producers." In *Residential Location and Urban Housing Markets*, ed. Gregory K. Ingram. New York: National Bureau of Economic Research, 1977.   Discusses landlord's choice of quality level, based on costs and benefits (rent) of different quality levels.

Kain, John, and William Apgar. "Simulation of Housing Market Dynamics." *Journal of the American Real Estate and Urban Economics Association* 7 (1979), pp. 505–38.   A simulation model in which landlords choose a quality level consistent with profit maximization.

Abandonment

Muth, Richard F. "The Demand for Non-Farm Housing." In *The Demand for Durable Goods*, ed. Arnold Harberger. Chicago: University of Chicago Press, 1960, pp. 29–96.

Peterson, George. "The Effect of Federal Taxes on Urban Form." In *The Prospective City*, ed. Arthur Solomon. Cambridge, Mass.: MIT Press, 1979.   Discusses the effects of federal taxes on abandonment.

Sterlieb, George, and Robert Burchell. *Residential Abandonment: The Tenement Landlord Revisited*. New Brunswick, N.J.: Rutgers University Press, 1973.

White, Michelle. "Property Taxes and Urban Housing Abandonment." *Journal of Urban Economics* 20 (1986), pp. 312–30.   Explores the effects of inflexible property taxation on the frequency of abandonment and concludes that the property tax encourages abandonment.

Supply Elasticities

De Leeuw, Frank, and Nkanta Ekanem. "The Supply of Rental Housing." *American Economic Review* 61 (1971), pp. 806–17.

Grieson, Ronald E. "The Supply of Rental Housing: Comment." *American Economic Review* 63 (1973), pp. 433–36.

Mason, John M. "The Supply Curve for Housing." *Journal of the American Real Estate and Urban Economics Association* 7 (1979), pp. 362–77.

Ozanne, L., and Raymond Struyk. "The Price Elasticity of Supply of Housing Services." In *Urban Housing Markets: Recent Directions in Research and Policy*, ed. L. S. Bourne and J. R. Hitchcock. Toronto: University of Toronto Press, 1978.   Estimates the supply elasticity of used housing.

Smith, Barton A. "The Supply of Urban Housing." *Quarterly Journal of Economics* 90 (1976), pp. 389–406.

The Hedonic Approach

Brown, H. James. "Micro Neighborhood Externalities and Hedonic Housing Prices." *Land Economics* 56 (1980), pp. 125–41.

Crecine, John; Otto Davis; and John Jackson. "Urban Property Markets: Some Empirical Results and Their Implications for Municipal Zoning." *Journal of Law and Economics* 10 (1967), pp. 79–100.

De Salvo, Joseph S. "Benefits and Costs of New York City's Middle-Income Housing Program." *Journal of Political Economy* 83 (1975), pp. 791–805.   Found that housing projects for middle-income housing increased the values of nearby properties by about 5 percent. Also estimated the welfare losses from using public housing instead of cash transfers as 45 percent of the program costs.

Freeman, A. Myrick, III. "The Hedonic Approach to Measuring Demand for Neighborhood Characteristics." In *The Economics of Neighborhood*, ed. David Segal. Orlando: Academic Press, 1979.

Kain, John F., and John M. Quigley. "Measuring the Value of Housing Quality." *Journal of the American Statistical Association* 65 (1970), pp. 532–38.

Kain, John F., and John M. Quigley. *Housing Markets and Racial Discrimination: A Microeconomic Analysis.* New York: National Bureau of Economic Research, 1975.   Chapter 9 is a hedonic study of the St. Louis housing market.

King, Thomas. "The Demand for Housing: Integrating the Roles of Journey to Work, Neighborhood Quality, and Prices." In *Household Production and Consumption*, ed. Nester Terlecky. New York: National Bureau of Economic Research, 1975.   A hedonic study of housing.

King, Thomas. "The Demand for Housing: A Lancastrian Approach." *Southern Economics Journal* 43 (1976), pp. 1077–87.   A hedonic study of housing prices.

Mills, Edwin S. "Housing Policy as a Means to Achieve National Growth Policy." In *Housing in the Seventies: Working Papers* vol. 1. Washington, D.C.: U.S. Government Printing Office, 1976.   Suggests that neighborhood effects are relatively small, between 5 and 15 percent of the amount invested in a dwelling.

Straszheim, Mahlon. *An Economic Analysis of the Urban Housing Market.* New York: National Bureau of Economic Research, 1975.   A hedonic study of housing prices.

Straszheim, Mahlon. "Estimation of the Demand for Urban Housing Services from Household Interview Data." *Review of Economics and Statistics* 55 (1973), pp. 1–8.   A hedonic study of housing prices.

Demand Elasticities

Ellwood, David, and Mitchell Polinski. "An Empirical Reconciliation of Micro and Grouped Estimates of the Demand for Housing." *Review of Economics and Statistics* 61 (1979), pp. 199–205.

Ihlanfeldt, Keith R. "Property Tax Incidence on Owner-Occupied Housing: Evidence from the Annual Housing Survey." *National Tax Journal* 35 (1982).

Mayo, Stephen K. "Theory and Estimation in the Economics of Housing Demand." *Journal of Urban Economics* 10 (1981), pp. 95–116.

Polinski, Mitchell. "The Demand for Housing: A Study in Specification and Grouping." *Econometrica* 45 (1977), pp. 447–62.

Filtering

Brueggeman, William B. "An Analysis of the Filtering Process with Special Reference to Housing Subsidies." In *Housing in the Seventies: Working Papers* vol. 2. Washington, D.C.: U.S. Government Printing Office, 1976, pp. 842–56.   Discusses the process through which subsidies for high-quality housing generate benefits for the occupants of low-quality housing.

Grisby, William. *Housing Markets and Public Policy.* Philadelphia: University of Pennsylvania Press, 1963.   Discusses the filtering process.

Kain, John F., and William C. Apgar. "Simulation of Housing Market Dynamics." *Journal of the American Real Estate and Urban Economics Association* 3 (1975), pp. 508–38.

Lowry, Ira S. "Filtering and Housing Standards: A Conceptual Analysis." *Land Economics* 36 (1960), pp. 362–70.

Ohls, James C. "Public Policy Toward Low Income Housing and Filtering in Housing Markets." *Journal of Urban Economics* 2 (1975), pp. 144–71.

Sweeney, James L. "A Commodity Hierarchy Model of the Rental Housing Market." *Journal of Urban Economics* 1 (1975), pp. 288–323.

Neighborhood Dynamics

Downs, Anthony. "Key Relationships Between Urban Development and Neighborhood Change." *Journal of the American Planning Association* 45 (1979), pp. 462–72.

Grisby, William; Morton Baratz; and Duncan Maclennan. *The Dynamics of Neighborhood Change and Decline.* Philadelphia: University of Pennsylvania, 1984.   Discusses the theories of neighborhood decline.

Heilbrun, James. "On the Theory and Policy of Neighborhood Consolidation." *Journal of the American Planning Association* 45 (1979), pp. 417–27.   Advocates a resettlement program for central cities under which households would be moved to certain neighborhoods. The remaining neighborhoods would be cleared for new development.

Stegman, Michael A. "The Neighborhood Effects of Filtering." *Journal of the American Real Estate and Urban Economics Association* 5 (1977), pp. 227–41.   Discusses the effects of new construction on the demand for central-city housing. Advocates the reorientation of federal programs away from policies that encourage the production of new suburban housing.

Stegman, Michael, and David Rasmussen. "Neighborhood Stability in Changing Cities." *American Economic Review* 70 (1980), pp. 415–19.

Taxes and Home Ownership

Gordon, Roger H.; James R. Hines; and Lawrence Summers. "Notes on the Tax Treatment of Structures." National Bureau of Economic Research, Working Paper no. 1896, 1986.

Hendershott, Patric H., and James Shilling. "The Economics of Tenure Choice, 1955–79." In *Research in Real Estate*, ed. C. Sirmans. Greenwich, Conn.: JAI Press, 1982, pp. 105–33.

King, Mervyn A., and Don Fullerton, ed. *The Taxation of Income from Capital: A Comparative Study of the United States, the United Kingdom, Sweden, and West Germany.* Chicago: University of Chicago Press, 1984. Estimates that rental housing is subsidized more heavily than owner-occupied housing.

Rosen, Harvey S. "Housing Decisions and the U.S. Income Tax: An Econometric Analysis." *Journal of Public Economics* 67 (1979), pp. 1–23.

Struyk, Raymond. *Urban Homeownership.* Lexington, Mass.: D. C. Heath, 1976. Explores the effects of mortgage subsidy on home ownership. Suggests that households are responsive to changes in the relative costs of ownership.

White, Larry J., and Michelle J. White. "The Tax Subsidy to Owner-Occupied Housing: Who Benefits." *Journal of Public Economics* 7 (1977), pp. 111–26.

CHAPTER 14

Housing Policies

This is the second of two chapters on the urban housing market. This chapter discusses three types of housing policies. The first is housing assistance: the federal government uses several policies to improve the housing conditions and decrease the housing costs of poor households. Second, the federal government uses a number of community-development programs to support local efforts to improve housing conditions and revitalize neighborhoods. Third, under a rent-control policy, a local government sets a maximum price for rental housing.

There are two distinct types of housing-assistance programs. The first type operates on the supply side of the housing market: the government either builds new housing for the poor (public housing) or subsidizes private developers to build and manage low-income housing. The second type of assistance policy operates on the demand side of the market: the government hands out coupons that can be used to rent existing housing. During the 1980s, the focus of federal housing policy shifted from supply policies to demand policies. In 1980, about 188,000 households were added to housing-assistance programs, with about 130,000 housed in new dwellings and 58,000 receiving housing coupons. In 1986, 99,000 households were added, with only 13,000 housed in new dwellings. In other words, there has been a fundamental policy shift from the traditional supply approach to the demand approach.

HOUSING CONDITIONS AND RENT BURDENS

The original goal of federal housing policy was to provide "a decent home and a suitable environment for every U.S. family." Have these objectives been met? Are most citizens living in decent houses in safe neighborhoods?

Table 14–1 shows the number and percent of households (renters and owners) that experienced housing problems in 1983. The definitions of housing problems come from the U.S. Department of Housing and Urban Development (HUD). A dwelling is considered "inadequate" if it has (a) incomplete plumbing or kitchen facilities, (b) structural problems (e.g., cracked walls, leaking roof, broken plaster), (c) deficiencies in common areas (stairwells, hallways), or (d) unsafe heating or electrical systems. A dwelling is "crowded" if there is more than one person per room. A household is "cost burdened" if it spends more than 30 percent of its gross income on housing.

TABLE 14–1   Condition of Housing Stock, 1983

	Number	Percent Households
All households		
Inadequate	7,561	8.9
Crowded	2,230	2.6
Cost burdened	14,425	17.0
Total with problems	24,216	28.5
Very poor households		
Inadequate	3,805	16.6
Crowded	926	4.0
Cost burdened	10,368	45.2
Total with problems	15,009	65.8
Metropolitan residents		
Inadequate	4,241	7.3
Crowded	1,570	2.7
Cost burdened	11,204	19.3
Total with problems	17,015	29.3
Black households		
Inadequate	2,053	22.4
Crowded	472	5.0
Cost burdened	2,196	24.0
Total with problems	4,721	51.4
Female-headed households		
Inadequate	2,722	11.6
Crowded	445	1.9
Cost burdened	7,088	30.3
Total with problems	10,255	43.8

SOURCE: Iredia Irby, "Attaining the Housing Goal," U.S. Department of Housing and Urban Development, Division of Housing and Demographic Analysis, July 1986, p. 16.

These categories are mutually exclusive: each household is counted only once.

Three conclusions can be drawn from Table 14–1. First, overcrowding is a minor problem: only 2.6 percent of all households live in overcrowded housing, and only 5 percent of black households (the group with the most severe overcrowding problems) are overcrowded. Second, affordability seems to be a larger problem than housing conditions: for every group except black households, the number of cost-burdened households is at least double the number living in inadequate housing. Third, the most severe housing problems are experienced by black households and very poor households (defined as households with income less than half the median area income). Almost two thirds of poor households have some sort of housing problem. Over half of black households experience problems: one in four black households lives in inadequate or overcrowded housing, and an additional one in four is cost burdened.

In the last several decades, there has been considerable progress in improving the condition of the housing stock. The percentage of urban households in overcrowded housing dropped from 13.5 percent in 1950 to 2.7 percent in 1983. The percentage of urban households living in "substandard" housing (defined differently than "inadequate" housing) dropped from 21.9 percent in 1950 to 1 percent in 1983. Despite this progress, many urban households continue to have housing problems.

In the last two decades, the fraction of income spent on housing has increased for most households. Between 1970 and 1983, the median rent-income ratio rose over 0.20 (the median renter household spent 20 percent of its income on housing) to 0.29. Over the same period, the median rent-income ratio in central cities increased from 0.21 to 0.31; the ratio for female-headed households increased from 0.27 to 0.44; and the ratio for the very poor rose from 0.35 to 0.40. The rent-income ratios rose over this period because real income declined while housing rents rose.

SUPPLY-SIDE POLICY—PUBLIC HOUSING

In 1987, about 1.3 million households lived in public housing. The number of public housing units increased from 478,000 in 1960 to 1.2 million in 1980. Since then, the number of occupied units has increased slowly, reflecting the shift toward demand-side policies. Public housing is built and managed by local public housing authorities. The federal government is involved in four ways:

1. **Capital subsidies.** Public housing is built with tax-exempt bonds. After the federal government pays off the bonds, the project becomes the property of the local housing authority.

2. **Operating subsidies.** Originally, the public-housing program was based on the notion that the local housing authority would charge enough rent to cover the project's operating costs. During the 1960s, operating costs rose rapidly while the average income level of tenants decreased. As a result, the rent-income ratios of public-housing tenants increased to relatively high levels. The federal government intervened, setting a maximum rent-income ratio of 0.25. To cover the difference between the tenant contribution and the project's operating costs, the federal government provided operating subsidies. In 1981, the maximum rent-income ratio was raised to 0.30. By 1984, operating subsidies covered about 40 percent of operating costs and cost the federal government a total of $1.6 billion per year.

3. **Modernization subsidies.** The federal government also provides subsidies for the repair and renovation of old housing projects. In 1984, the federal budget for modernization programs was $1.4 billion.

4. **Tenant selection.** The federal government places restrictions on what type of households qualify for public housing. One rule specifies that households are eligible for public housing only if their income is less than 80 percent of the median income of the area. In 1974, Congress directed local housing authorities to admit households from every income group within the eligible income range. The idea was to integrate the projects with respect to income, thus preventing large concentrations of the poorest households. In 1981, Congress reversed itself, directing the housing authorities to allocate the bulk of units (75 percent of units built before 1981 and 95 percent of units built after 1981) to households with "very low" income (less than half the median area income).

Public Housing and Housing Consumption

Figure 14–1 shows the effects of public housing on the housing consumption of recipients. The horizontal axis measures housing consumption (measured as the quantity of housing services generated by the dwelling), and the vertical axis measures the monthly consumption of all other goods (in dollars). The original budget line is drawn under the assumptions that (*a*) monthly income is $500 and (*b*) the price of housing is 25 cents per unit of

FIGURE 14–1   Public Housing Increases Housing Consumption

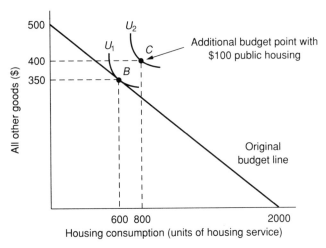

Income is $500 and the price of housing is 25¢ per unit of housing service. With the original budget line, the household chooses point *B* (600 units of housing service and $350 on other goods). Public housing (apartments generating 800 units of service) costs $100, so point *C* (800 units and $400 of other goods) is in the new budget set. Public housing allows the household to increase consumption of both housing and other goods.

housing service per month. Given the household's preferences for housing (as represented by the negatively sloped indifference curves) the household chooses point B, spending $150 on housing (occupying a 600-unit dwelling) and $350 on other goods.

Suppose that the typical public dwelling is an apartment that generates 800 units of housing service and is provided to the poor for $100. Public housing adds point C to the household's budget set: the household can consume an 800-unit apartment and have $400 left to spend on other goods. Given the household's indifference curves, utility is maximized at point C, so the household moves into public housing. The public-housing program increases housing consumption (from 600 to 800 units of housing service) and decreases housing costs (from $150 to $100).

Will public housing always increase housing consumption? Figure 14–2 shows the choices of a household with the same income as the household in Figure 14–1, but different tastes for housing. In the absence of public housing, the household lives in a 1,000-unit apartment (point D). The household spends $250 on housing (1,000 units times 25 cents per unit), leaving $250 for other goods. If the household moves into public housing, it will be forced to occupy a dwelling with fewer units of housing service (800 units), but the household will also have an additional $150 to spend on other goods. Public housing will increase utility if the additional $150 worth of nonhousing goods

FIGURE 14–2   Public Housing Decreases Housing Consumption

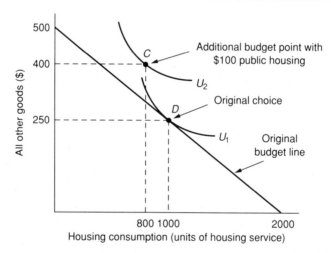

The household starts at point D (1,000 units of housing service and $250 of other goods). Public housing adds point C to the budget set. If the household occupies public housing, it will decrease its housing consumption (from 1,000 to 800) and increase its consumption of other goods (from $250 to $400).

is worth the sacrifice of 200 units of housing service. Given the indifference curves in Figure 14–2, utility is higher at point C than at point D, so the household accepts the offer of public housing and decreases its housing consumption.

Public Housing and Recipient Welfare

Would the household be better off with cash instead of subsidized public housing? Consider first the possibility that the cost of public housing is the same as the cost of private housing (25 cents per unit). It will cost the government $200 to build and maintain the 800-unit apartment, so the subsidy per dwelling is $100 ($200 less the $100 rent charged to tenants). The alternative to public housing is a $100 cash payment to the household. In Figure 14–3, a $100 cash payment shifts the recipient's budget line upward by $100. The household will choose point E instead of point C and will achieve a higher utility level.

This conclusion is not a result of an arbitrary placement of the indifference curves, but from basic microeconomic principles. The household will

FIGURE 14–3   Public Housing versus Cash Payment

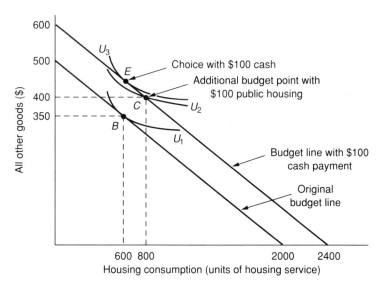

The alternative to $100 worth of public housing (800 units of housing service at a price of $100 instead of $200) is a $100 cash payment. Under public housing, the household chooses point C. The $100 cash payment shifts the budget line up by $100, and the household chooses point E. Utility is higher under the cash payment because the household can decide how to spend the money.

prefer the cash because it provides more consumption options. The cash allows the household to choose point C (the public-housing point) or any other point along the new budget line. The household will be better off with the cash if it chooses any point except C (i.e., if it does not occupy an 800-unit dwelling). If the objective of public policy is to maximize the household's utility, a cash payment will be superior to public housing.

How much is public housing worth to the tenant? The value of public housing can be measured by answering the following question: What cash payment will make the household indifferent between the cash and a $100 housing subsidy? In other words, what cash payment would move the household to indifference curve U_2? In Figure 14–4, a $75 payment shifts the budget line outward and the household maximizes utility at point F. Because the household reaches the indifference curve U_2, it will be indifferent between $75 in cash and the $100 housing subsidy. Studies by Kraft and Olsen (1977), Barton and Olsen (1976), and Murray (1975) suggest that tenants receive a benefit of about 75 cents per dollar spent on public housing. More recently, Smeeding (1982) estimated that the benefit per dollar is 80 cents.

FIGURE 14–4   Monetary Value of Public Housing

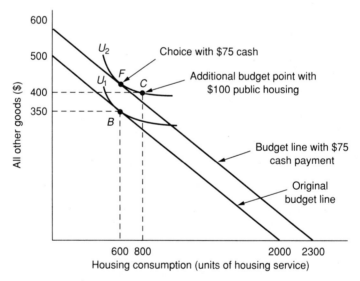

Public housing ($100 for an 800-unit apartment) is equivalent to a $75 cash payment. Under public housing, the household chooses point C. A $75 payment will allow the household to choose point F, which is on the same indifference curve as point C. The household is indifferent between $100 public housing and a cash payment of $75.

Production Costs of Public Housing.   How does the cost of new public housing compare to the cost of private housing? Public housing is more expensive for two reasons. First, the private sector can build new low-income housing more efficiently than the public sector: Weicher (1979) cites a number of studies showing that new public housing costs more than new private housing. Second, there is a plentiful supply of used low-quality housing, so even the least costly new housing costs more than used housing. According to the National Housing Review (1974), the cost of new public housing is about 33 percent higher than the cost of used private housing.

What are the implications for the efficiency of public housing? If new public housing costs one third more than used private housing, the government will spend \$266 (not \$200) to provide a new 800-unit apartment. Therefore, the government's cost of getting to point C in Figure 14–3 (the public housing option) is \$166 (\$266 less the \$100 rent paid by tenants), but the cost of getting to point E (the cash option) is only \$100. The cash option generates a larger increase in utility for three fifths of the cost.

Efficiency of Public Housing.   What is the bang per buck of public housing? In other words, what is the recipient benefit per dollar spent on public housing? As shown in Figure 14–4, recipients receive a benefit of \$75 from public housing, so the "bang" from public housing is \$75. If the government spends \$266 to build the apartment and collects \$100 in rent from the tenant, the government's cost is \$166. Therefore, the bang per buck is 45 cents (\$75 divided by \$166).

The Market Effects of Public Housing

Figure 14–5 shows the short-run market effects of public housing. In the short run, the supply of low-income housing from the private sector is perfectly inelastic: 500 dwellings are provided, regardless of price. At the initial equilibrium (point B), the price is \$250 per dwelling per month. If the local housing authority builds 200 new public-housing dwellings, the demand curve for private low-income housing shifts to the left by 200 dwellings: the 200 households housed in public housing leave the private housing market. As the poor move into public housing, they vacate private dwellings, causing excess supply that decreases the price of housing from \$250 to \$150 (point C). In the short run, all low-income households gain from the public-housing program: some households occupy subsidized public housing, and others pay lower prices for private low-income housing.

What happens to the private market over time? In Figure 14–5, the intermediate-run supply curve (the supply curve over a 5-year period) is positively sloped. The decrease in the price of housing caused by public housing decreases the profitability of private dwellings, so fewer low-quality dwellings are supplied. The supply response takes two forms:

FIGURE 14–5   Short-Run and Long-Run Effects of Public Housing on the Market
for Low-Income Housing

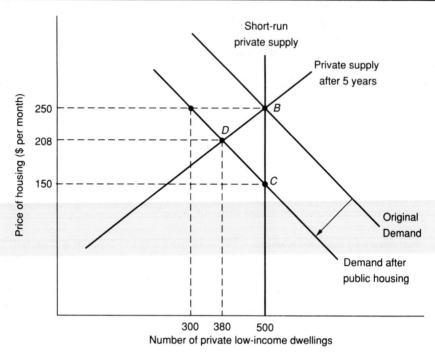

Public housing decreases the demand for private low-income housing by 200 households. In the short run, the supply of private housing is fixed, so the price of private
dwellings drops from $250 to $150. Over a five-year period, the decrease in the price
of private housing decreases the quantity of housing supplied from 500 to 380, and
the price rises to $208. The longer the period of time, the greater the displacement of
private housing and the smaller the net decrease in price.

1. **More retirement.** As explained in Chapter 13 (Why Is Housing
Different?), a decrease in the price of low-quality dwellings makes economic profits negative for some dwellings, so more dwellings will be retired from the housing market. The retired dwellings will be converted to
another use or abandoned.

2. **Slower downward filtering.** As the price of low-quality housing
decreases relative to the price of medium-quality housing, landlords hold
their dwellings in the medium-quality submarket for a longer period of
time.

In other words, more dwellings drop out of the low-quality submarket and
fewer dwellings filter down into the low-quality submarket. As the number of

low-quality dwellings decreases, the market price rises. The exit process continues until the price is high enough to restore zero economic profits (normal accounting profits). In Figure 14–5, a total of 120 private dwellings are withdrawn from the low-quality market (500 – 380) and the price rises from $150 to $208. Because public housing displaces private housing, there is a net increase in supply of only 80 dwellings.

Ohls (1975) used a computer model of the housing market to explore the effects of public housing on the filtering process. He divided the housing stock into 60 quality levels, and allocated housing in each level to the city's households: the highest-quality dwellings were occupied by the wealthy and the lowest by the poor. Under a public-housing policy, the bottom fifth of the population was removed from the private-housing market, causing the following changes:

1. The amount of new private construction decreased: the decrease in the demand for used low-quality housing decreased the incentive to build new housing.
2. Fewer dwellings filtered down to the low-quality submarket: the low-quality submarket became less lucrative, so the filtering rate decreased.
3. The retirement rate increased: the decrease in the demand for low-quality dwellings decreased the incentive to keep low-quality dwellings on the market, so the retirement rate increased.

In general, the private market responded by building fewer dwellings, slowing the filtering process, and increasing the retirement rate.

SUPPLY-SIDE POLICY—SUBSIDIES FOR PRIVATE HOUSING

An alternative to public housing is the subsidization of private housing. There are two subsidy programs for new low-income rental housing, Section 236 and Section 8. A third program, Section 235, provides interest subsidies to poor home owners. Under both rental programs, the federal government subsidizes landlords who build new housing for poor households. Both subsidy programs have the same market effects as public housing: they decrease the demand for low-quality private dwellings, lowering the equilibrium price of private housing. The decrease in price lowers the quantity of private dwellings supplied.

Section 236

Under the Section 236 program (started in 1968), the government contracts with a private developer to build low-income housing. The government pays the landlord an annual subsidy to cover the difference between the rental payments of tenants and the costs of building and operating the property.

The tenant's monthly rent is determined by the household's income. The **basic rent** is defined as the rent that would have prevailed if the project had been financed with money borrowed at a 1 percent interest rate. The tenant's rent is either the basic rent or 30 percent of household income, whichever is greater: if the basic rent is more than 30 percent of income, the household pays the basic rent; if the basic rent is less than 30 percent of household income, the household pays 30 percent of its income. The government pays the landlord the difference between the tenant contribution and **market rent**, which is defined as the rent required to cover all the landlord's costs.

A simple example will show how income affects the rental payment and the federal subsidy. Suppose that the market rent is $300 and the basic rent is $200. For a household with a monthly income of $500, the basic rent is more than 30 percent of its income ($150), so the household will pay the basic rent. The federal government will pay the difference between the market rent and basic rent, or $100. For a household with income of $800, the basic rent is less than 30 percent of its income, so the household will pay $240 (30 percent of its income) to the landlord and the government will pay the remaining $60.

Section 8—New Housing

Under the Section 8 program (started in 1974), private developers and local housing authorities submitted plans for low-income housing to the Department of Housing and Urban Development (HUD). If HUD approved a particular project, it signed a 20-year contract to provide annual payments to the landlord to cover the difference between tenants' rental payments and the landlord's costs. The subsidy per eligible tenant equals the difference between the **fair market rent** and the rent actually paid by low-income tenants. Under the contract, the developer was guaranteed the fair market rent on all units occupied by eligible households.

The tenant's rental payment depends on its income. To qualify for assistance, the household must live in a new dwelling that satisfies minimum physical standards and rents for no more than the fair market rent, defined as the rent that would be charged for a standard dwelling. The eligible household pays 30 percent of its income toward housing. The subsidy to the landlord equals the gap between the tenant's payment and the fair market rent:

$$\text{Fair market rent} = \text{Subsidy} + 0.30 \cdot \text{Income} \qquad (14-1)$$

For example, if the fair market rent is $400 and household income is $600, the household pays $180 in rent (30 percent of $600) and the subsidy is $220 ($400 − $180).

The Section 8–New Housing program was eliminated in 1983. The program was ended in large part because it was so expensive: in 1982, the average annual subsidy for a new Section 8 dwelling was over $6,000.

DEMAND-SIDE POLICY—CONSUMER SUBSIDIES

The supply-side housing policies help the poor by building more low-income housing. An alternative approach is to give subsidies directly to the poor and let them choose their own housing. Under a demand-side policy, low-income households are given housing coupons that can be redeemed for housing. Like the food-stamp program, the housing-coupon program allows the poor to make their own consumption choices. Coupons have two advantages over public housing. First, under some circumstances, the coupons are equivalent to cash. As shown earlier in the chapter, a cash payment generates a larger increase in utility than an equal expenditure on public housing. Second, the coupons can be spent on used dwellings, which are typically less expensive than new dwellings. There are two types of housing-coupon programs: rent certificates and housing vouchers.

Rent Certificates—Section 8–Existing Housing

Under the Section 8–Existing Housing program (started in 1975), poor households are issued rent certificates that can be used to rent existing housing. To qualify for assistance, household income must be less than 80 percent of the area's median family income. Under legislation passed in 1981, the bulk of funds are allocated to households with "very low" income (less than half the median area income). In 1988, about 780,000 households received rent certificates.

There are two restrictions on the housing choices of recipients. First, the rental dwelling must meet minimum physical standards for size and quality. Second, the household cannot spend more than the fair market rent, defined by HUD as a reasonable rent for a standard low-income dwelling. The eligible household pays 30 percent of its income toward housing and receives a rent certificate to cover the difference between its contribution and the actual rent:

$$\text{Subsidy} = \text{Actual rent} - 0.30 \cdot \text{Income} \qquad (14\text{--}2)$$

For example, suppose that the fair market rent is $400 and the household's income is $600. The household's contribution will be $180, and the subsidy equals the difference between the actual rent (up to a maximum of $400) and $180. If the actual rent is $350, the subsidy will be $170.

Figure 14–6 shows the household's choice between housing and other goods under the rent-certificate program. Household income is $600 per month, and the fair market rent is $400. The original budget line *AB* shows the initial trade-off between spending on housing and other goods: every dollar of spending on housing decreases spending on other goods by one dollar. The certificate program adds the points between *C* and *D* to the budget set: the household receives a subsidy equal to the gap between its actual spending on housing (its monthly rent) and 30 percent of its income ($180). Therefore, it can consume $420 worth of nonhousing goods and between $180 and $400 worth of housing. If the household rents an apartment for $181, it receives a subsidy of $1; if it rents an apartment for $400, it receives a subsidy of $220. Because the government pays the difference between actual rent and $180, an increase in housing consumption does not decrease the consumption of other goods as long as rent is less than the fair market rent. If the household spends more than the fair market rent ($400), it is ineligible for the certificate program, so it is stuck with the original budget line.

How will the certificate program affect the household's budget choice? In the absence of moving costs, a move from E to D will increase utility. It makes sense to go all the way to D because between points C and D, the opportunity cost of additional housing is zero: the tenant contribution to housing is fixed at $180 and the government pays any increase in rent. If moving costs are relatively large, however, the household will move straight up from E to F. In this case, the increase in utility is not large enough to offset moving costs, so the household stays in its original residence and spends the entire subsidy on other goods.

One of the surprising results of the rent-certificate program was that relatively few households moved to dwellings that rented for the fair market rent. In Figure 14–6, most households moved from point E to F, not E to D. This occurred despite the fact that the entire increase in rent would have been covered by the subsidy. Most households stayed in their existing dwelling and used the subsidy to cut their housing costs. This result suggests that moving costs are relatively large.

Housing Vouchers

The housing voucher program was started on an experimental basis in 1983. The eligibility requirements for housing vouchers are similar to those for rent certificates: most of the vouchers go to very poor households. To qualify for a voucher, the household must occupy a dwelling that meets the government's minimum quality standards. A voucher differs from a rent certificate in one important respect: the recipient can use the certificate to rent any dwelling that meets minimum physical standards. In 1988, about 156,000 households received vouchers.

The face value of the voucher is based on household income and the fair market rent. The formula is

$$\text{Face value} = \text{Fair market rent} - 0.30 \cdot \text{Income} \qquad (14-3)$$

Figure 14–7 shows the household's choice between housing and other goods under the voucher program. Household income is $600 and the fair market rent is $400, so the face value of the voucher is $220 ($400 − $180). The voucher program shifts the budget line outward from AB to FG. The voucher program gives the household more options than the rent-certificate program

FIGURE 14–6   Effects of Section 8 Rent Certificate on Housing Consumption

With the original budget line *AB*, the household chooses point *E*, spending $300 on rent and $300 on other goods. The rent-certificate program with a fair market rent of $400 adds points between *C* and *D* to the budget set: the government pays the difference between actual rent and 30% of income ($180), so the household's opportunity cost of spending beyond $180 is zero. In the absence of moving costs, the household will switch to point *D* because it generates higher utility. If moving costs are relatively large, the household will choose point *F*.

because the voucher is equivalent to a cash transfer. In the absence of moving costs, the household with the choices shown in Figure 14–7 will increase spending on housing from $300 (point *E*) to about $345 (point *H*), leaving $175 of the subsidy to spend on other goods. If moving costs are relatively large, the household will choose point *J* and spend the entire subsidy on other goods.

The voucher household also has the option of spending more than the fair market rent. In other words, the household has access to points along the budget segment *DG*. In contrast to the rent-certificate program, the voucher program allows the household to spend as much as it wants on housing.

In 1988, the budgetary costs of housing vouchers exceeded the costs of rent certificates by about $23 per recipient (Mariano 1989). The reason is simple: under the voucher program, the voucher covers the gap between the fair market rent and 30 percent of income, while the rent certificate covers the gap between the household's *actual rent* and 30 percent of income. As long as the actual rent is less than the fair market rent, the subsidy will be larger under the voucher. In Figure 14–7, the two programs will have equal budgetary costs only if all rent-certificate households choose point *D*. If a rent-certificate

FIGURE 14–7   Effects of Housing-Voucher Program on Housing Consumption

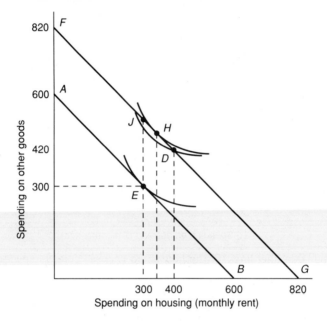

With the original budget line *AB*, the household chooses point *E*, spending $300 on rent and $300 on other goods. The voucher program with a fair market rent of $400 shifts the budget line outward to *FG*: the household receives a voucher worth $220 (the difference between the rent standard and 30% of income). In the absence of moving costs, the household will switch to point *H* and will be better off than it would be under a rent-certificate program (point *D*). If moving costs are relatively large, the household will choose point *J*.

recipient pays less than the fair market rent, the savings go to the government, so the certificate program costs less than the voucher program.

Market Effects of Consumer Subsidies

What are the market effects of rent certificates and housing vouchers? Consider a city with the following characteristics:

1. The city has poor families and middle-income families.

2. To qualify for a housing voucher, a poor household must occupy a moderate-quality dwelling (one that generates at least 800 units of housing service).

3. The poor households initially live in low-quality dwellings (which generate only 600 units of housing service).

4. Middle-income households live in moderate-quality dwellings (800 units of housing service) and medium-quality dwellings (1,000 units of housing service).

   Figure 14–8 shows the short-run effects of the coupon program on the moderate-quality submarket. The voucher program shifts the demand curve outward, increasing the market price from $250 (point B) to $350 (point E). Because the supply of moderate-quality housing is fixed in the short run, the vouchers simply bid up the price of housing. Who gains and who loses in the short run? Although voucher recipients pay more for housing, they also have more money to spend on housing. In contrast, nonrecipients (middle-income

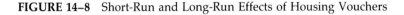

FIGURE 14–8 Short-Run and Long-Run Effects of Housing Vouchers

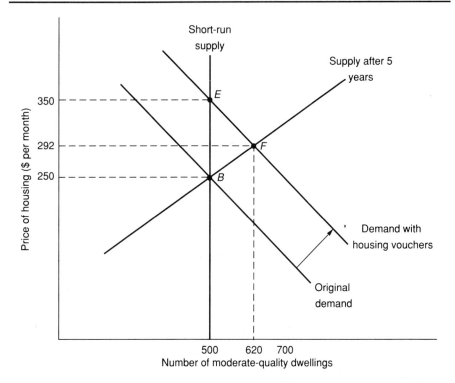

The housing-voucher program increases the demand for moderate-quality dwellings. In the short run, the supply of moderate-quality housing is fixed, so the price increases from $250 to $350. Over a five-year period, the increase in the price of housing increases the quantity supplied from 500 to 620, and the price drops to $292. The longer the period of time, the greater the increase in the quantity supplied and the smaller the net increase in price.

households) will pay higher housing prices without the benefit of housing vouchers.

What happens to the moderate-quality market after five years? Figure 14–8 shows the intermediate-run supply curve (the supply curve over a five-year period). The increase in price increases the profitability of moderate-quality dwellings, increasing the quantity supplied for three reasons:

1. **Downward filtering.** Dwellings filter down more rapidly from the medium-quality submarket to the more lucrative moderate-quality submarket.

2. **Increased maintenance.** The owners of moderate-quality dwellings will spend more on maintenance and repair to keep their dwellings in the market for a longer period of time: downward filtering is slowed.

3. **Upward filtering.** Dwellings from the low-quality submarket are upgraded to serve the more lucrative moderate-quality submarket.

For these three reasons, the quantity of moderate-quality dwellings supplied increases as the price increases. In equilibrium (point *F*), the price of moderate-quality housing is $292 and the number of dwellings is 620.

How does the voucher program affect the medium-quality submarket? The increase in the price of moderate-quality dwellings increases the price of medium-quality dwellings for two reasons. First is the demand effect: the increase in the relative price of moderate-quality dwellings causes some consumers to switch to the medium-quality submarket. The demand for medium-quality dwellings increases, so the market price increases. Second is the supply effect: the increase in the relative price of moderate-quality dwellings hastens the filtering of medium-quality dwellings downward to the moderate-quality submarket. In combination, the increase in demand and decrease in supply increase the market price of medium-quality dwellings. Because of the interactions between the housing submarkets, the voucher program increases the prices of both types of housing.

Ohls (1975) used a computer model of the housing market to explore the effects of consumer subsidies on the filtering process. As explained earlier, his model divides the housing stock into 60 quality levels, with the wealthy occupying the highest quality dwellings and the poor occupying the lowest quality dwellings. Under his consumer-subsidy program, the government provides a 50 percent housing subsidy for the poorest fifth of the population. The subsidy program caused the following changes in the market:

1. The poorest households upgraded to higher quality housing, moving from quality level 5 to 8. The typical recipient moved from quality level 8 to 11.

2. The increase in the demand for moderate-quality housing stimulated new construction (at the high-quality level) because the market for used housing became more lucrative.

3. Filtering down to the moderate-quality range sped up, and filtering down from the moderate-quality range slowed.

The Experimental Housing-Allowance Program

An alternative to a housing voucher is a housing allowance. A housing allowance is a cash payment, the size of which equals the gap between a given fraction of household income (e.g., 30 percent) and the fair market rent. To qualify for a housing allowance, the household must occupy a dwelling that meets minimum quality standards. A housing allowance will be equivalent to a housing voucher if (a) the two programs have the same quality standards, (b) the face value of the voucher equals the allowance payment, and (c) the household's rent exceeds the face value of the voucher. If the household spends more than the voucher value on housing, the household can substitute the voucher for its own spending on housing, freeing up an amount of cash equal to the face value of the voucher.

Under the Experimental Housing Allowance Program (EHAP), the federal government conducted a number of experiments with housing allowances. The **demand experiments** offered housing allowances to a small sample of poor renter households in two cities (Phoenix and Pittsburgh). The purpose of these experiments was to examine the effects of the allowance program on eligible households. The most important policy issues concerned participation rates (how many households would participate), the mobility of participants (how many recipients would move to higher-quality dwellings), and housing consumption (how much would housing consumption increase).

The demand experiments generated three conclusions about the responses of eligible households:

1. **Low participation rates.** Between 40 percent and 45 percent of the eligible households participated in the allowance programs. Participation rates were sensitive to the quality standards: the stricter the standards, the lower the participation rate.

2. **Small changes in housing consumption.** On average, between one quarter and one third of the allowance payment was used to increase housing consumption, and the remainder was spent on other goods. In other words, most of the allowance money was used to decrease rent burdens. The estimated income elasticity of demand of allowance recipients was relatively low (between 0.20 and 0.44 for renters and about 0.45 for owner-occupiers).

3. **Mobility.** Relatively few households changed dwellings. In Pittsburgh, 40 percent of allowance recipients moved over a two-year period, compared to 35 percent of households in a control group. In Phoenix, 63 percent of recipients moved, compared to 53 percent of the control households. The allowance program did not encourage integration with respect to race or income.

The general conclusion is that the housing allowances caused relatively small changes in housing choices. Recipients spent most of the money on nonhousing goods, and few moved from their original dwellings.

The **supply experiments** offered allowances to all poor households in two counties (Brown County, Wisconsin, and St. Joseph County, Indiana). The purpose of the supply experiments was to examine the effects of housing allowances on the market price of housing. The principal question was whether a citywide assistance program would increase housing prices.

The allowance program did not cause any measurable price increases in the two cities involved in the supply experiment. Because participation rates were relatively low and recipients spent a relatively small fraction of their allowances on housing, the rightward shift of the demand curve was relatively small. To the extent that the demand for housing increased, the supply of housing was sufficiently elastic to accommodate the increased demand without any measurable price effects. The supply of housing was relatively elastic because the two experimental sites had relatively high vacancy rates. The same result would not have occurred in a city with lower vacancy rates. In such a city, the shift of the demand curve would have bid up the price of housing.

What are the lessons from the supply experiment? As pointed out by Kain (1981), the supply experiment tested the effects of one type of allowance program, one with minimal housing quality standards and relatively low participation rates. Because the allowance program increased the housing consumption of a small number of households by relatively small amounts, it is not surprising that housing prices did not rise. If a national housing allowance program had higher participation rates, larger allowance payments, and more stringent housing standards, it would shift the housing demand curve by a larger amount and would probably increase housing prices. Kain cites studies by the National Bureau of Economic Research and the Urban Institute that suggest such an allowance program would increase prices in some housing submarkets. Other analysts disagree with Kain: they predict that a national allowance program would be similar to the EHAP program, and would have similar effects.

SUPPLY VERSUS DEMAND POLICIES

What are the trade-offs associated with supply-side policies (public housing) and demand-side policies (housing vouchers)? From the perspective of the recipient, the voucher program has two advantages over subsidized public housing. First, the voucher is equivalent to an income transfer, so it generates a larger increase in utility per dollar spent on housing programs. Second, the voucher allows tenants to occupy relatively inexpensive used housing, so a fixed assistance budget will provide more housing.

The disadvantage of the voucher program is that it increases the price of housing. The recipient will be better off under the voucher program if the program causes a relatively small increase in the price of housing. This will occur if the elasticity of supply is relatively large. As explained in Chapter 13 (Why Is Housing Different?), little is known about the intermediate-run and long-run elasticities of supply of housing. Unless one knows something about the individual housing submarkets in a city, it will be difficult to predict the effects of a voucher program on the price of housing.

What about taxpayers and nonrecipients? Two factors contribute to public support of public housing over housing vouchers. First, taxpayers seem to care about the housing consumption of recipients, not necessarily their utility levels. If public housing generates a larger increase in housing consumption, most taxpayers would consider it to be a superior policy. Second, nonrecipients pay a higher price for housing under a demand-side policy and a lower price under a supply-side policy. For these two reasons, taxpayers and nonrecipients may prefer public housing over housing vouchers even if recipients would be better off under the voucher program.

COMMUNITY DEVELOPMENT AND URBAN RENEWAL

There are dozens of programs and polices that fit under the term *community development*. The legislated mandate for federally supported community development calls for, "Systematic and sustained action by the federal, state, and local governments to eliminate blight, to conserve and renew older areas, to improve the living environment of low- and moderate-income families, and to develop new centers of population growth and economic activity." The two principal purposes of community development policies are to (*a*) revitalize declining areas of the city and (*b*) improve the housing of poor households. Community-development policies are neighborhood-oriented in the sense that they concentrate spending in relatively small geographical areas.

Urban Renewal

Urban Renewal, the first community-development program in the United States, was established under the Housing Act of 1949 and was eventually dropped in 1973. The national government provided local governments with the power and the money to demolish and rebuild parts of their cities. Local agencies acquired property under the right of eminent domain, cleared the site of "undesirable" uses (e.g., low-income housing and small businesses), and then either built a public facility or sold the site to a private developer. The local agencies charged the developer less than the cost of acquiring and clearing the site, and the federal government covered two thirds of the losses of local governments. The private developer built housing (usually for middle-income and high-income households), government buildings, or commercial establishments.

According to the Congressional Research Service, Urban Renewal had the following effects:

1. **Demolition.** A total of 600,000 dwellings were demolished, displacing about 2 million people, most of whom were poor.

2. **New housing.** A total of 250,000 new dwellings were built, most of which were occupied by middle-income and high-income households.

3. **Public facilities.** The total floor space of new public facilities was 120 million square feet.

4. **Commercial facilities.** The total floor space of new commercial facilities was 224 million square feet.

5. **Property assessments.** The assessed value of property on renewed sites increased by 360%.

In sum, Urban Renewal generated both costs and benefits. It displaced poor households, but also provided housing for middle-income and wealthy households, allowed the construction of commercial and public facilities, and increased tax revenue.

Was Urban Renewal worthwhile? The critics of the program focus on the demolition aspects of the program, pointing out that 2 million poor people were displaced. The defenders of the program focus on the rebuilding aspects of the program, pointing out that the new commercial developments provided jobs for the poor residents of the central city.

Recent Community-Development Programs

More recent federal community-development programs have avoided many of the problems of the Urban Renewal program. The newer programs are executed on a smaller scale, so they displace fewer households, and they place a greater emphasis on providing housing for the poor.

Table 14–2 shows the 1987 budget for community development. The total budget was over $3.5 billion, with about $2 billion used for Community Development Block Grants (CDBGs). The CDBG program is an entitlement program, with funds allocated to cities and states on the basis of population and other factors. The allocation formula gives relatively large grants to cities with relatively old and overcrowded housing, high poverty rates, and slow growth rates. The second largest program is the State and Small Cities Program, which gives money to states, which then distribute the money to small cities that are ineligible for CDBG funds. The third largest allocation goes to Urban Development Action Grants (UDAGs), which are used to leverage private investments in community development. Under the UDAG program, which was recently abandoned, the federal government provided small subsidies to transform slightly unprofitable private development projects into profitable ones. The fourth largest allocation is for rental rehabilitation: these grants subsidize the renovation of low-income rental housing. The fifth largest allocation is for emergency shelter: these grants subsidize shelters for the homeless.

Cities can spend their community-development grants on a wide variety of projects. Under the Carter administration, cities were required to spend a

TABLE 14–2   Community-Development Budget of Department of Housing and
Urban Development, 1987

Program	Funding ($ million)
Community development block grants	
Housing rehabilitation	876
Jobs programs	254
Public works	536
Public services	242
Assistance to homeless	46
Total	1,954
State and small cities program	883
Urban development action grants	325
Rental rehabilitation	200
Emergency shelter grants	60
Other	133
Total	3,555

SOURCE: U.S. Department of Housing and Urban Development, *1988 Community Development Programs: State Reports,* pp. 1–4.

large fraction of the grants on projects that directly benefited poor households and low-income neighborhoods. Under the Reagan administration, many of these restrictions were dropped. The projects funded by the various funding programs can be divided into four types:

1. **Improved housing.** Some programs support local projects that renovate buildings, enforce building codes, and build new low-income housing.

- The Boston Housing Partnership used $8.5 million in CDBG funds to acquire and rehabilitate 700 rental units.
- The city of Cleveland joined with a nonprofit organization and a private developer to build a 183-unit rental housing project, using $4.4 million in federal funds ($1.7 million from CBDG and $2.7 million from UDAG) to leverage $9.9 million from private and other sources.

2. **Renewed infrastructure.** Some programs support projects that improve streets, roads, and water and sewage facilities.

- In Fort Worth, Texas, the Main Street Project used $2.6 million in UDAG funds to improve the street's infrastructure (new curbs, gutters, sidewalks, and street lighting). As part of the renovation program, private developers agreed to build a $48 million hotel.
- The city of Oshkosh, Wisconsin, used $600,000 of CDBG and UDAG funds to expand its airport to accommodate increased traffic.

3. **Job development.** Some programs support projects that encourage economic development and job creation.

- In St. Louis, the Union Station was renovated with $10.2 million in CDBG and UDAG money and $126 million in other public and private funds. The station was developed into a hotel-retail-entertainment complex that produced 2,000 new jobs, over 50 percent of which were filled by minorities. The project rejuvenated a part of the city that had been dormant for 15 years.

- Salt Lake City is using a $1.1 million UDAG grant to support the construction of a downtown auto mall, using the grant to leverage $4.7 million in private financing.

- Baltimore used $10 million in UDAG funds to support the revitalization of its Inner Harbor. Private investment in office space, retail space, and a hotel totaled $73.4 million and produced 1,600 jobs.

4. **Responsive public services.** Some programs support public services for the elderly, the homeless, and children.

- Orange County, California, used $892,000 in CDBG funds to support the construction of a $7.5 million facility to provide emergency services for abused, abandoned, or neglected children.

- Phoenix used $361,000 in CDBG funds to build a recreation center for the handicapped.

- Fort Worth, Texas, used $106,000 in CDBG funds to start a neighborhood youth project designed to curtail gang activity.

These examples show that community-development funds are spent on a wide variety of projects.

What are the effects of community-development programs? The programs that support housing projects supplement federal housing programs (public housing, subsidized new construction, housing vouchers). The difference is that the city has more control over the spending of community-development funds. Other community-development programs support economic-development projects and can be evaluated as alternative means of promoting local economic growth. The costs and benefits of economic-development programs are discussed in Chapter 6 (Economic Growth).

RENT CONTROL

During World War II, the federal government instituted a national system of rent control. Following the war, New York City was the only city to retain rent control. During the 1970s, rent control returned to dozens of cities, including Boston, Cambridge, Los Angeles, Washington, D.C., Albany, Berkeley, and Santa Monica.

Market Effects of Rent Control

What are the market effects of rent control? Consider a city with the following characteristics:

1. All households live in identical apartments.
2. The equilibrium rent is $600 per month.
3. The equilibrium number of apartments is 90.
4. The apartments are made of stone and do not deteriorate over time.
5. The city sets a maximum rent of $400.

Figure 14–9 shows the short-run effects of rent control. The short run is defined as the period of time over which the supply of housing is fixed at 90 dwellings. In the short run, rent control does not affect the supply of housing,

FIGURE 14–9   Short-Run and Long-Run Effects of Rent Control

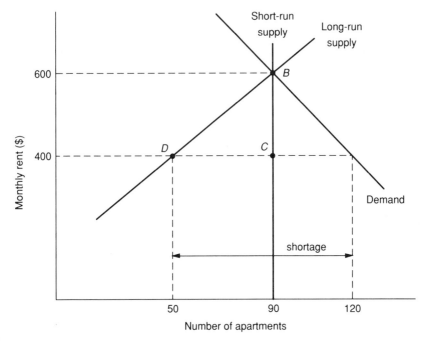

In the short run, the supply of apartments is fixed, so rent control (which sets the maximum rent at $400) simply transfers income from landlords to tenants: the market moves from point *B* to *C*. In the long run, the decrease in price decreases the quantity supplied: the market moves from point *C* to point *D*. In the long-run equilibrium, the shortage (the excess of quantity demanded over quantity supplied) is 70 apartments.

so the market moves from point B to C. Rent control simply transfers $200 per month ($600 − $400) from the landlord to the tenant.

In the long run, the supply of apartments depends on the price of rental housing. As rent decreases, some landlords will convert their property to more lucrative uses: some apartment buildings will be converted to condominiums, and other buildings will be demolished to make way for commercial land uses. In Figure 14–9, rent control decreases the number of apartments from 90 to 50. As the price of rental housing decreases, the market moves downward along the long-run supply curve. The supply response to rent control depends on the long-run elasticity of supply. The more elastic the supply, the larger the decrease in the quantity of housing supplied.

Rent control causes a shortage of housing. At the controlled price of $400, the quantity of apartments demanded is 120, compared to a supply of only 50 apartments. There are too many tenants chasing too few apartments. In such a market, tenants will spend relatively large amounts of time and money searching for apartments. For tenants, rent control brings good news and bad news: although rent control decreases the rent, it also increases search costs.

Rent control produces winners and losers. The city's population can be divided into four groups:

1. **Nonmovers.** Some households live in the city when rent control is implemented and occupy the same apartment forever. These households are winners in the rent-control game: they pay a lower price for the same apartment.

2. **Successful searchers.** Some people move to the city after rent control is implemented. They may spend several months to find an apartment. The full cost of a rent-controlled apartment is the sum of the rent ($400 per month) and the opportunity cost of search time. The full cost of a rent-controlled apartment may exceed the full cost of an uncontrolled apartment ($600 per month and small search costs). In general, if search costs are relatively large, the benefits of rent control (decreased rent) will be smaller than the costs (increased search costs), so successful searchers will be losers in the rent-control game.

3. **Displaced households.** Some tenants are displaced when apartments are converted or demolished and are unsuccessful in their search for a new apartment. In Figure 14–9, the number of dwellings decreases by 40 (from 90 to 50), so 40 households are displaced. The displaced households are obviously losers.

4. **Landlords.** Rent control decreases the annual rental income per apartment from $7,200 ($600 times 12 months) to $4,800. Because the market value of an apartment building reflects its income-earning potential, the announcement of the rent-control program decreases the market value of the city's apartment buildings. If Wilma owns an apartment

building when rent control is announced, she pays for rent control in the form of a decreased market value. She cannot escape the effects of rent control by selling the building to someone else: once prospective owners hear about rent control, they will be willing to pay less for the building. According to Smith and Tomlinson (1981), Toronto's rent-control program decreased the market value of apartment buildings by about 40 percent over a five-year period (1975–1980).

Olsen (1972) estimated the effects of New York City's rent-control program on tenants and landlords. Ignoring search costs, he estimated that the occupants of controlled units experienced a 3.4 percent increase in real income. On the other hand, landlords experienced losses in real income about twice as large as the total gain of tenants.

Deterioration and Maintenance

One of the assumptions of the simple model of the rent-control city is that apartments are made of stone, so dwellings do not deteriorate over time. This is clearly unrealistic. Suppose that housing is subject to physical deterioration: to maintain a dwelling at a given service level, the landlord must spend money on routine maintenance and repair. Suppose that in the initial equilibrium, the typical $600 apartment generates 1,000 units of housing service (Q=1,000).

Rent control discourages routine maintenance, so apartments will deteriorate more rapidly. In an uncontrolled city, landlords will spend money to keep their apartments at a service level high enough to justify a $600 rent. If the apartment deteriorates to Q=900, tenants would be unwilling to pay $600 rent for the dwelling. In the rent-control city, there is no incentive to keep the apartment at Q=1,000 because the landlord cannot charge $600 for the dwelling. Landlords will decrease their spending on repair and maintenance, thus allowing apartments to deteriorate to a service level consistent with the $400 rent. Under a rent-control program, tenants may eventually get what they pay for.

Studies of rent-control cities show that landlords do indeed cut back on maintenance and repair. The Rand Corporation studied the effects of rent control in New York City (1970) and concluded that rent control decreased the quality and quantity of rental housing. Between 1960 and 1967, the inventory of "sound" housing increased by 2.4 percent, the inventory of "dilapidated" housing increased by 44 percent, and the inventory of "deteriorating" housing increased by 37 percent. Between 1965 and 1967, 114,000 dwellings were retired from the housing stock. A study of Cambridge, Massachusetts, found that spending on maintenance decreased by $50 per apartment per year (Navarro, 1987).

Housing Submarkets

One of the assumptions of the rent-control model is that all households live in identical apartments. If there are housing submarkets, the analysis changes in two ways.

Consider first the possibility that there are two rent-controlled submarkets. There are large apartments (equilibrium rent of $600 and controlled rent of $400) and small apartments (equilibrium rent of $300 and controlled rent of $200). Rent control inhibits movement between the two markets because search costs are relatively large. Suppose that a household would like to move from a large apartment to a small one. In the rent-control city, there are two options. First, the household could stay in its large apartment, paying $400 per month. Second, the household could spend time and money searching for a small apartment (which rents for $200). If search costs are relatively high, the household will be better off staying in its original apartment.

Consider next the possibility that some of the dwellings in the city are not subject to rent control. Rent control decreases the supply of housing in the controlled sector, causing some of the displaced households to move into the uncontrolled submarket. As they do, they bid up the price of housing in the uncontrolled market. Therefore, part of the costs of rent control are borne by households living in uncontrolled dwellings.

Controlling the Supply Response to Rent Control

Rent control decreases the quantity and quality of rental housing. Cities have developed a number of policies to diminish this supply response.

1. **Rent adjustments.** Most rent-control laws allow periodic increases in rent, with the allowable increase tied to some price index (e.g., the consumer price index [CPI]). Rent adjustments weaken rent control and diminish the negative supply effects of the controls. In most rent-control cities that use rent adjustments, controlled rents rise slower than the costs of building and maintaining rental housing. In New York City, controlled rents rose by 110 percent between 1943 and 1968, while the operating costs of rental housing increased by 285 percent (de Salvo and Woodfill 1971). In Toronto, controlled rents increased by 39 percent between 1975 and 1980, while operating costs of rental housing increased by 75 percent (Smith and Tomlinson 1981).

2. **Exemption of new housing.** Most rent-control laws exempt new construction from controls. If new housing is exempt from controls, the quantity of new housing produced may be unaffected by rent control. In fact, tenants displaced from the controlled market will increase the demand for new rental housing, stimulating the supply of new rental housing. It is possible that new housing will make up for the loss in housing stock caused by rent control. But there are two reasons to suspect that

new housing will not offset the effects of rent control. First, new housing is typically a small part of the housing market, so it would take a relatively large increase in the supply of new housing to counteract the effects of rent control. Second, builders and owners are likely to be skeptical about the city's promise to never impose rent control on new rental housing. If builders suspect that today's new housing will become tomorrow's rent-control housing, they may be reluctant to supply new housing.

3. **Restrictions on conversions.** Many cities restrict the conversion of rental housing to condominiums. If successful, these restrictions limit the conversion of rental housing to other uses, diminishing the supply effects of rent control.

4. **Subsidies for new construction.** Public policies encourage the building of new dwellings to replace the dwellings lost as a result of rent control. The city of Toronto offered low-interest construction loans to housing firms. In the United States, one of the purposes of public housing is to replace the dwellings lost because of rent control.

5. **Vacancy decontrol.** In some cities, rent is fixed during a tenancy, but can be changed when a new tenant moves into the dwelling. This provision increases the landlord's rental income, weakening rent control. It also increases the incentive for long-term occupancy.

Another way to decrease the supply effect of rent control is to cheat. Tenants and landlords often find ways to violate the spirit of rent-control laws. Landlords charge tenants "key money" (e.g., $5,000 for a key to the apartment) or nonrefundable security deposits. To the extent that landlords use indirect payments to increase the net price of housing, the negative supply response to rent control will be reduced. Tenants also collect bribes for rent-controlled apartments: when a tenant vacates a controlled apartment, he can charge the new tenant a finder's fee. The fee is often implicit: in California, old tenants reportedly sold bean-bag chairs to new tenants, charging hundreds of dollars for chairs that sold for just a few dollars in thrift stores. Tenant bribery does not increase the supply of housing, but simply transfers income from the new tenant to the existing one.

Alternatives to Rent Control

In many cities, rent control is viewed as an indirect form of income redistribution. The idea is to take money from wealthy landlords and give it to poor tenants. At best, rent control is a blunt instrument for redistribution. Rent control helps all of the occupants of rent-controlled dwellings, rich and poor alike. Moreover, a poor person who occupies a controlled dwelling will be worse off under rent control if the search costs are larger than the savings in rent.

Suppose that a city wants to redistribute income from the wealthy to the poor. What are the alternatives to rent control? The first option is to finance income redistribution with a land tax. Because the supply of land is perfectly inelastic, the land tax will not affect the supply of land or the supply of housing. Therefore, the land tax will not cause the same supply problems as rent control. The second approach is to leave income redistribution to the federal government. Local attempts at income redistribution are likely to be frustrated by the movement of households into and out of the city. If the city gives the proceeds of a land tax to its poor residents, poor people from other cities are likely to migrate to the city, diluting the effects of the redistribution program. Because international mobility is less than intercity mobility, a national redistribution program does not suffer from this problem.

SUMMARY

1. The condition of the U.S. housing stock has improved considerably over the last several decades. Nonetheless, about two thirds of poor households experience some sort of housing problem, usually inadequate housing or high housing costs. Over half of black households experience housing problems.

2. The rent-income ratio is a measure of the affordability of housing. For the population as a whole, the median ratio increased from 0.20 in 1970 to 0.31 in 1983; for poor households, the median ratio rose from 0.35 to 0.40.

3. In 1987, about 1.3 million households lived in public housing. Public housing is built and managed by local housing authorities. The federal government specifies who is eligible for public housing and provides subsidies for capital costs, operating costs, and modernization.

    a. Public housing may increase or decrease housing consumption, depending on the recipient's willingness to trade off consumption of housing and other goods.

    b. Public housing produces a relatively small increase in recipient welfare per dollar because (i) the monetary value of public housing is about 75 percent of its market value and (ii) public housing costs more than used private housing.

    c. In the short run, the supply of private housing is fixed, so public housing decreases the market price of housing by a large amount.

    d. Over time, the decrease in the price of housing decreases the quantity of private dwellings supplied as more dwellings are retired and fewer dwellings filter down to the low-quality submarket. The more elastic the supply, the greater the displacement of private housing and the smaller the net decrease in market price.

4. There are two subsidy programs for new, low-income rental housing, Section 236 and Section 8. Both programs have the same market effects of public housing: they decrease the price of private housing and decrease the quantity supplied.

a. Under the Section 236 program, the household pays 30 percent of its income or the basic rent, whichever is larger, and the government pays the landlord the difference between the tenant contribution and the market rent.

b. Under the Section 8 program, the household pays 30 percent of its income and the government pays the difference between the tenant contribution and the fair market rent.

5. There are two types of consumer subsidies: Section 8 rent certificates and housing vouchers.

a. The rent certificates cover the difference between the actual rent and 30 percent of household income, and can be used on dwellings that rent for less than the fair market rent.

b. The face value of a housing voucher equals the gap between fair market rent and 30 percent of household income and can be used on any dwelling satisfying minimum physical standards.

c. Both subsidy programs shift the demand curve outward, increasing the market price in the short run. Over time, the quantity of housing increases as (i) fewer dwellings are retired and (ii) more dwellings filter down from higher quality submarkets. The larger the supply elasticity, the smaller the net increase in price.

6. The Experimental Housing Allowance Program (EHAP) tested a program of housing allowances (cash payments to poor households). The demand for housing increased by a relatively small amount because (i) participation rates were relatively low, (ii) few households changed dwellings, and (iii) only a small fraction of the allowance payment was spent on housing. The small shift of the demand curve caused no measurable increases in housing prices.

7. There are dozens of policies and programs that fit under the term *community development*. The two principal purposes of such policies are to (i) revitalize declining areas of the city and (ii) improve the housing of poor households.

8. Under the Urban Renewal program, the federal government subsidized the replacement of low-income housing with middle-income and high-income housing, public facilities, and commercial establishments.

9. More recent community-development programs support local projects that improve low-income housing and local infrastructure, stimulate economic development, and develop new public services for citizens who are handicapped, elderly, or disadvantaged.

10. Rent control has the following effects on the housing market.

a. The supply of dwellings decreases, causing a housing shortage that increases search costs.

b. Spending on maintenance and repair decreases, so individual dwellings produce lower quantities of housing services.

c. Consumer mobility decreases, and consumers make inefficient housing choices.

11. Rent-control cities use a number of policies to control the decrease in supply caused by rent control, including rent adjustments, exemption of new housing, restrictions on conversion, subsidies for new construction, and vacancy decontrol.

EXERCISES AND DISCUSSION QUESTIONS

1. In Figure 14–2, the offer of $100 public housing decreased housing consumption. Suppose that the government increases the rent on an 800-unit dwelling from $100 to $150.
   a. Using a graph similar to Figure 14–2, show the budget point with (*i*) $100 public housing and (*ii*) $150 public housing.
   b. Assume that the household starts with housing consumption of 1,000 units. Draw a set of indifference curves such that the household accepts the offer of $100 public housing, but is indifferent between its original choice and $150 public housing.

2. Suppose that the household in Figure 14–2 starts with housing consumption of 1,200 units of housing service instead of 1,000. Is this household more or less likely to decrease its housing consumption to get public housing? Explain.

3. Figure 14–3 shows that the consumer prefers cash to free public housing. The figure was drawn under the assumption that a system of cash transfers would not increase the price of housing.
   a. Redraw the budget line under the assumption that the cash transfers increase the price of housing from $0.25 to $0.50.
   b. Draw a set of indifference curves such that the consumer prefers free public housing (with no change in price) to the cash transfer (with the associated increase in price).

4. Comment on the following statement of Mr. Taxpayer: "I support public housing rather than cash transfers because I want to be sure that the recipients of public assistance increase their housing consumption. If we give them cash, they will spend the money on something else."

5. According to Mr. Wizard, a realtor in Modville, "If my assumptions are correct, the long-run market effects of public housing are nil. The building of 200 public-housing dwellings will affect neither the equilibrium price of housing nor the quantity of housing."
   a. What are Mr. Wizard's assumptions?
   b. Use Mr. Wizard's assumptions to predict the long-run market effects of housing vouchers.

6. In the early days of Section 8 rent certificates, the recipient received 25 percent of the savings associated with renting a dwelling for less than the fair market rent. Draw Figure 14–6 and add the budget line under the early version of the rent-certificate program.

7. Explain the following quote from a housing official: "Our housing-assis-

tance budget is $3 billion. If we use vouchers instead of rent certificates, we will serve 9,500 fewer households."

8. Suppose that you are interested in maximizing the welfare of the poor. You must choose between cash payments and free housing. What data do you need? Explain how you would use the data.

9. Suppose that the poor households of city H are enrolled in a federal housing-allowance program. You are a middle-income renter in the city.
   a. Will you be helped or harmed by the allowance program?
   b. If you will be harmed, what variables determine how much you will be harmed? In other words, what are the relevant elasticities and how does the cost you incur vary with the elasticities?
   c. How would your answer to (a) change if you owned your home?

10. Contrast the effects of rent control in two cities. In city R, the elasticity of supply of housing is 5.0 (i.e., a 10 percent increase in the price of housing increases the quantity of housing by 50 percent). In city S, the supply of housing is less elastic: the supply elasticity is 0.40.

11. Cheating on rent control is common. If you were a prospective tenant in a rent-controlled city, would you encourage your prospective landlord to cheat?

REFERENCES AND ADDITIONAL READINGS

Description of Federal Housing Policies

Aaron, Henry J. "Rationale for a Housing Policy." In *Federal Housing Policies and Programs*, ed. J. Paul Mitchell. New Brunswick, N.J.: Center for Urban Policy Research, 1985. Discusses the frequently cited justifications for federal housing policies.

Jacobs, Barry G.; Kenneth R. Harney; Charles L. Edson; and Bruce S. Lane. *Guide to Federal Housing Programs*. 2d ed. Washington, D.C.: Bureau of National Affairs, 1986. A detailed description of federal housing policies (public housing, housing subsidies, consumer subsidies, and community development).

Mariano, Ann. "The Voucher Controversy Drags On." *Washington Post* (February 18, 1989). Discusses the budgetary costs of vouchers and rent certificates.

Mitchell, J. Paul. "The Historical Context for Housing Policy." In *Federal Housing Policies and Programs*, ed. J. Paul Mitchell. New Brunswick, N.J.: Center for Urban Policy Research, 1985. A historical sketch of federal housing policy.

Struyk, Raymond J.; Margery A. Turner; and Makiko Ueno. *Future U.S. Housing Policy: Meeting the Demographic Challenge*. Washington, D.C.: Urban Institute, 1983. Discusses the implications of demographic changes (changes in family structure and the aging of society) for federal housing policy.

Struyk, Raymond J.; Neil Mayer; and John Tuccillo. *Federal Housing Policy at President Reagan's Midterm*. Washington, D.C.: Urban Institute, 1983. Explains the changes in federal housing policies (assisted housing, community development, and housing finance) during the early 1980s.

Weicher, John. "Urban Housing Policy." In *Current Issues in Urban Economics*, ed. Peter Meiszkowski and Mahlon Straszheim. Baltimore: The Johns Hopkins Press, 1979.

Condition of the Housing Stock

Irby, Iredia. "Attaining the Housing Goal." U.S. Department of Housing and Urban Development, Division of Housing and Demographic Analysis, July 1986. Describes the condition of the housing stock in 1983.

Supply versus Demand Policies

Maisel, Sheman. "The Agenda for Metropolitan Housing Policies." In *American Domestic Priorities—An Economic Appraisal*, ed. John M. Quigley and Daniel L. Rubinfeld. Berkeley: University of California Press, 1985. Discusses housing policies in the middle 1980s.

Olsen, Edgar. "Housing Programs and the Forgotten Taxpayer." *The Public Interest* 66 (1982), pp. 97–109. Discusses alternative housing policies from the perspective of taxpayers.

Welfare Effects of Public Housing

Aaron, Henry, and George M. von Furstenberg. "The Inefficiency of Transfers in Kind: The Case of Housing Assistance." *Western Economic Journal* 9 (1971), pp. 184–91. Estimates a welfare loss from public housing of between 10 percent and 18 percent.

Barton, David M., and Edgar O. Olsen. "The Benefits and Costs of Public Housing in New York City." Institute for Research of Poverty, Discussion Paper 373-76. Madison: University of Wisconsin, 1976. Estimates the welfare loss from public housing (relative to cash transfers) as 25 percent of program costs.

Kraft, John, and Edgar O. Olsen. "The Distribution of Benefits from Public Housing." In *The Distribution of Benefits from Public Housing*, ed. F. Thomas Juster. Studies in Income and Wealth, vol. 41. New York: National Bureau of Economic Research, 1977. Estimates the welfare losses from using public housing instead of cash transfers as 27 percent of the program costs.

Murray, Michael P. "The Distribution of Tenant Benefits in Public Housing." *Econometrica* 43 (1975), pp. 771–88. Estimates the welfare losses from using public housing instead of cash transfers as 16 percent to 20 percent of the program costs.

Muth, Richard F. *Public Housing: An Economic Evaluation*. Washington, D.C.: American Enterprise Institute, 1973. Estimates the welfare losses from using public housing instead of cash transfers as 45 percent of the program costs. Argues for the replacement of traditional housing programs with rent certificates, which would operate in the same way as food stamps.

National Housing Review. *Housing in the Seventies*. Washington, D.C.: U.S. Government Printing Office, 1974. Discusses the equity and efficiency effects of housing programs.

Smeeding, Timothy M. "Alternative Methods for Evaluating Selected In-Kind Transfer Benefits and Measuring Their Effect on Poverty." U.S. Bureau of the Census, Technical Paper no 50. Washington, D.C.: U.S. Government Printing Office, 1982. Estimates the value of in-kind transfers to the recipients. Estimates that $1 of public housing is worth 80 cents to the typical recipient.

Smolensky, Eugene. "Public Housing or Income Supplements: The Economics of Housing for the Poor." *Journal of the American Institute of Planners* 34 (1968), pp. 94–101.

Market Effects of Public Housing

Ohls, James C. "Public Policy Toward Low Income Housing and Filtering in Housing Markets." *Journal of Urban Economics* 2 (1975), pp. 144–71. Uses a computer model to simulate the effects of public housing on the filtering process.

Experimental Housing Allowance Program (EHAP)

Aaron, Henry J. "Policy Implications: A Policy Report." In *Do Housing Allowances Work*, ed. Katherine Bradbury and Anthony Downs. Washington, D.C.: Brookings Institution, 1981. Compares the effect of allowances to cash transfers and construction subsidies. Discusses the value of social experiments such as EHAP.

Allen, Garland E.; Jerry J. Fitts; and Evelyn S. Glatt. "The Experimental Housing Allowance Program." In *Do Housing Allowances Work*, ed. Katherine Bradbury and Anthony Downs. Washington, D.C.: Brookings Institution, 1981. A description of the housing allowance experiments.

Downs, Anthony, and Katherine Bradbury. "Conference Discussion." In *Do Housing Allowances Work*, ed. Katherine Bradbury and Anthony Downs. Washington, D.C.: Brookings Institution, 1981. A summary of the discussion of a conference on EHAP.

Frieden, Bernard J. "Housing Allowances: An Experiment that Worked." *The Public Interest* 59 (1980), pp. 15–35. A summary of the results of the allowance experiment.

Hanushek, Eric A., and John M. Quigley. "Consumption Aspects." In *Do Housing Allowances Work*, ed. Katherine Bradbury and Anthony Downs. Washington, D.C.: Brookings Institution, 1981. Discusses the responses of EHAP participants to housing allowances, focusing on the effects of housing consumption and the quality of housing.

Kain, John F. "A Universal Housing Allowance Program." In *Do Housing Allowances Work*, ed. Katherine Bradbury and Anthony Downs. Washington, D.C.: Brookings Institution, 1981. Discusses the implications of EHAP for a national housing-allowance program. Suggests that EHAP was not a true test of a national program because participation rates and housing-quality standards were relatively low.

Mills, Edwin S., and Arthur M. Sullivan. "Market Effects." In *Do Housing Allowances Work*, ed. Katherine Bradbury and Anthony Downs. Washington, D.C.: Brookings Institution, 1981. Discusses the market effects of the EHAP supply experiments.

Rossi, Peter H. "Residential Mobility." In *Do Housing Allowances Work*, ed. Katherine Bradbury and Anthony Downs. Washington, D.C.: Brookings Institution, 1981. Discusses the effects of EHAP on household mobility.

Straszheim, Mahlon R. "Participation." In *Do Housing Allowances Work*, ed. Katherine Bradbury and Anthony Downs. Washington, D.C.: Brookings Institution, 1981. Discusses the factors that explain the relatively low participation rates in EHAP.

Struyk, Raymond J., and Mac Bendick. *Housing Vouchers for the Poor*. Washington, D.C.: The Urban Institute, 1981.   A detailed description of the Experimental Housing Allowance Program.

Rent Controls

Lett, Monica. *Rent Control: Concepts, Realities and Mechanisms*. New Brunswick, N.J.: Rutgers University Press, 1976.   A general description of rent-control policies.

Navarro, Peter. "Rent Control in Cambridge, Massachusetts." *The Public Interest* 91 (1988), pp. 83–100.

Olsen, Edgar. "An Econometric Analysis of Rent Control." *Journal of Political Economy* 80 (1972), pp. 1081–100.

Rand Corporation. "The Effects of Rent Control on Housing in New York City." In *Rental Housing in New York City: Confronting the Crisis*. New York: Publication no. RM-6190-NYC, 1970.

Smith, Lawrence B., and Peter Tomlinson. "Rent Control in Ontario, Roofs or Ceilings." *American Real Estate and Urban Economics Journal* 9 (1981), pp. 93–114.

Urban Renewal

Anderson, Martin. *The Federal Bulldozer*. Cambridge, Mass.: MIT Press, 1964.   Argues that Urban Renewal destroyed low-income housing, displacing poor households.

Davis, Otto, and Andrew B. Whinston. "The Economics of Urban Renewal." In *Urban Renewal: The Record and the Controversy*, ed. James Q. Wilson. Cambridge, Mass.: MIT Press, 1966, pp. 50–67.

Rothenberg, Jerome. *Economic Evaluation of Urban Renewal*. Washington, D.C.: Brookings Institution, 1967.

Weicher, John. *Urban Renewal: National Program for Local Problems*. Washington, D.C.: American Enterprise Institute, 1973.

Weiss, Marc A. "The Origins and Legacy of Urban Renewal." In *Federal Housing Policies and Programs*, ed. J. Paul Mitchell. New Brunswick, N.J.: Center for Urban Policy Research, 1985.   Discusses the politics of Urban Renewal and housing policies.

Community Development

U.S. Department of Housing and Urban Development. *1988 Community Development Programs: State Reports*.   Shows HUD's community-development budget and describes how cities and states have used federal community-development funds.

PART FOUR

Urban Problems and Local Government

In contrast with the federal government, whose urban policies are primarily redistributional in nature, local governments are involved in resource allocation. Local governments build streets, provide mass transit, run public schools, and manage the criminal-justice system. Local spending programs are supported by taxes on property, income, and retail sales. Part Four of this book discusses the efficiency and distributional effects of local spending and tax policies. Chapter 15 provides an overview of local government decision making, exploring the issues of what to produce and how much to produce. Chapter 16 deals with local revenue sources, examining the incidence of local taxes and local responses to intergovernmental grants.

Chapters 17 through 20 examine several spending programs of local government. The first two chapters discuss urban transportation. Chapter 17 explores three problems caused by automobiles: congestion, pollution, and highway accidents. Chapter 18 deals with mass transit, showing how commuters choose between driving a car and riding mass transit, and how planners choose a transit system. Chapter 19 considers the spatial aspects of education, showing how the fragmented system of local government causes spatial inequalities in educational spending and achievement. It also discusses policies designed to offset spending and achievement inequalities, including intergovernmental grants and desegregation. Chapter 20 presents the economic approach to crime and crime fighting, discussing the optimum amount of crime and the alternative means of controlling crime.

CHAPTER 15

Decision Making
in Local Government

A community is like a ship: everyone ought to be prepared to take the helm.

Ibsen

This chapter provides an overview of the activities of the local public sector. It discusses the economic rationale for local government and explores two types of decisions concerning local government: what to produce and how much to produce. The decision about what to produce is made by state governments. The states have empowered local governments to provide schools, public-safety services, and transit systems. This chapter explains why these goods are produced by local governments instead of by private firms or higher levels of government. The decision about how much to spend on local public goods is made by local voters. The policy question is whether citizens' votes on budget elections and mayoral races lead to an efficient level of local public goods. Citizens have another option for expressing their preferences for local services: they can vote with their feet, moving to the local jurisdiction that provides the best combination of public services and taxes. The policy question is whether foot voting increases or decreases the efficiency of local government.

This chapter examines two additional issues concerning local spending. The first concerns the optimum size of local government. Suppose that a metropolitan area consolidated all of its local governments (municipalities, school districts, water districts, sewage districts) into a single metropolitan government. Will the metropolitan government be more or less efficient than the original fragmented system of local government? The second issue concerns the rising costs of local public goods. Are rising costs caused by inefficient local governments, or by other factors beyond the control of local governments?

LOCAL GOVERNMENT FACTS

As shown in Table 15–1, there are over 82,000 local governments in the United States. In terms of total expenditures, the most important types of local government are municipalities (36 percent of local government expenditures) and school districts (29 percent of local expenditures). Table 15–2 shows the per capita spending of local governments and municipalities. The largest spending category of local government is education, with spending of

TABLE 15–1   Types of Local Government

Type of Government	Number of Units (1982)	Total Expenditures (1985–86)	Percent of Total Local Expenditure
County	3,041	96,787	22
Municipal	19,076	158,835	36
Township	16,734	13,785	3
School district	14,851	129,655	29
Special district	28,588	44,664	10
Total	82,290	443,726	100

Definitions:
1. Municipality: a municipal corporation provides general local government for a specific concentration of population.
2. Township: serves the inhabitants of an area defined without regard to population concentrations.
3. Special district: independent, special-purpose governmental unit.

SOURCE: U.S. Bureau of Census, *Government Finances in 1986.* (Washington D.C.: Government Printing Office, 1987), pp. 1–7.

$634 per capita, about 42 percent of total spending. The spending of municipalities is more evenly divided, with the largest expenditures on police protection ($86 per capita), education ($78), highways ($59), sewerage ($52), and fire protection ($46).

Local governments derive their taxing and spending powers from state governments. There is considerable variation in the amount of power delegated to local governments. One measure of the relative importance of local government is the ratio of local spending to state spending: the larger the ratio, the greater the spending power of localities. In 1985, the average ratio was 0.75: local spending was about 75 percent of state spending (Advisory Commission on Intergovernmental Relations 1987). Some of the states with relatively low spending ratios were Alaska (0.05), Hawaii (0.25), New Mexico (0.29), Delaware (0.37), Massachusetts (0.43), and Kentucky (0.43). Some of the states with relatively high spending ratios were New York (1.27), New Hampshire (1.12), Texas (1.04), and Colorado (1.04).

There are two distinct trends in local spending during the postwar period. The first trend is the increase in spending between 1950 and 1976: over this period, local spending rose from about 5 percent to 9.2 percent of GNP. Three factors contributed to the steady growth during the postwar period. First, increases in real income increased the demand for many of the services provided by local governments. Second, the postwar baby boom increased the number of children attending local public schools. Third, for reasons described later in the chapter, the costs of providing local public services in-

TABLE 15–2   Per Capita Expenditures of Local Governments

	Annual Spending per Capita in 1984	
Expenditure Category	All Local Governments	Municipalities
Education services		
Education	$634	$78
Libraries	11	9
Social services		
Public welfare	82	39
Hospitals	88	34
Health	30	11
Transportation		
Highways	80	59
Other	27	22
Public safety		
Police protection	80	86
Fire protection	40	46
Other	27	13
Environment and housing		
Natural resources	9	0
Parks and recreations	35	34
Housing and community development	42	35
Sewerage	54	52
Sanitation	24	24
Administration and finance	165	98
General expenditure	81	77

SOURCE: U.S. Bureau of Census, *City Government Finance in 1986.* (Washington, D.C.: Government Printing Office, 1987), p. 5.

creased. The second trend in local spending is the decrease in the relative importance of local government in the last 10 years: between 1976 and 1986, local spending dropped from 9.2 percent to 7.9 percent of GNP. Since the middle 1970s, real income has increased at a relatively slow rate and the number of school children has increased slowly. As a result, the local sector has shrunk in relative terms.

THE ROLE OF GOVERNMENT

What is the role of local government in the market economy? This question can be answered by asking two separate questions. First, what is the role of government in the market economy? Second, how does local government fit into the general scheme of government involvement?

Musgrave and Musgrave (1980) distinguish between three types of government policies. The first is stabilization policy: the government uses monetary and fiscal policy to control unemployment and inflation. The second type of policy is income redistribution: the government uses taxes and transfers to alter the distributions of income and wealth. The third policy is resource allocation: the government makes decisions about what to produce and how to produce it. When the government actually produces a particular good or service, it makes these resource-allocation decisions directly. When the government subsidizes or taxes private activities, it influences the resource-allocation decisions of the private sector.

How do local governments fit into this three-part scheme of governmental activity? The responsibility for stabilization policy has been assumed by the national government for two reasons. First, although each local government could print its own money and execute its own monetary policy, such a system would be chaotic. Instead, the national government prints the money and manages monetary policy. Second, because a large fraction of local income is spent on goods produced outside the local area, local monetary and fiscal policies would be relatively weak and ineffective. Consider a city that tries to stimulate the local economy by cutting its taxes without decreasing spending on local public goods. This deficit-spending policy will be ineffective because a large fraction of the tax cut will be spent on imports, so the tax cut will have a relatively small local multiplier effect. Fiscal policy is more effective at the national level because, given that a relatively small fraction of national income is spent on imports, a national tax will have a relatively large multiplier effect.

Consider next the redistribution role of government. Local attempts to redistribute income will be frustrated by the mobility of taxpayers and transfer recipients. Suppose that a city imposes a tax on its wealthy citizens and uses the tax revenue to finance transfer payments to the poor. To escape the tax, some wealthy households will leave the city, and total tax revenue will fall. At the same time, some poor households will migrate to the relatively generous city, and the transfer payment per recipient will drop. In combination, the fleeing of the wealthy and the migration of the poor will weaken the city's redistribution program: there will be less money to transfer to more poor households. A national redistribution program would be more successful because there is less mobility between nations than between cities.

RESOURCE ALLOCATION—LOCAL GOVERNMENT

The third role of government is resource allocation. As shown in Table 15–2, local governments are responsible for the provision of several goods and services, including education, highways, police and fire protection, parks, and sewers. Under what conditions can government provision of these goods be justified on efficiency grounds? There are three possibilities. First, the good may be produced under conditions that generate a natural monop-

FIGURE 15–1   Natural Monopoly in Sewage Services

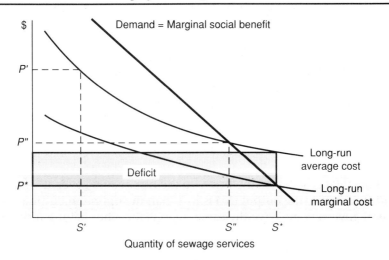

Quantity of sewage services

Sewage service is a natural monopoly: scale economies generate a negatively sloped long-run average-cost curve. The optimum output is where the demand curve intersects the marginal-cost curve. Since the optimum price is less than the average total cost, the sewage system will generate a deficit. The government could provide sewage service itself, covering the deficit with general tax revenue. Alternatively, the government could regulate a private sewage authority.

oly. Second, the good may generate positive externalities. Finally, the good may have the characteristics of a local public good.

Natural Monopoly

A natural monopoly occurs if the production of a particular good is subject to relatively large scale economies. In Figure 15–1, the long-run average total cost curve for sewage services is negatively sloped over a wide range of output, reflecting the fact that (a) there are substantial fixed costs associated with setting up a sewage system and (b) the marginal cost of adding another customer is relatively small. Because the average-cost curve is negatively sloped, the marginal cost is less than the average cost (the marginal cost pulls down the average cost as quantity increases). Sewage service is a natural monopoly in the sense that a single sewage authority (providing S^* units of service) could serve the city at a lower average cost than several sewage authorities (e.g., five firms, each supplying S' units).

What is the optimum level of sewage service? The basic efficiency rule is that an activity should be increased to the point at which the marginal social benefit of the activity equals the marginal social cost. In Figure 15–1, the demand curve, which shows consumers' willingness to pay for different levels of sewage service, is also the marginal social benefit curve. The optimum output (S^*) is the output at which the demand curve intersects the marginal-cost curve. One problem with an output of S^* is that a firm producing this output would lose money: to get consumers to purchase S^* units of sewage service, the firm would charge a price of P^*, which is less than the average total cost of producing S^*. The deficit is shown by the shaded area.

The government has several options. First, it can provide the service itself, charge a price of P^*, and cover the deficit with general tax revenue. Second, it can get a private firm to provide sewage service. If the government forces the firm to charge a price of P^*, subsidies will be required to cover the deficit. A final option is to allow the private firm to charge P'' instead of P^*. At P'', average total cost equals the price, so the firm would cover all of its costs. Under this scheme, the output (S'') is less than the optimum output.

Local governments have the same options for other natural monopolies. Chapter 18 (Mass Transit) discusses the pricing and regulation of mass transit. For other natural monopolies (water systems, cable television networks, telephone networks), the government has the option of producing the service itself or regulating a private producer.

What level of government should operate or regulate a natural monopoly? Should sewage and transit services be run by local, metropolitan, regional, state, or national governments? The appropriate level of government depends in part on the extent of scale economies: the greater the scale economies, the larger the political jurisdiction required to realize the scale economies associated with providing the services. As explained later in the chapter, the optimum level of government depends on other factors as well. In general, local governments are responsible for the provision and regulation of services for which scale economies are exhausted at the local level.

Externalities

One of the roles of government is to internalize externalities. An externality occurs if one person's consumption of a good generates benefits or costs for other people. The basic efficiency rule is that an activity should be increased to the point at which the marginal social benefit equals the marginal social cost. An externality causes a divergence between private and social benefits or private and social costs, so individual consumers, who base their decisions on private benefits and costs, will make choices that are inefficient from the social perspective. When this occurs, government intervention may promote efficiency.

Education Externalities.   Figure 15–2 shows the private and social benefits of education. Education generates private benefits (for the student himself) and external benefits (for the student's fellow workers and citizens). As a person becomes more educated, he becomes a better team worker: he under-

FIGURE 15–2   Externalities in the Consumption of Education

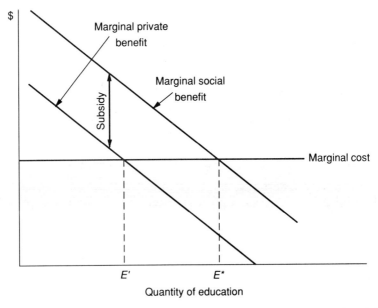

There are externalities in the consumption of education, so the marginal social benefit exceeds the marginal private benefit. In the absence of government involvement, the student will choose E' (where the marginal private benefit equals the marginal cost). The optimum level of education is E^*, which the student will choose if the government provides a subsidy equal to the gap between the marginal private benefit and the marginal social benefit.

stands instructions more readily and is also more likely to suggest ways to improve production. In other words, education generates workplace externalities. In addition, a more educated citizen makes better choices on election day, generating external benefits for his fellow citizens. Because education generates workplace and civic externalities, the marginal social benefit of education exceeds the marginal private benefit. In the absence of government intervention, the worker-citizen will ignore these external benefits, choosing E' units of education instead of the optimum amount (E^*).

The government has two options to solve the externality problem. The first is to take responsibility for providing the good. A system of free compulsory education may encourage citizens to consume more education. Alternatively, the government could subsidize education, encouraging citizens to consume more education while allowing them to choose their own schools. In Figure 15–2, a subsidy equal to the gap between the private and social benefit of education would increase consumption to E^* units of education. As discussed in Chapter 19 (Education), there is heated debate over whether the government should provide public schools *and* subsidize private education through tuition tax credits and education vouchers.

What level of government should deal with education externalities? Should the public school system (or education subsidies) be managed by local, metropolitan, regional, state, or national governments? One factor in determining the optimum level of government is the geographical extent of the externalities. If people throughout the country benefit from the education of children in a particular school, national participation in education decisions (national schools or a national subsidy) may promote efficiency. If the benefits are confined to a particular city, local decision making may be efficient. As explained later in the chapter, there are other factors that affect the optimum level of government.

Public Safety Externalities.   There are two types of externalities from spending on police services, a positive externality and a negative one. Both externalities result from the fact that criminals are mobile: they can move freely from one jurisdiction to another. The positive externality occurs when one municipality uses its police force to capture a criminal: by doing so, the municipality generates benefits for surrounding municipalities, so the marginal social benefit of police spending exceeds the marginal local (municipal) benefit. The negative externality occurs when one municipality's crime-fighting activities cause criminals to victimize people in surrounding municipalities. In other words, the police chase criminals from one municipality to another. In this case, the police just move crime around, so the marginal local benefit of police spending exceeds the marginal social benefit.

What is the optimum level of government for police protection? One factor is the geographical extent of the positive and negative externalities, which depends on the mobility of criminals. The greater the mobility of criminals, the larger the optimum jurisdiction. As explained later in the chapter, there are other factors that affect the optimum level of government. The typical response to the positive and negative externalities of police spending is to provide police services through municipal government.

The other public-safety service, fire protection, also generates externalities. Fires can spread from one house to another, so the marginal social benefit of fire protection exceeds the marginal private benefit. In most metropolitan areas, fire protection is provided by local governments. Some municipalities contract with private firms to provide fire protection. For the trade-offs between public and private production, see Savas (1982) and Stevens (1984).

Characteristics of a Local Public Good

A local public good has three characteristics. First, it is **nonrivalrous** in consumption: several people consume the same good at the same time. Second, it is **nonexcludable**: it is impossible or impractical to exclude some people (e.g., those who do not pay for the good) from consuming the good. Third, the benefits of the good are confined to a relatively small geographical area.

Nonrivalrous Consumption (Joint Consumption).   Consider first the issue of rivalry in consumption. A private good (e.g., a hot dog) can be consumed by only one person. In contrast, a public good can be consumed by many people at the same time. For example, hundreds of people can watch a parade without interfering with each other's enjoyment of the parade. In other words, a parade is subject to **joint consumption**: everyone can consume the good at the same time. The parade will be a **pure local public good** if the marginal cost of an additional parade viewer is zero. This will occur if an additional viewer does not decrease the enjoyment of other parade viewers.

Many of the goods provided by local governments are semirivalrous. If the number of consumers becomes large enough, an individual consumer's benefit decreases. For example, if the city does not set up bleachers for parade viewers, tall people will block the views of short people. This is a problem only if the number of parade viewers is large enough that short citizens do not get a front-row view. In this case, the parade is an **impure** or **congestable public good**. Other examples of impure public goods are city streets and highways: during the peak travel periods, travel speeds decrease as traffic volume increases, so the benefit of using the highway decreases as the number of consumers increases.

Nonexcludability.   The second characteristic of a local public good is that it would be impractical to exclude some people from consuming the good. In other words, the good is nonexcludable. Consider the parade example. Although it may be possible to charge everyone for watching the parade and exclude those who don't pay, it would be very costly to do so. The government would have to first empty the streets and buildings along the parade route and then admit people who paid a parade-viewing fee. If some people promised to not watch the parade, they might be permitted to enter a building along the route, but the government would have to find a way to prevent them from sneaking a look. Such a scheme would obviously be impractical.

What about streets and public parks? One way to charge people for using city streets would be to set up a system of toll booths, one on each corner. Such a system would be costly: the city would have to hire a large number of toll collectors, and road users would incur substantial time costs in stopping at every corner to pay the tolls. Chapter 17 (Autos and Highways) describes a high-technology, low-cost system for charging drivers for using streets and highways. There is little political support for such a system, so streets are likely to remain nonexcludable. The same argument applies to parks. Although it might be possible to install fences and turnstiles in city parks, such a system would be costly.

Localized Benefits.   The third characteristic of a local public good is that its benefits are confined to a relatively small geographical area. Unlike national defense, which generates benefits for the entire nation, most of the benefits of city parks and streets go to local citizens. The appropriate size of the jurisdiction is determined by the "localness" of the public good (the geographical extent of the benefits from the public good): the more extensive the benefits, the larger the jurisdiction required to contain all the beneficiaries.

The Optimum Quantity of a Local Public Good

What is the optimum level of a local public good? According to the basic efficiency rule, the optimum level of an activity is the amount at which the marginal social benefit equals the marginal social cost. To determine the optimum level, one must determine the marginal social benefit of the local public good.

Consider a three-person city that must decide how many acres of public parks to provide. In Figure 15–3, the marginal-benefit curves show how much each citizen is willing to pay for different park sizes: Sam has a low demand for parks and prefers relatively small parks (MB_s); Marian has a medium demand (MB_m); Bertha has a high demand and prefers big parks (MB_b). Suppose that city parks have the following characteristics.

1. **No congestion.** In the relevant range of park use, park acreage is nonrivalrous: park usage is low enough that there is no congestion.

2. **No intercity spillovers.** The parks do not generate benefits or costs for people outside the city.

If these two conditions are satisfied, the park is a pure local public good. The social benefit of a given park size is the sum of the marginal benefits of Sam, Marian, and Bertha: if there is no congestion, the three citizens do not affect their fellow citizens' enjoyment of the park; if there are no spillovers, there are no other potential beneficiaries to worry about. For A_s acres of land, the marginal social benefit is $103 (Sam's marginal benefit is $20, Marian's is $30, and Bertha's is $53). The marginal social benefit curve is the vertical sum of the individual marginal-benefit curves.

At the optimum, the marginal social benefit of park acreage equals its marginal social cost. In Figure 15–3, the marginal cost is $60 per acre, so the optimum acreage is A^*. For any amount less than A^*, citizens in the city would be willing to pay more than $60 per additional acre, so an increase in size would increase social welfare. For example, suppose the city starts at A_s. At this point, the willingness to pay for parks (from the social-benefit curve) is $103 and the cost is only $60, so an increase in park acreage would generate a net gain of $43. Similarly, for any amount exceeding A^*, the willingness to pay would be less than the social cost, so a smaller park would be more efficient.

FIGURE 15–3   Optimum versus Equilibrium Provision of a Local Public Good

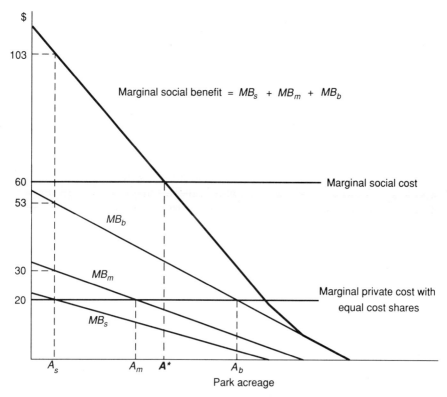

The marginal social benefit of park acreage is the sum of the private benefits of three citizens. The optimum park acreage is A^* (the amount where the marginal social benefit equals the marginal social cost). If every household faces a cost of $20 per acre, the preferred sizes are A_s, A_m, and A_b. Under majority voting, the preferred size of the median voter (A_m) will be chosen.

DECISION MAKING—THE MEDIAN-VOTER RULE

   Local governments must decide how much of local public goods to provide. Will the government provide the optimum amounts of local public goods? One approach to local decision making is to hold an election and let voters choose how much to spend on local public goods. Will voters make efficient choices?

   To continue the park example, suppose that the city divides park costs equally between its three citizens. If the marginal cost is $60 per acre, every citizen will pay $20 per acre of park land. What are the preferred park sizes for the three citizens? The preferred park size of a particular voter is the acreage such that the marginal private cost equals the marginal private benefit. In Figure 15–3, the marginal private cost is the horizontal line at $20. For Sam, the cost curve intersects the benefit curve at a park size of A_s acres, so his preferred size is A_s acres. For the other two citizens, the preferred sizes are A_m and A_b.

Suppose that the city holds a series of elections in which citizens vote for one of two proposed park sizes. In an election between A_s and A_m, there will be one vote for A_s (Sam's), but two votes for A_m (Marian's and Bertha's), so A_m will win the election. A_m will also win an election against A_b: both Sam and Marian will vote for A_m. A_m will win both elections because it is the preferred budget of the median voter (the voter that splits the rest of the voting public into two equal halves). The preferred budget of the median voter wins an election against a smaller size (as Bertha joins the median voter to make the vote 2–1) and a larger size (as Sam joins the median voter to make the vote 2–1). This is the **median-voter result**: if the spending level for a public good is determined by a majority vote, the winning budget will be the preferred budget of the median voter.

In Figure 15–3, the size chosen by voters (A_m) is less than the optimum size (A^*). Is this an artifact of the election sequence, or would A_m win a direct election against the optimum park size? In an election between A_m and A^*, Sam would join Marian in voting for A_m because A_m is closer to Sam's preferred size. Therefore, A_m will defeat the optimum size in a direct election.

The power—and inefficiency—of the median-voter result can be shown by considering the effects of changes in Bertha's preferences. Suppose that her marginal-benefit curve shifts upward by 100 percent: for every park size, her willingness to pay for parks doubles. Because the marginal social benefit curve is the vertical sum of the individual marginal private benefit curves, the social-benefit curve would also shift upward and the optimum park size would increase by a large amount. Nonetheless, voters will still choose A_m: Sam will join with Marian to defeat any size above A_m. The same is true of changes in the other (nonmedian) benefit curve MB_s. The voting outcome depends only on the position of the median voter's marginal-benefit curve.

Benefit Taxation

Majority voting is inefficient because the costs of the public good are divided equally among the three voters. An alternative approach is to allocate park costs according to the willingness to pay for parks: the greater the citizen's willingness to pay, the higher his tax liability. This is the **Lindahl approach** to local decision making (named after Erik Lindahl): according to the **benefit principle**, tax liabilities are based on the benefits received from public goods.

Figure 15–4 shows how benefit taxes work. Suppose that the government knows the marginal-benefit curves of its citizens, and announces that Sam's tax liability per acre is $9, Marian's is $16, and Bertha's is $35. Given

FIGURE 15–4   Benefit Taxation Generates Unanimous Support for the Optimum Level of the Local Public Good

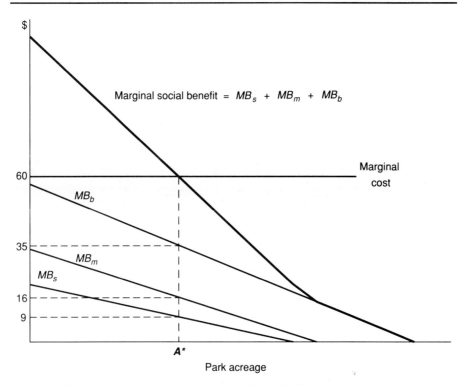

Park acreage

Using the benefit principle of taxation, each household pays a tax per acre equal to its marginal benefit at the optimum park size (A^*). If the government is clever enough to figure out the benefits of individual taxpayers, there will be unanimous support for the optimum park size.

these private costs, all three citizens have the same preferred park size, A^*, which also happens to be the optimum size. In this case, the government is clever enough to figure out how much individual citizens are willing to pay for different levels of the local public good, and it sets each citizen's tax equal to his or her marginal willingness to pay. Sam (who prefers small parks) agrees to a larger park because he faces a lower tax liability: he pays $9 per acre instead of $20. Bertha (who prefers big parks) gets a larger park at a cost: she pays $35 per acre instead of $20. Under benefit taxation, citizens with larger benefits pay higher taxes.

Is the benefit principle practical? One problem with this approach is that the government doesn't know the shapes of the marginal-benefit curves, so it can't estimate the appropriate taxes for individual citizens. Moreover, there is little incentive for taxpayers with relatively high benefits to reveal their willingness to pay for local public goods: in doing so, they would be volunteering to pay higher taxes. It may be rational for high demanders to hide their true preferences in the hope that someone else will pay for the public good. This is the **free-rider problem**: citizens may understate their willingness to pay in an attempt to get a free ride.

Budget Elections and the Median Voter

The median-voter result is applicable to a wide variety of election formats. For example, if a school district holds a series of elections to determine its budget, the winning budget will be the preferred budget of the median voter. To show this, consider a school district with the following characteristics:

1. **Citizens' preferences.** Citizens have different preferences for school spending. Table 15–3 shows the preferred budgets for seven voters in the school district. Voter A's preferred budget is $49, voter B's is $56, and so on.

2. **Series of elections.** The school board proposes a budget and holds an election in which citizens vote "yes" or "no." If a given budget proposal fails to receive a majority of votes, the school board will decrease its proposed budget by $10 and hold another election. This process continues until a majority of citizens vote in favor of the budget.

Under this election scheme, the school district will choose the largest budget receiving majority support.

Suppose that the school board starts with a budget of $90. The voters know that if the $90 budget fails, the board will propose an $80 budget in the second election. A citizen will vote "yes" if the $90 budget is better than an $80 budget (i.e., if the citizen's preferred budget is greater than $85). For example, voter F will vote against the $90 budget because an $80 budget is closer

TABLE 15–3   The Median Voter in a Series of School Budget Elections

Voter	Preferred Budget	Vote with $90 Budget	Vote with $80 Budget	Vote with $70 Budget
A	$49	N	N	N
B	$56	N	N	N
C	$63	N	N	N
D	$70	N	N	Y
E	$77	N	Y	Y
F	$84	N	Y	Y
G	$91	Y	Y	Y

to his preferred budget ($84). G is the only voter who will vote for the $90 budget, so the first budget proposal will lose by a vote of 6–1. The second proposal ($80) will fail by a vote of 4–3: only citizens with preferred budgets greater than $75 (E, F, and G) will vote "yes."

A proposed budget of $70 will win the election by a vote of 4–3. All citizens with a preferred budget greater than $65 (citizens D, E, F, and G) will vote for the $70 budget. The $70 budget proposal will be successful because it's the preferred budget of the median voter. A $70 budget splits the voters into two equal halves, with half (E, F, G) preferring a larger budget and half (A, B, C) preferring a smaller budget. By threatening to propose a smaller budget in the next election, the school board convinces citizens with preferred budgets above the median budget (E, F, G) to vote for the $70 budget; combined with the vote of the median voter (D), this generates a majority in favor of the proposed budget.

In this example, the school district decreases its proposed budget in $10 steps, from $90 down to the preferred budget of the median voter. The same result would occur if the board decreased the proposed budget in steps of $1. Similarly, the same result will occur if the school district reverses the direction of the budget sequence: if it starts out with a low budget and works its way upward, the median voter will still be decisive.

The Median Voter in a Representative Democracy

In a **representative democracy**, decisions about budgets are made by elected officials. Citizens make budgetary decisions indirectly, by electing people whose budget philosophies are consistent with their own preferences. For example, a citizen will vote for the mayoral candidate whose expressed position on the city budget is closest to the citizen's preferred budget.

The budget choices in a representative democracy can be explained with a model of a city that provides a single local public good (police services). The city has the following characteristics:

1. **Two candidates.** There are two candidates for mayor, Penny (a low spender) and Buck (a big spender).

2. **Single issue.** The only issue in the election is the police budget, which is set by the mayor.

3. **Citizen choice.** Every citizen votes for the candidate whose proposed police budget is closest to the citizen's preferred budget.

4. **Distribution of preferences.** Figure 15–5 shows the distribution of budget preferences. The horizontal axis measures the police budget and the vertical axis measures the number of votes for a given budget. For example, 10 citizens have a preferred budget of $2, 15 have a preferred budget of $3, and so on. The distribution of budget preferences is symmetric, and the median budget (the budget that splits the rest of the voters into two equal halves) is $6.

FIGURE 15–5 The Median Voter Result in a Representative Democracy

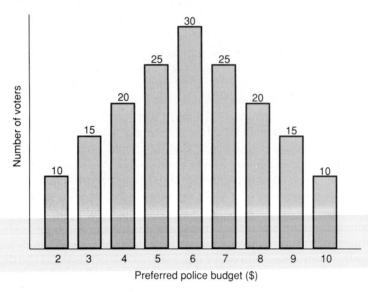

Citizens have different preferences for the police budget. If Penny proposes a budget of $4 and Buck proposes a budget of $8, the election will result in a tie vote: the two candidates will split the votes of citizens with $6 preferred budgets; Penny will get the votes of those with lower preferred budgets; and Buck will get the votes of those with higher budgets. By moving toward the median budget, Penny will increase her chance of being elected. In equilibrium, both candidates will propose the budget of the median voter ($6).

Suppose that the candidates start out with different proposed police budgets: Penny proposes a budget of $4, and Buck proposes $8. Citizens with preferred budgets less than or equal to $5 will vote for Penny (70 votes), and those with preferred budgets greater than or equal to $7 will vote for Buck (70 votes). The two candidates will split the 30 voters with a preferred budget of $6 (halfway between the two proposed budgets), so each candidate will get a total of 85 votes.

Penny could increase her chance of being elected by increasing her proposed budget. Suppose that she proposes $5 instead of $4. She will pick up all 30 votes of the citizens with a $6 preferred budget (Penny's $5 proposal is closer than Buck's $8 one), and she will win the election by a vote of 100 (10 + 15 + 20 + 25 + 30) to 70 (25 + 20 + 15 + 10). If Buck responds by decreasing his proposed budget to $7, the election will result in a tie vote again. Penny and Buck will continue to revise their proposed budgets until each candidate's budget is close to the budget of the median voter ($6).

This example shows that the median-voter result occurs in a representative democracy. In equilibrium, both candidates propose a budget equal to the preferred budget of the median voter. Since both candidates have virtually the same proposed budget, it doesn't matter which candidate actually wins the election. In either case, the median voter determines the size of the police budget.

Implications of the Median-Voter Rule

There are four implications from the median-voter rule:

1. **Inefficient voting outcome.** There is nothing that guarantees that the preferred budget of the median voter is the optimum budget (the budget at which the marginal social cost of spending equals the marginal social benefit).

2. **Predicting election outcomes.** To predict the outcome of an election, one needs to (a) identify the median voter and (b) estimate his or her preferred budget. As a practical matter, it may be difficult to identify the median voter. One approach is to assume that the desired spending on local public goods depends only on income. Under this assumption, the median voter is the voter with the median income. To the extent that desired spending depends on other variables (household size, age, political philosophy), this approach will generate inaccurate predictions.

3. **Estimating the income elasticity.** Differences in income cause differences in spending on local public services. These differences can be used to compute the income elasticity of demand for local public services. Consider two cities: city S has a small police budget ($100 per capita) and a low median income ($1,000), and city L has a large police budget ($125 per capita) and a high median income ($1,200). Assume that the "price" of police services (the opportunity cost of money spent on police) is the same in the two cities. The income elasticity of demand for police services is defined as the percentage change in the police budget divided by the percentage change in income. City L, with 20 percent higher income, has a 25 percent larger police budget, so the income elasticity of demand is 1.25 (25 percent divided by 20 percent). Inman (1979) summarizes the results of empirical studies based on the median-voter model. As shown in Table 15–4, the income elasticities for most local goods are less than 1.0.

4. **Estimating price elasticity.** If there is variation across communities in the price of local public goods, the median-voter model can also be used to estimate the price elasticity of demand for public goods. To plot the demand curve for local spending, one needs information on price (the opportunity cost of local spending) and quantity (the local spending level). The price elasticity can then be computed from the demand curve. As shown in Table 15–4, the demands for local public goods are price-inelastic: the price inelasticities are all less than or equal to 1.0 (in absolute

TABLE 15-4   Income and Price Elasticities of Demand for Local Public Goods

Public Good or Service	Price Elasticity	Income Elasticity
Total expenditures	−0.23 to −0.56	0.34 to 0.89
Education	−0.07 to −0.51	0.24 to 0.85
Parks and recreation	−0.19 to −0.92	0.99 to 1.32
Public safety (police and fire)	−0.19 to −1.0	0.52 to 0.71
Public works	−0.92 to −1.0	0.79

SOURCE: Robert Inman, "The Fiscal Performance of Local Governments," in *Current Issues in Urban Economics*, ed. Peter Mieszkowski and Hahlon Straszheim (Baltimore: The Johns Hopkins Press, 1979), pp. 270–321.

value). Some of the implications of these elasticities will be discussed in Chapter 16 (Local Government Revenue).

Qualifications of the Median-Voter Model

The median-voter model has a number of unrealistic assumptions. Although the model provides a useful framework for thinking about local-government decisions, it should be used with caution. Three assumptions limit the model's applicability:

1. **Ideology.** The politicians in the model care only about winning elections, so they slavishly adhere to voter preferences. An alternative assumption is that candidates base their positions on ideology. An ideological candidate uses an election campaign to persuade voters that the candidate's positions are the correct ones; such a candidate is a leader, not a follower. In a model with ideological candidates, there is no reason to expect that the choice of the median voter will prevail.

2. **Single issue.** There is a single issue in the simple median-voter model. If there are several election issues (e.g., the police budget, the park budget, policies for the homeless), candidates offer package deals to voters. Unless the same citizen is the median voter on every issue, the winning budget will not be the preferred budget of the median voter.

3. **All citizens vote.** In the median-voter model, all citizens vote. In the typical budget election, only a fraction of eligible voters actually cast ballots. A rational citizen will abstain from voting if the costs of voting (the time and monetary costs of becoming informed and going to the polls) exceed the benefits. The benefits of voting will be relatively small if (*a*) the two proposed budgets are so close to one another that it makes little difference which person is elected (indifference) or (*b*) the proposed budget of the best candidate is so far from the citizen's preferred budget that the citizen is alienated from the election process (alienation). If some citizens abstain from voting, the median-voter result will not necessarily occur.

DECISION MAKING—THE TIEBOUT MODEL

Most metropolitan areas in the United States have dozens of municipalities, school districts, and other local governments. A model developed by Tiebout (1956) shows the role of consumer choice in the development of our fragmented system of local governments. The idea is that people vote with their feet, choosing the local government that provides the best combination of taxes and local public goods. One of the implications of the Tiebout model is that interjurisdictional mobility (voting with feet) may prevent the inefficiencies associated with majority voting.

The Simple Model

There are five assumptions in the simple version of the Tiebout model:

1. **Jurisdictional choice.** A household "shops" for a local government and chooses the jurisdiction that provides the ideal level of local public goods. The model assumes that there are enough jurisdictions to ensure that every household finds the perfect jurisdiction.

2. **Information and mobility.** All citizens have access to all relevant information about the alternative jurisdictions, and moving is costless.

3. **No interjurisdictional spillovers.** There are no spillovers (externalities) associated with local public goods: all the benefits from local public goods accrue to citizens within the local jurisdiction.

4. **No scale economies.** The average cost of production is independent of output.

5. **Head taxes.** Local governments impose head taxes to pay for public goods: if you have a head, you pay a tax.

Citizens in the Tiebout world sort themselves into municipalities and school districts according to their demands for local public goods. People with relatively low demand for parks will choose a municipality with a relatively small park budget (and a relatively low head tax). Citizens with relatively high demand for parks will choose a municipality with a relatively large park budget. Citizens vote with their feet: if they are dissatisfied with their current municipality, they move to another one.

Efficiency Effects of the Tiebout Process

The simple Tiebout model suggests that shopping and sorting increase the efficiency of local government. As explained earlier in the chapter, majority voting will generate an inefficient level of local spending if the desired budget of the median voter differs from the optimum budget. One of the reasons for this inefficiency is that local citizens have different preferences for local public goods, so they disagree about the appropriate spending level.

Under the Tiebout process, households sort themselves into homogeneous communities, so citizens agree on how much to spend.

The efficiency effects of the sorting process can be explained with a model of a region that starts with three identical municipalities. Each community has three citizens, one Sam-type citizen (who wants a small park), one Marian-type (medium-size park), and one Bertha-type (big park). In other words, each municipality is heterogeneous with respect to the demand for parks. As shown in Figure 15–3, each heterogeneous municipality will choose A_m (the choice of the median voter), which is less than the optimum park size.

Suppose that the Tiebout process causes households to sort themselves into homogeneous municipalities. One municipality has three Sams (municipality S); one has three Marians (municipality M); one has three Berthas (municipality B). Figure 15–6 shows the spending choices in municipality S. The

FIGURE 15–6   Citizens in a Homogeneous Municipality Choose the Optimum Spending Level

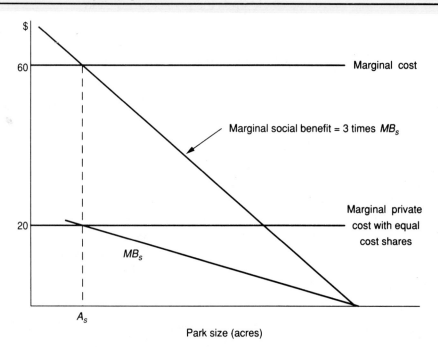

Municipality S has three Sam-type households (who want a small park), so the marginal social benefit curve is three times the marginal private benefit curve. If costs are divided equally between the three citizens, they all agree to a park size of A_s acres. The inefficiencies of majority voting are eliminated by sorting of households into homogeneous municipalities.

marginal social benefit curve is three times the marginal-benefit curve of Sam and intersects the marginal-cost curve at a park acreage of A_s. If costs are divided equally between the three households, the marginal private benefit equals the marginal private cost at the optimum budget (A_s). All three households have the same preferences for parks, so there is unanimous support for the optimum park size.

The same analysis applies to decision making in the two other homogeneous communities. In each municipality, every household has the same marginal-benefit curve, so an equal sharing of park costs will cause unanimous support for the optimum park size. In municipality M, the three Marians vote for a medium-size park. In municipality B, the three Berthas vote for a big park. The potential inefficiencies of majority voting are avoided by the sorting of households into homogeneous communities.

Tiebout Model with Property Taxes

Hamilton (1975) made the Tiebout model more realistic by introducing property taxes into the model. His model assumes that local governments finance their spending programs with a property tax, not a head tax. Consider a municipality with the following characteristics:

1. Every household demands $500 worth of park spending.
2. There are two income groups: the wealthy live in $75,000 houses and the poor live in $25,000 houses.
3. Under a head tax, every household pays $500 in local taxes to support the parks.

Suppose that municipality switches from the head tax to a one percent property tax. Under the property tax, each wealthy household will pay $750 in taxes (up from $500) and each poor household will pay $250 (down from $500).

How does the property tax affect location choices? The wealthy, who now pay $750 for $500 worth of parks, will try to decrease their taxes. One option is to set up a new municipality for wealthy households. If every household in the new wealthy municipality owns a house worth $75,000, a property tax of 0.667 percent will generate a tax bill of $500 per household. In other words, if the wealthy households form an exclusive municipality, they will again pay $500 in taxes for $500 worth of parks.

How do the wealthy establish their exclusive suburb? If it were legal, they might simply outlaw houses worth less than $75,000, thus guaranteeing that every household would pay at least $500 in taxes. Because this is illegal, they use **large-lot zoning**: the municipality establishes a minimum lot size for every dwelling. Since land and housing are complementary goods, the municipality can control housing consumption by controlling land consumption. One rule of thumb is that the market value of land is about one fifth of the total property value (the value of the structure and the land). If the price of land

is $30,000 per acre, a half-acre lot ($15,000 worth of land) will generate a property value of $75,000 (five times $15,000). Therefore, a minimum lot size of
half an acre will meet the target property value.

What about the poor people who remain in the original municipality?
The wealthy households will eventually be replaced by poor households in
less expensive housing. The average property value in the original municipality will decrease, requiring an increase in the tax rate to generate $500 of taxes
per household. If the average property value falls to $25,000, the property tax
rate will rise to 2 percent.

The switch from the head tax to the property tax causes households to
sort themselves with respect to housing consumption. There is one community for households with a large demand for housing and one for households
with a small demand for housing. This sorting occurs because tax liabilities
are based on housing consumption. If the municipalities were to tax Spam instead of housing, citizens would sort themselves into two communities, one
where people consume large quantities of Spam and one where people consume small quantities.

The switch from a head tax to a property tax increases the equilibrium
number of municipalities. Citizens sort themselves with respect to two characteristics: the demand for local public goods and the demand for housing.
The equilibrium number of municipalities depends on the number of housing
types and the number of public-good types. Suppose that there are three income groups, rich, middle-income, and poor, and three types of houses, large
(occupied by the wealthy), medium (middle-income), and small (poor). Suppose further that for each income group, there are two different levels of demand for public goods: some households in each income group have relatively high demands for local public goods, and others have relatively low
demands. Given these assumptions, there will be six communities: three
high-spending municipalities (one with large houses, one with medium
houses, and one with small houses) and three low-spending municipalities. If
local governments used a head tax instead of a property tax, there would be
only two municipalities, a high-spending one and a low-spending one.

Capitalization and the Tiebout Model

Most municipalities are not homogeneous with respect to property values. In other words, the sorting of households with respect to property values
is imperfect: there are some small houses in municipalities where most of the
houses are large. A small house surrounded by large houses will have a lower
tax liability than a small house surrounded by small houses because the large-
house community will have a lower property tax rate. In the example above, a
$25,000 house surrounded by $75,000 houses might have a tax rate of 0.667
percent, compared to a tax rate of 2 percent for a small house surrounded by
small houses.

As explained in Chapter 13 (Why Is Housing Different?), the market price of housing depends on the characteristics of the dwelling and the site. Among the relevant site characteristics are the local tax liability and the quality of public services. Everything else being equal, a dwelling with a lower tax liability will command a higher price: the small house in the large-house (low tax) municipality will cost more than an equivalent house in a small-house (high tax) municipality. In equilibrium, the consumers of small houses must be indifferent between the small houses in the two communities, and they will bid up the price of the small house in the low-tax community until the price difference is large enough to offset the tax difference. In other words, lower taxes are **capitalized** into the market value of the small house.

The capitalization of taxes diminishes the incentive for free riding. If the small-house buyer moves to a community with a relatively large tax base and a low tax rate, the household will pay a premium for the small house. In other words, the benefits of low taxes will be offset by higher housing costs.

Evidence of Shopping and Sorting

There is a good deal of evidence that citizens shop for municipalities and school districts. Using data for the New York metropolitan area, Oates (1969) estimated the relationship between house value, taxes, and school expenditures. He found that communities with relatively low tax rates had higher property values. This result suggests that people shop for school districts, bidding up the price of housing in areas with favorable combinations of taxes and local public goods. In other words, differences in taxes and expenditures are capitalized into house values.

There is also evidence that citizens sort themselves with respect to their demands for local public goods. Gramlich and Rubinfeld (1982) examined the tastes for local public goods in different metropolitan areas. In a metropolitan area with a single large municipality, households have no opportunity for shopping, so the single municipality will contain households with a wide variety of demands for local public services. In contrast, in a metropolitan area with a large number of jurisdictions, each household can pick the municipality that provides the preferred level of public services, so households will sort themselves into homogeneous communities. Using data from questionnaires, Gramlich and Rubinfeld concluded that the greater the number of municipalities to choose from, the more homogeneous the demand for local public goods within each municipality.

The Tiebout process is primarily a suburban phenomenon. In the suburbs, households can choose from dozens of municipalities and school districts. In the central city, there is typically a single large jurisdiction. One reason for the suburbanization of population is that the only option for central-city foot voters is to move to a suburban municipality. If large central-city governments were broken up into smaller municipalities, central-city residents would be able to vote with their feet without moving to the suburbs.

Critique of the Tiebout Model

Like any simple model, the Tiebout model can be criticized on a number of grounds. Some of the model's assumptions are unrealistic. For example, the model assumes that households are perfectly informed and perfectly mobile, so they can easily change jurisdictions if they become dissatisfied with their local government. This is clearly unrealistic: information about alternative locations is costly to acquire, and moving costs are large. As explained in Chapter 13 (Why Is Housing Different?), most households tolerate some dissatisfaction with their dwelling because moving is costly. In the context of the Tiebout model, a household that is unhappy with its local government will change jurisdictions only if the benefits from moving to a different jurisdiction are large enough to offset moving costs. Although the shopping and sorting predicted by the Tiebout model certainly occurs, the matching of households and jurisdictions is by no means perfect.

Another assumption of the Tiebout model is that there are enough local governments to allow every household to pick the ideal jurisdiction. In the Tiebout world, every household finds a local government that spends exactly the right amount on every public good. This is clearly unrealistic: there are simply not enough local jurisdictions to provide every household with its ideal level of every public good. This problem is complicated by the use of the property tax: if local governments use a property tax instead of a head tax, households must also sort themselves with respect to house value. If there are not enough jurisdictions to allow every household to choose the ideal jurisdiction, citizens will compromise on their ideal tax-spending package, choosing a jurisdiction that comes closest to their ideal package. Households will then express their preferences for local public goods in local budget elections: after the household votes with its feet, it starts voting with ballots.

A final criticism of the Tiebout model concerns its efficiency implications. The model suggests that the fragmented system of local government is efficient because the sorting of households allows each household to consume its ideal level of local public goods. A key assumption of the model is that local public goods do not generate interjurisdictional externalities: all the benefits and costs of local public goods are confined within the local jurisdiction, regardless of the size of the jurisdiction. In the Tiebout world, even a one-person jurisdiction is efficient: the model assumes that all the benefits of spending on police, fire protection, sewage, and education would be confined to the single person in the jurisdiction. Under this assumption, there is no real difference between local public goods and private goods. Therefore, the household's choice of a jurisdiction, however small it might be, is just as efficient as its choice of private goods.

The goods provided by local governments are indeed different from private goods. Some goods provided by local governments generate externalities for people in surrounding areas. When a small municipality uses its police force to capture a criminal, people outside the municipality benefit. The municipality will ignore these external benefits and will therefore spend too little on police services. If a child educated in one city moves to another city as an adult, workers and citizens in the second city benefit from the education program of the first. An individual city will ignore the benefits of its education program on outsiders and will therefore spend too little on education. In general, because the goods provided by local governments generate externalities, the fragmented system of local governments generated by the Tiebout process may be inefficient.

THE OPTIMUM LEVEL OF GOVERNMENT

Under the federal system of government, the responsibility for providing public goods is divided between the federal, state, and local governments. Some goods, such as defense and space exploration, are provided at the national level. Others, such as education and police protection, are provided at the local level. Why are some public goods provided by local governments instead of state or federal governments?

Oates (1972) discusses the advantages and disadvantages of the local provision of public goods.

1. **Diversity in demand.** A system of small local governments allows communities to choose different levels of spending on public goods (public safety, education, libraries). Because local governments can accommodate the diverse demands for public goods, they promote efficiency.

2. **Externalities.** If the local jurisdiction is not large enough to contain all the people affected by its spending programs, there are externalities (benefit spillovers). Under a system of small local governments, local voters will ignore the benefits that accrue to people outside the jurisdiction and will therefore make inefficient choices.

3. **Scale economies.** If there are scale economies in the provision of public goods, a system of small local governments will have relatively high production costs.

The local provision of a public good will be efficient if the advantages outweigh the disadvantages. In other words, local government will be efficient if (*a*) diversity in demand is relatively large, (*b*) externalities are relatively small, and (*c*) scale economies are relatively small.

Demand Diversity versus Externalities

The Tiebout model can be used to show the trade offs between diversity in demand and externalities. As explained earlier, the fragmented system of local government will be efficient if the benefits and costs of local-government spending are confined to the people within the jurisdiction. What happens if there are interjurisdictional spillovers?

Inefficiencies from Externalities.   If there are benefit spillovers, a local government will spend less than the optimum amount on local public goods. This is shown in Figure 15–7: the marginal social benefit of parks equals the marginal local benefit (the benefit to citizens within the municipality) plus the marginal external benefit (the benefit to people outside the municipality). The municipality will choose the level at which the marginal local benefit equals the marginal cost (A_s). The optimum level is where the marginal social benefit equals the marginal social cost (A^*). Because the municipality ignores the spillover benefits of its parks, it spends less than the optimum amount on parks. The inefficiency occurs because the municipality is too small to contain all the beneficiaries of its spending programs.

The same analysis applies to other local public goods that generate externalities. If a student educated in one school district eventually leaves the school district, workers and citizens outside the school district will benefit from its education program. When the police capture a criminal, potential victims in surrounding municipalities benefit, so the social benefit of police

FIGURE 15–7 Interjurisdictional Externalities and Local Decision Making

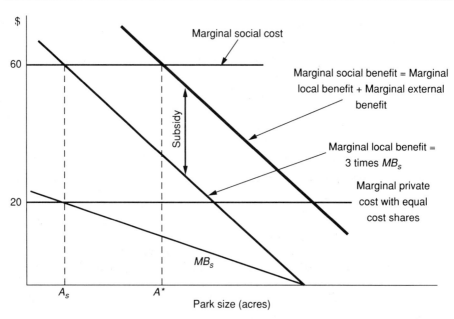

If municipal spending generates benefits for people outside the municipality, the marginal social benefit exceeds the marginal local benefit. The optimum spending level is A^*. Local voters, basing their decisions on local benefits and costs, will choose less than the optimum spending level (A_s). A subsidy equal to the gap between the local benefit and the social benefit will cause the municipality to choose the optimum spending level.

spending exceeds the local benefit. If households cross municipal borders to use the services of other local governments, the social benefit of these services exceeds the local benefit. These interjurisdictional spillovers cause inefficient choices by municipalities and school districts.

One solution to the spillover problem is a system of subsidies from a higher level of government. If the municipality receives a subsidy equal to the marginal external benefit of the public good, it will base its spending decisions on the marginal social benefit of the good. In Figure 15–7, the subsidy would increase the municipality's benefit to the marginal social benefit, so the municipality would increase its spending to the optimum level. Chapters 16 (Local-Government Revenue) and 19 (Education) explore the effects of various types of intergovernmental grants on local spending.

Metropolitan Consolidation.   An alternative response to the externality problem is metropolitan consolidation. The idea is that the jurisdiction could be expanded to include all the people affected by local government policies. For example, a metropolitan area could consolidate all of its municipalities, school districts, and special districts into a single metropolitan government. Under a metropolitan government, a single governmental unit would make spending decisions for the entire metropolitan area.

What are the trade-offs associated with metropolitan consolidation? Figure 15–8 shows the effects of consolidating three municipalities: S is full of Sam-type voters who prefer small parks; M is full of Marian-type households who prefer medium-sized parks; B is full of Bertha-type voters who prefer big parks. Under the municipal system, there are spillovers: in each community, the marginal local benefit of spending is less than the marginal social benefit, so each municipality spends less than the optimum amount. For example, in community S, the marginal local benefit equals the marginal cost at a spending level S', which is less than the optimum level S^*. Similarly, M and B spend less than the optimum amounts ($M' < M^*$ and $B' < B^*$).

Suppose that a metropolitan government is formed and holds a series of elections to determine how much to spend on parks. The metropolitan government is large enough to contain all the spillovers associated with local spending, so local voters will base their votes on the social benefits of local spending. For example, citizens in community S will base their votes on the marginal social benefits (MSB_s), not the marginal local benefits (MLB_s). Similarly, citizens in communities M and B will base their votes on MSB_m and MSB_b. Given the marginal-cost curve, the preferred budgets for the three types of households will be S^*, M^*, and B^*. According to the median-voter model, the winning budget will be the preferred budget of the median voter, or M^*.

The spending under the metropolitan government is inefficient because it chooses a single spending level for all households. The actual spending (M^*) exceeds the optimum level for low-demand households (S^*) and falls short of the optimum level for high-spending households (B^*). Under the

FIGURE 15–8   Municipal versus Metropolitan System of Government

There are two options for local decision making. Under the municipal system, each community chooses its own level of spending, ignoring interjurisdictional spillover benefits. Municipality S chooses S', M chooses M', and B chooses B'. In each of the municipalities, spending falls short of the optimum spending level (S^*, M^*, B^*). Under a metropolitan government, the median voter (Marian in community M) will pick the metropolitanwide spending level (M^*). The metropolitan spending level exceeds the optimum in community S ($M^* > S^*$) and falls short of the optimum in community B ($M^* < B^*$).

metropolitan government, externalities are internalized, so each type of household wants to spend the optimum amount. However, because a single spending level must be picked, two of the three communities are forced to compromise on their ideal spending levels.

Is the metropolitan system superior to the municipal system? The municipal system accommodates diversity in demand, but suffers from the externality problem. The metropolitan system solves the externality problem, but requires two of the communities to compromise on their ideal spending packages. It's not clear from Figure 15–8 which of the two systems of government is more efficient. Under both systems, the actual spending differs from the optimum combination (S^*, M^*, B^*) by large amounts: the municipal system generates a spending package of S', M', and B', and the metropolitan system generates a spending package of M^* in all three communities.

If the diversity in demand is large relative to externalities, the municipal system will be more efficient than the metropolitan system. In Figure 15–9, interjurisdictional externalities are relatively small, so the gaps between the local and social-benefit curves are relatively small. Therefore, under municipal decision making, the gaps between the equilibrium and optimum spending amounts will be relatively small. For example, the small-park municipality spends S', which falls short of the optimum spending S^* by a relatively small

FIGURE 15–9   The Municipal System Is Efficient if Diversity in Demand Is Large
Relative to Externalities

If externalities are relatively small, municipal decision making will be relatively efficient: the gaps between the equilibrium and optimum spending amounts ($S^* - S'$; $M^* - M'$; $B^* - B'$) will be relatively small. If the diversity in demand is relatively large, metropolitan decision making will be relatively inefficient: the gaps between the equilibrium and optimum spending amounts ($M^* - S^*$; $B^* - M^*$) will be relatively large. If externalities (spillovers) are small relative to diversity in demand, the municipal system will be more efficient than the metropolitan system.

amount. Similarly, the gaps between M^* and M' and between B^* and B' are relatively small. In contrast, because diversity in demand is relatively large, the compromises associated with metropolitan government are relatively large. The gaps between M^* (the budget chosen under majority rule) and the optimum budget of community S ($M^* - S^*$) is relatively large. Similarly, the gap between M^* and B^* is relatively large. Therefore, the municipal system is more efficient than the metropolitan system.

Metropolitan government will be more efficient than municipal government if interjurisdictional spillovers are large relative to diversity in demand. In this case, the advantages of small local government (the ability to accommodate diverse demands for local public goods) will be relatively small and the disadvantages (the inefficiencies associated with externalities) will be relatively large. Therefore, a metropolitan system of government will be more efficient.

Demand Diversity versus Scale Economies

There is also a trade off between demand diversity and scale economies. Consider a metropolitan area with a single local public good (fire protection) and two municipalities. The metropolitan area has the following characteristics:

1. **Diversity in demand.** The demand for fire protection is relatively high in municipality H and relatively low in municipality L.

2. **No externalities.** The benefits of fire protection do not cross municipal borders.

3. **Scale economies.** The average cost of fire protection decreases as the number of fire trucks increases. Therefore, a metropolitan fire department can produce fire protection at a lower average cost than a municipal fire department.

4. **Uniformity.** Under a metropolitan government, the two municipalities will have identical fire-protection programs.

Under a system of municipal governments, each municipality will make its own decision on fire protection. The decisions will be based on the local benefits and costs of fire protection. Suppose that municipality L, with its relatively low demand for fire protection, provides four fire trucks. In Figure 15–10, the average cost of its fire-protection program is $180. If municipality H provides eight fire trucks, its average cost will be $120.

Suppose that the two municipalities merge to form a metropolitan government. Suppose that each community gets six fire trucks (the average number of fire trucks that would occur under municipal government). The metropolitan government provides a total of 12 fire trucks, so the average cost of fire protection is $100. The switch to metropolitan government brings good news and bad news. The good news is that the average cost of fire protection decreases: in L, the average cost decreases from $180 per truck to $100; in H, the average cost decreases from $120 to $100. The bad news is that both municipalities must compromise on their ideal level of fire protection, with H getting too few trucks (six instead of eight) and L getting too many (six instead of four). Metropolitan consolidation will be efficient if the savings in production costs are large relative to the losses resulting from the uniform provision of fire protection. In other words, consolidation will be efficient if scale economies are large relative to the diversity in demand for fire protection.

What are the facts on scale economies in the provision of local public goods? There have been dozens of studies of the relationship between production costs and jurisdiction sizes. The evidence suggests that there are moderate scale economies in the provision of water and sewage services. Because these services are capital-intensive, the average production cost decreases as population increases. In contrast, most studies of other local public goods (police protection, fire protection, schools) suggest that scale economies are exhausted at a population of about 100,000.

An alternative to metropolitan consolidation is a **metropolitan federation.** Under a federated government, a metropolitan government would be

FIGURE 15–10   Scale Economies versus Diversity in Demand

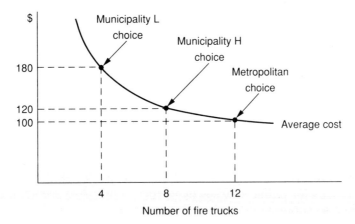

If there are scale economies in the provision of fire protection, the average-cost curve will be negatively sloped. With municipal fire departments, municipality L chooses four fire trucks (at an average cost of $180) and municipality H chooses eight fire trucks (at an average cost of $120). If the two fire departments are consolidated into a single metropolitan department (12 fire trucks), the average cost decreases to $100.

responsible for the provision of goods with large scale economies (e.g., water and sewage systems, sanitation, highways, transit). Municipalities would continue to provide goods with relatively small scale economies (e.g., schools, police and fire protection, parks). The Toronto area established a federated government in 1954.

Another alternative to metropolitan consolidation is to contract with another level of government to provide public services. According to a recent survey conducted by the U.S. Advisory Commission on Intergovernmental Relations (ACIR 1985), over half of all U.S. cities provided some public services under intergovernmental contracts (under which one unit of government arranges with another to provide a public service) and over half used joint-service contracts (under which two or more governmental units join to produce a public service). Both types of arrangements allow a relatively small jurisdiction to realize scale economies in the provision of public services.

Arguments for Metropolitan Consolidation

Should local governments be consolidated into metropolitan governments? Four arguments have been advanced in support of metropolitan consolidation.

Prevention of Suburban Exploitation.   According to the suburban exploitation hypothesis, suburban commuters do not pay their fair share of the costs of central-city public services. Consider the workers who commute from their suburban homes to the city. Although they use city services (streets, water, fire protection, police protection), they pay their property taxes to suburban governments. Do these commuters exploit central-city residents by using city services without paying for them?

The exploitation hypothesis ignores the fact that commuters pay taxes to the city. As shown in Chapter 16 (Local-Government Revenue), 43 percent of municipal tax revenue comes from sales and income taxes, meaning that suburbanites who work and shop in the city center pay taxes to city governments. For large cities (populations greater than 300,000), sales and income taxes generate over half of municipal tax revenue. In addition, most cities have user fees for public services (e.g., tolls, admission prices for zoos and museums), so suburbanites pay directly for some city services. Most studies of the exploitation hypothesis suggest that suburbanites pay close to their share of the costs of city services (see Bradford and Oates 1974 for a review of these studies).

Exploitation of Scale Economies.   Another argument advanced in favor of consolidation is that a metropolitan government could exploit scale economies in the provision of public services, so it could produce public services at a lower cost. The scale-economy argument is incomplete. The switch to metropolitan government will require communities to compromise on their ideal levels of public goods, so the cost savings from scale economies must be compared to the welfare losses resulting from the uniform provision of public goods. For metropolitan consolidation to be efficient, scale economies must be large relative to the diversity in demand.

Equalization of Tax Rates.   Under a system of fragmented local government, municipalities with large tax bases often have relatively low tax rates. Under a metropolitan government, there would be a single property tax base and thus a single tax rate. Therefore, the switch from a municipal system to a metropolitan government would increase tax rates in relatively wealthy communities and decrease tax rates in relatively poor communities.

To what extent will the equalization of tax rates redistribute income from the wealthy to the poor? Consider a metropolitan area with two municipalities, one with middle-income households (who own their homes) and one with poor households (who live in rental housing). Suppose that the poor community has a low tax base and a high tax rate and the middle-income community has a large tax base and a low tax rate. Metropolitan consolidation will increase property taxes in the middle-income community and decrease taxes in the poor community.

The changes in tax liabilities will affect housing prices and property values in the two communities. In the poor community, the tax cut will increase the profitability of housing, so the supply of housing will increase and the price of housing (monthly rent) will fall. Therefore, tenants will benefit from the tax cut. Property owners will also benefit: the decrease in the tax on rental housing will increase the net income from rental property, increasing market values. This is the capitalization process: changes in tax liabilities are capitalized into property values. In the middle-income community, home owners will face higher tax liabilities, so their property values will fall.

Who gains and who loses as a result of the equalization of taxes? Tenants and landlords in the poor community gain: the tenants pay lower rent, and the landlords have higher property values. Home owners in the middle-income community lose because their property values fall. To predict the distributional effect of the equalization of tax rates, one needs information on the income levels of tenants, landlords, and home owners. If landlords in the poor community are relatively wealthy, the equalization of tax rates could actually increase income inequality.

Equalization of Spending.   Under the fragmented system of local government, spending varies within the metropolitan area, reflecting variation in income and the demands for public services. The consolidation of local government would equalize spending on local public goods: all communities, wealthy and poor, would spend the same amount on local public goods.

Bradford and Oates (1974) explored the possible effects of metropolitan consolidation in northeastern New Jersey. They predicted the effects of consolidating 58 local jurisdictions (5 central cities and 53 suburban governments) into a single metropolitan government.

Bradford and Oates evaluated the trade-offs associated with the equalization of education spending. Their results can be explained with a model of a metropolitan area with two school districts, a wealthy one and a poor one. Before consolidation, the wealthy community spends $3,000 per pupil on education and the poor one spends $2,600. Suppose that under the consolidated government, spending is equalized at $2,800 per pupil: spending increases by $200 in the poor district and decreases by the same amount in the wealthy district. According to Bradford and Oates, the extra $200 of education spending is worth only about $130 to the typical poor household: the household would be indifferent between receiving $200 in educational spending and $130 in cash. In contrast, the typical wealthy household would be indifferent between losing $200 in educational spending and giving up $230 in cash. Therefore, the equalization program produces a $130 benefit (to poor households) at a cost of $230 (to wealthy households).

Using the Bradford-Oates numbers, the equalization program seems foolish. Both the poor and the wealthy would be better off if the government used cash transfers—not education spending—to redistribute income. For example, if the government took just $130 from the wealthy and gave it to the poor, the poor would be just as well off, but the wealthy would be better off by $100 ($230 − $130).

This simplistic analysis is deceptive. As pointed out by Bradford and Oates, these calculations ignore the external benefits of education. As explained earlier in this chapter, education generates externalities, so individual households will spend less than the optimum amount on education. The question is whether the external benefits of the equalization program are large enough to offset the private costs. If the equalization program increases the educational achievement of the poor by a relatively large amount and there are large external benefits from the additional achievement, the apparent inefficiency of the equalization program will disappear: the equalization program would not be foolish, but would in fact promote efficiency.

Another possible justification for the equalization program is that education may be a **merit good**, defined as a good that is assumed to be systematically undervalued by consumers. If individuals do not make rational choices concerning education, their willingness to pay for education will understate the true private value of education. In the example above, perhaps the poor don't realize that they would actually receive a benefit of $190 from the increase in education spending. If so, it wouldn't take much of an external benefit to make the equalization program socially efficient. The notion of a merit good can also be stated in terms of the willingness to donate: if the donors (the people in the wealthy school district) make decisions for the recipients (in the poor district), they may be willing to donate more. They may be willing to give only $50 in cash, but $200 in extra education. If so, everyone will be better off under the equalization program than under a cash-transfer program.

THE GROWTH IN LOCAL SPENDING

As mentioned earlier in the chapter, local spending rose from 5 percent of GNP in 1950 to 9.2 percent in 1976. This section explores some of the reasons for this rapid growth in local public spending. Total spending equals the unit cost times the quantity of output, so increases in spending are caused by increases in unit cost, increases in quantity, or increases in both cost and quantity.

Increases in Labor Cost—The Baumol Model

Baumol argues that rising labor costs have contributed to increases in local spending (1967). The Baumol model can be explained with a model of an economy that produces manufactured goods (e.g., watches) and personal services (e.g., haircuts, public education). The labor market has the following characteristics:

1. **Manufacturing productivity.** The productivity of manufacturing workers is increasing over time, a result of innovations that allow the substitution of capital for labor.

2. **Service productivity.** The productivity of service workers (bar-

bers and teachers) is constant. A haircut is a nonstandardized good: every head has a different shape, and every customer wants a unique haircut. Since a barber cannot be replaced by a machine, productivity is constant. Like the barber, the teacher provides a nonstandardized output: every child enters the classroom with a different set of skills and educational needs and requires personal attention. In addition, every child requires a different educational output. Given the difficulty of capital substitution, teacher productivity is constant.

3. **Worker mobility and wages.** Workers move costlessly between manufacturing and service jobs. In equilibrium, all workers earn the same daily wage.

4. **Fixed labor supply.** The total supply of workers is fixed.

Figure 15–11 shows the market for labor in the two-sector economy. The demand curves for both manufacturing and services are negatively sloped. In the initial equilibrium, the wage is $13, one quarter of the workers (25 workers) are employed in manufacturing (point B), and the other 75 workers are employed in services (point C).

Suppose that the productivity of manufacturing workers increases. An increase in productivity shifts the demand curve for manufacturing workers to the right: at every wage, more workers will be demanded. In the short run,

FIGURE 15–11   Effects of Increased Manufacturing Productivity on Wages in the Service Sector

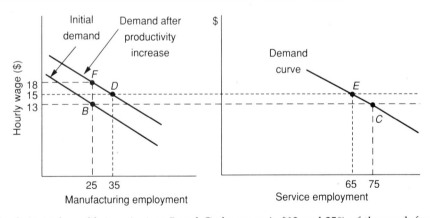

In the initial equilibrium (points B and C) the wage is $13 and 25% of the work force is in manufacturing. An increase in manufacturing productivity shifts the demand curve for manufacturing workers upward, causing excess demand for labor. As the manufacturing wage rises, service workers move to the manufacturing sector, causing a labor shortage in the service sector that increases wages. At the new equilibrium (points D and E), the wage is $15 and 35% of work force is in manufacturing.

the supply of manufacturing workers is fixed, so the manufacturing wage rises to $18 (point *F*).

In the long run, the increase in the manufacturing wage will cause some service workers to switch to manufacturing jobs. As the quantity of manufacturing workers increases, the manufacturing wage drops: the market moves downward along the new demand curve from point *F* toward point *D*. In addition, the decrease in the number of service workers causes a shortage of service workers, so the service wage increases: the market moves up the service demand curve from point *C* toward point *E*. Equilibrium is restored when two conditions are satisfied. First, total employment in the two sectors equals the fixed supply of labor (100 workers). Second, workers are indifferent between the two types of jobs. The second condition will be satisfied if the two sectors pay the same wage. These two equilibrium conditions are satisfied at points *D* and *E*.

What are the implications for the prices of manufacturing goods and services? Because the productivity of manufacturing workers is increasing over time, the increase in the wage is offset by increases in labor productivity, so production costs and market prices do not change. In contrast, the wages of service workers are rising while their productivity is constant, so production costs and market prices will increase over time. In other words, the price of haircuts and the unit cost of education will increase over time.

Other local public goods share the personal-service features of haircuts and education. Consider the costs of police protection. Police officers interview witnesses and look for clues at the scene of the crime. Neither of these tasks can be performed by a machine, so the growth in police productivity will be relatively slow. The same is true for fire fighting: every fire presents a different set of circumstances, preventing the sort of capital substitution that occurs in the manufacturing sector. If the productivities of police and fire fighters are constant, an increase in wages (caused by an increase in the wage of manufacturing workers) will increase the costs of police and fire protection.

Other Reasons for Rising Labor Costs

The Baumol model suggests that the labor costs of government increase because the government provides personal-service goods, not because public servants are lazy or greedy. There are two other possible reasons for increases in labor costs:

1. **Competition and innovation.** The nature of the public sector discourages innovation. Unlike a firm in a competitive market, the local government is shielded from competition, so there is less incentive to develop new labor-saving techniques. If this view is correct, the monopoly status of local government prevents innovations that would increase labor productivity and decrease unit costs.

2. **Union power.** Most government workers are represented by pow-

erful labor unions. If unions use their power to increase the wages of government workers, public servants will be overpaid relative to their private-sector counterparts, increasing the costs of government. Freeman (1985) examined the wages of private and government employees. He compared the wages of public and private workers with similar qualifications (education, work experience, personal characteristics). He found that state and local administrators earn about 5 percent more than equally qualified private-sector workers, and public school teachers earn about 6 percent less than equally qualified private workers. On balance, it appears that the differences between private and government wages are relatively small. Freeman did not include pension plans in his analysis. Since public pension plans are generally more generous than private plans, the inclusion of pension benefits would increase public-sector wages relative to private-sector wages.

Increases in Quantity

An increase in local spending may be caused, in part, by an increase in the quantity of local services demanded. The Baumol model provides a useful framework for analyzing changes in the quantity of local public goods.

Under what circumstances will the quantity of education demanded increase over time? The demand for education changes over time for two reasons. The first is the **income effect.** The increase in worker productivity increases the real income: the total output of the economy increases, increasing the purchasing power of its citizens. As real income increases, the demands for all normal goods, including education, increase. In Figure 15–12, the demand curve for education shifts to the right: at every price, more education is demanded. At P', the quantity of education increases from E_1 to E_3.

The **substitution effect** causes movement upward along the new demand curve. Because the productivity of manufacturing workers increases while the productivity of teachers is constant, the price of education increases relative to the price of other goods. As a result, consumers will substitute manufactured goods for education (and other personal-service goods), thus decreasing the quantity of education demanded. In Figure 15–12, the price of education increases from P' to P'', and the substitution effect causes movement upward along the new demand curve from point C to D.

Figure 15–12 shows a net increase in the quantity of education demanded from E_1 to E_2. The income effect (the outward shift of the demand curve) dominates the substitution effect (the upward movement along the new demand curve), so the equilibrium quantity of education increases. This will occur if the income elasticity of demand for education is large relative to the price elasticity of demand for education. Total spending on education increases: the community consumes more education (E_2 instead of E_1) at a higher unit cost (P'' instead of P').

Another possibility is that the quantity of education demanded will de-

FIGURE 15–12   Changes in Quantity of Education Demanded

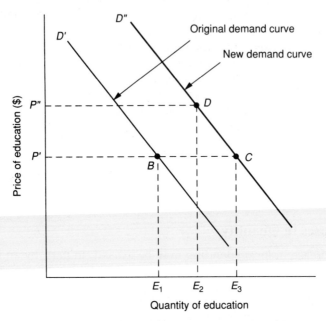

An increase in the productivity of manufacturing increases real income, shifting the demand curve for education outward, increasing the quantity of education demanded (the income effect, a move from point B to C). Since education is a personal-service good, the unit cost (price) of education increases from P' to P'', decreasing the quantity of education demanded (the substitution effect, a move from point C to D). Since the income effect is large relative to the substitution effect, the net effect is an increase in the quantity of education demanded (point B to D).

crease over time. If the income effect is small relative to the substitution effect (if the income elasticity is small relative to the price elasticity), the outward shift of the demand curve would be small relative to the movement up the new demand curve, and the quantity of education demanded would decrease. If this happens, total expenditures on education may either increase or decrease. If the decrease in the quantity demanded is large enough to offset the increase in unit cost, total expenditures would decrease. But if the decrease in quantity demanded is relatively small, total expenditures would increase.

Taxpayer Revolt—Expenditure Limits

As mentioned earlier, the share of GNP spent on local government has decreased since 1976. The decrease in the relative importance of local spending was caused in part by new restrictions on local taxes and spending. By 1981, a total of 30 states had tightened restrictions on local tax rates, tax revenue, and spending. According to Aronson and Hilley (1986), there is evidence that tax and expenditure limits have decreased local spending in several states, including Arizona, California, Colorado, Indiana, Iowa, and New Jersey.

Aronson and Hilley discuss the responses of local governments to tax and expenditure limitations. Local governments have mitigated the effects of the limitations in four ways:

1. Local governments have shifted to user fees and taxes that are not subject to restrictions (income, sales, and business taxes).
2. Some local governments have evaded the spending limits by transferring some spending programs to special districts.
3. Some state governments have increased intergovernmental grants.
4. In cases where limits apply to specific spending categories, some localities have moved programs from restricted categories to unrestricted ones.

The debate over tax and spending limitations has been spirited. The supporters of limitations view local governments as inefficient monopolies. According to this view, the limitations will force local governments to "cut out the fat" by increasing productivity and decreasing wages. According to Courant, Gramlich, and Rubinfeld (1987), many of the people who vote for tax and spending limitations hold this view.

Some of the critics of tax and spending limitations believe that the Baumol model is applicable to the local public sector. They believe that the cost of local services has increased because of rising productivity in the private sector, not because public workers are lazy and wasteful. According to this view, there is little fat in the local public budget, so the spending limitations will decrease the quantity of local public services. Another concern is that local tax limitations may increase state involvement in local budget choices, so local citizens will have less control over tax and spending policies.

SUMMARY

1. There are over 82,000 local governments in the United States, including municipalities, school districts, counties, and special districts. Municipalities are responsible for about 35 percent of local government spending, and school districts are responsible for about 30 percent. The largest spending program is education (42 percent of local spending).
2. The national government is responsible for stabilization and redistribution policies.
3. Local governments are involved in resource allocation for three types of goods.

   a. Natural monopoly. Local governments either produce or regulate the private production of goods produced by natural monopolies (water, sewage, transit).

b. Externalities. One option is for the government to provide goods that generate externalities. Another option is to internalize the externality with a subsidy.

c. Local public goods. A local public good is nonrivalrous and nonexcludable, and its benefits are confined to a relatively small geographical area. For the optimum quantity, the marginal social benefit (the sum of the marginal private benefits) equals the marginal cost.

4. The median-voter model predicts that the government will adopt the preferred budget of the median voter (the voter that splits voters into two halves, with one half preferring a smaller budget and the other half preferring a larger budget).

a. Majority rule will not necessarily produce the optimum level of spending.

b. The median voter is decisive in both a direct democracy and a representative democracy.

c. Economists have used the median-voter model to estimate the elasticities of demand for local public goods.

5. The inefficiencies resulting from majority rule could be eliminated by the use of Lindahl taxes (taxes equal to the citizen's marginal benefit from the local public good).

6. According to the Tiebout model, citizens shop for jurisdictions and sort themselves with respect to their demands for local public goods. Because the Tiebout model assumes that there are no externalities, the Tiebout process is just as efficient as shopping for private goods.

7. The property tax increases the equilibrium number of communities: households sort themselves with respect to both the demand for local public goods and housing consumption.

a. The wealthy (consumers of large houses) use large-lot zoning to exclude the poor (consumers of small houses) from wealthy communities.

b. Differences in taxes are capitalized into property values, so a small house in a wealthy community (with a low tax rate) costs more than a small house in a poor community (with a high tax rate).

8. There is a good deal of evidence for the Tiebout process.

a. Citizens shop for local governments and sort themselves into relatively homogeneous communities.

b. Most of the jurisdictional shopping is in the suburbs: central-city governments are large, so shopping opportunities in the central city are limited.

9. There are three trade offs associated with the local provisions of public goods.

   a. Local governments promote efficiency if there is diversity in demand for public goods.

   b. Local governments inhibit efficiency if the benefits or costs of public goods spill over into other jurisdictions (externalities).

   c. Local governments inhibit efficiency if there are scale economies in the production of public goods.

   d. Local provision is efficient if the diversity in demand is large relative to externalities and scale economies.

10. Metropolitan consolidation has been advocated as a way to prevent suburban exploitation, exploit scale economies, equalize tax rates, and equalize spending.

11. The Baumol model suggests that increases in the labor cost of personal services (e.g., haircuts and education) result from rising productivity in manufacturing, which pulls up the wages of all workers.

   a. Other theories of rising labor costs focus on the monopoly power of local governments and labor unions.

   b. The quantity of public services demanded will increase if the income effect (from rising productivity) is large relative to the substitution effect (from rising unit costs).

12. Between the late 1970s and 1981, a total of 30 states tightened restrictions on local tax rates, tax revenue, and spending. Local governments have avoided some of the restrictions.

EXERCISES AND DISCUSSION QUESTIONS

1. Why do we have public libraries? Why don't people rent books from firms, just as they rent trucks, rototillers, and videos? If we have U-Haul, why not U-Read; if we have Captain Video, why not Captain Book?

2. The figures showing the marginal social benefit of local parks assume that there is no congestion in the use of the parks. In other words, the good is literally nonrivalrous.

   a. Draw a new MSB curve under the assumption that congestion occurs for some park sizes.

   b. What are the implications for the optimum park acreage? Does it increase or decrease?

3. In the example shown in Table 15–3, the school board started with a budget of $90 and works its way downward until a majority of voters votes

"yes." Would the same outcome result if it started with a budget of $10 and works upward?

4. In the example shown in Table 15–2, the winning budget is $70. Explain the effects of the following changes on the winning budget. In each case, use as the starting point the distribution of voters shown in Table 15–3.

   a. Four elderly voters move into the school district. The elderly voters have preferred budgets of $20, $25, $30, and $35.

   b. In response to "A Nation at Risk," a report critical of educational programs, the desired spending of every household increases by $5.

5. Consider the effect of private schools on the local school election. Suppose that households F and G (in Table 15–3) enroll their children in private schools. Use the example shown in Table 15–3 to predict the effects of a new private school on the public school budget under the following two cases.

   a. F and G abstain from voting in the school election.

   b. F and G vote in the election. Their preferred budgets drop by $40 ($44 instead of $84 and $51 instead of $91).

6. Comment on the following: "If the median-voter model is correct, it's silly to mess around with elections. We should hire Mr. Gallup to identify the median voter and find out his or her preferred budget. Such a system will be cheaper than a series of budget elections."

7. You are the campaign manager for Dick Tracy, who is running for mayor. His opponent has committed herself to spending $500 per capita on police services. You must decide how much Dick will propose for the police budget. What information would you collect, and how would you use it?

8. The conventional head tax is a fixed amount per head: if you have a head, you pay a $500 tax. Suppose that the head tax is based on head weight: the heavier your head, the larger your tax. Would you expect the switch from the conventional head tax to the head-weight tax to increase or decrease the equilibrium number of municipalities?

9. In Metro, there are three types of houses: E (expensive), M (medium), and C (cheap). A recent survey suggests that there are three types of preferences for fire protection: H (high), I (intermediate), and L (low).
   Mr. Wizard, an economic consultant to the city, recently made the following statement: "If my assumptions are correct, the shopping and sorting from the Tiebout process will generate three municipalities."

   a. Assume that Mr. Wizard's reasoning is correct. What are his assumptions?

   b. Suppose that the equilibrium number of municipalities turns out to be nine, not three. Where did Mr. Wizard go wrong? What set of assumptions would have given him the correct prediction?

10. Consider a metropolitan area in which all households demand the same spending per pupil on public education. Education is produced with constant returns to scale. Because schools are financed with the property tax, there are dozens of school districts. According to Peabody, a fiscal analyst in Metro, "If my assumptions are correct, if we replace the property tax (a tax on market value) with a tax based on square footage (e.g., $2 per square foot of living space per year), the equilibrium number of school districts will decrease to one."
    What are Peabody's assumptions?

11. Under the traditional public school system, parents must send their children to the neighborhood school. In recent years, many people have suggested that parents should have the option of sending their children to the public school of their choice, not necessarily the closest one. Suppose that this change is implemented. Discuss the effects on the Tiebout shopping and sorting process. Would there be more or less income segregation?

12. In the example of the Tiebout model with a property tax, wealthy households established an exclusive suburb with a property tax rate of 0.667 percent, spending of $500, and a minimum lot size of 0.50 acres. Discuss the effects of the following changes on the property tax rate and the minimum lot size.

    a. The market value of houses is $100,000 instead of $75,000.

    b. The market value of land is $50,000 instead of $30,000 (and the market value of houses is $100,000).

13. Consider a metropolitan area with three school districts, East, West, and North. The optimum spending is $500 in East, $900 in West, and $700 in North. If the districts make independent decisions, spending will be $450 in East, $850 in West, and $650 in North. In other words, there are externalities in the provision of education, causing each district to spend too little. Suppose that the three districts are consolidated into a single metropolitan school district.

    a. Assume that there are no scale economies in the provision of schools. Will the metropolitan school district be more or less efficient than the original arrangement?

    b. How would your answer to (a) change if the expenditures under independent decision making were $200 (East) and $600 (West)?

    c. How would your answer to (a) change if there are scale economies in the provision of education?

14. Consider a metropolitan area with two municipalities, Sportville (high demand for parks) and Slothburg (low demand for parks). The provision of parks is subject to scale economies (the cost per acre of parks is lower under metropolitan management) and generates externalities. Suppose that

the two municipalities are consolidated into a single metropolitan government. Under what circumstances will total expenditures on parks decrease?

15. Consider a metropolitan area with two municipalities, each of which has a small police force. The only activity of the police is chasing criminals. In other words, the police chase—but never capture—the criminals.

    a. Suppose that the provision of police services is subject to scale economies. If the two municipal police forces are consolidated into a single metropolitan force, will total expenditures on police services increase, decrease, or stay the same?

    b. If you don't have enough information to answer the question, describe the information you need and explain how you would use it.

16. In the city of Crewville, everyone gets crew cuts: the output of the barber is standardized. The output of the teacher is also standardized: the only objective is to teach children how to add and subtract. Will the costs of haircuts and education increase (over time) relative to the costs of manufactured goods?

17. Consider the cost of admission to a performance by a popular rock band. Would you expect the relative cost of admission to increase over time (relative to the price of manufactured goods)?

18. The example shown in Figure 15–6 assumes that all citizens vote in the mayoral election. Suppose that some citizens refuse to vote if the proposed budgets of the two candidates are not very far apart: some citizens abstain because of indifference. Specifically, suppose that if the difference between the candidates is less than $1, only 50 percent of citizens (of all budget preferences) will vote.

    a. Will Buck increase his chances of being elected if he increases his proposed budget from $6 (the median budget) to $7? Demonstrate with a graph.

    b. Will the median-voter result persist?

19. The example shown in Figure 15–6 assumes that all citizens vote in the mayoral election. Suppose that some citizens refuse to vote if the proposed budget of the closest candidate is too far from their preferred budget: some citizens abstain because of alienation. Specifically, a voter abstains if the difference between the closest candidate and the citizen's preferred budget is greater than $3.

    a. Suppose that Penny decreases her proposed budget to $4. Using a graph like Figure 15–6, show her gains and losses. Does she increase or decrease her chances of being elected?

    b. Will the median-voter result persist if there is alienation?

REFERENCES AND ADDITIONAL READINGS

Overview

Advisory Commission on Intergovernmental Relations. *Significant Features of Fiscal Federalism, 1987 Edition.* Washington, D.C.: Government Printing Office, 1987.

Inman, Robert P. "The Fiscal Performance of Local Governments: An Interpretive Review." In *Current Issues in Urban Economics,* ed. Peter Meiszkowski and Mahlon Straszheim. Baltimore: The Johns Hopkins Press, 1979, pp. 270–321. Discusses various models of decision making in the local public sector, including the median-voter model and the dominant-party model. Summarizes studies of the price and income elasticities of demand for local public goods and the elasticity of local expenditures with respect to intergovernmental aid.

Musgrave, Richard A., and Peggy B. Musgrave, *Public Finance in Theory and Practice,* 3rd ed. New York: McGraw-Hill, 1980.

U.S. Bureau of Census, *City Government Finances in 1986.* Washington, D.C.: Department of Commerce, 1987.

The Role of Local Government in Federal System

Break, George. *Financing Government in a Federal System.* Washington, D.C.: Brookings Institution, 1980.

Oates, Wallace. *Fiscal Federalism.* New York: Harcourt Brace Jovanovich, 1972. Analyzes the division of responsibilities between different levels of government, focusing on spillovers, scale economies, and diversity in demand.

Olson, Mancur. "The Principle of Fiscal Equivalence: The Division of Responsibilities Among Different Levels of Government." *American Economic Review* 59 (1969), pp. 479–87. Argues that the federal system is required in order to control benefit spillovers.

Stigler, George J. "The Tenable Range of Functions of Local Government." In *Private Wants and Public Needs,* ed. Edmund S. Phelps. New York: Norton, 1965.

The Median-Voter Model

Barr, J. and Davis, O. "An Elementary Political and Economic Theory of Local Governments." *Southern Economic Journal* 33 (1966), pp. 149–65.

Bergstrom T., and R. Goodman. "Private Demand for Public Goods." *American Economic Review* 63 (1973), pp. 286–96. Derives the conditions under which the chosen budget is equal to the preferred budget of the median-income family.

Black, D. "On the Rationale of Group Decision-Making." *Journal of Political Economy* 56 (1948), pp. 88–95.

Downs, Anthony. *An Economic Theory of Democracy.* New York: Harper & Row, 1956. Chapters 3, 8, and 14 discuss the rational voter and the median-voter model.

Edelson, N. "Budgetary Outcomes in a Referendum Setting." In *Property Taxation and the Finance of Education,* ed. R. Lindholm. Madison: University of Wisconsin Press, 1974.

Hotelling, Harold. "Stability in Competition." *Economic Journal* 39 (1929), pp. 41–57. The basis for the median-voter model. Shows why politicians are like ice cream vendors.

Inman, Robert. "Testing Political Economy's 'As If' Proposition: Is the Median Voter Really Decisive?" *Public Choice* 33 (Winter 1978). pp. 45–65. Tested the median-voter model for local public schools and found that the decisive voter was in fact the median-income home owner (among households whose children attended public schools). The chosen budget moved away from the preferred budget of the median voter as the number of renters, elderly, and private-school families increased.

Rubinfeld, D. "Voting in a Local School Election: A Micro Analysis." *Review of Economics and Statistics* 59 (1977), pp. 30–42.

The Tiebout Model of Interjurisdictional Mobility

Bewley, T. "A Critique of Tiebout's Theory of Local Public Expenditures." *Econometrica* 49 (1981), p. 713–40. Discusses the conditions under which the Tiebout process is efficient.

Eberts, Randall W., and Timothy J. Gronberg. "Jurisdictional Homogeneity and the Tiebout Hypothesis." *Journal of Urban Economics* 10 (1981), pp. 227–39. Discusses the problems caused by a limited supply of local jurisdictions.

Hamilton, Bruce W. "Zoning and Property Taxation in a System of Local Governments." *Urban Studies* 12 (1975), pp. 205–11. Discusses the role of zoning in maintaining the Tiebout equilibrium under property-tax finance.

————. "Capitalization of Interjurisdictional Differences in Local Tax Prices." *American Economic Review* 66 (1976), pp. 743–53. Explores the roles of zoning and capitalization in attaining a Tiebout equilibrium in a community whose citizens have different demands for housing.

Hamilton, Bruce W.; Edwin S. Mills; and David Puryear. "The Tiebout Hypothesis and Residential Income Segregation." In *Fiscal Zoning and Land Use Controls*, ed. Edwin S. Mills and Wallace Oates. Lexington, Mass.: D.C. Heath, 1975. Discusses the effects of the fragmented system of local government on income segregation.

Henderson, J. V. "Theories of Group, Jurisdiction, and Size." In *Current Issues in Urban Economics*, ed. Peter Meiszkowski and Mahlon Straszheim. Baltimore: The Johns Hopkins Press, 1979, pp. 235–69. Discusses the allocation of population among local communities.

Oates, Wallace E. "On the Use of Local Zoning Ordinances to Regulate Population Flows and the Quality of Local Services." In *Essays in Modern Labor Market Analysis*, ed. Orley Ashenfelter and Wallace Oates. New York: John Wiley & Sons, 1977, pp. 201–19.

Pack, H., and J. Pack. "Metropolitan Fragmentation and Local Public Expenditure." *National Tax Journal* 31 (1978), pp. 349–62. Discusses the problems associated with a limited supply of local jurisdictions.

Tiebout, Charles. "A Pure Theory of Local Expenditures." *Journal of Political Economy* 64 (1956), pp. 416–24. The original statement of the Tiebout model.

Tests of the Tiebout Model

Gramlich, Edward M., and Daniel L. Rubinfeld. "Microestimates of Public Spending Demand Functions and Test of the Tiebout and Median-Voter Hypothesis." *Journal of Political Economy* 90 (1982), pp. 536–60.   Found relatively small differences in the demands for local public goods within municipalities in metropolitan areas where there are many local jurisdictions.

Oates, Wallace E. "The Effects of Property Taxes and Local Public Spending on Property Values: An Empirical Study of Tax Capitalization and the Tiebout Hypothesis." *Journal of Political Economy* 77 (1969), pp. 957–70.   Estimates the effects of local taxes and expenditures on property values. Provides evidence that households shop for local jurisdictions.

Zodrow, George *The Tiebout Model After Twenty-Five Years.* New York: Academic Press, 1983.   A collection of papers on the Tiebout model.

Municipal versus Metropolitan Government

Bahl, Roy, and David Puryear. "Regional Tax Base Sharing: Possibilities and Implications." *National Tax Journal* 29 (1976), p. 328–35.

Bollens, John C., and Henry J. Schmandt. *The Metropolis.* New York: Harper & Row, 1982.   Describes the metropolitan-federation form of government, under which some public services are provided by a metropolitan government and others are provided by small local governments.

Bradford, David, and Wallace E. Oates. "Suburban Exploitation of Central Cities and Government Structure." In *Redistribution Through Public Choice*, ed. Harold Hochman and George Peterson. New York: Columbia University Press, 1974,   pp. 33–90. Discusses the suburban exploitation hypothesis and predicts the effects of metropolitan consolidation on tax rates, expenditure levels, and income segregation.

Greene, Kenneth V., and Thomas J. Parliament. "Political Externalities, Efficiency, and the Welfare Losses from Consolidation." *National Tax Journal* 33 (1980), pp. 209–17.   A study of the efficiency effects of metropolitan consolidation.

Reschovsky, Andrew. "An Evaluation of Metropolitan Area Tax Base Sharing." *National Tax Journal* 33 (1980), pp. 55–66.   Describes the experience with tax-base sharing in Minneapolis–St. Paul.

Scale Economies in the Provision of Local Public Goods

Advisory Commission on Intergovernmental Relations. *Intergovernmental Service Arrangements for Delivering Local Public Services: Update 1983.* Washington, D.C.: 1985. A survey of the use of intergovernmental and joint-service contracts in the provision of local public services.

Gardner, John L. "City Size and Municipal Service Costs." In *Urban Growth Policy in a Market Economy*, ed. George S. Tolley, Philip E. Graves, and John L. Gardner. New York: Academic Press, 1979, pp. 51–61.   Examines the relationship between public-service costs and city size, controlling for the fact that the demand for public services depends on income, which varies across cities. Concludes that cost per family increases with city size and decreases as population density increases.

Gyimahbrempong, K. "Economies of Scale in Municipal Police Departments—The Case of Florida." *Review of Economics and Statistics* 69 (1987), pp. 352–56.

Hines, Lawrence G. "The Long Run Cost Function of Water Production for Selected Wisconsin Communities." *Land Economics* 45 (1969), pp. 133–40. Detects scale economies in the provision of water services.

Hirsch, Werner "Expenditure Implications of Metropolitan Growth and Consolidation." *Review of Economics and Statistics* 41 (1959), pp. 234–35. Estimated the degree of scale economies for police, fire protection, and public schools. Did not detect scale economies for police services or public schools. Found scale economies for fire protection up to a population of about 100,000.

Neutze, G. M. *Economic Policy and the Size of Cities.* Canberra: Australian National University, 1965. Discusses scale economies in the provision of urban services.

Walzer, Norman. "Economies of Scale and Municipal Police Services: The Illinois Experience." *Review of Economics and Statistics* 54 (1972), pp. 431–38. Suggests that there are small scale economies in the provision of police services for small cities (up to 140,000 population).

Rising Costs of Government and the Tax Revolt

Aronson, J. Richard and John L. Hilley, *Financing State and Local Governments* (Washington, D.C.: Brookings Institution, 1986).

Baumol, William. "The Macroeconomics of Unbalance Growth: The Anatomy of Urban Crisis." *American Economic Review* 65 (1967), pp. 414–26.

Bradford, David F.; R. A. Malt; and Wallace E. Oates. "The Rising Cost of Local Public Services: Some Evidence and Reflections." *National Tax Journal* 22 (1969), pp. 415–26.

Brennan, Geoffrey. "Tax Limits and the Logic of Constitutional Restrictions." Chapter 6 in *Tax and Expenditure Limitations*, ed. Helen Ladd and Nicholas Tideman. Washington, D.C.: The Urban Institute, 1987, pp. 121–38.

Courant, Paul; Edward Gramlich; and Daniel Rubinfeld. "Why Voters Support Tax Limitation Amendments: The Michigan Case." Chapter 3 in *Tax and Expenditure Limitations*, ed. Helen Ladd and Nicholas Tideman. Washington, D.C.: The Urban Institute, 1987, pp. 37–72.

Freeman, Richard B., "How Do Public Sector Waste and Employment Respond to Economic Conditions?" National Bureau of Economic Research, Working Paper no. 1653, Cambridge Mass., 1985.

Musgrave, Richard. "Leviathan Cometh—Or Does He?" Chapter 5 in *Tax and Expenditure Limitations*, ed. Helen Ladd and Nicholas Tideman. Washington, D.C.: The Urban Institute, 1987, pp. 77–120.

Privatization

Savas, E. S. *Privatizing the Public Sector.* Chatham, N.J.: Chatham House, 1982. Argues for shifting the responsibility for providing some public services to the private sector.

Stevens, Barbara J. *Delivering Municipal Services Efficiently: A Comparison of Municipal and Private Sector Delivery: Summary.* U.S. Department of Housing and Urban Development, no. RP 3744. June 1984.   Compares the costs of providing municipal services by local governments and by private firms (through the contracting process). Concludes that government costs were substantially higher.

CHAPTER 16

Local-Government Revenue

The thing generally raised on city land is taxes.

Charles Dudley Warner

In contrast with the previous chapter, which discusses local-government spending, this chapter explores the revenue side of local government. The first part of the chapter examines the economic effects of local taxes. When a government imposes a tax, the people who pay the tax have the incentive to change their behavior to avoid the tax. By doing so, they shift the tax to someone else. The policy question is: After taxpayers have fully adjusted to the new tax, who actually pays the tax? The second part of the chapter explores the role of intergovernmental grants. The principal question is: How do local governments respond to state and federal grants? Do they spend all of the grant on additional local public goods, or do they use the grant to cut local taxes?

Table 16–1 shows the revenue sources for different types of local governments. For local governments as a whole, 40 percent of total revenue comes from intergovernmental grants, 37 percent comes from local taxes, and the remaining 23 percent comes from user charges and general revenue. School districts are heavily dependent on intergovernmental grants, receiving about 55

TABLE 16–1 Revenue Sources of Local Governments, 1985–1986

| | Percent of General Revenue From | | | |
Type of Government	Intergovernmental Grants	Local Taxes	Charges and General Revenue	Total
County	37%	37%	26%	100%
Municipal	30	42	28	100
Township	29	56	15	100
School district	55	37	8	100
Special district	29	15	57	100
All local government	40	37	23	100

SOURCE: U.S. Bureau of Census, *Government Finances in 1986* (Washington, D.C.: U.S. Government Printing Office, 1987), p. 7.

FIGURE 16–1   Percent of Local Tax Revenue from Various Sources, 1984

SOURCES: U.S. Bureau of Census, *Census of Governments* (Washington, D.C.: Department of Commerce, 1987); U.S. Bureau of Census, *City Government Finances in 1984–85* (Washington, D.C.: Department of Commerce, 1987).

percent of their revenue from the federal and state governments. For municipal governments, 30 percent of revenue comes from grants, 42 percent from local taxes, and 28 percent from user charges and general revenue. In contrast, special districts are heavily dependent on user charges, receiving about 57 percent of their revenue from charges and general revenue.

Figure 16–1 shows the relative importance of local taxes. In 1984, the property tax generated about three fourths of all local tax revenue. Municipalities are less dependent on the property tax: for municipalities as a whole, the property tax generated about half of tax revenue; for large municipalities (population greater than 300,000), the property tax generated only about 41 percent of tax revenue. The second largest revenue source is the sales tax: it generated 16 percent of local tax revenue and 29 percent of municipal tax revenue. The third largest source is the local income tax, which generated 6 percent of local taxes and 14 percent of municipal taxes.

WHO PAYS THE RESIDENTIAL PROPERTY TAX?

The property tax is a tax on residential, commercial, and industrial property. This section considers the effect of the residential property tax, using a model of a residential city to explore the market effects of the tax. The analysis focuses on two principal questions about the residential property tax. First, how do property owners respond to the tax? Second, to what extent do property owners pass on the tax to consumers, landowners, and other property owners?

It will be useful to divide rental housing into two components: the dwelling itself (the structure) and the land that comes with the dwelling. The annual rent on the residential property is the sum of dwelling rent and land rent. For example, an annual rent of $5,000 can be broken down into $4,000 of dwelling rent and $1,000 of land rent. Similarly, the market value of residential property is the sum of the market values of the dwelling and the land. As explained in Chapter 7 (Introduction to Land Rent and Land Use), the market value of property equals the present value of the rental income from the property. If the market interest rate is 10 percent, the market value of the dwelling will be $40,000 ($4,000/0.10), the market value of the land will be $10,000 ($1,000/0.10), and the market value of the residential property (both dwelling and land) will be $50,000.

The residential property tax is an annual tax based on the market value of the property. For example, under a 2 percent property tax, the owner of a $50,000 property would pay $1,000 per year in taxes. This can be broken down into an $800 tax on the dwelling itself (2 percent of a market value of $40,000) and a $200 tax on the land (2 percent of a market value of $10,000).

Consider the city of Taxville, where all land is used for rental housing. The city has the following characteristics:

1. **Identical dwellings.** The city has 900 identical rental housing units.
2. **Housing inputs.** There are two inputs to housing: land and improvements (the dwelling). Every dwelling occupies a quarter-acre lot.
3. **Capital mobility.** Dwellings are immobile in the short run, but can be moved from one city to another in the long run.
4. **Household mobility.** The population of the city is fixed: households can neither leave nor enter the city.
5. **Property tax.** The annual property tax (2 percent of market value) is paid in legal terms by the landlord (property owner).

Who Pays the Land Portion of the Property Tax?

Consider first the effect of the land portion of the property tax. Figure 16–2 shows the city's land market. The supply of land is perfectly inelastic, with a fixed supply of 900 quarter-acre lots. The demand curve intersects the supply curve at point *B*, generating an annual rent of $1,000 per lot. If the market interest rate is 10 percent, market value of land will be $10,000 per lot (1,000/0.10).

Will landowners be able to shift the land tax onto land consumers? The 2 percent property tax increases the landlord's tax liability by $200 per year.

FIGURE 16–2   Land Market and Land Tax

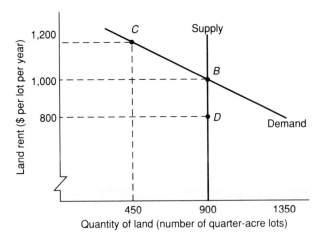

In the initial equilibrium, land rent is $1,000 per lot per year. A 2% property tax generates a tax of $200 per lot (2% of the market value of $10,000). Since the supply of land is fixed, annual land rent is unaffected by the tax. If the landowner tried to pass on the $200 annual tax to consumers, the net cost of land would rise to $1,200 (point C) and the quantity supplied (900) would exceed the quantity demanded (450). The surplus of land would cause rent to fall back to $1,000.

Suppose that the landlord increased land rent from $1,000 per year (point *B*) to $1,200 (point *C*). At point *C*, the quantity of land demanded (450 lots) will be less than the fixed supply (900 lots), so some land will be vacant. The excess supply of land will cause landowners to cut prices to attract consumers. The price cutting will continue until the gap between supply and demand is eliminated. In equilibrium, land rent falls to $1,000 and the net return to landlords drops to $800 ($1,000 less the $200 tax). Because the supply of land is fixed, the land tax is ultimately borne by landowners. The decrease in net rental income lowers the market value of land from $10,000 to $8,000 ($800/0.10). Therefore, people who own the land when the tax is announced bear the burden of the land tax.

Who Pays the Improvement Tax—The Traditional View

The traditional analysis of the property tax examines the effects of the property tax on the city that imposes the tax. The traditional view is based on partial-equilibrium analysis. The analysis is "partial" in the sense that it ignores the effect of the tax on other markets and other cities.

Figure 16–3 shows the market for improvements (dwellings) in the taxing city. In the long run, the supply of dwellings is assumed to be perfectly

FIGURE 16–3   Partial-Equilibrium Effects of Improvements Tax

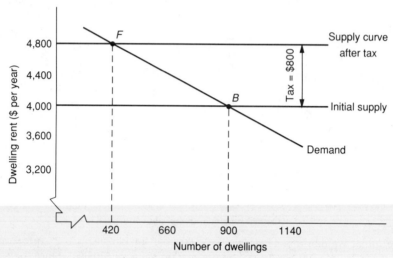

Before the improvement tax, B is the equilibrium point (rent = $4,000 per year). A 2% property tax increases the tax liability of landlords by $800 (2% of the market value of $40,000), so the supply curve shifts up by $800. Dwelling rent increases to $4,800 per year, and the number of dwellings drops to 420 (point F).

elastic: the city is assumed to be a small part of a national market for dwellings, so the market price is unaffected by events in the city. Given the supply and demand curves, the initial equilibrium (point B) generates a dwelling rent of $4,000 per year and 900 dwellings. If the market interest rate is 10 percent, the market value of the rental dwelling is $40,000.

Why is the long-run supply curve perfectly elastic? One way to picture the long run is to imagine that landlords can put wheels on their dwellings and roll them to other cities. Although landlords do not literally move their dwellings from place to place, they can decrease the supply of housing in other ways. As explained in Chapter 13 (Why Is Housing Different?), landlords can (*a*) decrease their investment in repair and maintenance, (*b*) abandon the dwellings, (*c*) convert property to other uses, and (*d*) not respond to increases in the demand for housing. Therefore, landlords can decrease the effective supply of housing without actually moving their dwellings to another location. The house-on-wheels metaphor captures the idea that landlords can decrease the supply of housing in the long run.

A 2 percent property tax generates an annual tax of $800 per dwelling. Because the landlord pays the improvement tax (in legal terms), the tax shifts the long-run supply curve up by the amount of the tax: the supply curve is a marginal-cost curve, and the tax increases the marginal cost of rental property by $800 per dwelling per year. The market moves from point B to F: the equilibrium rent rises by the full amount of the tax (from $4,000 to $4,800), and the quantity of dwellings drops from 900 to 420. Net rental income remains at $4,000: the landlord collects $4,800 in rent and pays $800 in taxes, leaving $4,000 in net income. The tenant pays the entire tax: the annual cost of rental housing rises by $800 (2 percent of the market value of the dwelling).

The improvement tax is borne by consumers because the supply of dwellings is perfectly elastic. The city is a small part of the national market for dwellings, so it takes the national rent of $4,000 as given: if the city's landlords were to receive anything less than $4,000 in net rental income, they would roll their dwellings out of town. In fact, the decrease in the supply of dwellings (from 900 to 420) increases dwelling rent to restore the original net rental income of $4,000.

Who Pays the Residential Property Tax—The New View

Partial-equilibrium analysis explores the effects of the property tax on the markets for land and improvements in the taxing city. General-equilibrium analysis explores the effects of the property tax on markets outside the city, providing a new view of the property tax.

A Simple General-Equilibrium Model.   Suppose that Taxville shares a region with Notax, a residential city without a property tax. The region has the following characteristics:

1. **Fixed supply of dwellings.** The total number of dwellings in the region is fixed at 1,800. This assumption will be dropped later in the section.

2. **Capital mobility.** In the short run, dwellings cannot be moved between cities. In the long run, dwellings can be moved between the two cities at zero cost.

3. **Household mobility.** Households are immobile in the sense that they cannot move from one city to another. This assumption will be dropped later in the chapter.

4. **Equilibrium price.** Landlords move their dwellings to the city with the highest return (the highest net return). In equilibrium, the net return on dwellings is the same in the two cities.

The regional dwelling market is shown in Figure 16–4. Each city has a negatively sloped demand curve, and the initial equilibrium occurs with points B (in Taxville) and K (in Notax). The equilibrium price of dwellings is $4,000, and each city has 900 dwellings.

The Effects of the Improvement Tax.   In the short run, the supply of dwellings in each city is fixed. The 2 percent property tax ($800 per year) de-

FIGURE 16–4 General-Equilibrium Effects of Improvement Tax

The initial (pretax) equilibrium consists of points *B* and *K*. A 2% improvement tax increases the landlord's tax liability by $800 per dwelling per year. In the short run, dwellings are immobile, so dwelling rent is fixed at $4,000 and landlords pay the tax. In the long run, landlords move their dwellings to the nontaxing city, increasing dwelling rent in the taxing city (movement upward along the demand curve) and decreasing rent in the nontaxing city (moving down the demand curve). In long-run equilibrium, landlords receive the same net (posttax) return, so Taxville rent exceeds Notax rent by the amount of the tax: with points *D* and *M*, Taxville rent is $4,400 (net landlord return = $3,600) and Notax's rent is $3,600. The tax is shifted to property owners in the nontaxing city.

creases the net rental income in Taxville from $4,000 (point B) to $3,200 (point T). The property tax is borne by landlords because the supply of dwellings is perfectly inelastic. In the nontaxing city, rent stays at $4,000.

In the long run, landlords will move their dwellings to the more lucrative market in Notax. Suppose that landlords move 120 dwellings from Taxville to Notax. In Figure 16–4, the Taxville market moves from point B (900 dwellings) to point C (780 dwellings), causing the rent on Taxville dwellings to rise from $4,000 to $4,200. The net income of Taxville's landlords increases from $3,200 ($4,000 rent less $800 tax) to $3,400 ($4,200 less $800). Taxville's loss is Notax's gain: the Notax market moves from point K to point L (an increase of 120 dwellings, from 900 to 1,020), and rent drops from $4,000 to $3,800.

Is the dwelling market in equilibrium with points C and L? Equilibrium occurs when two conditions are satisfied. First, the total number of dwellings in the two cities must equal 1,800 (the fixed supply). Second, landlords must have no incentive to move their dwellings from one city to another: the net rental income must be the same in the two cities. For points C and L, the first condition is satisfied (780 + 1,020 = 1,800), but the second condition is violated: the net income in Taxville ($3,400) is still less than net income in Notax ($3,800). Therefore, there will be additional movement up the Taxville demand curve and down the Notax demand curve. The movements along the demand curves will continue until both equilibrium conditions are satisfied. Equilibrium occurs with points D and M: there are 660 dwellings in Taxville and 1,140 in Notax, and the net income is $3,600 per rental dwelling.

There are two lessons from the general-equilibrium analysis.

1. **Landlords pay the tax.** The tax decreases net rental income in both cities to $3,600. The movement of dwellings to the untaxed city decreases rent in the untaxed city (to $3,600) and increases rent in the taxing city (to $4,400). The tax is paid by landlords throughout the region, not just landlords in the taxing city.

2. **Consumer effects.** Consumers in Taxville lose (they pay $4,400 instead of $4,000), and consumers in Notax gain (they pay $3,600). The changes in housing costs offset one another, so the tax does not change the average rent in the region.

The general-equilibrium analysis suggests that the improvement tax is paid by landlords (the owners of dwellings). Because the total (regional) supply of dwellings is perfectly inelastic, landlords are unable to escape the tax. On the other side of the market, housing consumers, as a class, escape the tax: the losses of Taxville households are offset by the gains of Notax households. The improvement tax causes zero-sum changes in rent, so housing consumers are no worse off as a result of the tax.

Changing the Assumptions

The simple general-equilibrium model has a number of unrealistic assumptions. How does the analysis change when these assumptions are dropped?

More than Two Municipalities.   One of the key assumptions of the simple model is that only two municipalities share a fixed supply of dwellings. An alternative assumption is that Taxville is one of 100 cities in a region and shares a fixed supply of dwellings with 99 other cities.

When Taxville imposes a property tax, dwellings will be moved to 99 other cities, not just to Notax. Suppose that 240 dwellings leave Taxville (the market moves from point B to point D in Figure 16–4), so that each of the other 99 cities gets about 2.4 additional dwellings. Each city will experience a relatively small increase in dwellings, so each city will experience a relatively small decrease in dwelling rent (e.g., from $4,000 to $3,996). Given the small decrease in rent, there will still be a gap between the net income on dwellings in Taxville ($4,400 − $800 = $3,600) and net income elsewhere ($3,996). Therefore, point D in Figure 16–4 is not an equilibrium point in the 100-city case.

Dwellings will continue to leave Taxville until the income gap is closed. Given the small price effect of the movement of dwellings out of the taxing city, a large number of dwellings must leave the city: the market will move a relatively long distance up Taxville's demand curve. In equilibrium, the market will end up near point F (dwelling rent is $4,800, and a total of 480 dwellings have left the taxing city). Suppose that 475 dwellings leave Taxville, meaning that the other 99 cities each gain about 4.8 dwellings. Dwelling rent will be $4,792 in Taxville and $3,992 in the other 99 cities. At this rent, the net income of Taxville landlords ($3,992 = $4,792 − $800) equals the net income of landlords in other cities.

The 100-city case has the same aggregate effects as the 2-city case. The tax is paid by landlords: every landlord in the 100-city region receives $8 less per dwelling. The only difference is that there are 50 times as many dwellings in the 100-city case (100 cities full of dwellings instead of 2 cities), so the decrease in equilibrium rent in the nontaxing cities is one fiftieth as large ($8 instead of $400). In the taxing city, the tax increases dwelling rent by a relatively large amount because a large number of dwellings leave the city.

Tax in Both Cities.   The simple model assumes that the property tax is imposed in only one city. Suppose that both cities impose a 1 percent improvement tax. In the short run, the improvement taxes decrease the net income of landlords to $3,600. Because both cities impose a tax, there is no incentive for landlords to move their dwellings to the other city. Therefore, the short-run effect is the same as the long-run effect: the tax decreases net income, but does not affect the market rent. Landlords pay the improvement tax, just as they did in the single-tax case. Because the tax does not cause the movement of dwellings from one city to another, it does not change the equilibrium rent, so housing consumers escape the tax.

Variable Supply of Dwellings.   The simple model assumes that the total supply of dwellings is fixed. Although the tax decreases income from rental property, it does not decrease the total supply of dwellings. If the total supply of dwellings decreases as net rental income decreases, the analysis will change in three ways:

1. **Withdrawal of dwellings.** Only some of the dwellings that leave Taxville will end up in the untaxed city. Some of the dwellings will be withdrawn from the regional housing market. Suppose that one third of the dwellings that leave Taxville are transferred to the untaxed city, and two thirds are withdrawn from the regional market. In Figure 16–4, equilibrium will occur with points E and L (compared to D and M if the total supply of dwellings is fixed). The quantity of dwellings in Taxville decreases to 540 (a reduction of 360), while the quantity of dwellings in Notax increases to 1,020 (an increase of only 120), and 240 dwellings are retired from the market.

2. **Landlords lose less.** The withdrawal of dwellings increases net rental income. At points E and L, dwelling rent will be $3,800 in Notax and $4,600 in Taxville. The net income for landlords in both cities will be $3,800 (compared to $3,600 with a fixed supply of dwellings). The tax causes a smaller decrease in rental income because landlords respond to the tax by decreasing the supply of dwellings.

3. **Tenants pay part of the tax.** The withdrawal of dwellings shifts part of the tax to housing consumers. The tax increases dwelling rent to $4,600 in Taxville and decreases rent in Notax to $3,800. In other words, the loss of Taxville tenants (rent increase of $600) exceeds the gain of Notax tenants (rent reduction of $200). The tax harms Taxville tenants by more than it helps Notax tenants, so the tenant class is worse off. Because landlords decrease the supply of dwellings, they can shift part of the improvement tax to housing consumers.

Mobile Consumers.   One of the assumptions of the simple model is that tenants are immobile. When dwelling rent increases in the taxing city, none of the households leave the city. What happens if households can move to the nontaxing city?

If households can move costlessly between the two cities, they will leave the taxing city as long as it has a higher housing rent. If the market is at points D and M in Figure 16–4, housing rent (the sum of dwelling rent and land rent) will be $5,400 in the taxing city ($4,400 for the dwelling plus $1,000 for the land) and $4,600 in the untaxed city ($3,600 plus $1,000). When households leave the taxing city, the demand for Taxville land will decrease, decreasing land rent and housing rent. For example, if land rent drops to $900, housing rent will decrease to $5,300. At the same time, the migration of households to the untaxed city will bid up land rent, increasing housing rent: if land rent increases to $1,100, housing rent will increase to $4,700. In other words, migration from the taxing city to the untaxed city will narrow the difference between housing rents in the two cities. In locational equilibrium, the two cities will have the same housing rent. For example, if land rent drops to

$600 in the taxing city and rises to $1,400 in the untaxed city, housing rent will be $5,000 in both cities ($4,400 plus $600 in the taxing city and $3,600 plus $1,400 in the untaxed city).

The migration of households causes capital gains and losses for landowners. If the annual rent on Taxville land drops from $1,000 to $600, the market value of the land will drop from $10,000 to $6,000. In contrast, if rent on Notax land rises to $1,400, its market value will increase to $14,000. The migration of households eliminates the intercity differences in housing costs and replaces them with differences in the market value of land. In other words, the migration of households shifts the tenant benefits and costs of the improvement tax to landowners.

SUMMARY—WHO PAYS THE RESIDENTIAL PROPERTY TAX?

The different views and models of the property tax are cleverly designed to baffle students. Who actually pays the property tax? The incidence of the land tax is straightforward: given the perfectly inelastic supply of land, the tax is paid by landowners. The incidence of the improvement tax is not so easily summarized. The incidence of the tax depends on one's perspective.

The Local Effects of a Local Tax

Tom is the mayor of a small city in a nation of 100 cities. To predict the effects of his city's improvement tax, he should use the partial-equilibrium model. Because his city is small, it will not affect the national market for dwellings, so the assumption of a perfectly elastic supply of dwellings is a good approximation of reality. Using the partial-equilibrium model, Tom would predict that a 2 percent improvement tax will increase dwelling rent by the full amount of the tax ($800): the tax will be borne entirely by housing consumers.

Tom's analysis is not literally correct, but it is a good approximation. In one of the examples in the previous section, an improvement tax in a 100-city region increased dwelling rent in the taxing city by $792 and decreased dwelling rent in the rest of the region by $8. Because Tom doesn't care about people outside his city, he can ignore the effects of the tax on outsiders. From Tom's perspective, all that matters is that his citizens pay about $800 more for dwelling rent.

Table 16–2 shows the distribution of the property tax burden from the local perspective (the traditional view). In computing the numbers, Pechman (1985) assumes that (*a*) the land tax is borne entirely by landowners and (*b*) the improvement tax is borne entirely by housing consumers. In other words, the computational results are based on partial-equilibrium analysis. Since the income elasticity of demand for housing (or improvements) is slightly less than 1.0, the improvement tax is regressive: the ratio of tax to income decreases as

TABLE 16–2   Property Tax Incidence, Local and National Perspectives

	Property Tax as Percent of Income	
Income ($)	Local Perspective (partial equilibrium)	National Perspective (general equilibrium)
0– 5,000	7.9%	1.0%
5,000– 10,000	3.0	0.6
10,000– 15,000	2.4	0.9
15,000– 20,000	2.1	0.9
20,000– 25,000	2.1	1.0
25,000– 30,000	2.1	1.2
30,000– 50,000	2.2	1.4
50,000–100,000	2.3	2.2
100,000–500,000	2.2	3.9
500,000–1 million	2.2	5.2
Over 1 million	2.3	5.8

SOURCE: Joseph A. Pechman, *Who Paid the Taxes, 1966–85?* (Washington, D.C.: Brookings Institution, 1985), Table 3–1, p. 56.

income increases. In contrast, land ownership rises rapidly with income, so the land portion of the property tax is progressive. In combination, the two components of the tax cause the property tax to be highly regressive for incomes less than $20,000 and roughly proportional for incomes above $20,000.

The National Effects of a Local Tax

Bertha, the president of a nation of 100 cities, wants to estimate the national effects of a property tax imposed by a single city. She should use the general-equilibrium model. Under the assumption of a fixed national supply of dwellings, the improvement tax will be paid by capitalists in the form of a lower return on capital (lower net income from rental property). The tax will cause zero-sum changes in housing costs: consumers outside the taxing city gain at the expense of consumers in the taxing city.

Table 16–2 shows the distribution of the property tax burden from the national perspective (the new view). In computing the numbers, Pechman (1985) assumes that (*a*) the land tax is borne entirely by landowners and (*b*) the improvement tax is borne entirely by capitalists. In other words, the computational results are based on general-equilibrium analysis. Because capital and land ownership increase rapidly with income, the property tax is progressive for incomes above $5,000: the tax burden as a fraction of income increases with income.

What if Bertha assumes that the supply of capital is not fixed? If the supply is not perfectly inelastic, part of the tax will be shifted to housing consumers. The price of housing will increase by a relatively large amount in the taxing city and will decrease by a relatively small amount in the other 99 cities. As a result, the average cost of housing will increase.

The Effects of a National Tax

Sam is the president of a nation in which all 100 cities have the same property tax. He wants to estimate the effect of the improvement tax. Because all cities impose the tax, the improvement tax does not cause any movement of capital between cities. Under the assumption of a fixed national supply of capital, the tax is borne entirely by capitalists. The tax does not affect the cost of housing because there is nowhere for the dwellings to move. Under the assumption that the supply of capital is not perfectly inelastic, the tax will be split between housing consumers and capitalists, with the consumers' share increasing as the elasticity of supply of capital increases.

Summary of Incidence Results

Table 16–3 summarizes the results of the analysis of the property tax. It shows who pays the tax under different assumptions about the type of tax (a tax in a small city versus a national tax), household mobility, and the response of landlords to the tax (fixed versus variable supply of dwellings). It also lists the welfare effects for three types of jurisdictions: the taxing city, the nontaxing city, and the nation.

ADMINISTERING THE PROPERTY TAX

Because the property tax is based on the value of the property, the local government must periodically assess the value of the property. The annual tax liability of a piece of property is

$$\text{Tax} = \text{Nominal tax rate} \cdot \text{Assessed value} \qquad (16\text{--}1)$$

The assessed value is

$$\text{Assessed value} = \text{Assessment ratio} \cdot \text{Market value} \qquad (16\text{--}2)$$

If the assessment ratio is 25 percent, a house with a market value of $120,000 will receive an assessed value of $30,000. If the nominal tax rate is 10 percent, the tax liability is $3,000 (10 percent of the assessed value). The **effective tax rate**, defined as the tax liability divided by market value, is only 2.5 percent ($3,000 divided by $120,000). The effective tax rate is less than the nominal tax rate because the assessed value is less than the market value.

Most local governments systematically underassess property. According to the Census of Governments, the average assessment ratio was 0.40 in 1981, meaning that the typical property was assessed at 40 percent of its market value. If all property in a jurisdiction is subject to the same assessment ratio, underassessment does not affect tax liabilities or effective tax rates, but simply

TABLE 16–3   Who Pays the Property Tax?

Tax Imposed by a Small City
  Welfare effects in the taxing city
    1. Immobile households: consumers pay higher dwelling rent.
    2. Mobile households: landowners receive lower land rent.
  Welfare effects in a nontaxing city
    1. Immobile households: consumers pay lower dwelling rent.
    2. Mobile households: landowners receive higher land rent.
  National welfare effects
    1. Landlords (capitalists) receive lower net rental income.
    2. Immobile households
      a. Fixed supply of dwellings: zero-sum changes in dwelling rent.
      b. Variable supply of dwellings: net increase in dwelling rent.
    3. Mobile households
      a. Fixed supply of dwellings: zero-sum changes in land rent.
      b. Variable supply of dwellings: net decrease in land rent.
Tax Imposed by All Cities (A National Property Tax)
  Welfare effects in the taxing cities
    1. Fixed supply of dwellings: housing consumers and landowners unaffected by
      the tax.
    2. Variable supply of dwellings: dwelling rent increases and land rent decreases.
  National welfare effects
    1. Landlords (capital owners) receive lower net rental income.
    2. Fixed supply of dwellings: landlords pay the entire tax.
    3. Variable supply of dwellings: tax shared by capitalists, consumers, and land-
      owners.

requires a higher nominal tax rate to generate the same tax revenue. In other words, a local government can offset a low assessment ratio with a higher nominal tax rate.

In most jurisdictions, assessment ratios also vary from one piece of property to another. Some of the variation is caused by random assessment errors, a reflection of the imperfections of the assessment process. Assessment errors are systematic if the assessment ratio varies systematically with property value. In many cities, the assessment ratio is inversely related to property value: as property value increases, the assessment ratio decreases. This practice of regressive assessment has been documented by Engle (1975), Black (1977), Ihlanfeldt (1982), and Netzer (1980).

Table 16–4 illustrates the effects of regressive assessment. There are three households, poor, middle-income, and wealthy. Each household owns a home with a market value equal to three times its income. The nominal tax rate is 10 percent. Under a proportional assessment scheme, all properties are assessed at 50 percent of market value and tax liabilities are proportional to income. The poor household pays a 10 percent tax on an assessed value of

TABLE 16–4   Systematic Assessment Errors

	Poor	Middle-Income	Wealthy
Income ($)	20,000	30,000	40,000
Market value of house ($)	60,000	90,000	120,000
Proportional assessment			
Assessment ratio (%)	50	50	50
Assessed value ($)	30,000	45,000	60,000
Nominal tax rate (%)	10	10	10
Tax liability ($)	3,000	4,500	6,000
Effective tax rate (%)	5	5	5
Tax as fraction of income (%)	15	15	15
Regressive assessment			
Assessment ratio (%)	60	50	40
Assessed value ($)	36,000	45,000	48,000
Nominal tax rate (%)	10	10	10
Tax liability ($)	3,600	4,500	4,800
Effective tax rate (%)	6	5	4
Tax as fraction of income (%)	18	15	12

$30,000, generating a tax liability of $3,000, which is 15 percent of its $20,000 income. The other households also pay 15 percent of their income in property taxes, so the property tax is a proportional tax. Note that this example adopts the traditional view of the property tax: housing consumers pay the tax.

Under a regressive assessment policy, the poor, who occupy low-value housing, face an assessment ratio of 60 percent, compared to assessment ratios of 50 percent for middle-income households and 40 percent for the wealthy. The switch to regressive assessment increases the tax liability of the poor from $3,000 to $3,600 and decreases the tax liability of the wealthy from $6,000 to $4,800. Under regressive assessment, the property tax is regressive. The fraction of income spent on property taxes is a decreasing function of income: the poor pay 18 percent of their income on the property tax, while the middle-income households pay 15 percent and the rich pay 12 percent.

There are two reasons for regressive assessment practices. First, assessors do not always keep up with changes in property value: unless property is reassessed as it increases in value, the assessment ratio will decrease over time. Because market values typically rise more rapidly in wealthy neighborhoods, the assessment ratio of high-income housing decreases relatively fast over time (see Engle 1975). Second, assessors sometimes discriminate against multifamily properties, assessing them at higher rates than single-family properties. Because a large fraction of the poor live in multifamily buildings, the poor face higher effective tax rates. This phenomenon is discussed by Aaron (1975) and Netzer (1980).

THE TAX ON COMMERCIAL AND INDUSTRIAL PROPERTY

The model of Taxville assumes that the city has only residential property, so the property tax is effectively a tax on residential property. This section discusses the effects of the general property tax (a tax on residential, commercial, and industrial property) in cities with all three types of property.

The General Property Tax

The analysis of the land portion of the general property tax is straightforward. Because the supply of land is perfectly inelastic, the tax is paid entirely by landowners. The land tax does not affect land rent, but simply decreases the annual rental income by the amount of the tax. The decrease in net rental income decreases the market value of the land.

What about the tax on improvements? Suppose that a city imposes a 2 percent tax on residential, commercial, and industrial structures. In the short run, the supply of structures is fixed, so the tax decreases the net income of the city's landlords. In the long run, landlords will move their structures to Notax, the other city in the region. The movement of capital will increase the rent on structures in the taxing city and decrease it elsewhere. For example, rent in the taxing city might rise from $4,000 to $4,400 and decrease elsewhere to $3,600. The changes in structure rents will change the prices of consumer goods: the price of consumer goods will increase in the taxing city and decrease elsewhere. The changes in structure rents will also equalize net property income at $3,600.

Differential Tax Rates

Most jurisdictions impose the same nominal tax rate on residential and business property. Because assessment ratios differ across property types, however, effective tax rates often differ. Consider a city with the following characteristics.

1. There are two types of structures: houses and pizza parlors.
2. The city starts with the same effective tax rates on pizza parlors and houses.
3. The total capital in the city (the total number of structures) is fixed.
4. Structures can be used as either houses or pizza parlors.
5. In the initial equilibrium, the annual rent on a structure is $4,000.

Suppose that the city cuts the property tax rate on pizza parlors and increases the tax rate on housing. The change in tax policy is revenue-neutral: the loss of revenue from pizza parlors equals the gain in tax revenue from residences. The new tax policy causes the following changes in the city:

1. **Transfer of capital.** Landlords will move capital from the residential sector to the more lucrative pizza sector.

2. **Increased dwelling rent.** The movement of capital out of the housing sector will increase dwelling rent.

3. **Decreased pizza prices.** The movement of capital into the pizza sector will decrease the price of pizza.

Who gains and who loses? The change in tax policy is revenue-neutral, so landlords, as a class, are not affected by the change in tax policy. Housing consumers lose because the price of housing increases, and pizza consumers gain because the price of pizza decreases. This general-equilibrium analysis suggests that differences in effective tax rates are reflected in differences in consumer prices. If a city taxes residential property at a higher rate than business property, its citizens pay more for housing but less for other goods.

What if nonresidential goods are consumed by people outside the city? The taxation of property used in the production of exports will increase the export price, so part of the city's tax burden will be borne by consumers outside the city. This is known as **tax exporting**: the city uses tax revenue from outsiders to pay for local government. Suppose that a large fraction of the city's pizza is consumed by outsiders. If the city wants to decrease the local tax burden, it could cut the residential tax rate and increase the tax rate on commercial property (including pizza parlors). Although pizza prices will increase, partly offsetting the decrease in housing costs, local consumers will be better off because a larger fraction of local taxes will be shifted to outsiders.

What are the limits to tax exporting? The taxation of exports will decrease the city's commercial tax base. Consumers will respond to the increase in price by decreasing the quantity of exports demanded. In addition, export firms will have the incentive to move to cities with lower taxes. As the volume of exports decreases, the amount of commercial property will decrease. Because taxation decreases the city's tax base, there are limits to tax exporting. Tax exporting is more likely in a city that (*a*) sells a product with relatively inelastic demand, and (*b*) has a unique production advantage that makes it the dominant locational choice for export firms.

THE TIEBOUT MODEL AND THE PROPERTY TAX

The Tiebout model, introduced in the previous chapter, suggests that citizens shop for municipalities and school districts. In equilibrium, households sort themselves with respect to (*a*) the demand for public goods and (*b*) housing consumption. This section discusses the implications of the Tiebout process for the incidence of the property tax.

Consider Metro, a metropolitan area with the following characteristics:

1. **Local public good.** Municipalities provide a single public good (parks).

2. **Income and house value.** Half the households are wealthy and have $100,000 houses. Half are poor and have $50,000 houses.

3. **Park demands.** Half the households in each income group want a large park budget ($2,000), and half want a small park budget ($200).

4. **Municipalities and zoning.** Households can set up new municipalities, using large-lot zoning to establish minimum house values.

As shown in Table 16–5, households will sort themselves with respect to park demands and property values, forming four municipalities. There are two wealthy communities, one with a large park budget (tax rate = 2.0 percent) and one with a small park budget (tax rate = 0.20 percent). Similarly, there are two poor municipalities.

Because the households in Metro sort themselves into homogeneous communities, the property tax is a user fee, not a conventional tax. The tax liability of a particular household depends on its park consumption, not on its housing consumption (property value). Every household pays a tax equal to its desired park budget, regardless of its property value: the poor pay a higher tax rate to generate the same park budget as their counterparts in the wealthy community; the low spenders pay a lower tax rate than their counterparts in the high-spending municipalities. In the Tiebout world, there is no link between property value and property tax liability. Instead, the tax liability depends strictly on park consumption.

In the Tiebout world, an increase in housing consumption will not affect property taxes. Suppose that a few of the wealthy, high-spending households decide to buy $200,000 homes. They will form a new community of high-spending households with $200,000 houses and will finance their $2,000 park program with a 1 percent property tax. The doubling of housing consumption cuts the property tax rate in half, so property taxes remain at $2,000. In general, a change in housing consumption will cause the household to move to a community where other households have (*a*) the same demand for public goods and (*b*) the same housing consumption.

In the Tiebout world, a discussion of the incidence of the property tax is meaningless. If households are sorted into homogeneous communities, the property tax is a user fee, and every household gets exactly what it pays for. The incidence of a $200 tax liability is the same as the incidence of a $1 paid for a hot dog: you pay the $1 to get the hot dog; you pay the $200 tax to get $200 worth of parks. Since the consumer's tax liability is independent of housing choice, the property tax is a user fee, not a conventional tax.

How realistic is the Tiebout model? The conditions required for Tiebout equilibrium are unlikely to be satisfied. There are simply not enough local

TABLE 16–5 Tiebout Sorting and the Property Tax

Municipality	Property Value ($)	Park Budget ($)	Tax Rate (%)
Wealthy—Large Budget	100,000	2,000	2.0
Wealthy—Small Budget	100,000	200	0.20
Poor—Large Budget	50,000	2,000	4.0
Poor—Small Budget	50,000	200	0.40

governments to allow households to sort themselves into perfectly homogeneous communities. The Tiebout model is clearly inapplicable to central cities where a single municipality serves a large and diverse population. Therefore, the central-city property tax is not a user fee, but a conventional tax. In the suburbs, where there is more sorting of households with respect to demands for public services and housing consumption, the property tax is closer to a user fee.

OTHER TAXES

Property taxes generate less than half of municipal tax revenue. As shown in Figure 16–1, the sales tax raises 29 percent of municipal tax revenue and the income tax raises 14 percent of municipal revenue. Larger cities rely to a greater extent on the municipal income tax: the income tax generates 22 percent of tax revenue in cities with populations greater than 300,000. This section discusses the incidence of the municipal sales tax and income tax.

Municipal Sales Tax

Who pays the municipal sales tax? According to the theory of tax incidence, the distribution of the tax burden depends on the elasticities of supply and demand: the relatively inelastic side of the market will pay a relatively large share of the tax.

Figure 16–5 shows the effects of a 25 percent general sales tax. The market starts at point B, with an equilibrium price of $8 and an equilibrium quantity of 30 units. The tax is paid, in legal terms, by the city's merchants: their costs increase by 25 percent, shifting the supply curve upward. The equilibrium net price (the price charged by the merchant plus the tax) will rise to $9.00, and total sales will decrease to 25 units (point C). Merchants charge consumers $9 and pay the government $1.80 in taxes, leaving them with $7.20. In this example, consumers pay about 55 percent of the tax (the $1 increase in price divided by the $1.80 tax).

How does a change in the elasticity of demand affect the distribution of the tax burden? Suppose that the demand curve in Figure 16–5 becomes more elastic: its slope decreases, and it pivots around point B. The flatter demand curve (shown by the dashed line) intersects the posttax supply curve at a lower net price, so consumers pay a smaller fraction of the tax. A relatively elastic demand means that consumers can more easily change their behavior, so they are better able to escape the tax.

How does a change in the supply elasticity affect the distribution of the tax burden? Suppose the initial supply curve in Figure 16–5 is horizontal (perfectly elastic). The sales tax will again shift the supply curve up by the amount of the tax, and the posttax supply curve will intersect the demand curve at a price equal to the original price plus the tax. In other words, if supply is perfectly elastic, consumers bear the entire tax. In general, the more elastic the

FIGURE 16–5   Effects of Municipal Sales Tax

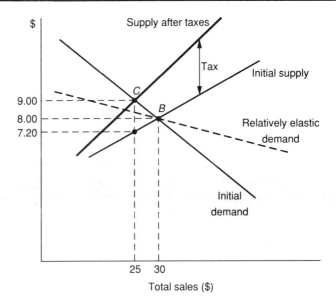

Before the sales tax, B is the equilibrium point. A 25% sales tax shifts the supply curve upward by 25%, generating a new equilibrium at point C. The consumer price rises from $8 to $9, and the net revenue of the merchant (price less tax) drops from $8 to $7.20.

supply curve (the flatter the curve), the smaller the supplier burden and the larger the consumer burden.

The sales tax also affects the urban land market. As the city's sales volume decreases, the demands for all inputs (labor, land, capital) decrease: merchants need fewer laborers, machines, buildings, and land. In the short run, the prices of these inputs will fall. In the long run, inputs that are mobile (e.g., labor and capital) will leave the taxing city, and the prices of these mobile inputs will recover. In contrast, land is immobile, so the tax-induced decrease in the demand for land will cause a long-term decrease in the price of land. Therefore, part of the sales tax will be borne by landowners. Although merchants receive a lower net price ($7.20 instead of $8), they can still make zero economic profit (normal accounting profit) because they pay less for land.

This discussion of the city's input markets shows the link between the tax policy and economic development. The sales tax increases the net price of the city's products, so the city will produce less output and use less capital, labor, and land. In other words, the tax decreases output and employment. The local economy is particularly sensitive to changes in taxes because firms and households can easily move between jurisdictions. Because of the high de-gree of intercity mobility, a relatively small change in tax rates can cause relatively large changes in the level of economic activity.

Municipal Income Tax

The income tax generates about one sixth of municipal tax revenue. Table 16–6 shows the importance of municipal income tax for several large cities. For the four Ohio cities in the table, the municipal income tax generates well over two thirds of municipal taxes. For the other cities listed in the table, the contribution ranges from 29 percent (New York City) to 65 percent (Phila-delphia). For all large cities, the income tax generated 21 percent of municipal taxes in 1984, up from 17 percent in 1972.

Who pays the municipal income tax? It will be useful to compare the mu-nicipal income tax to a national income tax. Figure 16–6 shows the effect of a national income tax. In the initial equilibrium (point B), the wage is $8 and the quantity of labor is N_o. Suppose that the federal government imposes an in-come tax of $2 per hour, which is paid, in legal terms, by the employer. The tax shifts the demand curve down by $2, decreasing the market wage (paid to employees) from $8 to $6.10. The net cost of labor (the wage plus the employ-er's tax liability) rises from $8 to $8.10. Workers pay almost the entire tax be-cause the supply of labor is relatively inelastic.

TABLE 16–6   Local Income Taxes as Percent of Local Taxes in Selected Cities

City	Percent of Taxes from Income Tax	
	1972	1984
Baltimore	14%	20%
Cincinnati	58	69
Cleveland	48	75
Columbus	78	86
Detroit	35	49
Kansas City	37	31
New York City	21	29
Philadelphia	63	65
Pittsburgh	17	30
St. Louis	29	31
Toledo	75	84
All large cities (pop > 300,000)	17	21

SOURCE: J. Richard Aronson, and John L. Hilley, *Financing State and Local Governments* (Washington, D.C.: Brookings Institution, 1986), Table 8–6, p. 151.

FIGURE 16–6 Effects of a National Income Tax

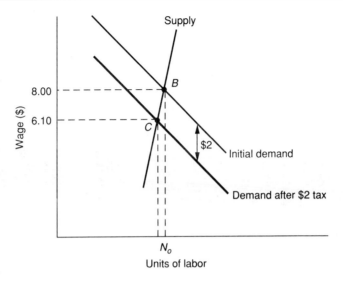

The initial equilibrium is point *B*. A $2 labor tax (paid by the employer) shifts the demand curve down by the amount of the tax, generating a new equilibrium at point *C*. The equilibrium wage (paid to laborers) drops from $8 to $6.10, meaning that workers pay about 95% of the $2 tax.

Figure 16–7 shows the effect of a municipal income tax. Because laborers can move easily from one municipality to another, the municipal supply curve is more elastic than the national supply curve. When the municipality imposes a $2 income tax, the demand curve shifts down by $2, decreasing the market wage from $8 to $7. Compared to the national income tax, the municipal tax causes a smaller decrease in the market wage ($1 instead of $1.90) because it is easier for workers to escape the municipal tax by leaving the jurisdiction. Because intercity migration is less costly than international migration, laborers bear a smaller fraction of the municipal tax.

The municipal income tax increases the net cost of labor from $8 to $9. In other words, the demander's share of the tax is $1. If all firms make zero profit, who actually pays this part of the tax? The tax is paid by the owners of immobile resources, that is, people who own inputs that cannot be moved to other cities with the fleeing laborers. As the level of economic activity in the taxing city decreases (the number of laborers decreases from M' to M''), the demand for land decreases, thus lowering the price of land. Although firms pay a higher net wage ($9 instead of $8), they also pay less for land, so they can still make zero economic profit.

FIGURE 16–7   Effects of Municipal Income Tax

The initial equilibrium is point *D*. A $2 labor tax (paid by the employer) shifts the demand curve down by the amount of the tax, generating a new equilibrium at point *E*. The equilibrium wage (paid to laborers) drops from $8 to $7, meaning that suppliers pay only about half of the $2 tax. Workers pay a smaller portion of the municipal tax because the municipal supply of labor is more elastic than the national supply.

INTERGOVERNMENTAL GRANTS

As shown in Table 16–1, intergovernmental grants provide about 40 percent of local government revenue. Between 1950 and 1980, the relative importance of intergovernmental grants grew, rising from 32 percent of local revenue to 44 percent. Since then, the fraction of revenue from grants has decreased, reaching 40 percent in 1985. The municipal spending programs that are most heavily dependent on intergovernmental grants are education (52 percent of spending from grants), welfare (76 percent), and housing and community development (62 percent) (see U.S. Bureau of Census 1985).

Table 16–7 shows the amounts and types of grants from the federal and state governments. In 1984, the federal government provided about 14 percent of the grants to local governments and about 29 percent of the grants to municipalities. The two largest federal grant programs were for housing and community development (about 4.5 percent of total local grants) and education (1.03 percent of local grants). Between 1972 and 1987, the federal government provided general (unrestricted) grants under the revenue-sharing program. State governments provided about 86 percent of grants to local governments and about 71 percent of grants to municipalities. About two thirds

TABLE 16–7   Federal and State Grants to Local Governments, 1984–85

Source and Type of Grant	All Local Governments		Municipalities	
	Amount ($ thousands)	% of Total	Amount ($ thousands)	% of Total
Federal government				
Education	1,516	1.03%	251	0.73%
Public welfare	392	0.27	280	0.81
Health and hospitals	307	0.21	98	0.28
Highways	288	0.20	167	0.49
Housing and community Development	6,635	4.51	3,426	9.96
General revenue sharing	4,424	3.00	2,358	6.85
Other	6,870	4.67	3,233	9.39
Total federal	20,432	13.88	9,813	28.52
State government				
Education	81,187	55.13	5,936	17.25
Public welfare	14,840	10.08	4,475	13.00
Health and hospitals	3,555	2.41	621	1.80
Highways	6,270	4.26	2,477	7.20
General support	11,801	8.01	7,085	20.59
Other	9,171	6.23	4,006	11.64
Total state	126,824	86.12	24,600	71.48
Total state and federal	147,256	100.00	34,413	100.00

SOURCE: U.S. Bureau of the Census, *City Government Finances in 1984–85* (Washington, D.C.: U.S. Government Printing Office, 1986).

of the state money was spent on education. Chapter 19 (Education) discusses several types of intergovernmental grants for education.

Why Intergovernmental Grants?

Why don't local governments pay their own way, supporting their spending programs with local taxes? There are two principal reasons. First, intergovernmental grants can be used to internalize interjurisdictional spillovers, as discussed in Chapter 15 (Decision Making in Local Government). Second, local tax instruments are relatively inflexible, causing mismatches between local tax revenue and local expenditures.

The Mismatch Problem.   The mismatch problem occurs if the desired spending on local public goods rises faster than the tax base. Figure 16–8 shows the mismatch problem for a city with the following characteristics:

1. Local public goods are financed with the residential property tax.
2. Income is rising twice as fast as property values.

3. The desired spending on local public goods is proportional to income: the income elasticity of demand for local public goods is 1.0.

At the start of the decade, the desired spending equals the average property tax liability. Because income increases at twice the rate as property values, the desired spending increases twice as fast as the average tax liability. By the end of the decade, there is a $50 gap between desired spending and taxes. The mismatch occurs because (*a*) property values are relatively sluggish and (*b*) the tax rate is fixed.

There are two possible responses to the mismatch problem. The obvious response is to increase the tax rate. The alternative approach is to transfer surplus federal tax revenue to the local government. The federal income tax will generate a surplus if (*a*) the income tax has a progressive rate structure and (*b*) federal spending is a constant fraction of income. In Figure 16–8, a federal transfer of $50 per capita would solve the local mismatch problem.

The Tax Revolt and Intergovernmental Grants. The mismatch model provides a useful framework for analyzing the property tax revolt in the state of California. In 1978, Californians voted overwhelmingly for Proposition 13, which established a maximum property tax rate of 1 percent. One of the rea-

FIGURE 16–8 Mismatch between Desired Spending and Tax Revenue

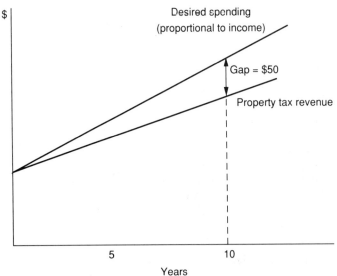

If income rises twice as fast as property values, the desired spending rises twice as fast as property tax revenue. The gap between tax revenue and desired spending grows to $50 by the end of the decade. An increase in the tax rate would close the gap.

FIGURE 16–9   Mismatch and Proposition 13

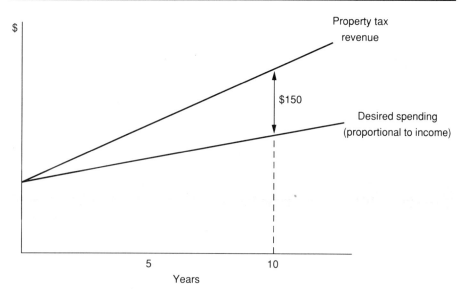

If property values increase twice as fast as income, tax revenue will increase twice as fast as desired spending. The gap between taxes and desired spending grows to $150 by the end of the decade.

sons for the revolt was that there was a mismatch between desired spending and tax liabilities.

Figure 16–9 shows the California situation in the decade preceding the passage of Proposition 13. In the 1960s and 1970s, rapid population growth caused rapid increases in property values. The figure is drawn under the assumption that property values increased twice as fast as income (and desired spending). Proposition 13, which cut the tax rate to 1 percent, cut local tax revenue to the point at which most local governments experienced large budget shortfalls. The state government, which had built up a large surplus, used intergovernmental grants to rescue the local governments.

Unconditional Grants

An unconditional grant is a lump-sum grant with no strings attached. An example of an unconditional grant is general revenue sharing, a program under which the federal government provided unrestricted grants to localities. The local response to an unconditional grant can be predicted by examining the effects of the grant on the preferences of the median voter.

Responses to Unconditional Grant. Figure 16–10 shows the budget lines and indifference curves of Marian, the median voter in city G. The city provides a number of local public goods and pays for them with local taxes: for every dollar spent on public goods, there is $1 of taxes, so there is one less dollar to spend on private goods. The indifference curves, which show Marian's subjective trade-off between public and private goods, are convex, reflecting the diminishing marginal rate of substitution between public and private goods. Given the initial budget line (*AB*) and her indifference curves, Marian's utility is maximized at point *E*. According to the median-voter model (described in Chapter 15, Decision Making in Local Government), the city will choose the preferred budget of the median voter, so the city will spend $25 per household on public goods, leaving Marian $45 for private goods.

Suppose that the state gives the city an unconditional grant of $20 per

FIGURE 16–10 Effects of a $20 Unconditional Grant

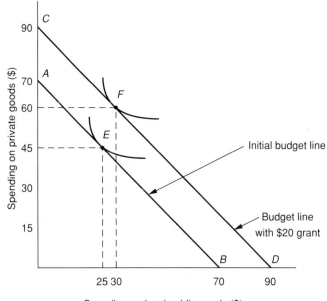

Spending on local public goods ($)

An unconditional grant of $20 per capita shifts the budget line of the median voter from *AB* to *CD*. The utility-maximizing combination of public and private goods moves from point *E* to point *F*. Spending on local public goods increases by $5, and spending on private goods increases by $15. The local government responds to the grant by cutting local taxes, allowing citizens to spend three fourths of the grant on private goods.

household. The city makes the following announcement to its citizens: "The state has just given us $20 per household. Tell us how much to spend on public services, and we'll cut taxes to distribute the rest of the grant to you." The grant shifts Marian's budget line upward, from AB to CD, increasing her desired spending on public goods to $30 (point F). The city, adhering to the preferences of the median voter, increases its budget by $5 and cuts taxes, thus distributing the rest of the grant ($15) to its citizens. The tax cut allows Marian to increase private consumption to $60.

The Flypaper Effect. One of the predictions of the median-voter model is that an unconditional grant has the same effect on local spending as an equal increase in per capita income. In fact, there is conclusive evidence that cities spend a relatively large fraction of an unconditional grant on public goods, meaning that a grant is not equivalent to an increase in income. This phenomenon is known as the **flypaper effect**: the grant money sticks where it first hits (the local government).

Some of the theories of the flypaper effect assume that city officials either confuse or deceive their citizens. In a model developed by Filimon, Romer, and Rosenthal (1982), the objective of city bureaucrats is to maximize the city budget. If bureaucrats do not publicize the grant, citizens are unlikely to demand tax cuts, so a large fraction of the grant can be used to increase government spending.

Lump-Sum Conditional Grants

The money from a **conditional grant** or **categorical grant** must be spent on a specific program. As shown in Table 16–7, conditional grants are provided for education, public welfare, health and hospitals, highways, housing, and community development. There are program-specific grants within each expenditure group. For example, the $1.5 billion in education grants is composed of specific grants for remedial reading, school libraries, special education, and other programs.

Response to Conditional Grant. Suppose that the state gives the city a lump-sum grant of $20 per capita for special-education programs. Figure 16–11 shows Marian's preferences for special education and all other goods. "Other goods" includes private goods and other local public goods. The grant shifts Marian's budget line from AB to AGD. Point G is in the new budget set because Marian could spend all of her own money on other goods and use the $20 grant to support special education. As spending on special education increases above $20, there is a dollar-for-dollar trade-off between spending on special education and other goods, so the slope of the budget line is 1.0.

The grant increases Marian's desired spending on both special education and other goods. If the city adheres to the preferences of the median voter, spending on special education will increase from $25 to $30 and spending on other goods will increase from $45 to $60. One quarter of the grant is spent on special education, and three fourths is spent on other goods.

The city can spend part of the grant on other goods because it decreases its own contribution to special education. Before the grant, $25 of local tax money was spent on special education. After the grant, spending on special education is $30, and the city can pay for its special-education program with the $20 grant and $10 of local tax money. The grant frees up $15 worth of local tax money, which can be spent on other local public goods and private goods.

Equivalence to Unconditional Grant? In Figure 16–11, the conditional grant is equivalent to an unconditional grant. Because the city's desired spending exceeds the grant, the city can replace its own spending on special education with the grant: in effect, the grant has no strings attached. In graphic terms, the budget lines of the two grants are identical as long as the desired

---

FIGURE 16–11 Effects of a $20 Conditional Grant

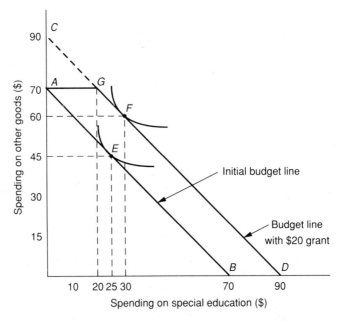

A conditional grant of $20 per capita shifts the budget line of the median voter from *AB* to *AGD*. The utility-maximizing combination moves from point *E* to point *F*: one fourth of the grant is spent on special education. The city uses the grant to decrease its contribution to special education, providing more money to spend on other goods. Because the desired spending on special education exceeds the grant, the conditional grant is equivalent to an unconditional grant.

spending exceeds the grant (i.e., as long as the city chooses a point to the right of G).

The conditional grant will not be equivalent to the unconditional grant if the desired spending on special education is less than $20. Suppose that the city starts with spending of $5 on special education and the desired spending increases to $10 under the unconditional grant. In other words, the city moves to a point midway along the segment CG. In contrast, the city is likely to choose point G under the conditional grant. Since the city wants to spend less than $20 on special education, it cannot substitute the conditional grant for its own spending on special education, so a conditional grant is not equivalent to an unconditional grant. The conditional grant generates a lower utility level for citizens but a larger increase in spending on special education.

Matching Grants

Under a matching grant, the government contributes $m for every $1 of local spending on a program. One possibility is a one-for-one matching grant: every $1 of local spending generates $1 in grant money, so $1 of local spending buys $2 worth of local public goods. There are two types of matching grants, open-ended and closed-ended.

Open-Ended Matching Grants.   Figure 16–12 shows the effect of a one-for-one matching grant for special education. The grant decreases the slope of Marian's budget line from 1.0 to 0.50: instead of a dollar-for-dollar trade-off, Marian gets $2 worth of special education for every $1 she diverts from other goods. Given the new budget line, Marian's optimum point moves from point E to point H. If the city adheres to the preferences of the median voter, spending on special education will increase from $25 to $40 and spending on other goods will increase from $45 to $50. Half of the city's $40 special-education budget comes from the state government, so the local contribution to special education is $20, leaving $50 for spending on other goods. In other words, the city spends one quarter of the matching grant on other goods.

The matching grant provides a greater stimulus to special education than an equivalent lump-sum conditional grant. Although the state spends the same amount on each type of grant ($20), the matching grant increases spending on special education to $40, while the lump-sum grant increases spending to only $30 (see Figure 16–11). The matching grant has a relatively large stimulative effect because it has both an income effect and a substitution effect. Both grants increase real income by $20 per capita, increasing the demand for all normal goods, including special education (the income effect). The matching grant also has a substitution effect: the matching grant cuts the relative price of special education in half (from 1.0 to 0.50), causing the substitution of special education for other goods. Since the matching grant has a substitution effect as well as an income effect, it increases spending by a larger amount.

The information in Figure 16–12 could be used to plot two points on the

FIGURE 16–12 Effects of Open-Ended Matching Grant

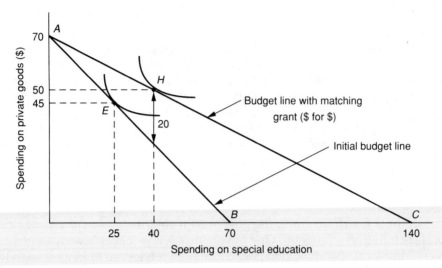

An open-ended matching grant shifts the budget line of the median voter from *AB* to *AC*. The utility-maximizing combination moves from point *E* to point *H*: three fourths of the grant is spent on special education. The matching grant decreases the opportunity cost of spending on special education, providing a greater stimulus to special education than an equivalent lump-sum grant.

city's demand curve for special education. Before the matching grant, the "price" of special education is $1: there is a dollar-for-dollar trade-off between special education and other goods. At a price of $1, the quantity of special education demanded is 25 (point *E*). The matching grant decreases the price to $0.50 and increases the quantity demanded to 40 (point *H*). Because the grant does not affect the other determinants of demand (income and other prices), points *E* and *H* identify two points on the demand curve: ($1, $25) and ($0.50, $40).

Closed-Ended Matching Grants. Under a closed-ended matching grant, the government specifies a maximum grant. In Figure 16–13, the maximum grant is $30: the government provides matching funds up to a total of $30. The budget line has a kink at the point at which the grant limit sets in. Given a one-for-one matching grant, the kink occurs when spending on special education (the sum of city spending and grant money) reaches $60. For spending above $60 (below point *D*), every additional dollar spent on special education decreases local spending on other goods by $1, so the slope of the budget line is 1.0.

FIGURE 16–13   Effects of Closed-Ended Matching Grant

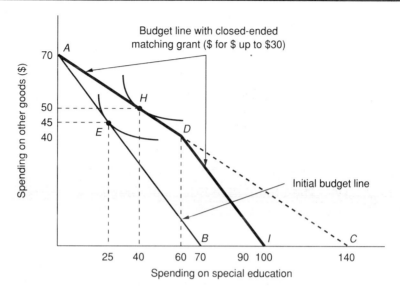

A closed-ended matching grant shifts the budget line of the median voter from AB to ADI. The utility-maximizing combination moves from point E to point H. Since the desired spending level ($40) is less than the limit ($60), the grant limit is irrelevant and the closed-ended grant is equivalent to the open-ended grant. If desired spending exceeded the limit, the city would spend less under the closed-ended grant than under the open-ended grant.

In Figure 16–13, the city's response to the closed-ended grant program is the same as its response to the open-ended program. Since the desired spending level ($40) is less than the limit, the grant limit is irrelevant. Therefore, the closed-ended grant is equivalent to the open-ended grant.

The two grants are not equivalent if the desired spending under the open-ended grant exceeds $60. In Figure 16–13, the open-ended budget line is the line ADC and the closed-ended budget line is ADI. If the desired spending under the open-ended grant exceeds $60, the city will choose a point along the segment DC. In this region, the open-ended budget line (segment DC) lies above the closed-ended budget line (segment DI). Spending will be larger under the open-ended grant for two reasons. First, real income is higher under the open-ended grant, producing an income effect that increases spending on all normal goods, including special education. Second, the opportunity cost of special education is lower under the open-ended grant, producing a substitution effect that reinforces the income effect.

Block Grants

Under a block-grant program, dozens of conditional grants are consolidated into a single general grant. For example, all grants for education (for special education, remedial reading, kindergartens, libraries) could be consolidated into a single block grant for education. The block grant is a compromise between unconditional and conditional grants. Although the city is forced to spend the entire education block grant on education, it can decide how to allocate the money between special education, remedial reading, kindergartens, and libraries. This greater flexibility is welcomed by local officials, but is often opposed by state and federal officials because they lose some control over grant money.

Summary—The Stimulative Effects of Grants

As explained earlier in the chapter, local governments use intergovernmental grants to increase local spending and cut local taxes. The tax cuts allow local citizens to spend part of the grant on private goods. The empirical question is: What fraction of grant money is used for additional local spending, and how much is used to cut taxes? Inman (1979) summarizes the results of several studies of the local response to grants. He concludes that local-government spending increases by about 30 cents per dollar of grant money, leaving 70 cents per dollar for tax relief.

CAPITALIZATION AND THE REDISTRIBUTIVE EFFECTS OF GRANTS

Intergovernmental grants are often used to promote income redistribution. Grants are targeted to two types of communities: those with a relatively large number of low-income households and those with relatively high tax rates.

Grants to Low-Income Communities

Consider a state with two cities, a wealthy one and a poor one. In the poor city, all households rent housing for $400 per month. In an attempt to redistribute income from the rich to the poor, the state imposes a tax on the wealthy city and uses the tax revenue to support a $100 grant (per household) to the poor city. Suppose that the poor city responds to the grant by cutting its income tax by $100 per household.

Figure 16–14 shows the effect of the grant program on the housing market in the poor city. The decrease in local taxes increases the relative attractiveness of the city, causing migration to the city that shifts the demand curve for housing upward. The equilibrium price of housing increases from $400 to $435. Because the grant increases the price of housing, the net benefit per household is only $65 ($100 less the $35 increase in rent).

FIGURE 16–14   Grant to Poor City and the Price of Housing

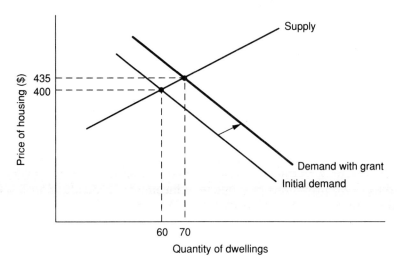

A grant to a poor community increases the relative attractiveness of the community, increasing the demand for housing and housing prices. The grant is capitalized into housing prices, so some of the benefits of the grant go to property owners.

The intergovernmental grant is a blunt instrument for income redistribution for two reasons. First, the grant is tied to a location, not to a poor household. The grant increases the market value of land and housing in the poor city, generating benefits for landlords. In other words, the grant is capitalized into housing and land prices. Second, although part of the grant goes to households in the recipient city, all households in the city benefit, not just poor households.

Grants to High-Tax Communities

Under some grant programs, the size of the grant depends on local tax effort. A city with relatively high tax rates receives a relatively large grant. Is this equitable?

Suppose that there are two cities in a region, North and South. North has harsh winters, so the city has high taxes to support large expenditures on highway maintenance. In contrast, South has mild winters and a relatively low tax rate. In equilibrium, people must be indifferent between living in the two cities, so the differences in tax rates will be capitalized into property values. Although the residents of North will pay high taxes, they will also be able to buy inexpensive land and housing. Similarly, the low taxes in South will be offset by relatively high prices for land and housing.

Suppose that highway grants are based on local tax effort, so that North receives a larger highway grant. Is the grant policy equitable? Before the highway grant, households were indifferent between the two cities, with differences in tax rates capitalized into housing prices. Because citizens in the two cities achieve the same utility level before the grant, a larger grant to North does not necessarily promote fairness. On the contrary, the relatively large grant to North increases property values in the city, generating capital gains for property owners.

TAX EXPENDITURES—IMPLICIT GRANTS

The federal government uses its tax code to influence local-government spending. Two provisions of the federal income-tax code affect local spending: the deductibility of local taxes and the exemption of interest from municipal bonds. In recent years, there have been several proposals to eliminate both of these provisions. These reform proposals have precipitated heated debate.

Deductibility of Local Taxes

Federal taxpayers can deduct local and state taxes on income and property from their taxable income. Consider a city with the following characteristics:

1. Marian, the median voter in the city, itemizes her deductions on her federal tax form.
2. Marian has a marginal tax rate of 28 percent.
3. All local taxes are deductible.

Figure 16–15 shows Marian's spending choices. In the absence of the deduction for local taxes, the opportunity cost of $1 of public spending is $1 of private spending, so her budget line is AB. The deductibility of local taxes decreases the opportunity cost of local spending to 72 cents on the dollar: every dollar of local taxes decreases Marian's federal tax liability by 28 cents, so she gives up only 72 cents worth of private goods to consume $1 worth of local public goods. The deduction shifts the budget line from AB to AC, shifting Marian's preferred point from E to F. If the city adheres to the preferences of its median voter, it will choose point F.

The deduction for local taxes is equivalent to an open-ended matching grant. This can be seen by comparing figures 16–15 and 16–12. The deduction is an example of a **tax expenditure**: the federal government stimulates local spending indirectly by cutting taxes with the expectation that part of the tax cut will be spent on local public goods. Instead of giving the locality an intergovernmental grant of $20 per capita, the federal government gives local

FIGURE 16–15   Deductibility of Local Taxes and Local Spending

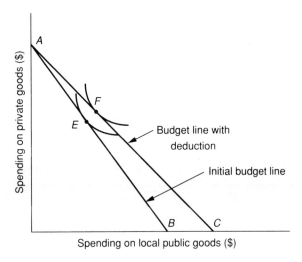

The deduction for local taxes decreases the opportunity cost of local spending, increasing the desired spending of the median voter. The deduction is equivalent to an open-ended matching grant.

citizens a $20 tax cut. In other words, the federal government uses local taxpayers as intermediaries in its subsidization of local spending.

The stimulative effect of the federal tax deduction varies across cities. If the median voter in a middle-income city has a marginal tax rate of 15 percent, the city's federal subsidy is 15 cents per dollar of local spending. If the median-income voter in a higher income city has a marginal tax rate of 28 percent, the city's federal subsidy is 28 cents per dollar. If the median voter in a low-income city does not itemize deductions, the city's federal subsidy is zero.

Exemption of Interest on Local-Government Bonds

Because the interest earned on bonds issued by local government is not subject to the federal income tax, local governments can pay bondholders a relatively low interest rate. Consider Bill, whose marginal tax rate is 28 percent. Suppose that the market interest rate for private bonds is 12 percent. Since Bill declares his interest earnings on private bonds as taxable income, every $1 of interest income increases his federal tax liability by 28 cents. Therefore, the net return on private bonds is about 9 percent, not 12 percent. If the interest on local-government bonds is not taxable, the net return on a government bond is equal to its gross return. The local government can compete with private bonds by setting the interest rate on government bonds at about 9 percent. The tax exemption allows local governments to finance their capital projects at a fraction of the cost of private projects, so it stimulates local spending. The exemption is another example of a tax expenditure: the federal government stimulates local spending by giving up tax revenue, not by providing money directly to local governments.

FISCAL DISTRESS OF CITIES

Since the early 1970s, many cities have experienced serious fiscal problems. The most sensational episode was the near default of New York City in 1975. The most severe fiscal problems have been experienced by large, older cities in the northeastern and north-central states. There are several sources of fiscal distress:

1. **Decrease in tax base.** As discussed in Chapter 10 (Suburbanization of Population and Employment), a large number of manufacturers, retailers, and office firms have moved from the central city to the suburbs. The suburbanization of employment and population decreases the city's tax bases (income, property, sales) and tax revenue.

2. **Increase in production costs.** As the population of a city falls, the costs of urban services do not fall proportionately. The reason is simple: if a city invests in plants and equipment for a city of 5 million, it pays the same capital costs for its streets, transit systems, schools, and fire stations even if its population drops to 4 million. A decrease in population increases per capita costs because there are fewer "capitas" to pay the costs.

3. **Inflexible labor force.** In some cities, labor unions are powerful enough to prevent layoffs when the city's population decreases. If a city maintains a constant work force as it shrinks, a fiscal squeeze is inevitable.

Peterson (1976) examined the sources of fiscal distress in declining cities. He compared declining cities with growing cities and concluded that declining cities had (a) larger public expenditures per capita, (b) more municipal employees per capita, (c) higher municipal wages, and (d) declining real-tax bases. Why do declining cities have higher wages? According to Peterson, cities used the large federal grants of the 1960s and 1970s to increase the wages of municipal workers. When the federal grants were reduced in the middle 1970s, the cities were left with overpaid workers.

SUMMARY

1. In 1984, 37 percent of local revenue came from taxes on property, income, and sales and 40 percent came from intergovernmental grants. The rest of local money came from user fees and charges.

2. The property tax is a tax on land and improvements (capital). Since the supply of land is fixed, the land tax is borne by landowners. There are two perspectives on the incidence of the improvement tax.
   a. The traditional view takes a partial-equilibrium approach, focusing on the effect of the improvement tax on the taxing jurisdiction. The supply of dwellings is perfectly elastic, so the tax is paid by housing consumers.
   b. The new view takes a general-equilibrium approach, focusing on the effect of the tax on people both inside and outside the taxing jurisdiction. Landlords throughout the region pay the tax, and consumers outside the taxing city gain at the expense of consumers in the taxing city.

3. The incidence of the improvement tax depends on one's perspective.
   a. A mayor should use the partial-equilibrium model (the traditional view) to estimate the effects of the city's property tax. From the local perspective, the tax is paid by local housing consumers.
   b. The president of the nation should use the general-equilibrium model to estimate the national effect of one city's tax. Because the tax causes zero-sum changes in housing rent, the president can ignore the effects on housing consumers. The tax is paid by the nation's capitalists.
   c. If all cities in the nation have the same property tax rate, the tax is paid by capitalists. There are no housing-price effects because there is nowhere for capitalists to move their capital.

4. The simple model of the property tax assumes that the national supply of capital is fixed. If the supply of capital decreases as the net return decreases, capitalists shift part of the tax onto housing consumers in the form of higher housing prices.

5. The simple model assumes that households are immobile. If they can leave the taxing jurisdiction, interjurisdictional differences in housing costs will be replaced with interjurisdictional differences in land prices.

6. Assessment practices cause differences between nominal and effective property tax rates.
   a. Because of underassessment, the nominal property tax rate exceeds the effective tax rate.
   b. Some cities systematically overassess low-value property and underassess high-value property, so the poor face a relatively high effective tax rate.

7. The analysis of the general property tax (on residential, commercial, and industrial property) is the same as the analysis of the residential property tax.
   a. According to the general-equilibrium model, the tax depresses the return on capital. In addition, consumer prices increase in the taxing city and decrease elsewhere.

    b. If a city imposes a higher effective tax rate on residential property, consumers will pay more for housing but less for other goods (e.g., pizza, clothes).

8. In the Tiebout world, a household's property tax bill is independent of its housing consumption: households sort themselves into homogeneous communities, so a household's tax bill depends only on its consumption of public goods.

9. Taxes on sales and income are paid in part by landowners.
       a. The municipal sales tax is paid by consumers (who pay higher prices) and landowners (who receive less rent).
       b. The municipal income tax is paid by laborers (who receive lower wages) and landowners. Because labor is more mobile between municipalities than between nations, labor's share of a municipal income tax is smaller than its share of a national income tax.

10. The states provide the bulk of grants to local governments (86 percent of all grants). Grants are used to internalize externalities and solve the mismatch problem (desired spending rising faster than tax revenue).

11. The local response to an intergovernmental grant can be predicted by examining the effects of the grant on the budget choices of the median voter.
       a. Local governments respond to a grant by cutting local taxes, so part of the grant is spent on private goods.
       b. If citizens don't know about grants, government spending may increase by a relatively large amount (the flypaper effect).
       c. A conditional grant is equivalent to an unconditional grant if the desired spending exceeds the grant: the local government can replace its own spending with the grant money, so the conditional grant is the same as a cash payment.
       d. A matching grant has a relatively large stimulative effect because it has both a substitution effect and an income effect.

12. Under a block-grant program, dozens of conditional grants are consolidated into a single general grant.

13. Intergovernmental grants are capitalized into property values, so part of a grant to a low-income community ends up in the pockets of property owners. Similarly, a grant to a high-tax community generates benefits for property owners.

14. The federal government uses tax expenditures to stimulate local spending. Taxpayers act as intermediaries in the stimulation of local spending.
       a. The deduction for local taxes decreases the opportunity cost of government spending.
       b. The exemption of interest on local bonds decreases the cost of government borrowing.

15. The fiscal distress of cities was caused in part by economic decline, which decreased tax bases and increased average production costs.

EXERCISES AND DISCUSSION QUESTIONS

1. Consider the new view of the property tax. Discuss the long-run effects of Taxville's property tax on the following individuals.
   a. Ms. Partial rents a house in Taxville.
   b. Mr. Wash is a traveling salesman who rents one dwelling in Taxville and one in Notax.
   c. Ms. Capitalist owns five dwellings in Taxville.
   d. Mr. Capitalist owns five dwellings in Notax.

2. In the Taxville example, a 2 percent property tax decreased net rental income by $400 in each city. Suppose that the region has four cities instead of just two.
   a. By how much will the property tax increase dwelling rent in the taxing city?
   b. By how much will the tax decrease net rental income?

3. Choose the word in parentheses that makes the following statement correct, and then explain your choice:
   As the moving costs of households decrease, the tax-induced increase in Taxville's dwelling rent (*increases, decreases*).

4. Mr. Javelin is the economic forecaster of the city of Drip, Oregon. You are his research assistant and do all of his computations. The city is considering a tax of $2 per raincoat. In estimating the revenue from the raincoat tax, you make the following assumptions.
   i. The supply of raincoats to the city is perfectly elastic.
   ii. The current price of raincoats is $20, and the current quantity of raincoats demanded is 1,000 per week.
   iii. The price elasticity of demand for raincoats is -2.0.

   a. Estimate the tax revenue from the raincoat tax.

   b. When Mr. Javelin sees your computations, he says: "Those revenue projections look pretty low. You know, the state imposed a $2 raincoat tax several years ago and it raised $39,000 per week. Since about 5 percent of the state's raincoats are bought in Drip, I would expect that we would raise about 5 percent of the revenue raised by the state tax. If your revenue projection is less than $1,950, it's wrong."
   Is Mr. Javelin correct? If so, what is your mistake? If not, what is wrong with his analysis?

5. The city of Tinytown is one of 10 municipalities in a large metropolitan area. Compare the incidence of a Tinytown income tax to the incidence of a metropolitan income tax.

6. Suppose Collegetown eliminates its tax on pizza parlors and increases its tax on residential property. Under what conditions will the change in tax policy decrease the tax liability of Joe College?

7. Consider a school district (E) with a total budget of $500,000. The district is currently spending $250,000 on special-education programs for disadvantaged students (SE programs). There are three types of federal grants for SE programs:

    Grant A: Unconditional grant of $100,000 to the school district.

    Grant B: Categorical grant (money to be spent on SE programs) of $100,000. To ensure that the categorical grant is spent on SE, the federal government gives 100,000 marked dollar bills to E. On each dollar bill is written: "This dollar must be spent on special education."

    Grant C: Categorical matching grant (dollar for dollar) with a maximum subsidy of $100,000. For each $1 spent by E on SE, the federal government gives E $1.

    a. Use diagrams to illustrate the district's responses to the three types of grants.

    b. How would the district's responses differ if the pregrant expenditures on SE were only $50,000?

8. The state of Grantland has experimented with different types of matching grants for education. The state picked four identical school districts and used three different matching grants. The results are as follows:

School District	Type of Grant	Educational Spending
E	none	$50
F	$1 grant for $1 local	70
G	$0.33 grant for $1 local	60

    a. Map the demand curve for education—different combinations of price (opportunity cost) and quantity (educational spending).

    b. Using the data for school districts E and F, compute the price elasticity of demand for education.

9. If the flypaper effect occurs, will the deductibility of local taxes still be equivalent to a matching grant? Which policy will generate a larger increase in local-government spending?

10. The discussion of the mismatch between local tax revenue and desired spending assumes that the desired spending on local public goods is proportional to income, that is, the income elasticity of demand for public spending is 1.0. Another implicit assumption is that the unit cost of local

public goods is constant. Draw the spending and tax lines for the following two cases:

   a. The income elasticity of demand for local spending is 2.0. Does the larger income elasticity generate a larger or a smaller gap between desired spending and tax revenue?

   b. The income elasticity of demand for local spending is 1.0, but the unit cost of local public goods increases by 25 percent over the course of the decade. Do rising costs generate a larger or a smaller gap between desired spending and tax revenue?

11. Consider the distributional effects of intergovernmental grants. In the example in the chapter, the $100 grant to the poor city decreased the city's income taxes, generating benefits for both tenants (the poor) and landowners. Suppose that instead of cutting taxes, the city increases spending on schools, police, fire protection, and parks. Will the benefits of the grants still be shared by tenants and landowners?

REFERENCES AND ADDITIONAL READINGS

Revenue Facts

U.S. Bureau of Census, *Census of Governments*. Washington, D.C.: Department of Commerce, 1987.

U.S. Bureau of Census. *City Government Finances in 1984–85*. Washington, D.C.: Department of Commerce, 1987.

Property Tax Incidence

Aaron, Henry J. *Who Pays the Property Tax? A New View*. Washington, D.C.: Brookings Institution, 1975. Chapter 3 discusses the traditional and new views of the property tax.

Boskin, Michael. "Taxation, Saving, and the Rate of Interest." *Journal of Political Economy* 86 (1978), pp. S3–S28. Estimates that the supply of savings is responsive to the rate of return, with an elasticity between 0.20 and 0.60.

Meiszkowski, Peter. "The Property Tax: An Excise Tax or a Profits Tax?" *Journal of Public Economics* 1 (1972), pp. 73–96. Discusses the new view of the property tax.

Pechman, Joseph A. *Who Paid the Taxes, 1966–1985?* Washington, D.C.: Brookings Institution, 1985. Estimates the incidence of the property tax under the traditional view and the new view.

Property Tax: Administration and Reform

Aaron, Henry J. *Who Pays the Property Tax? A New View*. Washington, D.C.: Brookings Institution, 1975. Chapter 4 discusses the administrative problems of the property tax, including assessment errors. Chapters 5 and 6 discuss reform proposals.

Aronson, J. Richard, and John L. Hilley. *Financing State and Local Governments* (Washington, D.C.: Brookings Institution, 1986. Chapter 7 discusses some of the assessment problems associated with the property tax.

Black, David E. "Property Tax Incidence: The Excise-Tax Effect and Assessment Practices." *National Tax Journal* 30 (1977), pp. 429–34. Discusses the effects of regressive assessment practices on the incidence of the property tax.

Engle, Robert F. "De Facto Discrimination in Residential Assessments: Boston." *National Tax Journal* 28 (1975), pp. 445–51. Shows that assessment ratios are inversely related to market values.

Ihlanfeldt, Keith. "Property Tax Incidence on Owner-Occupied Housing: Evidence from the Annual Housing Survey." *National Tax Journal* 35 (1982), pp. 89–97. A study of regressive assessment in Philadelphia and Atlanta.

Netzer, Richard. *Real Property Tax Policy for New York City*. New York: New York University, 1980. Shows that assessment ratios are relatively low for one-family and two-family houses.

Peterson, George E. *Property Tax Reform*. Washington, D.C.: The Urban Institute, 1973.

Income and Sales Taxes

Aronson, J. Richard, and John L. Hilley. *Financing State and Local Governments*. Washington, D.C.: Brookings Institution, 1986. Chapter 8 discusses the local sales tax, the income tax, and user fees.

Intergovernmental Grants: Reasons, Types, and Effects

Aronson, J. Richard, and John L. Hilley. *Financing State and Local Governments*. Washington, D.C.: Brookings Institution, 1986. Chapter 3 discusses federal intergovernmental grants, and Chapter 4 discusses state grants.

Courant, Paul N.; Edward M. Gramlich; and Daniel Rubinfeld. "The Stimulative Effect of Intergovernmental Grants, or Why Money Sticks Where It Hits." In *Fiscal Federalism and Grants-in-Aid*, ed. Peter Meiszkowski and William Oakland. Washington, D.C.: The Urban Institute, 1979. Discusses the flypaper effect.

Gramlich, E. M. "Intergovernmental Grants: A Review of the Empirical Literature." In *The Political Economy of Fiscal Federalism*, ed. Wallace E. Oates. Lexington, Mass.: Lexington Books, 1977. Reviews the literature on the effects of grants on local spending. Concludes that matching grants are more stimulative than lump-sum grants, and a categorical grant has a larger stimulative effect than an equivalent increase in private income.

Ornstein, Norman J. "Chipping Away at the Old Blocks." *The Brookings Bulletin* 18 (1982), pp. 11–15. Discusses the reasons for categorical and block grants.

U.S. Bureau of the Census. *City Government Finance in 1984–85*. Washington, D.C.: U.S. Government Printing Office, 1986.

Tax Limitation Movement: Proposition 13

Aronson, J. Richard, and John L. Hilley. *Financing State and Local Governments*. Washington, D.C.: Brookings Institution, 1986. Chapter 12 discusses revenue and expenditure limits and the responses of local governments to the limits.

Ladd, Helen F. "An Economic Evaluation of State Limitations on Local Tax and Spending Powers." *National Tax Journal* 31 (1978), pp. 1–18.   Explores the reasons behind tax revolts.

Ladd, Helen F., and Julie Boatwright Wilson. "Why Voters Support Tax Limitations: Evidence from Massachusetts' Proposition 2 1/2." *National Tax Journal* 35 (1982), pp. 137–40.

Oakland, William. "Proposition 13: Genesis and Consequences." *National Tax Journal* 32 (1979), pp. 387–409.   Discusses the reasons for the tax revolt in the state of California.

Rabushka, A., and P. Ryan. *The Tax Revolt.* Stanford: Hoover Institution, 1982.   Discusses the attempts by citizens to control government spending by tax and expenditure limitations.

Tax Expenditures

Ladd, Helen F. "Federal Aid to State and Local Governments." In *Federal Budget Policy in the 1980's,* ed. Gregory V. Mills and John L. Palmer. Washington, D.C.: The Urban Institute, 1984.   Discusses the role of tax expenditures in intergovernmental finance.

Fiscal Distress of Cities

Bradbury, Katharine L.; Anthony Downs; and Kenneth A. Small. *Urban Decline and the Future of American Cities.* Washington, D.C.: Brookings Institution, 1982.   Discusses the reasons for the economic problems of cities.

Humphrey, Nancy; George Peterson; and Peter Wilson. *The Future of Cleveland's Capital Plant.* Washington, D.C.: The Urban Institute, 1979.   Discusses the fiscal problems of Cleveland.

Inman, Robert P. "The Fiscal Performance of Local Governments: An Interpretive Review." In *Current Issues in Urban Economics,* ed. Peter Meiszkowski and Mahlon Straszheim. Baltimore: Johns Hopkins University Press, 1979, pp. 270–321.

Oakland, William H. "Central Cities: Fiscal Plight and Prospects for Reform." In *Current Issues in Urban Economics,* ed. Peter Meiszkowski and Mahlon Straszheim. Baltimore: The Johns Hopkins Press, 1979, pp. 322–58.   Discusses the sources of central-city fiscal distress, suggesting that fiscal distress is caused in large part by the attempt of local governments to redistribute income. Suggests that intergovernmental grants should be designed to compensate local governments for the money spent on high-cost, low-revenue citizens.

Peterson, George E. "Finance." In *The Urban Predicament,* ed. William Gorham and Nathan Glazer. Washington, D.C.: The Urban Institute, 1976.   Provides a comprehensive analysis of the reasons for the fiscal crises of large cities and suggests ways to avoid future problems.

Reischauer, Robert; Peter Clark; and Peggy Cuciti. *New York City's Fiscal Problem.* Washington, D.C.: Congressional Budget Office, 1975.   A detailed discussion of the fiscal problems experienced by New York City.

CHAPTER 17

Autos and Highways

The home is where part of the family waits until the others are through with the car.

Herbert Prochnow

This is the first of two chapters on urban transportation. This chapter discusses the most popular travel mode, the automobile, which is used by about 83 percent of U.S. commuters. It examines three transportation problems caused by the automobile: congestion, air pollution, and highway accidents. This chapter explains why a certain level of congestion is efficient, and explores alternative policies to decrease congestion to its optimum level. The second problem is air pollution, which is controlled by federal government through its auto emissions policies. The policy question is whether other pollution-control polices such as pollution taxes or gas taxes might be more efficient in controlling pollution. The third transportation problem is auto safety. Traffic accidents injure and kill people and also disrupt traffic flow, contributing to the congestion problem. The policy question is: How do government policies affect highway death rates and accident rates?

Table 17–1 shows commuting patterns and auto usage in U.S. cities in 1980. About one third of workers commute within central cities, and about one fifth commute from a suburban residence to a central-city job. The most frequent commuting trip is from a suburban residence to a suburban job, a trip made by about 40 percent of commuters. Over four fifths of commuters travel to work by car, truck, or van, and about three fourths of these commuters drive to work alone. The private vehicle is most popular among people who commute to or from the suburbs: it is used by about 90 percent of the workers who commute from the suburbs to the city center, about 91 percent of the workers who commute from the central city to the suburbs, and about 88 percent of the workers who commute from one suburb to another.

CONGESTION—EQUILIBRIUM VERSUS OPTIMUM TRAFFIC VOLUME

Most cities suffer from traffic congestion during the morning and evening rush hours. Consider a city with the following characteristics:

1. **Radial highway.** There is a two-lane highway from the suburbs to the city center (a distance of 10 miles). There is one person per vehicle.

TABLE 17–1   Commuting Patterns and Auto Use

Type of Commute Trip	Percent of All Trips	Percent Using Car, Truck, or Van	Percent Driving Alone	Percent in Carpools
Central city to central city	33.1	72.4	56.1	16.3
Central city to suburb	6.8	91.3	69.2	22.1
Suburb to central city	20.1	90.3	68.1	22.2
Suburb to suburb	40.1	87.5	69.7	17.8
Total	100	83.3	64.9	18.5

SOURCE: U.S. Bureau of Census, *1980 Census of Population: Journey To Work—Metropolitan Commuting Flows* (Washington, D.C.: U.S. Government Printing Office, 1984).

2. **Monetary travel cost.** The monetary cost of auto travel is 20 cents per mile.

3. **Time cost.** The opportunity cost of travel time is 10 cents per minute.

The total cost of a commuting trip is the sum of the monetary and time costs of the 10-mile trip. The monetary cost is $2 (10 miles times 20 cents per mile). The time cost depends on travel time: a trip that takes 30 minutes has a time cost of $3 (30 minutes times 10 cents per minute); a 20-minute trip has a time cost of only $2. Therefore, the total cost of a 30-minute trip is $5.00 ($2 plus $3), and the total cost of a 20-minute trip is $4.

The Demand for Urban Travel

Consider first the demand side of the urban travel market. Figure 17–1 shows the demand curve for travel along the radial highway. The horizontal axis measures the number of vehicles per lane per hour. The vertical axis measures the cost of the commuting trip, the sum of the monetary and time costs of the 10-mile trip. The demand curve shows, for each trip cost, how many travelers will use the highway. For example, if the trip cost is $12.80, there will be 1,200 people for whom the benefit of the trip exceeds the cost, so there will be 1,200 vehicles per lane per hour. As the cost of the trip decreases, there are more people for whom the benefit exceeds the cost, so the city moves downward along the travel-demand curve: there are 1,400 vehicles at a cost of $9.14, and 1,600 vehicles at a cost of $5.48.

The demand curve is a marginal-benefit curve. For each traffic volume, it shows how much the marginal traveler is willing to pay for the highway trip. Suppose that the city starts with a trip cost of $9.15 and a traffic volume of 1,399. If the trip cost decreases to $9.14, traffic volume increases to 1,400, meaning that the 1,400th driver is willing to pay $9.14 to make the trip: at any cost above $9.14, the trip would not be worthwhile. The demand curve shows that the marginal benefit of the 10-mile trip decreases from $12.80 for the 1,200th driver to $1.82 for the 1,800th driver.

FIGURE 17–1 Congestion Externalities and the Congestion Tax

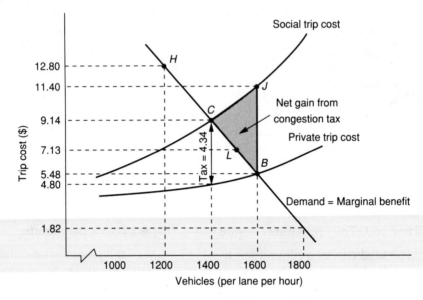

Drivers use the highway as long as the marginal benefit (shown by the demand curve) exceeds the private trip cost, so the equilibrium traffic volume is 1,600 vehicles per lane per hour. At the optimum, the marginal benefit equals the marginal social cost (the social trip cost). The equilibrium volume (1,600) exceeds the optimum volume (1,400) because drivers ignore the external costs of their trips. A congestion tax of $4.34 will "internalize" the congestion externality, generating the optimum traffic volume.

The Private and Social Costs of Travel

Table 17–2 shows the relationships between traffic volume and travel time. Column B lists the trip time (the travel time per driver) for different traffic volumes. For traffic volumes up to 400 vehicles per lane per hour, there is no congestion: everyone travels at the legal speed limit of 50 miles per hour, and the 10-mile trip takes 12 minutes. For traffic volume above 400 vehicles, the computations are based on the following formula:

$$\text{Trip time} = 12.0 + 0.001 \cdot (\text{Volume} - 400) + 0.000015 \cdot (\text{Volume} - 400)^2 \tag{17–1}$$

When the 401st driver enters the highway, the congestion threshold is crossed. As the highway becomes crowded, the space between vehicles decreases and drivers slow down to maintain safe distances between cars. As more and more drivers enter the highway, travel speeds decrease and travel times in-

TABLE 17–2   Traffic Volume, Travel Time, Travel Costs, and Congestion Externalities

A	B	C	D	E	F	G	H
Traffic Volume (vehicles)	Trip Time (minutes)	Increase in Travel Time per Driver (minutes)	Increase in Total Travel Time (minutes)	External Trip Cost ($)	Private Trip Cost ($)	Social Trip Cost ($)	Marginal Benefit (Demand)
200	12.00	0	0	0	3.20	3.20	31.10
400	12.00	0	0	0	3.20	3.20	27.44
600	12.80	0.007	4.20	0.42	3.28	3.70	23.78
800	14.80	0.013	10.40	1.04	3.48	4.52	20.12
1,000	18.00	0.019	19.00	1.90	3.80	5.70	16.46
1,200	22.40	0.025	30.00	3.00	4.24	7.24	12.80
1,400	28.00	0.031	43.40	4.34	4.80	9.14	9.14
1,600	34.80	0.037	59.20	5.92	5.48	11.40	5.48
1,800	42.80	0.043	77.40	7.74	6.28	14.02	1.82
2,000	52.00	0.049	98.00	9.80	7.20	17.00	

crease: the trip takes 12.8 minutes if there are 600 vehicles, 22.4 minutes for 1,200 vehicles, and 52.0 minutes for 2,000 vehicles.

Columns C and D show the effects of the marginal driver on the travel times of other drivers. For low traffic volumes (below 400 vehicles), an additional driver does not affect speeds or travel times. For volumes above 400 vehicles, however, an additional driver slows traffic and increases travel times. For example, the 600th driver increases the travel time *per driver* by 0.007 minutes (Column C): when the driver enters the highway, the trip time increases from 12.793 to 12.80. The increase in total travel time is simply the extra time per driver (0.007) times the number of other drivers (599), or 4.20 minutes (Column D). This is the **congestion externality:** the marginal driver slows traffic and increases travel time, forcing other drivers to spend more time on the road. The congestion externality increases with traffic volume: the 1,200th driver increases travel time by 30 minutes (0.025 minutes times 1,199), and the 1,600th driver increases travel time by 59.20 minutes (0.037 times 1,599).

The **external trip cost** equals the monetary value of the congestion externality. The figures in column E are based on the assumption that the opportunity cost of travel time is 10 cents per minute. For the 600th driver, the external trip cost equals the increase in total travel time (42 minutes) times 10 cents per minute, or $0.42. The external trip cost increases with traffic volume, rising to $3.00 for the 1,200th driver, $5.92 for the 1,600th driver, and $9.80 for the 2,000th driver.

Columns F and G show the private and social cost of travel. The **private trip cost** is the travel cost incurred by the individual commuter, defined as the sum of the monetary cost ($2.00) and the private time cost. To compute the private time cost, multiply the trip time by the opportunity cost of travel time:

the opportunity cost is 10 cents per minute, so the private time cost is $1.20 for a volume of 200 vehicles, $1.28 for 600 vehicles, and so on. Therefore, the private trip cost is $3.20 for 200 vehicles, $3.28 for 600 vehicles, and so on. The **social trip cost** is the sum of the private trip cost (column G) and the external trip cost (column E). Figure 17–1 shows the cost curves for private trip cost and social trip cost. The social-cost curve lies above the private-cost curve, with the gap between the two curves equal to the external trip cost.

Equilibrium versus Optimum Traffic Volume

What is the equilibrium number of drivers? A driver will use the highway if the marginal benefit of the trip (from the demand curve) exceeds the private trip cost. In Figure 17–1, the demand curve intersects the private trip cost curve at 1,600, so the equilibrium number of vehicles is 1,600 and the equilibrium private trip cost is $5.48. The 1,601st driver does not use the highway because the marginal benefit of using the highway is less than the private trip cost.

What is the optimum number of drivers? The basic efficiency rule is that an activity should be increased as long as the marginal social benefit exceeds the marginal social cost; at the optimum level, the marginal benefit equals the marginal cost. In Figure 17–1, the marginal social benefit is shown by the demand curve and the marginal social cost is shown by the social trip cost curve. The demand curve intersects the social trip cost curve at a volume of 1,400, so the optimum traffic volume is 1,400 vehicles. For the first 1,400 drivers, the social benefit of travel exceeds the social cost, so their use of the highways is efficient. For the 1,401st driver, the social cost exceeds the benefit, so his use of the highway is inefficient.

The equilibrium volume exceeds the optimum volume because drivers ignore the costs they impose on other drivers. An additional driver slows traffic, forcing other drivers to spend more time on the road. Suppose that Carla, the 1,599th driver, has a private benefit of $5.49. From Column F in Table 17–2, the private trip cost for 1,599 vehicles is about $5.48, so Carla will use the highway. Her use of the highway is inefficient because the benefit of the trip ($5.49) is less than the social cost of the trip ($11.40, equal to the sum of Carla's private cost of $5.48 and the external trip cost of $5.92). Because Carla ignores the $5.92 worth of external cost, she makes an inefficient choice.

THE POLICY RESPONSE—CONGESTION TAX

The government could use a congestion tax to generate the optimum traffic volume. A tax equal to the external trip cost would internalize the congestion externality, generating the optimum number of drivers. In Figure 17–1, a congestion tax of $4.34 per trip would shift the private trip cost curve upward by $4.34, decreasing the equilibrium number of drivers from 1,600 to 1,400. The 1,401st driver would not use the road because the benefit of the trip

($9.13) would be less than the full cost of the trip ($9.14, the sum of the $4.80 private cost and the $4.34 congestion tax). Because the congestion tax closes the gap between private and social costs, drivers base their travel decisions on the social cost of travel. Therefore, the highway will be used efficiently.

Benefits and Costs of Congestion Taxes

From the perspective of the individual traveler, the imposition of congestion taxes generates good news and bad news. People who continue to use the highway after the tax pay the tax, but also have lower time costs because the tax decreases traffic volume and travel times. People who stop using the highway avoid the tax, but forgo the benefits associated with using the highway. In other words, there are costs and benefits for both types of people. Do the benefits outweigh the costs?

A key consideration in the evaluation of the congestion tax is the disposition of the revenue generated by the congestion tax. The government will not throw the tax revenue away, but will presumably use it to finance public services or to decrease other local taxes. In fact, as explained later in the chapter, the total revenue from the congestion tax will be just enough to pay for the optimum highway. Therefore, the government could substitute congestion taxes for the gasoline tax, which is currently used to finance highways. To simplify matters, suppose that the government redistributes the tax revenue, in equal shares, to all of the households who use the highway before the congestion tax is imposed. In Figure 17–1, the pretax traffic volume is 1,600, so there are 1,600 highway users. The total tax revenue is $6,076 (1,400 vehicles at $4.34 per vehicle), so the transfer per household is $3.79 ($6,076/1,600).

Table 17–3 shows the costs and benefits for two travelers. Helen has a relatively large willingness to pay for highway use, so she uses the highway

TABLE 17–3 Benefits and Costs of Congestion Taxes

Citizen	Congestion Tax	Tax Refund	Net Transfer	Travel Time Savings	Loss of Consumer Surplus	Net Benefit
Helen (H)	$4.34	$3.79	− $0.55	$0.68	—	+ $0.13
Louis (L)	—	3.79	+ 3.79	—	1.65	+ 2.14

Definitions
1. Total tax revenue = Tax per driver times volume: 1,400 times $4.34 = $6,076.
2. Transfer payment = Total tax revenue divided by number of citizens: $6,076/1,600 = $3.79.
3. Net transfer = Refund − congestion tax (if any).
4. Consumer surplus loss = Willingness to pay (from demand curve) − private trip cost (before congestion tax).

even after the congestion tax is imposed. In Figure 17–1, her position on the demand curve is shown by point H. Louis has a relatively small willingness to pay, so he stops using the highway after the tax is imposed (point L in Figure 17–1). What are the benefits and costs for the two travelers?

1. Helen pays a tax of $4.34 and receives a refund of $3.79, for a 55 cent net increase in taxes. The congestion tax decreases the private trip cost from $5.48 (at a volume of 1,600) to $4.80 (at a volume of 1,400), for a savings of 68 cents. The net benefit is 13 cents—a benefit of 68 cents less a tax increase of 55 cents.

2. Louis doesn't use the highway after the congestion tax is imposed. Before the tax, his benefit from using the highway equaled the gap between his willingness to pay (from the demand curve) and the private trip cost. This gap is his **consumer surplus** from using the highway. From Figure 17–1, Louis was willing to pay $7.13 for a trip with a private trip cost of $5.48, so his consumer surplus was $1.65 ($7.13 − $5.48). After the congestion tax, Louis does not use the highway, so he loses this surplus. Because the tax also provides a transfer payment of $3.79, Louis is better off after the congestion tax by $2.14: the transfer payment more than offsets his loss of consumer surplus.

In this example, both citizens benefit from the imposition of congestion taxes. A more rigorous analysis of the benefits and costs would show that some people in the city would be harmed by the congestion-tax policy: for some travelers, the savings in travel costs and the transfer payment would not be large enough to offset the congestion tax or the loss in consumer surplus.

A more rigorous analysis would also show that the benefits of the winners will exceed the costs of the losers. In other words, the move from the equilibrium to the optimum will generate a net gain for society. In Figure 17–1, the net gain is shown by the shaded area, the area between the demand curve (the marginal-benefit curve) and the social trip-cost curve. To explain this, suppose the city starts with the equilibrium volume (1,600 vehicles) and somehow persuades the 1,600th driver to not use the road. What are the benefits and costs of diverting the driver? On the benefit side, total travel costs decrease by the social trip cost of the 1,600th driver (about $11.40 at point J). On the cost side, the driver loses the benefits of the highway trip; the willingness to pay for the trip is shown by the demand curve (about $5.48 at point B). The net benefit from diverting the driver is the difference between the social trip cost and the willingness to pay ($5.92). The social gain from diverting the 1,599th driver is slightly lower than this because the social trip cost is lower (the city starts lower on the cost curve) and the willingness to pay is higher (the city starts further up the demand curve). The net gain to society from moving from the equilibrium (point B) to the optimum (point C) is the sum of the differences between the social trip cost and the willingness to pay (from the demand curve) for the 1,600th through the 1,401st drivers. In other words, it is the area between the two curves, shown by the area of triangle *CJB*. Because there is a net gain from the move to the optimum point, the government could, in principle, redistribute income from the winners to the losers to ensure that everyone is made better off by the congestion tax.

Peak versus Off-Peak Travel

To be efficient, the congestion tax must vary across time and space, with a higher tax on relatively congested highways. The most congested highways are the ones leading to and from employment centers. Most congestion occurs during the morning and evening rush hours. According to Straszheim (1979), about a quarter of all trips are made during the morning and evening rush hours. McConnell-Fay (1986) reports that 64 percent of the trips from homes to workplaces in the San Francisco Bay area occur between 6:30 and 8:30 A.M. and 57 percent of the workplace-home trips occur between 4:30 and 6:30 P.M. Figure 17–2 shows the demand curves and congestion tolls for the peak period and the off-peak period. Given the high volume of traffic during the peak period (V_p, compared to V_o during the off-peak period), the peak-period congestion toll is higher.

FIGURE 17–2   Congestion Tax during Peak and Off-Peak Periods

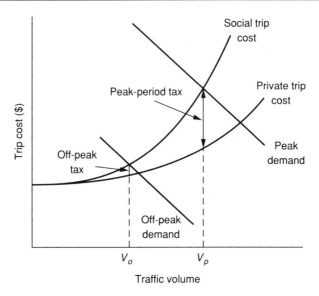

During the off-peak period, the demand for travel is relatively low, generating a low traffic volume (V_o, compared to V_p during the peak period), so the optimum congestion tax is relatively low.

Estimates of Congestion Taxes

What is the optimum congestion tax? In a study of the San Francisco Bay area, Keeler and Small (1975, 1977) estimated congestion taxes for different locations and times. Pozdena (1988) has recently updated the Keeler and Small estimates. He estimates that during the peak travel periods, the congestion tax would be 65 cents per mile on central urban highways, 21 cents per mile on suburban highways, and 17 cents per mile on fringe highways. During the off-peak periods, the taxes would be between 3 and 5 cents per mile at all locations. Because the Bay area is more congested than most metropolitan areas, the optimum congestion taxes would be lower in most other metropolitan areas.

Suppose the Bay area implemented such a system of congestion tolls. How much would different types of commuters pay for travel during the peak periods? Consider first a suburban commuter who travels to a job in the central city, traveling seven miles on suburban highways and three miles on central urban highways. The commuter's one-way congestion bill would be $3.42 (seven miles times 21 cents plus three miles times 65 cents), so the daily congestion tax would be $6.84. For a suburban commuter who travels eight miles to a job in another suburb, the one-way congestion tax would be $3.36 (16 miles times 21 cents per mile).

Implementing the Congestion Tax

How would the government collect the congestion tax? One possibility is to install toll booths on every road and collect the tax directly from drivers. This option is impractical because the collection process will slow traffic, causing more congestion. The high-technology version of toll booths is a vehicle-identification system (VIS). Under a VIS, every car is equipped with an electronic device that allows sensors along the road to identify the car as it passes. The system records the number of times a vehicle uses the congested highway and sends a congestion bill to the driver at the end of the month. For example, a driver who travels 10 miles along a congested highway 20 times per month would pay a monthly congestion bill of $86.80 (20 times $4.34).

Why haven't cities used the VIS to impose congestion taxes? The systems are relatively inexpensive, so the opposition is not based on the costs of installing and running the system. Some people oppose VIS because they oppose congestion taxes of any form. A common complaint is that congestion taxes would be "regressive" (the poor would pay a larger fraction of their income for taxes). There is no evidence to support this view. Even if congestion taxes were regressive, the government could presumably adjust other taxes to offset the undesirable distributional effects of tolls. Other people oppose VIS because they are troubled by the potential threat to civil liberties: the information gathered from VIS might be used by an inquisitive government to spy on its citizens.

ALTERNATIVES TO A CONGESTION TAX— TAXES ON AUTO USE

Given the practical difficulties in imposing a congestion tax, a number of alternative policies have been proposed. One set of policies discourages auto use by increasing the cost of auto travel. Three of the pricing options are gasoline taxes, parking taxes, and congestion-zone taxes. How effective are these policies compared to the congestion tax?

To evaluate the efficacy of the alternative policies, it will be useful to discuss the four ways that the congestion tax decreases traffic volume.

1. **Modal substitution.** The tax increases the cost of auto travel relative to carpooling and mass transit (buses, subways, light rail), causing some travelers to switch to these other travel modes.

2. **Time of travel.** The tax will be highest during the peak travel periods, causing some travelers to travel at different times. Because work and study schedules are relatively inflexible, commuters and students would be less likely to change their travel times than other travelers (e.g., shoppers). Nonetheless, firms would have a greater incentive to change work schedules to allow their workers to avoid costly travel during the peak period. The institution of "flex-time" and the rearrangement of shift times would allow some workers to change their travel times to avoid congestion taxes.

3. **Travel route.** The congestion tax will be highest on the most congested routes, causing some travelers to switch to alternative routes.

4. **Location choices.** The congestion tax increases the unit cost of travel (travel cost per mile), causing some commuters to decrease their commuting distances. Some workers may move closer to their jobs, and others may switch to jobs closer to their residences.

These four changes cause the city to move up the travel demand curve as the cost of travel increases. In Figure 17–1, the congestion tax decreases traffic volume from 1,600 to 1,400 because it changes travel modes, times, routes, and distances.

Gasoline Tax

One alternative to the congestion tax is a gasoline tax. The idea is that if travel is more expensive, traffic volume will decrease. The problem is that the gas tax increases the costs of all automobile travel, not just travel along congested routes during peak periods. In contrast with the congestion tax, which changes travel times and routes, the gas tax does not encourage drivers to switch to other travel times or routes.

Suppose the government wants to use the gasoline tax to decrease the peak-period traffic volume to its optimum level. What is the required gasoline tax? To have the same effect as the congestion tax in Figure 17–1, the gas tax must increase the cost of travel by 43.4 cents per mile ($4.34 per 10-mile trip). If the typical car gets 25 miles per gallon of gasoline, the required gas tax will be $10.85 per gallon (43.4 cents times 25). Such a gasoline tax is obviously infeasible. Even if it were feasible, it would be inefficient because it also increases the cost of off-peak travel by 43.4 cents per mile.

Parking Tax

A number of cities use parking taxes to discourage driving to CBD jobs. In an experiment in Madison, Wisconsin, a tax surcharge of $1 was imposed on drivers who arrived at parking garages during the peak travel period (7 A.M. to 9 A.M.) and left their cars for more than three hours. As explained by Parody (1984), the surcharge decreased traffic volume because (a) some commuters switched to carpools and mass transit and (b) some travelers changed their travel times. In Washington, D.C., the government increased parking costs for its employees, causing some workers to switch to carpools and mass transit (Miller and Everett 1982). In Ottawa, Canada, the government increased parking rates for government employees from zero to 70 percent of the commercial rate, causing (a) a 23 percent decrease in the number of workers driving to work, (b) a 6 percent increase in the auto occupancy rate (from 1.33 to 1.41), and (c) a 16 percent increase in bus ridership (DiRenzo, Cima, and Barber 1981).

There are three potential problems with using parking taxes to decrease congestion. The first is that the taxes must be imposed only on peak-period commuters: drivers who travel during the off-peak period should be exempt from the tax. As shown by the Madison experiment, this problem can be solved by imposing a surcharge for drivers who arrive at parking garages during the peak travel period. Second, in contrast with the congestion tax, which increases the unit cost of travel and decreases travel distances, the parking tax does not depend on the distance traveled. Therefore, there will be less incentive for commuters to economize on travel costs by living closer to their workplaces. Third, because much of the congestion problem is caused by cars that do not park in congested areas, the tax will not force all peak-period travelers to pay for their congestion.

Shoup (1980) suggests that the subsidization of parking by private employers contributes to the congestion problem. Using data from the 1970s, he shows that over 90 percent of commuters parked for free. Shoup estimates that if private parking subsidies were eliminated, about 20 percent of drive-alone commuters would switch to some sort of ride sharing or mass transit. A recent study of Los Angeles (Willson 1988) suggests that subsidies are widespread and large. Only 14 percent of employers in the city did not offer any subsidies, and the median subsidy was $3.71 per day (compared to a median parking cost of $5 per day). If employers replaced the parking subsidies with cash payments, the increase in parking costs would encourage some workers to carpool or use mass transit.

Congestion Zones and Permits

A third congestion policy involves the establishment of congestion zones, defined as areas where access would be limited to drivers who paid a special fee. Under a scheme proposed for London in 1974, all vehicles using the inner streets between 8 A.M. and 6 P.M. were to pay a flat fee (Altshuler 1979). The proposal generated heated debate and was never implemented. Singapore implemented a congestion-zone scheme in 1975. To drive in the central area of the city between 7:30 and 10:15 A.M., auto drivers must buy a permit costing about $1.30 per day. Travel within the control area is free to buses, motorcycles, and carpools.

Singapore's zoning policy generated some interesting results. During the morning hours, auto traffic in the control zone decreased by 74 percent and travel speeds increased by 22 percent (Altshuler 1979). Many commuters drove their cars to the edge of the control area and then rode buses to their downtown workplaces. During the afternoon rush hours (when driving permits were not required), the changes in traffic volume and travel speeds were relatively small. Some commuters took public transit to central-city workplaces in the morning, but were picked up at the end of the day by family members. Through traffic, which used circumferential routes during the morning control period, resumed its radial travel pattern in the afternoon.

ALTERNATIVES TO AUTO TAXES

The congestion policies discussed so far decrease congestion by increasing the cost of driving. There are several alternative approaches. One option is to increase the carrying capacity of the highway, and another is to subsidize transit ridership.

Capacity Expansion and Traffic Design

One response to the congestion problem is to widen the highway to increase its carrying capacity. Figure 17–3 shows the effects of such a policy on travel times and traffic volume. The wider road reaches the congestion threshold at a higher traffic volume and has a lower private trip cost at all volumes above the original congestion threshold ($V = 400$). The decrease in trip costs increases traffic volume as the city moves down the demand curve from point D to E.

Under what conditions will the widening of the highway be efficient? One way to measure the total benefit is with consumer surplus. As explained earlier, consumer surplus equals the excess of the willingness to pay (from the demand curve) over the actual cost of travel. The widening of the highway decreases the trip costs of all drivers, so it increases consumer surplus. The increase in consumer surplus is shown as the shaded area in Figure 17–3. For the original drivers (volume = V_o), the consumer surplus per driver increases by the savings in private-trip cost ($C_w - C_o$). The increase in their consumer

FIGURE 17–3   Effects of Widening the Highway

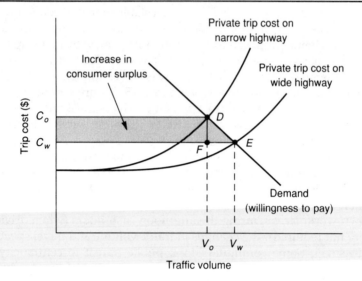

The widening of the highway shifts the private trip cost to the right: the congestion threshold increases, and trip cost is lower at every traffic volume above the original threshold volume. The decrease in trip cost increases traffic volume from V_o to V_w. The benefit of the widening is the shaded area (the increase in consumer surplus).

surplus is the rectangular area with a width of $(C_w - C_o)$ and a length of V_o. The decrease in trip cost also increases traffic volume from V_o to V_w. The consumer surplus of the new drivers equals the area of the triangle DEF. The benefits of widening the highway will exceed the cost if the increase in consumer surplus (the sum of the rectangle and the triangle) exceeds the cost of widening the highway. This analysis ignores pollution costs, which are discussed later in the chapter.

The city could also improve the flow of traffic on the existing highway. Street lights can be synchronized to keep traffic flowing at a steady speed. The use of one-way streets and restrictions of on-street parking increase the carrying capacity of streets. Some cities have placed stoplights on expressway on-ramps, thus smoothing the flow of vehicles onto expressways. In the language of transportation engineers, the ramp lights decrease the "turbulence" caused by entering vehicles, increasing travel speeds. In Los Angeles, the installation of such a system on the Harbor Freeway increased average travel speeds from 15 miles per hour to 40 miles per hour. A similar system in Dallas increased travel speeds from 14 to 30 miles per hour.

Subsidies for Transit

Another alternative to the taxation of auto travel is the subsidization of mass transit (buses, subways, commuter trains, light rail). Transit and autos are substitute travel modes, so a decrease in the cost of transit will cause some consumers to switch from autos to transit. In other words, a transit subsidy will decrease the auto volume, narrowing the gap between the equilibrium and optimum traffic volumes.

Figure 17–4 shows the interactions between the auto and transit markets. Under a system of optimum congestion taxes, the auto market reaches point B, with traffic volume of A^* (where the demand curve intersects the social-trip cost curve), and the transit market reaches point Q, with ridership of T^* (where the demand curve intersects the marginal social cost curve). In the presence of congestion taxes, both markets are at their optimum points, defined as the points at which the marginal social benefit (from the demand curve) equals the marginal social cost.

What if there are no congestion taxes? The auto market will reach point C, where the demand curve intersects the private trip cost curve, generating an equilibrium traffic volume of A'. The underpricing of auto travel will shift the demand curve for transit (a substitute good) downward. The equilibrium will move to point R, with ridership of T'. If auto travel is underpriced, the auto volume exceeds the optimum volume and transit ridership is less than the optimum ridership.

A small transit subsidy will move both markets closer to their optimum points. In the transit market, the subsidy decreases the cost of transit, causing movement down the demand curve to point S: ridership increases to T'', closing about two thirds of the gap between the equilibrium and the optimum volume. In the auto market, the decrease in the price of transit shifts the auto demand curve downward, moving the market from point C to point D. The equilibrium volume decreases from A' to A'', closing about one quarter of the gap between the equilibrium and the optimum volume. The subsidy narrows —but does not eliminate—the gaps between the optimum and equilibrium volumes: A^* is still less than A'' and T' is still less than T^*.

Would it be possible to eliminate both the auto gap and the transit gap? In Figure 17–4, the transit gap is closing faster than the auto gap: the subsidy closes two thirds of the transit gap, but only one quarter of the auto gap. In other words, the subsidy increases transit ridership by more than it decreases auto volume. This occurs because in addition to diverting some drivers from cars to transit, the subsidy also attracts new travelers to transit. For example, suppose that the subsidy causes 250 drivers to switch from autos to transit ($A' - A'' = 250$) and also generate 280 new travelers. The total increase in transit ridership will be 530 ($T'' - T' = 530$), the sum of the diverted auto drivers and the new transit riders. Because the transit gap is closing faster than the auto gap, if the city decides to eliminate the transit gap, it will be left with an

FIGURE 17–4 Effects of Transit Subsidies on Auto Volume and Transit Ridership

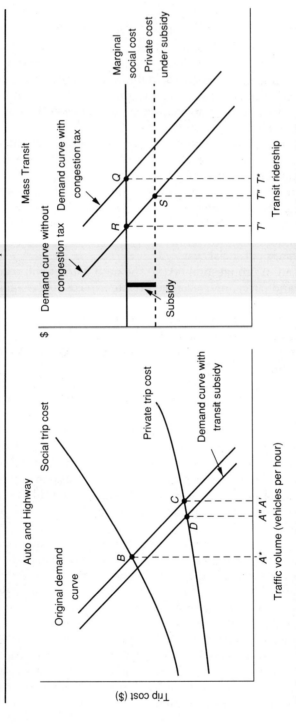

In the optimum situation, auto drivers pay a congestion tax, so auto volume is A^* and transit ridership is T^*. If there is no congestion tax, the auto volume is A' and the transit ridership is T' (the underpricing of auto travel shifts the demand curve for transit downward). A transit subsidy increases transit ridership to T'' and decreases auto volume to A'' (the subsidy shifts the auto demand curve downward). The subsidy narrows the transit gap faster than it narrows the auto gap.

auto gap. Alternatively, if it decides to eliminate the auto gap, it will "overshoot" the transit gap: transit ridership will exceed the optimum ridership. The city can close one—but not both—gaps.

The fundamental problem of the transit subsidy is that it underprices transit, increasing ridership above its optimum level. In the absence of congestion taxes, a transit subsidy may improve the efficiency of the transportation system, but the subsidy will never be as efficient as a system of congestion taxes. The policy question is whether the benefits of the transit subsidy (the diversion of drivers from underpriced and congested roads) are larger or smaller than the costs (excessive transit ridership).

HIGHWAY PRICING AND TRAFFIC VOLUME IN THE LONG RUN

This section shows how the government could pick both the optimum traffic volume and the optimum road width. The long-run analysis of highway pricing and investment has four steps:

1. Derive the average total cost curves for different highway widths.
2. Derive the long-run cost curves (average and marginal).
3. Pick the optimum traffic volume and road width.
4. Pick the congestion tax that generates the optimum traffic volume on the optimum road.

Average Total Cost for Two-Lane and Four-Lane Highways

The average total cost of travel is the sum of the trip cost and the **average road cost.** Figure 17–5 shows the trip-cost curves for both a two-lane and a four-lane highway: the cost curves are horizontal up to the point at which congestion sets in; the congestion threshold is V_2 vehicles per hour for the two-lane highway and V_4 vehicles for the four-lane highway. The average road cost equals the total cost of building the highway divided by the number of trips.

The average total cost curves are U-shaped. An increase in traffic volume has two effects on average total cost. First, an increase in volume spreads construction costs over more drivers, so the average road cost decreases (the road-cost effect). Second, an increase in volume may increase congestion, increasing travel times and the trip cost (the trip-cost effect). At traffic volumes below the congestion threshold (V_2 for the two-lane highway and V_4 for the four-lane highway), there is no trip-cost effect, so the average total cost curve is negatively sloped. At high traffic volumes, the average road cost is relatively low and congestion is severe, so the trip-cost effect dominates the road-cost effect. Therefore, the average total cost curve is positively sloped. In Figure 17–5, the average total cost curve for the two-lane highway reaches its

FIGURE 17–5   Average Cost for Two- and Four-Lane Highways

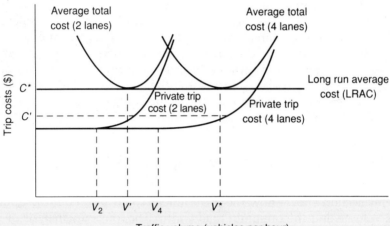

The average total cost of travel is the sum of private trip cost and average road cost. The average total cost curves are U-shaped. If there are constant returns to scale in road-building, the two average total cost curves reach the same minimum cost C^*, but the four-lane highway reaches this cost with twice the traffic volume (V^* instead of V'). The long-run average cost is composed of the minimum points of the average total cost curves.

minimum point at a volume of V' drivers, indicating that the road-cost effect dominates for volumes up to V' drivers and the trip-cost effect dominates for higher volumes. For the four-lane highway, the trip-cost effect dominates for volumes above V^* drivers.

The cost curves in Figure 17–5 are drawn under the assumption of constant returns to scale in highway building. According to Keeler and Small (1977) and Kraus (1981), this is a reasonable assumption. Constant returns to scale mean that a doubling of construction costs (to build four lanes instead of two) will double the carrying capacity of the highway. The congestion threshold of the four-lane highway (V_4) is double that of the two-lane highway (V_2). Similarly, it takes twice as many drivers on the four-lane road to reach a given private trip cost: to reach the private trip cost C', the four-lane highway requires twice the traffic volume. The two total-cost curves reach the same minimum cost (C^*), but the four-lane highway reaches this point with twice the traffic volume (V^* instead of V').

Long-Run Average-Cost and Marginal-Cost Curves

The long-run average cost curve (LRAC) shows the minimum average total cost for each traffic volume. The curve is mapped by answering the following question: for a given traffic volume, what is the average total cost of the *most efficient* highway? Figure 17–5 shows two points on LRAC: for a volume of V' drivers, the two-lane highway minimizes average cost at an average cost of C^*; for a volume of V^* drivers, the four-lane highway minimizes average cost at the same cost. LRAC is made up of the minimum points of the average total cost curves for different highway widths, so it indicates the average total cost under the assumption that the government builds the optimum highway for each traffic volume. Given the assumption of constant returns to scale, LRAC is horizontal, with an average total cost (the sum of average road cost and average trip cost) of C^*. The long-run marginal cost curve (LRMC) shows the marginal social cost of an additional driver, including the cost of widening the road to accommodate the new driver. In Figure 17–5, LRAC is horizontal (a result of constant returns to scale), so LRMC is the same as LRAC (if the average is constant, the marginal equals the average).

Optimum Volume and Road Width

For the optimum traffic volume, the marginal benefit of travel equals the long-run marginal cost of travel. In Figure 17–6, the demand curve shows the marginal benefit of travel and LRMC shows the long-run marginal cost of

FIGURE 17–6   Optimum Road Width and Congestion Tax

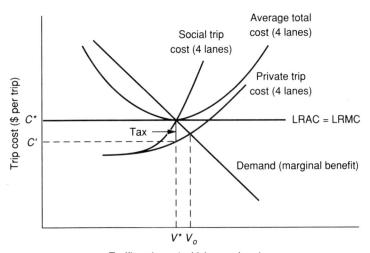

Traffic volume (vehicles per hour)

The optimum traffic volume (V^*) is the volume such that the marginal benefit of travel (shown by the demand curve) equals the long-run marginal cost of travel (LRMC). The four-lane highway minimizes the average total cost of travel for V^* drivers, so the optimum road width is four lanes. The appropriate price of travel is C^*, so a congestion tax of T is added to the private trip cost of C'. The congestion tax equals the average road tax, so congestion taxes pay for the optimum road.

travel. The two curves intersect at V^*, so the optimum traffic volume is V^* drivers. From Figure 17–5, the four-lane highway generates the minimum average total cost for a volume of V^* drivers, so the optimum road width is four lanes.

How does the city persuade the optimum number of drivers to use the highway? From the demand curve, a total of V^* drivers will use the road if the cost of the trip is C^*. Drivers will face a cost of C^* only if the city imposes a congestion tax. If the city builds a four-lane road but does not impose a congestion tax, there will be V_o drivers (volume at which the demand curve intersects the private trip cost curve) instead of V^*. If the government adds a congestion tax of $(C^* - C')$, the traffic volume will be V^* (volume at which the demand curve intersects the social trip cost curve).

Congestion Tolls Pay for the Optimum Road

If there are constant returns to road building, the revenue from the congestion tax will cover the cost of building the road. In Figure 17–6, the congestion tax equals the gap between the social trip cost and the private trip cost $(C^* - C')$. Because the long-run average cost is the sum of the private trip cost and the average road cost, the gap between the LRAC and the private trip cost is the average road cost $(C^* - C')$. Because the congestion tax equals the average road cost, a system of congestion tolls will pay for the optimum road.

Is this a fluke, or is there something systematic about congestion tolls and road costs? The expressions for average road cost and the congestion tax are as follows:

$$\text{Average road cost} = \text{Average total cost} - \text{Private trip cost} \qquad (17\text{–}2)$$

$$\text{Congestion tax} = \text{Social trip cost} - \text{Private trip cost} \qquad (17\text{–}3)$$

Therefore, the average road cost will equal the congestion tax if the average total cost (ATC) equals the social trip cost (STC). STC is actually the short-run marginal cost of driving: it shows the increase in social cost from one additional driver. The marginal-cost curve (STC) intersects the ATC curve at its minimum point. If the government builds the optimum highway, the market will reach the minimum point of some ATC curve, so STC will equal ATC. Therefore, the average road cost will equal the congestion tax, meaning that the revenue from congestion taxes will pay for the road.

The revenue from a congestion tax provides an important signal to policy makers. If tax revenue exceeds the total cost of building the road, the road should be widened. In other words, any surplus tax revenue should be spent on widening the road. Suppose that the city builds a two-lane highway and imposes a congestion tax of $4.34 (see Figure 17–1). If the total revenue from the tax ($4.34 times 1,400 drivers) exceeds the total cost of building the road, the road should be widened.

Who Pays for Highways?

Highways are financed through various user fees. Auto drivers pay federal and state taxes on gas, oil, and auto parts. In addition to these normal user taxes, truck drivers also pay user fees based on mileage and weight.

Since the early 1970s, user taxes have failed to cover the costs of building and maintaining roads (Meyer and Gomez-Ibanez 1981). During the 1960s, revenue from user taxes exceeded highway costs by about 25 percent. During the 1970s, revenue from the gas tax did not keep pace with inflation because the gas tax is a fixed amount per gallon, not a fixed percentage of the price. By 1975, there was a deficit of about 25 percent. Urban road users actually paid more than their share of highway costs: the tax revenue collected from urban road users exceeded the costs of urban roads by about 14 percent. In contrast, rural travelers paid only about 56 percent of the costs of rural roads.

CONGESTION AND LAND-USE PATTERNS

This section explores the effects of congestion externalities and congestion taxes on urban land-use patterns. It uses the concepts developed in Part 2 of the book (Land Rent and Urban Land-Use Patterns) to show how a system of congestion taxes would change residential land use and city size. The land-use effects can be divided into partial-equilibrium effects and general-equilibrium effects.

Partial-Equilibrium Effects

The congestion tax increases the slope of the residential bid-rent function. The congestion tax increases the unit cost of commuting: in Figure 17–1, the congestion tax adds 43.4 cents per mile to commuting costs. As explained in Chapter 8 (Land Use in the Monocentric City), an increase in the unit cost of commuting increases the slopes of the housing-price function and the residential bid-rent function. Figure 17–7 shows three residential bid-rent functions. The relatively flat curve (R_o) is the initial bid-rent function (before the imposition of the congestion tax). After the congestion tax is imposed, the bid-rent function will shift to R_c if (*a*) the government throws the tax money away and (*b*) the congestion tax does not change traffic volume or travel times. Under these two assumptions, the congestion tax decreases the bid rent at all locations, with the gap between R_o and R_c increasing with distance to the city center: the longer the commuting distance, the larger the decrease in the bid rent for land.

The third bid-rent function, R_e, shows the actual partial-equilibrium effect of the congestion tax. It lies above R_c for two reasons. First, if the government uses the congestion tax revenue to cut other taxes, residents will be willing to pay more for housing and land at all locations. Second, the congestion tax will decrease traffic volume, increasing travel speeds and decreasing

FIGURE 17–7   Partial-Equilibrium Effects of Congestion Taxes

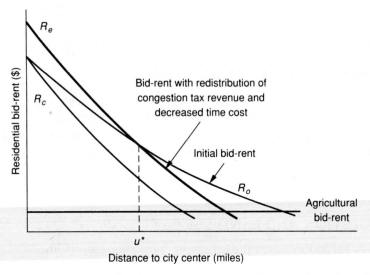

The imposition of congestion taxes shifts the bid-rent function from R_o to R_t if the tax revenue is not redistributed to the city's households. The redistribution of tax revenue (combined with the decreases in travel times caused by decreases in traffic volume) shifts the bid-rent function upward from R_c to R_e. The bid rent rises above the original bid rent for distances up to u^* miles, and drops below the original bid rent for locations beyond u^*.

travel times. The decrease in time costs lowers the unit cost of travel, partially offsetting the effects of the congestion tax on the slope of the bid-rent function. By comparing R_e to the original bid-rent function R_o, we can see that the congestion tax increases land rent within u^* miles of the city center and decreases land rent beyond u^*. Locations near the city center become more attractive because the congestion tax bill will be relatively low, so the bad news (increase in congestion taxes) is dominated by the good news (decrease in other taxes and lower time costs). For locations far from the city center, land rent falls because the large congestion tax decreases the relative attractiveness of these locations. To summarize, the congestion tax increases the relative attractiveness of locations close to the city center and increases the slope of the bid-rent function.

Figure 17–8 shows the effect of congestion taxes on the residential density function. The density function shows population density (people per acre) at different locations. As explained in Chapter 8 (Land Use in the Monocentric City), density increases as one approaches the city center. Land is more expensive near the city center, and people economize on the relatively expensive land by consuming less of it (they live in smaller dwellings on less

FIGURE 17–8   Congestion Taxes and Residential Density

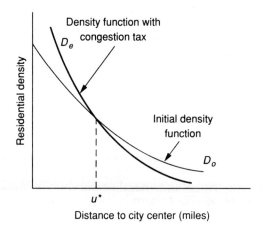

The congestion tax increases residential density up to u^* miles from the city center (locations where land rent rises) and decreases density beyond u^* (locations where land rent falls).

land). The congestion tax shifts the density function from D_o to D_e: in locations where land rent rises (distance less than u^*), households will consume less land, so density will increase; beyond u^*, where land rent falls, households will consume more land, so density will decrease.

The change in the density function shows that the congestion tax generates a more compact city. After the tax, the city has a larger fraction of its population living within a given distance of the city center, so it has shorter commuting distances and travel times. As explained earlier in the chapter, the congestion tax causes the city to move up its travel demand curve: the increase in travel cost decreases traffic volume. One reason for the decrease in traffic volume is that workers in the more compact city have shorter commuting distances.

General-Equilibrium Effects

Figures 17–7 and 17–8 show the partial-equilibrium effects of the congestion tax. In other words, they show the effects of the congestion tax on the residential land market, ignoring the effects on other markets in the city. As explained in Chapter 9 (General-Equilibrium Land Use), general-equilibrium analysis examines the effects of changes in the land market on the city's labor market.

Does the congestion tax increase or decrease total labor supply? The tax will increase total labor supply because it increases the efficiency of the city's transportation system and increases the welfare of city residents. As shown in the example in Table 17–3, the congestion tax makes both Helen (the typical highway user) and Louis (the typical nonuser) better off. In Figure 17–1, the net gain from the congestion tax is the shaded area *CJB*. Because the congestion tax generates a net gain for city residents, it increases the relative attractiveness of the city, increasing total labor supply.

How does the congestion tax affect the labor market and the city's wage? The initial increase in total labor supply will cause excess supply of labor, so the city's wage will fall. Firms will respond to the wage cut by increasing the quantity of labor demanded, narrowing the gap between labor supply and demand. The wage will continue to drop until labor supply equals labor demand. Equilibrium will be restored with a lower wage and a larger work force.

How will the city look after general equilibrium is restored? One way to answer this question is to use a computer to generate two pictures of the urban economy, one before the congestion tax and one after the economy has adjusted to the new tax. An urban general-equilibrium computer model allocates different plots of land in a hypothetical city to firms and households. If a particular allocation does not satisfy the conditions for general equilibrium, the computer tries a different one. This groping process continues until an equilibrium allocation of land is found. The computer model can be designed to compute a pretax equilibrium and a posttax equilibrium. To see the general equilibrium effects of the congestion tax, one compares the before and after pictures of the urban economy.

Sullivan (1983) used a computer model to simulate the effects of congestion taxes in a monocentric city. The results of the study are listed in Table 17–4. The hypothetical city has an initial population of 518,000 and a wage of $6.00 per hour. The average commuter travels 3.72 miles to work and spends 3.73 hours per week commuting. As shown in the second column of the table, the congestion tax increases the city's population and decreases its wage. The changes in population and wages are relatively large because the hypothetical city is highly congested, much more so than the typical U.S. city. The congestion tax causes households to move closer to their workplaces: the average commuting distance drops from 3.72 miles to 3.42 miles, and the average weekly commuting time drops by 0.32 hours. Another change occurs in the transportation network: the decrease in traffic volume allows the city to build narrower roads, so it uses less of its land for highways (16.2 percent instead of 17.9 percent).

The analysis of congestion taxes provides an important lesson about urban problems and policies. Congestion is truly an urban problem in the sense that the largest cities usually have the most severe congestion. Nonetheless, a city that imposes a congestion tax is likely to grow, not shrink. Because the congestion tax internalizes the congestion externality, it improves the efficiency of the city's transportation network and thus increases the relative attractiveness of the city. The lesson is that solving an urban problem is likely to cause economic growth, not decline.

TABLE 17–4   General-Equilibrium Effects of Congestion Taxes

Variable	Initial City	Congestion Tax City
Population	518,000	561,000
Wage ($ per hour)	6.00	5.31
Commute distance (miles)	3.72	3.42
Commuting time (hours per week)	3.73	3.41
Percent of land used for transportation	17.9	16.2

SOURCE: Arthur M. Sullivan, "The General Equilibrium Effects of Congestion Externalities," *Journal of Urban Economics* 14 (1983), pp. 80–104.

AUTOS AND AIR POLLUTION

Another urban transportation problem is air pollution. Autos and trucks contribute to air pollution in a number of ways.

1. **Photochemical smog.** Smog results from the combination of hydrocarbons, nitrogen oxides, sunlight, and heat. In the typical city, autos and trucks generate about 40 percent of hydrocarbons and about 40 percent of nitrogen oxides. For healthy people, smog causes physical discomfort, coughing, and nausea. For people who suffer from respiratory disease, smog causes more serious health problems.

2. **Carbon monoxide.** About 83 percent of carbon monoxide is generated by motor vehicles. In high concentrations, carbon monoxide decreases the breathing capacity and alertness of healthy individuals and causes pain and discomfort for people who suffer from cardiovascular disease.

3. **Lead.** About 88 percent of lead comes from motor vehicles. If lead is absorbed into the blood at high concentrations, it can cause serious health problems.

4. **Suspended particulates.** About 9 percent of particulate matter comes from motor vehicles. Some particulates cause respiratory problems, and others are suspected of causing cancer.

5. **Nitrogen oxides.** Autos and trucks generate about two fifths of nitrogen oxides. The experts disagree about the health effects of nitrogen oxides.

Although everyone agrees that automobiles and trucks are important sources of air pollution, there is disagreement about what should be done about the problem.

The Economic Approach—Effluent Fees

The economic approach to air pollution starts with a description of the externality problem. Drivers base their travel decisions on the marginal private cost of driving, which is less than the marginal social cost because autos and trucks generate air pollution. The externality occurs because drivers ignore the costs of pollution generated by their vehicles. The pollution externality causes people to (a) drive cars that generate a relatively large amount of pollution per mile driven and (b) drive too many miles. To an economist, the obvious response is to force people to pay for pollution, that is, to internalize the externality.

One approach would be to install a monitoring device in every car. Such a device would measure the car's emissions and allow the government to tax the car owner for the air pollution caused by the car. For example, if the estimated pollution cost per unit of carbon monoxide is one cent, the monthly bill would be $2 for a vehicle that emits 200 units per month and $3 for a vehicle that emits 300 units. Such a scheme is obviously impractical, but it illustrates the basic objective of the policy: drivers should pay for the pollution their cars generate. The trick is to estimate how much pollution each car generates.

An alternative approach is to impose a one-time pollution tax on automobiles. The government could estimate (a) the lifetime emissions of a particular car model and (b) the cost per unit of pollution. The pollution tax for a particular model would be equal to the product of total emissions and the unit cost. For example, if a certain type of car is expected to emit 5,000 units of carbon monoxide (CO) over its lifetime and the unit cost of CO is one cent, its CO tax would be $50. If the same car is expected to emit 400 units of lead and the unit cost of lead pollution is 50 cents, its lead tax would be $200. The car's total pollution tax would equal the sum of the taxes for CO, lead, nitrogen oxides, hydrocarbons, and particulates. Under this scheme, car buyers would pay more for cars that generate more pollution, so consumers would have the incentive to buy cleaner cars.

Another approach is to use a gasoline tax to increase the private cost of auto travel. The tax would increase the cost per mile driven, so it would decrease the total miles driven and decrease air pollution. The problem with the gas tax is that every driver would pay the same tax, regardless of how much pollution his or her car generated. In other words, there would be no practical way to impose a higher tax on cars that generate more pollution. Such a tax would decrease pollution by decreasing miles driven, not by persuading people to drive cleaner cars.

What is the marginal external cost of auto driving? Straszheim (1979) summarizes the results of a number of studies of auto-related air pollution. In the 1970s, the cost of auto pollution was between 0.50 and 0.80 cents per mile driven. Since then, auto emissions rates have decreased as a result of federal emissions policy, pulling down the cost per mile driven. Between 1970 and 1983, hydrocarbon emissions per mile dropped by two thirds, carbon monoxide dropped by three fifths, and nitrogen oxides dropped by one third (Crandall, Gruenspecht, Keeler, and Lave 1986). During this same period, the price level rose, pulling up the pollution cost per mile. The net effect of inflation and falling emission rates is a moderate increase in the cost per mile driven. If the cost per mile is 1 cent and the typical car gets 25 miles per gallon, the appropriate gasoline tax would be about 25 cents per gallon.

Transit Subsidies

An alternative approach for controlling auto pollution is to subsidize mass transit. Although both autos and mass transit generate air pollution, the pollution per passenger is lower on mass transit. If there are no pollution taxes, auto travel will be underpriced relative to transit. As explained earlier in the section on congestion externalities, the underpricing of autos will generate an excessive traffic volume (the equilibrium auto volume will exceed the optimum volume) and too little transit ridership (the equilibrium transit ridership will be less than the optimum ridership). One response to the underpricing of autos is to subsidize transit, the substitute good.

As shown in Figure 17–4, transit subsidies can be used to move the auto and transit markets closer to their optimum points (A^* and T^*). As explained for the case of congestion externalities, the basic problem with transit subsidies is that they decrease the cost of transit below the marginal social cost, causing too much transit travel. The excessive amount of travel is costly because society's productive resources (labor, capital, fuel) will be used inefficiently: transit will use an excessive number of drivers, mechanics, and buses, and will consume an excessive amount of fuel. If the pollution cost per auto passenger exceeds the pollution cost per transit rider by a wide margin, there will be large air-quality benefits from transit subsidies. The real question is whether the air-quality benefits dominate the resource costs of the policy.

Regulatory Policy

The Environmental Protection Agency (EPA) has adopted a two-part strategy for controlling air pollution. First, the EPA has established emissions standards for autos and trucks. The standards control four pollutants: nitrogen oxides (NOX), carbon monoxide (CO), hydrocarbons (HC), and lead. Second, the EPA has established standards for ambient air quality, specifying maximum concentration (parts per million) for NOX, lead, CO, sulfur oxides (SOX), and particulate matter.

Emissions Policy.   The national emissions policy started with the Motor Vehicle Pollution Control Act of 1965. In 1963, the state of California set maximum emission levels for CO, HC, and NOX. The emissions standards were first applied to the 1966 model year. In 1965, the federal government extended the California standards to the rest of the nation, with the standards applied to the 1968 model year. In 1970, the amendments to the Clean Air Act mandated 90 percent reductions in CO, HC, and NOX by 1975. Automakers were unable to meet the deadlines for the emissions standards, so the EPA relaxed the standards and extended the deadlines. By 1980, new-car emissions of HC and CO had been reduced to the target levels. The NOX emissions proved more difficult to control: by 1980, they had been reduced by half.

The emission program has decreased auto emissions considerably. Although the total miles driven increased between 1970 and 1983, total emissions decreased. In 1983, the volume of hydrocarbons generated per mile was only 33 percent of the corresponding figure for 1970 (Crandall, Gruenspecht, Keeler, and Lave 1986). The 1983 figure for carbon monoxide was 40 percent of the 1970 figure, and the 1983 figure for nitrogen oxides was 65 percent of the 1970 figure.

Costs and Benefits of Emissions Policy.   What are the benefits of the emissions policy? Freeman (1982) estimated the benefits that would occur if all auto-related pollution was eliminated. He divides the benefits of cleaner air into health benefits (e.g., decreased risk for cardiac patients), the reduction of damage to vegetation (e.g., increased crop and forest yields), and aesthetic benefits (e.g., increased visibility). He estimated that the total benefit from eliminating air pollution from autos would be about $8.3 billion per year (in 1984 dollars).

What are the costs of the emissions policy? Crandall, Gruenspecht, Keeler, and Lave (1986) estimated that the national emissions standards added $1,601 to the cost of a 1984 car, including $592 in additional equipment and $1,009 in additional fuel and maintenance costs. Based on this figure, they estimate that the total cost of the U.S. emissions standards was about $16.8 billion per year. In other words, the total cost of the 1984 emissions policy, which decreased but did not eliminate auto pollution, was about twice the estimated benefit that would occur if all auto-related pollution were eliminated ($8.3 billion).

It's important to note that there is a great deal of uncertainty about the health effects of air pollution. Therefore, it is difficult to estimate the benefits of pollution abatement, and Freeman's estimates should be used with caution. In addition, the estimates do not take into account the greenhouse effect or the depletion of the ozone, two phenomena which scientists are only beginning to explore. Nonetheless, the available evidence suggests that the costs of the current emissions program far outweigh the benefits we know about and can quantify.

Ambient Air-Quality Standards.   As part of the 1970 amendments to the Clean Air Act, EPA established standards for ambient air quality. The individual states were made responsible for meeting the standards. In response, most states issued permits for stationary sources of pollution, but did little to control mobile sources (autos and trucks).

In the early 1970s, it became clear that many cities would not satisfy the EPA air-quality standards by 1975. To prevent widespread violations of the standards, the EPA granted two-year extensions to the 1975 deadline. In addition, the EPA drafted plans to regulate auto traffic in cities that were expected to continue to violate the standards. The EPA plan for Los Angeles, for example, would have decreased auto traffic by 84 percent. The plans for three other cities called for reductions of at least 50 percent. The EPA planned to decrease traffic by imposing parking taxes and decreasing the supply of parking slots. The resulting public outcry forced the EPA to abandon these plans.

The 1977 amendments to the Clean Air Act were weak and ineffective. The deadline for meeting the EPA standards was extended ten years, to 1987. The EPA directed the cities that violated the air-quality standards to develop plans to implement inspection and maintenance programs for auto emissions. Many cities developed plans but did not implement them and were subject to trivial penalties. EPA got the cities to do the paperwork, but was less successful in getting the cities to meet its criteria for pollution control.

The 1977 amendments did include one innovative feature for the control of stationary pollution sources. In cities where the EPA standards were exceeded, new pollution sources were allowed if two conditions were satisfied. First, the new sources had to adopt the most effective abatement technology. Second, existing sources had to decrease their emissions to ensure that there was a net improvement in air quality. This policy set the stage for the development of a market for pollution rights, in which new firms purchase pollution rights from existing firms. Because this "offset" policy mimics a system of effluent fees, it will generate efficient abatement activity.

AUTO SAFETY

The third transportation problem is auto safety. Traffic accidents generate two types of costs. First, people involved in accidents are often injured or killed: traffic accidents kill about 50,000 people per year and injure another 2 million people. About a third of the deaths and about three fifths of the injuries occur in urban areas. Second, traffic accidents during rush hours disrupt traffic flows and contribute to the congestion problem.

This section explores the effects of various public policies on auto safety and traffic accidents. Federal safety legislation requires automakers to install a number of safety features (e.g., seatbelts, shatterproof windshields). One policy issue concerns the effects of these regulations on highway death rates and accident rates. Another issue concerns the effects of congestion and pollution policies on traffic safety. For example, policies that encourage the switch to smaller cars will decrease the congestion problem (smaller cars take up less space on the highway) and the pollution problem (small cars use less fuel and generate less pollution). Unfortunately, smaller cars are less safe (injuries are more severe in collisions involving small cars), so there are trade-offs between safety, congestion, and pollution.

The Effects of Safety Regulations

The Vehicle Safety Act of 1966 established safety standards for new cars. Automakers were forced to install head restraints, padded dashboards, seatbelts, shatterproof windshields, dual braking systems, and collapsible steering columns. Most of the standards were met in the 1968 model year. Figure

17–9 shows the trend in highway deaths per 100 million vehicle miles. The death rate decreased between 1947 and 1961, increased from 1961 to 1965, and then decreased from 1965 to 1983. In other words, highway death rates have decreased steadily since the safety standards were implemented.

The data on highway death rates raise two questions. First, to what extent did the safety regulations contribute to the decrease in highway death rates? Crandall, Gruenspecht, Keeler, and Lave (1986) have studied the effects of various factors on highway death rates. They estimate that safety regulations decreased the number of highway fatalities by about 30 percent, saving about 20,000 lives per year.

The second question concerns the response of drivers to safety regulations. Peltzman (1975) argues that because safety regulations make people feel safer, they drive more recklessly and are therefore involved in more collisions. This is the **theory of risk compensation.** This theory suggests that safety regulations generate benefits (greater safety in the event of a collision) and costs (more collisions). If the regulations increase the number of collisions, the death rates of nonoccupants (pedestrians and bicyclists) will increase. In addition, an increase in the number of accidents will increase the congestion problems on crowded urban highways.

The Optimum Speed. To understand a driver's response to safety equipment, consider Duke, who lives in Hazard City. Every Saturday night, Duke must decide how fast to drive from his suburban home to the dance hall

FIGURE 17–9 Highway Deaths per 100 Million Vehicle Miles

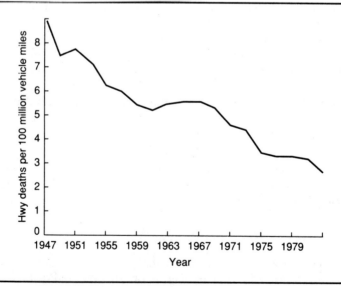

SOURCE: Crandall, Robert W., Howard K. Gruenspecht, Theodore E. Keeler, and Lester B. Lave, *Regulating the Automobile* (Washington, D.C.: Brookings Institution, 1986), p. 46.

in the city center. The benefit of fast driving is that he will spend less time on the road, giving him more time to dance with Betty Lou. Figure 17–10 shows the marginal-benefit curve for speed. The curve indicates how much Duke benefits from a one-unit increase in speed. For example, when his speed increases from 45 m.p.h. to 46 m.p.h., he can spend more time dancing, and he is willing to pay $16 for the additional dance time. The benefit curve is negatively sloped, reflecting the diminishing marginal utility of dancing.

Table 17–5 shows the expected costs of crashing at different speeds. As the speed increases, the probability of crashing increases: the probability is only 0.001 for a speed of 45 m.p.h., but rises to 0.011 for a speed of 55 m.p.h. Faster driving also causes more damage to Duke and his car. If he crashes at a speed of 45 m.p.h., his total crash costs (medical bills plus auto-repair costs) will be $2,000. If he crashes at a speed of 55, his total crash costs will be $12,000. The **expected crash cost** is the probability of crashing times total crash costs. The expected crash cost rises from $2 for a speed of 45 m.p.h. (0.001 times $2,000) to $132 for a speed of 55 m.p.h. (0.011 times $12,000). The **marginal cost of speed** is the change in the expected crash cost for a one-unit increase in speed. An increase in speed from 45 m.p.h. to 46 m.p.h. increases the expected crash cost from $2 to $6, so the marginal cost of speed is $4 for a speed of 46 m.p.h. The marginal cost of speed increases with the speed, reaching $22 for a speed of 55 m.p.h.

FIGURE 17–10   Optimum Speed and Safety Regulations

The optimum speed is the speed at which the marginal benefit of speed (value of decreased travel time) equals its marginal cost (the increase in expected accident costs). In the absence of safety regulations, Duke chooses point *A* (50 m.p.h.). Safety regulations decrease the expected costs of collisions, shifting the marginal-cost curve downward, increasing the optimum speed to 52 m.p.h. (point *B*).

TABLE 17–5   Crash Costs and Optimum Speed

Speed (m.p.h.)	Probability of Crash	Crash Cost ($)	Expected Crash Cost ($)	Marginal Cost of Speed ($)	Marginal Benefit of Speed ($)
45	0.001	2,000	2	0	17
46	0.002	3,000	6	4	16
47	0.003	4,000	12	6	15
48	0.004	5,000	20	8	14
49	0.005	6,000	30	10	13
50	0.006	7,000	42	12	12
51	0.007	8,000	56	14	11
52	0.008	9,000	72	16	10
53	0.009	10,000	90	18	9
54	0.01	11,000	110	20	8
55	0.011	12,000	132	22	7

What is the optimum travel speed? Duke will increase his speed as long as the marginal benefit of speed (the value of the increase in dance time) exceeds the marginal cost (the increase in the expected crash cost). In Figure 17–10, the optimum speed (where the marginal-benefit curve intersects the marginal-cost curve) is 50 m.p.h. Table 17–5 shows that a speed of 50 m.p.h. generates a marginal cost and a marginal benefit of $12 and an expected crash cost of $42.

What are the effects of safety regulations on the expected crash costs? Suppose that Duke is forced to buy a car with seatbelts and a shatterproof windshield. If he crashes in his new car, he is less likely to suffer serious injuries, so the expected cost of crashing at each speed decreases. In Figure 17–10, the decrease in the expected crash cost shifts the marginal-cost curve downward, increasing his optimum speed from 50 m.p.h. to 52 m.p.h. Because the safety regulations protect Duke in an accident, they cause him to take more risks, so the probability of crashing increases. The net effects of the safety regulations are smaller than they would be if his speed did not change: he has lower injury costs if he crashes, but he is also more likely to crash.

Evidence of Risk Compensation.   Peltzman (1975) uses two observations to support his theory of increased risk taking. First, collision rates were higher than expected in the years following the implementation of safety regulations. Second, pedestrian death rates were also higher than expected. If people drive faster and more recklessly in their safer cars, they take more risks for themselves and others and may kill more pedestrians.

The results of Crandall, Gruenspecht, Keeler, and Lave (1986) also support the risk-compensation theory. The death rates for pedestrians and bicyclists are inversely related to an index of safety features, suggesting that drivers in safe cars take more risks and endanger others. Because the decrease in driver deaths exceeds the increase in nondriver deaths, safety regulations produce a net decrease in highway deaths.

Small Cars and Safety

A second safety issue concerns the costs and benefits of shifting to a fleet of smaller cars. A greater reliance on small cars would provide some relief from transportation problems because small cars use less fuel and generate less air pollution. In addition, small cars take up less space on streets and highways, so a switch to smaller cars would increase the carrying capacity of the road system, reducing congestion. On the other hand, travel in small cars is less safe. The policy issue is whether the decreases in energy consumption, pollution, and congestion are worth the cost (the increase in traffic injuries and deaths).

The occupants of small cars are more likely to suffer serious injuries in a collision. The state of New York has estimated the injury rates for different car types (Meyer and Gomez-Ibanez 1981). In a collision between two large cars (weight exceeding 3,500 pounds), the rate of serious injury is 5.2 per hundred million vehicle miles. In a collision between a large car and a small car (weight less than 2,000 pounds), the injury rate is 3.7 for the occupants of the large car and 13.8 for the occupants of the small car. The combined injury rate for such a collision is 8.8. In a collision between two small cars, the injury rate is 9.7 for the occupants of each car. In other words, a collision between two small cars is more lethal than a collision involving a small and a large car.

Are small cars more or less likely to be involved in collisions? Studies of the accident rates of different car sizes have generated mixed results: some studies found higher collision rates for small cars, while others found no significant differences in accident rates. Overall, it appears that small-car occupants are just as likely to be involved in collisions and more likely to suffer serious injuries. Therefore, travel in small cars is more dangerous than travel in large cars.

A shift toward a small-car fleet will increase injury and death rates. As the fraction of small cars increases, the fraction of collisions involving small cars will increase, increasing the rate of serious injury. According to Meyer and Gomez-Ibanez (1981), if the percent of small cars in the fleet increased from 20 percent to 70 percent, the percent of accidents considered "dangerous" (between a large and a small car or between two small cars) would increase from 50 percent to 95 percent, causing a large increase in traffic death rates. These numbers suggest that there are considerable costs associated with the switch to smaller cars. The policy question is whether the benefits (less congestion and pollution) are greater than the costs.

Meyer and Gomez-Ibanez point out two additional factors that must be taken into account in predicting the safety effects of small cars. First, about 37 percent of urban traffic deaths involve pedestrians and bicyclists. If small cars are less lethal for pedestrians and bicyclists, there would be fewer pedestrian and bicycle deaths. Second, about 11 percent of urban traffic deaths result from single-car crashes (which occur when a car hits a fixed object). Since small cars are about as safe as large cars in this type of accident, a shift to small cars will not increase the number of single-car fatalities.

The switch to small cars is also likely to change driving habits. A driver who switches to a smaller, more dangerous car is likely to drive more cautiously to mitigate the risk of serious injury. If Duke switches to a small car, his expected injury cost would increase, shifting his marginal-cost curve upward. As a result, he will decrease his speed, partly offsetting the increase in the severity of accidents by decreasing the probability of crashing. In addition, Duke would be more likely to fasten his seatbelt, thus decreasing the severity of injuries.

SUMMARY

1. The three most popular commuting trips are between suburbs (40 percent of commuters), within the central city (33 percent), and from a suburb to the central city (20 percent). About 4 in 5 workers (and 9 in 10 suburbanites) commute by auto, truck, or van.

2. The demand for travel depends on the private cost of travel, the sum of the monetary and time costs of the trip: the higher the trip cost, the fewer the drivers.

3. Auto travel is subject to congestion externalities.
    a. The external cost of travel is the time cost imposed on other drivers: the marginal driver slows down traffic, forcing other drivers to spend more time on the highway.
    b. The social trip cost is the sum of the private trip cost and the external trip cost.
    c. Drivers base their travel decisions on private—not social—costs, so the equilibrium volume exceeds the optimum volume.
    d. A congestion tax internalizes the congestion externality, generating the optimum traffic volume.
    e. The congestion tax would be higher during peak travel periods and along more congested routes.
    f. Estimates for the San Francisco Bay area suggest that the congestion tax for travel during the peak period would be 65 cents per mile on central highways, 21 cents per mile on suburban highways, and 17 cents per mile on fringe highways.

4. One way to implement congestion taxes is with a vehicle identification system, under which every car is equipped with an electronic device that allows sensors along the road to identify the car as it passes.

5. There are several alternatives to the congestion tax.

    a. The gas tax is inappropriate because it would be the same on all routes at all times.

    b. Experiences with parking taxes suggest that they decrease traffic volume by encouraging auto drivers to carpool and take mass transit. One problem is that the tax is not based on distance traveled.

    c. The supply response to congestion is to increase highway capacity. The benefit of capacity expansion equals the increase in consumer surplus.

    d. A transit subsidy would cause some auto drivers to switch to transit, decreasing the congestion problem. The problem is that the subsidies may increase transit ridership above the optimum level.

6. In the long run, the optimum road width and traffic volume are determined simultaneously.

    a. The optimum volume is where the demand (marginal benefit) curve intersects the long-run marginal-cost curve.

    b. A congestion tax will generate the optimum traffic volume.

    c. The congestion tax will pay the full costs of the optimum highway. If the revenue from congestion taxes exceeds the cost of the road, the road should be widened.

7. The congestion tax will increase the efficiency of the city's transportation system, decrease commuting distances, and increase city size.

8. Autos and trucks generate several types of air pollution, including smog, carbon monoxide, lead, suspended particulates, and nitrogen oxides.

    a. One response to the pollution problem is to impose pollution taxes on new cars.

    b. Another option is to impose a gasoline tax.

    c. A third option is to subsidize transit, a policy that decreases pollution but also increases transit ridership above its optimum level.

    d. The EPA sets emission standards for carbon monoxide, hydrocarbons, and nitrogen oxides. Emissions controls have decreased total emissions despite an increase in total miles driven. The estimated cost of the current emissions policy, which decreases but does not eliminate auto pollution, is about twice the estimated benefit of eliminating all auto pollution.

9. There are trade-offs associated with safety regulations: the regulations decrease death rates of accident victims in autos, but increase death rates of nonoccupants (pedestrians and bicyclists), and increase collision rates.

10. A shift toward small cars is likely to increase injury and death rates: small-car collisions are more lethal than large-car collisions, and small cars are just as likely to be involved in accidents. The policy question is whether the benefits of small cars (less pollution and congestion) are greater than the safety costs.

EXERCISES AND DISCUSSION QUESTIONS

1. Suppose that the relationship between traffic volume and travel time is

   $$\text{Trip Time} = 12.0 + 0.001 \cdot (\text{Volume} - 400) + 0.00001 \cdot (\text{Volume} - 400)^2$$

   The marginal benefit (demand) is $22.12 for a volume of 200 and drops by $0.48 for every additional 200 drivers.
   a. Use this equation to derive a table like Table 17–2.
   b. What is the equilibrium traffic volume? What is the optimum volume?
   c. What is the appropriate congestion tax?

2. In estimating the congestion tax for peak-period travel, Keeler and Small (1977) assumed that the imposition of a congestion tax would not affect traffic volume.
   a. Depict graphically the model of auto travel underlying this assumption.
   b. Did Keeler and Small overestimate or underestimate the congestion tax? In other words, if the assumption of a fixed traffic volume is dropped, will the estimated congestion tax increase or decrease?

3. Consider the following quote from Peabody and Associates, a transportation consulting firm: "According to the Peabody principle, an increase in highway capacity increases traffic volume by an amount sufficient to leave private trip cost unchanged."
   a. Use a graph to depict a situation in which the Peabody principle is correct.
   b. Use a graph to depict a situation in which this principle is incorrect.
   c. Choose the word in parentheses that makes the following statement correct: "As the price elasticity of demand for highway travel (increases, decreases), the Peabody principle becomes a more accurate prediction of reality." Explain your choice.
   d. Suppose that the Peabody principle is nearly correct (capacity expansion causes a small reduction in private trip cost). Does this mean that investments in highway expansion are socially inefficient? Explain, using a graph.

4. A city has announced plans to widen a radial highway. The demand curve for the typical traveler is

   $$T = 40 - P$$

   where T is the number of trips per month and P is the cost per trip (in cents). For example, if the cost is 10 cents, the typical traveler will make 30 trips per month. If the new highway is built, the cost per trip would decrease from 30 cents to 20 cents and the taxes of the typical traveler would increase by $1.25 per month. Will the typical traveler support the construction of the new highway? Explain.

5. In Figure 17–3, the widening of the road decreased trip costs and increased traffic volume.

   a. Compute the increase in consumer surplus if $C_o = \$5$, $C_w = \$4$, $V_o = 1{,}600$, and $V_w = 1{,}800$. If the widening project costs $\$1{,}400$, is it worthwhile?

   b. How would your answer change if every auto using the stretch of highway generates $\$2$ worth of air pollution?

   c. What is the lesson from this exercise?

6. Consider a city that has both a congestion problem (it does not have a congestion tax) and an auto pollution problem (drivers do not pay for the pollution they generate).

   a. Draw the private trip cost curve and the social trip cost curve. How do your cost curves differ from those in Figure 17–1?

   b. Label the optimum volume V^* and the equilibrium volume V'.

   c. Suppose that the city builds a light-rail transit system and subsidizes light-rail fares. Depict graphically a situation in which the subsidized light-rail system generates the optimum auto volume (V^*).

   d. Does the fact that the light-rail system generates the optimum auto volume mean that it is an efficient policy?

7. Using the data in Table 17–5, compute the effects of the following events on Duke's optimum speed. Illustrate your answers with a graph (like Figure 17–9).

   a. Betty Lou is grounded by her parents for make-up violations, leaving Duke without his favorite dance partner. The marginal benefit of speed decreases by $\$9$ for every speed.

   b. The normal country-western band is replaced by Adam Smith and the Invisible Hands, a punk-rock band. Although Duke and Betty Lou enjoy slam dancing, it generates one quarter of the utility of the two-step (a country-western dance).

   c. The legal speed limit decreases to 46 m.p.h. The expected cost from speeding tickets increases by $\$3$ for every 1 m.p.h. over the speed limit: $\$3$ for 47 m.p.h., $\$6$ for 48 m.p.h., $\$9$ for 49 m.p.h., and so on.

   d. Highway improvements cut the probabilities of crashing in half.

8. Consider Duchess, a resident of Hazard City. She has the same marginal-benefit curve as Duke (Table 17–5), but her marginal-cost curve is horizontal.

   a. Suppose that the marginal cost of speed without air bags is $\$14$. What is her optimum speed?

   b. Suppose that an air-bag system would decrease the marginal cost of speed to $\$8$. If the air-bag system costs $\$300$, should Duchess buy the system?

9. Traffic accidents cause congestion because disabled vehicles block traffic. In Los Angeles, some transport planners have proposed that disabled ve-

hicles be lifted off the highway by helicopter. In other words, the city would buy a fleet of helicopters and use them to clear up accident scenes. Evaluate the merits of this proposal. Under what circumstances will it be an efficient policy?

REFERENCES AND ADDITIONAL READINGS

General

Kraft, Gerald, and Thomas A. Domencich. "Free Transit." In *Readings in Urban Economics*, ed. Matthew Edel and Jerome Rothenberg. New York: Macmillan, 1972, pp. 459–80.   Reports estimates of the elasticities of demand for auto travel.

Meyer, John R., and José A. Gómez-Ibáñez. *Autos, Transit and Cities*. Cambridge, Mass.: Harvard Univ. Press, 1981.

U.S. Bureau of the Census. *1980 Census of Population: Journey to Work—Metropolitan Commuting Flows*. Washington, D.C.: U.S. Government Printing Office, 1984.

Congestion

Altshuler, Alan A. *The Urban Transportation System*. Cambridge, Mass.: Joint Center for Urban Studies of MIT and Harvard, 1979. Chapter 9 (pp. 317–73).   Discusses auto congestion and alternative policy responses.

Keeler, Theodore E., and Kenneth A. Small. "Optimal Peak-Load Pricing, Investment and Service Levels on Urban Expressways." *Journal of Political Economy* 85 (1977). Develops a long-run model of highway pricing and investment and uses the model to estimate optimum congestion taxes.

Keeler, Theodore E.; Kenneth A. Small; George S. Cluff; and Jeffrey K. Finke. "Optimal Peak-Load Pricing, Investment and Service Levels on Urban Expressways." Institute of Urban and Regional Development, Working Paper no. 253. Berkeley: University of California, 1975.   Develops a long-run model of highway pricing and investment and uses the model to estimate optimum congestion taxes.

McConnell-Fay, Natalie. "Tackling Traffic Congestion in the San Francisco Bay Area." *Transportation Quarterly* 40 (1986), pp. 159–70.   A planner's view of the congestion problem and alternative policy responses.

Meyer, John R., and José A. Gómez-Ibáñez. *Autos, Transit and Cities*. Cambridge, Mass.: Harvard Univ. Press, 1981. Chapter 11, pp. 185–229.

Pozdena, Randall J. "Unlocking Gridlock." *Federal Reserve Bank of San Francisco Weekly Letter* (December 1988). pp. 1–5.   Updates the Keeler et al. (1975) estimates of congestion tolls.

Sullivan, Arthur M. "The General Equilibrium Effects of Congestion Externalities." *Journal of Urban Economics* 14 (1983), pp. 80–104. Uses a general-equilibrium computer model to simulate the effects of optimum congestion externalities on land rent, land use, and city size.

Vickrey, William S. "Pricing in Urban and Suburban Transport." In *Urban Economics: Readings and Analysis*, ed. Ronald E. Grieson. Boston: Little, Brown, 1973, pp. 106–18. Reprint. *American Economic Review* 53 (1963), pp. 452–65.

Walters, A. A. *The Economics of Road User Charges.* Baltimore: The Johns Hopkins Press, 1968. Chapters 2 and 3.

Watson, Peter L., and Edward P. Holland. "Congestion Pricing—The Example of Singapore." In *Urban Transportation Economics, Special report 181.* Washington, D.C.: Transportation Research Board, 1978, pp. 27–30. Reprint. *Finance and Development* 13 (March 1976), pp. 20–24.

Williams, Stephen R. "Getting Downtown, Relief of Highway Congestion through Pricing." In *Urban Economic Issues,* ed. Stephan Mehay and Geoffrey Nunn. Glenview, Ill.: Scott, Foresman, 1984. Discusses the efficiency and equity effects of congestion tolls and describes Singapore's congestion policy.

Wohl, Martin. "Congestion Toll Pricing for Public Transport Facilities." In *Public Prices for Public Products,* ed. Selma Mushkin. Washington, D.C.: The Urban Institute, 1972, pp. 245–46.

Parking Taxes and Other Alternatives to Congestion Taxes

DiRenzo, J.; B. Cima; and E. Barber. *Parking Management Tactics Volume 3: Reference Guide.* Washington, D.C.: U.S. Department of Transportation, 1981. Reports the results of the increase in parking costs in Ottawa, Canada.

Kulash, Damian. *Parking Taxes as Roadway Prices: A Case Study of San Francisco Experience.* Washington, D.C.: The Urban Institute, 1973, pp. 25–28.

McElhiney, Paul T. "Evaluating Freeway Performance in Los Angeles." *Traffic Quarterly* 14 (July 1960), pp. 296–312.

Miller, Gerald K., and Carol T. Everett. "Raising Commuter Parking Prices—An Empirical Study." *Transportation* 11 (1982), pp. 105–29. Examines the result of an increase in parking costs for government employees in Washington, D.C.

Mohring, Herbert. "The Benefits of Reserved Bus Lanes, Mass Transit Subsidies, and Marginal Cost Pricing in Alleviating Traffic Congestion." Chapter 6 in *Current Issues in Urban Economics,* ed. Peter Meiszkowski and Mahlon Straszheim. Baltimore: The Johns Hopkins Press, 1979, pp.165–95.

Parody, Thomas E. "Implementation of a Peak-Period Pricing Strategy for CBD Parking." *Transportation Quarterly* 38 (1984), pp. 153–69. Describes the results of an experiment with peak-period parking taxes in Madison, Wisconsin.

Willson, Richard W. "Parking Subsidies and the Drive-Alone Commuter: New Evidence and Implications." Paper presented at the annual meeting of the Transportation Research Board, 1988. Reports the results of a survey of parking subsidies in Los Angeles.

Highway Investment

Downs, Anthony. "The Law of Peak Hour Expressway Congestion." In *Urban Problems and Prospects,* 2d ed. ed. Anthony Downs. Skokie, Ill.: Rand McNally, 1976, pp. 185–99. Reprint. *Traffic Quarterly* (July 1962), pp. 393–409.

Keeler, Theodore E., and Kenneth A. Small. "Optimal Peak-Load Pricing, Investment and Service Levels on Urban Expressways." *Journal of Political Economy* 85 (1977), pp.

1–25. Develops a long-run model of highway pricing and investment and uses the model to estimate optimum congestion taxes.

Keeler, Theodore E.; Kenneth A. Small; George S. Cluff; and Jeffrey K. Finke. "Optimal Peak-Load Pricing, Investment and Service Levels on Urban Expressways." Institute of Urban and Regional Development, Working Paper no. 253. Berkeley: University of California, 1975. Develops a long-run model of highway pricing and investment and uses the model to estimate optimum congestion taxes.

Kraus, Marvin. "Scale Economies Analysis for Urban Highway Networks." *Journal of Urban Economics* 9 (1981), pp. 1–22.

Mohring, Herbert. "Urban Highway Investments." In *Measuring Benefits of Government Investments*, ed. Robert Dorfman. Washington, D.C.: Brookings Institution, 1965.

Auto Safety

Altshuler, Alan A. *The Urban Transportation System*. Cambridge, Mass.: Joint Center for Urban Studies of MIT and Harvard, 1979. Chapter 7, pp. 210–51.

Case, H. W.; A. Burg; and J. D. Baird. "Vehicle Size and Accident Involvement: A Preliminary Study." *Journal of Safety Research* 5 (1973), pp. 26–35.

Crandall, Robert W.; Howard K. Gruenspecht; Theodore E. Keeler; and Lester B. Lave. *Regulating the Automobile*. Washington, D.C.: Brookings Institution, 1986. Chapter 3 explores the costs of safety regulations. Chapter 4 discusses the effects of safety regulations on highway death rates. Chapter 7 discusses the conflicting goals of regulations on auto safety, auto emissions, and fuel economy.

Meyer, John R., and José A. Gómez-Ibáñez. *Autos, Transit and Cities*. Cambridge, Mass.: Harvard Univ. Press, 1981, Chapter 13, pp. 254–76.

Peltzman, Sam. *Regulation of Automobile Safety*. Washington, D.C.: American Enterprise Institute, 1975. Explores the effect of auto safety regulation on driver behavior.

Auto Pollution

Ackerman, Bruce. "Clean (Cough) Air." *New York Times*. August 20, 1977, p. 21.

Altshuler, Alan A. *The Urban Transportation System*. Cambridge, Mass.: Joint Center for Urban Studies of MIT and Harvard, 1979. Chapter 6, pp. 172–209.

Crandall, Robert W.; Howard K. Gruenspecht; Theodore E. Keeler; and Lester B. Lave. *Regulating the Automobile*. Washington, D.C.: Brookings Institution, 1986. Chapter 5 discusses the effects of emissions policy on air pollution. Chapter 3 explores the costs of emissions controls. Chapter 7 discusses the conflicting goals of regulations for auto safety, auto emissions, and fuel economy.

Freeman, A. Myrick. *Air and Water Pollution Control: A Benefit-Cost Assessment*. New York: John Wiley & Sons, 1982. Estimates the benefits and costs of air pollution programs.

Gómez-Ibáñez, José A., and Gary R. Fauth. "Downtown Auto Restraint Policies: The Costs and Benefits for Boston." *Journal of Transport Economics and Policy* 14 (1980), pp. 133–53.

Meyer, John R., and José A. Gómez-Ibáñez. *Autos, Transit and Cities*. Cambridge, Mass.: Harvard Univ. Press, 1981, Chapter 9. pp. 149–70.

Mills, Edwin S., and Lawrence J. White. "Government Policies toward Automotive Emissions Control." In *Approaches to Controlling Air Pollution*, ed. Ann F. Friedlaender. Cambridge, Mass.: MIT Press, 1978, pp. 348–409.

National Academy of Sciences and National Academy of Engineering, *Air Quality and Automotive Emission Control*. Vol. 4, *The Costs and Benefits of Automobile Emission Control*. Report prepared for the Senate Committee on Public Works. Washington, D.C.: U.S. Government Printing Office, 1974.

Straszheim, Mahlon R. "Assessing the Social Costs of Urban Transportation Technologies." In *Current Issues in Urban Economics*, ed. Peter Meiszkowski and Mahlon Straszheim. Baltimore: The Johns Hopkins Press, 1979. Reviews the literature on the externalities associated with automobiles and highways.

CHAPTER 18

Mass Transit

While real trolleys in Newark, Philadelphia, Pittsburgh, and Boston languish for lack of patronage and government support, millions of people flock to Disneyland to ride fake trains that don't go anywhere.

Kenneth T. Jackson

This chapter addresses six questions about urban mass transit, devoting one section to each question. First, what are the facts on transit ridership? Second, how do commuters choose a travel mode, and why do so few commuters use mass transit? Third, how does the cost of a bus system compare to the cost of a heavy-rail system and the cost of an auto-based system? Third, how do the costs of the new light-rail systems compare to the costs of alternative transit systems? Fifth, why do most transit systems generate large operating deficits? Finally, should the private sector play a greater role in the provision of mass transit?

MASS TRANSIT FACTS

Table 18–1 shows the commuting patterns and transit ridership in U.S. metropolitan areas. Public transit, which includes buses, streetcars, subways, elevated trains, and railroads, is most popular among workers who commute within the central city, being used by 15.8 percent of such commuters. Transit is less popular among workers who commute from a suburban residence to a central-city job: only 8 percent of these commuters use transit. For the most frequent commuting trip (from suburb to suburb), only 1.5 percent of commuters use public transit.

Table 18–2 shows the trends in transit ridership in the United States. Between 1950 and 1980, the total number of transit trips decreased by 50 percent. Transit ridership reached its low point in the early 1970s and has increased since then. The trolley coach (a bus powered by overhead electric wires) reached its peak in 1950 and has declined since then. The use of light-rail systems (streetcars) decreased steadily between 1940 and 1980, but has recently staged a recovery: systems have recently been built or restored in Portland, San Jose, Sacramento, Buffalo, San Diego and Pittsburgh. In Canada, there are new light-rail systems in Edmonton and Calgary.

There is substantial variation in transit ridership between metropolitan areas. In 1980, the percentage of workers riding transit was 45 percent in New York, but no more than 18 percent in any other metropolitan area. In the 25

TABLE 18–1 Commuting Patterns and Public Transit Use

| | Percent of | Percent Using | | |
Commute Pattern	Trips	Public Transit	Bus or Streetcar	Heavy Rail
Central-city residents				
Job in central city	33.1	15.8	10.0	5.8
Job in suburb	6.8	5.5	4.9	0.6
Suburban residents				
Job in central city	20.1	8.0	5.0	3.0
Job in suburb	40.1	1.5	1.4	0.1
Total	100.0	7.8	5.2	2.6

Definitions:
1. Public transit: buses, streetcars, subways, elevated trains, and railroad.
2. Heavy rail: subways, elevated trains, and railroad.

SOURCE: U.S. Bureau of Census, 1980 *Census of Population. Journey to Work. Characteristics of Workers* (Washington, D.C.: U.S. Government Printing Office, 1984).

largest metropolitan areas, there were 4 areas with transit ridership between 15 and 18 percent (Chicago, San Francisco–Oakland, Washington, D.C., and Boston) and 4 with transit ridership between 10 and 15 percent (Philadelphia, Baltimore, Pittsburgh, Cleveland, and New Orleans). In the remaining 16 large metropolitan areas, less than 10 percent of commuters took mass transit. Among the areas with the lowest transit ridership were Detroit (3.7 percent), Dallas (3.4 percent), Houston (3 percent), and San Diego (3.3 percent).

What are the elasticities of demand for mass transit? By how much does transit ridership increase when transit fares decrease or transit service improves? There are four general conclusions from empirical studies of transit ridership:

1. **Price elasticity.** The demand for transit is price-inelastic, with an elasticity between -0.20 and -0.50 (Beesely and Kemp 1987). A common

TABLE 18–2 Public Transit Ridership, 1940–1980 (numbers in thousands)

Year	Total Rides	Heavy Rail	Light Rail	Trolley Coach	Motor Bus
1940	13,098	2,382	5,943	534	4,239
1950	17,246	2,264	3,904	1,658	9,420
1960	9,395	1,850	463	657	6,425
1970	7,332	1,881	235	182	5,034
1980	8,228	2,290	107	45	5,731

SOURCE: American Public Transit Association, *Transit Fact Book* (Washington, D.C., 1981).

rule of thumb is that a 10 percent increase in fares will decrease ridership by about 3.3 percent, meaning that the price elasticity is -0.33.

2. **Time elasticities.** The demand for transit is more responsive to changes in travel times than changes in fares. For the **line-haul** portion of the trip (time spent in the vehicle), Domencich, Kraft, and Valette (1972) estimate an elasticity of -0.39: a 10 percent increase in line-haul time will decrease ridership by about 3.9 percent. For access time (time spent getting to the bus stop or transit station), they estimate an elasticity of -0.71.

3. **Value of travel time.** Commuters value time spent in the transit vehicle at about one third to one half the wage: the typical commuter would be willing to pay about a third or a half of his hourly wage to avoid an hour on the bus or train. The value of time spent walking and waiting is two to three times larger: the typical commuter would be willing to pay about his hourly wage to avoid an hour of walking or waiting time.

4. **Noncommuting trips.** The elasticities of demand for noncommuting travel are higher than the elasticities for commuting trips.

There are three principal implications from these empirical results. First, an increase in transit fares will increase total fare revenue. A fare increase will decrease ridership by a relatively small amount, so total revenue (fare times ridership) will increase. Second, a simultaneous improvement in service and fares may increase ridership. Suppose that a transit authority increases the frequency and speed of buses and finances the improved service with increased fares. Because people are more sensitive to changes in time costs than changes in fares, ridership may increase. Third, service improvements that decrease walking and waiting time (more frequent service, shorter distances between stops) will generate larger increases in ridership than service improvements that decrease line-haul time.

CHOOSING A TRAVEL MODE—THE COMMUTER

This section considers modal choice from the perspective of the commuter. The commuter chooses the mode that minimizes the total cost of travel, which is defined as the sum of time and monetary costs. Suppose that a commuter has three travel options: the automobile, the bus, and a fixed-rail transit system such as San Francisco's Bay Area Rapid Transit (BART) or Washington, D.C.'s Metro.

The commuting trip can be divided into three parts. The **collection phase** involves travel from the home to the main travel vehicle. The auto mode has no collection cost because the driver uses his own vehicle. The bus mode has a moderate collection cost because the rider must walk from his home to the bus stop. The fixed-rail system has the highest collection cost because there is usually a relatively long average distance between transit stations, so the riders must either walk a long distance or take another mode (e.g., auto or bus) from his home to the transit station. The **line-haul phase** is the part of the trip spent on the main travel vehicle. The heavy-rail mode has the shortest line-haul time because it has an exclusive right-of-way and thus avoids rush-hour congestion. Although the bus and the auto both travel on congested streets and highways, the auto is faster because the bus must stop to pick up passengers along the way. The **distribution phase** involves travel from the end of the vehicular trip (at the downtown transit station, parking garage, or bus stop) to the workplace. If parking is available near the workplace, the auto will have the shortest distribution time, followed by the bus and the fixed-rail system.

An Example of Modal Choice

Table 18–3 lists the monetary and time costs of the three travel modes for Carla, a commuter who travels 10 miles from her suburban home to a job in the central city. The computations are based on the assumption that Carla values the time spent on the transit vehicle at one third her wage rate and values time spent walking and waiting at her wage rate. If her wage is $18 per hour, she is willing to pay $6 to avoid one hour of in-vehicle time and $18 to avoid one hour of walking and waiting time. Therefore, the cost of walking and

TABLE 18–3   Costs of Travel Modes and Modal Choice

	Auto	Bus	BART
Collection cost			
Collection time (minutes)	0	10	15
Cost per minute ($)	0.30	0.30	0.30
Collection time cost ($)	0.00	3.00	4.50
Line-haul cost			
Line-haul time (minutes)	40	50	30
Cost per minute ($)	0.10	0.10	0.10
Line-haul time costs ($)	4.00	5.00	3.00
Distribution cost			
Distribution time (minutes)	0	5	9
Cost per minute ($)	0.30	0.30	0.30
Distribution time cost ($)	0.00	1.50	2.70
Monetary cost ($)	2.00	1.00	1.50
Parking cost ($)	3.00	0.00	0.00
Total time cost (minutes)	4.00	9.50	10.20
Total monetary cost ($)	5.00	1.00	1.50
Total cost ($)	9.00	10.50	11.70

waiting time is 30 cents per minute, and the cost of in-vehicle time is 10 cents per minute.

1. **Collection time cost.** Carla walks to the bus stop or the BART station. Since the bus stop is closer to her home, the bus has lower collection costs.

2. **Line-haul time cost.** BART is the fastest mode (it operates on an exclusive right-of-way), followed by autos (which travel on congested streets) and buses (which travel on congested streets and stop to pick up passengers).

3. **Distribution cost.** Carla parks her auto in a company parking lot under her office building, so the distribution cost of the auto trip is zero. The bus stop is relatively close to the office, so the bus has lower distribution costs than BART.

4. **Monetary cost.** The monetary cost of the auto trip is $0.20 per mile, or $2.00. The bus fare is $1, and the BART fare is $1.50. Half of the $6.00 daily parking cost is allocated to the morning commute.

The cost of driving is less than the cost of the bus and BART. Although the monetary cost of driving exceeds the monetary cost of the bus by $4, the lower time cost of the auto more than offsets its higher monetary cost. Similarly, the auto is more expensive but faster than BART. The largest difference in time costs is for collection and distribution costs, where the auto has a cost advantage of $4.50 over the bus ($3.00 for collection + $1.50 for distribution) and $7.20 over BART ($4.50 + $2.70). Since the auto has a lower cost than both the bus and BART, Carla will drive to work.

What would it take to persuade Carla to switch from her auto to mass transit? There are several possibilities.

1. **Subsidized transit.** If the bus and BART were free, Carla would still drive. To get her to switch to the bus, she would have to be paid a bribe of 50 cents per bus ride. A larger bribe ($1.20) would be required to get her to switch to BART. In general, transit fares must decrease by relatively large amounts to offset the time advantages of the automobile.

2. **Line-haul time.** If the line-haul time of the bus decreased from 50 minutes to less than 35 minutes, Carla would ride the bus. She would take BART if its line-haul time decreased to less than 3 minutes.

3. **Collection and distribution time.** Carla would ride the bus if the collection and distribution time of the bus decreased from 15 minutes to less than 10 minutes and would switch to BART if its collection and distribution time decreased from 24 minutes to less than 15 minutes.

4. **Auto monetary cost.** Carla would ride the bus if the unit cost increased from 20 cents to 36 cents per mile. As reported in Chapter 17 (Autos and Highways), estimates of the congestion tax are in the range of 21 to 65 cents per mile for rush-hour traffic, so the imposition of a conges-

tion tax would cause her switch to the bus. Similarly, if the city imposed a pollution tax of at least 16 cents per mile, Carla would stop driving.

5. **Parking cost.** Carla would ride the bus if the parking cost rose to at least $4.50 ($9 per day).

6. **Wage.** If Carla's wage dropped to $13, the bus would be less costly than the auto, and if her wage dropped to $10, BART would be less costly than the auto. As the wage decreases, the opportunity cost of travel time decreases, increasing the relative attractiveness of the modes with relatively low monetary costs and high time costs.

To summarize, to get Carla to switch to transit, the changes in either monetary costs or line-haul time costs would have to be relatively large. On the other hand, she would switch to transit with relatively small changes in collection and distribution time costs. These conclusions are consistent with the transit elasticities discussed earlier in the chapter.

What type of commuters will take mass transit instead of driving? There are five possibilities.

1. **Proximity to stops and stations.** A person who lives near a bus stop or a rail station has relatively low collection costs for transit and is more likely to take the bus or BART.

2. **Low opportunity cost.** For a person who has a low opportunity cost of travel time (a worker with a low wage, a student, a retired person), the time costs of travel are relatively low. As a result, the advantages of transit (lower monetary cost) dominate the disadvantages (longer commuting time). Such a person is more likely to choose transit.

3. **Low walking cost.** A person who enjoys walking will have relatively low collection and distribution costs and is therefore more likely to choose transit.

4. **Disutility of driving.** A person who dislikes the hassle and anxiety of driving is more likely to choose transit. In terms of the numerical example, such a person will have a relatively high cost for in-vehicle auto time and is more likely to take the bus or BART. In contrast, a person who considers driving a form of athletics will buy a pair of gloves and drive to work.

5. **No automobile.** Many of the poor do not have access to an auto, so their only option is to use public transit.

Transit Service and Modal Choice

How do changes in transit design and scheduling affect ridership? Transit ridership will increase when service improvements decrease the time costs of transit. As explained earlier, commuters are most responsive to changes in collection and distribution time (walking and waiting time).

Designing the Bus System.   Consider first the bus system. The bus company affects time costs in two ways. First, it chooses the bus headway, the period of time between buses on the bus route. As the headway decreases, riders spend less time waiting at the bus stop, so their time costs decrease. Second, the bus company chooses the frequency of stops in the residential collection area. An increase in the frequency of stops decreases walking distances and collection costs. Similarly, the more frequent the stops in the downtown distribution area, the lower the distribution costs. An increase in the frequency of stops also increases line-haul (in-vehicle) time: more time is spent picking up and dropping off passengers, so the trip takes a longer time.

Designing the Fixed-Rail System.   Consider next the design of a fixed-rail system. San Francisco's BART provides a nice illustration of the trade-offs associated with the design of a rail transit system. There are two basic design trade-offs.

1. **Mainline versus integrated system.** BART is considered a mainline system because it relies on other transit systems to collect its riders from residential neighborhoods. Riders must either walk, drive, or ride a bus to the BART station. The alternative to the mainline system is an integrated system, under which commuters make the entire commute trip on a single transit mode.

2. **Spacing between stations.** BART has widely spaced stations (about 2.5 miles apart), so there are few stops on the way to the city center. As a result, travel time from the suburban station to the downtown station (line-haul time) is relatively short and in-vehicle time costs are relatively low. On the other hand, the average commuter must travel a relatively long distance from his home to one of the widely spaced transit stations, so collection costs (by foot, bus, or car) are relatively high.

BART was designed to compete with the line-haul portion of the automobile trip. It achieves this objective, providing comfortable, speedy service from the suburban stations to the city center. There is a trade-off, however: collection costs are relatively high because BART is a mainline system with widely spaced stations. Because walking and waiting time is more costly to commuters than in-vehicle time, the negative attribute (high collection costs) dominates the positive one (comfortable and speedy line-haul travel), so the full cost of a BART trip is relatively high. As a result, BART has diverted a relatively small number of auto commuters.

Bus and Car-Pool Lanes.   Another design issue concerns the treatment of high-occupancy vehicles (HOV), such as car pools and buses. When a city establishes a "diamond" lane for the exclusive use of buses and carpools, the line-haul times of buses and car pools will decrease. Under the diamond-lane approach, buses and carpools have the advantages of the fixed-rail system (shorter line-haul times) without the disadvantages (high collection and distribution costs). As a result, some drivers will switch to a bus or a carpool. Because the elasticity of transit demand with respect to line-haul time is moderate (−0.39), there will be a moderate diversion of auto traffic.

What are the effects of diamond lanes on commuters who continue to drive? There is good news and bad news. The good news is that because some auto drivers are diverted to buses and carpools, there will be less auto traffic. In Figure 18–1, the diamond lane shifts the demand curve to the left, decreasing trip costs for the original trip-cost curve. The bad news is that there are fewer lanes for the remaining autos: the diamond lane decreases the amount of road space, so the congestion threshold decreases and the trip-cost curve shifts to the left. In this example, the shift of the demand curve is small relative to the shift of the cost curve, so the trip cost increases from $5 to $6. If shift of the demand curve were relatively large, the trip cost would decrease.

Figure 18–1 accurately depicts recent experiences with diamond lanes. The first experiment with diamond lanes occurred along the Santa Monica Freeway in Los Angeles. The diamond lanes increased the average trip costs of a vociferous group of auto commuters, and the experiment was short-lived.

FIGURE 18–1   Diamond Lanes and Auto Trip Costs

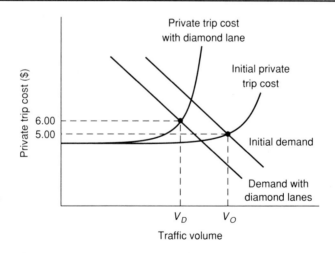

The addition of diamond lanes (reserved for buses and carpools) affects travel in nondiamond lanes in two ways. There are fewer vehicles in nondiamond lanes, so the demand curve shifts to the left. In addition, there are fewer lanes, so the trip-cost curve shifts to the left. If a relatively small number of vehicles are diverted to the diamond lanes, the net cost of travel in nondiamond lanes will increase. In this example, the cost increases from $5 to $6.

The city of Boston experienced similar problems when it set up diamond lanes along the Southeast Expressway.

Some cities have built new lanes for buses and carpools. Among the cities that have built new diamond lanes are Miami (along Interstate 95), Washington, D.C. (along the Shirley Expressway), and Los Angeles (along the San Bernardino Freeway). By building new lanes instead of taking away auto lanes, these cities did not impose any explicit costs on auto drivers, so there was little opposition to the diamond lanes. The new diamond lanes do, however, impose an implicit cost on drivers: if the new lanes were opened to auto traffic, the trip-cost curve would shift to the right, decreasing travel times for auto commuters.

CHOOSING A SYSTEM—THE PLANNER'S PROBLEM

This section discusses modal choice from the perspective of a transportation planner. The planner must decide what type of transportation system to build, choosing one of three options: an auto-based highway system, an integrated bus system, and a fixed-rail system like BART or Metro. Estimates of the costs of these alternative systems are provided by a study of transportation options in the San Francisco Bay area (by Keeler, Merewitz, Fisher, Small, and Associates 1975).

Keeler et al. estimated the costs of three different commuting systems: an auto-based system, an integrated bus system, and BART (with feeder buses). The principal conclusions of their study are shown in Figure 18–2. The horizontal axis measures the number of commuters travelling through a transportation corridor during the one-hour peak period. The vertical axis measures the long-run average cost of a typical commuting trip (a six-mile line-haul and additional time spent in residential collection and downtown distribution). The cost curves show that the bus system is more efficient than the auto system for volumes above 1,100 passengers per hour and is more efficient than BART for all traffic volumes. The auto system is more efficient than BART for volumes up to about 22,000 passengers per hour.

Costs of the Auto System

The cost of the auto system is the sum of the driver's time costs, the auto operating costs, and the public costs of highways and auto traffic. The public costs include the cost of building the optimum road system. As explained in the previous chapter, the revenue from the optimum congestion tax equals the cost of building the optimum road, so congestion taxes can be used to both internalize congestion externalities and pay for the roads. Also included in the public costs are the costs of air and noise pollution.

The average-cost curve for the auto system is horizontal for two reasons. First, Keeler et al. assume that the average operating cost and the average pollution cost (cost per mile) do not depend on traffic volume. Second, the trip

FIGURE 18–2   Costs of Alternative Transit Systems

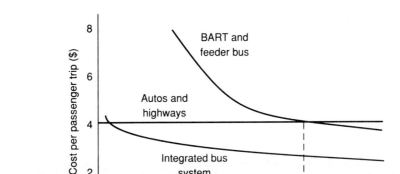

The average cost of auto traffic is independent of auto volume, but the average costs of an integrated bus system and BART decrease as volume increases. The bus system is more efficient than BART for all volumes studied and more efficient than an auto-based system for volumes exceeding 1,100.

time (and private trip cost) does not depend on traffic volume: as volume increases, the road is widened to accommodate the increased traffic, so travel speeds are constant. Given constant returns to scale in highways, a doubling of highway capacity doubles traffic volume without changing the trip time. Using data for 1972, Keeler et al. estimate that the full cost of an auto trip with a six-mile line-haul segment was $4.15.

Costs of the Bus System

The cost of the integrated bus system is the sum of time costs, agency costs, and the public costs of the bus system. The agency costs include both operating costs and capital costs. Included in the public costs are (a) the costs of modifying the roadway to accommodate buses and (b) pollution costs.

The average-cost curve is negatively sloped for two reasons. First, as ridership increases, the fixed costs of administering the bus system are spread over more riders. Second, as ridership increases, collection and distribution times decrease. An increase in ridership decreases headways (the time between buses) and decreases the space between bus stops, so riders spend less time walking to and waiting for the bus. In addition, an increase in ridership allows a bus to fill up with a shorter collection route. Less time is spent picking up passengers, so in-vehicle time decreases. According to Keeler et al., if the traffic volume along the corridor exceeds 1,100 passengers, the express bus system is less costly than the auto system.

Costs of BART

The BART option involves a mainline heavy-rail system and feeder buses to bring commuters to the BART stations. The time cost of the BART option is the sum of walking, waiting, and in-vehicle time costs. The agency cost is the sum of the operating and capital costs of the feeder buses and the mainline system. Given the substantial investment in tracks and right-of-ways, the capital costs of the BART option are large.

The BART cost curve is negatively sloped for three reasons. First, the system has substantial fixed costs, which are spread over more riders as ridership increases. Second, as ridership increases, headways decrease, so commuters spend less time waiting for trains. Third, an increase in bus ridership decreases the time and monetary costs of feeder-bus service.

BART is more costly than the bus system for three reasons. First, because it is a mainline system with widely spaced stations, its collection and distribution costs are relatively high. Second, its capital costs are very large. According to Webber (1976), BART could have purchased enough buses to carry all of its passengers for only $40 million (one fortieth of BART's $1.6 billion capital costs). Third, BART has surprisingly high operating costs: in 1975, the operating cost was 15.7 cents per passenger mile, compared to 13.6 cents for a bus. Most planners were surprised to discover that the large investment in capital equipment did not generate much savings in operating costs.

System Choice

The Keeler et al. study provides important information for transit planners. For all corridor volumes studied (up to 30,000 passengers per hour), BART was more costly than an integrated bus system. At a peak volume of 30,000 passengers per hour, BART is 50 percent more costly than the bus system. In 1984, BART's peak ridership through the transbay tube was 15,300 passengers per hour. The lesson for planners is clear: with the possible exceptions of New York City and Chicago, which have corridor volumes exceeding 30,000 passengers per hour, an integrated bus system is likely to be more efficient than a modern heavy-rail system like BART.

Experiences with new heavy-rail systems in other metropolitan areas have been similar to the BART experience. To cover its operating and capital costs, the Washington, D.C. Metro system would have to charge a one-way fare of $8 (Gordon and Richardson 1988). Ridership on the new systems in Atlanta, Miami, and Baltimore have fallen well short of the projected levels. The problems with heavy-rail systems should not be surprising in light of Keeler et al.'s conclusion that the corridor volume must exceed 30,000 to make a heavy-rail system competitive with a bus system.

LIGHT RAIL

In recent years, many medium-sized cities have built light-rail transit systems. Light rail is the modern version of the trolley (streetcar) system that was popular in the late 1800s and early 1900s. The first modern light-rail system opened in Edmonton in 1978. Since then, new systems have opened in San Diego, Calgary, Buffalo, Portland, Vancouver, Sacramento, and San Jose. Many other cities are planning to build new systems or extend old streetcar and trolley systems.

How does light rail compare to buses and heavy rail? Gomez-Ibanez (1985) has studied the costs and performance of new light-rail systems in San Diego, Edmonton, and Calgary and comes to the following conclusions:

1. **Capital costs.** The capital costs of light rail include the costs of the vehicles, the track, and the power distribution system. These costs make light-rail more costly than a bus system, which uses less expensive vehicles and travels along regular streets and highways. Light rail is much less costly than heavy rail: the cost per mile is between $7 million and $20 million per mile, compared to $50 million to $200 million per mile for heavy rail. Light rail is less expensive because it typically uses surface streets (instead of requiring subways or elevated guideways) and is designed for lower speeds.

2. **Operating costs.** Compared to a bus system, light rail has lower labor costs because it needs fewer operators: a three-car train can be operated by one person and can carry about 10 times as many riders as a standard bus. Because light rail has higher maintenance costs for its vehicles and its right-of-way, however, its total operating costs are equal to or greater than the operating costs of an equivalent bus system.

3. **Performance.** Most light-rail systems consist of one or two radial rail lines, with feeder buses for the collection and distribution phases of the transit trip. Like the heavy-rail systems, the light-rail systems have higher collection and distribution costs than bus systems. Light rail has shorter line-haul times and provides a more comfortable ride than the bus.

Table 18–4 compares the costs of the San Diego light-rail system to the bus routes it replaced. The total cost per light-rail passenger was $3.11, compared to $1.16 for the bus system. Light rail has moderately higher operating costs and much higher capital costs. The light-rail system seems to have increased transit ridership: ridership in the area served by the system increased

TABLE 18–4   Comparison of San Diego's Light-Rail and Bus Systems

	Bus Systems	Light-Rail Systems
Costs per passenger		
Operating costs ($)	0.82	1.02
Capital costs ($)	0.34	2.09
Total costs ($)	1.16	3.11
Ridership (thousands per year)	3,398	4,845
Cost per new light-rail passenger ($)		5.47

SOURCE: Jose A. Gomez-Ibanez, "A Dark Side to Light Rail?" *American Planning Association Journal* 51 (Summer 1985), pp. 337–51.

from 3.4 million to 4.8 million per year. According to Gomez-Ibanez, much of the increased ridership was caused by population growth in the corridor served by light rail. If one assumes that the entire increase in ridership was caused by the introduction of the light-rail system, the cost per additional transit rider was $5.74. The San Diego experience suggests that although light rail may increase ridership, it does so at a relatively high cost.

SUBSIDIES FOR MASS TRANSIT

In 1985, passenger fares covered only about 39 percent of the operating costs of mass transit. As shown in Figure 18–3, the remainder of operating costs were covered by local governments (providing 22 percent of revenue), state governments (13 percent), the federal government (12 percent), and other sources (13 percent). Can transit subsidies be justified on efficiency grounds?

Justification for Transit Subsidies

There are two justifications for the subsidization of mass transit. First, there are substantial scale economies in the provision of transit, so transit systems have the characteristics of a natural monopoly. As explained in Chapter 15 (Decision Making in Local Government), the subsidization of a natural monopoly promotes efficiency. Figure 18–4 shows the long-run average-cost and marginal-cost curves for a transit system. The curves are negatively sloped because (a) there are substantial fixed costs associated with setting up the system and (b) the marginal cost of adding another rider is relatively small. The optimum ridership (R^*) is where the marginal social benefit (from the demand curve) equals the long-run marginal cost. To generate this level of ridership, the price must be P^*, which is less than the average total cost. The deficit asso-

FIGURE 18–3 Transit Revenue Sources, 1982

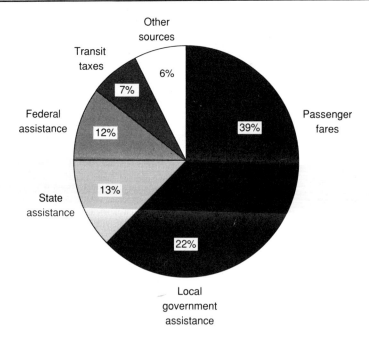

ciated with marginal-cost pricing is shown by the shaded area. If the transit system were forced to cover all its costs, it would charge a price of P' and generate ridership of R', which is less than the optimum ridership.

The second justification for transit subsidies is explained in Chapter 17 (Autos and Highways). Auto travel is underpriced because drivers do not pay the external costs associated with highway congestion and air pollution. Therefore, transit will be overpriced relative to auto travel, and transit subsidies can be used to offset the artificially low price of autos. As explained in Chapter 17, there are trade-offs with transit subsidies: although the subsidies discourage auto use and thus decrease congestion and pollution, they also cause the underpricing of transit and urban travel in general, leading to an excessive amount of travel. The policy question is whether the benefits of the subsidy (decreased congestion and air pollution) exceed the costs (too many resources used in transit and transportation).

How large a transit subsidy would be required to offset the underpricing of auto travel? Suppose that the appropriate congestion tax is, on average, 43 cents per mile and the pollution cost is 1 cent per mile. If the typical auto commute is 10 miles, the commuter avoids $4.40 worth of taxes per round trip. A transit subsidy of this amount would eliminate the artificial cost advantage of the automobile.

FIGURE 18–4   Transit Subsidies for Natural Monopoly

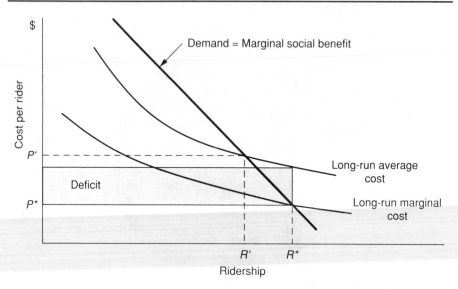

Mass transit is a natural monopoly: scale economies generate a negatively sloped long-run average-cost curve. The optimum output is where the demand curve (the marginal-benefit curve) intersects the marginal-cost curve. At the optimum ridership (R^*), price (P^*) is less than the average total cost, so the system will generate a deficit. The system would cover its cost at a price of P', but ridership (R') would be below the optimum level.

Reasons for Transit Deficits

Table 18–5 shows recent trends in transit revenues and costs. All dollar figures are in 1980 dollars. In 1965, the fare-box ratio (the ratio of fare revenue to operating cost) was 0.99, meaning that transit riders covered most of the operating costs of transit. By 1980, the fare-box ratio decreased to 0.42, meaning that transit riders paid only 42 percent of operating costs.

One reason for the growth in the transit deficit is that operating revenue decreased over time. Between 1965 and 1980, operating revenue per vehicle mile decreased from $1.72 to $1.23 (in 1980 dollars). Three factors contributed to the decline in revenue. First, the average passenger fare decreased from 47 cents in 1965 to 40 cents in 1980. Second, total ridership decreased slightly, from 8.25 billion to 8.23 billion. Third, the total vehicle miles increased from 2.01 billion miles to 2.09 billion miles. Because the number of riders decreased while vehicle miles increased, the number of riders per vehicle mile dropped. Since there were fewer riders paying lower fares, revenue per vehicle mile decreased.

The primary reason for the growth of the deficit is rising costs. Between

TABLE 18–5   Transit Revenue, Costs, and Deficits, 1960–1980

	1960	1965	1970	1975	1980
Fare-box ratio	1.02	0.99	0.86	0.54	0.42
Revenue					
Operating revenue per vehicle mile ($)	1.71	1.72	1.77	1.33	1.23
Fare per passenger ($)	0.46	0.47	0.54	0.47	0.40
Passengers (millions)	9,345	8,253	7,332	6,972	8,235
Cost					
Operating cost per vehicle mile ($)	1.65	1.72	2.06	2.67	2.98
Vehicle miles (millions)	2,143	2,008	1,883	1,990	2,093
Employees (thousands)	156	145	138	160	187
Vehicle miles per employee	13,737	13,848	13,645	12,438	11,193
Passengers per employee	59,904	56,917	53,130	43,575	44,519
Federal funds (million $)	0	27	299	1,608	3,367

SOURCE: Gordon J. Fielding, *Managing Transit Strategically* (San Francisco: Jossey-Bass, 1987), Tables 2 and 3, pp. 24–25.

1965 and 1980, the operating cost per vehicle mile increased from $1.72 to $2.98 (in 1980 dollars). Operating costs increased because of rising wages, increased energy costs, and decreased labor productivity. One of the reasons for rising wages is explained in Chapter 15 (Decision Making in Local Government): the Baumol model shows that the wages of service workers will rise despite constant productivity because of rising productivity (and wages) in manufacturing.

The simple facts on labor productivity are startling. Between 1965 and 1980, total transit employment increased from 145,000 to 187,000. Since the number of vehicle miles increased by a smaller amount, the number of vehicle miles per employee decreased from 13,848 to 11,193. While the number of transit workers increased, the number of transit riders decreased, so the number of passenger rides per transit worker decreased from 56,917 to 44,519.

Why did the number of passengers per employee decrease? According to Fielding (1987), an important factor was an increase in the fraction of transit trips taken during the peak period. To explain the peaking problem, consider a city where transit ridership is uniform throughout the day: the city can serve its transit riders with a single bus running all day. Suppose that all the riders suddenly decide to travel during two rush hours: traffic volume during the two rush hours quadruples. The city will no longer be able to serve its transit riders with a single bus and a single bus driver, but will be forced to buy three more buses and hire more drivers.

What are the effects of the shift to peak ridership on the city's labor productivity and labor costs? Consider first the possibility that the city hires part-time drivers. If the city hires drivers by the hour, productivity does not change: the city will hire four part-time drivers instead of one full-time driver. On the other hand, if the city must hire four full-time drivers (who will be idle for six hours per day), its labor productivity will decrease and its labor costs will rise. In other words, if the shift to peak-period travel is combined with restrictive work rules that prevent part-time workers and split shifts, labor productivity will decrease and labor costs will increase.

Pickrell (1983) examined the relative importance of five factors that contributed to the growth of the transit deficit between 1970 and 1980. The factors, and their contributions to the growing deficit, are as follows:

1. Decrease in fares: responsible for 28 percent of the growth in deficit.
2. Increase in wages: 25 percent.
3. Decrease in labor productivity: 18 percent.
4. Increase in transit mileage: 16 percent.
5. Increase in energy cost: 12 percent.

Pickrell's results suggest that many factors contributed to the growing deficit. It's important to note that two of the contributing factors (the decrease in fares and the increase in mileage) were integral parts of transportation policy: in an attempt to divert commuters from polluting autos on congested highways, the government improved transit service while keeping fares relatively low. As explained in the previous chapter, an alternative policy would be to force auto drivers to pay the full cost of travel, including the costs of congestion and air pollution.

History of Federal Assistance

Federal assistance to mass transit grew from only $27 million in 1965 to $2.84 billion in 1985 (Fielding 1987). The Urban Mass Transit Act of 1964 established a program of capital subsidies for transit. For the first several years, most of the federal money was used to purchase unprofitable bus companies. Later, the money was used to invest in new capital equipment (buses, rail vehicles, tracks, and right-of-ways). Before 1973, the federal government paid two thirds of the cost of new transit projects. In 1974, the federal contribution increased to four fifths of the project cost. These capital subsidies create a bias toward capital-intensive transit systems (rail systems), and caused some cities to choose rail systems over less expensive bus systems.

Federal assistance for operating costs started with the National Mass Transportation Act of 1974. By 1984, a total of $5.3 billion of operating assistance was provided by all levels of government, with about half of the money coming from local governments, one third from state governments, and one sixth from the federal government. Federal operating subsidies were originally allocated to cities on the basis of total population. This allocation scheme caused large cities to receive relatively small subsidies per transit rider. Suppose that every city receives a one-cent subsidy per citizen. A large city in which 25 percent of the population uses transit would receive a subsidy of four cents per transit rider. A small city in which 2 percent of the population uses transit would receive a subsidy of 50 cents per rider. To solve this problem, allocations are now based primarily on transit ridership.

Since 1983, a portion of the revenue from the federal gasoline tax has been funnelled to mass transit. When the gas tax was increased by five cents per gallon, one cent of the increase was earmarked for a mass-transit fund. In 1984, a total of $1.2 billion was generated by this tax. The money was used to support bus systems ($300 million), existing rail systems ($500 million), and new transit systems ($400 million). A city receiving money from the transit fund must either use the money for mass transit or lose it. This creates an incentive to undertake transit projects when other projects (e.g., highway improvements) might be more efficient.

DEREGULATION—THE PRIVATE PROVISION OF TRANSIT

In most cities, mass transit is provided by the public sector. To shield the public transit system from competition, private transit activity (e.g., taxis and private bus service) is heavily regulated. Given the large deficits generated by public transit authorities, an obvious question is whether private industry could provide transit services more efficiently. There are two possible strategies for transit deregulation: the private provision of transit services through service contracts and free entry into the mass-transit market.

Contracting for Transit Services

Under the first type of deregulation, the local transit monopoly would be granted to a private firm instead of a government agency. Under a contracting arrangement, the local government first specifies the service characteristics of the transit system (e.g., headways, travel times, location of bus stops, fares) and then accepts bids from private firms for the transit service. The transit monopoly is granted to the firm that provides the service at the lowest cost.

The experiences with contracting arrangements are discussed by Lave (1985), Echols (1985), and Rosenbloom (1985). The city of Tidewater, Virginia, contracted for bus service to low-density areas. The private transit company provided the same transit service at a fraction of the cost of public bus service. Along one route, the deficit per passenger decreased from $4.75 to $1.63. Other cities using transit contracts have had similar experiences: the typical private bus company provides transit service for about half the cost of the public bus system. Contracts are also used for subsidized dial-a-ride services: in 1983, the city of Phoenix paid a local taxi company $104,425 to provide dial-a-ride services on Sundays, about one sixth the cost of using city buses for Sunday service.

Private firms provide transit services for lower costs for three reasons. First, they pay lower wages. Second, they have more flexible work rules. They have split shifts and use part-time workers, so they don't pay idle workers during the off-peak periods. Third, they use minibuses on low-density routes. In Phoenix, the private bus company uses minibuses with operating costs of $1.22 per mile, compared to $2.86 per mile for the standard bus.

Entry and Competition

Most cities grant monopoly power to the local transit authority and protect the transit authority from competition. There are two rationales for restricting entry:

1. **Cross-subsidization.** The city sets a single transit fare and then forces the transit authority to cover all routes, including some unprofitable ones. For some routes, fare revenue exceeds costs, providing a surplus that is used to subsidize service along unprofitable routes. If entry were allowed, a new firm could underprice public transit along the lucrative routes. The transit authority would make less money along the profitable routes, destroying the cross-subsidization scheme.

2. **Scale economies.** As explained earlier, there are substantial fixed costs in providing mass transit, so transit service is a natural monopoly. Although fixed-rail systems are certainly natural monopolies, the case is not so clear for bus systems. Walters (1982) and Morlok and Viton (1985) suggest that scale economies in bus transit are exhausted at a ridership level well below the volume of the typical medium-sized city.

Some cities allow private bus companies to compete with the public bus authority. The experiences with private bus companies are discussed by Johnson and Pikarsky (1985) and Walder (1985). In the city of Chicago, commuter bus clubs provide subscription bus service. In 1981, the full cost (including vehicle cost) of a private bus trip was $1.15, compared to a partial cost (excluding vehicle cost) of $1.44 for a public bus trip. In New York City, private commuter vans that travel from Staten Island to Manhattan charge the same fare as the public bus, but cover all of their costs and take less time to make the trip.

Would deregulation increase fares along some routes? Under deregulation, a route would not be served unless its total revenue exceeds its total cost. Therefore, transit fares along low-volume routes are likely to increase. If policy makers are concerned about poor households along low-volume routes, they could give money to the poor to offset the higher fares. Another option is to provide explicit subsidies for service along low-volume routes, a strategy adopted by Phoenix and other cities.

A second proposal for deregulation is to allow taxis to serve as transit vehicles. Under current regulations, a taxi cannot serve as a common carrier: the taxi can carry an individual or a small group of people travelling together, but cannot carry strangers in transit. If taxis were deregulated, they could pick up customers along routes of their own choice, serving as flexible transit vehicles.

The proposals for taxi deregulation have revived the jitney concept. Between 1915 and 1920, private cars were used as transit vehicles. The fare was five cents and the slang word for a nickel was "jitney," so the private vehicles were called jitneys. Most jitneys operated only during rush hours, so the jitney drivers could work at another job during the off-peak hours. Some jitneys operated as carpools: the driver posted his workplace on his windshield and picked up riders along his way to work. Other jitney drivers started out without a specific destination and then modified their routes as they picked up passengers. If taxis were deregulated to serve as common carriers, they would operate much like the jitneys of the early 1900s.

Summary—Flexible Transit?

The advocates of deregulation imagine a more competitive, flexible, and efficient transit system. The elimination of the public bus monopoly would lead to entry and competition. There would be a greater variety of transit vehicles: large buses would service high-volume routes, minibuses and vans would service low-volume routes, and jitneys would provide flexible transit service.

TRANSPORTATION AND LAND-USE PATTERNS

Part 2 of this book (Land Rent and Urban Land-Use Patterns) discusses the effects of changes in transportation technology on urban land-use patterns. For example, the development of the internal-combustion engine allowed the development of new travel modes (the car and the truck) that were more flexible and less costly than streetcars and horse-drawn wagons. The new modes decreased the reliance of firms and households on the central area of the city, allowing the decentralization of employment and residents. This section discusses two types of changes in transportation: an increase in gasoline costs and the construction of fixed-rail transit systems.

Gasoline Prices

Suppose that the real cost of gasoline increases. How will the increased cost of auto travel affect housing and land prices? As explained in Part 2 of the book, an increase in transportation costs will increase the slopes of the housing-price function and the residential bid-rent function. Studies by Small (1986) and Coulson and Engle (1987) confirm these theoretical predictions: an increase in the price of gasoline increases the relative attractiveness of locations near employment centers, so land and housing near employment centers increase in price.

How will an increase in the cost of gasoline affect the distributions of employment and population? The changes are likely to be relatively small for two reasons. First, the cost of gasoline is a relatively small part of the cost of travel. Second, other responses to an increase in gasoline prices (buying more fuel-efficient cars, carpooling, switching to public transit) allow drivers to decrease travel costs without changing their residences or workplaces. For these two reasons, the change in the prices of housing and land will be relatively small. Even if the changes in price were relatively large, it would be a long time before we would see large changes in population density near employment centers because structures last a long time and are costly to demolish. Small (1985) estimated that a $1 per gallon increase in the price of gasoline would cause a relatively small number of suburban households to move to the central city.

Fixed-Rail Systems and Land Use

How do fixed-rail systems affect land rent and land use? Dewees (1976) examined the effect of Toronto's subway on housing prices near the new transit stations and concluded that the subway increased the price of housing within one third of a mile of the stations. The largest increases in prices occurred for the locations closest to the stations.

Do fixed-rail systems affect land-use patterns? Webber (1976) studied the effects of BART on land-use patterns in the San Francisco Bay area. His conclusions are as follows:

1. There was a boom in downtown office construction during the construction of BART. The office boom was caused by several factors, and it is impossible to identify BART's contribution.

2. There is no evidence that downtown office development would have been any slower if transit authorities had expanded bus service instead of building BART.

3. There has been little development of activities around the suburban train stations.

In a different study, Dyett and Escudero (1977) concluded that BART caused some clustering of activities within the central city. In summarizing the results from several studies of the effects of rail systems on land-use patterns, Altshuler (1979) made two observations:

1. In a growing economy, rail transit contributes to the clustering of activities near downtown stations. These clustering effects are usually negligible outside the CBD.

2. Investment in rail transit is sensible only if it is combined with more powerful land-use instruments such as zoning and property taxation. If the government uses its zoning and tax policies to generate high-density development, rail transit provides an efficient means of delivering a large number of workers to high-density areas.

In general, there is evidence that fixed-rail systems cause small changes in the spatial distribution of employment. The primary effect of mass transit has been an increase in downtown employment.

SUMMARY

1. Mass transit is most popular among workers who commute within the central city (used by 15.8 percent of commuters) and least popular among workers who travel from one suburb to another (used by 1.5 percent).
2. Transit ridership is relatively unresponsive to changes in monetary costs (fares), but responsive to changes in time costs, especially waiting and walking costs. Commuters value in-vehicle time at about one third the wage rate, and value collection and distribution time at about the wage rate.
3. The time cost of a trip is the sum of collection costs, in-vehicle costs, and distribution costs. Commuters choose the mode that minimizes the sum of monetary and time costs. Mass transit typically has lower monetary costs than autos, but higher collection, distribution, and time costs.
4. There are trade-offs associated with bus service: a decrease in the headway or an increase in the frequency of stops decreases collection and distribution costs, but increases line-haul costs.
5. There are two basic trade-offs in the design of a fixed-rail system like BART.
   a. A mainline system forces commuters to use other travel modes in the collection and distribution phases of the trip. An alternative is an integrated system, which allows commuters to take the entire trip on a single mode.
   b. A system with widely spaced stations has shorter line-haul times but higher collection and distribution costs.
   c. BART is a mainline system with widely spaced stations. Because its collection and distribution costs are relatively high, a relatively small number of commuters have switched from autos to BART.
6. Diamond lanes cause a moderate number of commuters to switch from autos to buses. The decrease in the number of auto lanes increases congestion, increasing the time cost of auto commuters.
7. A study of alternative transport systems for the San Francisco Bay area generated the following conclusions.
   a. For all corridor volumes studied, BART was more costly than an integrated bus system.
   b. For corridor volumes exceeding 1,100 vehicles per hour, an integrated bus system was less costly than an auto-based system.
8. In 1985, passenger fares covered only about 39 percent of the operating costs of transit. Transit subsidies can be justified on efficiency grounds

because transit is a natural monopoly and automobile travel is under-priced. Transit deficits have increased over the last few decades, a result of decreases in fares and productivity and increases in wages, energy costs, and transit mileage.

9. Deregulation of transit could take two forms: the private provision of transit through service contracts and free entry into the transit market. Contracting arrangements have decreased the costs of providing transit services in a number of cities. Free entry could involve private buses or taxis serving as common carriers.

10. Increases in gasoline prices change housing and land prices, but do not cause large changes in location patterns.

11. Fixed-rail systems have increased land rent for locations near transit sta-tions, but have caused relatively small changes in location patterns. If the government uses its zoning and tax policies to generate high-density de-velopment, rail transit can provide an efficient means of delivering work-ers to the high-density areas.

EXERCISES AND DISCUSSION QUESTIONS

1. Fill in the blanks in the following table.

	Auto	Bus	BART
Collection cost			
Collection time (minutes)	0	12	16
Cost per minute ($)	0.20	0.20	0.20
Collection time cost ($)	——	——	——
Line-haul cost			
Line-haul time (minutes)	30	40	20
Cost per minute ($)	0.15	0.15	0.15
Line-haul time costs ($)	——	——	——
Monetary cost ($)	3	1.5	2
Distribution cost			
Distribution time (minutes)	0	4	11
Cost per minute ($)	0.20	0.20	0.20
Distribution time cost ($)	——	——	——
Parking cost	4	0	0
Total time cost	——	——	——
Total monetary cost	——	——	——
Total cost	——	——	——

2. Buster the transport planner must pick the distance between bus stops (D). Suppose that a 10 percent increase in D would decrease line-haul time by three minutes per rider and increase collection and distribution

time by two minutes per rider. Will the increase in D increase or decrease ridership?

3. Marta the transportation planner must pick a headway (the time between trains) for a light-rail system. A 10 percent decrease in the headway will increase operating costs by $0.20 per rider and decrease waiting time by one minute per rider. Assume that total ridership is fixed.

   a. Why does the decrease in headway increase operating costs?

   b. Under what circumstances would the decrease in the headway be efficient from the social perspective?

   Suppose that ridership is not fixed and the circumstances you specified in (b) are met.

   c. If the transit authority decreases the headway and increases fares to pay for the higher operating costs, will total ridership increase or decrease?

4. The cost curves in Figure 18–2 were derived by Keeler et al. under a number of assumptions about the disutilities of walking, waiting, and in-vehicle time. Show how the curves will shift for the following changes:

   a. Decrease in the disutility of walking and waiting time.

   b. Increase in the disutility of line-haul time.

5. In drawing the cost curves in Figure 18–2, Keeler et al. assumed that the disutility of time spent riding a bus is the same as the disutility of time driving a car.

   a. Based on your own preferences, is this a realistic assumption?

   b. Draw a new set of cost curves consistent with your preferences.

6. In drawing the cost curves in Figure 18–2, Keeler et al. assumed that the interest rate was 6 percent. Draw a new set of cost curves under the assumption that the interest rate is 12 percent.

7. In Weather City, the winters are cold and the summers are hot and humid. In Mild City, the winters and summers are mild. Except for the differences in weather, the two cities are similar. Would you expect the distance between bus stops to be longer or shorter in Mild City?

8. The city of Congestville is examining alternative policies to deal with its congestion problem. One of the options is free rush-hour bus service. Depict graphically the effects of free bus service on auto congestion and auto trip costs.

9. In the city of Phoenix, private companies provide bus services on low-volume routes at a fraction of the cost of the public bus agency. In New York City and Chicago, private companies provide bus service on high-volume (peak-period) routes at a fraction of the cost of the public bus agency. If private firms can underprice the public sector on high-volume and low-volume routes, what, if anything, should be the role of the public sector in the provision of transit services?

10. Suppose that the purpose of cross-subsidization is to increase the welfare of people along low-volume routes. Discuss some alternative means of improving their welfare.

REFERENCES AND ADDITIONAL READINGS

General

Altshuler, Alan A. *The Urban Transportation System*. Cambridge, Mass.: Joint Center for Urban Studies of MIT and Harvard, 1979.

American Public Transit Association. *Transit Fact Book*. Washington, D.C., 1981.

Cervero, R. "Efficiency and Equity Impacts of Current Transit Fare Policies." *Transportation Research Record* 790 (1981), pp. 7–15.

Cherwony, W., and S. R. Mundle. "Peak-Base Cost Allocation Models." *Transportation Research Record* 663 (1978), pp. 52–56.

Dewees, Donald. "Travel Cost, Transit, and Urban Motoring." *Public Policy* 24 (Winter 1976), pp. 59–79.

Kemp, Michael A., and Melvyn D. Cheslow. "Transportation." In *The Urban Predicament*, ed. William Gorham and Nathan Glazer. Washington, D.C.: The Urban Institute, 1976, pp. 321–24.

Lave, Charles A. "The Demand for Urban Mass Transportation." *Review of Economics and Statistics* 52 (1970), pp. 320–23.

———. "Transportation and Energy: Some Current Myths." *Policy Analysis* 4 (Summer 1978), pp. 297–315.

Meyer, John R., and José A. Gómez-Ibáñez. *Autos, Transit and Cities*. Cambridge: Harvard Univ. Press, 1981.

Meyer, John; John Kain; and Martin Wohl. *The Urban Transportation Problem*. Cambridge, Mass.: Harvard Univ. Press, 1965.

Mohring, Herbert. *Transportation Economics*. Cambridge, Mass.: Ballinger, 1976.

U.S. Bureau of the Census. *1980 Census of Population: Journey to Work—Characteristics of Workers*. Washington, D.C.: U.S. Government Printing Office, 1984.

Buses and Scale Economies

Mohring, Herbert. "Optimization and Scale Economies in Urban Bus Transportation." *American Economic Review* 62 (1972), pp. 591–604.

———. "Minibuses in Urban Transportation." *Journal of Urban Economics* 14 (1983), pp. 293–317.

Morlok, Edward K., and Philip A. Viton. "The Comparative Costs of Public and Private Providers of Mass Transit." Chapter 10, pp. 233–50. In *Urban Transit: The Private Challenge to Public Transportation*, ed. Charles Lave. Cambridge, Mass.: Ballinger, 1985.

Walters, A. A. "Externalities in Urban Buses." *Journal of Urban Economics* 11 (1982). Discusses the advantages of small buses.

Demand Elasticities

Beesley, Michael E. "The Value of Time Spent Travelling: Some New Evidence." In *The Demand for Travel: Theory and Measurement*, ed. Richard Quandt. Lexington, Mass.: D. C. Heath, 1970.

Beesley, Michael E., and Michael A. Kemp. "Urban Transportation." Chapter 26. In *Handbook of Regional and Urban Economics*. Vol. 2 of Urban Economics, ed. Edwin S. Mills. Amsterdam: North Holland, 1987.

Domencich, Thomas, and Daniel McFadden. *Urban Travel Demand*. Amsterdam: North Holland, 1975.

Domencich, T.; G. Kraft; and J. Valette. "Estimation of Urban Passenger Travel Behavior." *Highway Research Record* No. 238 (1968).

Kemp, Michael A. "Some Evidence of Transit Demand Elasticities." *Transportation* 2 (1973).

Kraft, Gerald, and Thomas A. Domencich. "Free Transit." In *Readings in Urban Economics*, ed. Matthew Edel and Jerome Rothenberg. New York: Macmillan, 1972, pp. 459–80.

Lago, Armando M.; Patrick Mayworm; and J. Matthew McEnroe. "Transit Service Elasticities." *Journal of Transport Economics and Policy* 15 (1981), pp. 99–119.

Meyer, John, and Mahlon R. Straszheim. *Pricing and Project Evaluation*. Vol. 1 of *Techniques of Transport Planning*. Washington, D.C.: Brookings Institution, 1971. Chapter 7.

Improving Mass Transit

Fielding, Gordon J. *Managing Public Transit Strategically: A Comprehensive Approach to Strengthening Service and Monitoring Performance*. San Francisco: Jossey-Bass, 1987.

Hamer, Andrew Marshall. *The Selling of Rail Rapid Transit*. Lexington, Mass.: D.C. Heath, Lexington Books, 1976, pp. 61–67, 75–77.

Kain, John F. "How to Improve Urban Transportation at Practically No Cost," *Public Policy* 20 (Summer 1972), pp. 335–58.

————. "Toward Better Urban Transport Pricing: Using What Is Known and Exploring What Is Not Known." In *Urban Transportation Pricing Alternatives*, ed. Washington, D.C.: Transportation Research Board, 1976.

Meyer, John R., and José A. Gómez-Ibáñez. *Improving Urban Mass Transportation Productivity*. Washington, D.C.: U.S. Department of Transportation, Urban Mass Transportation Administration, 1977.

Webber, Melvin W. "The Bart Experience—What Have We Learned?" *The Public Interest* (Fall 1976), pp. 79–108.

Transit Deficits

Hilton, George. *Federal Transit Subsidies*. Washington, D.C.: American Enterprise Institute for Public Policy Research, 1974.

Pickrell, Don H. "The Causes of Rising Transit Operating Deficits." *Transportation Research Record* 915 (1983), pp. 18–24.

Pucher, John; Anders Markstedt; and Ira Hirshman. "Impacts of Subsidies on the Costs of Urban Public Transport." *Journal of Transport Economics and Policy* 17 (1983); pp. 155–76.

Comparative Costs of Different Systems

Keeler, Theodore E.; L. Merewitz; P. Fisher; K. Small. *The Full Costs of Urban Transport.* Institute of Urban and Regional Development Monographs no. 21, part 3. Berkeley: University of California, 1975. Estimates the costs of alternative travel modes.

Straszheim, M. "Assessing the Social Costs of Urban Transportation Technologies." Chapter 7 in *Current Issues in Urban Economics*, ed. Peter Meiszkowski and Mahlon Straszheim. Baltimore: The Johns Hopkins Press, 1979, pp. 196–232.

Public Transit: Monopoly and Regulation

Glaister, Stephen. "Competition on an Urban Bus Route." *Journal of Transport Economics and Policy* 19 (1985), pp. 65–81.

Gomez-Ibanez, Jose A. "A Dark Side to Light Rail?" *Journal of the American Planning Association* 51 (1985), pp. 337–351. Compares the costs of new light rail systems to the costs of conventional bus systems.

Gordon, Peter, and Harry Richardson. "Notes from Underground: The Failure of Urban Mass Transit." *The Public Interest* 94 (1989), pp. 77–86.

Hilton, George W. "The Rise and Fall of Monopolized Transit." Chapter 2. In *Urban Transit: The Private Challenge to Public Transportation*, ed. Charles Lave. Cambridge, Mass.: Ballinger, 1985.

Kemp, Michael A., and Ronald F. Kirby. "Government Policies Affecting Competition in Public Transportation." Chapter 12. In *Urban Transit: The Private Challenge to Public Transportation*, ed. Charles Lave. Cambridge, Mass.: Ballinger, 1985.

Lave, Charles A. "The Private Challenge to Public Transportation—An Overview." Chapter 1. In *Urban Transit: The Private Challenge to Public Transportation*, ed. Charles Lave. Cambridge, Mass.: Ballinger, 1985.

Savas, E. S. "Municipal Monopolies vs. Competition in Delivering Public Services." *Urban Analysis* 2 (1974), pp. 93–116.

Wilson, James Q. "The Dead Hand of Regulation." *The Public Interest* 49 (Fall 1977), pp. 39–58.

Cost Comparisons: Public versus Private Transit

Echols, James C. "Use of Private Companies to Provide Public Transportation Services in Tidewater, Virginia." Chapter 4. In *Urban Transit: The Private Challenge to Public Transportation*, ed. Charles Lave. Cambridge, Mass.: Ballinger, 1985.

Giuliano, Genevieve, and Roger F. Teal. "Privately Provided Commuter Bus Services: Experiences, Problems, and Prospects." Chapter 7. In *Urban Transit: The Private Challenge to Public Transportation*, ed. Charles Lave. Cambridge, Mass.: Ballinger, 1985.

Johnson, Christine M., and Milton Pilarsky. "Toward Fragmentation: Transportation in Chicago." Chapter 3 in *Urban Transit The Private Challenge to Public Transportation*, ed. Charles Lave. Cambridge, Mass.: Ballinger, 1985.

Morlok, Edward K., and Philip A. Viton. "The Comparative Costs of Public and Private Providers of Mass Transit." Chapter 10. In *Urban Transit: The Private Challenge to Public Transportation*, ed. Charles Lave. Cambridge, Mass.: Ballinger, 1985(a).

————. "Recent Experience with Successful Private Transit in Large U.S. Cities." Chapter 6, pp. 121–148. In *Urban Transit: The Private Challenge to Public Transportation*, ed. Charles Lave. Cambridge, Mass.: Ballinger, 1985(b).

Pagano, Anthony M. "Private Sector Alternatives for Public Transportation." *Transportation Quarterly* 38 (1984), pp. 433–47.

Rosenbloom, Sandra. "The Taxi in the Urban Transport System." Chapter 8 in *Urban Transit: The Private Challenge to Public Transportation*, ed. Charles Lave. Cambridge, Mass.: Ballinger, 1985.

Simpson, Anthony U. "Implications of Efficiency Incentives on Use of Private Sector Contracting by the Public Transit Industry." Chapter 13. In *Urban Transit: The Private Challenge to Public Transportation*, ed. Charles Lave. Cambridge, Mass.: Ballinger, 1985.

Walder, Jay H. "Private Commuter Vans in New York." Chapter 5, pp. 101–18. In *Urban Transit: The Private Challenge to Public Transportation*, ed. Charles Lave. Cambridge, Mass.: Ballinger, 1985.

Taxis and Jitneys

Eckert, Ross, and George Hilton. "The Jitneys." *Journal of Law and Economics* 15 (1972), pp. 293–325.

Kirby, Ronald F. *Paratransit: Neglected Options for Future Mobility.* Washington, D.C.: The Urban Institute, 1974.

Rosenbloom, Sandra. "Taxis, Jitneys, and Poverty." *Transaction* 7 (1970), pp. 47–54.

Wohl, Martin. "The Taxi's Role in Urban America: Today and Tomorrow." *Transportation* 4 (1975).

Transportation Systems and Land Use

Anas, Alex, and Leon N. Moses. "Transportation and Land Use in the Mature Metropolis." In *The Mature Metropolis*, ed. C. L. Leven. Lexington, Mass.: D.C. Heath, Lexington Books, 1978, p. 161.

Cather De Leuw and Company. "Land Use Impacts of Rapid Transit: Implications of Recent Experience." Washington, D.C.: U.S. Department of Transportation, August 1977.

Coulson, N. Edward, and Robert F. Engel. "Transportation Costs and the Rent Gradient." *Journal of Urban Economics* 21 (1987), pp. 287–97.

Dewees, D. N. "The Effect of a Subway on Residential Property Values in Toronto." *Journal of Urban Economics* 3 (1976), pp. 357–69. Estimates the effects of Toronto's subway on property values along the transit line and around the transit stations.

Dyett, Michael V., and Emilio Escudero. "Effects of BART on Urban Development." 1977. Mimeo.

Goldstein, Gerald, and Leon Moses. "Transport Controls, Travel Costs, and Urban Spatial Structure." *Public Policy* 23 (Summer 1975), pp. 355–80.

Heenan, Warren G. "The Economic Effect of Rapid Transit on Real Estate Development." *Appraisal Journal* 36 (April 1968), pp. 213–24.

Hilton, George W. "Rail Transit and the Pattern of Modern Cities: The California Case." *Traffic Quarterly* 21 (July 1967), pp. 379–93.

Small, Kenneth A. "The Effects of Gasoline Shortages on Philadelphia Housing Prices." *Journal of Urban Economics* 19 (1986), pp. 371–81.

Small, Kenneth. "Transportation and Urban Change." In *The New Urban Reality*, ed. P. Peterson. Washington, D.C.: Brookings Institution, 1985, pp. 197–223.

Smerk, George M. "The Streetcar: Shaper of American Cities." *Traffic Quarterly* 21 (October 1967), pp. 569–84.

Warner, Samuel B., Jr. *Streetcar Suburbs: The Process of Growth in Boston, 1870–1900.* Cambridge, Mass.: Harvard Univ. Press, 1932.

Future Transit Systems

Anderson, Edward J. *Personal Rapid Transit.* Minneapolis: University of Minnesota, Department of Audio Visual Extension, 1972.

Anderson, Edward J., ed. *Personal Rapid Transit II.* Minneapolis: University of Minnesota, Department of Audio Visual Extension, 1974.

Fisher, Ronald J. "Megatrends in Urban Transport." *Transportation Quarterly* 38 (1984).

Kain, John F. "The Unexplored Potential of Freeway Rapid Transit in Regional Transportation Planning: An Atlanta Case Study." In *Unorthodox Approaches to Urban Transportation: The Emerging Challenge to Conventional Planning*, ed. Andrew Hamer. Atlanta: Georgia State University, Bureau of Business and Economic Research, 1972, pp. 38–51.

Skinner, Robert E., Jr., and Thomas B. Deen. "Second Generation U.S. Rail Transit Systems: Prospects and Perils." *Transportation* 8 (1980).

Benefit-Cost Analysis

Beesley, M. E. *Urban Transport: Studies in Economic Policy.* London: Butterworths, 1973.

Foster, C. D., and M. E. Beesley. "Estimating the Social Benefit of Constructing an Underground Railway in London." *Journal of the Royal Statistical Society* 126 (1963), pp. 46–92.

Meyer, John, and Mahlon R. Straszheim. *Pricing and Project Evaluation.* Vol. 1 of *Techniques of Transport Planning.* Washington, D.C.: Brookings Institution, 1971. Chapters 11, 12.

Peterson, Thomas C. "Cost-Benefit Analysis for Evaluating Transportation Proposals: Los Angeles Case Study." In *Urban Economic Issues*, ed. Stephan Mehay and Geoffrey Nunn. Glenview, Ill.: Scott, Foresman, 1984. Critique of a cost-benefit study that was used to justify the construction of a fixed-rail transit system in Los Angeles.

CHAPTER 19

Education

Human history becomes more and more a race between education and catastrophe.

H. G. Wells

This chapter explores some of the spatial aspects of elementary and secondary education. Given the large number of school districts in most metropolitan areas, households can choose from a wide variety of schools, each of which provides a different combination of teaching philosophies, educational quality, and tax costs. As explained in Chapter 15 (Decision Making in Local Government), the Tiebout process causes households to sort themselves geographically with respect to desired spending on local public goods, property values, and income. This chapter explains how this sorting process contributes to inequalities in educational spending and achievement. It also discusses the effects of various public policies on spending and achievement inequalities.

What's special about education? Spending inequalities also occur for other local public goods: poor municipalities also spend less on parks, recreation, and fire protection. Education is special for two reasons. First, a good education is necessary for economic survival. A person with an inferior education is unlikely to find a well-paying job and is therefore more likely to be poor. Moreover, such a person is more likely to turn to crime. One approach to solving the problems of poverty and crime is to improve the educational opportunities for poor children in the central city. A second reason for the special treatment of education is that societies use their educational systems to transmit their values from generation to generation.

The remainder of the chapter is organized as follows. The first section discusses the education production function, which is used by researchers to estimate the relative importance of various inputs to the education process. The most important factors in educational achievement are the student's home environment and the intelligence and motivation of his fellow students. The second section explains the effects of the Tiebout sorting process on the educational system, showing how the sorting process causes inequalities in educational spending, segregation with respect to race and income, and inequalities in educational achievement. The third and fourth sections discuss two policy responses to these inequalities: grants can be used to equalize educational spending, and desegregation can be used to integrate students with respect to race and income. The question is whether these policies actually

577

decrease spending inequalities and segregation. The final section explores the effects of subsidies for private schools (education vouchers) on the educational system.

THE EDUCATION PRODUCTION FUNCTION

The production function for education summarizes the relationship between the inputs to the educational process and the output (achievement). The production-function approach can be used to estimate the relative importance of the various inputs to the education process.

Inputs and Outputs of the School

What is the output of a school? The purpose of education is to develop cognitive, social, and physical skills. The basic cognitive skills (reading, writing, mathematics, logic) are necessary for employment and participation in a democracy. Cognitive skills also increase the enjoyment of leisure activities: they allow people to read books, understand jokes, and compute bowling scores. Schools also develop social skills: they teach children how to exchange ideas and make group decisions. Finally, schools develop physical skills: they teach children how to exercise and play games.

Education is different from other production activities because the output (educational achievement) is difficult to measure. While tests have been developed to measure basic cognitive skills, it is virtually impossible to accurately measure social and physical skills. Consequently, any empirical study of schools can, at best, measure only one component of the output of schools. Because empirical studies ignore social and physical skills, they provide an incomplete picture of the education process and must be interpreted with caution.

The production-function approach explores the contributions of different inputs to the cognitive achievement of students, with cognitive achievement usually measured by scores on standardized achievement tests. Suppose that achievement is defined as the change in the test score of a particular child over a one-year period. If the output of the school is defined as the change in the test score, the production function can be written as

$$\text{Achievement} = f(C, E, T, H, P) \qquad (19\text{--}1)$$

where

C = the school curriculum
E = the quantity of instructional equipment of the school
T = the quantity of labor input (teacher) per student
H = the home environment of the child
P = the average achievement level of other students in the class.

Achievement depends on five inputs: the school's curriculum and educational equipment, the classroom teacher, the home environment, and the achievement level of the child's classmates.

The five inputs to the production function can be divided into three groups.

1. **School resources.** The school has control over three inputs: curriculum, instructional equipment, and classroom teachers. Under the supervision of the local school district, the school designs a curriculum, purchases instructional equipment (building, books, science labs, computers), and hires teachers. An increase in the number of teachers decreases class size, increasing the teacher input per student.

2. **Home environment.** Educational achievement is influenced by the home environment of the child in three ways. First, parents set the rules of the household, establishing an environment that is either favorable or unfavorable to education. For example, an unfavorable environment is one in which children watch television instead of reading books or doing their homework. Second, parents can motivate their children by encouraging reading, helping with homework, and rewarding success. Third, parents can provide instructional materials such as books and home computers, thus encouraging independent learning. The quality of the home environment depends in part on the income and education level of the parents. The children of wealthy and educated parents typically learn more because they usually receive more encouragement and assistance at home and also pick up verbal and quantitative skills in everyday interactions with their parents. In contrast, children from poor and less educated families typically learn less because there is often less encouragement of achievement and less learning from parents. In addition, children living in poverty are often malnourished, inhibiting their ability to learn.

3. **Peer group effects.** The final input to the production process is the peer group of the child. A child will learn more if he or she is surrounded by smart and motivated children. Smart peers promote achievement because of cooperation (children learn from one another) and competition (children compete with one another). Motivated peers promote achievement because the teacher can spend less time disciplining and motivating students, and more time teaching them. In addition, an unmotivated student provides an undesirable role model for other students.

The Coleman Report

Which inputs to the production process are the most important? Using the production-function approach, educators and economists have estimated the contributions of the various inputs to the education process. The Coleman report (1966) was the first attempt to estimate the education production function. The conclusions of the report are as follows:

1. The most important inputs are the home environment of the student and the characteristics of the peer group.
2. High-income families have more favorable home environments, so children from wealthy families learn more than children from poor ones.
3. Children from wealthy families provide a more favorable peer group, so children with wealthy classmates learn more than children with poor ones.
4. School inputs (curriculum, instructional equipment, teachers, and class size) do not affect achievement.

The Coleman report shocked the education community. The report was disturbing and perplexing for three reasons. First, it implies that schools don't matter, that educational achievement is determined by factors beyond the control of educators. This was a surprise to teachers and educators, who assumed that they contributed to the education process. Second, the report suggests that education cannot be used to lift children out of poverty. If achievement depends exclusively on the child's home environment and peer group, children in poor areas are trapped: they receive inferior education precisely because they come from poor families (with inferior home environments) and live in poor neighborhoods (with inferior peer groups). If school resources do not affect achievement, the government cannot counteract the effects of inferior home and peer environments by spending more money on the schools of poor students. Third, the report suggests that teachers do not matter, that all teachers are equally effective, regardless of education, experience, innate intelligence, and motivation. In other words, a teacher is a standardized input like a blackboard: put one in the classroom and he or she works just as well as any other teacher.

To put the conclusions of the Coleman report in perspective, suppose that you are a parent choosing a school for your child. What questions would you ask about a prospective school? According to the Coleman report, you need to ask only one question: What is the average income level of students in the school? It would be senseless to ask questions about curriculum, instructional equipment, and teachers because, according to the Coleman report, these inputs do not affect achievement.

The Coleman report precipitated a flood of criticism. As several researchers pointed out, the statistical methods of the report were flawed. There are two basic problems with the statistical methods.

1. **Unit of observation.** Coleman chose the school, not the individual student, as the unit of observation. The report explored the relationship between the average achievement level of a school and the average school inputs (e.g., average class size, average level of teacher experience, average income) and found that schools with different input levels

did not have different achievement levels. The alternative approach is to examine the relationship between the achievement level of an individual child and the quantities of inputs experienced by that child (e.g., the size of the child's class, his teacher's experience and education level, the income level of his family). Because Coleman used school-wide data, his approach obscures important differences between students in a given school and may have generated inaccurate assessments of the relative importance of the various education inputs.

2. **Robustness of results.** The second problem is that Coleman's results are not robust. In other words, they change with small changes in the statistical methodology. His results are sensitive to the order in which the various inputs (home environment, peer environment, and school resources) are incorporated into the statistical analysis. If the home variables enter the analysis before the school variables, it appears that school inputs don't matter. If, however, the school variables are entered first, it appears that school inputs affect achievement. Because Coleman's results are sensitive to the order in which inputs are included in the study, his results are of questionable validity.

Other Studies of the Production Function

Researchers did more than criticize the statistical methods of the Coleman report. Using superior data and more sophisticated statistical methods, they generated new estimates of the education production function. The new results cast doubt on some of the conclusions of the Coleman report. The results of these new studies are by no means definitive, so many issues remain unresolved. There is a consensus emerging, however, on the influences of the home environment, the peer group, and teachers.

Home Environment and Peer-Group Effects. Most researchers agree that the home environment has an extraordinary effect on achievement. Wealthy and well-educated parents provide a more favorable home environment. Researchers also agree about the effects of the peer group: a student learns more if he or she is surrounded by smart and motivated students. There is some evidence that the largest peer-group effects are experienced by low achievers: the students at the bottom of the class have the most to gain from adding smart and motivated students to the class. There is also evidence that these peer effects are most important in the middle and upper grades (grades 5 through 12).

The Effectiveness of Teachers. There is also agreement that teachers matter. Contrary to the conclusions of the Coleman report, teachers are not like blackboards, but in fact vary in effectiveness. The most effective teachers are the ones that are smart, motivated, innovative, and flexible.

While researchers agree that some teachers are more effective than others, they do not agree on what makes a teacher effective. In looking for teacher characteristics that explain differences in effectiveness, researchers have focussed on the teacher's education level (years of postgraduate study), communication skills (verbal ability), and experience (years of teaching). The results of the studies are as follows:

1. **Education level.** There is no evidence that graduate education increases teacher productivity. It appears that students do not learn more from teachers with advanced degrees.

2. **Verbal skills.** The most effective teachers have superior communication skills. Students learn more from teachers that score high on standard tests of verbal ability.

3. **Experience.** There is some disagreement about the effects of experience on teaching skills. Murnane (1975, 1983, 1985) suggested that teaching effectiveness increases for the first few years of teaching and then levels off. In contrast, Hanushek (1971, 1981) suggested that teaching skills are independent of teaching experience. Summers and Wolfe (1977) found that low achievers learn more from inexperienced—but enthusiastic— teachers, while high achievers learn more from experienced teachers. Given these conflicting results, the link between teacher experience and effectiveness is still an open question.

Curriculum and Instructional Equipment.   There is evidence that curriculum matters. One of the most important factors in the highly publicized decline in SAT test scores during the 1970s and 1980s was the relaxation of graduation requirements: under the smorgasbord approach to education, students were allowed to choose from a wide variety of courses, many of which were not academic in nature. The typical student took fewer rigorous academic courses, and academic achievement declined. This is the "twinkie" effect: students skipped the meat and vegetable courses (academic courses) and filled up on the twinkie courses.

Researchers agree that differences in achievement are not caused by differences in instructional equipment. In other words, students do not learn more in schools that spend a relatively large amount on books, projectors, and buildings. This does not mean that achievement would be unaffected if we returned to the days of log schoolhouses and shared books. It means that, given the current levels of spending on books and buildings, small changes in spending will not affect achievement.

Class Size.   There is some disagreement about the effects of class size on achievement. As Hanushek (1981) pointed out, there have been 112 studies of the relationship between class size and achievement, with 9 studies finding a negative relationship, 14 studies finding a positive relationship, and 89 studies finding no significant relationship. Summers and Wolfe (1977) suggested that low achievers learn more in small classes and high achievers learn more in large classes. Given these conflicting results, the link between class size and achievement is still an open question. The issue is not whether class size matters at all, but whether small changes from the current class size will affect achievement. No one doubts that achievement would decline if the average class size increased from 20 to 60 students.

THE TIEBOUT PROCESS AND INEQUALITIES IN ACHIEVEMENT

How does the Tiebout sorting process affect educational spending and educational achievement? Under the Tiebout process, households sort themselves with respect to three characteristics: desired spending on schools, property values, and peer-group characteristics. Consider first the sorting with respect to education spending. The desired spending on education will vary across households, reflecting differences in income and preferences for education. Households will sort themselves into high-spending and low-spending school districts. In this case, spending inequalities result from the simple fact that the wealthy will spend more on education, just as they spend more on clothes, cars, and housing. The spending inequalities will cause inequalities in educational opportunity: the low-spending school districts will have less money for teachers, so they will have lower achievement levels.

Because local schools are financed with the property tax, households will also sort themselves with respect to property values. Because housing is a normal good (positive income elasticity), the sorting with respect to house value causes sorting with respect to income. Suppose that all the households in a city, wealthy and poor, have the same desired spending on education. Under the property tax, the city will have two school districts, one for the wealthy (who live in large houses) and one for the poor (small houses). Although the two school districts have the same per pupil spending, achievement will be higher in the wealthy school district for two reasons. First, the average income level will be higher in the wealthy district, so the average achievement level will be higher. Second, the wealthy district will have a better peer environment, so a given child will learn more in the wealthy school district. Income segregation deprives poor students of the possible benefits from being surrounded by smart and motivated students.

Consider finally the effects of student peer groups on location choices. Parents care about educational achievement, not simply educational spending. Given the importance of the peer group in achievement, the household will look for a school with smart and motivated students. In practical terms, this means that the household will look for a neighborhood full of high-income, well-educated parents who provide a favorable home environment. The shopping for a good peer group will reinforce income segregation. Suppose that a poor household has the same desired spending on education as middle-income households and occupies a house with the same market value (same tax liability). In the absence of peer-group effects, middle-income house-holds would welcome the poor household into their school district. However, because the poor student is likely to have a below-average achievement level, middle-income households have an incentive to exclude the child from their school. In general, the peer-group effect adds another item to the household's shopping list, increasing the pressures for segregation with respect to in-come, race, and social status. As a result, it widens the spatial inequalities in educational achievement. Poor households are denied access to schools that provide favorable peer environments.

Spending Inequalities

By how much does educational spending vary across school districts? Ta-ble 19–1 shows the variation in per pupil spending within states, listing the numbers of states with different degrees of spending inequalities. The spend-ing ratios in the left-hand column are computed as follows. For each state, school districts are ranked with respect to per pupil expenditures: if a state has 80 school districts, its school districts are ranked first through eightieth. The high-spending quartile is composed of the top 25 percent school districts (the top 20 of 80), and the low-spending quartile is composed of the bottom 25 percent school districts (bottom 20 of 80). The state's **quartile spending ratio** is computed as the average per pupil spending in the high-spending quartile (the top 20 districts) divided by the average per pupil spending in the low-spending quartile (the bottom 20 districts). In three states, the quartile spend-ing ratio was over 1.50, meaning that spending in the top 20 districts was 50 percent higher than spending in the bottom 20 districts. The spending ratio was greater than 1.20 for a total of 26 states.

TABLE 19–1   Intrastate Spending Inequalities

Quartile Spending Ratio	Number of States
1.51–1.60	3
1.41–1.50	4
1.31–1.40	5
1.21–1.30	14
1.11–1.20	14
1.00–1.10	5
Total	45

Quartile spending ratio (in 1975) = average spending of the top 25% school districts divided by average spending of the lowest 25% school districts.
Data unavailable for Alabama, Alaska, Louisiana, Montana, and Vermont.

SOURCE: L. Brown, A. Ginsberg, J. Killalea, R. Rosthal, and E. Tron, "School Finance Reform in the Seventies: Achievements and Failures," *Selected Papers in School Finance, 1978* (Washington, D.C.: U.S. Department of Health, Education, and Welfare, 1978), p. 61.

FIGURE 19-1   Percent of Minority Students in Schools with Different Degrees of Segregation, 1986

Integrated
(Less than 50% minority)

30%

46%

Highly segregated
(80–100% minority)

24%

Moderately segregated
(50–79% minority)

SOURCE: Bradley Shiller, *The Economics of Poverty and Discrimination* (Englewood Cliffs, N.J.: Prentice-Hall, 1989), p. 141.

Segregation and Achievement Inequalities

How segregated is the U.S. school system? Figure 19–1 shows the percentages of minority students (blacks, Hispanics, and other minorities) in schools with different degrees of segregation. Almost half of minority students (46 percent) attended highly segregated schools (where over 80 percent of the students were minorities). About a quarter (24 percent) of minority students attended schools that were moderately segregated (between 50 percent and 80 percent of the students were minorities). Only 30 percent of minority students attended schools in which they were a minority of the student body.

According to a recent report from the Department of Education (1987), classrooms are even more segregated than schools. Under the **ability-tracking system**, students are segregated with respect to ability and achievement: the high achievers are put in one class, and the low achievers are put in another class. Because minority students often fall behind white students in the early grades, ability tracking in the later grades contributes to racial segregation within the schools.

How does the educational achievement of blacks and Hispanics compare to that of whites? At age nine, black and Hispanic students are, on average, 25 percent behind their white counterparts in reading, science, and math; by age 17, the achievement gap grows to 30 percent (National Center for Education Statistics 1982). Figure 19–2 takes a closer look at the reading scores of 9-, 13-, and 17-year-olds between 1970 and 1980. Although blacks and Hispanics from all three ages scored lower than whites, the gaps in achievement narrowed somewhat between 1970 and 1980. The largest absolute and relative gains occurred for 9 year olds: the gap between the black and white scores decreased from 16.7 points (49.7 versus 66.4) to 9.7 points (59.6 versus 69.3).

FIGURE 19–2   Reading Scores by Race, 1970–1980

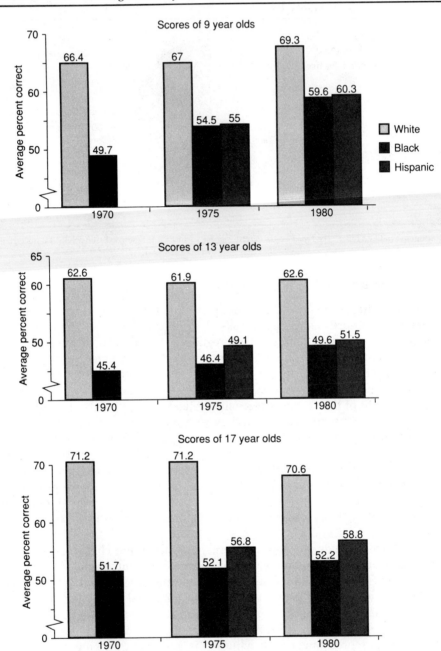

Two other measures of educational achievement are the completion rates for high school and college. According to the Department of Education (1986), in 1985, only 63 percent of blacks had completed high school by age 19 (up from 56 percent in 1974), compared to 77 percent of whites (up from 76 percent in 1974). Although the gap in high school completion rates has narrowed, it is still large. In 1986, only 11 percent of Hispanics and 12 percent of blacks between ages 24 and 29 had completed at least four years of college, compared to 23 percent of whites (Schiller 1989).

PROGRAMS TO DECREASE SPENDING INEQUALITIES

Under the traditional system of education finance, school districts finance their education programs with the local property tax. Therefore, spending per pupil depends on local property values, which of course vary across school districts. In response to spending inequalities, states have developed a number of programs that redistribute money to school districts with relatively low tax bases. Figure 19–3 shows the contributions of the three levels of government to local education. In 1985, state governments provided about half of the funds for education.

FIGURE 19–3   Sources of Education Funding: 1930–1985

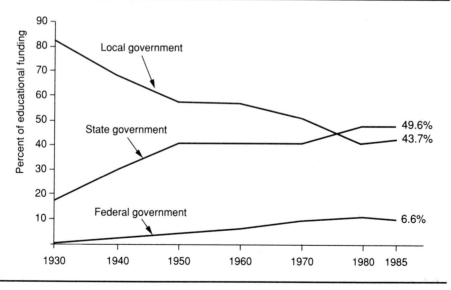

SOURCE: U.S. Department of Education, *The Condition of Education: A Statistical Report* (Washington, D.C.: Government Printing Office, 1986), p. 55.

Flat Grants

At the turn of the century, thirty-eight states distributed funds to local school districts in the form of flat grants. Under a system of flat grants, the state gives each school district a fixed amount per student, thus guaranteeing a minimum level of spending.

Figure 19–4 shows the tax-spending options of two school districts before and after a program of flat grants. The horizontal axis measures the local property tax rate, and the vertical axis measures spending per pupil. The wealthy district has $60,000 of property per student, so per-pupil spending increases by $600 for every one percent of property tax. The poor district has $30,000 per student, so a given tax rate raises half as much tax revenue. The poor district might choose point P, spending $900 per pupil with a tax rate of 3 percent, while the wealthy district might choose point W, spending $1,200 per pupil with a tax rate of only 2 percent. In other words, children in poor school districts often receive less education while their parents pay relatively high tax rates.

FIGURE 19–4   Tax-Spending Options for Different Tax Bases with and without a Flat Grant

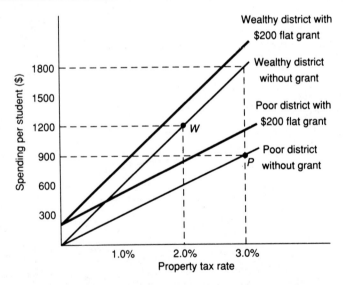

The tax-spending lines show education spending for different tax rates. The wealthy district has twice as much property value per student, so a given tax rate generates twice as much revenue per student. At point W, the wealthy district has a tax rate of 2% and spends $1,200 per student. At point P, the poor district has a tax rate of 3% and spends only $900 per student. A $200 flat grant shifts the tax-spending lines upward by $200.

FIGURE 19–5 Flat Grant and Spending per Student

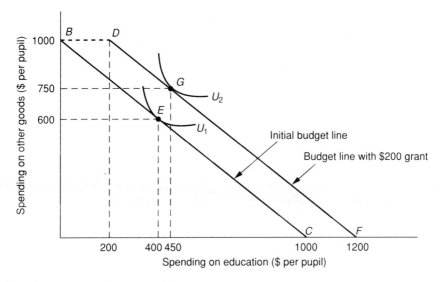

A $200 flat grant shifts the budget line of the median voter from *BC* to *BDF*, and the utility-maximizing point moves from *E* to *G*. One fourth of the grant is spent on education, and the remaining $150 is spent on other goods. The school district cuts taxes, allowing citizens to spend part of the grant on other goods.

A flat grant of $200 will shift the spending lines up by $200, providing both districts with more tax-spending options. Before the grant, a 1 percent tax generates $600 in the wealthy district and $300 in the poor district. After the grant, the same tax rate generates $800 in the wealthy district and $500 in the poor district.

How does a flat grant affect spending in the two school districts? Suppose that each school district adopts the preferred budget of its median voter, as explained in Chapter 15 (Decision Making in Local Government). Figure 19–5 shows the budget lines and indifference curves of Marian the median voter. The horizontal axis measures education spending per pupil, and the vertical axis measures spending on other goods (on a per pupil basis). The budget line *BC* shows the trade-off between education and other goods: Marian has a total of $1,000 per pupil to spend on education and other goods, and every dollar spent on education decreases spending on other goods by one dollar. Before the flat grant, Marian chooses point *E*. If the school district adopts the preferred budget of the median voter, its initial spending on education will be $400 per student.

The flat grant shifts Marian's budget line outward from *BC* to *BDF*. Point *D* is in the new budget set because Marian can use the grant to get $200 worth of education while spending all of her own money ($1,000) on other goods. The points along the line connecting *D* and *F* are in the new budget set: starting from point *D*, Marian still faces a dollar-for-dollar trade-off between education and other goods. The shift of the budget line moves Marian's utility-maximizing point from *E* to *G*. If the school district adopts the preferred budget of the median voter, the flat grant increases education spending by $50 (to $450) and spending on other goods by $150 (to $750).

How does the school district increase spending on other goods? The district can fund its $450 spending program with the $200 grant and $250 of local tax revenue. The grant decreases the local contribution to education from $400 to $250, so the school district cuts local taxes by $150. Therefore, its citizens can spend $150 of the grant on other goods. From the perspective of local citizens, the flat grant is equivalent to an increase in consumer income, which increases the demand for all normal goods, including education and other goods. In cutting taxes, the school district is simply responding to the demands of its citizens.

Will a system of flat grants narrow the gap between the spending of wealthy and poor communities? Because every school district receives the same $200 grant, spending on education will increase in every district. The grant program will decrease spending inequalities only if the wealthy school district spends a smaller fraction of its $200 grant on education. This will occur if citizens in the wealthy school district have a relatively low income elasticity of demand for education. There is no reason to think that wealthy citizens will have a lower income elasticity.

Foundation Grants

In the 1920s, some states switched from flat grants to foundation grants. Under the foundation program, the education grant is inversely related to the property wealth of the school district. The grant for a particular school district is

$$\text{Grant} = \text{Transfer rate} \cdot (\text{Threshold property value} - \text{Property value per student}) \qquad (19\text{--}2)$$

If the district's property value per student is less than the threshold property value, the district is eligible for a foundation grant. The grant is computed as the transfer rate times the gap between the threshold and the actual property value. For example, suppose that the threshold property value is $80,000 and the transfer rate is 0.01. A school district with property value per student of $30,000 has a property-value gap of $50,000 ($80,000 − $30,000) and will receive $500 per pupil (0.01 times $50,000). Similarly, a school district with property value per student of $60,000 will receive $200 per pupil.

The only difference between the foundation grant and the flat grant is that the foundation grant is a decreasing function of the local tax base. In contrast with the flat grant, which is the same for all school districts, the foundation grant decreases as the local tax base increases. In Figure 19–4, the foundation plan in the example above would shift the tax-spending line of the poor school district up by $500 and shift the tax-spending line of the wealthy district up by only $200. The two tax-spending lines would intersect at a 1 percent tax rate: if both districts were to impose a 1 percent tax, they would each spend $800 on education. The poor district would combine its $500 grant with $300 of local taxes, and the wealthy community would combine its $200 grant with $600 of local taxes. For tax rates below 1 percent, the poor district would spend more than the wealthy district; for tax rates above 1 percent, the poor district would spend less than the wealthy district.

In most states, foundation plans have caused relatively small changes in spending inequalities. The foundation plans have failed to significantly narrow spending inequalities for two reasons. First, most foundation programs provide relatively small grants. Second, school districts typically spend only a small fraction of their grants on education, using the rest of the grant to increase spending on other goods. Because foundation plans do not stimulate education spending by very much, they have had relatively small effects on spending inequalities.

The Legal Mandate to Equalize Expenditures

State courts became involved in the financing of education in the 1970s. In response to persistent inequalities in education spending, parents from poor school districts sued state governments, claiming that the spending inequalities violated state constitutions. In a number of states, the courts ruled in favor of the parents, finding that inequalities in educational spending violated the equal-protection clauses of state constitutions. Education is considered a fundamental right of citizens of some states, meaning that all citizens in the state are to receive the same quality of education. The courts developed the **principle of fiscal neutrality**: The quality of education may **not** be a function of the wealth of the local community. In other words, children from poor school districts must receive the same quality of education as children from wealthy school districts. The courts directed state governments to equalize spending on primary and secondary education.

Serrano v. Priest. The most frequently cited court case is *Serrano v. Priest*, decided in 1974 by the California Supreme Court. When John Serrano complained about the low quality of the local high school's education program, the school's principal suggested that Mr. Serrano move his family to a school district where per pupil spending was higher. Instead of moving, Mr. Serrano sued the state of California, arguing that spending inequalities were unconstitutional.

To illustrate the spending disparities, Serrano cited the difference between two school districts in the Los Angeles area, Beverly Hills and Baldwin Park. As shown in Table 19–2, Beverly Hills used its larger property tax base

TABLE 19–2   Taxes and Spending in Baldwin Park and Beverly Hills in 1968

	Baldwin Park	Beverly Hills
Property value per student	$16,000	$200,000
Educational spending per student	$ 595	$ 1,244

SOURCE: James Guthrie, "United States School Finance Policy 1955–1980," in *School Finance Policies and Practices*, ed. James Guthrie (Cambridge, Mass.: Ballinger, 1980), p. 14.

to spend more per student. The property tax rate in Baldwin Park was over twice the rate in Beverly Hills. In ruling in favor of Serrano, the court ruled that the property tax system violated the equal-protection clause of the state's constitution. The court ordered the state legislature to develop a financing system under which per pupil spending would vary by no more than $100.

Courts in other states have produced similar decisions. Between 1971 and 1973, there were 51 court actions in a total of 31 states. By 1985, 36 states had been ordered to reform their school-finance systems.

Limits on Reform.   Two court cases established the limits on education-finance reform. In *McInnis* v. *Ogilvie*, the plaintiffs argued that the constitution guarantees the right to equal educational *outcomes* rather than equal educational *spending*. They argued that government should eliminate inequalities in educational achievement by spending more on low-achieving students to bring them up to the level of high achievers. The court ruled against the plaintiffs, arguing that there was no practical way to enforce an equal-achievement standard. Given this decision, the objective of reform efforts is to equalize spending, not achievement.

Another case, *San Antonio Independent School District* v. *Rodriguez*, established the limits for federal involvement in school finance. The court ruled that education is not a fundamental right guaranteed to U.S. citizens. This ruling is based on the fact that education is not mentioned in the U.S. Constitution. Consequently, the equal-protection clause of the U.S. Constitution does not apply to education, and variation in per-pupil spending is not proscribed by the U.S. Constitution. There are two implications from the *San Antonio* decision. First, any reform of the school-finance system must come from state governments. Second, although the court system may promote equalization of spending within individual states, the courts will do nothing to promote equalization of spending across states.

The Guaranteed Tax-Base Plan

The court cases of the 1970s demonstrated that the conventional grant programs had failed to reduce spending inequalities to tolerable levels. In response to court orders, states adopted new programs to decrease spending inequalities. Under the **guaranteed tax-base** (GTB) plan (also called district power equalizing), every school district has access to the same *effective* tax base. If the guaranteed tax base is $50,000 per student, every school district will receive $500 for every percent of the local tax rate: $500 for a one percent tax rate, $1,000 for a 2 percent tax rate, and so on. Every school district has the same taxing power, regardless of its local tax base.

GTB Plan and the Poor School District.   Figure 19–6 shows the effect of a guaranteed tax base on the tax-spending options of a poor school district. The upper line is the guaranteed tax revenue for different local tax rates, given a guaranteed tax base of $50,000 per student. The lower line is local tax revenue, given a local tax base of $30,000 per student. The state grant is the difference between the guaranteed tax revenue and local tax revenue. For a 1 percent local tax, the school district is guaranteed a total of $500. The local district raises $300 locally, and the state provides the $200 difference between guaranteed revenue and local revenue. For a 3 percent tax, the district receives a total of $1,500 ($900 from local taxes and $600 from the state).

The GTB plan decreases the opportunity cost of spending on education. Before the grant program, there is a dollar-for-dollar trade-off between spending on education and spending on other goods: every dollar spent on educa-

FIGURE 19–6   Guaranteed Tax Base: Poor School District

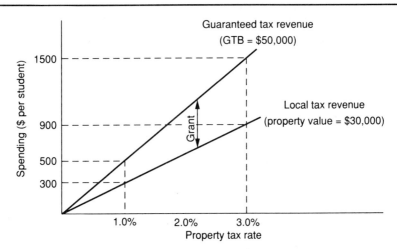

Under a guaranteed tax base (GTB) plan, all school districts have access to the same effective tax base. If the GTB is $50,000 per student, the district is guaranteed tax revenue of $500 for every 1% of local tax rate. If the district imposes a 3% tax rate, it is guaranteed a total of $1,500 of tax revenue, so the state supplements the $900 of local revenue with a $600 grant. In this case, the GTB plan decreases the opportunity cost of education spending from $1 to 60¢.

tion requires one dollar of local taxes, so every dollar of education decreases spending on other goods by one dollar. Under the GTB plan, the trade-off is 1 dollar for 60 cents. In Figure 19–6, the district can increase spending on education from $0 to $500 by imposing a 1 percent tax. A 1 percent tax generates $300 of local tax revenue and a $200 grant, so the district gives up only $300 worth of other goods to get $500 worth of education. On average, the school district can get a dollar of education by sacrificing only 60 cents worth of other goods. The GTB program is equivalent to a matching grant with a matching rate of two thirds ($300 of local taxes generates a $200 grant).

How does the GTB plan affect the choices of the median voter? In Figure 19–7, the plan pivots Marian's budget line from BC to BD. The slope decreases because the grant decreases the opportunity cost of education spending from $1 to 60 cents. Marian chooses point F instead of point E. If the school district adheres to the preferences of the median voter, it increases school spending from $400 to $500.

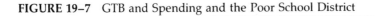

A GTB grant has a larger stimulative effect than a flat grant because the GTB grant has both an income effect and a substitution effect. Like a flat grant, the GTB grant increases Marian's real income, increasing her desired spending on all normal goods, including education (the income effect). The GTB grant also decreases the opportunity cost of education spending from $1

FIGURE 19–7   GTB and Spending and the Poor School District

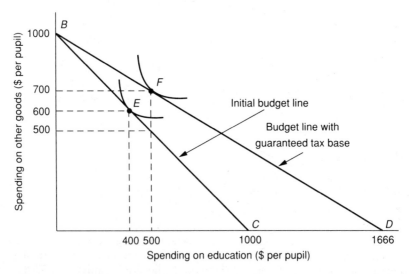

The GTB plan shifts the budget line of the median voter from BC to BD. The opportunity cost of education spending decreases, causing both an income effect and a substitution effect. Desired spending on education rises from $400 to $500.

to 60 cents, causing Marian to substitute education for other goods (the substitution effect). In Figure 19–5, a $200 flat grant increases education spending by $50 (from $400 to $450), while in Figure 19–7, a $200 GTB grant increases spending by $100 (from $400 to $500).

GTB Plan and the Wealthy School District.

GTB Plan and the Wealthy School District.   How would the GTB plan affect the tax-spending options of a wealthy school district? Suppose that the wealthy district has $60,000 of property value per student, compared to a guaranteed tax base of $50,000. The local tax revenue will exceed the guaranteed tax revenue: the surplus tax revenue is $100 for a 1 percent tax, $200 for a 2 percent tax, and so on. Under a pure GTB plan, the state would collect this surplus tax revenue.

The GTB plan increases the opportunity cost of education spending in the wealthy district. If the district imposes a 1 percent tax, it raises $600 of local tax revenue, decreasing spending on other goods by $600. Since $100 of the $600 tax revenue is collected by the state, only $500 is left for local education. On average, the district must give up $1.20 worth of other goods to get $1 worth of education, so the GTB plan increases the opportunity cost of education from $1 to $1.20.

In the wealthy district, the income and substitution effects of the GTB plan combine to decrease spending on education. The GTB plan decreases the real income of the median voter, decreasing the desired spending on all normal goods, including education (the income effect). It also increases the opportunity cost of education, causing the median voter to substitute other goods for education (the substitution effect). If the school district adheres to the preferences of its median voter, it will decrease education spending.

GTB as an Equalization Tool.   Compared to the foundation plan, the pure GTB plan is a more powerful equalization tool. The GTB is more powerful for two reasons. First, the GTB plan has a Robin Hood feature: it takes from wealthy school districts and gives to poor ones. The resulting income effects decrease spending in wealthy districts and increase spending in poor ones. Second, the GTB plan increases the opportunity cost of education in wealthy districts and decreases the opportunity cost in poor districts. The resulting substitution effects reinforce the income effects, narrowing the spending gaps.

Would a pure GTB plan equalize spending on education? The GTB plan provides each school district with the same effective tax base. If every community chooses the same tax rate, education spending would be the same in all districts. If, however, communities chose different tax rates, spending inequalities would persist. Under a pure GTB plan, any remaining differences in education spending are the result of differences in tax *rates*, not differences in tax *bases*.

Most states with GTB plans have adopted an impure version of GTB.

School districts are allowed to raise and spend more than the guaranteed tax revenue. In the language of local government, states do not "recapture" or "recycle" the surplus tax revenue of wealthy school districts. Because the impure GTB plan does not recapture surplus tax revenue, it is a relatively weak equalization tool: the plan increases spending in poor school districts, but does not decrease spending in wealthy school districts. According to Carroll (1979), GTB plans have had relatively small effects on spending inequalities.

Michigan's Equalization Plan

Michigan adopted an equalization plan that combined the features of a foundation plan and a GTB plan. The state's 531 school districts were divided into three groups:

1. **GTB districts.** About one third of the school districts were included in a GTB plan. These districts had tax rates less than 2.2 percent and tax bases less than $38,000 per student. The guaranteed tax base was $38,000.

2. **Foundation districts.** About three fifths of the school districts were included in a foundation plan. These districts had tax rates greater than 2.2 percent and tax base less than $38,000 per student. The transfer rate was 2.2 percent and the threshold property value was $38,000.

3. **Ineligible districts.** The remaining school districts had tax bases greater than $38,000 per student, and received no state aid.

The Michigan program had a relatively small effect on spending inequalities. Three factors contributed to its limited effect. First, only about one third of the school districts—those eligible for the GTB plan—experienced significant changes in state support. The districts eligible for foundation grants continued to receive about the same level of state support. Second, the state did not recapture the surplus tax revenue of the relatively wealthy school districts, so the plan did not decrease the spending of wealthy districts. Third, the GTB school districts increased their spending on education by relatively small amounts. The Michigan program failed to equalize spending because it caused relatively small effects in only about one third of the state's school districts.

The California Equalization Program

Under the California equalization plan, the state has equalized expenditures by assuming complete control of education finance. The state of California responded to the *Serrano* decision by establishing spending limits for local school districts. The state limited the rate at which each district could increase its per-pupil spending. Because the state allowed low-spending districts to increase their spending more rapidly than high-spending districts, the spending limits narrowed the spending gaps over time. Until 1979, a school district could override its spending limit if it received the approval of two thirds of its voters. Starting in 1979, the spending limits could not be exceeded under any circumstances.

The state's equalization plan received a boost from the tax revolt. In 1978, California voters approved Proposition 13, which imposed strict limits on local property tax rates. The state made the following offer to every school district: if the district imposed a property tax of 1 percent (the maximum allowable under Proposition 13), the state would make up the difference between local tax revenue and the district's state-imposed spending limit. If the school district agreed to the deal, its actual spending would equal its maximum spending. Since every school district accepted the state's offer, the state is now in full control of education spending: every school district spends the maximum amount allowed by the state.

The California plan has sharply reduced spending inequalities. The *Serrano* decision directed the state to decrease spending inequalities to no more than $100 per student. The court would be satisfied, for example, if all school districts spent between $3,000 and $3,100 per student. Figure 19–8 shows the

FIGURE 19–8   Percent of California Students within $100 Spending Interval, 1974–1984

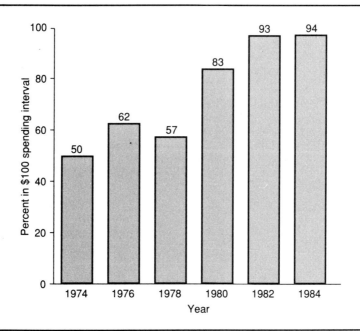

SOURCE: California Department of Education, *Selected Financial and Related Data for California Public Schools, K-12, 1984–85* (Sacramento, 1986).

trend in spending inequalities. The vertical axis measures the percentage of students that fell within a $100 spending interval (in 1975 dollars) in a given year. Between 1974 and 1984, the percentage of students in the $100 interval increased from 50 percent to 94 percent. The equalization program increased the state's support of education: the state's share of education spending increased from about 40 percent in 1974 to about 65 percent in 1984.

DESEGREGATION POLICY

What causes racial segregation in the schools? One reason for segregation is racial prejudice. Some white parents are unwilling to let their children be educated with racial minorities, regardless of the achievement level of the minority children (and their peer-group effects). Others use race as a signal about the likely achievement level of students: if minority children have, on average, a lower achievement level, a simple way to produce a more favorable peer group is to exclude all racial minorities.

Racial segregation can be accomplished in a number of ways. The first approach is to use explicit segregation, a method used in many southern cities until the early 1970s. A more subtle approach, used by many northern cities, is to manipulate attendance boundaries to send most black children to predominantly black schools. The third approach is to set up neighborhood schools and let households sort themselves with respect to race: households interested in sending their children to white schools can move to wealthy suburban school districts that exclude blacks. A final approach to segregation is to send white children to private schools, which are often too expensive for black households.

Court-Ordered Desegregation

In *Brown* v. *Board of Education of Topeka* (1954), the Supreme Court declared that explicit racial segregation is unconstitutional. The *Brown* case reversed *Plessy* v. *Ferguson* (1896), which established the constitutionality of "separate but equal" schools. The *Brown* decision required the desegregation of schools in areas where local governments pursued a policy of explicit segregation. Most cities forced to desegregate their schools under the *Brown* decision were in the South.

The mandate for desegregation was extended in the 1970s to northern cities that used attendance boundaries and other subtle techniques to promote segregation (Clotfelter 1979). The courts ordered several large northern and western cities to desegregate their schools. The objective was to integrate the schools to the extent that would have occurred in the absence of earlier government policies that had encouraged segregation. In other words, the court did not require each city to develop a truly integrated school system, only one in which government policy had a neutral effect. The segregation that results from the individual location choices of households (the Tiebout shopping process) is considered constitutional.

How did white households respond to forced desegregation? One of the lessons from the history of desegregation policy is that it often increases rather than decreases segregation. Some of the powerful forces behind segregation are not neutralized by court-ordered desegregation, and households can take a number of actions to counteract desegregation plans. There are two responses that weaken or reverse the effects of desegregation: households can move from the integrating school district to all-white school districts, or parents can enroll their children in private schools.

Moving to Another School District

Consider first the possibility of moving to another school district. In the South, many central cities had marble-like spatial distributions of households: black areas were interspersed within white areas. The cities used explicit segregation to send whites and blacks living in the same area to different schools. When the courts outlawed explicit segregation, many central-city white families moved to the predominantly white suburbs to keep their children in all-white schools.

Clotfelter (1979) examined the various responses to desegregation in Baltimore and Atlanta and came to the following conclusions.

1. The fleeing of whites to the suburbs decreased the demand for central-city housing and decreased central-city housing prices. In stable but changing neighborhoods, the price of central-city housing decreased by about 4.7 percent for every 10 percent increase in the proportion of blacks in local public schools.

2. Families with school-age children were the most likely to move to the suburbs when central-city schools were integrated.

The same phenomenon occurred in other cities that used busing to integrate their schools: some white households moved from desegregating school districts to predominantly white school districts.

Switching to Private Schools

Another option for parents in a desegregating school district is to enroll their children in private schools. To evaluate the effects of desegregation on private-school enrollment, it will be useful to develop a model of the household's choice between private and public schools.

The Choice between Public and Private Schools.   In choosing between public and private schools, parents face a trade-off between the consumption of education and other goods. Private schools charge tuition, but also provide a better education, on average, than a public school. Parents will send a child

FIGURE 19–9   Desegregation Causes Switch from Public to Private Education

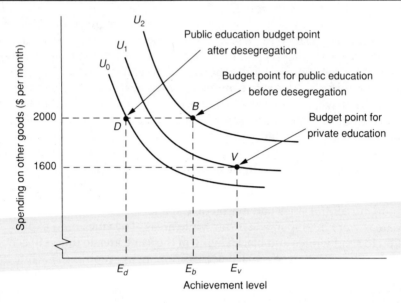

Before desegregation, the budget point for public education is B and the budget point for private education is V. Private education provides a higher achievement level (E_v instead of E_b), but also costs \$400. Given the shape of its indifference curves, the household is not willing to sacrifice \$400 worth of other goods to increase achievement by ($E_v - E_b$), so it chooses public education. Desegregation decreases achievement in public schools (the budget point shifts from B to D), so utility is higher in the private school.

to a private school only if the increase in educational achievement is worth the sacrifice of other goods.

Figure 19–9 shows the options faced by the Smith family. The horizontal axis measures the consumption of education (measured by the achievement level of the child) and the vertical axis measures consumption of other goods (in dollars). The family faces a binary choice: it chooses either a public-school education *or* a private-school education, not a mixture of the two. Therefore, the budget set consists of two points, V (private education) and B (public education). If the family has \$2,000 to spend on education and other goods, the public-school option is point B: if the family chooses public education, it receives E_b units of free public education, leaving \$2,000 for other goods. If private-school tuition is \$400, the family could get E_v units of private education at a cost of \$400, leaving \$1,600 to spend on other goods (point V).

The Smiths will choose public education over private education. The household's negatively sloped indifference curves (U_1 and U_2) reflect its subjective trade-off between education and other goods. The indifference curves show that the family is willing to sacrifice only a small amount of noneducation goods to increase educational achievement. Given the indifference curves and the budget points, the utility level from public education (U_2) exceeds the utility level from private education (U_1), so the family will choose public education. The benefit of increased achievement (from E_b to E_v) is outweighed by the loss of $400 worth of other goods.

Differences in Achievement?   Why do students in private schools learn more than their counterparts in public schools? According to Murnane (1986), private schools are superior in part because they have more favorable peer-group effects. As discussed earlier in this chapter, a particular student learns more if he is surrounded by smart and motivated classmates, and the smartest and most motivated students come from high-income families. Because a large fraction of private-school children come from high-income families, the peer groups in private schools are superior to the peer groups in public schools. According to Murnane, the favorable peer-group effects explain over half of the difference between the achievement levels of public and private students.

Murnane quantifies the peer-group effect by predicting student test scores under different circumstances. The first question he poses is *"How would the test score of the typical public-school student change if the student transferred from the public school to a private school?"* The answer is that the student's score would increase from 24.4 to 26.1. By transferring to a private school, the typical student would experience a 7 percent increase in achievement. The second question posed by Murnane is *"How would the test score of the typical public-school student change if the student, along with his public-school classmates, transferred from the public school to a private school?"* The answer is that the student's score would increase from 24.4 to 25.1, an increase of about 2.9 percent. If the student brings his public-school peers along with him to the private school, he experiences less than half the achievement gain that would occur if he left his public-school peers behind.

Murnane's results suggest that a large part of the difference between public and private school is caused by peer-group effects. A student in a private school is surrounded by smarter and more motivated students, so he learns more. The other half of the achievement difference is presumably caused by differences in curriculum, teachers, educational methods, and discipline. An important advantage of private schools is that they have more flexibility in expelling troublemakers.

Desegregation and Private Schools.   How does desegregation affect the household's choice between private and public schools? Suppose that desegregation enrolls more poor children in the public schools and decreases the average achievement level of public schools. In Figure 19–9, the budget point for public education would shift to the left, from B to D. For the Smiths, who chose the public school before desegregation, the utility generated by the public school will now be less than the utility from private schools: the achievement gap is larger, so the increase in achievement generated by a switch from the public to the private school is now worth the $400 sacrifice of other goods. In this case, desegregation causes a switch to a private school.

There is conclusive evidence that desegregation causes "white flight" to private schools. Clotfelter (1976) hypothesizes the following relationship

$$E = f(S, I, B) \qquad\qquad (19-3)$$

where

E = Proportion of whites enrolled in private schools
S = Family size
I = Household income
B = Percentage of public school students who are black.

Using data from Mississippi, he concluded that white enrollment in private schools increased with the number of blacks in public schools. The relationship is especially strong when black enrollment in public schools exceeds 50 percent. For B less than 50 percent, a one-unit increase in B (one percentage point increase) raised E by 0.40 percentage points; for B greater than 50 percent, a one-unit increase in B raised E by 2.8 percentage points. In other words, the **tipping point** (where the relationship between B and E suddenly becomes much stronger) is about 50 percent.

Tiebout-Based Segregation

The segregation that results from the individual location choices of households (the Tiebout shopping process) is considered constitutional. What sort of government actions would diminish this type of segregation? In other words, what policies will diminish the incentives for households to sort themselves with respect to income and race?

One approach would be to consolidate local school districts into a metropolitan school district or a state-wide school authority. Such a policy would generate a uniform spending level and a single tax base, so there would be less incentive for households to sort themselves with respect to desired school spending and property values. As explained in Chapter 15 (Decision Making in Local Government), there are some trade-offs with this policy: to the extent there is diversity in demand for education, the large jurisdiction—with its uniform provision of education—may be less efficient than a system of smaller jurisdictions. Moreover, as pointed out by Bradford and Oates (1974), such a policy would not eliminate segregation because parents will still seek schools that provide favorable peer groups for their children. Middle-income households will still have an incentive to exclude poor children from their neighborhoods and their schools because the poor have lower average achievement levels.

A less drastic approach would be to use intergovernmental grants to equalize spending. This policy has an advantage over the consolidation approach because it gives the local school district greater control over how to spend its fixed budget. Such a policy would eliminate the incentive for fiscally based sorting (sorting with respect to desired spending levels and property values), but would not affect the sorting motivated by peer-group effects. As explained earlier in the chapter, state governments have tried a number of grant programs, none of which has narrowed spending gaps significantly. The only equalization policy that worked was the California program, under which the state assumed complete control of education funding.

Is there any way to diminish the sorting motivated by peer-group effects? Suppose that state grants were tied to students (they traveled with the student to his school) and were inversely related to the income level of the student. By admitting a low-income student, a school would increase its grant revenue, and the school could use the extra money to improve its education program (e.g., decrease class sizes, hire better teachers). Such a scheme would decrease the incentive for middle-income and wealthy households to exclude poor students, so it would promote integration. Even if it failed to integrate the schools, a school full of poor (highly subsidized) students could at least use the extra money to provide a better education program.

PUBLIC SUBSIDIES FOR PRIVATE EDUCATION— EDUCATION VOUCHERS

Should the government subsidize students who attend private as well as public schools? The advocates of private-school subsidies view the public-school system as an inflexible and inefficient monopoly. They argue that a subsidy for private education would force public schools to compete with private schools for students. As a result, public schools may become more concerned about efficiency and more responsive to parental concerns. Would the public support of private schools lead to greater inequalities in educational achievement?

Under a voucher system, every child would be issued a coupon that could be used to pay for either public or private education. The typical voucher proposal has the following features:

1. The state gives each child an educational voucher with a face value equal to the current per-pupil spending in public schools (e.g., $2,500).
2. The family uses the voucher to pay for tuition at a qualifying school, either public or private. The school redeems the voucher with the state government.
3. Public schools charge a tuition of $2,500, making public education effectively free.

4. To qualify for the voucher program, a school must teach basic cognitive skills and civics and must admit students without regard to race, sex, or religion.

5. The family is free to supplement the voucher with its own funds, so the child is free to attend a school charging more than $2,500 in tuition.

6. The government collects and disseminates information on the teaching methods, curriculum, and test scores of qualifying schools.

The voucher proposal involves a mixture of subsidies and regulations. The subsidies would place private and public schools on equal footing with respect to governmental support. The regulations would prevent explicit racism and sexism and force private schools to teach basic cognitive skills and civics. The government's information program would help parents choose among the alternative schools.

The debate over education vouchers has been spirited. Like most policy proposals, the voucher plan has some good points and some bad points. Because a true voucher plan has never been tried, there is a great deal of uncertainty about the possible effects of such a plan. The obvious response is to experiment with voucher systems in one or more school districts.

The advocates of education vouchers stress two points in their arguments for vouchers.

1. **Competition.** The voucher plan would allow private schools to compete more effectively for students. Competition will improve the efficiency of the education system, increasing the educational achievement per dollar spent.

2. **Diversity.** The voucher plan would encourage diversity in educational philosophy and methods, providing parents with more options.

Voucher advocates argue that vouchers would break up the public-school monopoly, leading to greater efficiency and wider consumer choice.

The opponents of education vouchers stress four points in their arguments against vouchers.

1. **Unequal educational opportunities.** Under a voucher system, wealthy families may supplement the voucher with their own money, sending their children to expensive (and high-quality) schools. The children from poor families would receive inferior education.

2. **Income segregation.** Under the voucher system, there would be low-cost schools (patronized by poor families) and high-cost schools (patronized by wealthy families). The education system may become more stratified with respect to income.

3. **Pluralist decision making.** Children educated in a stratified education system would be less aware and tolerant of other viewpoints and lifestyles, so decision making in today's pluralist society would become more difficult.

4. **Occupational choices.** Children educated in a stratified system would be more likely to choose the same occupation and social status as their parents: the education system would inhibit occupational and social mobility between generations.

The opponents of vouchers consider the public-school system a necessary component of a pluralist democratic society. Education in public schools forces children from different social classes to interact, resulting in citizens who are more tolerant and flexible. If the voucher system generated a more stratified education system, children from different social classes would not have the opportunity to interact, so children would not develop the traits needed to manage a pluralist democracy.

There are clearly trade-offs associated with the voucher scheme. The vouchers would improve the efficiency of the school system by fostering competition between schools and providing more choice. The vouchers may also increase inequalities in education spending, causing greater inequalities in educational achievement. In addition, they may increase income segregation, causing the school system to produce citizens who are less tolerant of alternative viewpoints and lifestyles. Given the lack of experience with voucher plans, these trade-offs cannot be quantified, so it is difficult to make an informed policy decision.

SUMMARY

1. The production function summarizes the relationship between education inputs and achievement.
   a. There are five inputs to education: curriculum, educational equipment, teachers, the home environment, and the peer group.
   b. The home environment has an extraordinary effect on achievement.
   c. A child learns more when surrounded by smart and motivated peers.
   d. Teachers vary in effectiveness. Teacher productivity increases with communication skills, but is not affected by graduate education. Some researchers suggest that productivity increases for the first few years of teaching, while others suggest that productivity is independent of teaching experience.
   e. The link between class size and achievement is still an open question. If there is a negative relationship, it seems to be a weak one.
2. Under the Tiebout process, households sort themselves with respect to three characteristics: desired spending on schools, property values, and peer-group characteristics.
3. Education spending varies considerably across school districts, a result of differences in desired spending and property tax bases.
4. U.S. schools are highly segregated: in 1986, almost half of minority students attended schools in which over 80 percent of the students were mi-

norities. Under the ability-tracking system, classrooms are even more segregated than the schools.

5. Blacks and Hispanics have relatively low achievement levels: at age 17, they are about 30 percent behind white students. In the last few decades, the test scores of blacks and Hispanics have increased relative to whites, with the largest improvements experienced by 9-year-olds. In 1985, the high school completion rate was 63 percent for blacks, compared to 77 percent for whites.

6. The traditional education grants (flat grants and foundation grants) are lump-sum grants. Under a flat-grant program, the state gives the same per pupil grant to every school district. Under a foundation plan, the grant is inversely related to the district's tax base per pupil.
   a. The grant increases spending on education and also decreases taxes, so households can spend part of the grant on other goods.
   b. Foundation plans have had small effects on spending inequalities because the grants are small and school districts spend a relatively small fraction of their grants on education.

7. In the 1970s, many state courts declared that intrastate spending inequalities were unconstitutional. The states responded by developing new grant programs.
   a. Under the guaranteed tax base (GTB) plan, every school district has access to the same effective tax base.
   b. The pure version of GTB would decrease spending inequalities by a relatively large amount because it (i) decreases the tax base of wealthy districts and increases the tax base of poor districts and (ii) increases the opportunity cost of education in the wealthy district and decreases the opportunity cost in the poor district.
   c. Most states have adopted an impure version of GTB, under which wealthy districts keep the excess of local taxes over the guaranteed tax revenue.

8. In California, the state government has assumed complete control of education finance and has virtually eliminated spending inequalities.

9. The Supreme Court outlawed segregation based on explicit and implicit government actions and ordered many cities to desegregate their school systems.
   a. Many white households moved from central-city school districts to all-white school districts in the suburbs.
   b. Other white households switched to private schools.

10. In choosing between public and private schools, parents face a trade-off between the consumption of education and other goods.
    a. Achievement is higher in private schools, a result of more favorable peer groups and other factors.

b. Desegregation will cause some households to switch to private schools if the integration of public schools decreases achievement.

11. Under a voucher system, every child is issued a coupon to pay for either public or private education. The voucher plan has advantages and disadvantages.

a. Competition among schools would increase, improving efficiency and increasing consumer choice.

b. Spending inequalities may increase, violating the principle of equal education opportunity.

c. Income segregation may increase, causing the school system to produce citizens who are less tolerant of alternative viewpoints and lifestyles.

EXERCISES AND DISCUSSION QUESTIONS

1. According to Summers and Wolfe (1977), low achievers learn more in small classes and with inexperienced teachers, while high achievers learn more in large classes with experienced teachers. Why?

2. Consider two teacher characteristics: verbal ability (V) and graduate training (G). The following combinations of V and G generate a teacher with the same teaching ability (holding other inputs constant).

V	20	30	40	50	60	70
G	70	50	35	25	20	18

a. Using the data above, map the isoquant for teacher ability, with V on the horizontal axis and G on the vertical axis.

b. Explain the shape of the isoquant: Is it flat or steep, and why?

c. Suppose that the school district starts with the teacher combination $V = 30$ and $G = 50$. The school pays $20 for every additional unit of G and $10 for every additional unit of V. If the objective of the school is to minimize the cost of teachers for its current ability level, what should it do?

3. The objective of the state of Egalitaria is to equalize educational opportunity (defined as the same average achievement level in every school). Comment on the following: "To achieve its objective, the state must equalize educational spending. In other words, it must spend the same amount per student in every school."

4. Your task is to predict the effects of a state's foundation plan on a school district and the state budget. The transfer rate (t) is two percent, and the maximum property value per student (V') is $60,000. The income elasticity of demand for education is + 0.50.

a. Fill in the blanks in the following table

	District E	District F
Tax base (per pupil)	40,000	50,000
Initial spending (per pupil)	600	800
Tax rate	_____	_____
Foundation grant	_____	_____
Initial income of median voter	1,600	2,000
Percentage change of median-voter income	_____	_____
New (postgrant) spending (per pupil)	_____	_____
Local contribution to education (per pupil)	_____	_____
New tax rate	_____	_____

b. If each school district has 1,000 students, how much does the foundation plan cost the state?

c. What is the bang (increase in education spending) per buck of the foundation grant in E?

5. Suppose that a school has a tax base per student of $40,000 and per-pupil spending of $600.

   a. Draw the district's tax-spending line and label its chosen point "A."

   b. Suppose the state gives the school district a foundation grant of $400. Using the same graph, draw the new tax-spending line. The district responds by increasing its spending to $800. Label its new chosen point "B."

   c. Suppose that the state offers the school district a GTB plan under which the guaranteed tax base is $80,000. Map the new tax-expenditure line. If the school district must choose between the foundation plan and the GTB plan, which plan will it choose?

6. Compute the price elasticity of demand for education given the following facts:

   i. The local school district has a property value per student of $30,000.

   ii. The state institutes a guaranteed tax base plan with GTB = $40,000.

   iii. As a result of the GTB, the school district increases spending per student from $2,000 to $2,100.

7. Suppose that you are the budget analyst for the state government. Your task is to estimate the fiscal impact of a GTB plan. Assume the following:

   i. The price elasticity of demand for education is −0.80.

   ii. The guaranteed tax base is $40,000.

   iii. The typical school district has 100 students, a property tax base of $30,000 per student, and initially spends $600 per student.

   Compute the effects of the GTB on the following.

   a. Spending per pupil.

   b. The local contribution to education (per pupil) and the local tax rate.

c. The state contribution to education (per pupil) and the total budgetary cost of the GTB plan.

d. The bang (increase in education spending) per buck (budgetary cost).

8. Use the median-voter model (see Chapter 15) to predict the effects of desegregation on spending (per pupil) on public schools. Will spending increase or decrease?

REFERENCES AND ADDITIONAL READINGS

Overview

Garms, Walter I.; James W. Guthrie; and Lawrence C. Pierce. *School Finance: The Economics and Politics of Public Education.* Englewood Cliffs, N.J.: Prentice-Hall, 1978. Chapter 3 discusses the reasons for government intervention in education. Chapter 4 discusses the roles of the federal, state, and local governments.

Murnane, Richard J. "An Economist's Look at Federal and State Education Policies." In *American Domestic Priorities: An Economic Appraisal,* ed. John Quigley and Daniel Rubinfeld. Berkeley and Los Angeles: University of California, 1985. Discusses a number of issues in public education, including trends in achievement scores, merit pay for teachers, the restrictive effects of state-certification requirements, and curriculum reforms.

Education Facts

Brown, L.; A. Ginsberg; J. Killalea; R. Rosthal; and E. Tron. "School Finance Reform in the Seventies: Achievements and Failures." *Selected Papers in School Finance, 1978.* Washington, D.C.: U.S. Department of Health, Education, and Welfare, 1978.

Congressional Budget Office. *Trends in Educational Achievement.* Washington, D.C.: U.S. Congress, 1986. Reports trends in test scores.

National Assessment of Educational Progress. *Three National Assessments of Science: Changes in Achievement, 1969–77.* Denver: Education Commission of the States, 1978. Reports trends in science test scores for 9-, 13-, and 17-year-olds.

————. *Has Title I Improved Education for Disadvantaged Students? Evidence from Three National Assessments on Reading.* Denver: Education Commission of the States, 1981(a). Evaluates the effects of federal support programs.

————. *Three Assessments of Reading: Changes in Performance, 1970–1980.* Denver: Education Commission of the States, 1981(b). Reports trends in reading test scores for 9-, 13-, and 17-year-olds.

————. *The Third National Mathematics Assessment: Results, Trends, and Issues.* Denver: Education Commission of the States, 1982. Reports trends in math test scores for 9-, 13-, and 17-year-olds.

National Center for Education Statistics. *Digest of Education Statistics, 1982.* Washington, D.C.: U.S. Government Printing Office, 1982. Documents the differences in achievement between whites, blacks, and Hispanics.

Schiller, Bradley. *The Economics of Poverty and Discrimination.* Englewood, N.J.: Prentice-Hall, fifth edition, 1989.

U.S. Department of Education. *1986 Elementary and Secondary School Civil Rights Survey: National Summaries.* Washington, D.C.: U.S. Government Printing Office, 1987. Shows that classrooms are more segregated than schools.

————. *The Condition of Education: A Statistical Report, 1983, 1985, 1986.* Washington, D.C.: U.S. Government Printing Office.   Reports the facts on education including information on student performance, fiscal resources, teacher characteristics, public opinion of the schools, and governance.

Production Function

Brown, B. "Achievement, Costs, and the Demand for Public Education." *Western Economic Journal* 10 (1972), pp. 198–219.   Suggests that an increase in the teacher-pupil ratio does not affect achievement, but an increase in teacher quality (experience and training) increases achievement.

Brown, B., and D. Sachs. "The Production and Distribution of Cognitive Skills Within Schools." *Journal of Political Economy* 83 (1975), pp. 571–94.

Coleman, James S.; E. Q. Campbell; C. J. Hobson; J. McPartland; A. M. Mood; F. D. Weinfield; and R. L. York. *Equality of Educational Opportunity.* Washington, D.C.: U.S. Government Printing Office, 1966.   The controversial "Coleman report" which was interpreted to mean that schools and teachers did not matter.

Hanushek, Eric A. "Throwing Money at Schools." *Journal of Policy Analysis and Management* 1 (1981), pp. 19–41.   Summarizes the results of estimates of the production function, focussing on the effects of teachers on achievement. Concludes that people with relatively high verbal skills are better teachers. Suggests that spending more money on schools will not increase achievement; argues for the development of direct performance incentives.

————."The Economics of Schooling: Production and Efficiency in Public Schools." *Journal of Economic Literature* 24 (1986), pp. 1141–77.   A survey of research on education, focussing on the production and efficiency aspects of education. Discusses the results of studies of the education production function.

Murnane, Richard J. *The Impact of School Resources on the Learning of Inner City Children.* Cambridge, Mass.: Ballinger, 1975.   Surveys the results of previous studies of the education production function and provides new estimates of the production function. Concludes that teacher experience matters for the first few years of teaching.

Summers, Anita, and Barbara Wolfe. "Do Schools Make a Difference?" *American Economic Review* 67 (1977), pp. 639– 52.   Estimates the education production function, showing that achievement depends on teacher characteristics and class size, with different effects on high achievers and low achievers.

Teachers: Productivity and Class Size

Armor, David et al. *Analysis of the School Preferred Reading Program in Selected Los Angeles Minority Schools.* Santa Monica: Rand Corporation, 1976.   A study of reading achievement in minority elementary schools. Suggests that school principals have the information and ability to identify effective teachers.

Eberts, Randall W., and Joe Stone. "Wages, Fringe Benefits, and Working Conditions: An Analysis of Compensating Differentials." *Southern Economic Journal* 52 (1985), pp. 274–79. Estimates the responsiveness of teacher salaries to changes in working conditions, including changes in class size.

Hanushek, Eric, A. "Teacher Characteristics and Gains in Student Achievement: Estimates Using Micro Data." *American Economic Review* 61 (1971), pp. 280–88. Estimates the education production function, showing that achievement depends on the general ability of teachers (as measured by scores on verbal tests) and how recently the teacher received formal training.

Murnane, Richard J. "Understanding the Sources of Teaching Competence: Choice Skills, and the Limits of Training." *Teachers College Record* 84 (1983), pp. 564–69. Discusses the evidence about which teacher characteristics affect achievement and explores the policy implications of these findings.

Decline of Test Scores

Advisory Panel on the Scholastic Test Score Decline. *On Further Examination.* New York: College Entrance Examination Board, 1977. Discusses some of the reasons for the decline in SAT scores during the 1960s and 1970s.

Harnischfeger, Annegret, and David E. Wiley. *Achievement Test Score Decline: Do We Need to Worry.* Chicago: Cemrel, 1975.

————. *Time and Learning in California Schools.* Sacramento: California Testing Program, 1984. Suggests that achievement depends on the number of academic courses completed.

Spending Inequalities

Berne, Robert, and Leanna Stiefel. *The Measurement of Equity in School Finance.* Baltimore: The Johns Hopkins Press, 1984.

Coons, John E.; William H. Clune; and Stephen D. Sugarman. *Private Wealth and Public Education.* Cambridge, Mass.: Harvard Univ. Press, 1970. Developed the notion of "fiscal neutrality."

Guthrie, James W. "United States School Finance Policy 1955–1980." Chapter 1. In *School Finance Policies and Practices.* Cambridge, Mass.: Ballinger, 1980. Relates the history of school finance, focussing on court cases that forced states to reform their financing policies.

McDonald, M. Brian. "Educational Equity and the Fiscal Incidence of Public Education." *National Tax Journal* 33 (1980), pp. 45–54. Shows that there is an inverse relationship between income and the net benefits from education.

Equalization Policies

Bradford, David, and Wallace E. Oates. "Suburban Exploitation of Central Cities and Government Structure." In *Redistribution Through Public Choice,* ed. Harold Hochman and George Peterson. New York: Columbia University Press, 1974.

California Department of Education. *Selected Financial and Related Data for California Public Schools, K-12, 1984-85.* Sacramento: State of California, 1986.

Carroll, Stephen J. *The Search for Equity in School Finance: Summary and Conclusions.* Santa Monica: Rand Corporation, 1979. Discusses the reasons why GTB plans have not had a significant effect on spending inequalities.

Courant, Paul N.; Edward M. Gramlich; and Daniel Rubinfeld. "The Stimulative Effect of Intergovernmental grants, or Why Money Sticks Where It Hits." In *Fiscal Federalism and Grants-in-Aid,* ed. Peter Meiszkowski and William Oakland. Washington, D.C.: The Urban Institute, 1979. Discusses the flypaper effect of intergovernmental grants.

Gramlich, E. M. "Intergovernmental Grants: A Review of the Empirical Literature." In *The Political Economy of Fiscal Federalism,* ed. Wallace E. Oates. Lexington, Mass.: Lexington Books, 1977. Reviews the literature on the effects of grants on local spending. Concludes that matching grants are more stimulative than lump-sum grants and the categorical grant has a larger stimulative effect than an equivalent increase in private income.

Neenan, William B. "Fiscal Relations Between State of Michigan and Southeastern Michigan." In *Financing the Metropolis,* ed. Kent Mathewson and William B. Neenan. New York: Praeger, 1980.

Public versus Private Schools

Barzel, Y. "Private Schools and Public School Finance." *Journal of Political Economy* 81 (1973), pp. 174–86. Analyzes the exit of wealthy households to private schools when the achievement level of public schools decreases.

Coleman, James S.; Thomas Hoffer; and Sally Kilgore. *Achievement in High School: Public and Private Schools Compared.* New York: Basic Books, 1981. Shows that students in private schools have higher test scores than students in public schools. Also suggests that achievement depends on the number of academic courses completed.

Inman, Robert. "Optimal Fiscal Reform of Metropolitan Schools: Some Simulation Results." *American Economic Review* 68 (1978), pp. 107–22. Discusses the choice between private and public schools and the implications for education finance.

Murnane, Richard J. "Comparisons of Private and Public Schools: The Critical Role of Regulations." Chapter 4. In *Private Education: Studies in Choice and Public Policy,* ed. Daniel C. Levy. Oxford: Oxford University Press, 1986.

————."Comparisons of Private and Public Schools: What Can We Learn?" Chapter 5. In *Private Education: Studies in Choice and Public Policy,* ed. Daniel C. Levy. Oxford: Oxford University Press, 1986.

School Problems: Desegregation and Busing

Clotfelter, Charles T. "The Effect of School Desegregation on Housing Prices." *Review of Economics and Statistics* 57 (1975), pp. 446–51. Shows that desegregation in the South decreased the demand for central-city housing, decreasing housing prices.

————. "School Desegregation, Tipping, and Private School Enrollment." *Journal of Human Resources* 11 (1976), pp. 28–50. Shows that an increase in black enrollment increases the proportion of whites enrolled in private schools.

————. "School Desegregation as Urban Public Policy." In *Current Issues in Urban Economics*, ed. Peter Meiszkowski and Mahlon Straszheim. Baltimore: The Johns Hopkins Press, 1979, pp. 359–88. Describes the evolution of desegregation policy, explores the "white flight" phenomenon, and discusses the effects of desegregation on achievement.

Coleman, James, and Sara Kelly. "Education." In *The Urban Predicament*, ed. William Gorham and Nathan Glazer. Washington, D.C.: The Urban Institute, 1976. Analyzes racial segregation in schools between 1968 and 1973.

Giles, Michael W.; Douglas Gatlin; and Everett F. Cataldo. "White Flight and Percent Black: The Tipping Point Re-Examined." *Social Science Quarterly* 56 (1975), pp. 85–92. Using data for Florida, estimates that the tipping point for white enrollment in private schools is about 30 percent black enrollment in public schools.

Education Vouchers

Bridge, Gary. "Citizen Choice in Public Services." In *Alternatives for Delivering Public Services*, ed. E. S. Savas. Boulder, Colo.: Westview Press, 1977. Suggests that parents are likely to pick education programs for their children that prepare them for the same type of occupation.

Coons, John E., and Stephen D. Sugarman. *Education by Choice: The Case for Family Control.* Berkeley and Los Angeles: University of California, 1978. Discusses the voucher program, arguing that a voucher system would provide better education because parents and students would have greater opportunity for educational choice.

Levin, Henry M. "Educational Vouchers and Social Policy." In *School Finance Policies and Practices*, ed. James W. Guthrie. Cambridge Mass.: Ballinger, 1980. Relates the history of the voucher proposal and describes the features of the most recent proposals. Discusses the role of integrated classrooms for the promotion of occupational mobility and the functioning of a pluralist democracy and suggests that a voucher scheme is likely to cause a stratification of the education system.

CHAPTER 20

Crime and Punishment

I don't worry about crime on the streets; it's the sidewalks I stay off of.

Johnson Letellier

This chapter presents the economic approach to crime and crime prevention. The economic approach assumes that both criminals and victims are rational in the sense that they base their choices on the expected benefits and costs of alternative actions. A rational person will commit a property crime if the expected benefit of the crime exceeds the expected cost. Similarly, potential victims use their resources to prevent crime if the expected benefit of crime prevention exceeds the expected cost. The economic approach leads naturally to a discussion of the optimum amount of crime: because crime is costly to prevent, it will be rational to allow some crime to occur.

Why study crime? The analysis of crime is an important part of urban economics for three reasons. First, most crime occurs in metropolitan areas, and crime rates are highest in central cities. Second, households are sensitive to crime rates, so their location decisions are affected by local crime rates. In other words, crime affects the spatial distribution of people within and between cities. Because households are attracted to areas with low crime rates, the price of housing is negatively related to the crime rate. Third, suburbanization is caused, in part, by relatively high crime rates in central cities: many households have moved to the suburbs to escape central-city crime.

CRIME FACTS

Most crime data come from the FBI's *Uniform Crime Reports*. The FBI collects data from local police departments on seven **index crimes**. The index crimes are divided into personal crimes and property crimes.

1. **Personal crime.** The victim of a personal crime is placed in physical danger. For some personal crimes, the criminal's objective is to injure the victim (e.g., homicide, rape, aggravated assault). For other personal crimes, the objective is to steal property, but the criminal uses force to coerce the victim (e.g., robbery).

2. **Property crime.** Property crimes are crimes of stealth, not force. Examples are burglary (illegal entry of a building), larceny (purse snatching, pocket picking, and bicycle theft), and auto theft.

The FBI data provide a partial picture of the crime sense. Among the crimes omitted in the *Uniform Crime Reports* are disorderly conduct, shoplifting, arson, employee theft, and drug-related offenses (possession and sale of narcotics, public drunkenness, drunk driving).

Table 20–1 lists crime rates for the seven index crimes for the last few decades. The crime rates are expressed as the number of crimes per 100,000 population. Most of the reported index crimes are economically motivated. In 1986, the four economic crimes (robbery, burglary, larceny, and auto theft) made up about 91 percent of total reported crimes. The total crime rate rose from 1,870 in 1960 to 5,950 in 1980 and then fell to 5,480 in 1986.

Because the FBI data include only the crimes that are reported to the police, it may be deceptive. In 1986, estimated reporting rates were 54 percent for robberies, 46 percent for assaults, 27 percent for personal larceny, 50 percent for burglary, 27 percent for household larceny, and 71 percent for auto theft. The reporting rate for auto theft is relatively high because most people insure their cars against theft and must submit a police report with their insurance claim. Given the low reporting rates for most crimes, a change in the FBI crime rate could be caused by a change in actual crime or a change in reporting rates.

Since 1973, the Justice Department has collected crime data from its semiannual victimization surveys. The survey suggests that crime rates decreased between 1973 and 1985. The percentage reductions of property crime were 25 percent for robbery, 32 percent for burglary, 25 percent for larceny, and 25 percent for auto theft.

TABLE 20–1   FBI Index Crimes, 1960–1986

	Number of Crimes per 100,000 People			
	1960	*1970*	*1980*	*1986*
Personal crime				
Murder	5.0	7.8	10.2	8.6
Rape	9.5	18.6	36.8	37.5
Aggravated assault	85.2	176.9	298.5	346.1
Robbery	59.5	187.2	251.1	225.1
Property crime				
Auto theft	182	457	502	508
Larceny	1,024	2,124	3,167	3,010
Burglary	504	1,152	1,684	1,345
Total index crimes	1,870	3,949	5,950	5,480

SOURCE: U.S. Federal Bureau of Investigation, *Uniform Crime Reports for the United States 1986* (Washington, D.C.: U.S. Government Printing Office, 1987).

The Victims of Crime

Who are the victims of crime? Victimization rates vary with income, place of residence, and race.

1. **Crime and income.** Table 20–2 shows victimization rates for different income levels. The victimization rates for personal crimes (rape, robbery, and assault) decrease as income increases: the poor are more likely to be assaulted and robbed. The victimization rate for burglary is highest for the lowest income group. In contrast, the incidence of auto theft increases with income.

2. **Crime and place of residence.** Figure 20–1 shows victimization rates for different residential locations. Crime rates are higher in metropolitan areas than in nonmetropolitan areas and higher in central cities than in suburbs. The largest difference in crime rates is for robbery: the

FIGURE 20–1   Crime Rates and Place of Residence

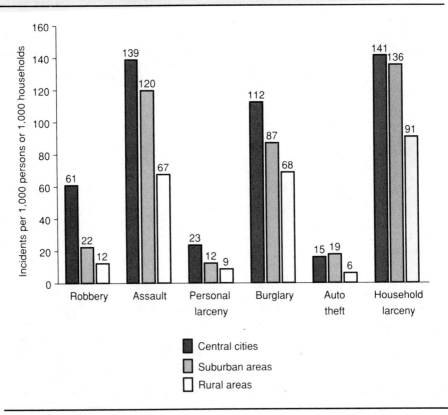

SOURCE: U. S. Bureau of Justice, *Criminal Victimization in the U.S.*, 1985 (Washington, D.C.: U.S. Government Printing Office, 1987). pp. 34–35, 44–45.

TABLE 20–2   Victimization Rates and Income, 1985

	Victimization Rate: Incidents per 1,000 Persons or 1,000 Households Annual Income ($ thousands)						
	0–7.5	*7.5–10*	*10–15*	*15–25*	*25–30*	*30–50*	*Over 50*
Personal crime							
Rape	2.2	1.1	0.7	0.1	0.4	0.6	0.4
Robbery	8.8	7.4	5.4	4.7	4.7	3.5	3.2
Assault	41.1	25.4	25.7	23.2	23.9	18.2	21
Household crime							
Burglary	86.3	60.4	67	58.7	53.9	58.4	55.9
Vehicle theft	10.7	15.4	14.1	14	12.7	15.6	21.1

SOURCE: U.S. Bureau of Justice, *Criminal Victimization in the United States, 1985* (Washington, D.C.: U.S. Department of Justice, 1987) Table 14.

central-city robbery rate is over five times the rural rate and almost three times the suburban rate. Crime is concentrated in cities for three reasons. First, poverty is concentrated in cities. Because a large fraction of criminals come from poor households, the cities have a large supply of potential criminals. Second, wealth is concentrated in cities, and criminals are attracted by urban loot. Third, population density is higher in cities, providing criminals with a large concentration of targets.

3. **Crime and race.** Figure 20–2 shows the victimization rates for whites and blacks. Except for personal larceny, blacks are victimized more frequently than whites: the robbery rate for blacks is about 2.5 times the robbery rate for whites; the black burglary rate is about 1.5 times the white rate; and the black auto-theft rate is 1.7 times the white rate. For personal larceny, whites are victimized more frequently than blacks, but the difference is relatively small.

Crime and the Price of Housing

Crime rates vary across space, causing variation in the price of housing. Gray and Joelson (1979) studied the relationship between crime rates and property values in Minneapolis. In 1970, the burglary rate varied considerably across the city's census tracts, from 1 percent of dwellings per year in the lowest crime tract to 14 percent in the highest. A one-unit increase in the crime rate (an additional percentage point of dwellings burglarized) decreased the average property value by $336. The vandalism rate varied from less than one incident to 30 incidents per 1,000 population. A one-unit increase in the vandalism rate (an additional incident per 1,000 population) decreased the average property by $117. In another study, Thaler (1978) esti-

FIGURE 20-2   Victimization Rates and Race, 1985

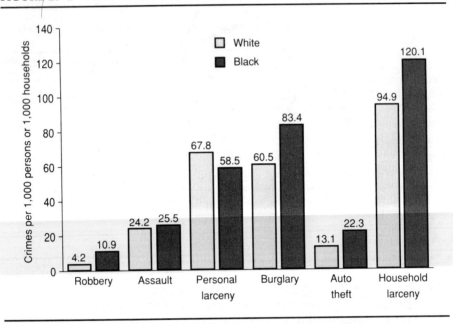

SOURCE: U. S. Bureau of Justice, *Criminal Victimization in the U.S.*, 1985 (Washington, D.C.: U.S. Government Printing Office, 1987). pp. 16, 28.

mated the elasticity of property values with respect to crime rates as −0.067: a 10 percent increase in the crime rate decreased the market value of housing by about 0.67 percent.

The Costs of Crime

Criminal activity imposes two types of costs on society. The direct costs are the costs incurred by the physical victims of crime: the victims of personal crimes are injured or killed, and the victims of property crime lose their property. The indirect costs are the costs incurred by potential victims in their efforts to prevent crime: people spend money on locks, guard dogs, and other prevention measures, and also pay taxes to support society's crime-prevention programs (the police, the court system, and prisons). The opportunity cost of crime prevention is the value of the resources in alternative uses: if there were less crime to prevent, locks could be melted into plows, lawyers could build bridges, and prison cells could be converted to condominiums.

Reynolds (1986) has estimated the direct and indirect costs of personal and property crime, using data from several sources. He estimated the nationwide cost of crime in 1983 and then divided the nationwide cost by the number of households to get the crime cost per household. As shown in Table 20-3, Reynolds estimated that the cost of crime was $2,323 per household in 1983.

TABLE 20–3   The Costs of Crime in 1983

	Cost per Household ($ per year)
Direct costs	
Personal losses	
Homicide	$ 72
Rape	89
Assault	192
Robbery (cost of injury)	82
Property losses	
Burglary	93
Larceny-theft	81
Robbery (property losses)	8
Motor-vehicle theft	56
Business losses	
Arson	22
Shoplifting	300
Employee theft	125
Business fraud	600
Indirect costs	
Prevention costs	
Businesses	81
Households	106
Criminal justice system	
Police	200
Courts and legal services	87
Corrections	87
Opportunity cost of imprisonment	50
Total cost	$2,323

Direct Costs.   There are three types of direct costs from crime: personal losses, property losses, and losses from business crime.

1. **Personal losses.** To estimate the social costs of crimes against people, one must place dollar figures on the costs of injuries and death. Reynolds assumed that the cost per homicide was $300,000, the cost per rape was $30,000, the cost per serious assault was $12,000, and the injury cost per robbery was $6,600. As shown in Table 20–3, the estimated annual cost per household ranges from $72 for homicide to $192 for assault.

2. **Property losses.** Property losses occur as a result of burglary, larceny, robbery, and motor-vehicle theft. The estimated value of property losses in 1983 was $238 per household.

3. **Business crime.** There are four types of business crimes. Arson generated losses of $1.8 billion, or $22 per household. Reynolds assumed

that the loss from shoplifting was two percent of retail sales, or $300 per household, and the loss from employee theft was $125 per household. Business fraud, which generated total losses of $600 per household, includes credit-card theft (losses of $1 billion per year), securities theft ($8 billion), bad checks ($2 billion), insurance fraud ($4 billion), mail and bank fraud ($1 billion), deceptive practices ($18 billion), bribes and kickbacks ($6 billion), and fencing stolen property ($7 billion).

Indirect Costs.   There are two types of indirect costs: prevention costs and the costs of the criminal justice system. According to Reynolds, the total indirect cost was $611 per household in 1983.

1. **Prevention costs.** Reynolds estimated that firms spent a total of $6.5 billion on crime-prevention measures in 1983. Most of this money was spent on private security guards. Households spent an additional $8.5 billion on prevention measures, so the total cost of crime prevention was $15 billion or $187 per household.

2. **Criminal justice system.** Reynolds estimated that spending on police, courts, and corrections facilities was $374 per household. Another cost of the criminal justice system is the opportunity cost of time spent in prison. Reynolds assumed that each prisoner could have produced $10,000 worth of goods if he or she were gainfully employed. Based on this assumption, the opportunity cost of imprisonment was $50 per household. The total cost of the criminal justice system was $424 per household.

THE RATIONAL CRIMINAL AND THE SUPPLY OF CRIME

The economic model of crime assumes that the criminal commits a crime if the expected benefit of the crime exceeds its expected cost. The model of the rational criminal is relevant for economically motivated crimes (property crimes), but not for crimes of passion or violence.

A Numerical Example of Burglary

Consider Boris, who must decide whether to spend a day planning and executing a burglary. Boris will commit the burglary if the expected net benefit of burglary exceeds the expected benefit of spending the day in some legal activity. The costs and benefits of the two activities are listed in Table 20–4.

1. **The expected loot** (*EL*). The expected value of the burglary loot is the probability that Boris succeeds in the burglary (P_s) times the monetary value of the loot:

$$EL = P_s \cdot Loot \qquad (20-1)$$

TABLE 20–4 Expected Benefits and Costs for a Burglary

Burglary Activity	Benefits and Costs
Expected loot	
Loot	$ 600
Probability of success (P_s)	0.80
Expected loot ($EL = P_s \cdot Loot$)	480
Expected cost	
Probability of imprisonment ($P_i = P_a \cdot P_p$	0.02
Opportunity cost of prison time	
Daily wage (W)	$ 40
Expected workdays per year (D)	150
Forgone income per year ($I = W \cdot D$)	$6000
Cost of lost freedom per year (F)	$2000
Opportunity cost per year ($C = I + F$)	$8000
Expected Cost ($EC = P_i \cdot C$)	$ 160
Expected benefit of burglary ($B = (EL - EC)$)	$ 320
Legal activity	
Daily income if employed (W)	$ 40
Net return from burglary ($R = B - W$)	$ 280

If the probability of success is 80 percent and the resale value of the stolen property is $600, the expected value of the loot is $480.

2. **Expected cost** (EC). On the cost side, Boris faces the possibility of being sent to prison for committing the burglary. The expected cost of the burglary is the probability of being imprisoned (P_i) times the opportunity cost of time spent in prison.

   a. **Probability of imprisonment.** The probability of being imprisoned is determined by the police and the court system. The probability of imprisonment (P_i) is the probability of being arrested (P_a) times the probability of being sentenced to prison once arrested (P_p).

$$P_i = P_a \cdot P_p \tag{20-2}$$

   In the 1970s, about 16 percent of index crimes resulted in an arrest, so P_a is about 0.16 (Wilson and Boland 1976). In the 1970s, about 13 percent of arrestees were sent to prison, so P_p is about 0.13 (Wilson and Boland 1976). If Boris faces similar chances of arrest and sentencing, the probability of being imprisoned is about 0.02 (0.16 times 0.13).

   b. **The opportunity cost of prison time.** The opportunity cost of time spent in prison equals the annual opportunity cost times the length of the prison sentence. Suppose that Boris is a relatively low-skilled worker who can find work only about 150 days per year and is paid $40 per day. For every year in prison, he gives up $6,000 in income (150 times $40).

Another cost of imprisonment is the loss of liberty and freedom. If he values his freedom at $2,000 per year, the annual opportunity cost of prison is $8,000 ($6,000 in foregone wages plus $2,000 in lost freedom). If the prison sentence for burglary is one year, the opportunity cost of imprisonment is $8,000.

   c. **Expected cost** (*EC*). The expected cost is $160 (the probability of being imprisoned [0.02] times the opportunity cost of imprisonment for burglary [$8,000]).

3. **Expected benefit from burglary** (*B*). The expected benefit from burglary is the expected loot ($480) less the expected cost ($160), or $320.

4. **Net return from burglary** (*R*). The alternative to burglary is to spend the day in a legal job. The net return from a burglary is the expected benefit of the burglary ($320) less the money Boris could earn in a legal job ($40), or $280. The net return is positive, so if Boris bases his decision exclusively on the expected benefits and costs of burglary, he will commit the burglary.

Morality and Aversion to Crime?   Most people have an underlying aversion to committing crime. For the typical person, crime is unattractive at any price. For other people, the net return of crime must be high enough to overcome their underlying aversion to crime. One way to incorporate the aversion to crime into the benefit-cost analysis is to estimate a person's **anguish cost**, defined as the cost associated with engaging in antisocial activity. If Gabriel has a strong aversion to crime, his anguish cost may be $10,000, meaning that he will commit a crime only if the net return exceeds $10,000. If Lucifer is less averse to crime, his anguish cost may be only $10, so he will commit a crime if the net return exceeds $10. Returning to the example in Table 20–4, Boris will commit the burglary if his anguish cost is less than the net return of the burglary ($280).

Who Commits Crimes?   The model of the rational criminal provides three reasons why some people commit crime. First, some people are relatively skillful at committing crime and escaping punishment. For such people, the expected loot is relatively large and the expected cost is relatively low, so the expected benefit of crime is relatively high. Second, some people have relatively low opportunity costs of time spent committing crime and time spent in prison, so the expected cost of crime is relatively low. For example, the poor may have lower opportunity costs because they are unemployed or earn low wages. Third, some people have less respect for society and are less averse to committing crime, so they need a relatively small net return to make crime worthwhile. For most people, the moral anguish associated with crime is large enough to make crime unattractive at almost any price.

The Crime-Supply Curve

The model of the rational criminal can be used to derive the supply curve for burglary. The supply curve shows the relationship between the net return or "price" of burglary and the number of burglaries committed.

FIGURE 20–3   Boris's Supply Curve of Crime

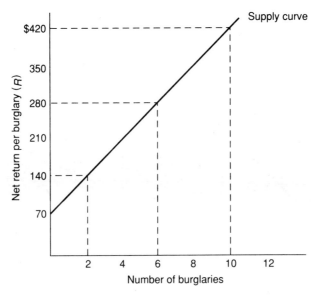

The supply curve shows the number of burglaries that Boris will commit for different net returns (R) per crime. Boris's anguish cost is $70: he will not commit a burglary unless R is at least $70. If R is $280, he will commit six burglaries per month.

Figure 20–3 shows the individual supply curve. The horizontal axis measures the number of burglaries that Boris commits per month, and the vertical axis measures the net return (R) per burglary. The supply curve is drawn under the assumption that the anguish cost is $70: Boris will commit burglaries only if the price exceeds $70. As R increases, Boris commits more burglaries: for R = $140, he commits 2 burglaries per month; for R = $420, he commits 10.

The aggregate supply of crime is the sum of the crimes committed by individual criminals. Figure 20–4 shows the supply curves of Boris and Natasha. Natasha has a greater aversion to crime than Boris: she must have a net return of at least $210 per burglary to offset her anguish costs. Because Natasha enters the crime scene when R exceeds $210, her supply curve intersects the vertical axis at $210.

The aggregate supply curve is the horizontal sum of the supply curves of individual criminals. For a given price, the aggregate supply of burglary equals the sum of the crimes committed by the two criminals. The aggregate supply curve is kinked at $210: for R less than Natasha's anguish cost, Natasha commits no burglaries, so the aggregate supply curve is the same as Boris's; for R greater than Natasha's anguish cost, the aggregate supply curve is the Boris supply plus the Natasha supply. For example, if R = $280, Boris commits six burglaries and Natasha commits two, so the aggregate supply is

FIGURE 20–4   Aggregate Supply of Crime: Boris and Natasha

The aggregate supply of crime is the sum of the crimes committed by individual criminals. If R is $280, Boris will commit six burglaries and Natasha will commit two, for a total of eight burglaries. If R rises to $420, the total supply increases to 16 (10 by Boris and 6 by Natasha).

eight burglaries. If R rises to 420, the number of crimes rises to 16 (6 by Natasha and 10 by Boris).

As explained later in the chapter, society has some control over the net return to crime. When the net return to crime decreases, the number of crimes decreases (society moves down the supply curve) for two reasons. First, each criminal commits fewer offenses. Second, some criminals exit from the crime business because the net return of crime falls short of their anguish costs. Marginal criminals "go straight" if the return of crime is not high enough to offset their underlying aversion to crime.

Shifting the Supply Curve

The position of the aggregate supply curve is determined by the number of potential criminals. An increase in the number of criminals means that there are more individual supply curves to sum, so the aggregate supply curve (the horizontal sum of the individual supply curves) shifts to the right. At a given net return, more people will commit burglaries, so the total supply of burglaries will be higher.

The aggregate supply curve is also affected by changes in the underlying aversion to crime. Suppose that someone persuades Boris and Natasha that crime is evil. As Boris and Natasha become more averse to crime, their anguish costs increase, shifting their individual supply curves upward. In Figure 20–5, Boris would require a net return of $280 to overcome his aversion to crime and Natasha would require a net return of $560. The increase in the aversion to crime shifts the aggregate supply curve upward: the number of crimes at each R decreases.

The aggregate supply curve is also affected by the age distribution of the population. Young males commit more than their share of crimes. Therefore, a society with a relatively large number of young males will have relatively high crime rates. Recent shifts in the age distribution of the U.S. population have decreased the proportion of young males. As the proportion of the population in the crime-prone years decreased, crime rates fell.

OPTIMUM AMOUNT OF CRIME

Because crime prevention is costly, the optimum amount of crime is positive. In other words, it will be rational to tolerate some crime. How much crime should be allowed?

FIGURE 20–5   Shift in Supply from Increased Aversion to Crime

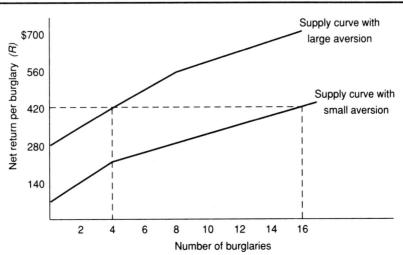

An increase in the aversion to crime shifts the individual supply curves upward, shifting the aggregate supply curve upward. For R = $420, the number of burglaries decreases from 16 to 4.

Victim Costs and Prevention Costs

The social costs of crime can be divided into **victim costs** and **prevention costs**. The victims of property crime lose property and are sometimes injured in the process. Figure 20–6 shows total victim costs as a function of the number of burglaries. The victim-cost curve is positively sloped and linear, reflecting the assumption that the victim cost per burglary is independent of the number of burglaries: for example, if the number of burglaries doubles, total victim costs also double.

Although society can decrease crime by decreasing the net return to burglary, crime prevention is costly. There are a number of options for crime prevention:

1. **Hardening the target.** Victims can decrease the expected loot by decreasing the probability of successful burglary (e.g., by installing locks and guard dogs).

2. **Increased probability of arrest.** The police can increase the expected cost of crime by increasing the probability of arrest (e.g., by hiring more police officers).

3. **Increased probability of imprisonment.** The criminal justice system can increase the expected cost of crime by increasing the probabilities

FIGURE 20–6   The Optimum Number of Burglaries

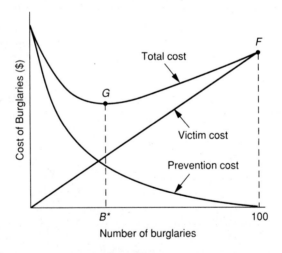

The total social cost of burglaries equals the sum of the costs incurred by victims and the cost of prevention. Victim cost increases at a constant rate if the cost per crime is constant. The prevention cost increases rapidly as the number of burglaries decreases, a result of diminishing marginal returns. Total cost is minimized at B^*.

of conviction and punishment (e.g., by hiring more investigators to gather evidence on crime).

4. **Increased severity of punishment.** The criminal justice system can increase the expected cost of crime by lengthening prison sentences (e.g., by building more prison cells.).

5. **Increased value of legal opportunities.** Society can increase the attractiveness of legal activity by increasing the job skills of potential criminals, thus increasing their legal wages. As the opportunity cost of crime increases, the net return to burglary decreases.

In Figure 20–6, the prevention-cost curve is negatively sloped. All of these preventive measures are costly, so the larger the number of crimes prevented (the fewer the burglaries committed), the higher the prevention cost. The prevention-cost curve increases in slope as the number of burglaries decreases, reflecting the assumption of diminishing marginal returns to crime prevention: as prevention efforts increase and the number of crimes decreases, it becomes progressively more difficult to prevent more crime. For example, it is relatively easy to decrease the number of burglaries from 100 to 99, but more difficult to decrease the number from 11 to 10.

The total cost of crime is the sum of the victim costs and the prevention costs. In Figure 20–6, the total-cost curve is U-shaped, reflecting the trade-offs between victim and prevention costs. Suppose that a city starts with zero prevention costs, so it has 100 burglaries per day, and the total cost of crime is the victim cost (i.e., the city starts at point F). The city could decrease the number of burglaries and decrease victim costs by spending a small amount on prevention (e.g., hardening targets, lengthening prison sentences, improving legal opportunities). By doing so, it would decrease the total cost of crime: starting from point F, the savings in victim costs would exceed the increase in prevention costs, so the city would move down the total-cost curve. The total costs of crime are minimized at point G, so the optimum crime rate is B^*.

How does the city persuade burglars to commit the optimum number of burglaries (B^*)? The city would use its crime-prevention resources to decrease the net return to burglary to the point at which burglars commit B^* burglaries per day. In other words, the city picks the point on the burglary supply curve and invests resources to bring the net return down to the necessary level.

Marginal Costs and Variation in Optimum Crime Levels

The optimum crime rate can also be derived from the marginal-cost curves underlying the total-cost curves in Figure 20–6. In Figure 20–7, the lower horizontal line shows the marginal victim cost for burglary, defined as the increase in victim costs per additional burglary (the slope of the total victim-cost curve in Figure 20–6). This cost curve is horizontal because the cost per burglary victim is assumed to be constant. The negatively sloped

FIGURE 20-7   Marginal Victim and Prevention Costs and the Optimum Crime Level

The optimum crime level is where the marginal victim cost equals the marginal prevention cost (B^* for burglaries and A^* for armed robberies). The optimum number of robberies is smaller because robbery has higher victim costs.

curve shows the marginal prevention cost, defined as the change in prevention cost per unit change in the number of burglaries (the slope of the total prevention-cost curve in Figure 20–6). It is negatively sloped because of diminishing returns to crime prevention: the first unit of crime prevention (decreasing the number of burglaries from 100 to 99) has a relatively low marginal cost; the last unit of crime prevention (decreasing the number of burglaries from one to zero) has a high marginal cost.

The optimum amount of crime is shown by the intersection of the two marginal-cost curves (marginal victim cost and marginal prevention cost). Starting with 100 burglaries, the marginal cost of prevention exceeds the marginal victim cost, so it is sensible to deter the 100th crime. Prevention will be efficient as long as the marginal victim cost exceeds the marginal prevention cost, so the optimum crime rate for burglary is B^*.

The marginal-cost curves explain why optimum crime rates vary across crimes. Suppose that burglary and armed robbery have the same prevention costs but different victim costs: the victims of armed robbery are often injured during the crime, so robbery has a higher marginal victim cost. In Figure 20–7, the optimum crime rate for robbery (A^*) is less than the optimum crime rate for burglary (B^*): more resources are invested in robbery prevention because the savings in victim costs per robbery are higher. Optimum crime rates also differ because of differences in prevention costs: crimes with higher marginal prevention costs have higher optimum crime rates, everything else being equal.

The same arguments can be used to explain why crime rates vary within a metropolitan area. The relatively high crime rates in some central-city areas can be explained by two factors. First, these areas have large concentrations of poor and unemployed people, so the opportunity cost of crime is relatively low and the number of potential criminals is relatively large. The plentiful supply of criminals will generate a relatively high marginal prevention cost, so the area will have a relatively high optimum crime rate. Second, the poor may be willing to pay a relatively small amount to avoid being victimized. The poor have less money to spend on all goods, including housing, food, and police protection. In Figure 20–7, a low willingness to pay for crime prevention would be shown as a relatively low victim-cost curve, so the optimum crime rate would be relatively high.

CRIME-PREVENTION ACTIVITIES

This section discusses some of the details of crime prevention, exploring the effects of various approaches to preventing crime. The first part of this section considers "carrot" policies: by increasing the value of legal opportunities, the government rewards people who choose legal activities over crime. The second part of the section shows how potential victims can protect themselves from crime. The final part examines "stick" policies: by increasing the certainty and severity of punishment, the government deters crime.

Increasing the Value of Legal Opportunities

One approach to preventing crime is to increase the value of legal opportunities. This can be accomplished in a number of ways, including education, job training, and government employment. Chapter 12 (Poverty and Public Policy) describes several programs that provide education and training to the poor. The discussion generated three general conclusions about the effects of the various antipoverty policies on crime rates.

1. Because crime rates are lower among teenagers who stay in school longer and get better grades, programs that increase the amount of schooling and increase scholastic achievement decrease crime rates. For example, the Perry Preschool Program increased high school completion rates and decreased arrest rates: compared to a control group, program participants had higher high school completion rates (67 percent versus 49 percent) and lower arrest rates (by a margin of 40 percent).

2. Some of the youth job-training programs (e.g., Job Corps and Youth Employment Demonstration Projects Act) increase earnings and decrease crime rates.

3. The job-training programs for ex-addicts and ex-offenders have had mixed results. For example, the National Supported Work Demonstration decreased the crime rates of ex-addicts, but had relatively small effects on ex-offenders.

What is the relationship between unemployment and crime? Freeman (1983) summarizes the evidence from dozens of studies and comes to two basic conclusions. First, although there is a positive relationship between crime and unemployment, the relationship is relatively weak. Second, the crime rates of first-time offenders are relatively sensitive to the unemployment rate. This conclusion is consistent with the results of Fleisher (1966) and Phillips, Votey, and Maxwell (1972), both of whom found a strong relationship between youth unemployment and crime rates. A similar conclusion was reached by the National Bureau of Economic Research (NBER) study of youth unemployment (discussed in Chapter 12): teenage crime rates were higher in cities with fewer legal opportunities.

Victims as Crime Fighters

Potential victims can discourage crime by decreasing the thief's expected benefits from the crime. There are two strategies for decreasing the expected loot: hardening the target and decreasing the market value of the stolen property.

Hardening the Target. The potential victim can harden the target by investing in protective devices. Alice's options for protecting her bike are listed in Table 20–5. If she does not spend any money on protection, there is a 30 percent chance that her $100 bike will be stolen, so her expected loss from theft is $30 (0.30 times $100). If she locks her bike with a flimsy lock, the probability of theft drops to 10%; if she locks her bike with a sturdy lock, the probability drops to 2 percent. If she hires an armed guard, the probability of theft is zero.

What is the optimum level of protection? Alice's objective is to minimize the total cost of protecting her bike, equal to the sum of protection costs and the expected loss from theft. She minimizes total cost with the flimsy lock: her protection cost is $11 and the expected loss is $10, for a total cost of $21. Although a sturdy lock would decrease the probability of theft, the marginal benefit of the additional protection (the $8 decrease in the expected loss) is less than the marginal cost (the $13 increase in protection cost). Alice will tolerate a 10 percent chance of having her bike stolen because the marginal cost of additional protection exceeds the marginal benefit.

The optimum level of protection depends on the value of the item being protected. If Alice replaces her $100 bike with a $200 bike, she will upgrade her protection to a sturdy lock: the switch to the more expensive bike doubles the expected loss from theft, so the marginal benefit of the sturdy lock ($16) exceeds its marginal cost ($13). In general, people with more property to protect spend more money on protection.

How do people and firms harden crime targets? Most people lock their cars and houses, and some install burglar alarms. Purchasers of expensive car stereo systems can buy plastic covers that make the stereos look cheap and

TABLE 20–5   Protective Measures for $100 Bicycle

Protective Action	Protection Cost	Probability of Theft	Expected Theft Cost	Total Cost
No protection	$ 0	0.30	$30	$30
Flimsy lock	11	0.10	10	21
Sturdy lock	24	0.02	2	26
Armed guard	80	0.00	0	80

unattractive. Most businesses keep their valuables in safes and install alarms to deter robbers. Convenience stores keep their money in timed safes, so clerks (and thieves) have access to a limited amount of cash.

Protection and Insurance.   How does insurance affect Alice's spending on protective measures? Suppose that she insured her $100 bicycle against theft and there are no costs associated with filing a claim (no transactions costs and no deductible payment). If so, the total cost of leaving her bike unprotected is zero: every time her bike is stolen, she collects $100 from her insurance company and then buys a new bike. Therefore, Alice will leave her bike unprotected.

This is the **moral-hazard problem**. If Alice buys insurance, she reduces her own protective measures and is more likely to be victimized. The moral-hazard problem explains why many people do not lock their cars: according to the FBI, 80 percent of stolen cars are left unlocked and 40 percent have the keys in the ignition. The moral-hazard problem also explains why most insurance policies have deductibles: the deductible increases the property owner's expected loss from theft, encouraging the owner to invest in protection measures. Recently, some insurance companies have tried to control the moral-hazard problem by providing free home-security systems to their policyholders.

Market Value of Loot.   Potential victims can also decrease the resale value of stolen property. As the resale value of the stolen property decreases, the net return from theft decreases, discouraging crime. A potential victim can decrease the likelihood of being victimized by making his property less valuable to criminals.

The resale value depends on how easily the loot can be identified as stolen property. A person who purchases stolen property is subject to prosecution for receiving stolen goods. Given the risks associated with buying stolen goods, a consumer is willing to pay less for a good that is easily identified as "hot." The more readily the stolen goods can be identified, the lower the resale value. The typical criminal sells his loot to a fencing operation and is paid between 20 percent and 50 percent of the legal market value of the goods.

Suppose that Natasha can steal either a hundred-dollar bill or an original painting with a legal market value of $100. Which will she steal? The resale value of the painting will be less than $100 because the purchaser of the painting could be arrested for the possession of stolen property. In contrast, the "resale" value of the cash is equal to its face value: given the number of hundred-dollar bills in circulation, it would be impossible to find and punish the person who "buys" the stolen hundred-dollar bill. Natasha will steal the cash, not the painting.

How do potential victims facilitate the identification of stolen goods? In the wild West, ranchers branded their cattle to discourage cattle rustling. More recently, ranchers have experimented with implanting microchips into cow hides to locate and identify stolen cattle. Many communities have developed programs under which residents mark their possessions with identification numbers (social security numbers, driver license numbers) to discourage burglary. Participants in "Operation Identification" place warning labels in conspicuous places to inform potential burglars that "all items of value have been marked for ready identification."

The Police

The primary responsibility of the police is to arrest criminals. In the 1970s, the **arrest ratio**, defined as the number of arrests divided by the number of index crimes, was about 0.16 (Wilson 1985). In other words, only about 16 percent of index crimes led to an arrest, so criminals faced a one-in-six chance of being arrested for a crime. Changes in the arrest ratio affect crime rates. One rule of thumb is that the elasticity of property crime with respect to the probability of arrest is about -0.50: a 10 percent increase in the arrest ratio decreases the number of crimes by about 5 percent (see Ehrlich 1973; Wilson and Boland 1976; Bartel 1979; Witte 1980).

Police Patrol.   The police spend a lot of time patrolling streets and sidewalks. The idea behind patrol is that the police should be in a position to respond quickly when crime occurs. Does patrol deter crime? A number of studies have shown that car patrol does not have a significant effect on crime rates. In a famous experiment in Kansas City, the city increased patrolling activity in some neighborhoods and decreased patrolling in others. There were no significant changes in either arrest ratios or crime rates in any of the neighborhoods, which suggests that patrolling does not decrease crime. Other experiments have come to the same conclusion (Sherman 1983).

Why doesn't car patrol work? One reason is that crime victims are slow to report crimes to the police. According to Sherman, the typical victim takes about 50 minutes to report the crime to police. Suppose that an increase in patrolling could decrease the response time of police (defined as the period of time between receiving a report of the crime and arriving on the scene) from 10 minutes to 2 minutes. If the typical victim takes 50 minutes to report the crime, the police could arrive on the crime scene 52 minutes after the crime is committed instead of 60 minutes. In either case, the criminal's trail is already cold, so the increase in response time is unlikely to increase the arrest ratio. On the other hand, if the victim took only 1 minute to report the crime, an increase in patrolling could make a difference: the police would arrive 3 minutes after the crime instead of 11 minutes, so they would have a better chance of capturing the criminal.

What about foot patrol? A number of studies have shown that foot patrol can increase arrest ratios and deter crime. Police on foot patrol are constantly gathering information about the people and businesses in their territories. The foot-patrol officer knows who is arguing with whom, who is suddenly living beyond his means, and whose children are running amok. As a result, the foot-patrol officer is better equipped to prevent crimes and to solve crimes once they occur.

Police Investigation. In addition to arresting criminals, police gather information for public prosecutors and the courts. The success of investigations is measured by the **clearance rate**, defined as the fraction of arrests that result in convictions. According to Forst (1983), about 32 percent of felony arrests result in conviction. The most important investigative task is to find eyewitnesses to the crime. One rule of thumb is that if the police provide two eyewitnesses to a crime, a conviction is virtually guaranteed.

Under the traditional investigative system, crimes are investigated by police detectives rather than patrol officers. The patrol officer usually makes the arrest, prepares a report on the crime, and then hands over the investigation to a detective.

Some police forces have experimented with alternative investigative systems. Under a **community-service system**, each police officer is assigned a small territory and is responsible for both making arrests and investigating crimes. Instead of simply filing a report about the crime, the arresting officer finds eyewitnesses and gathers other evidence for prosecutors. The idea behind this system is that the local patrol officer has a great deal of information about his territory that would be useful in the investigation. There is some evidence that the community-service approach increases clearance rates.

Other cities have experimented with different incentive systems. Under the traditional system, police rewards are based on the number of arrests, not on clearance rates or local crime rates. If police were rewarded for increasing clearance rates and decreasing crime rates, they might have a greater incentive to follow up arrests by gathering information and finding eyewitnesses. The city of Orange, California, has experimented with a system under which police salaries depend on crime rates (see Reynolds 1986).

The Court System. Forst (1983) shows how the court system handles a typical set of 100 felony arrests. His results are summarized in Figure 20–8. Only 9 of 100 felony arrests result in a prison sentence. The process by which the 100 arrests are whittled down to 9 imprisonments is as follows:

FIGURE 20–8 Typical Disposition of 100 Felony Arrests, 1974–1980

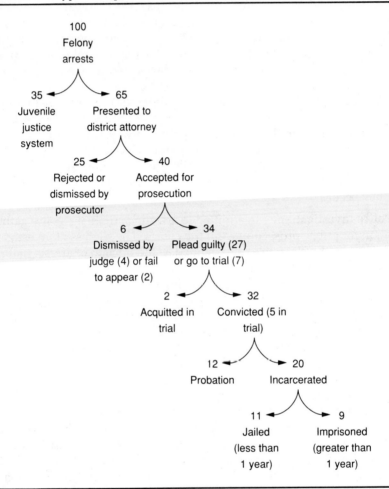

SOURCE: Brian Forst, "Prosecution and Sentencing," Chapter 10 in *Crime and Public Policy*, ed. James Q. Wilson, San Francisco: Institute for Contemporary Studies, 1983, pp. 165–182.

1. **Juvenile cases.** About one third of the offenses are committed by juveniles and are handled by the juvenile justice system. Little is known about the disposition of these cases.

2. **Dismissed by prosecutor.** Of the 65 cases presented to the district attorney, 25 are dropped: most cases are dropped because of weak evidence; a small number of cases are dropped because the offense is trivial. Only about 1 percent of cases are dropped because of violations of rules concerning arrest procedures and evidence.

3. **Dismissed by judge.** Of the 40 cases accepted by the district attorney, 4 are dismissed by the judge, usually because the evidence is insufficient or the offense is trivial.

4. **Disappearing defendant.** Two cases are eventually dropped because the defendant disappears after being released on bond, personal recognizance, or third-party custody.

5. **Plea bargaining.** Of the 34 remaining cases, 27 of the defendants plead guilty, usually to lesser charges.

6. **Trial acquittal.** Of the seven cases that go to trial, two result in acquittal and five result in a guilty verdict.

7. **Probation.** Of the 32 defendants found guilty (27 from plea bargains and 5 in trials), 12 receive probation (supervised release).

8. **Jail versus prison.** Twenty convicts are incarcerated. Eleven serve time in jails (receiving sentences of less than one year), and 9 are imprisoned (receiving sentences of more than one year).

Plea Bargaining.   As shown in Figure 20–8, of the 32 cases that result in conviction, only 5 cases are actually decided by a trial. The other 27 cases are resolved through the **plea-bargaining process**.

The district attorney has broad powers to negotiate with the accused over the criminal charge and the resulting punishment. Under the plea-bargaining process, the district attorney reduces the criminal charge and the accused pleads guilty to the lesser charge. The plea bargain generates benefits for both sides: the district attorney gets a certain conviction, and the defendant receives a relatively light sentence. In addition, both parties avoid the costs of a criminal trial.

Table 20–6 provides a simple example of the plea-bargaining process. Suppose that Bonnie is accused of armed robbery, a crime that carries a three-year prison sentence. Given the evidence in the case, both Bonnie and the district attorney (D.A.) agree that there is a 50 percent chance that a criminal trial will produce a guilty verdict. Therefore, the expected penalty from the armed robbery charge is 1.5 years (3 years times 0.50). The alternative to a trial on the robbery charge is a plea of guilty to petit larceny, a crime that carries a one-year prison sentence.

Should Bonnie accept the plea bargain? Suppose that a criminal trial would cost Bonnie $1,000 in legal fees, but the plea bargain would cost only $200. She would be better off with a guilty plea for two reasons. First, she saves $800 in legal costs ($1,000 − $200). Second, the expected prison sentence is shorter (1 year versus 1.5 years). If the D.A. offers this plea bargain, Bonnie will accept it.

Should the D.A. offer the plea bargain or pursue a trial on the robbery charge? Suppose that a criminal trial would cost taxpayers $2,000, but the plea bargain would cost only $300. From the perspective of law-abiding citizens

TABLE 20–6   Plea Bargaining

	Armed Robbery	*Petit Larceny*
Penalty	3 years	1 year
Probability of conviction	0.50	1.0
Expected penalty	1.5 years	1.0 years
Court costs	$2,000	$300
Defense costs	$1,000	$200

who wish to see Bonnie punished for her crime, the plea bargain produces good news and bad news. The good news is that the plea bargain saves taxpayers $1,700. The bad news is that the plea bargain decreases Bonnie's expected prison time by half a year. If society is willing to give up half a year of punishment to save $1,700, the D.A. will offer the plea bargain.

Under what circumstances will Bonnie and the D.A. not agree to a plea bargain, but instead bring the case to trial? Suppose that both sides are optimistic about their chances of winning the court battle. Bonnie assumes that the probability of a guilty verdict is very low (10 percent), so the expected penalty from a robbery trial is 0.30 years, compared to a certain penalty of one year under the proposed plea bargain. She will demand a trial if she is willing to pay at least $800 (the increase in legal costs if the case goes to trial) to decrease her expected prison term by 0.70 years. If the D.A. assumes that the probability of a guilty verdict is very high (90 percent), the expected penalty from a trial is 2.7 years, compared to a certain penalty of one year under the proposed plea bargain. The D.A. will seek a trial if the extra 1.7 years in expected punishment is worth at least $1,700. In this example, Bonnie's case will go to trial because the two parties disagree about the likely outcome of the trial.

Proof of Guilt.   In any justice system, two types of errors are inevitable. First, some innocent people will be found guilty and will be punished for crimes they did not commit (a **false positive result**). Second, some guilty people will be found innocent and will escape punishment (a **false negative result**).

The U.S. courts have developed a set of rules that place the burden of proof on the shoulders of the prosecutors. To convict a person of a crime, the state must prove the person's guilt "beyond a reasonable doubt." Under the reasonable-doubt rule, the accused is presumed innocent until proven guilty and close cases are decided in favor of defendants. The rule decreases the frequency of false positives (fewer innocents are convicted), but increases the frequency of false negatives (more guilty people are acquitted). In other words, the courts err on the side of innocence rather than guilt.

Court systems in other countries err on the side of guilt rather than innocence. If the accused is presumed guilty until proven innocent, the burden of proof is on the shoulders of the accused. Under this type of rule, close cases are decided in favor of the state. The adoption of this rule would increase the number of false positives (more innocents would be convicted) and decrease the number of false negatives (fewer guilty would be acquitted).

The Principle of Marginal Deterrence

The penalties for various crimes are determined by legislators, prosecutors, and judges. Legislatures pass laws that establish minimum and maximum penalties, providing guidelines for prosecutors and judges. In the plea-bargaining process, the prosecutors negotiate with suspects over criminal charges and penalties, and then pass on their recommendations to judges, who usually accept the plea bargains. If a case goes to trial and the defendant is found guilty, the presiding judge sets the penalty.

In determining the penalties for different crimes, legislators and judges are guided by the **principle of marginal deterrence**. According to this principle, the penalty for a particular crime should depend on the seriousness of the crime, with greater penalties for more serious crimes.

A Numerical Example.   The principle of marginal deterrence can be explained with a simple example. Suppose that a state initially has a one-year penalty for burglary and a two-year penalty for armed robbery. Robbery carries a greater penalty because robbery has higher social costs: the victims of robbery are often injured or killed, while the victims of burglary simply lose their property.

Emil is a career criminal who must decide whether to commit a robbery or a burglary. He will commit the crime that provides the larger net benefit. His options are shown in Table 20–7. Robbery generates a greater expected loot ($2,000 versus $1,700), but also carries a higher expected prison cost ($1,600 versus $800). The expected net benefit of burglary ($900) exceeds the net benefit for armed robbery ($400), so Emil will commit burglary rather than robbery.

The state's penalties for robbery and burglary provide a marginal deterrent for robbery, the more serious crime. In deciding on the level of crime, Emil weighs the marginal benefits and marginal costs associated with upgrading from burglary to robbery. The marginal benefit of upgrading is the increase in the expected loot ($300). The marginal cost is the increase in the expected prison cost ($800). Since the marginal benefit is less than the marginal cost, Emil sticks with burglary. Society deters Emil from the more serious crime by imposing a larger penalty on robbery.

Suppose that the state passes a law that equalizes the penalties for burglary and robbery at two years. The increase in the burglary penalty decreases the expected net benefit from burglary to $100 ($1,700 − $1,600), but does not affect the net benefit from robbery. Since the net benefit of robbery now ex-

TABLE 20–7   Marginal Deterrence

	Armed Robbery	Burglary (1 year Penalty)	Burglary (2 years Penalty)
Expected loot	$2,000	$1,700	$1,700
Probability of punishment	0.10	0.10	0.10
Prison sentence	2 years	1 year	2 years
Annual opportunity cost of prison	$8,000	$8,000	$8,000
Expected prison cost	$1,600	$ 800	$1,600
Net benefit	$ 400	$ 900	$ 100

ceeds the net benefit of burglary, Emil will switch to robbery. The equalization of penalties eliminates the marginal deterrent: the marginal benefit of moving from burglary to robbery is still $300, but the marginal cost of upgrading (the increase in the expected prison cost) is zero. If Emil receives the same penalties for the two crimes, he will commit the more lucrative crime. The equalization of penalties eliminates the marginal deterrent, so Emil switches to the crime with higher social cost.

The General Effects of Equalizing Penalties.   Figure 20–9 shows the effects of increasing the burglary penalty on the number of burglaries and robberies. Suppose that initially the two crimes have the same net return (R'). Given the two supply curves, there will be B' burglaries and A' armed robberies. If the state increases the penalty for burglary, the net return will drop to R'', decreasing the number of burglaries to B''. The decrease in the net return of burglary will cause some criminals to upgrade to robbery, so the robbery supply curve will shift to the right. The net return to robbery is still R', so the number of robberies will increase to A''. Because the increase in the burglary penalty weakens the marginal deterrent, some criminals upgrade to the more serious crime.

The increase in the burglary penalty decreases the total number of crimes: the decrease in the number of burglaries (from B' to B'') exceeds the increase in the number of robberies (from A' to A''). This occurs because the increased penalty causes some burglars to stop committing crimes. In other words, only some of the burglars who change their behavior shift to robbery.

Is society better or worse off under the higher burglary penalty? It depends on the social costs of the two crimes. Because victims are often injured or killed in robberies, the social cost of robbery exceeds the social cost of burglary. According to Phillips and Votey (1979), the social cost of the typical armed robbery is about $5,400 and the social cost of the typical burglary is only about $900. In Figure 20–9, the increase in the number of robberies is about one fourth the decrease in burglaries. If the social cost of robbery is six

FIGURE 20–9   Responses to an Increase in the Burglary Penalty

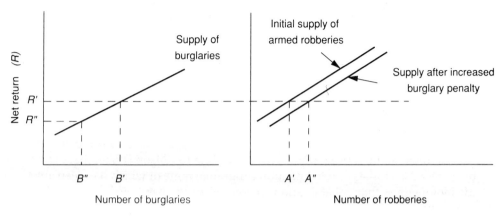

In the initial equilibrium, both burglary and robbery have a net return of R', so there are B' burglaries and A' robberies. A decrease in the net return of burglaries to R'' decreases the number of burglaries to B'' (movement down the supply curve) and increases the number of robberies to A'' (shift of the supply curve and unchanged net return to robbery). The increase in robberies is less than the decrease in burglaries because some burglars "go straight."

times the social cost of burglary, the total social cost of crime will increase. In this case, the increase in the burglary penalty increases the social costs of crime.

There are two lessons from the discussion of marginal deterrence. First, because stiffer penalties provide a marginal deterrent, an increase in the penalty for one crime will cause some criminals to upgrade to a higher level crime. Second, policy makers could use this approach to estimate 'the effects of changes in penalties on the social cost of crime. To do so, they would need information on the social costs of different crimes and the criminals' responses to the change in penalties. The principal questions are: how many criminals would be deterred; how many would upgrade to higher level crime; how many would downgrade to lower level crime?

The Prison System

The prison system has four functions. The first is the **rehabilitation** function, which is based on the idea that society can use education and counselling to persuade convicts to "go straight." The second function is **deterrence**: by punishing convicts, society makes the threat of punishment credible, discouraging other people from committing crime. The third function is **incapacitation**: prisons isolate criminals from their potential victims, decreasing crime by taking criminals out of circulation. A final function is **retribution** or revenge: law-abiding citizens like to see criminals punished for their actions. This section discusses the first three prison functions.

The Rehabilitation Function. According to the popular view, it is possible to rehabilitate convicts. Education and counselling programs are designed to provide convicts with the skills and the desires to become lawful citizens. The success of a particular rehabilitation program is measured by its effect on the **recidivism rate**, defined as the percentage of convicts that are arrested for another crime after they leave prison. The overall recidivism rate is about 80 percent: four fifths of convicts are arrested after they leave prison.

Do rehabilitation programs work? According to Wilson (1975), there have been over 200 studies of rehabilitation programs, none of which has been able to demonstrate that rehabilitation decreases recidivism rates. The studies evaluated the effects of several types of rehabilitation schemes, including education and job-training programs, work-release programs, and counselling programs. The rehabilitation programs did not affect the recidivism rates of either juveniles or adults. Given the results of these studies, there is good reason to be pessimistic about the prospects for using rehabilitation to reduce crime.

Why doesn't rehabilitation work? First, it is difficult to change the antisocial attitudes that make criminals relatively receptive to crime. Second, by the time a criminal reaches the rehabilitation stage (i.e., by the time the criminal is imprisoned), he is firmly committed to crime. If the probability of being imprisoned for a particular crime is 2 percent, the typical criminal has committed 50 crimes by the time he is imprisoned. Third, it is difficult to make legal opportunities more profitable than crime: crime pays, and it is difficult to increase the job skills of an adult criminal.

The **parole system** is based on the principle of rehabilitation. Under the parole system, a convict stays in prison until the parole board declares that he is "rehabilitated." The rehabilitated convict is released and serves the remainder of his prison term under the supervision of a parole officer. A parolee cannot get married or own a car and must receive the approval of his parole officer before borrowing money or changing residence.

Most parole boards have large caseloads and base most parole decisions on simple rules of thumb. One popular rule is that a convict is released after serving either three years or one third of the prison sentence, whichever is shorter. Studies of the parole system have generated mixed results. In some states, parolees have lower rates of recidivism than convicts who serve out their entire sentence. In other states, there is no measurable difference between the recidivism rates of parolees and other convicts.

The Deterrence Function. A number of studies have shown that the threat of imprisonment decreases crime rates. An increase in either the probability of imprisonment or the length of the prison term increases the expected cost of crime, thus decreasing the number of crimes.

There is evidence that an increase in the *certainty* of punishment provides a greater deterrent than an increase in the *severity* of punishment. In other words, an increase in the probability of imprisonment deters more crime than an increase in the length of the prison term. For example, Bartel (1979) estimates that the elasticity of the supply of crime with respect to the probability of punishment is about -0.30: a 10 percent increase in the chance of imprisonment decreases the crime rate by 3 percent. On the other hand, the elasticity of supply with respect to the length of imprisonment is close to zero.

Why don't longer prison sentences deter crime? Although an increase in the penalty may discourage crime by increasing the expected cost of crime, it may simultaneously encourage crime for three reasons.

1. **Hardening the criminal.** Perhaps a long prison sentence hardens the convict, making antisocial behavior more likely. In Figure 20–10, a longer prison term decreases the net return to crime from R^* to R', causing movement down the initial supply curve (from point C to D) and decreasing the number of crimes from B^* to B'. If criminals are hardened by longer prison terms, their anguish costs will decrease, shifting the supply curve to the right and causing a move from point D to E. The net effect is a small decrease in the crime rate (from B^* to B'').

FIGURE 20–10 Effects of Increased Punishment on Crime

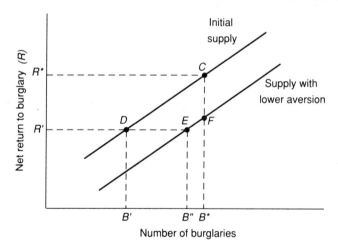

Number of burglaries

The increase in the severity of punishment decreases the net return from R^* to R', causing a move from point C to D. If a longer prison term hardens the criminal, his aversion to crime will decrease, shifting the supply curve to the right and causing a move from point D to E: crime rises close to its original level (B'' is close to B^*). If the criminal also learns more in prison, he will have a higher probability of success when he gets out, causing a move from E to F (increasing the crime rate to its original level).

2. **Prison schooling.** If prison allows a criminal to learn the tricks of the trade from other criminals, a longer prison term means more education and a more skillful criminal. The postprison probability of success will increase, increasing the net return from crime. In Figure 20–10, the prison-schooling effect causes a move from point E to F, restoring the original crime level (B^*).

3. **Discount rates.** If criminals are present-oriented, they are more concerned with instant gratification than the long-term consequences of crime (imprisonment). The perceived cost of an additional year in prison (e.g., four years instead of three) will be small relative to the benefits of today's crime. In formal terms, if criminals have large discount rates, the perceived cost of an additional year of imprisonment will be relatively small in present-value terms, so it will have a relatively small deterrent effect.

The Incapacitation Function.   The third function of the prison system is to take criminals out of circulation. An obvious way to reduce crime is to lock up potential criminals. The practical policy issue is whether the benefit of incapacitation (the decrease in crime) exceeds the cost (the cost of running the prison). If each prisoner costs the state about $18,000 per year, the question is whether a one-year prison term decreases the social costs of crime by at least $18,000. If the victim cost per burglary is $900, incapacitation will be worthwhile if the burglar would have committed at least 20 burglaries per year. If the victim cost per armed robbery is $5,400, incapacitation will be worthwhile if the robber would have committed four robberies per year.

Wilson and Boland (1976) estimated the effects of increased prison sentences on crime rates. They estimated the effects of a mandatory two-year prison sentence on felony crime rates. Underlying their computations (shown in Table 20–8) are the following assumptions:

1. **Probability of conviction.** The probability of being convicted for a felony crime is 10 percent.

2. **Base sentencing policy.** The basis for comparison is a situation in which no convicted felons spend time in prison.

3. **Mandatory sentence.** The new sentencing policy is that every person convicted of a felony will spend two years in prison.

4. **Incapacitation effect.** The rehabilitation and deterrence effects of prisons are ignored. The changes in crime rates are caused exclusively by the incapacitation effect.

As shown in Table 20–8, the switch to the mandatory two-year sentence decreases crime rates by different amounts, depending on the number of crimes the typical criminal commits. If the typical criminal commits five crimes per year, the change to two-year sentences will decrease the crime rate

TABLE 20–8 Incarceration and Crime Rates

Crimes per Offender	Percent Reduction from Two-Year Sentence
5	50.0%
10	66.7
20	80.0
50	90.9

SOURCE: James Q. Wilson and Barbara Boland, "Crime," in *The Urban Predicament*, ed. William Gorham and Nathan Glazer (Washington, D.C.: The Urban Institute, 1975) p. 207.

by 50 percent. If the typical convict commits 20 crimes per year, the decrease in crime is 80 percent. The table shows that the more prolific the criminal, the stronger the incapacitation effect.

To achieve the crime reductions listed in Table 20–8, society would have to spend more on police, courts, and prisons. To increase the probability of conviction to 10 percent, more would have to be spent catching and prosecuting criminals. If all convicts are sent to prison for two years, prison expenditures must increase. Would the additional spending be worthwhile? If the typical criminal commits a large number of offenses, the reduction in crime would be relatively large, so the benefits of the incapacitation program may exceed its cost.

ILLEGAL COMMODITIES

The fact that a product is illegal does not prevent people from consuming it. Simon and Witte (1977) estimated the sales volume of a number of illegal goods and services. Their upper-bound estimates for 1974 are as follows: $11.6 billion was spent on heroin, $9.1 billion on cocaine, $5.2 billion on marijuana, $2.2 billion on illegal gambling, $3.2 billion on loan-sharking, $14.8 billion on prostitution, and $16.7 billion on other illegal goods. These figures suggest that, on average, households spent about $785 per year on illegal goods and services.

Why are some goods outlawed? First, lawmakers assume that consumers are irrational about some products: a gambler is unable to make rational choices in the heat of a gambling frenzy, and a drug user is incapable of rational thought in the middle of a drug trip. Second, the consumption of certain goods is assumed to be contagious. Society protects itself from a drug "epidemic" for the same reasons that it protects itself from a polio epidemic. Third, drug addiction is often passed from parent to child, through either physiological or psychological means. By outlawing certain drugs, the government protects children from drug dependence. Fourth, lawmakers assume that drug use leads to unemployment, poverty, and welfare dependence.

644 Chapter 20 Crime and Punishment

Product Illegality and Production Costs

A firm selling an illegal product differs from a lawful firm in two ways. First, there are large penalties if the illegal activity is discovered by the police. The participants may be fined or imprisoned, and the assets of the firm may be seized. Second, contracts with illegal enterprises are not legally enforceable, so creditors cannot be certain that they will be paid for services rendered. These two characteristics make the production costs of the illegal firm relatively high.

To compensate for the risk of engaging in illegal activity, the illegal firm must pay its workers a wage premium. Just as a coal miner is paid more than a person in a safe and clean job, a worker in an illegal enterprise is paid more than a person in a legal job. In addition, the firm pays a relatively high wage to prevent "squealing." If workers earn relatively high wages, they have more to lose if the firm's illegal activity is discovered, so they have a greater incentive to conceal the firm's activities.

The threat of punishment also affects the way that a firm organizes its production process. To maintain secrecy, the firm controls the flow of information about its activities. One way to control information is to segment the work force into small work groups and limit the information that passes from one group to another. For example, heroin passes through many groups on the way from the poppy field to the consumer (importer, processor, wholesaler, distributor), and each group has little knowledge of the activities of the other groups in the chain. These evasion techniques add to production costs.

The illegal activity also has relatively high capital costs. A loan to an illegal enterprise is relatively risky for three reasons. First, contracts are not legally enforceable, so lenders can never be certain that they will be repaid. Second, given its desire for secrecy, the illegal firm cannot provide the lender with financial information. Since the lender cannot assess the profitability of the illegal enterprise, the loan is relatively risky. Finally, given the risk of confiscation, the illegal firm does not have any real collateral, so the lender may be unable to collect if the borrower defaults on the loan. Because a loan to an illegal enterprise is relatively risky, the lender will charge a relatively high interest rate, so production costs will be relatively high.

Product Illegality and Price

Figure 20–11 shows the effect of product illegality on the market for drugs. Suppose that a particular drug is suddenly declared illegal. The costs of producing and distributing the drug will increase, shifting the supply curve to the left: at every price, less will be supplied. The illegal status of the drug also affects the demand curve. The total cost of consuming the illegal drug equals the sum of the market price and the expected penalty for consuming the drug. For example, if there is a 2 percent chance of a $1,000 penalty for drug consumption, the expected penalty will be $20 per dose (0.02 times

FIGURE 20–11   Effects of Product Illegality on Price and Quantity

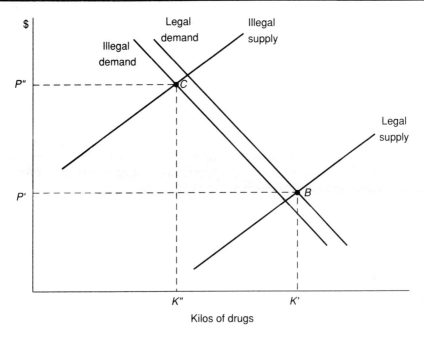

If a commodity is declared illegal, the costs of producing and selling the good increase, shifting the supply curve upward. Consumer penalties increase the net cost of consuming the good, shifting the demand curve downward. The equilibrium moves from point B to C. The supplier penalty is large relative to the consumer penalty, so the supply shift is larger than the demand shift, and the price of the good increases from P' to P''. The equilibrium quantity decreases from K' to K''.

$1,000). When the product is declared illegal, the demand curve shifts downward by the expected penalty. The penalty for drug consumption is like a tax: it shifts the demand curve by the amount of the implicit tax.

If enforcement efforts are concentrated on the supply side of the drug market, the prohibition of drugs will increase the market price. In Figure 20–11, the shift of the supply curve is larger than the shift of the demand curve, reflecting the assumption that the expected penalty for the production and sale of drugs is large relative to the expected penalty for consumption. The price rises from P' to P'', and the equilibrium quantity decreases from K' to K''. By declaring the drug illegal, the government increases the price and decreases the quantity consumed.

What are the implications for the consumers of illegal goods? Consumers pay higher prices for the illegal goods and services. The typical heroin addict, for example, pays about $60 per day for his habit, about 30 times the amount he would pay if heroin were legal. The same analysis applies to other types of illegal goods. The patrons of loan sharks pay higher interest rates because the loan shark must be compensated for the risk of imprisonment and the costs of concealing his activities. Similarly, gamblers face lower odds (lower expected returns) because bookies face higher risks and incur large concealment costs.

Drugs and Property Crime

There is a positive correlation between drug use and criminal activity. According to Wilson (1975), between 25 percent and 67 percent of property crime is committed by drug addicts. Despite this high correlation, the causal link between drug consumption and crime is not fully understood. Although there is evidence that some addicts support their drug habits with property crime, it is unclear just how much addict crime is committed solely to support drug habits.

Will the enforcement of drug laws increase total property crime? In Figure 20–11, the illegality of drugs increases price and decreases the quantity consumed. The increase in price is relatively large because (a) the leftward shift of the demand curve is relatively small and (b) the demand curve is relatively steep (the price elasticity of demand for drugs is relatively low). Because the price rises by a relatively large amount, total expenditures on drugs (price times quantity) will increase. If drug addicts support their habits with property crime, the increase in total expenditures will increase property crime.

Silverman and Sprull (1977) have estimated the effects of changes in drug prices on property crime. They estimate that the price elasticity of demand for heroin is about -0.27, meaning that a 50 percent increase in the price of heroin would decrease the quantity of heroin demanded by about 13 percent and increase total drug expenditures by about 30 percent. Because only part of property crime is drug-related, the resulting increase in property crime (14 percent) is less than the increase in drug expenditures.

There are two implications from this analysis. First, there is often a trade-off between drug control and property crime. Because a supply-side policy increases total expenditures on drugs, property crime is likely to increase. Although drug-enforcement policies decrease drug consumption and thus decrease the social costs associated with drug abuse, they also increase property crime. The difficult policy question is whether the benefits (the decrease in the social costs of drug abuse) exceed the costs (increased property crime). The second implication is that demand-side policies do not have the same trade-offs. Because a demand-side policy simply shifts the demand curve downward, decreasing both the price and quantity of drugs, it decreases total expenditure on drugs and thus decreases drug-related property crime.

SUMMARY

1. The facts on crime are collected by the FBI (from local police departments) and the Justice Department (from victimization surveys).

2. Victimization rates vary with income, place of residence, and race. Victimization rates are generally higher for the poor, racial minorities, and the residents of central cities.

3. The direct costs of crime include injury costs and property losses. The indirect costs include protection costs and the costs of running the criminal justice system. According to one study, the total cost of crime in 1983 was $2,323 per household.

4. The optimum amount of crime is the amount such that the marginal victim cost equals the marginal protection cost. Crimes differ in victim costs and prevention costs, so optimum crime rates vary.

5. A rational person will commit a property crime if the net return to crime is large enough to offset his underlying aversion to crime.
   a. The expected benefit depends on the monetary value of the loot and the probability of success.
   b. The expected cost depends on the probability of imprisonment, the opportunity cost of prison time, and the length of the prison sentence.
   c. The opportunity cost of crime is the income forgone in a legal job.
   d. The net return is the expected benefit less the expected cost and the opportunity cost.
   e. Crime is rational if the net return exceeds the anguish cost.

6. The supply curve for crime shows the relationship between the net return and number of crimes. Society determines the net return of crime and picks a point on the supply curve.
   a. Investments in education and job training increase the value of legal opportunities.
   b. Potential victims can decrease the expected benefit of crime by hardening the target and decreasing the resale value of the loot.
   c. The police can increase the expected cost of crime by arresting more criminals.
   d. The courts can increase the expected cost of crime by increasing the likelihood and severity of punishment.

7. The supply curve of crime shifts as a result of demographic and social changes.
   a. As the share of the population in the crime-prone years increases, the supply curve shifts to the right.
   b. Social changes that increase the underlying aversion to crime shift the supply curve upward.

8. Police are responsible for arresting criminals and investigating crimes.
   a. The arrest ratio is the fraction of crimes that lead to an arrest, currently about 0.16. The elasticity of crime with respect to the probability of arrest is about −0.50.
   b. The success of police investigation is measured by the clearance ratio, the fraction of arrests that lead to conviction. The most important investigative task is to find eyewitnesses to the crime.

    c. Although an increase in car patrol decreases the police response time, it does not affect arrest rates and crime rates because victims are slow to report crimes. Foot patrol is more effective because the police gather information about people and potential criminals on their beats.

9. The courts are responsible for determining guilt and setting penalties.
    a. Only about 9 in 100 felony arrests result in prison sentences. Many cases are dropped because the offenses are trivial or the evidence is insufficient. About one third of arrests lead to convictions, but most convicts receive probation or short jail terms.
    b. Most criminal cases are resolved through plea bargaining: the district attorney reduces the criminal charge, and the accused pleads guilty to the lesser charge. From the perspective of society, plea bargaining is efficient if the benefits (the savings in court costs) exceed the cost (the decrease in the punishment of convicts).
    c. Two types of errors are inevitable in the criminal justice system: a false positive occurs when an innocent person is found guilty, and a false negative occurs when a guilty person is found innocent. In the United States, the state must prove the case beyond a reasonable doubt, a rule that decreases the number of false positives and increases the number of false negatives.

10. According to the principle of marginal deterrence, penalties should be scaled to the severity of the crime, thus providing a marginal deterrent for more serious crimes. An increase in the penalty for a particular crime causes some criminals to switch to other crimes. An increase in the penalty for burglary causes criminals to upgrade to robbery, downgrade to larceny, or abandon crime.

11. The prison system has four purposes: rehabilitation, deterrence, incapacitation, and retribution.
    a. Contrary to popular opinion, rehabilitation does not seem to work.
    b. Deterrence works. An increase in the certainty of punishment is a greater deterrent than an increase in the severity of punishment.
    c. Incapacitation is an efficient policy if the prisoner would commit a large number of crimes if he were free.
    d. Retribution (revenge) is not amenable to economic analysis.

12. Illegal goods are relatively expensive because firms must compensate their workers and lenders for extra risks and must spend money on concealment.

13. Policies that decrease the supply of illegal drugs increase their prices. If drug addicts support their habits with property crime, an increase in total expenditures will increase total property crime, partly offsetting the benefits associated with decreased drug abuse.

EXERCISES AND DISCUSSION QUESTIONS

1. Consider Boris, a potential burglar who weighs the benefits and costs of burglary. Fill in the blanks in the following table:

Loot	$1,000
Probability of success	0.70
Expected loot	_____
Probability of being imprisoned	0.03
Wage per day	$ 20
Workdays per year	100
Forgone income per year	_____
Loss of freedom per year	$3,000
Opportunity cost per year	_____
Length of prison term	2 years
Expected penalty cost	_____
Expected benefit from burglary	_____
Daily income if employed	_____
Net return from burglary	_____

2. Consider Boris, whose benefit-cost analysis of burglary is shown in Table 20–5. The net return of burglary depends on the probability of success (P_s), the value of the loot, and the probability of imprisonment (P_i). Compute the values of these variables such that Boris is indifferent between burglary and a legal job. In computing the threshold values for each variable, assume that the values of other variables are the same as in Table 20–5.
   a. What is the threshold value of P_s?
   b. What is the threshold value of *Loot*?
   c. What is the threshold value of P_i?

3. Choose the word in parentheses that makes the following statement correct and explain your choice. "As the net return to burglary increases, the elasticity of supply of crime (*increases, decreases*)."

4. Consider a city where several industries generate toxic wastes. Waste generators either discard their wastes at a legal disposal site or dump their wastes illegally. To combat illegal disposal, the city adopts the following policy: The city will spend $Z on a program that will increase the probability of convicting illegal dumpers. The program will be financed with a unit tax on legal disposal.
   a. Under what conditions will the volume of illegal disposal decrease?
   b. How would your answer to (a) differ if the policy were to be financed with a residential property tax?

5. Suppose that Alice purchases an insurance policy for her bike. Complete the following table, assuming that her policy has a $20 deductible.

Protective Action	Protection Cost	Probability of Theft	Expected Theft Cost	Total Cost
No protection	$ 0	0.30		
Flimsy lock	11	0.10		
Sturdy lock	24	0.02		
Armed guard	80	0.00		

6. A number of insurance companies have started offering free burglar alarms with their home owner insurance policies. Evaluate the merits of such a policy. Would you expect such firms to make more or less profit than firms that do not provide alarms?

7. Sympacity is considering a policy under which every victim of crime would be compensated for victim costs. The city would cover the property losses from crime and would also compensate victims for injuries suffered as a result of crime.
Evaluate the efficiency and equity effects of the city's policy.

8. Recall the Bonnie example, shown in Table 20–6. You are negotiating with the D.A. over the length of the prison term for petit larceny. Suppose that Bonnie's opportunity cost of prison time is $8,000 per year. What is the maximum larceny term she will accept? In other words, what larceny term will make her indifferent between facing a criminal trial on armed robbery and a plea bargain for larceny?

9. Monty, a former district attorney, was recently elected the governor of a state in which the only crimes are burglary and robbery. In the election campaign, he said: "I have been making deals with criminals all my professional life, and I'm sick of it. If I'm elected governor, I will stop the let's-make-a-deal approach to the criminal justice system. I will replace the plea-bargaining process with a set of required penalties, one for burglary and one for robbery."
   a. Suppose that you are Monty's crime advisor and must develop the penalties. How would you do it? What information would you collect, and how would you use it?
   b. Is this a wise policy? Is it efficient?

10. Consider a state where an increase in the severity of punishment has a smaller deterrent effect than an increase in the likelihood of punishment. Specifically, the elasticity of supply of crime with respect to the length of imprisonment (e_s) is -0.10, and the elasticity of supply with respect to the probability of imprisonment (e_c) is -0.50. Critically appraise the fol-

lowing statement: "Since e_c exceeds e_s, we should shorten prison terms and increase the number of convicts who spend time in prison. This change in policy will not affect the total cost of the criminal justice system because the total demand for prison cells will not change. Because the new policy will decrease crime rates at no cost, it will be worthwhile."

11. Critically appraise: "The social cost of robbery is about nine times the social cost of burglary. Given the principle of marginal deterrence, the length of the prison term for robbery should be nine times the length of the prison term for burglary."

12. Consider the analysis of marginal deterrence shown in Figure 20–9. Under what circumstances (what values for the social costs of burglary and robbery) would the increased penalty for burglary decrease the total social costs of crime?

13. The property losses from business fraud (white-collar crime) totaled $600 per household in 1983, compared to losses of $90 for robbery, $93 for burglary, and $56 for auto theft. Yet white-collar crime receives less attention than other types of property crime.
Why do you suppose white-collar crime receives such little attention?

14. Suppose that your city has a fixed budget to allocate among 10 police precincts. You are responsible for allocating the budget.
    a. Your allocation decisions should be guided by some crime-fighting objective. What is your objective?
    b. What information would you collect, and how would you use it?

15. Consider a city with an active heroin market. The city is described by the following assumptions:
    i. The supply curve of heroin is vertical (perfectly inelastic) at 200 kilos.
    ii. The initial equilibrium price is $40. The price elasticity of demand is -0.25.
    iii. The city will spend $500 on a drug policy that will shift the supply curve to the left by 5 percent (from 200 to 190). The drug policy will not affect the demand curve.
    iv. There are two types of social costs from heroin. First, the consumption of heroin generates a social cost of $150 per kilo: the citizens of the city are willing to pay $150 for every one-kilo reduction of heroin. Second, heroin consumers support their habits with property crime.
    a. Is the drug program efficient?
    b. Choose the word in parentheses that makes the statement correct and explain your choice. "As the price elasticity of demand for heroin increases in absolute value, the efficiency of the drug policy (*increases, decreases*).

16. Comment on the following statement: "Our drug policy is inefficient. We should legalize drugs and tax drug producers. We can set the tax at a level

such that we have the same equilibrium drug consumption. By doing so, we will save all the money we currently spend on the enforcement of drug laws and the prosecution and punishment of drug dealers." What are the advantages and disadvantages of this policy?

REFERENCES AND ADDITIONAL READINGS

Crime Facts

Chaiken, Jan M., and Marcia Chaiken. "Crime Rates and the Active Criminal." In *Crime and Public Policy*, ed. James Q. Wilson. San Francisco, CA: Institute for Contemporary Studies, 1983.   Discusses recent trends in crime rates.

U.S. Bureau of Justice. *Criminal Victimization in the United States, 1985.* Washington, D.C.: U.S. Department of Justice, 1987.

_____. *Sourcebook of Criminal Justice Statistics, 1986.* Washington, D.C.: U.S. Government Printing Office, 1987.

U.S. Federal Bureau of Investigation. *Uniform Crime Reports for the United States 1986.* Washington, D.C.: U.S. Government Printing Office, 1987.

The Costs of Crime

Gray, Charles M., and Mitchell Joelson. "Neighborhood Crime and the Demand for Central City Housing." Chapter 3. In *The Costs of Crime*, ed. Charles M. Gray. Beverly Hills: Sage, 1979.   Explores the effects of crime on property values.

Reynolds, Morgan. *Crime by Choice: An Economic Analysis.* Dallas: Fisher Institute, 1986.   Estimates the costs of personal and property crimes.

Thaler, Richard. "Note on the Value of Crime Control—Evidence from the Property Market." *Journal of Urban Economics* 5 (1978), pp. 137–45.   Examines the effects of crime rates on property values.

The Rational Criminal

Cobb, William. "Theft and the Two Hypotheses." In *The Economics of Crime and Punishment*, ed. Simon Rottenberg. Washington, D.C.: American Enterprise Institute, 1973.

Deutsch, Joseph; Simon Hakim; and J. Weinblatt. "A Micro Model of the Criminal's Location Choice." *Journal of Urban Economics* 22 (1987), pp. 198–208.

Gunning, J. Patrick, Jr. "How Profitable Is Burglary." In *The Economics of Crime and Punishment*, ed. Simon Rottenberg. Washington, D.C.: American Enterprise Institute, 1973.

Herrnstein, Richard J. "Some Criminogenic Traits of Offenders." In *Crime and Public Policy*, ed. James Q. Wilson. San Francisco: Institute for Contemporary Studies, 1983.   Discusses the personal traits that predispose some people to crime (the traits that cause some people to have relatively low aversion to crime).

Krohm, Gregory. "The Pecuniary Incentives of Property Crime." In *The Economics of Crime and Punishment*, ed. Simon Rottenberg. Washington, D.C.: American Enterprise Institute, 1973.

Sesnowitz, Michael. "Returns to Burglary." *Western Economic Journal* 10 no. 4 (1972), pp. 477–81.

Crime, Demographics, and Culture

Blumstein, Alfred; Jacqueline Cohen; and Harold Miller. "Demographically Disaggregated Projections of Prison Population." *Journal of Criminal Justice* 8 (1980), pp. 1–26.   Predicts that crime rates will decline as the relative number of teenagers decreases.

Fox, James A. *Forecasting Crime.* Lexington, Mass.: Lexington Books, 1978.   Predicts crime rates on the basis of the age distribution and racial composition of the population.

Schapiro, Morton Owen, and Dennis A. Ahlburg. "Why Crime Is Down." *American Demographics* 8 (1986).

Wilson, James Q. "Crime and American Culture." *The Public Interest* 70 (Winter 1983), pp. 22–48.

Unemployment and Crime

Cook, Philip J., and Gary A. Zarkin. "Crime and the Business Cycle." *Journal of Legal Studies* 14 (1985), pp. 115–28.   Found that robbery and burglary rates rise by a small amount during recessions.

Fleisher, Belton. *The Economics of Delinquency.* Chicago: Quadrangle Books, 1966. Suggests that an increase in the unemployment rate increases the juvenile crime rate.

Freeman, Richard B. "Crime and Unemployment." In *Crime and Public Policy*, ed. James Q. Wilson. San Francisco: Institute for Contemporary Studies, 1983.   Reviews dozens of studies of the relationship between crime and unemployment. Concludes that there is a negative but weak relationship between the crime rate and the unemployment rate and that the link between the crime rate and sanctions (expected punishment) is stronger. Speculates that an improvement in labor-market conditions may deter first-time offenders.

Phillips, Llad; Harold Votey; and Harold Maxwell. "Crime, Youth, and the Labor Market." *Journal of Political Economy* 80 (1972), pp. 491–504.   Suggests that the crime rates of 18- and 19-year-old males are sensitive to labor-market conditions: the lower the labor-force participation rate, the higher the crime rate.

Wilson, James Q. and Philip J. Cook, "Unemployment and Crime: What Is the Connection?" *Public Interest* 79 (Spring 1985), pp. 3–8.   Discusses the relationship between unemployment rates and crime rates.

Victim as Crime Fighter

Balkin, S., and J. F. McDonald. "The Market for Street Crime—An Economic Analysis of Victim-Offender Interactions." *Journal of Urban Economics* 10 (1981), pp. 390–405. A discussion of the subtle interactions between potential victims and criminals.

Clotfelter, Charles D. "Urban Crime and Household Protective Measures." *Review of Economics and Statistics* 59 (1977), pp. 499–503. Discusses the effects of increased crime rates on the protective measures of potential victims.

————. "Explaining Unselfish Behavior—Crime and the Helpful Bystander." *Journal of Urban Economics* 8 (1980), pp. 196–212. Discusses altruistic behavior of witnesses to crime.

Clotfelter, Charles, and Robert D. Seeley. "The Private Costs of Crime." In *The Costs of Crime*, ed. Charles M. Gray. Beverly Hills: Sage, 1979, pp. 213–32. Discusses the private and social costs of private protection measures.

Wilson, James Q., and Barbara Boland. "Crime." Chapter 4. In *The Urban Predicament*, ed. William Gorham and Nathan Glazer. Washington, D.C.: The Urban Institute, 1976, pp. 179–230. Discusses how potential victims protect themselves from crime.

Police Issues

Carr-Hill, R., and N. Stern. "Theory and Estimation in Models of Crime and Its Social Control and Their Relations to the Concepts of Social Outputs." In *The Economics of Public Services*, ed. Martin Feldstein and Robert Inman. London: Macmillan, 1977. Discusses the issue of how to measure the output of crime enforcement.

————. "An Econometric Model of the Supply and Control of Recorded Offenses in England and Wales." *Journal of Public Economics* 2 (1973), pp. 289–318. Concludes that an increase in police and enforcement expenditures per capita increased reported (not actual) crime per capita.

Hakim, S.; A. Ovadia; E. Sagi; and J. Weinblatt. "Interjurisdictional Spillover of Crime and Police Expenditure." *Land Economics* 55 (1979), pp. 200–12.

Kelling, G. L.; T. Pate; D. Dieckman; and C. E. Brown. *The Kansas City Preventative Patrol Experiment: A Technical Report*. Washington, D.C.: The Police Foundation, 1974. Suggests that increases in patrol activity do not affect crime rates.

Levine, James. "The Ineffectiveness of Adding Police to Prevent Crime." *Public Policy* 23 (Fall 1975), pp. 523–45.

Mehay, Stephen. "Inter-Governmental Contracting for Municipal Police Services—An Empirical Analysis." *Land Economics* 55 (1979), pp. 59–72.

Phillips, Llad, and Harold Votey. "Crime and Control in California." *Journal of Legal Studies* 4 (1975), pp. 327–50. Estimates the effects of enforcement expenditures on crime. An increase in the number of law enforcement personnel increases the probability of conviction.

Pogue, Thomas F. "Effect of Police Expenditures on Crime Rates." *Public Finance Quarterly* 3 (1975), pp. 14–44. Finds no relationship between police spending and crime rates.

Sherman, Lawrence. "Patrol Strategies for Police." In *Crime and Public Policy*, ed. James Q. Wilson. San Francisco: Institute for Contemporary Studies, 1983. Discusses the efficacy of alternative police-patrol strategies.

Thaler, Richard. "Econometric Analysis of Property Crime—Interaction Between Police and Criminals." *Journal of Public Economics* 8 (1977), pp. 37–51.

Wilson, James Q. "The Police and Crime." Chapter 5. In *Thinking About Crime*, ed. New York: Basic Books, 1975. Discusses the efficacy of patrol in deterring crime and contrasts the traditional patrol approach to the community-service approach.

Evidence of Deterrence

Bartel, Ann P. "Women and Crime: An Economic Analysis." *Economic Inquiry* 42 (1979), pp. 29–51. The probabilities of arrest and conviction have significant deterrent effects on female property crime. The decrease in the number of preschool children accounts for over half of the increase in female property crime between 1960 and 1970.

Craig, Steven G. "The Deterrent Impact of Police: an Examination of a Locally Provided Public Service." *Journal of Urban Economics* 21 (1987), pp. 298–311. Discusses the effects of changes in clearance rates on the crime rate and the reporting rate.

Ehrlich, Issac. "The Deterrent Effect of Criminal Law Enforcement." *Journal of Legal Studies* 1 (1972), pp. 259–76.

————. "Participation in Illegitimate Activities." *Journal of Political Economy* 81 (1973), pp. 521–65.

Goldberg, I., F. C. Nold. "Does Reporting Deter Criminals—An Empirical Analysis of Risk and Return in Crime." *Review of Economics and Statistics* 62 (1980), pp. 424–31. Discusses the effects of increased reporting rates on the return to crime and the probability of being victimized.

Mathur, V. K. "Economics of Crime—Investigation of the Deterrent Hypothesis for Urban Areas." *Review of Economics and Statistics* 60 (1978), pp. 459–66. Discusses the deterrent effects of increases in the certainty and severity of punishment.

Myers, S. L. "Crime in Urban Areas, New Evidence and Results." *Journal of Urban Economics* 11 (1982), pp. 148–58. Examines the effects of increased penalties and increased income on crime rates.

Phillips, Llad. "Crime Control: The Case for Deterrence." In *The Economics of Crime and Punishment*, ed. Simon Rottenberg. Washington, D.C.: American Enterprise Institute, 1973.

Sjoquist, David L. "Property Crime and Economic Behavior: Some Empirical Results." *American Economic Review* 63 (1973), pp. 439–46. Found that an increase in the probability of arrest decreased crime rates for burglary, robbery, and larceny.

Tullock, Gordon. "Does Punishment Deter Crime?" *The Public Interest* (Summer 1974), pp. 103–11.

Viscusi, W. Kip. "The Risks and Rewards of Criminal Activity: A Comprehensive Test of Criminal Deterrence." *Journal of Labor Economics* 4 (1986), pp. 317–40.

Wilson, James Q., and Barbara Boland. "Crime." Chapter 4. In *The Urban Predicament*, ed. William Gorham and Nathan Glazer. Washington, D.C.: The Urban Institute, 1976, pp. 179–230. Overview of crime and crime prevention, including a summary of deterrent studies. Estimates that the elasticity of supply of burglaries with respect to the probability of arrest is -0.50.

Witte, Ann D. "Estimating the Economic Model of Crime with Individual Data." *Quarterly Journal of Economics* 94 (1980), pp. 57–84. Estimates deterrent effects and finds that increased certainty of punishment (larger probability of punishment) has a larger deterrent effect than increased severity (larger penalty).

Wolpin, V. "A Time Series Cross Sectional Analysis of International Variation in Crime and Punishment." *Review of Economics and Statistics* 62 (1980), pp. 1417–23. Compares the crime rates of the United States, Japan, and the United Kingdom.

Economics of the Courts

Forst, Brian. "Prosecution and Sentencing." In *Crime and Public Policy*, ed. James Q. Wilson. San Francisco: Institute for Contemporary Studies, 1983. Discusses how the criminal justice system processes a typical set of 100 criminal cases.

Landes, William. "The Bail System: An Economic Approach." *Journal of Legal Studies* 2 no. 1 (1973), pp. 79–105.

Rhodes, W. M. "Economics of Criminal Courts—Theoretical and Empirical Investigation." *Journal of Legal Studies* 5 (1976), pp. 311–430.

Schlesinger, Steven R. "Criminal Procedures in the Courtroom." In *Crime and Public Policy*, ed. James Q. Wilson. San Francisco: Institute for Contemporary Studies, 1983. Discusses the bail system and the exclusionary rule.

Stepan, Jan. "Possible Lessons from Continental Criminal Procedure." In *The Economics of Crime and Punishment*, ed. Simon Rottenberg. Washington, D.C.: American Enterprise Institute, 1973.

Optimum Penalties

Becker, Gary S. "The Case for Fines." *Journal of Political Economy* 76 no. 2 (1968), pp. 168–217.

Dickens, William T. "Crime and Punishment Again: The Economic Approach with a Psychological Twist." *Journal of Public Economics* 30 (1985), pp. 97–107. Discusses the effects of psychological factors on the deterrent effect of increased penalties.

Stigler, George. "The Optimum Enforcement of Laws." *Journal of Political Economy* 78 (May 1970), pp. 526–36. Discusses the principle of marginal deterrence.

Wilson, James Q. "Courts and Correction." In *Thinking About Crime*. New York: Basic Books, 1975. Advocates several reforms of the sentencing procedure, including (*a*) centralized sentencing management and uniform sentences, (*b*) some form of confinement for every crime (certain punishment), and (*c*) a shortening of prison and jail sentences. In other words, he advocates short but certain punishment.

Rehabilitation

Evans, Robert. "The Labor Market and Parole Success." *Journal of Human Resources* 3 no. 2 (1968), pp. 201–11.

Glaser, Daniel. "Supervising Offenders Outside of Prison." In *Crime and Public Policy*, ed. James Q. Wilson. San Francisco: Institute for Contemporary Studies, 1983. Discusses parole, halfway houses, counseling programs, and employment assistance.

Martinson, Robert. "What Works—Questions and Answers about Prison Reform." *The Public Interest* 35 (Spring 1974), pp. 22–54. Reviewed the results of 231 studies of the effects of rehabilitation programs on recidivism rates. Concluded that rehabilitation has no appreciable effect on recidivism.

Incapacitation

Greenberg, David F. "The Incapacitative Effects of Imprisonment: Some Estimates." *Law and Society Review* 9 (Summer 1975), pp. 541–80.

Greenwood, Peter. "Controlling the Crime Rate through Imprisonment." In *Crime and Public Policy*, ed. James Q. Wilson. San Francisco: Institute for Contemporary Studies, 1983. Discusses the trade-offs associated with selective incapacitation.

Shinnar, Reuel, and Shlomo Shinnar. "The Effects of the Criminal Justice System on the Control of Crime." *Law and Society Review* 9 (Summer 1975), pp. 581–611.

Wilson, James Q. "Dealing with the High-Rate Offender." *The Public Interest* 72 (Summer 1983), pp. 52–71.

Wilson, James Q., and Barbara Boland. "Crime." Chapter 4. In *The Urban Predicament*, ed. William Gorham and Nathan Glazer. Washington, D.C.: The Urban Institute, 1976, pp. 179–230. Estimates the incapacitation effect for different numbers of crimes per offender.

Prison Reform

Blumstein, Alfred. "Prisons: Population, Capacity, and Alternatives." In *Crime and Public Policy*, ed. James Q. Wilson. San Francisco: Institute for Contemporary Studies, 1983. Discusses alternative strategies for dealing with prison congestion, including new construction and selective incapacitation.

Conley, J. "Economics and the Social Reality of Prisons." *Journal of Criminal Justice* 10 (1981), pp. 25–35.

DiIulio, John J. "Prison Discipline and Prison Reform." *The Public Interest* 89 (Fall 1987), pp. 71–90.

Engel, Kathleen, and Stanley Rothman. "Prison Violence and the Paradox of Reform." *The Public Interest* 73 (Fall 1983), pp. 91–105.

Heroin and Property Crime

Becker, Gary S. "Should Drug Use Be Legalized?" *Business Week*, August 17, 1987, p. 22.

Clague, Christopher. "Legal Strategies for Dealing with Heroin Addiction." *American Economic Review* 63 no. 2 (1973), pp. 263–69.

————. "Controlling Criminogenic Commodities: Drugs, Guns, and Alcohol." In *Crime and Public Policy*, ed. James Q. Wilson. San Francisco: Institute for Contemporary Studies, 1983. Discusses the role of drugs, guns, and alcohol in criminal activity.

Moore, Mark. "Policies to Achieve Discrimination of the Effective Price of Heroin." *American Economic Review* 63 no. 2 (1973), pp. 270–77.

Silverman, L. P., and N. L. Sprull. "Urban Crime and the Price of Heroin." *Journal of Urban Economics* 4 (1977), pp. 80–103.   Discusses the interactions between drug policies and property crime.

Wilson, James Q. "Heroin." Chapter 7. In *Thinking About Crime*. New York: Basic Books, 1975.   Discusses the relationship between heroin addiction and property crime and examines the British system of legalized heroin.

Organized Crime

Allsop, Kenneth. *The Bootleggers: The Story of Chicago's Prohibition Era*. Arlington House, 1970.

Buchanen, James. "A Defense of Organized Crime?" In *The Economics of Crime and Punishment*, ed. Simon Rottenberg. Washington, D.C.: American Enterprise Institute, 1973.

Reuter, Peter, and Jonathan Rubinstein. "Fact, Fancy and Organized Crime." *The Public Interest* 53 (Fall 1978), pp. 45–67.

Rottenberg, Simon. "The Clandestine Distribution of Heroin, Its Discovery and Suppression," *Journal of Political Economy* 76 (January 1968), pp. 78–90.

Rubin, Paul. "The Economic Theory of the Criminal Firm." In *The Economics of Crime and Punishment*, ed. Simon Rottenberg. Washington, D.C.: American Enterprise Institute, 1973.

Schelling, Thomas C. "Economics and Criminal Enterprise." *The Public Interest* 7 (1967), pp. 61–78.

Miscellaneous

Gordon, David. "Capitalism, Class, and Crime in America." *Review of Radical Political Economy* 3 no. 3 (1971), pp. 51–75.

Kates, Don B., Jr. "The Battle Over Gun Control." *The Public Interest* 84 (Summer 1986), pp. 42–52.

Katzman, Martin. "The Economics of Defense Against Crime in the Streets." *Land Economics* 19 (1968), pp. 431–40.

Phillips, Llad, and Harold Votey. *Crime and Public Policy*. Beverly Hills: Sage, 1979.

Shoup, Carl. "Standards for Distributing a Free Governmental Service: Crime Prevention." *Public Finance* 19 (December 1964), pp. 383–401.   Discusses the trade-offs between efficiency and equity in the distribution of crime-fighting resources.

Thurow, Lester. "Equity versus Efficiency in Law Enforcement." *Public Policy* 18 no. 4 (1970), pp. 451–59.

Toby, Jackson. "Crime in the Schools." In *Crime and Public Policy*, ed. James Q. Wilson. San Francisco: Institute for Contemporary Studies, 1983.

Index

A

Aaron, Henry J., 478, 505
Ability tracking system, 585
Absolute advantage, 15
Accelerated depreciation of property, 363
Advanced Micro Devices, 56
Advisory Commission on Intergovernmental
　Relations, 416
Agricultural preserves, 280
Aid to Families with Dependent Children (AFDC),
　312, 315–18
　effects on labor supply, 318
　work incentives, 314, 316–18
Air pollution by automobiles, 270, 508
　ambient air quality standards, 534–35
　Clean Air Act, 533–35
　effluent fees, 531–32
　regulatory policy, 533–35
　transit subsidies, 533
Agglomerative economies, 13, 181
　marketing, 28–29
　production, 22–28
　　empirical estimates, 27–28
　　localization economies, 22–26
Alaska, 416
Albany, 4
Alonso, William, 207
Alonso-Muth theory of income segregation, 208,
　210–11
Altshuler, Alan A., 519, 568
Ambient air quality standards, 534–35
Aronson, J. Richard, 458, 484
Arrest ratio, 632
Arrow, Kenneth, 310
Aschauer, David A., 129
Ashenfelter, Orley, 313
Associated Home Builders, Inc. v. *City of Livermore*, 284
Atlanta, 257
Athens, Greece, 70, 71
Automobiles and highways
　air pollution; *see* Air pollution by automobiles
　commuting; *see* Commuting
　congestion; *see* Traffic congestion
　costs of auto transportation system, 556–60
　demand for urban travel, 509
　highway pricing, 523–27
　land use patterns, 527–31
　optimum traffic volume, 512, 525–26
　private and social costs of travel, 510–12
　safety, 535–40
　　optimum speed, 536–38
　　regulations, 535–39
　　small cars, 539–40
　suburbanization, 244–45, 253
　taxes
　　congestion, 510, 512–16, 527–31
　　gasoline, 517, 532
　　parking, 518

Automobiles and highways—*Cont.*
　transit subsidies, 521–23, 533
　usage in U.S. cities, 509

B

Baltimore, 79–80
　urban renewal, 300
Bane, Mary Jo, 312
Barber, E., 518
BART; *see* San Francisco Bay Area Rapid Transit
Bartel, Ann P., 632, 641
Bartik, Timothy J., 58, 59
Barton, David M., 384
Basic rent, 388
Bassie, Laurie, 313
Baumol model, 448–53, 563
Becker, Charles, 59
Becker, Gary S., 310
Beesley, Michael E., 549
Benefit principle, 426–28
Berkeley, California, 400
Berrueta-Clement, John R., 309
Berry, Brian J. L., 109
Bid-rent function, 164–71
　allocation between two competing uses, 170–72
　decrease in transport costs, 168–70
　manufacturers, 181–84
　office firms, 184–85, 186
　residential, 195–98, 251
Black, David E., 477
Black capitalism, 331
Blacks
　concentration in central city, 329
　discrimination, 310, 330
　dispersal policies, 330–31
　education, 329
　housing, 380
　poverty, 329
　underclass status, 331
　unemployment, 329, 331
Blanchard, Lois, 323
Blank, Rebecca M., 303, 318
Blinder, Alan S,. 303
Block grant, 496
Boland, Barbara, 621, 632, 642, 643
Boorstin, Daniel, 76
Boston, 79, 80, 400
Boston Housing Partnership, 399
Bradbury, Katherine L., 250
Bradford, David, 446, 447, 448, 602
British Corn Laws, 172
British Navigation Acts, 60
British woolen industry, 20–21
Brown, L., 584
Brown v. *Board of Education of Topeka*, 598
Buffalo, N.Y., 48
Building permits, 267–68
Buses, 549, 552–56
　costs, 557

H

I

T